Jonathan Torralba Torrón

THE METAPHYSICAL COMPASS

Finding your Way in a complex world full of conflicting worldviews

The Metaphysical Compass Project

For Ana María, who with her encouragement, advice, and tireless dedication to even the most mundane tasks has saved this project from being delayed for an indefinite period of time.

For Miguel and Ofelia, for their constant support, without which the author would not have been able to write this book.

For Xavier, for our interesting talks on everything metaphysical, from which the idea of writing the present book arose.

The Metaphysical Compass Project

This book is part of The Metaphysical Compass Project. Its aim is to investigate the metaphysical concepts behind the ubiquitous symbolism present in popular culture and to discuss the ancient narratives and worldviews being promoted.

Throughout this book, as well as the accompanying website (TheMetaphysicalCompass.com), we hope to provide context, knowledge, and guidance to help us navigate the complex landscape of conflicting worldviews brought about by globalization, in the process trading confusion for insight.

About Structure and Style

This book is divided into two parts: one of Analysis and another of Synthesis. Some of its chapters can be read independently, especially those in the first part (e.g., Chapter III). However, it is advisable to read the Synthesis section in sequential order to better understand the general argument of the book and the implications that can be derived for our own lives.

Since the book is based on the different answers given by various worldviews to the same set of limited metaphysical questions, some degree of repetition is unavoidable. However, the narrative of the book has been woven in such a way that the material is never repeated without providing additional insight from a different point of view or without unraveling an underlying implication. In this way, we have tried to avoid circularity by tracing a spiraling path of increasing depth.

Finally, the book uses a large number of capitalized terms in order to improve readability and memorability of complex words, even if they are not normally capitalized.

The Metaphysical Compass

Finding your Way in a complex world

full of conflicting worldviews

JONATHAN TORRALBA TORRÓN

TABLE OF CONTENTS

ANALYSIS SECTION

SYNTHESIS SECTION

Chapter IV. Comparing Worldviews: Similarities, Differences
and Recurrent Patterns   336

Chapter V. Metaphysics and Worldview Promotion in Popular Culture:
Modern Common Narrative Trends and their Underlying Influences   336

Chapter VI. Navigating the Complex Landscape of Current Worldviews:
Typology of Mysticism and the Solution to the Problem of the One and the Many 358

Chapter VII. Typology of Theistic Mysticism: Or Why Not All
Monotheistic Religions Are the Same   412

Appendixes 546

A Plurality of Choices:
Which Path Will You Take?

The Complexity of the Modern World

The Globalization of Metaphysical Confusion

THE WORLD HAS BECOME TOO COMPLICATED. Technology has changed the landscape of human beliefs. It has served both to educate and to confuse us. We now have more knowledge to digest, more concepts to grasp, more worldviews to evaluate. Knowledge has progressively become globalized.

The invention of the printing press was a key milestone for the globalization of knowledge, and modern computing has exponentially accelerated this process.

A few centuries ago a person had to decide if they believed what was handed down to them or if they rejected it (e.g., are you a believer or an atheist?). Maybe they also decided that a particular denomination of their religion was somewhat better than the others (e.g., Orthodox, Catholic or Protestant Christianity? Theravāda, Mahāyāna or Vajrayāna Buddhism? Shia or Sunni Islam?). More often than not, they might not even have been aware of all the different denominations of their own religion. Maybe they did not need to.

However, never in the past had an individual access to all of humanity´s worldviews and deepest beliefs. Neither did they have to analyze and decide which, if any, incompatible set of doctrines they followed and believed in.

Even just a few decades ago, without the existence of the internet and worldwide information sharing, most people continued living the life of their ancestors. They, with greater or lesser faith depending on the individual, mostly followed the set of beliefs handed down to them by their family and community. They may have argued about some aspects of their faiths (when has mankind not argued?), but the basic framework of a specific society´s beliefs was mostly fixed. This, in turn, allowed for greater behavior predictability, societal stability, and just an overall greater cohesion than we have now.

1. The Big Consequences of Small Variations in Beliefs

The consequences of small changes in abstract beliefs do not limit themselves to the realm of the mind, but also affect common everyday life.

Is God an impersonal force or a Person who we can have a personal relationship with? Each view has different implications on how we should live. This difference in behavior, in turn, will lead to the creation of different types of communities with different cultural patterns. In time, the traditions and symbolism used and propagated by each community will be radically different from each other based on their original assumptions and beliefs regarding who, or what, God is.

If God is a blind force (e.g., Deism) instead of a Person who possesses a will, morality, etc., then we are justified in living in a certain way. However, if He is a pre-existing Person who became incarnated in human form, and in fact we are made in His image (as Christian theology teaches), the implications and what is expected of us are very different.

Let´s see another example. In worldviews where it is believed that in the end we are all one with God or ultimate reality (e.g., Panentheism), we might become "liberated" or facilitate our own ascension (Self-Deification) by means of the application of the correct knowledge and the correct practice. In most Far Eastern worldviews this is thought to be possible because of the belief that we are, and always have been, one with ultimate reality itself, each one of us being a particular manifestation of the Ultimate of which we are not yet aware. In other worldviews, such as in Christianity, even though we are an important part of the process of salvation and we are expected to put effort towards it, we need God to collaborate with us in a synergistic fashion, because we alone are not enough. This, in turn, puts emphasis on humility and reliance on God, as well as on God´s transcendental aspect. The overall picture is quite different.

Two further classic examples follow. The first: is existence linear or cyclical? Cyclical time doctrines state that there exists an unavoidable succession of differentiated periods of time or ages, each successive one more ignorant and morally corrupt than the last, until a restoration takes place. One of the possible consequences of sharing this belief is that we might be tempted to stop trying to make the world a better place. It could even be argued that promoting degeneracy is instead a better thing to do in order to hasten the reappearance of a better age. If we have to fall to rise again we might as well do it sooner than later.

The second example involves the Indian doctrine of liberation (e.g., Buddhism, Hinduism). If liberation, for the majority of people, is gained after a multitude of lifetimes, we might be drawn to wait for better conditions to work on our liberation. We could devote this life to just acquiring merit by doing good deeds that would be "cashed out" in the next, not struggling to acquire wisdom or insight. However, if this is really the only life we get, we would be making the biggest possible mistake, with consequences beyond life and death, as we would not be getting another opportunity to further our spiritual progress.

Let´s see a last example. What do you believe to be the origin of evil? Is it related to matter and the "density" of the lower and unspiritual planes of reality? Is it due to ignorance? Maybe sin? The first cause is external to us as individuals, while the second is based on a cognitive deficiency and the third on our own wilful rebellion, made possible by the Fall of the original human person and archetype, Adam. Our belief in this matter has radical implications for the way we see the world, ourselves, and others, with different attitudes deriving from it.

Certain beliefs regarding this topic may even have created historically contradictory ways of acting. For example, in worldviews were matter is viewed as intrinsically evil (e.g., Gnosticism), the aim is to detach yourself completely from the world (not only from the passions or bad aspects of life, but also from the apparently good ones) while focusing on obtaining the right intellectual and ceremonial knowledge in order to be able to escape from this life, conceptualized as a prison for the soul. You might want to purify yourself completely of everything material, including sexual relations with a spouse. [In other worldviews (e.g., Christianity), where creation was initially deemed good by God, marital sex is thought as wholesome and without fault].

This idea that matter is intrinsically evil, however, can also justify the opposite behavior. If this world of matter is conceived as being originally bad you would be justified, not only in retreating ascetically from it, but also in abusing it. This could be done to obtain a feeling of saturation, detachment, and freedom from matter and desire (e.g., the Phibionite Gnostic sect and left hand paths of certain tantric and esoteric traditions, even though some of the later may consider matter altogether illusory).

Figure 1. Examples of faulty thinking. When evaluating our beliefs, we want them to be logically sound and coherent in order to avoid self-assertions and self-refuting arguments (e.g., "everything is relative"). Other beliefs may be able to justify radically opposite behaviors, therefore becoming useless to guide us in life.

You would even be theoretically justified in defiling nature or your own body, as you would consider matter as inherently evil and only the soul or spirit as worthy of being saved once liberated from this fleshly prison.

If ignorance is the root of evil, in turn, you should value knowledge above all else. This involves only the cognitive aspect of a person. In this case, striving for relative purity might be of help but, if the solution is mostly cognitive, the moral and behavioral aspects of the person are not emphasized. Hence, we could conceive of someone who has attained great power because they possess great knowledge that allows them to tap into primordial forces, but wields it for egotistical purposes (e.g., similar to some modern views on magic, which include white and black magicians).

However, if sin is the problem, repentance is key in order to turn in the right direction and stop "missing the mark" (which is the original meaning of the word sin). This would involve, especially, the willing and behavioral aspects of the person, in addition to knowledge. This view considers the person as a whole.

Finally, we may take a materialist approach and think that existence has no ultimate meaning and that everything sprouted from a statistically improbable fluctuation of the forces of the Universe, which we do not know where they come from.[1,2] In this case, the concept of evil might not even make sense to us. "Evil" could then be a somewhat useful relative human construction, variable in time and dependent on the social and cultural context.

––––––––––––––––

1. *"What men call chance is simply their ignorance of causes; if the statement that something had happened by chance were to mean that it had no cause, it would be a contradiction in terms."*

– Guénon, René (1927). The Crisis of the Modern World. Sophia Perennis, Ch. VI: The Social Chaos, p.70.

2. *"[Modern scientific] theories can necessarily never be more than hypothetical, since their starting-point is wholly empirical, for facts in themselves are always susceptible of diverse explanations and so never have been and never will be able to guarantee the truth of any theory."*

– Guénon, René (1945). The Reign of Quantity and the Signs of the Times. Sophia Perennis, Ch. 18: Scientific Mythology and Popularization, p. 120.

In this last scenario, we could argue that we are justified in doing everything that gives us satisfaction and saves us from pain, however "evil" it might seem to others. This would be so because the concept of evil itself would be relative for us and, therefore, there would be no ultimate truth or standard of behavior that we have to abide by.

In summary, our beliefs in particular metaphysical concepts can have drastic consequences in our outlook on life and how we plan the way we live. They can even affect how we evaluate others and what we feel for them.

2. Metaphysically Neutral Behavior Does Not Exist

So, we have seen that beliefs are not vague abstractions with no contact with reality. They have very real and tangible consequences in our lives.

Our actions may even be judged by others depending on their underlying presuppositions on how the world works and what reality and life really are. The same action may be labelled as murder or as morally neutral (even as morally good) by reading it through a different worldview or metaphysical lens (e.g., abortion of a baby conceived by rape).

This underscores the fact that metaphysical neutrality does not exist, and even atheists or agnostics are incapable of acting in a metaphysically neutral way.[3] We all carry our own metaphysical presuppositions on how reality works, who or what we are and what the ultimate truth is, even if we are not consciously aware of them.

We often feel very attached to our own values and feel that they define us (e.g., pro-life or pro-abortion), but we are not always aware of the metaphysical principles and presuppositions that are at their core,

---

3. "In short, the majority of men "without religion" still hold to pseudo religions and degenerated mythologies. There is nothing surprising in this, for, as we saw, profane man is the descendant of homo religiosus and he cannot wipe out his own history—that is, the behavior of his religious ancestors which has made him what he is today."

— Eliade, Mircea (1957). The Sacred and the Profane: The Nature of Religion. Harcourt Brace Jovanovich, Ch. IV: Human Existence and Sanctified Life, p. 209.

or where do they come from. Did we evaluate them personally? Do we know the alternatives? Or did we just accept a set of principles as part of our cultural heritage? Maybe we were unconsciously influenced by mass media? Have we just internalized a set of values transmitted by our school? In that case, the values transmitted may be different in different places, times or in institutions under different political regimes.

Given the importance of our core beliefs and presuppositions in how they shape our lives and even our connection with others, and the fact that they are rarely obvious (we usually have to dig deep to find them in us), it would be ill advised to not go on a journey of self-discovery and let them go unchallenged, influencing us from the shadows.

It would also be unwise to adopt an indifferent attitude towards our core beliefs and just follow the easy but dangerous path of being a follower of whatever trends are being put forth by the media (the fourth power) and whatever the educational institutions of the time (a part of the ruling state) promote.

Recapitulating, different sets of beliefs imply different approaches to how we live our lives and promote radically different behaviors. Most of the time, however, we are not even aware of what our core metaphysical presuppositions are. Especially when we are young and finding or ground in life, our core beliefs might come from cultural osmosis.

3. A Battle Between Conflicting Worldviews Being Waged in Our Minds

Now, going back to the complexity of our times, we now do not only have to decide if we think a particular denomination has the fullness of the truth (e.g., Orthodox, Catholic or Protestant Christianity? Shia or Sunni Islam? Theravāda or Mahāyāna Buddhism?).

We also have to evaluate which faith, if any, is closer to the truth and the correct path for us to follow. Is it one of the Abrahamic religions (Christianity, Judaism, Islam) or is it perhaps one of the Dharmic ones? (Buddhism, a specific variety of Hinduism, Jainism or Sikhism).

Furthermore, is the truth found in the exoteric religions that everyone knows or only in the esoteric schools that are part of these religions? (e.g., Kabbalah is the mystical tradition of Judaism, Sufism is the one derived from Islam).

Is the truth revealed to the initiates of these different mystical traditions the same? Maybe the truth was lost to time and all we can do is to get as close as possible by distilling the common denominator found in all these esoteric traditions while abandoning any particularity as something superfluous? (Perennialism).

This is a complex issue. In order to make sense of all of this, some people even create their own personal metaphysical system by mixing different beliefs that seem right to them in an incoherent and syncretistic[4] way that has no historical roots (e.g., New Age, Wicca).

Moreover, we now even have to decide which individual doctrines we believe in! Do we believe in a cyclical cosmology or in a linear one? What about reincarnation and past lives? Is God an absolute Monad (unity) or can He/It include multiplicity in Himself because He transcends the concept of number, which He created? Are we aware of the consequences of each different belief and how it sheds light on how we should live?

---

4. *"[...] if he then should wish to perform rites belonging to many different forms, claiming to use them concurrently as means and 'supports' of his spiritual development, he will not really be able to combine them except 'from the outside', which amounts to saying that what he accomplishes will be nothing else than syncretism, which consists precisely in this kind of mingling of disparate elements that nothing really unifies.*

[...] This situation is similar to that of someone who, hoping to secure his health the more effectively, makes use at one and the same time of many different medicines the effects of which neutralize and destroy each other [...]".

— Guénon, René (1946). Perspectives on Initiation. Sophia Perennis, p. 49.

Influenced by modern philosophy, we can go even further and ask ourselves, does Truth even exist? Can it even exist in principle? (e.g., Subjectivism).

Are post-modern philosophers right? Is truth a construct? What path should we follow, then?[5,6] Is Nietzsche´s will to power a worthy ideal to follow that will liberate us from both old gods and Nihilism?[7] Or maybe we should embrace selfishness, which is a virtue and nothing to be ashamed of, as Ayn Rand[8] proposed?

This is a lot of work! Do we even have to complicate our lives by thinking on these things? Maybe we can live in a hedonistic way, looking only after pleasure and avoiding pain (e.g., Epicureanism[9]), or just adopt a Stoic attitude against "Fate", trying not to fall into Cynicism.

------

5. *"Indeed, in many cases, discussion can be carried on indefinitely without arriving at any solution, which is the reason why almost all modern philosophy is built up on quibbles and badly-framed questions. Far from clearing up these questions, as it is commonly supposed to do, discussion usually only entangles or obscures them still further."*

— Guénon, René (1927). The Crisis of the Modern World. Sophia Perennis, Ch. V: Individualism, p. 66.

6. *"[...] the contentions of philosophers are often much more justifiable when they are arguing against other philosophers than when they pass on to expound their own views, and as each one generally sees fairly clearly the defects of the others, they more or less destroy one another mutually."*

— Guénon, René. The Reign of Quantity & the Signs of the Times (1945). Sophia Perennis, Ch. 14: Mechanism and Materialism, p. 93.

7. *"This world is the will to power—and nothing besides! And you yourselves are also this will to power and nothing besides!"*

— Nietzsche, Friedrich (c. 1960). The Will to Power. Vintage Books, p. 550.

8. *"Man—every man—is an end in himself, not the means to the ends of others. He must exist for his own sake, neither sacrificing himself to others nor sacrificing others to himself. The pursuit of his own rational self-interest and of his own happiness is the highest moral purpose of his life."*

— Rand, Ayn (June 17, 1962). "Introducing Objectivism". Los Angeles Times. Also in The Objectivist Newsletter.

9. *"Don't fear the gods; Don't worry about death; What is good is easy to get, and what is terrible is easy to endure."*

Or maybe it is better if we just forget about all this pretentious nonsense that comes from minds with too much available free time. We could then put our faith in the technical knowledge of a gifted few, while we keep pushing technology forward until we can upload our consciousness onto a more enduring non-biological substrate.

We could thus escape into a substrate-independent existence which would grant us something similar to an immanent "immortality", a continuous existence in this Universe. However, Functionalism must be true for this to be a possibility, and we would have to gamble on it.

This is what the "religious" or metaphysical side of Transhumanism is looking for,[10] like a modern version of Gnosticism resurrected in the language of the twenty-first century.

In summary, things are now more complex. They were never easy, but there was a time when a person could know much about a lot of things.

Now it is difficult to be an expert in even one small aspect of reality, especially regarding the biggest questions of life, as there is metaphysical, philosophical, theological, and scientific knowledge required to tackle the deeper questions of spirituality and meaning in our lives.

Never previously in history has humanity been confronted with so much metaphysical information and possibilities on what to believe, how to behave, and what to pursue as the aim of their life. However, never previously in history has humanity had at its disposal so many resources for learning and discussing these topics.

— Epicurus. The Epicurus Reader: Selected Writings and Testimonia. Hackett Publishing, p. VI.

10. "Contemporary philosopher Max More describes the goal of humanity as a transcendence to be `achieved through science and technology steered by human values.'"

— Kurzweil, Ray (2005). The Singularity is Near: When Humans Transcend Biology. Penguin Books, p. 548.

4. The Metaphysical Compass: A Tool to Help You Navigate this Complex Conceptual Landscape

Metaphysics is the branch of philosophy that deals with the first principles of things. That which goes beyond, or is prior, to physics. A compass is a navigation tool to find our way and avoid danger.

The Metaphysical Compass[11] is now born as another tool in the digital age that you can use to try to find your way in this exceedingly complex landscape of beliefs, doctrines, and symbols that we are faced with. Information overload and cognitive complexity is a unique battle that the digital generations will have to face, and we will need different tools to navigate ourselves in this sometimes obscure and serpentine path.

If you use this tool you will be confronted with your own self, with your own core beliefs and presuppositions that you probably did not know you had. Why do you believe what you do? Are you even aware of what you believe deep down? Do you behave like you do because of some *pre*-supposition on how reality works? You will also learn of the alternatives, and about the beliefs other people nowadays and throughout history have lived and died for.

Finally, you will discover that it seems the modern world is trying to push us towards certain worldviews and apart from others. You will be asked if you think this is for our own good or does not have our best interests in mind.

In the past, life may have been more physically demanding but, in general, it had meaning. Today, it is common to feel lost or unsure about our beliefs and embrace different worldviews in different periods of our life. We suffer from metaphysical anxiety, we could say, and it is not going away.

------

11. *The Metaphysical Compass Project comprises this book and a website (TheMetaphysicalCompass.com), as well as the accompanying social media. The website will be based on this book but will also include further periodic articles on symbolism, metaphysics, and worldviews.*

Pandora´s box has already been opened and the excessive amounts of information about conflicting worldviews, what to believe, and how to live our lives has sowed doubts and restlessness in vast amounts of people.

Therefore, *The Metaphysical Compass* exists as an invitation to enjoy ourselves while navigating and discovering additional layers of meaning in the tumultuous waters of this complex world. A world filled with ancient symbols, deep concepts, and different visions of the beyond.

Maybe you will find new meaning. Maybe your current worldview and beliefs will become more solid. In any case, hopefully you will end up knowing more about yourself and the world, about why you believe what you do, and about the different answers provided throughout time to the most fundamental questions of all.

Journeys of self-discovery are seldom easy, as they involve moving away from our comfort zone, but they are always fulfilling and full of meaning.

Recommended Reading

1. **Nihilism: The Root of the Revolution of the Modern Age.**
   Fr. Seraphim Rose.
2. **The Reign of Quantity & the Signs of the Times.**
   René Guénon.

Symbol and Ritual:
Road to Spiritual Initiation

Symbolic Patterns in Popular Culture

What Do they Mean and Why Do they Matter

1. What is a Symbol?

A SYMBOL CAN BE DEFINED IN MULTIPLE WAYS. THE simplest modern definition would be the representation of one thing using another. As such, it is used in artistic fields such as literature or cinema as a narrative device to enrich and give thematic cohesion and depth to a story. Symbols can also be used to convey complex meanings not easily transmitted otherwise. They can be repeatedly used as motifs to help convey the important themes of a story. They may also be used to provide hints regarding deeper meanings that are not explicitly shown.

A symbol, instead of being a completely abstract notion, teaches concepts in a sensorial way. Shapes, colors, and sounds can be used as supports through which we can achieve a higher understanding. In fact, this intrinsic usefulness and natural human attunement to symbolic and sensory learning has been used as an argument against theories that state that humanity is pure intellect (e.g., Descartes[1]), thus underestimating our physical dimension.

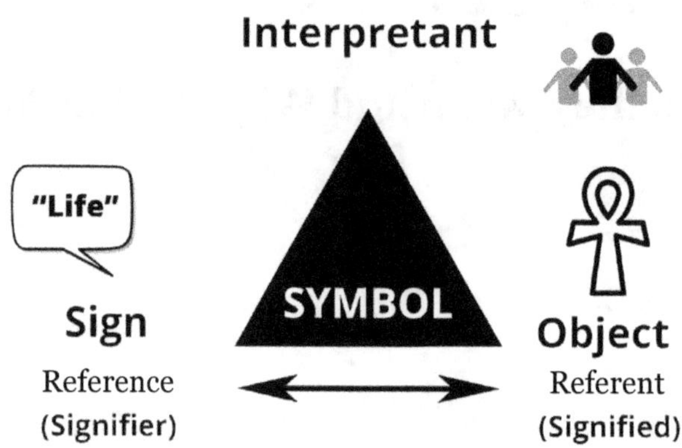

Figure 1. Symbol definition in the science of Semiotics. A symbol can be defined by the triadic relationship between sign, object, and interpretant. Sign interpretation can also depend on the context. In this example, the ancient Egyptian Ankh symbol is interpreted as a symbol of life.

---

1. *"One must take the human compound as it is, at once one and multiple in its real complexity; this is what tends to be forgotten, ever since Descartes claimed to establish a radical and absolute separation between soul and body. For a pure intelligence, assuredly, no exterior form, no expression is required in order to understand the truth, or even to communicate to other pure intelligences what it has understood insofar as it is communicable; but it is not so for man."*

– Guénon, René (1962). "Word and Symbol". Fundamental Symbols: The Universal Language of Sacred Science. Quinta Essentia, p. 7.

Modern popular culture is full of symbolic patterns that repeat themselves across different media, and a growing number of people are relying on their analysis to understand the deeper meaning of their favorite movies, books, music or video games. We live in an increasingly symbolic world but, as we will see, symbols have been a part of the human condition since the beginning. Due to their very nature, it could not have been otherwise.

SIGNS AND SYMBOLS

Signs have a clearly defined meaning. They point to something specific, like an instruction to follow (e.g., driving signs).

Although symbols also represent something else, they need some additional knowledge to be interpreted. Their meaning is not as standardized or easily exhausted as in a sign and a degree of intuition is required.

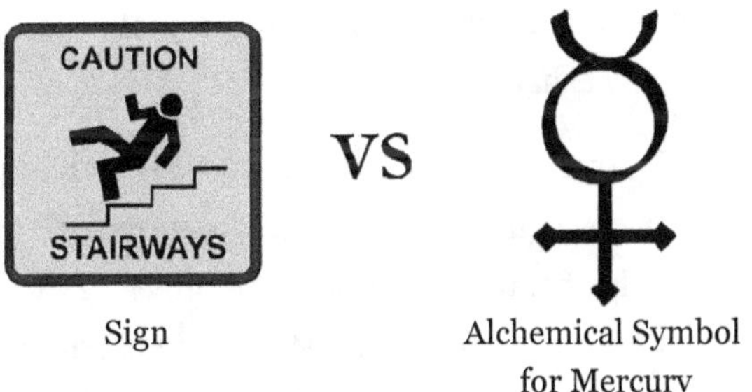

Sign

Alchemical Symbol
for Mercury

Figure 2. Comparison between a stereotypical sign and a symbol.

2. The Traditional Understanding of Symbolism

The roots of symbolism can be traced back to ancient times. All traditional cultures can be said to be symbolic. But the word traditional, in this context, has a special meaning that differs from the modern understanding of the term. Nowadays, tradition usually means just custom, habit or any inherited way of thinking and living.

In contrast, in a religious and metaphysical context, Tradition means the set of transcendental or divinely ordained principles that have been revealed to humanity in one way or another (e.g., via messengers, prophets or the Logos). Once codified, this knowledge is passed from generation to generation to remind us of our ultimate origin.

In the next sections we will delve deeper in the traditional view on various aspects of symbolism, including its ultimate purpose.

a. Symbolism and Language

Symbolism is synthetic, involves a certain degree of intuition, and is able to convey unlimited concepts. Language, on the other hand, is analytic and creates narrower limits for what is being signified. This makes common language more useful for applications were concrete and unambiguous knowledge is required. Symbolism, in turn, is the best option to transmit concepts and teachings that by their very nature cannot be completely exhausted by the rational aspect of the human mind.

This is why the transmission of metaphysical teachings in ancient traditions was done by using predominantly a symbolic language. It was considered as the best (and sometimes the only) way to transmit the higher truths of life so that they could at least be partially understood.[2] However, symbols were not considered as the whole truth they tried

---

2. *"Indeed, if one accepts that symbolism has its basis in the very nature of beings and of things, that it is in perfect conformity with the laws of this nature, and if one reflects that natural laws are in sum only an expression and as it were an exteriorization of the Divine Will, does this not justify the affirmation that symbolism is "non-human" in origin as the Hindus say; or, in other words, that its principle is beyond and higher than humanity?"*

"[...] The philosopher Berkeley was not wrong, therefore, when he said that the world is "the language that the infinite Spirit speaks to finite spirits."

– Guénon, René (1962). "Word and Symbol". Fundamental Symbols: The Universal Language of Sacred Science. Quinta Essentia, p. 7.

to represent. They were only thought of as a support, an aid, only to be used until the reality behind them was firmly grasped and they became unnecessary.

In short, symbols can be understood as catalysts of a special type of knowledge and were historically used as a kind of language useful to understand the deeper questions of life.

b. Symbolism and the Natural World

In many traditional worldviews, the Universe is the creation of the divine Intellect or Word, where all that can possibly exist is contained before time began.[3] Therefore, according to these worldviews, the whole of nature can be seen as a symbol of the transcendent or true reality. The real importance and meaning of the natural world would then be in its symbolic value, in helping us to get closer to our primordial reality, with symbols being able to represent certain divine ideas. Together, these symbols were thought to form a harmonious totality that, once correctly read, reflect the divine unity in our plane of existence.

———————————————

3. "We could adduce an immense weight of testimony offered by human faith and wisdom proving that the invisible or spiritual order is analogous to the material order. [...] Let us recall the saying of Plato, taken up later by the pseudo-Dionysius the Areopagite: 'What is perceptible to the senses is the reflection of what is intelligible to the mind'; and echoed in the Tabula Smaragdina: 'What is below is like what is above; what is above is like what is below', and also in the remark of Goethe: 'What is within is also without.'

However it may be, symbolism is organized in its vast explanatory and creative function as a system of highly complex relations, one in which the dominant factor is always a polarity, linking the physical and metaphysical worlds."

"[...] In his Letter number LV, St. Augustine shows that teaching carried out with the help of symbols feeds and stirs the fires of love, enabling Man to excel himself; he also alludes to the value of all things in nature—organic and inorganic—as bearers of spiritual messages."

— Cirlot, J.E. (1958). "Origin and Continuity of the Symbol". A Dictionary of Symbols. *Welcome Rain Publishers; Second edition, p. xvi.*

Even man himself is considered a symbol of the divine in most traditional worldviews (e.g., Adam and Eve being created in the image of God [Genesis 1:26-27] in Christianity, man partaking of the Buddha Nature in Mahāyāna Buddhism or the correspondence between macrocosm and microcosm in esoteric teachings).

In fact, this theory of correspondences where the material (inferior) plane of existence can represent a transcendent (superior) reality, is the real basis and justification of symbolism in the traditional mindset.[4]

The temporal world was thought to be the reflection of the eternal one,[5] and this really has to be so for us to be able to obtain at least some intuitive knowledge about the latter through symbols. Otherwise, there would be no adequate object that could signify any metaphysical truth. This would leave us perpetually in the dark and completely abandoned in our quest for truth.

------

4. *"All that exists, in whatever mode this may be, necessarily participates in universal principles, and nothing exists except by participation in these principles, which are the eternal and immutable essences contained in the permanent actuality of the Divine Intellect. Consequently, it can be said that all things, however contingent they may be in themselves, express or represent these principles in their own way and according to their order of existence, for otherwise they would be purely and simply nothingness. Thus, from one order to another, all things are linked together and correspond, to come together in total and universal harmony, for harmony is nothing other than the reflection of principal unity in the manifested world; and it is this correspondence which is the veritable basis of symbolism."*

— Guénon, René (1929). Spiritual Authority and Temporal Power; Cited in Fundamental symbols: the universal language of sacred science. Quinta Essentia, Introduction, p. 3.

5. *"The true basis of symbolism is, as we have said, the correspondence linking together all orders of reality, binding them one to the other, and consequently extending from the natural order as a whole to the supernatural order. By virtue of this correspondence, the whole of Nature is but a symbol, that is, its true significance becomes apparent only when it is seen as a pointer which can make us aware of supernatural or "metaphysical" truths [...]. The symbol must always be inferior to the thing symbolized, which destroys all naturalist concepts of symbolism."*

— Guénon, René; as quoted in Cirlot, J.E. (1958). "Definitions of the symbol". A Dictionary of Symbols. *Welcome Rain Publishers; Second edition, p. xxxi.*

c. Symbolism as a Means of Integration

J.E. Cirlot, in his *A Dictionary of Symbols*, summarizes as follows the position on symbolism of renowned historian of religions Mircea Eliade:[6]

1. Symbols have the mission of going beyond the limitations of man seen as a fragment, a piece of the All, while integrating this fragment into a wider totality (e.g., society, culture, the Universe).

2. The symbol, then, unites different planes of reality but without destroying the lower ones in the process. It is a union without confusion, because all the planes of reality are integrated into a wider system without being destroyed or fused together, therefore maintaining what makes them unique.

3. Given the above, if the All can appear contained within a significant fragment, it follows that each fragment is able to restate the All.

---

6. *"[...] In restoring the symbol to its status as an instrument of knowledge, our world is only returning to a point of view that was general in Europe until the eighteenth century and is, moreover, connatural to the other, non-European cultures, whether "historic" (like those of Asia or Central America for instance) or archaic and "primitive".*

[...] today we are well on the way to an understanding of one thing of which the nineteenth century had not even a presentiment - that the symbol, the myth and the image are of the very substance of the spiritual life, that they may become disguised, mutilated or degraded, but are never extirpated.

[...] The symbol reveals certain aspects of reality - the deepest aspects - which defy any other means of knowledge.

These degraded images present to us the only possible point of departure for the spiritual renewal of modern man. It is of the greatest importance, we believe, to rediscover a whole mythology, if not a theology, still concealed in the most ordinary, everyday life of contemporary man; it will depend upon himself whether he can work his way back to the source and rediscover the profound meanings of all these faded images and damaged myths."

– Eliade, Mircea (1961). Images and Symbols: Studies in Religious Symbolism. *Princeton University Press, p. 9.*

3. A Language Once Lost and Now Recovered

The idea of symbolism as a long-lost language is a common one.[7] However, as was discovered by a certain type of psychoanalysis, whenever the conscious layers of human consciousness are depleted of symbolic content, the unconscious is paradoxically overloaded with it as an automatic compensation mechanism.

This affirmation would be fully endorsed by the Swiss psychiatrist and founder of analytical psychology C.G. Jung [8, 9], who found that in each person there is a rich internal symbolic life. Jung abandoned the central thesis of his master, Sigmund Freud, for whom the key to human neurosis and inner psychic life was repressed sexual energy (libido). For Jung, the Collective Unconscious is instead composed of ancient symbolic archetypes pointing towards higher truths.

In Jung´s view, archetypes are not just images conjured by a repressed libido trying to sublimate a lower instinct in order to achieve some kind of release through other, more acceptable, means. Instead, they contain symbolic and spiritual value. Jung´s whole work is based on the discovery that each of us has inside a collection of ancient archetypical figures that we can integrate into our personality and use as guides to grow psychologically and spiritually.

---

7. *As can be seen in the titles of the books of famous authors, such as:* The Lost Language of Symbolism, *by Harold Bayley;* The Forgotten Language: An Introduction to the Understanding of Dreams, Fairy Tales and Myths, *by Erich Fromm.*

8. *"Modern man does not understand to what extent his 'rationalism' has placed him at the mercy of this underground psychic world. He freed himself from "superstition" (at least he believes so) but in doing so he lost his spiritual values to an alarming degree. His moral and spiritual traditions have disintegrated and he is paying for this collapse with a disarray and dissociation that is rampant throughout the world."*

– Jung, C.G (1964). Man and His Symbols. *Doubleday.*

9. *"The psychological mechanism that transforms energy is the symbol."*

– Jung, C.G. (1970). The Structure and Dynamics of the Psyche. *Collected Works, Volume 8, Part 1. Princeton University Press, p. 45.*

Jung was, and still is, an enormously influential figure. His ideas are especially strong in today´s popular culture (e.g., in movies: Star Wars; in video games: Persona).

His influence, as well as the undeniably regular and consistent presence of these ancient archetypes in most traditional mythologies, led the comparative mythologist Joseph Campbell to introduce the term Monomyth, which also has played an important role in modern movie making and other works of fiction.

George Lucas, for example, discusses this influence at great length in the authorized biography of Joseph Campbell, *A Fire in the Mind*:

"[...] It came to me that there really was no modern use of mythology... The Western was possibly the last generically American fairy tale, telling us about our values. And once the Western disappeared, nothing has ever taken its place. In literature we were going off into science fiction... so that's when I started doing more strenuous research on fairy tales, folklore, and mythology, and I started reading Joe's books.

Before that I hadn't read any of Joe's books... It was very eerie because in reading The Hero with a Thousand Faces I began to realize that my first draft of Star Wars was following classic motifs... So I modified my next draft according to what I'd been learning about classical motifs and made it a little bit more consistent... I went on to read The Masks of God and many other books."

Also named *The Hero's Journey*, the Monomyth is the common narrative template found in most mythologies and in its simplest form involves a hero who is called to go on an adventure, undergoes a real or symbolic death and rebirth by facing a series of existential challenges, and comes back home transformed into a leader and healer of men, having transcended his previous human limitations.

Symbolism has not always been held in high esteem, however, especially in modern times.

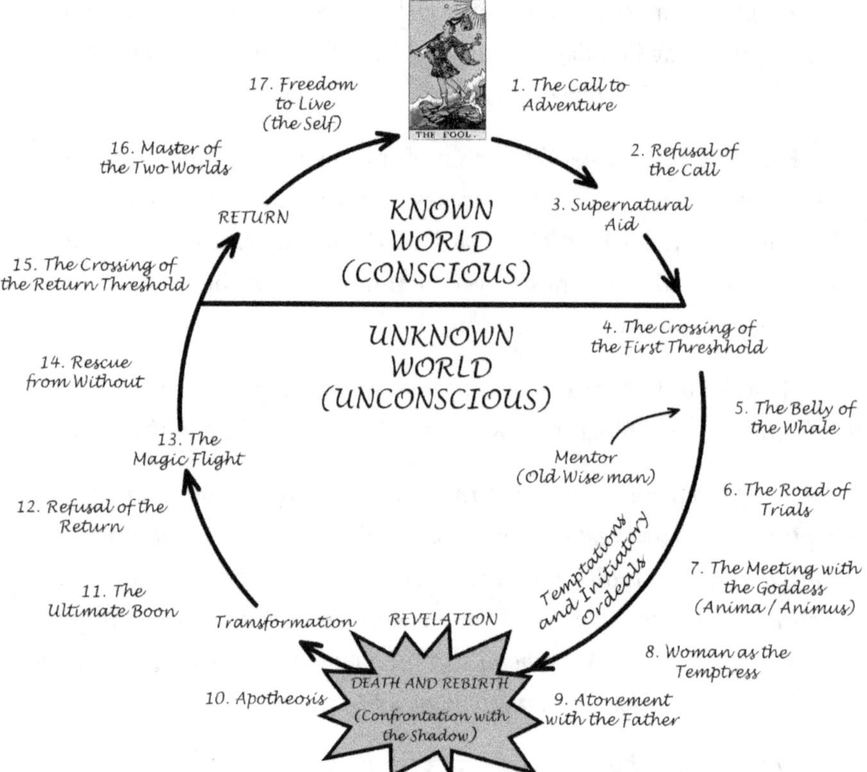

Figure 3. Diagram of the Hero´s Journey (or Monomyth) as viewed by Joseph Campbell. Numerous analogies with other esoteric systems of Self-Transcendence can be made. For example, with C.G Jung´s individuation process (in brackets: some of the principal Jungian archetypes); also with the Major Arcana of the Tarot and with the Magnum Opus of the Alchemists. In fact, Jung was heavily influenced by these initiatory and esoteric systems. Picture: anonymous (modified); Wikimedia Commons.

During the nineteenth century, it was mostly looked down and sent to the fringes of the acceptable. This was a time of constant and exciting scientific discoveries and technological inventions that greatly changed human life. Symbolism just seemed like a relic of a dark past that had not yet discovered Reason and the scientific mindset.

Nevertheless, the twentieth and twenty-first centuries, thanks to figures such as C.G. Jung and Joseph Campbell, saw a revival of interest in symbolic thought. This has culminated in today´s popular culture, which is oversaturated with it.

Most of us have been exposed to copious amounts of ancient symbolism since childhood. Be it via cartoons for children, fairy tales and folk literature, music videos, video games, comics or even public events like the Olympic Games´ opening ceremonies. Our current world is unmistakingly symbolic. Symbolism is now everywhere and it reaches farther than ever thanks to modern information technology. The only decision we can make regarding this fact is: do we want to actively learn more about those symbols to which we are unavoidably exposed to or do we prefer to passively consume them?

4. The Modern Dangers of Symbolism

Symbols present two main but opposite dangers: not taking them into consideration at all and overanalyzing them.

We have previously mentioned how mankind can suffer the consequences of completely removing the symbolic dimension from our life. Since symbols can not be erased, they are transferred to the unconscious layers of our minds. We will now speak of the other main danger, one particularly prominent in our times.

Symbols are demanding. They hide as well as reveal, each person obtaining a shallower or deeper understanding depending on their own capacity and previous knowledge. Because of that, it would be unwise to use them when the topic at hand can be discussed in a more straightforward manner, as symbols have also the potential to obscure.

Given this potential, there exists the danger of a dishonest use of symbolism. As previously mentioned, modern media is becoming increasingly symbolic. Nowadays, it seems that adding multiple layers of meaning to a work of art adds a certain aura of prestige, refinement, and depth to it. But we should also be weary of symbolism used in a pretentious and overcomplicated way, not looking to enlighten us but just at providing an appearance of depth that is not really there.

In a traditional world, symbols were only used to guide us. Today, they can be misused as a mere game. It may be entertaining to have to play a detective game to try to understand the possible meaning of what is shown, but if the real depth and meaning was not there from the beginning, it will be a waste of time. Modern films and TV shows are especially notorious for this pedantic use of symbolism.

This is another of the differences between modern times and traditional ones. This age is one of smoke and mirrors, where the truth is not easy to find and sometimes not even looked for.

Recommended Reading

1. **Fundamental Symbols. The Universal Language of Sacred Science.** *René Guénon.*
2. **Images and Symbols: Studies in Religious Symbolism.** *Mircea Eliade.*
3. **The Hero with a Thousand Faces.** *Joseph Campbell.*
4. **A Dictionary of Symbols.** *Juan Eduardo Cirlot [reference work].*

Ubiquitous Symbolism:
Are We Aware of its Meaning?

The Prominence of Symbolism in Modern Mass Media

Explanations Regarding its Use and Prevalence

5. Symbols in Contemporary Culture

NOW THAT WE HAVE SEEN HOW SYMBOLS WERE traditionally understood, we may wonder why are there so many of them in popular culture.

Why are your favorite movies filled with ancient symbols? And why are the same symbolic patterns and narrative templates used over and over at the expense of originality (and therefore, probably, of higher profits)?

Why do giant media conglomerates want to make us acquainted with ancient metaphysical teachings and the symbols that transmit them?

Are the multinational investment companies that at least partially own them (e.g., BlackRock, Vanguard[1]) suddenly interested in us having a rich and healthy spiritual life? Why would that be so?

A few explanations have been given in the past. What follows is a summary of the most prevalent. Each of us will have to ultimately decide, based on the available evidence, if for us the explanations below are worth believing in or not.

Do you believe in any or all of them? Are they exclusive or complementary? Are some of them a conspiracy theory or just an actual conspiracy? Do you totally or partially believe in them? Or maybe you just believe everything to be a coincidence without further meaning? Whatever the case, let´s briefly learn about them as a first step in discovering our own opinion on the matter at hand.

6. Possible Explanations for the High Volume and Consistency of Symbolic Content in Popular Culture

There exist a few theories that try to explain why popular culture is nowadays so full of symbolic content. Some of these theories are focused on symbols as transmitters of metaphysical and religious concepts. Others are centered around psychology, sociology, and how unconscious symbolic absorption can accelerate societal changes in one direction or another.

---

1. *"[...] It should be no surprise that Netflix, Microsoft, Comcast, Meta, Alphabet (Google), Amazon, Fox, Disney, Lionsgate, Roku, Paramount, AMC Networks, Warner Bros. Discovery, Nexstar and Live Nation all count Vanguard and BlackRock among their 2022 13G filers."*

— Variety.com (8 March 2023). Who Owns What? Top Investors Shuffle Their Securities Holdings in the Media and Entertainment Sector.

The same theory may be too far fetched for some persons while making complete sense for others. Our mission here is only to provide some knowledge and discussion, as well as to raise some relevant questions. It will correspond to each individual to discover and solidify their own position on these matters.

a. Popular Culture is an Oligopoly: Or How Only a Few Companies Own All the Media

The definition of an oligopoly is a situation in which a small number of organizations or companies has control over an area of business so that others have no share. Oligopolistic markets have homogenous products and few market participants, as no new players can enter the scene.

Ben Bagdikian[2] published the first edition of his book called *The New Media Monopoly* in 1983. Back then, he was called an alarmist regarding his warnings about the decreasing number of owners of mass media companies. Forty years have passed, and the book has reached its twentieth edition. Also, the number of corporations controlling most of America's media (newspapers, magazines, radio and television stations, book publishers, and movie companies) has been reduced from fifty to five, according to the most recent edition of the book.

This may not explain *why* symbolism is so prevalent in modern media, but it surely is a necessary step for the interest of a few to dominate the cultural landscape in an efficient and homogeneous way.

————————————

2. *"The American audience, having been exposed to a narrowing range of ideas over the decades, often assumes that what they see and hear in the major media is all there is. It is no way to maintain a lively marketplace of ideas, which is to say it is no way to maintain a democracy."*

[...] "The safest way to ensure diversity of opinion is diverse ownership."

— Bagdikian, Ben (1987). "The 50, 26, 20 . . . corporations that own our Media."

b. Psychological Manipulation

The previous section can, by itself, explain the homogeneity and regularity found in the symbolic patterns present in popular culture. The following theories, in contrast, try to explain the motives behind this.

They range from the psychological to the political or even the ritualistic. They have in common that they believe that symbolism is being used to reinforce subtle psychological manipulation techniques in order to steer society and human beliefs in a pre-determined direction. Obviously, without the knowledge or consent of the public being targeted by them.

b1. Predictive Programming

Predictive programming can be defined as a psychological conditioning technique in which the notions of already pre-planned societal changes that have yet to pass, most of them drastic, are implanted by the media in the mind of the public. If these are later put through, public resistance may be lessened due to the familiarity of the public with what they are facing. Even if unconsciously, the changes already implanted in seed form in the mind of the masses are seen as pertaining to the realm of the possible. Common examples include *The Simpsons´* frequently accurate future predictions or a 2016 episode of the *Legends of Chamberlain Heights* cartoon, where Kobe Bryant´s death in a helicopter crash seems to have been predicted four years prior to it really happening.

b2. Negative Priming

Negative priming is a concept that originally comes from the field of psychology. It can be defined as the creation of an implicit memory effect in which prior exposure to a stimulus unfavorably influences the response to the same stimulus afterwards.

It has been proposed that this well known psychological effect could be used to subtly condition unsuspecting spectators in order to generate aversion for specific ideas. It could be done by presenting a truth, but with the intention of leading the viewers to intentionally reject it through the way it is presented to them (e.g., in a horror movie context). Our unconscious association between this truth and a work of fiction could also play a role in undermining the value we assign to the core idea being targeted.

Symbols that represent a certain worldview could be used with this purpose in mind (e.g., a cross or some other symbol representative of a particular religion or belief).

b3. Subliminal Implantation

The use of subliminal imagery is nothing new. For example, the horror film *The Exorcist* effectively used subliminal images throughout the film, showing a demonic entity named Captain Howdy/Pazuzu in order to create an automatic and unconscious emotional response, thus increasing the fear caused by the movie.

The main idea behind it is that our brain can perceive and process the information presented to it even if it is shown for a period of time so short that our conscious mind cannot.

These unconscious manipulation techniques have also been associated with modern theories of magic (or magick), where the ritualistic implantation of seed ideas in the unconscious mind of the practitioner has a special power to make them become real.

According to some of these modern subjectivist worldviews (e.g., Chaos Magic), movies could be used as a forced mass ritual where certain notions would be implanted in the unconscious mind of a large number of unsuspecting viewers, thus bringing closer their manifestation in reality. Symbols could then be used as "instruments of power", due to their special connection with certain fundamental metaphysical truths.

Two ideas are especially important regarding this modern magical worldview. They are the following:

1. *For the unconscious mind there are no false notions.* If an idea has been implanted in the unconscious it is processed as existent and therefore as true, regardless of its real truth value, because it has already been able to create a memory.

2. *Reality is the manifestation of the consensus beliefs of the minds of the masses.* This implies that the manipulation of this consensus is able to change reality itself, with this being most effectively accomplished via the unconscious mind.

c. Social Engineering and the Overton Window

The Overton window is a political theory. It states that there exists a spectrum of acceptability of governmental policies and that politicians can act only within this acceptable range. However, the shifting of this acceptable range (the Overton window itself) is possible by persuading the public to expand it.

According to this theory, some ideas and practices that are viewed as completely unacceptable at a certain point in time can end up, not only being accepted, but actually being enforced and protected by laws and governmental policies. Some people fear worrying trends in mass media may imply that this technique is being slowly but purposefully used to make us tolerant to things now considered unacceptable.

d. Cultural Subversion and Demoralization

Yuri Bezmenov was a journalist and a former KGB informant. He is famous for having revealed the communist programme to take over a culture via psychological subversion, without the need of waging an actual physical war. This plan, he explained, included demoralization as one of the key steps needed for cultural take over.[3]

Some people think that symbolism may be purposefully being used as a form of mockery or taunting.[4] The final aim of this would be the demoralization of society in general and of the most vigilant persons of a given population in particular. This would crush them psychologically before any effective resistance could be formed.

e. Initiation

The last, but for us one of the most interesting of the proposed theories, is that we are being initiated. Or, at least, being prepared for a future initiation while laying the doctrinal building blocks that will be needed.

Mircea Eliade, the great historian of religions, defines initiation as:[5]

"[...] a body of rites and oral teachings whose purpose is to produce a decisive alteration in the religious and social status of the person to be initiated. In philosophical terms, initiation is equivalent to a basic change in existential condition; the novice emerges from his ordeal endowed with a totally different being from that which he possessed before his initiation; he has become another."

---

3. *"[...] Exposure to true information does not matter anymore. A person who is demoralized is unable to assess true information. The facts tell him nothing, even if I shower him with information, with authentic proof, with documents and pictures... he will refuse to believe it... That's the tragedy of the situation of demoralization."*

— Bezmenov, Yuri (1983). Interview, as quoted in "38 years ago, a KGB defector chillingly predicted modern America" (18 July, 2018); Big Think.

4. *See, for example: www.theguardian.com/politics/shortcuts/2022/oct/05/ dictator-chic-why-did-liz-truss-wear-the-same-outfit-as-a-fictional-fascist*

5. *Eliade, Mircea (1958). Rites and Symbols of Initiation. Harper Collins Publishers, p. X.*

Regarding the ultimate purpose of any initiation, he further explains:

"Initiation introduces the candidate into the human community and into the world of spiritual and cultural values. He learns not only the behavior patterns, the techniques, and the institutions of adults but also the sacred myths and traditions of the tribe, the names of the gods and the history of their works; above all, he learns the mystical relations between the tribe and the Supernatural Beings as those relations were established at the beginning of Time. Every primitive society possesses a consistent body of mythical traditions, a "conception of the world"; and it is this conception that is gradually revealed to the novice in the course of his initiation."

In this view, modern media would be using ancient metaphysical symbols and fictional psychodramas that follow initiatory narrative templates in order to prepare us and to make us acquainted with certain ancient metaphysical concepts.

This, in turn, would be the preliminary preparation needed for the future acceptance of a new or revived worldview by a higher percentage of the population.

As we have previously mentioned, the basic Monomyth template is already widely used in science fiction movies. As Eliade explains, this is also the basic template that any initiation follows:

"The majority of initiatory ordeals more or less clearly imply a ritual death followed by resurrection or a new birth. The central moment of every initiation is represented by the ceremony symbolizing the death of the novice and his return to the fellowship of the living. But he returns to life a new man, assuming another mode of being. Initiatory death signifies the end at once of childhood, of ignorance, and of the profane condition."

— Mircea Eliade (1958). Rites and Symbols of Initiation. Introduction.

7. Conclusion

Whatever our position may be regarding the different possible explanations discussed above regarding the consistent and recurrent use of symbolism in popular culture, the facts remain the same:

1. The symbolism and narrative templates currently employed in movie making and other media are ancient, and they contain metaphysical teachings regarding how reality ultimately works. These notions and beliefs are compatible with some worldviews, but not with others.

2. Their consistency and frequency implies centralized coordination, which is made possible by the consolidation of media ownership in a few hands.

Can it be just a fancy fad? A pretentious way of adding a false layer of depth into modern culture? In that case, it would be arguably better to use a more varied range of narratives in order to provide the public with a sense of novelty and variety. Instead, massive blockbusters prefer to face criticism and probably see profit reduced for rehashing already familiar stories.

Is this just because the top players in the industry are running short on creativity? It seems doubtful. After all, they have whole mythological pantheons and stories to choose from, as well as highly talented people working for them.

If profit is not the most important consideration in these cases, then delivering a specific message must be. So, what are the most common messages being delivered? What do the symbols tell us? What is the fruit of this informal symbolic teaching, if any, in our life and in our interpretation of reality?

Recommended Reading

1. **Perspectives on Initiation.** *René Guénon.*
2. **Initiation and Spiritual Realization.** *René Guénon.*
3. **Rites and Symbols of Initiation: The Mysteries of Birth and Rebirth.** *Mircea Eliade.*

All from One:

Do We Know the Implications of Prominent Metaphysical Beliefs?

Metaphysics: The Meaning Behind the Symbolism

What Symbols Teach Us Regarding Ultimate Truths

1. What is Metaphysics?

WE HAVE SEEN THAT SYMBOLS HAVE BEEN traditionally used for the transmission of metaphysical and religious concepts and doctrines. But, what exactly is metaphysics?

It can be defined as the discipline concerned with understanding the fundamental nature and structure of reality. It studies what lies beyond physics, the ultimate principles of existence itself.

Metaphysics (*what is the nature of reality?*) is one of the main branches of philosophy. It is usually classified as part of the "big four", which also includes epistemology (*how can we obtain knowledge in a rationally justified way?*), logic (*is our reasoning sound?*), and ethics (*based on our premises and beliefs, what is right and wrong behavior?*).

2. What Does Traditional Metaphysics Talk About?

Metaphysics addresses subjects such as: the nature of reality, existence, and being; identity; space, time, and change; cause and effect, necessity, and possibility; the nature of consciousness and the relationship between mind and matter. Therefore, the common objective and basic structure of tradition<xal metaphysical symbolic initiations includes the transmission of knowledge regarding:

- *Ultimate reality.* Is the highest metaphysical truth the existence of an underlying unity in the form of God, multiple gods, or an impersonal Principle, Law or Force? Maybe atoms and matter is all there is?

- *The structure of existence and Being itself.* Questions answered include: What is the nature of being? What are we in relation to God or the First Principle? How does time work? How did all that exists come to be?

- *The nature of evil.* Does evil exist? If so, why? What is its nature? Why and how did this plane of existence come to be perceived as having fallen from a superior state?

- *The amount of agency that we have in deciding our ultimate destiny.* How much are we conditioned by external influences? For example, is there a Fate that will determine our path in life or can our internal free will prevail over external circumstances? Are we the product of an unavoidable law of causality (causal determinism, e.g., karmic bonds) or can we overcome the consequences of our past actions?

- *What our ultimate aspiration and path in life should be.* Can we transcend our current limitations? How should we behave in order to get closer, or eventually go back, to God or to the One (the Source or Absolute)? Is it possible for us to achieve salvation or liberation? What are these states of being like?

a. The Problem of the Universal and the Particular: Different Approaches

Metaphysics differentiates between abstract and concrete, as well as between universal and particular, entities. This is best seen with an example:

- *Abstract universal:* greenness.

- *Concrete particular:* a green apple.

- *Abstract particular:* individual numbers, which are neither concrete objects nor universals, being particular entities which do not themselves occur inside time or space.

- *Concrete Universal:* notion crucial to Christian theology and also to G.W.F. Hegel´s school of Absolute Idealism. In short, a concrete universal is something that connects everything together, which the absolute idealists identified as the Absolute (an all-inclusive Mind). Christian theology, in contrast, emphasizes its Tri-Une God (and its incarnation in Jesus Christ) as the true concrete universal that solves the problem of unity (universality) and multiplicity (concreteness).

Regarding the Absolute, Christian theologians such as Cornelius Van Til argued that it presents problems that from a non-Christian starting point of view (axioms and presuppositions) are unsolvable.

For example, the Absolute, when viewed as a monadic unifying element, appears to swallow its source of plurality, our world ruled by chance. In addition, the existence of the latter seems to undermine the "absoluteness" of the Absolute (being its necessary counterpart which actualizes the former's potentiality).

In Christianity, Van Til emphasized, both unity and plurality are seen as equally fundamental[1], God Himself (the Trinity) being the underlying harmony between them. With creation having been modeled after its Creator, this is believed to be reflected in our world, too.

a1. The Possibility of Knowledge

The very possibility of us having knowledge, in fact, depends on the co-primacy of unity and multiplicity. This is so because, if only the plurality of the particular has primacy, we end up with unrelated entities of which nothing can be known in principle, as they become abstract particulars with nothing in common, a world unto themselves.

Furthermore, if absolute primacy is given instead to the unity of the universal, we have the same problem. Abstracting things into universal categories leads to them losing part of what makes them unique. If we aim for absolute abstract unity, we will obtain complete homogeneity instead. The loss of the particular means the loss of everything that makes each thing (or being, e.g., a person) what (or who) it is. This also makes knowledge impossible, since knowledge implies the existence of differentiated entities, contrary to absolute sameness (e.g., it is not possible to think about "personhood" without thinking about a specific person).

Either way we end up being unable to make any distinction between particulars so, again, nothing can be known in principle. What appeared to be two opposing positions turned out to be two sides of the same coin.

––––––––––––––––––

1. *Van Til, Cornelius (1955). The Defense of the Faith. P&R Publishing, p. 25-26.*

Therefore, even in our world, in order to be able to know anything, our reality must be such that its unity and plurality are related yet there is difference.[2]

If this is true for our plane of existence, it is to be expected that it is also true for the higher reality that gave birth to it, as a superior reality cannot have additional limitations compared to a lower one.

Christian apologists defend that, for the Tri-Une God, this is accomplished at all levels: in our reality (as we have mentioned through the previous example regarding knowledge), in the Godhead (the Trinity), and in Jesus Christ, the incarnation of the Logos and recapitulation of all that exists, who Himself is seen as the greatest possible symbol (icon) of the unity of the universal and the particular.

2.1. On God and Ultimate Reality: The Problem of the One and the Many

One of the main functions of traditional symbolism is to disclose who or what God or the highest Principle of our reality is believed to be.

This, in turn, depends on the solution we give to what became known as the problem of *the One and the Many,* or the tension between unity and multiplicity, the universal and the particular. The One understood, not as a numerical and mathematical concept, but as ultimate reality, the underlying Unity behind the apparent multiplicity of our world (for example: God, the Absolute or pure Being). By contrast, *the Many* refers to all particular objects or beings.

---

2. *Dialectics is the contrary belief that states that we should decide between one horn or the other of any specific dilemma. Its underlying presupposition is that difference means the same as contradiction or opposition, with one option always being better than the rest. It excludes the possibility of the existence of many equally good options. If something is good, everything else is bad by virtue of being different.*

THE PROBLEM OF AUTHORITY

What is the source of metaphysical knowledge?

This type of knowledge may be viewed as a revelation from God or the gods (for example, via the incarnation of God Himself, avatars or prophets) or as the hard-won collective experience of man, obtained through spiritual exercises, ritualistic endeavours or mere human reasoning. These experiences may be obtained with or without the help of psychoactive substances, understood as a way to shatter the barrier between the different planes of existence.

Further distinctions can be made between worldviews that conceptualize the One as a transcendent entity (eg., monotheistic religions), and the ones that view it as the immanent sum of all the different parts that constitute reality (e.g., Pantheism).

Common questions that underlie this metaphysical problem include: why do we perceive unifying categories in nature (e.g., the "treeness" in all different species of trees) instead of different objects with a vaguely similar collection of characteristics? Is this unity based on categories present in the very structure of our reality (Universals) or only in the human mind? If they exist, what is the origin of these categories?

Why do we experience our consciousness as a continuous self-awareness, a unity, from cradle to grave? Especially given that we go through states of being that are completely different from each other (e.g., infant and adult). Even the components that form our body, the cells, are replaced in time without our perceived unity being affected in the slightest (the Ship of Theseus paradox).

How are different sensorial stimulus integrated into a single consciousness (Unity of Consciousness problem) and why can some people experience one sensory modality as another (Synesthesia)? Does this not speak of an underlying unity?

What is the origin, then, of this underlying unity and stability that we perceive in our reality even though our Universe is one of constant flux and change?

Ancient philosophy begins with this question, which dominated both Eastern and Western thought throughout time. As we shall see later in *Chapter III*, both major religions and philosophical schools defined themselves primarily by the position they took in this matter. For, example, different schools of Hinduism were named for their emphasis in either unity, plurality or their interrelatedness, while Buddhism emphasized a different type of non-dual co-primacy, and Christianity found in its Tri-Une God the answer to this dilemma. In short, this question seems to be the most deeply rooted metaphysical concern of man across the ages.

It even plays a decisive influence in modern physics, with its metaphysical push for finding a unique "Theory of Everything". This theory, if found, would unify in mathematical language all the basic forces of the Universe. It would be like an intellectual return to the One. But why should there be a single unified theory? There is no scientific reason for reality to necessarily work this way.

We could say that we are hardwired to think about this metaphysical problem. It is a common "metaphysical human instinct". Even modern science cannot explain mankind´s need to find a solution to it. In fact, it does not make sense to have evolved this recurrent "hardwired metaphysical concern" in a Darwinist evolutionary context.

Why would humanity obsess over an abstract concept that does not increase its chances of survival? In fact, it can reduce them, as men have been willing to lose their life instead of abandoning their deeply felt position on this issue (e.g., martyrs). Why would men in every corner of the world and throughout history organize their life around a concept that does not increase their "fitness" level to their particular environment, using a Darwinist term?

Regarding these matters, science cannot help us. The scientific method, by definition, cannot provide the answer to any metaphysical concern, while modern Scientism can only explain them away.

2.1.1. The Consequences of Our Presuppositions Regarding the Problem of the One and the Many

This seems like an abstract problem detached from everyday life. However, as we will see, the presuppositions we hold regarding the dilemma between *the One and the Many* will determine to a great extent which kind of life we will lead, even if we are not aware of them.[3]

Let´s see a paradigmatic example: do we find the core meaning and value of a particular being to be in its own individuality and idiosyncratic characteristics? Or do we find it in its participation on a basic unified structure? (e.g., a family, a culture, a nation, a religion).

This dilemma is the main question we can ask ourselves, as well as the one on which every other one depends. The solution given to it serves as the foundation upon which all other metaphysical beliefs that constitute a certain worldview are based on.

----

3. *"The question which haunts the dialectical culture is this: how to have unity without totally undifferentiated and meaningless oneness? If all things are basically one, the differences are meaningless, divisions false, and definitions are sophistications, in that the tyranny, or destiny, of oneness is the truth of all being.*

But, if all things are basically many, and if plurality is ultimate, then the world dissolves into unrelated particulars and becomes, as some thinkers insist, not a universe but a multiverse, and every atom is in a sense its own law and being.

The first leads to the breakdown of differences and the liberty of atomistic individualism and particularity; the second is the breakdown of fundamental law into nihilism and the retreat of men and their arts into isolated and private universes."

– Rushdoony, R.J. (1971). The One and the Many: Studies in the Philosophy of Order and Ultimacy. Chalcedon/Ross House Books, Chapter 2: The Ground of Liberty; Introduction.

a. An Example: Realism and Nominalism

For instance, in worldviews that favor the Many and the value of individuals over an underlying unity, a nominalist position may be more easily held.

Nominalism is the metaphysical view that Universals and abstract objects do not actually exist other than as names or labels arbitrarily created and assigned by human ingenuity.

In views that embrace Nominalism, any unifying reality or concept such as God or the state might be seen as oppressive and limiting to each individual´s intrinsic value and desires.

The moral action in these worldviews would be to break free from the perceived tyrant and the radical affirmation of the individual, whatever he might be or represent. A nominalist belief underlies many modern worldviews, including Materialism, Empiricism, and Anarchism.

If the value of oneness is emphasized over that of particulars, however, one may be much more inclined to embrace a realist position. According to Realism, Universals exist, and they give form to particular aspects of reality. Most traditional worldviews share this belief (e.g., Platonic Realism), with Universals usually being seen as aspects of the One or the highest reality.

2.1.2. Historical Answers Provided to the Question of the One and the Many

The knowledge transmitted by the various worldviews on this topic is usually related to the concept of number. Are there many gods (Polytheism) or does only an absolute God exist (Monotheism, as for example in Abrahamic religions)?

a. Answers Based on Prioritizing the Many Over the One (or Metaphysical Pluralism)

This is the view that ultimate reality is made of a variety of irreducible entities, gods, laws or principles.

Usually, the existence of many different gods is believed. This can be seen, for instance, in Shamanism and many ancient mythological pantheons (e.g., the Babylonian, Mesopotamian, Greek, Roman, and Norse ones; in Japanese Shintō and other animistic worldviews).

Gods tend to be perceived as flawed and similar to human beings, but their good will can be propitiated. They can also be conceived as archetypes or particular aspects of reality. For example, Athena is seen as the goddess of practical reason (also of war and handicraft).

Recurrent symbols of Plurality: each god may have their own particular symbols. For example: Mjölnir pendants are symbols of the god of thunder Thor; the owl, the ever vigilant nocturnal animal that can see in the darkness, is in turn used as one of Athena´s primary symbols.

b. Dualistic Worldviews (or Metaphysical Dualism)

A particular case of the belief in ultimate multiplicity, where reality is composed of two primordial aspects or essences. Dualism can be either absolute or relative. In the first form, the two principles are held to exist from eternity. In the second, one of the two principles may presuppose or derive from the other. They can also be classified as antagonistic dualities involving opposites or as complementary ones.

b1. Involving Opposites and Conflict

This is when ultimate reality is believed to be composed of two Principles in conflict with each other. This conflict is usually presented in moral terms, such as the battle between good and evil (e.g., Zoroastrianism, Manichaeism). These powers may be seen as equals and in balance.

Many classic mythologies speak of two primordial beings (e.g., the battle of Marduk and Tiamat in the Babylonian creation myth; Indra´s battle with the demonic serpent Vritra in the Rig Veda). The antagonists are related to Chaos, night, emptiness, primordial energy, matter, pure possibility. They are usually depicted as dragons, serpents or demonic entities. The heroes, on the other hand, are usually represented by a sky or lightning god who subdues Chaos and thus becomes capable of bringing creation into being. This hero transforms pure potentiality into actuality.

Another possible way of classifying these types of dualistic views is by differentiating between dialectical and eschatological Dualism. The first involves an eternal tension between the two opposed Principles. It is usually associated with a cyclical view of time. Eschatological Dualism, in contrast, believes in a final resolution of the conflict at the end of time, with evil disappearing and history having a beginning and an end.

b2. Involving Complementarity

Where two Forces or Principles are believed to be the origin of all aspects of reality. They are the two halves of the same coin, whose interplay of forces brings everything into existence. Common examples are Mind and Matter or Spirit and Form (e.g., in Platonism, Descartes´ Mind-Body Dualism, and Sāṃkhya school of Indian philosophy).

Recurrent symbols of Duality: a circle made of black and white halves. It should be noted that the Yin and Yang symbol can be wrongly used for representing duality because, in Chinese non-dualist thought, Yin and Yang are both said to proceed from the Great Ultimate, Taiji.

c. Answers Based on Prioritizing the One Over the Many (or Metaphysical Monism)

The view that ultimate reality can be reduced to a single substance or essence and the appearance of plurality or multiplicity is only an illusion or a temporal situation that happened after a catastrophic event.

c1. Religious or Theistic Variations

Includes worldviews where a Supreme Being is believed to be the origin and end of all there is. God can be conceived in various ways. In theistic versions of the One, God is personal (such as in Islam and certain Hindu sects).

Depending on the worldview at hand, God can be involved with His creation or detached from it, being a God who does not intervene in the Universe after creating it (e.g. Deism).

God can be conceived as transcending His creation (e.g., monotheistic religions), but may also be conceptualized as an immanent "deity" identical with the totality of the Universe (Pantheism, which most would define, however, as primarily atheistic) or as being the totality composed of ultimate reality **plus** the whole of creation derived from It (theistic Panentheism).

c2. Non-Religious or Atheistic Variations

Where reality can be reduced to only one aspect other than God. This aspect can be material (e.g., primordial matter, atoms, a particular element such as fire or Aether) or immaterial, with the latter exemplified in positions such as "everything is mind, consciousness or soul" (e.g., Panpsychism, Animism).

Ultimate reality may also be seen as an impersonal Force or Principle (e.g., Chaos in older mythologies, the One in Neo-Platonism, Nirvana or Emptiness in Buddhism, and in most versions of Pantheism/Panentheism).

Recurrent symbols of Unity: the Sun and the circled dot.

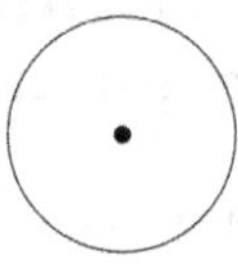

Figure 1. The circled dot symbolized the Monad or the Absolute for the Pythagoreans and later traditions.

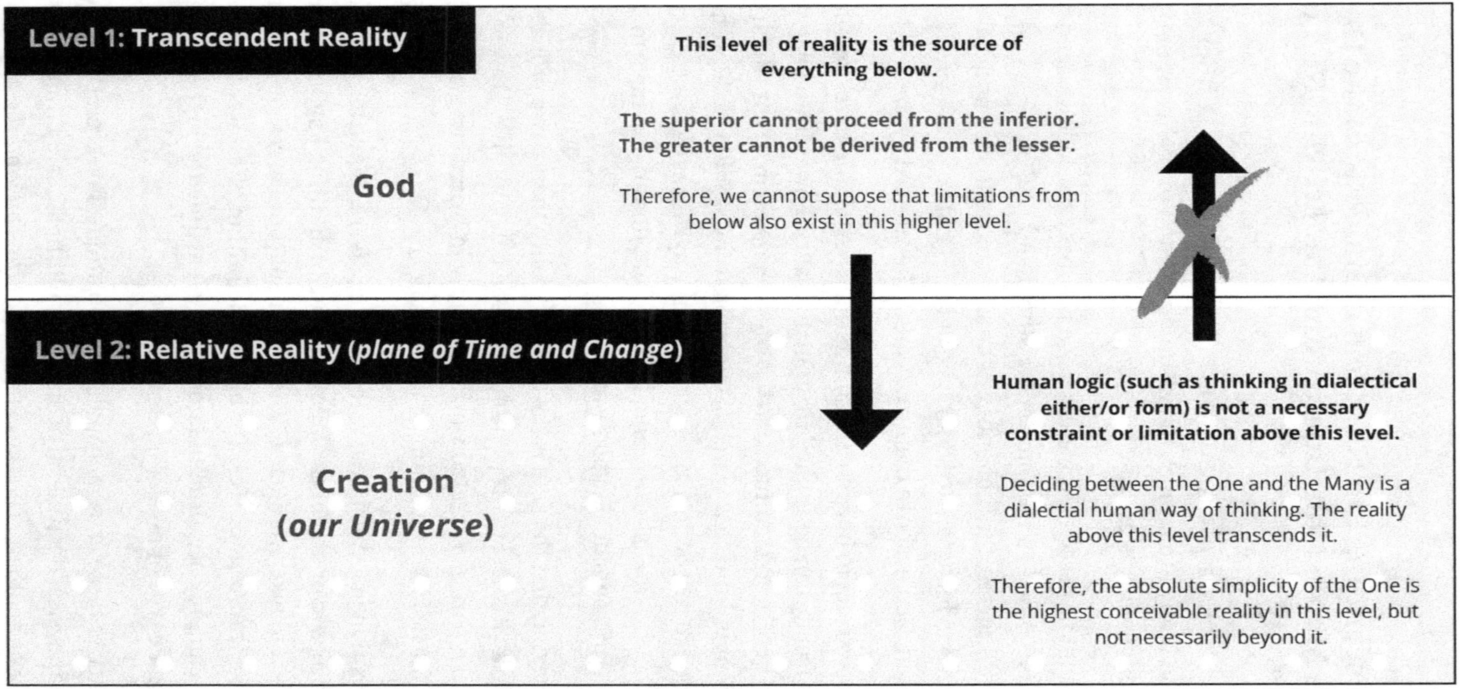

Figure 2. Diagram of how different levels of reality can interact with each other. The superior level is the ground and basis of existence of the inferior ones. The latter cannot condition or influence the former. To use a symbolic image we could say that water cannot rise higher than its source.

d. Transcending the Numerical Dialectic of the One and the Many: Non-Duality and the Tri-Une God of Christianity

The above mentioned solutions are dialectical in nature. **Either** the One **or** the Many are seen as the ultimate ground of reality. If one is true, the other will necessarily be wrong.

The solutions based on the Many have relatively few followers today. The solutions based on the One, on the other hand, still place on God or the highest Principle the limitations of human concepts such as number and the need to follow a particular type of logic (Either/Or) even when, by definition, God is above them and cannot be affected by them.

It seems wrong to imagine that limitations pertaining to the human reasoning faculty can be applied to ultimate reality, however we imagine Him/It to be. He created them, so He transcends them. That which is inferior cannot bind that which is superior. Why would the Supreme Reality need to reason in a created (human) way? Either/Or logic may be true in a now dualistic or "fallen" world, but, does it also have to be the whole truth outside this plane of existence?

By believing that the One is the highest reality there is we probably believe in the highest concept human reason can conceive. However, man is still a part of a created world currently in a dualistic state and, therefore, he is under the limits of its dialectical logic.

The position just discussed, without being aware, is putting its faith in human reason on top of the hierarchy by not allowing anything that transcends it to take precedence. The immanent (human reason) is then defining the transcendent (God) when, by definition, the lower levels of existence can only acquire full knowledge regarding the highest level through some type of revelation from above.

Contrary to these extremely polarized positions, however, there are other metaphysical doctrines that state that ultimate reality transcends, in one way or another, even the categories of *the One and the Many.*

Metaphysics: Solutions to the Problem of the One and the Many in the Godhead

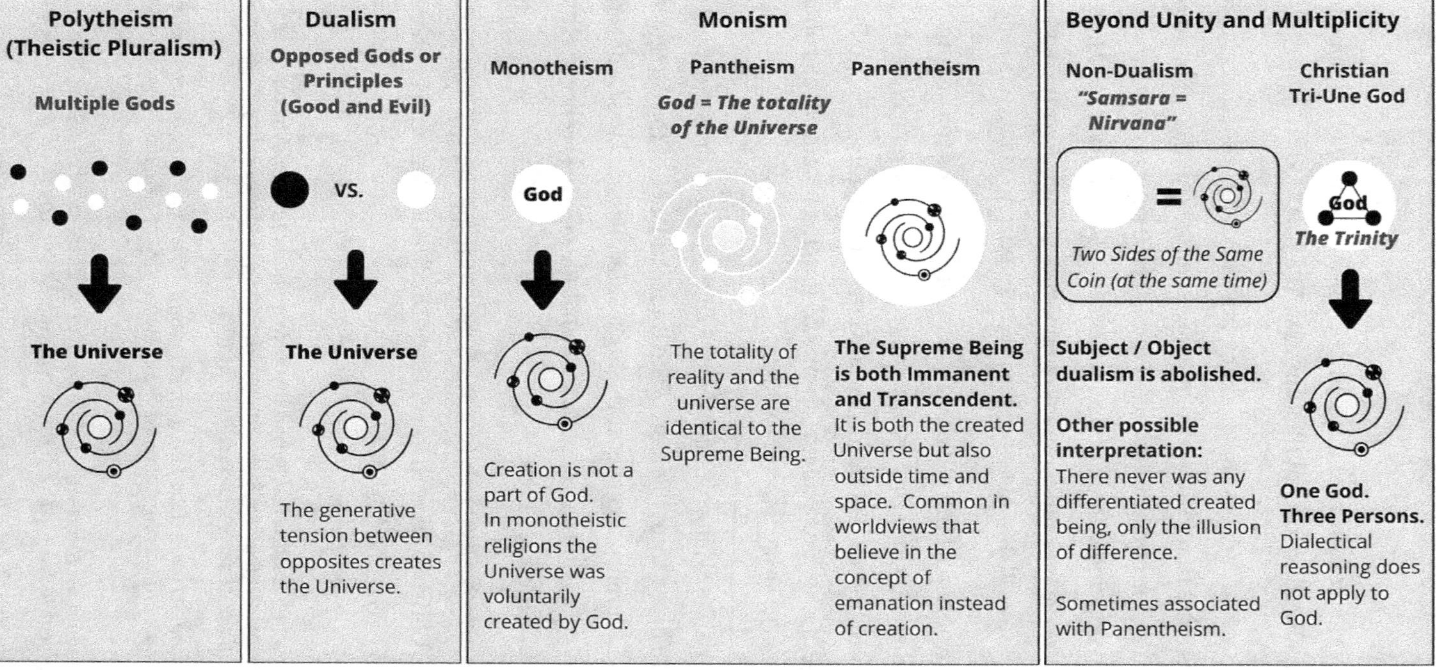

Figure 3. The most common historically proposed solutions to the dialectical problem of the One and the Many. The standard pluralistic, dualistic, and monistic solutions do not transcend this dialectical way of thinking. Non-Dualism might or might not depending on the interpretation, as it is sometimes classified as a type of Panentheism.

These are the Far Eastern concept of Non-Dualism (e.g., Mahāyāna or Vajrayāna Buddhism) and the Christian Tri-Une God.

There are differences among them, however. Non-dual consciousness teachings state that *"Saṃsāra equals Nirvana"*[4], which can be roughly translated as *"this apparently fallen world is the same as ultimate reality once correctly understood and experienced"*. *The One and the Many* are thus *"transcended"*, but in an immanent way. This is done by including this *"fallen"* world into Absolute Reality, but understood in a different way.

The problem of *the One and the Many* remains for persons who achieve liberation, however: at any single point in time enlightened people may **either** freely roam the different states of being that this reality has to offer (Plurality), **or** remain "absorbed" into the homogeneous oneness of the One (Unity).

In Christianity, in contrast, the Tri-Une God is at the same time One God and Three (Many) Persons. The transcendence of the categories of Unity and Plurality happens at the highest level, that of the Godhead. As a consequence, God does not need to include created reality in Himself in order to transcend them.

In addition, saved persons are believed to be deified (especially in Orthodox Christianity, with its concept of deification) instead of liberated, with God becoming *"All in all"*.[5]

---

4. *"Nothing of Samsara is different from Nirvana, nothing of Nirvana is different from Samsara. That which is the limit of Nirvana is also the limit of Samsara, there is not the slightest difference between the two."*

— *Nāgārjuna, as quoted in: Loy, David (1983). "The difference between samsara and nirvana". Philosophy East and West. University of Hawai'i Press, p. 355.*

5. *"Now when all things are made subject to Him, then the Son Himself will also be subject to Him who put all things under Him, that God may be all in all."*

— *1 Corinthians, 15:28. The Holy Bible. New King James Version.*

The problem of *the One and the Many*, then, is transcended at all levels, with all saved beings also partaking of this transcendence. Neither individuality nor oneness are sacrificed.

The Godhead, in non-dual solutions, remains an absolutely simple unity that can be experienced in multiple ways through the created world once the distinction between subject and object, creator and created is found to be an illusion. Everything created is a particular mode of existence of the Only Existent.

In Christianity, however, the Godhead is Tri-Une in itself. The difference between Creator and created is not abolished, but the created is elevated to the stature of the Creator, who loves them in their individuality and difference.

Non-dual teachings are sometimes understood as panentheistic.[6] This is not the case for the Christian God.

Symbols of Non-Dualism: Sri Yantra, mandalas, the Taiji in Taoism (as the generating principle behind everything), the Om syllabe and A letter in Hinduism and Dzogchen Buddhism, respectively.

---

6. *"At the outset, let me state that Buddhism is not atheistic as the term is ordinarily understood. It has certainly a God, the highest reality and truth, through which and in which this universe exists. However, the followers of Buddhism usually avoid the term God, for it savors so much of Christianity, whose spirit is not always exactly in accord with the Buddhist interpretation of religious experience.*

Again, Buddhism is not pantheistic in the sense that it identifies the universe with God. On the other hand, the Buddhist God is absolute and transcendent; this world, being merely its manifestation, is necessarily fragmental and imperfect.

To define more exactly the Buddhist notion of the highest being, it may be convenient to borrow the term very happily coined by a modern German scholar, "panentheism," according to which God is πᾶν καὶ ἕν (all and one) and more than the totality of existence."

— Shaku, Soyen (Reverend Zen Master) (1906). Zen For Americans. The God-Conception Of Buddhism, p. 26.

Symbols of the Christian Tri-Une God: the Shield of the Trinity, Borromean rings, Celtic Trinity knot.

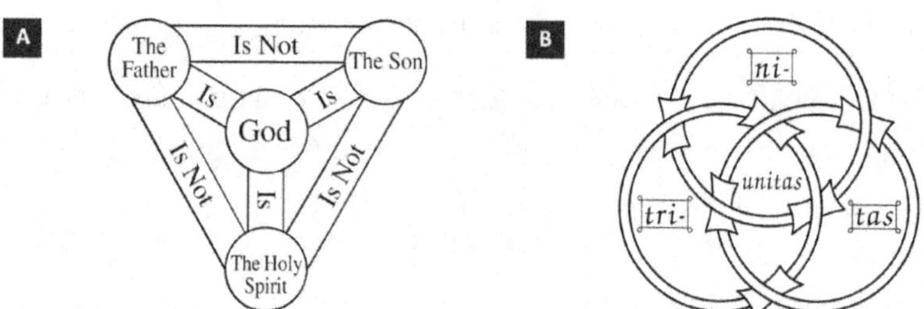

*Figure 4. **A:** the Shield of the Trinity or the Shield of Faith. **B:** Borromean rings (origin: Italian Borromeo family), used in the Middle Ages to represent the Trinity, although the symbol itself had been previously used by the Nordic and Germanic cultures.*

2.2. On the Structure of Reality, Being and Time

As we have seen, the solution offered by each worldview to the problem of *the One and the Many* is a central concern of symbolic initiations. However, it is not the only metaphysical subject that these initiations try to reveal. In the following sections we will briefly discuss the main metaphysical doctrines and concepts being taught to the initiate.

To begin with, let´s remark that traditional initiations focus on explaining not only who or what God or ultimate reality is, but also what is our relationship with the divine.

Who are we in relation to God? How was the world created? How does time work? The answers provided to these questions will condition what our main objectives in life should be and how they can be achieved.

2.2.1. Metaphysical Anthropology: Who Are We in Relation to God or Ultimate Reality?

a. Answers Based on the Many as Ultimate Reality (Metaphysical Pluralism)

For polytheistic mythologies we are little more than the plaything of the gods, who live a life of divine drama full of human-like passions and conflict among them. Mankind is usually caught in between and suffers the consequences. Sometimes it is considered that humans were only created as servants of the gods, as in the Babylonian creation myth.

This contrasts with Abrahamic monotheistic religions, for example, where it is believed that we were made in the image and likeness of God. This doctrine is especially important in Judaism and Christianity.

For dualist worldviews where two primordial principles are antagonistic to each other, such as in Zoroastrianism, man is considered as God's helper in the fight against evil. Through man's choices evil can and will be eliminated, establishing a new paradisiacal age.

b. Answers Based on the One as Ultimate Reality (Metaphysical Monism)

Nowadays the "doctrines of the One" have a much greater following than those of the Many, which are usually seen as primitive, unrefined or allegorical in character.

The following doctrines, in contrast, have achieved mainstream appeal. Thanks, in part, to modern media and the presence of these concepts in products conceived for worldwide mass consumption.

b1. Teachings Involving Contraries: The Paradigmatic Examples of Lurianic Kabbalah and Gnosticism

Are We Fragments of God?

According to certain worldviews, every human soul is just a fragment of God or of a higher entity close to God.

We will use the Jewish mystical tradition, the Kabbalah, as a paradigmatic example. In it, it is taught that every human soul is part of Adam Kadmon, the primordial man. In addition, and contrary to the main Abrahamic religions, this mystical tradition views Adam as an androgynous being equal in size with the Universe.[7]

The creation myth of Lurianic Kabbalah, a highly influential version of this tradition, is very illustrative:

In the beginning, God contracted part of His infinite light in order to partially conceal Himself so creation could take place. However, the "vessels" of the attributes of God (Sefirot) could not contain at this stage the fullness of the Divine Light and shattered. The realm of chaos or confusion was born, then, due to a catastrophic event in the Godhead itself.

After the shattering of the vessels the Divine Light was released and re-ascended back to God. The broken fragments of the vessels however, still animated by the sparks of Divine Light, descended and animated the four lower worlds that were successively emanated from the source. They comprise the realm of rectification. These shards became sparks of light trapped within that realm.

Through prayer and contemplation, especially of the main attributes of God, man is believed to be able to re-unify the scattered sparks of God´s light. Each liberated spark, which also represents the soul and seat of holiness of every being, is then reunited with God´s **essence**, thus going back to the One.

During the restoration of this fallen Universe man filters what is holy from what is profane. The physical world then, seen as the impure opposite of soul or spirit, is deprived of the light that supported its existence and is eventually destroyed.

---

7. *Androgyny is related with the concept of the unity of opposites, while equating Adam with the whole Universe implies in this case a panentheistic outlook, rather than a pantheistic one, since God is believed to transcend Adam.*

Another version of this doctrine is that of Gnosticism, where it is taught that within each person resides a portion of God: the Divine Spark. The purpose of life is then to achieve the release of this spark from the prison of this fallen material world so that it can return to God, its Source.

As for this purpose, persons can be classified in three categories:

- Material, or ruled by the body.

- Psychic, or ruled by the mind.

- Spiritual, or ruled by the spirit.[8]

The first ones are thought to be incapable of salvation, as no spark is found in them. Only the spiritual type can be sure of salvation, while the psychic person is capable of both ends, depending on his actions in life. Salvation is gained through the knowledge of the presence of the Divine Spark within the soul.

Symbols representing an Alienated Soul: sparks of light, shards of a broken vessel, pearl.

---

8. *"They conceive, then, of three kinds of men, spiritual, material, and animal… The material goes, as a matter of course, into corruption. The animal, if it make choice of the better part, finds repose in the intermediate place; but if the worse, it too shall pass into destruction.*

But they assert that the spiritual principles which have been sown by Achamoth, being disciplined and nourished here from that time until now in righteous souls (because when given forth by her they were yet but weak), at last attaining to perfection, shall be given as brides to the angels of the Saviour, while their animal souls of necessity rest for ever with the Demiurge in the intermediate place.

And again subdividing the animal souls themselves, they say that some are by nature good, and others by nature evil. The good are those who become capable of receiving the [spiritual] seed [and becoming pneumatic]; the evil by nature are those who are never able to receive that seed [and become hylic]."

— of Lyon, St. Ireneus (174-189 AD). Against Heresies or "On the Detection and Overthrow of the So-Called Gnosis". Ante-Nicene Fathers Volume 1. Christian Classics Ethereal Library, Ch. I. 7, 5.

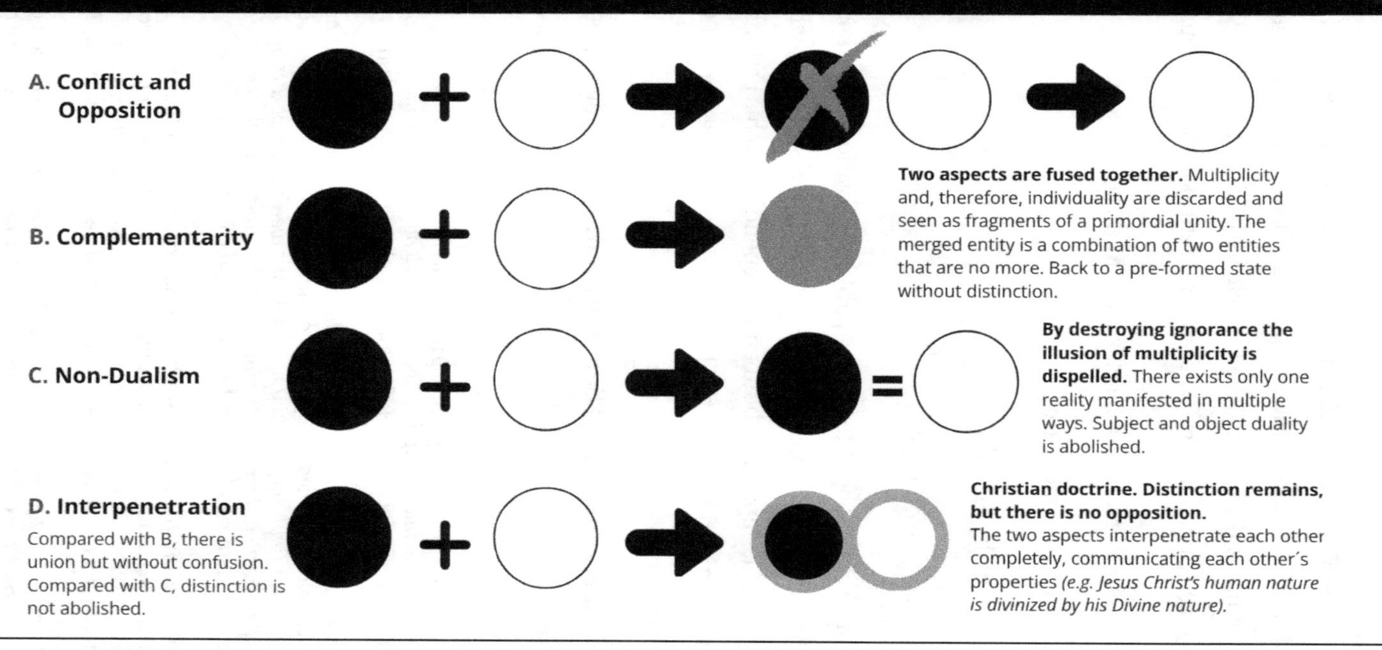

Figure 5. Traditional solutions to duality and multiplicity. Two different opposed aspects could, in order to solve their tension: **A.** Be reduced to only one aspect (good vs. evil; the good prevails); **B.** If the aspects are complementary, they can fuse into another primordial entity that does not preserve all their individuality but is and is not both and neither of them at the same time; **C.** Non-dual solutions do away with the perception of difference. There is only one reality, manifested in a myriad ways; **D.** Interpenetration is a Christian doctrine where two natures or beings share completely their properties without taking away the other´s. The classic example are the two natures of Jesus Christ, which are also a symbol of how the saved persons in the Eschaton are believed to be deified and united with God.

b2. Teachings Involving Complementaries: Alchemy

Another important metaphysical doctrine based in going back to the One through the reunification of spiritual fragments is that of the unity or coincidence of opposites (*Coincidentia Oppositorum*).

In it, a higher metaphysical reality is obtained through the union of two opposite entities, principles or qualities that nevertheless depend and presuppose each other.

The idea is that when these principles are separated, as in the material plane of existence where we currently live in, there is tension. The energy released by this tension is generative, bringing forth creation. However, to attain a higher state of being, this tension must be overcome by merging both complementary entities or principles back into a superior one that is neither one nor the other.

This concept has a special prevalence in Alchemy, were it was codified in the figure of the Rebis (meaning dual or double matter), the culmination of the Great Work of the Philosophers.

In this case, instead of the liberation of trapped souls that go back to the Source as drops of water into the ocean, the mystical reunion is thought to be accomplished inside each practitioner.

The Rebis represents the final state of being attained after the stages of putrefaction and purification have been completed. On these stages, opposing spiritual aspects of the practitioner are separated (dissolution stage), purified, and reintegrated (coagulation stage).

The state attained once these qualities have been reintegrated into a single, higher order, one is symbolized by the Divine Hermaphrodite. It signifies a union and reconciliation of opposing attributes that are in conflict in our profane world, such as spirit and matter, male and female. The birth of a higher-order entity is sought, one which transcends and is not limited by any dualistic concept. Once the pieces have been reintegrated, it is believed that the practitioner is then able to go back from a state of duality to the original state of absolute unity.[9, 10]

This ancient concept was widely popularized by important figures in different fields, such as Nicholas of Cusa (Catholic cardinal and theologian), Mircea Eliade (history of religions), Carl Jung (psychoanalysis), Henry Corbin (Islamic mysticism), and Gershom Scholem (Jewish mysticism), among others.[11]

This popular doctrine can also be found in worldviews where, after attaining insight into the true nature of reality, our lower

––––––––––––

9. *"Alchemists such as Gerhard Dorn, in his work 'The Speculative Philosophy,' referred to this next alchemical stage [inner healing] as Unus Mundus, where splits are healed, duality ceases, and the individual, the vir unus, unites with the World Soul."*

– Wikman, Monika (2004). Pregnant Darkness. Berwick, Maine: Nicolas-Hays, Inc, p. 59.

10. *"With the two of you then made one, you will have peace in union. ... O admirable efficacy of the fountain, which makes one from two and brings peace between enemies. ...It makes one man from Mind and Body."*

– Dorn, Gerhard (1567). The Speculative Philosophy of Gerhard Dorn: Magnum Opus Vol. 34., p. 70.

11. *In the field of philosophy, G.W.F. Hegel, an influential figure in modern Freemasonry and himself influenced by the Hermetic tradition, wrote:*

"The principles of the metaphysical philosophy gave rise to the belief that, when cognition lapsed into contradictions, it was a mere accidental aberration, due to some subjective mistake in argument and inference.

According to Kant, however, thought has a natural tendency to issue in contradictions or antinomies, whenever it seeks to apprehend the infinite. [...]

But here too Kant, as we must add, never got beyond the negative result that the thing-in-itself is unknowable, and never penetrated to the discovery of what the antinomies really and positively mean. That true and positive meaning of the antinomies is this: that every actual thing involves a coexistence of opposed elements. Consequently to know, or, in other words, to comprehend an object is equivalent to being conscious of it as a concrete unity of opposed determinations.[...]."

– Hegel, G.W.F. (1830). Logic. The Encyclopaedia of the Philosophical Sciences. Part One, IV. Second Attitude of Thought to Objectivity. Two: The Critical Philosophy, §48.

plane of existence is eventually discovered to be the same as the highest reality, hence becoming awakened. This view represents absolute unity through immanence, and is found in different non-dualist traditions (e.g., Mahāyāna Buddhism, including Zen Buddhism).

Symbols representing the Rebis: an hermaphrodite, the Sun (male) and Moon (female), the Red King and White Queen (Sacred Marriage motif).

b3. Are We Just Ignorant of Already Being The One?

The idea that we are fragments of ultimate reality that need liberation or re-unification is not the only solution proposed by the followers of the One to achieve absolute unity. We may already be there, but we are not aware of it.

This is the core message of most religions born in India and Far Eastern spirituality (e.g., Hinduism, Mahāyāna, and Vrajayana Buddhism). For example, the *Upanishads*, one of the most important and authoritative texts in all Hindu traditions, concludes with the formula that Ātman equals Brahman (e.g., *Brihadaranyaka Upanishad*, hymn 4.4.5). Or, in other words, that the individual self or soul is equivalent to the Universal Soul or Being. This means that we have already arrived at our destination even before starting our journey, we are just not aware of this fact.

In these views, our current ego is understood as one of many particular manifestations, masks or thoughts of God, and the Universe as His playground, where the Divine Play of Self-Discovery takes place.

This implies that, logically, our current ego has by necessity only two options: to disappear merged into the One (ego death), or to suffer self-inflation until it discovers that it has always been God. In most traditions, the way of the death of the ego is favored. Either way, what we currently are disappears to become something else.

This is especially true in worldviews, such as in the very popular in the West Advaita Vedānta, that conceptualize the Supreme Being

(Para Brahman) as an attribute-less and impersonal Absolute (Nirguṇa Brahman). In other traditional views (even in Hindu ones, such as in Vishishtadvaita Vedānta, Vaishnavism, Shaivism, and Shaktism), the Supreme is defined instead as possessing attributes (e.g., Saguṇa Brahman) and sometimes as a personal God. In these cases, an eventual absorption into the One may not be viewed as our ultimate end.

c. Answers Based on Transcending the Duality of the One and the Many

As we have seen, for some "non-dual" worldviews the highest state is one of absorption into an absolutely simple Unity. Therefore, for those systems of thought to "transcend" the One (Unity) and the Many (Plurality) dichotomy, the liberated individual would have to exist at the same time in this world of multiplicity and illusion (Saṃsāra) as well as in ultimate reality itself (e.g., Nirvana, Emptiness, Nirguṇa Brahman). This would be an immanent "transcendence". Even then, Saṃsāra would not be a perfect or elevated world, but would still be the same imperfect one that we all know. It would be, though, incapable of constraining a liberated soul, who would have gained absolute freedom in this cyclical realm of death and rebirth.

For Christianity, on the other hand, we are the adopted sons of God through the Incarnation, Death, Resurrection, and Ascension of the Logos, who corrected the original metaphysical catastrophe that saw our likeness disfigured. In this view, our particular individuality can then be, and in fact is, loved by a personal God.

While the Roman Catholic doctrines of **Absolute** Divine Simplicity and the Vision of God as the highest ideal achievable by man resemble the absorption into the One mentioned above for panentheistic and some non-dual systems, the ultimate end of a person is viewed differently in Eastern Orthodox Christianity.

Thanks to the doctrines of deification and Essence-Energies distinction, the Orthodox believe that saved persons receive the totality of the Uncreated Energies of God without having to lose their particular individuality in the process.

The duality of *the One and the Many* is, then, transcended not only by God but by each saved person as well. Not through an immanent solution that uses our "fallen" world as the source of multiplicity, like in the non-dual solutions mentioned above, but at the highest level. The source of multiplicity, in this case, is not intrinsically constrained to remain in a lower plane of existence. This can be so because the existence of distinction at the highest levels of reality is not viewed necessarily as an imperfection.

Christians believe that, in the Eschaton (the coming Age), God will be One and All there is, but He will give Himself fully to all. Each saved person will become then an instance of the All, but without losing their individual way of being the All. Personhood is in this view not abolished, but purified, perfected, and deified. This reality can be seen already pre-figured in the very structure of the Tri-Une God of Christianity, where the Many (the Three Persons of the Trinity) are One God.

2.3. On the Origin of the Universe

Other traditional metaphysical concepts taught via symbolic initiations involve how the world came to be. For many worldviews, the answer is through successive emanations from the One (e.g., Neo-Platonism, Gnosticism). In this view, all things flow from the highest reality, or First Principle. It is believed that each emanation is progressively less perfect than the previous one as it moves away from its Source.

For this doctrine there are no gaps in creation, with every level of reality being a continuous and necessary gradation from absolute perfection to absolute non-existence, the latter usually associated with matter as the lowest and most dense plane of existence.

Once the process of emanating has begun, successive emanations are believed to occur as part of an automatic process. This follows the notion that "nothing comes from nothing" (Parmenides), meaning that everything derives from a pre-existing substance, the logical implication being that everything can go back to the One by a process of reversal, or de-creation.

To the contrary, the theistic doctrine of creation out of nothing (Creatio Ex Nihilo; e.g., Abrahamic religions) explains that creation came to be through a divine creative act willed by God.

In this latter view there is a discontinuity between creation and God, as there is no belief in a continuous gradation of being. God´s will is enough to bring forth creation, and there is an unbridgeable chasm between it and the transcendence of God.

Therefore, this doctrine implies that no "process" of auto-deification can happen without God´s collaboration (synergy), as there is no continuity between creatures and their transcendent Creator.

Symbols representing Creation: the World Egg, the Cosmic Waters, embryo.

2.3.1. The Nature of Time

Time is traditionally considered to be either a linear or a cyclical phenomenon or aspect of reality.

a. Cyclical Time and the Doctrine of Differentiated Periods or Ages

The concept of cyclical time is prevalent in Indian religions (Hinduism, Jainism, Buddhism, and Sikhism), with popular and well known concepts such as reincarnation (or transmigration) and karmic bonds.

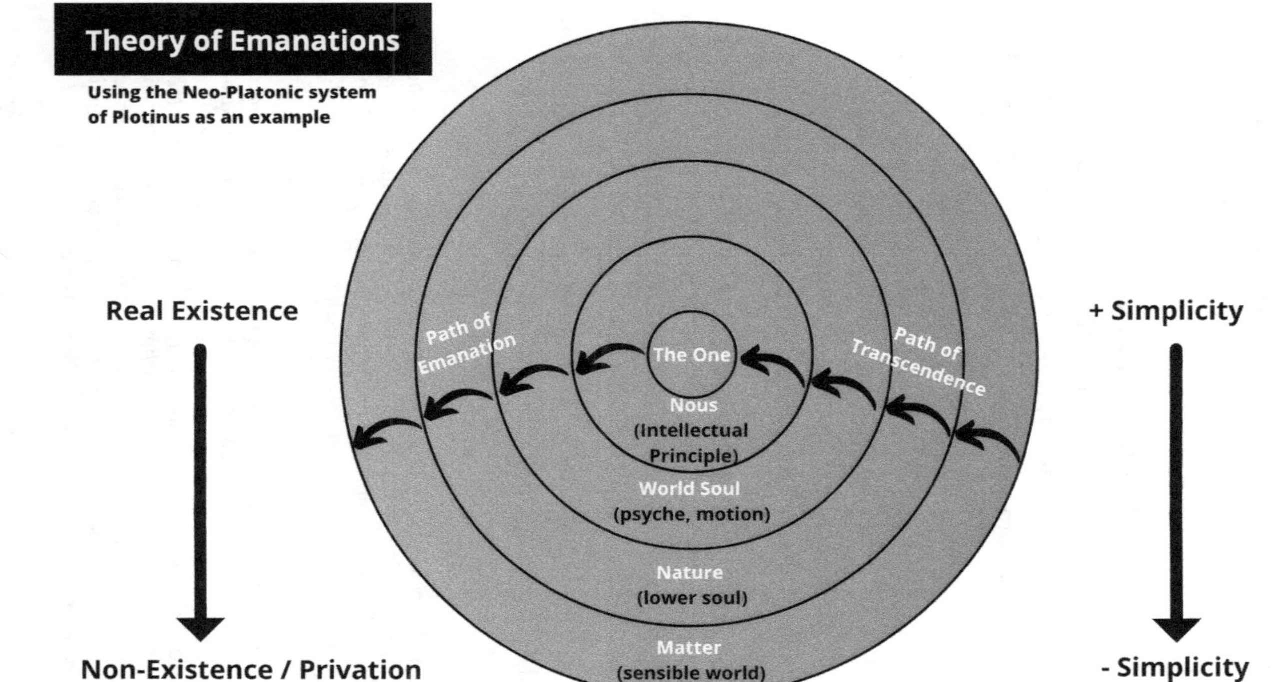

Figure 6. The concept of emanations as the source of creation using Plotinus´ Neo-Platonic system as an example. Each successive level of reality is more imperfect than the one before. The continuous gradation in the levels of reality implies the possibility of elevating oneself to higher levels, as no discontinuity is present. A discontinuity would mean that, for beings in a lower level to reach higher ones, they would need the help from a superior level. This implies a personal God.

In addition, there also were, and still are, numerous Western and near-Eastern proponents of reincarnation, such as the Orphic mystery religion, Platonism, Manichaeism, Gnosticism, Lurianic Kabbalah, and Theosophy.

The cyclical nature of all life (e.g., Saṃsāra) is a fundamental belief of these worldviews. According to it, individuals pass through a long series of deaths and rebirths until they are able to liberate themselves from the aimless wandering around this mundane existence, thus breaking the cycle.

Individuals are believed to re-incarnate in different places, including our world and the realms of the gods, demi-gods, animals, hungry ghosts, and different hells, depending on their actions in life (merit) and the wisdom and insight attained regarding the true nature of reality.

The cyclical nature of time, however, is not reserved only for living beings. In many traditional worldviews the world undergoes cycles consisting of different ages of increasing decadence and ignorance, until a new cycle begins anew and truth and virtue are restored again. The whole Universe itself is also believed to undergo continuous cycles of creation and destruction (e.g., Yuga and Kalpa).[12]

----

12.   *"The Hindu doctrine teaches that a human cycle, to which it gives the name Manvantara, is divided into four periods marking so many stages during which the primordial spirituality becomes gradually more and more obscured; these are the same periods that the ancient traditions of the West called the Golden, Silver, Bronze, and Iron Ages.*

We are now in the fourth age, the Kali-Yuga or "dark age", and have been so already, it is said, for more than six thousand years, that is to say since a time far earlier than any known to "classical" history. Since that time, the truths which were formerly within reach of all have become more and more hidden and inaccessible; those who possess them grow fewer and fewer, and although the treasure of "nonhuman" (that is, supra-human) wisdom that was prior to all the ages can never be lost, it nevertheless becomes enveloped in more and more impenetrable veils, which hide it from men's sight and make it extremely difficult to discover.

This is why we find everywhere, under various symbols, the same theme of something that has been lost—at least to all appearances and as far as the outer world is concerned—and that those who aspire to true knowledge must rediscover; but it is

Symbols representing Time: Ouroboros, a spiral, the Wheel of Time.

Figure 7. The Ouroboros dragon as a symbol of cyclical time. Note the dualities in the painting: winged dragon against ground serpent; two main branches in the tree, going in opposite directions; dead tree versus sprouting one. Picture: Zoroaster Clavis Artis, MS. Verginelli-Rota, vol. 2, p. 18.

2.4. On the Problem of Evil or Why This World Lost its Original Perfection

In traditional initiations, in addition to the knowledge pertaining to each tradition´s view on God and creation, the initiate is also given an explanation of why the perfection that existed before time was created was lost. How did we end up in an existence so full of struggle?

In theistic worldviews, this explanation necessarily has to take into consideration the fact of the existence of evil or suffering in a world

also said that what is thus hidden will become visible again at the end of the cycle, which, because of the continuity binding all things together, will coincide with the beginning of a new cycle."

— Guénon, René. The Essential René Guénon: Metaphysical Principles, Traditional Doctrines, and the Crisis of Modernity. World Wisdom and Sophia Perennis (2010), p. 3.

created by an All-powerful, All-Knowing, and All-Good God. This issue, which could seem at first sight contradictory, has therefore been named the "Problem of Evil" (Theodicy).

a. Evil as Matter and Non-Existence

Some worldviews, most of them believing in the concept of emanations explained before, consider that material existence is intrinsically flawed or evil, since it is the aspect of creation that is further away from God and borders on non-existence.

Thus, for example, many Gnostic texts do not speak of sin and repentance but deal with doctrines such as illusion and enlightenment. These concepts are typically found in "doctrines of the One"[13,14], even though Gnosticism is frequently misrepresented as a dualist worldview.

For other traditions, on the other hand, evil can have its usefulness and even be partially redeemable, as in the case of Lurianic Kabbalah.

This latter tradition considers that evil was created indirectly by God and it can be said to play a certain beneficial role. Here, the metaphorical "shells" surrounding holiness (Qlippoth), like a vessel containing a liquid, prevent the flow and the dissipation of the Divine Light of the Godhead.

---

13. "Then Matter is simply Alienism (the Principle of Difference)?

No: it is merely that part of Alienism which stands in contradiction with the Authentic Existents which are Reason-Principles.

So understood, this non-existent has a certain measure of existence; for it is identical with Privation, which also is a thing standing in opposition to the things that exist in Reason."

— Plotinus (270 AD). Enneads. Cambridge University Press, Ch: 2.4.16.

14. "There remains, only, if Evil exists at all, that it be situate in the realm of Non-Being, that it be some mode, as it were, of the Non-Being [...]."

— Plotinus (270 AD). Enneads. Cambridge University Press, Ch: 1.8.3.

Nevertheless, these "husks" also conceal God and are opposite to holiness. They comprise an inverted realm, called the Other Side, which serves as a mirror image to the realm of the Holy Attributes of God (Sefirot). It is believed that the completely unclean shells will be destroyed during the restoration of the world, while the redeemable ones will be purified and sublimated.

b. Evil as an Illusion or Ignorance

In most Indian religions and mystical traditions, "evil" also has its usefulness. It is seen as a consequence of universal laws of causality that take into consideration the moral aspects in life (Karma). The necessary consequence of causing harm to others is to suffer it oneself in this life or in future ones, in one way or another. These views are focused on direct causality and what can be learnt through suffering in order to grow in wisdom and advance towards detachment and liberation. Legalistic concepts such as justice and retribution are not emphasized, although they are prevalent in the popular interpretation of the doctrine of karmic law in the West.

Regarding the source of this "evil", in most Indian traditions ignorance or the Principle of Illusion (Māyā) are seen as the ultimate causes of all that can be considered malicious. However, Māyā´s origin is problematic.

If all there is really is an *absolutely* simple One (e.g., Nirguṇa Brahman in Advaita Vedānta), then the Principle of Illusion can logically only be **either** a part of the One **or** it does not exist at all. If we accept the first option, then Māyā is equal to Brahman ("God"), with the latter being the source of all evil. If, on the other hand, we accept the second solution, truth is not veiled in this world, meaning that our quest to be liberated from delusion is pointless and makes no sense.[15] The only

---

15. *Notice the dialectical way of reasoning even when thinking about ultimate reality, which may not be necessarily appropriate at that level, since human logical categories by definition cannot limit transcendent reality.*

alternative solution is to transform Advaita (which means non-dual) into a dualist philosophy, which is a contradiction in terms. This is what, apparently, has been proposed by some modern scholars:

"*Maya and Brahman together constitute the entire universe, just like two kinds of interwoven threads create a fabric. Maya is the manifestation of the world, whereas Brahman, which supports Maya, is the cause of the world.*" [16]

— Prakasatman

c. Evil as an Unavoidable Consequence of the Existence of Free Will

Other worldviews hold that the existence of evil is necessary for the existence of free will, and that God is able to use even evil itself to achieve a good end.

In Christianity, for example, evil is not willed by God as a mechanism for human development and growth. Instead, it is only tolerated as long as the world is in its current fallen state. Evil is not to be integrated into a totality, but is conceptualized as sin (which means missing the mark) and is seen as the consequence of the free will of created beings (angels and humans).

Nevertheless, even though God did not will evil into existence, He is able to use it to produce good fruits and lead us closer to Him, if we are able to learn from it. This nullifies (even mocks) evil itself, which cannot avoid being self-destructive as it has no ground for existence apart from being a negation of the good itself.

St. Irenaeus, for example, understood the existence of evil as necessary for human development in the current state of this world. He taught that through work and will we can shape our souls and become who we are

---

16. *Prakasatman. In Esther Abraham Solomon (1969). Avidyā: A Problem of Truth and Reality. Gujarat University, pp. 269-270.*

going to be for all eternity. Our current life would be, then, a soul-making process where we have the opportunity to develop as moral agents and achieve the likeness of God.

In order to be able to claim our progress in this process as really ours, though, God must remain at an "intellectual" distance from us. Free will can only be completely free if I am not constrained to believe in God, because of the multiple implications this would have.

The concept of evil and death eventually destroying themselves can be most clearly seen in the Eastern Orthodox Christian understanding of the Death of Jesus Christ, and is viewed as an unavoidable consequence of their lack of independent ontological existence. In this view, the swallowing of Life (the Logos) by Death results in the annihilation of the latter.

Other Christian interpretation of evil (very prominent in the West), later developed mainly by Augustine of Hippo, is that of Original Sin. However, there are important differences between the doctrine of Ancestral Sin as understood by the Church of the first two centuries and current Orthodox Christianity and the concept of Original Sin as understood by the Western Church.

Ancestral Sin is focused on death as the primary inheritance we received from the original human archetype and person, Adam. In this view, universal human nature was partially corrupted in the original archetype. Any further existence coming from him had to necessarily carry this injury, too. A compassionate personal God then sacrificed Himself to provide a way to heal this injury without violating human free will or compromising Divine Justice. A therapeutic view is emphasized. The concept of Original Sin, in contrast, gives primacy to inherited human guilt and a legalistic view of God´s Justice.

Figure 8. Orthodox Christian icon of the "Harrowing of Hades". It symbolically depicts Jesus Christ´s triumphant descent into Hell, bringing salvation to the souls held captive since the beginning of the world. The source of Life, the Logos, being affected by Death was an ontological and metaphysical impossibility that ended in the death of "Death" itself.

d. Evil as Unconscious or Repressed Traits of the Human Psyche

Jungian psychoanalysis transformed religious and metaphysical symbols and concepts into projections of unconscious human psychological realities (Psychological Reductionism).

According to this view, highly present in popular culture, our purpose should be to integrate repressed aspects of our personality into a totality, the Self. The Shadow,[17,18] represented in classical times by symbols of evil (e.g., the dragon) is the main antagonist in that process. However, once its existence as a part of ourselves is acknowledged, it is to be integrated into our whole personality in one way or another.

As can be seen, this is another version of the Union of Opposites doctrine discussed earlier. In fact, Jung was deeply influenced by Alchemy and other esoteric traditions (such as Gnosticism), and viewed his work as a rediscovery and reformulation of the truths of those ancient traditions in modern psychological terms.

Symbols of Evil: dragon, reptiles, symbols representing corruption (e.g., black goo [prevalent modern symbol]) or death (e.g., skull).

---

17. *"The enlargement of the light side of consciousness has the necessary consequence that the part of the psyche which is less light and less capable of consciousness is thrown into darkness to such an extent that sooner or later a rift occurs in the psychic system.*

At first, this is not recognized as such and is therefore projected – i.e. it appears as a religious projection, in the form of a split between the powers of Light and Darkness."

– Jung, Carl. The Symbolism of the Spirit. F.C.Econom (2000).

18. *"...this integration [of the shadow] cannot take place and be put to a useful purpose unless one can admit the tendencies bound up with the shadow and allow them some measure of realization – tempered, of course, with the necessary criticism. This leads to disobedience and self disgust, but also to self- reliance, without which individuation is unthinkable."*

– Jung, C.G. (1970). A Psychological Approach to the Dogma of the Trinity. Princeton University Press. Bollingen Series, Ch.6: Conclusion.

2.5. On Fate, Free Will and To What Extent Are We Conditioned in This Life

After discovering the deficiencies and limitations of our current state of being and its cause, it is only logical to ask ourselves: are we able to do something about it? This, with regard to the matters at hand, is the same as asking: do we have free will?

Traditional worldviews provide different answers revolving around the concept of Fate and its greater or lesser importance. Fate is defined as a power, often divinely inspired, that pre-determines the course of events in an unavoidable way. It is based on the belief that there exists a natural order in the cosmos.

Astrology, or the influence of the stars in our lives, is a natural consequence of studying this order. It is prominently featured in different systems of thought, especially in the most esoteric ones (e.g., Hermeticism), and is based on the theory of correspondences between all levels of reality.

A different doctrine with similar consequences is that of causal determinism. It includes, for example, the non-theistic Buddhist concept of dependent origination, which is a key doctrine shared by all Buddhist schools.

According to it, all phenomena (dharmas) come to be as a consequence and in complete dependence upon other previous phenomena, following a universal law. For traditions that believe in karmic cycles, for example, the amount of agency that we possess during a specific incarnation in this world is further limited by the consequences of our actions in past incarnations.

A science-based worldview that advocates for a hard materialistic determinism, in addition, despite being a completely different worldview, would have a similar outlook on this dilemma between Freedom and Necessity.

a. On Fatalism

More interesting is the question regarding how to deal with Fate in worldviews that believe in it. Should we accept it? Confront it? This, in turn, depends on whether we believe Fatalism to be true or not.

Fatalism is the belief that Fate not only exists, but it is also unchangeable by any human means. We are the spectators, not the active agents, of our own lives.

Followers of the concept of a fixed Fate include those of ancient religions such as the Summerian, Babylonian, Greek, Roman, and Norse ones. The Moirai, Parcae or Norns in Greek, Roman, and Norse mythology, respectively, are common symbolic beings representing a Fate that cannot be modified. This concept is also discussed by Stoicism and is accepted in certain aspects of Hinduism, too (caste system).

A theistic version of Fatalism is especially important in Islam. It is not, however, a biblical doctrine.[19] In Christianity, it is emphasized that we have the free will needed to battle the temptations and tendencies of our fallen nature, thus being capable of working out our own salvation.

a1. Rebellion Against Fate

Worldviews that believe in intermediate evil gods between us and the real God or highest reality (with Gnosticism being the paradigmatic example) are more inclined to believe that confronting Fate and the current order of things is justified. It may even be the only moral choice for such believers.

---

19. *"When tempted, no one should say, 'God is tempting me.' For God cannot be tempted by evil, nor does he tempt anyone; but each one is tempted when, by his own evil desire, he is dragged away and enticed."*

— James, 1:13-14. The Holy Bible. New King James version.

Non-theistic systems that believe in an impersonal First Principle or Force that can be manipulated for both good and evil (e.g., different modern occultist schools) can also fall into this category.

In such views, given that anyone with the correct knowledge or skill can tap into primordial forces and become an unjust tyrant, the fight against a "false destiny" imposed by such a tyrant would be justified.

b. Absolute Determinism is Untraditional

According to most traditional systems of thought, however, it is a misconception to believe that we do not have even a modicum of free will. Material causes cannot create thought, and even if we are conditioned by them, we are never compelled. Therefore, we are ultimately free to choose the Good, even if it implies fighting against powerful influences (e.g., animal-like instincts).

When the assertion that we are not free is made, it merely means that we do not choose the Good already known to the Intellect, instead being overcome by those influences.

c. Providence, Will and Destiny: Man as Mediator Between Heaven and Earth

In traditional worldviews[20], all action takes place through the powers of Providence, Will or Destiny.

On the macrocosmic side, this is translated in that man´s will is the mediator between Providence (free Nature) and Destiny (Nature bound by Necessity, which acts following its own laws). Said in other terms,

---

20. *See, for example, The Great Triad of René Guénon and the works of Fabre d'Olivet on Pythagoreanism and Chinese metaphysics.*

man is the mediator between Heaven and Earth, with Providence (the Principles or Ideas of the Divine Mind, the only truly free existent) acting on Nature through him as an intermediary.

On the microcosmic scale, on the other hand, man´s will is the central middle ground that links and unifies the intellectual (spirit), psychic (soul), and instinctive (body) aspects of his being.

By choosing the side of Providence, man becomes aligned with Freedom, detaching himself from bounded natural law and walking towards spiritual realization.

As Guénon stated: *"In uniting itself to Providence and consciously collaborating with it, the human will can become a counter-balance to destiny and finally neutralize it."* [21]

This alignment of mankind´s will with Providence (pole of spiritual Unity) is what defines a good action. Its alignment with Nature (pole of material Multiplicity), on the contrary, constitutes vice and depravity.

d. The Purification of the Will: The Common First Step in All Mystical Paths

A necessary first stage of the spiritual path, then, is the purification of the will. This process, in turn, requires inner vigilance to see and counter every pernicious influence that conditions it.

Eventually, these intruders masking our true Self become identified and controlled, the Intellect (Nous) becomes able to discern what is Good and, only then, the will becomes liberated, free to choose and follow it. This is accomplished by "cleaning" our mind and awakening to our spiritual capacities.

---

21. Guénon, René. *The Great Triad. Quinta Essentia*, p. 142.

e. Is Ultimate Reality Free? Necessity and Contingency Against Willed Creation

e1. The Notion of Freedom in the Religions of The One

Existence, for the religions of the One, is at the same time contigent and necessary. As René Guénon explained:

"*We said earlier that every possibility of manifestation must be manifested for the very reason that it is what it is, namely, a possibility of manifestation, so that manifestation is necessarily implied in principle by the very nature of particular possibilities. Thus manifestation, which as such is purely contingent, is nonetheless necessary in its principle, just as, although transitory in itself, it nevertheless possesses an absolutely permanent root in universal Possibility, this moreover being what constitutes all its reality.*"

— René Guénon. The Multiple States of the Being. Sofia Perennis, p. 86

From there, Guénon derives its proof regarding the existence of freedom. Since everything that is possible is real, freedom must also be real:

"*To prove freedom metaphysically, without encumbering oneself with all the usual philosophical arguments, it is sufficient to establish that it is a possibility, since the possible and the real are metaphysically identical. To this end we may first define freedom as the absence of constraint [...].*"

— René Guénon. The Multiple States of the Being. Sofia Perennis, p. 90

In Guénon´s perennialist worldview, freedom is synonimous with the highest reality, All-Possibility, ultimate Unity[22], which is free precisely because it is everything, being unlimited and containing it all.

---

22. "*[...] As soon as there is multiplicity, as is the case in the order of particular existences, it is evident that there can no longer be a question of any but relative freedom.[...]*"

Paradoxically, given that All-Possibility (the One, the Absolute) is compelled to manifest it all, it is therefore not free.

e2. The Notion of Freedom in Christianity

For Christianity, on the contrary, given that it rejects this dialectical opposition between Unity and Plurality, the solution is not found in neither absolute homogeneity nor in unchecked multiplicity.

The Christian Trinity, by being both One God and Many (three) Persons, is a personal deity that transcends this dichotomy and therefore does not need every possibility to become manifested. Instead, it willingly (and lovingly) conceives[23] and creates. This has serious implications:

1. The Tri-Une non-dialectical personal God of Christianity is free, able to create instead of being compelled to emanate.

2. Everything in creation can thus be said to be loved, even in its current fallen state, since it was conceived and willed by a God who cares.

The Orthodox concept of deification (Theosis), in addition, states that in the Eschaton man becomes One due to God becoming "All in all". Thus, a personal God makes it possible for us to retain our personality, becoming unique deified personifications (hypostases or particular modes of existence) of the common God we will carry within.

[…]A being will be free to the extent that it participates in this unity; in other words, it will be the more free as it has more unity in itself, or as it is more "one".[…]

[…] Whereas a relative freedom belongs to every being under any condition whatsoever, this absolute freedom can only belong to the being that, liberated from the conditions of manifested existence, whether individual or even supra-individual, has become absolutely "one", at the degree of pure Being, or "without duality", if its realization surpasses Being. It is then, but then only, that one can speak of a being "that is a law unto itself" because this being is then entirely identical with its sufficient reason, which is both its principial origin and its final destiny."

— René Guénon. The Multiple States of the Being. Sofia Perennis, pp. 91, 94-95.

23. Through the Logos and His Logoi, God´s thoughts and the Reasons for the existence of everything.

Figure 9. Nornir, by J. L. Lund (1844). A depiction of the three Norns that decide the fates (Wyrd) of everyone in Norse mythology. They were seen as either benevolent or malevolent, and represented the past, present, and future of each one. In other words, they represented time.

Instead of being disolved into a single homogeneous Monad, a communion[24] in love in which we become unique images of the One God. Only with Him as the center of our being is man "One", and the one who achieves this is said to have attained a Holy or True Will.

————————

24. *Including a communion of will.*

Symbols representing Fate: the Wheel of Fortune, the Zodiac, symbols representing the Moirai, Parcae or Norns (e.g., thread, spindle, scroll, scales).

2.6. On Salvation, Liberation or How to Transcend Our Current Limitations

The last question a traditional worldview can initiate us in is also the most important: how can we be saved or liberated? In some cases, it is even believed that it may be possible to achieve a higher state of divinization.

The answer to this question crucially depends on the view we hold regarding who or what God or ultimate reality is. It also depends on what we perceive the cause of evil or our current limitations to be. Finally, we must believe that we possess free will and that no fatalistic decree will inevitably prevent us from reaching our goal.

a. The Destiny of the Believers in a Plurality of Gods

We will begin by exploring the path for those following the solutions based on the Many.

In some of those pessimistic polytheistic worldviews, there is not much to do for most men in this life except to try to enjoy it while they can.

There is no promise or a clear understanding about the possibility of achieving a higher plane of existence in life or after death (for example in Hades, in the early Mycenaean period of Greek religion). Only in some cases may a better destiny await, usually for heroes (as can be found in the writings of Homer and Hesiod) or emperors (imperial cults).

In others worldviews, a life after death similar in character to our present human life awaits. For example, a life of glorious battle against the dark forces of the Universe awaits the chosen ones (Valhalla) in Norse religion, and to lead a life that is conducive to that desirable state is encouraged.

Later additions to the Greek religious views, due to the influence of the initiatory Mystery Cults (divided into Lesser and Greater Mysteries), included the reward for the virtuous (Elysium) and punishment for the wicked (Tartarus), solidifying the idea of a worthy an achievable life after death.

Similarly, the Egyptian conception of the afterlife included judgment and rewards for the virtuous, as well as punishment for the wicked (e.g., Feather of Maat, Anubis). Only Pharaohs, however, were considered as capable of being deified.

b. Henosis: Or How to Achieve Union with The One

For those looking to go back to the One, however, the following are some of the most widespread and important paths.

Henosis is a Greek term describing mystical oneness or union. It was used in Greek Mystery Religions and later by neo-platonic authors to signify re-unification with the One (Tὸ Ἕν), also called the Monad. It presents many similarities with other mystical traditions, such as Eastern philosophy[25], Hermeticism, and Sufism.

Plotinus, the father of Neo-Platonism, defined the process of Henosis as a reversal of normal consciousness through contemplation (or meditation, the term preferred by Eastern philosophies) with the objective of achieving a state free of any thought or perception.

This would mean transcending the sphere of Intellect (or Nous), which is characterized by duality or division. It was believed that once a state of

---

25. *Mar Gregorios, Paulos (2017). Neoplatonism and Indian Philosophy, SUNY Press.*

emptiness is achieved and the mind of the practitioner is dissolved into the absolute simplicity of the Monad, also called the Source, ultimate reality could be grasped.

Following Plotinus´greatest work, the Enneads, the process of unification would involve, roughly, the following steps:

- **Step 1.** *Catharsis.* Where any multiplicity in mind is abandoned, as it is interpreted as a contamination of mind´s original pure state. This includes any type of mental activity, such as thoughts or sensations.

- **Step 2.** *The withdrawal of the Intellect.* Where mind, once emptied, is surrendered to what lies behind it.

- **Step 3.** *Vision.* Where the adepts perceive a luminous vision of their real Self.

- **Step 4.** *Annihilation of the ego.*

- **Step 5.** *Union with the One.* A state where the practitioner´s subjective individuality completely ceases to be and becomes something else.

The Monad was viewed as an impersonal Principle, also called Force (Dynamis) by Plotinus. Everything was thought to be contained in it, all division and difference reconciled. The One is All and in all (Panentheism).

In a certain sense, this way of union with the One could be interpreted as trying to achieve Self-Deification (Apotheosis), as it all depends on the efforts of the adept without any active participation of a personal ultimate reality.

Union with the One, according to Neo-Platonists such as Iamblichus, could also be attained through Theurgy, which means divine working. The term was first mentioned in the *Chaldean Oracles.*[26]

---

26. *"For the theourgoí do not fall under the fate-governed herd".*

– *Des Places, E. Chaldean Oracles. Fragment 153 (Paris, 1971).*

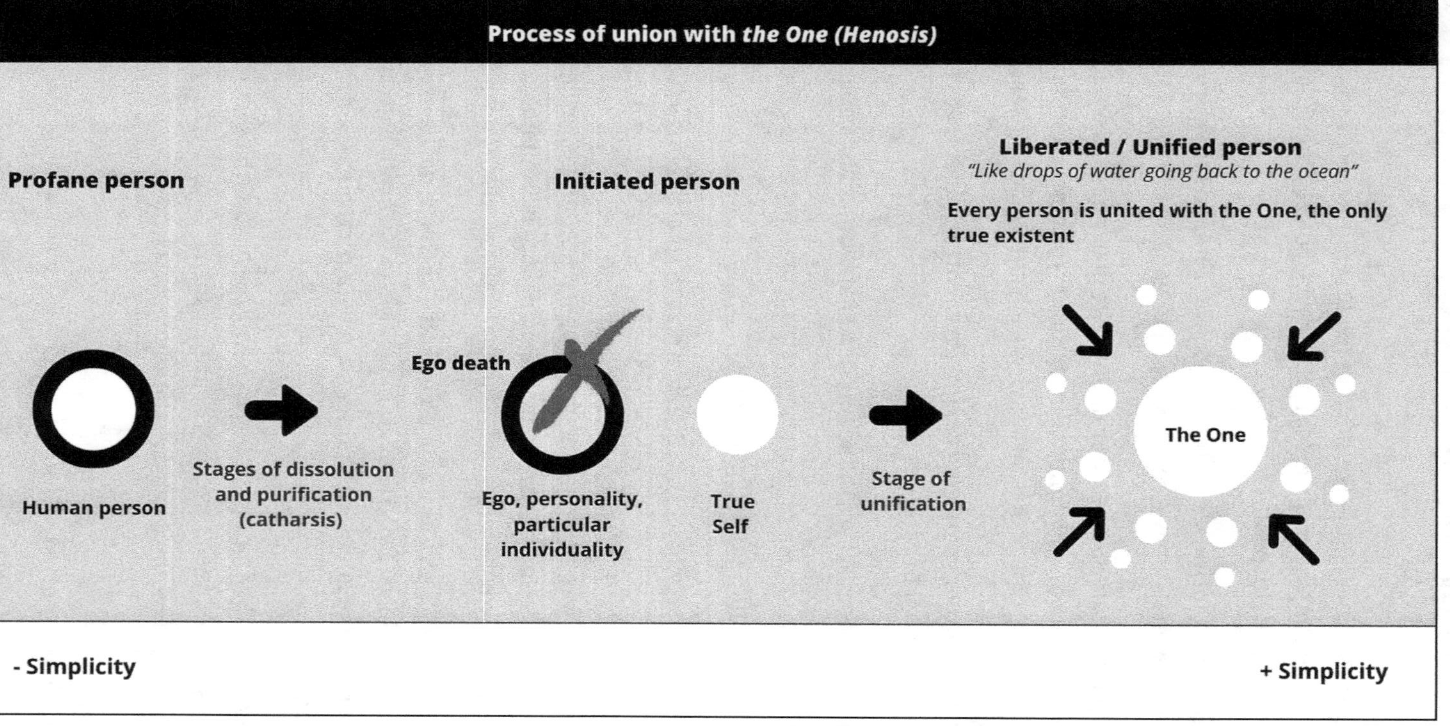

Figure 10. Main characteristics and comparison of the differences between the process of Henosis, or going back to the One, and the Orthodox Christian understanding of the union with God through Theosis (deification; Figure 11).

This process involves a series of ritual practices that mimic the actions of the demiurgic universal Mind as the creator of the Universe, but with the intention of reversing creation back into the One.

Rituals from earlier Mystery Religions were used to perfect and integrate the different aspects of the practitioner, and included the invocation or evocation of deities or "god forms" to help in this process of unification (similar to Buddhist Vajrayāna tantric practices).

b1. Yoga and Meditation: Eastern Paths of Liberation from Multiplicity and Union with The One

These Greek practices are not, however, unique. Extreme similarities can be found in the methods of all schools of thought that believe in an absolutely simple Monad as the highest reality, however it may be called (e.g., the One, Emptiness, Ein Sof).

We can include in this list Eastern meditation techniques. Even if their objective is conceived in negative form as a way to put an end and achieve liberation from the cycle of deaths and rebirths, their ultimate purpose can also be stated in positive terms as a union with the one true reality.

These techniques (skillful means) have been widely popularized in the West during the last decades. Popular methods include the different forms of Buddhist meditation: Samatha and Vipassana in Therevada Buddhism; Mindfulness and Zen meditation in Mahāyāna Buddhism; the many techniques involving deity visualizations or meditation on the ground of existence of Vajrayāna Buddhism.

Hindu Yoga, which means union, also follows the same pattern. Especially Rāja Yoga, of which the widely practiced physical (or Hatha) Yoga was originally conceived as a preparation for. Through this practice, the final achievable state of union with the unchanging ultimate reality is traditionally described as "existence, consciousness, and bliss" (Satcitananda).

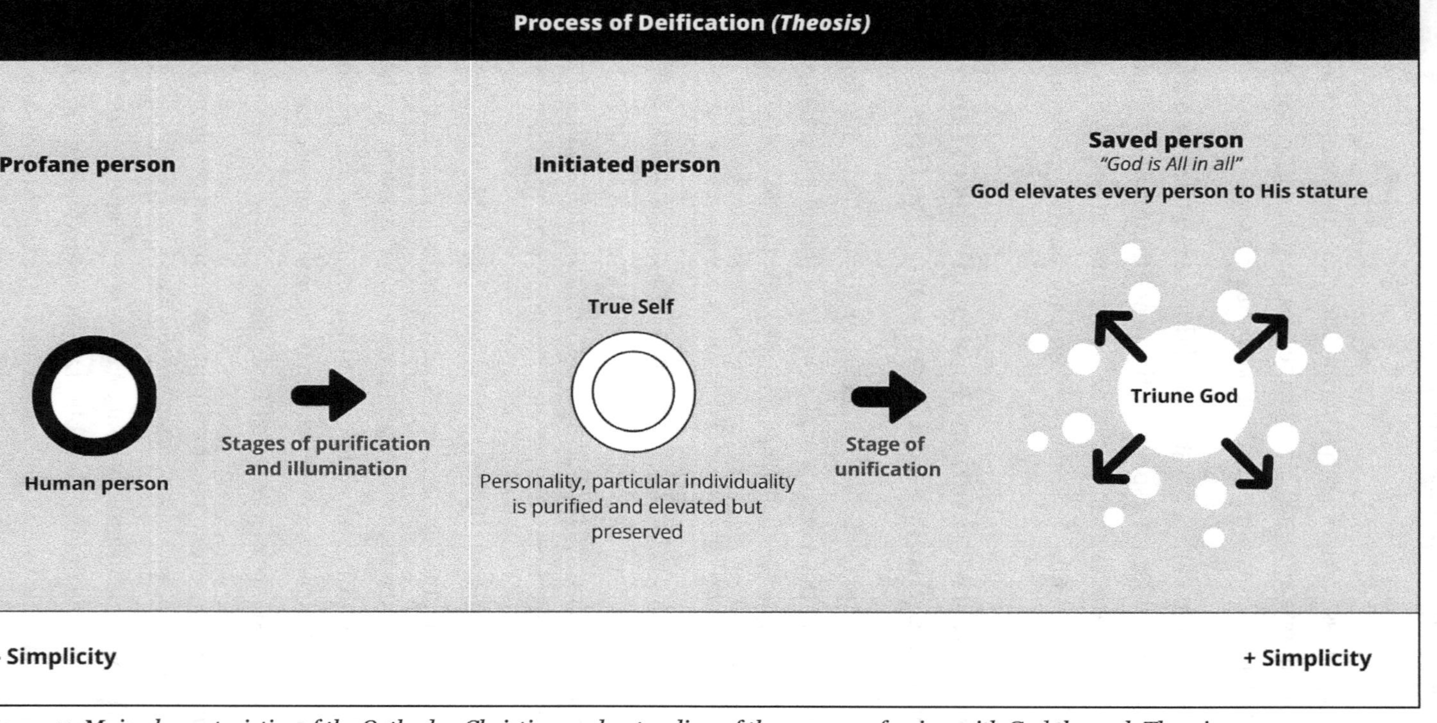

Figure 11. Main characteristics of the Orthodox Christian understanding of the process of union with God through Theosis.

Finally, the practices of mystical traditions such as Kabbalah (Jewish meditation) and Sufism also have to be mentioned. For example, Jewish Hasidic philosophy, which also teaches Kabbalah, utilizes the practice of "self-nullification" to achieve a state of mystic contemplation.

c. Salvation: Achieving Closeness to God in Monotheistic Religions

For Abrahamic religions (Judaism, Christianity, and Islam) man can be elevated to a state of existence closer to God by acting in this life according to His will and striving to lead a virtuous and moral existence.[27] In these worldviews, since mankind is conceived as being created in the image of God, the highest and most logical purpose for human beings is to try to restore the lost likeness and achieve the closest possible relationship with their personal God.

c1. Theosis: Collaborating in Synergy with God to Achieve Deification

The concept of Theosis or deification, taught by the Christian Orthodox Church (also found in the Latin rite of the Catholic Church) refers to the process of divinization that a saved person undergoes (usually) after death.

Both laymen and monastics are believed to be able to achieve deification if they lead a worthy life, struggling to recover the likeness of God. This is possible because deification is seen not as the end result of using a spiritual technique, but as a state of being that can only be granted by God when we work in synergy with Him.[28, 29]

---

27. *With some reservations regarding Judaism, since there is no exact description of Heaven in Jewish scripture, even though most orthodox Jews believe that following the Law will provide this reward.*

28. *"He was incarnate that we might be made god".*

– of Alexandria, St. Athanasius. On the Incarnation. St Vladimir's Seminary Press, p. 167.

29. *"A sure warrant for looking forward with hope to deification of human nature is provided by the Incarnation of God, which makes man God to the same degree*

Figure 12. Icon of the Ladder of Divine Ascent. It symbolizes the gateway towards Heaven and divinization (Theosis), with each rung representing a particular vice or virtue. Christ can be seen at the apex waiting to receive the righteous into His Kingdom.

On one side of the ladder there are harmful spiritual influences and passions in the form of demons. They try to drag the faithful off the ladder. On the other side there are angels (also representing virtues) that support them from falling.

The icon represents our journey and struggles in this life. It also implies that the higher someone ascends, the greater the fall they may potentially face. Therefore, humility and vigilance are imperative in order to grow spiritually and transform the passions into virtues, while safeguarding the fruits already obtained in our quest. Picture: late-12th-century Christian icon at Saint Catherine's Monastery, Mount Sinai.

The path for laymen to achieve deification includes: trying to overcome our passions (or at least reduce their influence in our life), participating in the Sacraments (conceived as vessels of divine grace or the Uncreated Energies of God), and repentance.

Repentance, in Eastern Orthodox Christianity, means aligning our will with God´s will, by "stopping going in the opposite direction". It is not the same as guilt.

Orthodox monastics, however, can follow the mystical path of Hesychasm to get closer to God and therefore to deification. This path includes the following stages:

- **Step 1.** *Catharsis, or purification of mind and body.* This includes the restraining of the passions and their transformation into their corresponding virtues. This initial step of purification, however, does not view the presence of a multiplicity of thoughts as intrinsically evil. They are only considered a problem if the thoughts themselves drive us away from God. Given the Tri-Une God of Christianity, who transcends the dialectical opposition between *the One and the Many,* multiplicity is not the enemy.

- **Step 2.** *Contemplation or illumination* (Theoria). This includes concentration and prayer (e.g., Jesus Prayer) and in some cases culminates in the vision of God.

---

as God Himself became man.

[...] Let us become the image of the one whole God, bearing nothing earthly in ourselves, so that we may consort with God and become gods, receiving from God our existence as gods.

For it is clear that He Who became man without sin (cf. Heb. 4:15) will divinize human nature without changing it into the Divine Nature, and will raise it up for His Own sake to the same degree as He lowered Himself for man's sake. This is what St. Paul teaches mystically when he says, "that in the ages to come he might display the overflowing richness of His grace (Eph. 2:7)."

— the Confessor, St. Maximus. Philokalia. Faber & Faber (1983), Volume 2, p. 178.

- **Step 3.** *Union with God.* In some cases, it is even believed that this state of being can be partially experienced in this life.

The difference between Theosis and Henosis or union with the One is that, in the former, created beings are not absorbed or fused with God´s Essence (Ousia). Instead, each person receives God´s full Uncreated Energies, the full actuality of *what* God is. Instead of having to undergo the annihilation of their ego (only its purification), the deified persons are elevated by God to His stature, but without supplanting Him. Both the personhood of God and that of the deified subjects is cherished and maintained.

Symbols of Ascension, Salvation, Purity or Rebirth: ladder, symbols of centrality (e.g., Cosmic Tree, mountain or column situated in the axis of the world [Axis Mundi]), lotus, the Phoenix.

Recommended Reading

1. **The One and the Many: Studies in the Philosophy of Order and Ultimacy.** *R.J. Rushdoony.*
2. **Man and His Becoming according to the Vedanta.** *René Guénon.*
3. **Traditional Forms and Cosmic Cycles.** *René Guénon.*
4. **God, History, and Dialectic. Volumes I and II.** *Joseph P. Farrell.*
5. **The Mystical Theology of the Eastern Church.** *Vladimir Lossky.*
6. **The Enneads.** *Plotinus.*
7. **Evil and the God of Love.** *John Hick.*

A Myriad Worldviews:
Do We Know All Our Options?

Worldviews: Where Metaphysics Leads Us To

Main Metaphysical Doctrines and their Implications

1. Worldviews (Implicitly or Explicitly) Guide Our Lives

WE HAVE NOW BECOME FAMILIARIZED WITH THE traditional metaphysical teachings that are transmitted through symbolic initiations. When put together forming a coherent vision of the world, we obtain a worldview. A worldview is seeing and interpreting "the whole picture" in a certain way. This includes believing that the world functions in a specific manner, and has implications for how we should live and behave towards God or the highest reality, as well as towards others.

A worldview also includes the whole knowledge, culture, and ethics of a particular community, and anyone interested in forming part of that group would need to share them. It is the glue that binds communities together, as they give meaning and direction to life. The very meaning and direction that is missing in our contemporary world.

Due to globalization and technological advances, we currently live in a world full of confusion. We now have to process extreme amounts of information coming from many conflicting worldviews and decide what we believe in and why.

We have lost our traditions, and an increasing number of people have become vulnerable to those who prey on the desperation of those who feel lost. It is not easy to filter the nuggets of valuable information contained among the noise (signal-to-noise ratio).

As a result, some people never commit to a coherent worldview. Instead, they pick metaphysical doctrines here and there from incompatible ones (Syncretism; e.g., New Age). However, this path cannot lead to a fulfilling spiritual life, as it lacks a coherent worldview that provides a solid structure, unity, and stability.

So, in this complicated landscape of beliefs, what do people around the world believe in? What gives meaning, coherence, and direction to their lives and hope beyond our current existence?

In the following sections we will briefly present the types of worldviews we can be confronted with, as well as their main representatives. These are:

• **Religious Worldviews:** showing us different paths towards a personal God or the impersonal Absolute.

• **Mystical Worldviews:** aiming at fusion with the Supreme.

• **Esoteric Worldviews:** based on secret knowledge and ritual, more reliant on personal practice and Self-Transcendence than on notions of a personal God.

- **Philosophical Worldviews:** a multitude of schools of thought and lifestances that aim at providing guidance on how to lead a good life based on human reason alone.

- **Worldviews based on Science and Technology:** that believe that every aspect of life can be explained through science alone (Scientism) or aim at transcending the human condition through knowledge and technology (Transhumanism).

We will put an emphasis on their doctrines pertaining to the metaphysical categories previously discussed, and especially on their proposed solution to the problem of *the One and the Many*.

2. Religious and Mystical Worldviews

2.1. Judaism

Judaism is a monotheistic and ethnic religion that follows the Old Covenant of Moses established between God and the ancient Israelites. Jews believe they were chosen to be "a light unto the nations".

Contrary to what many people may think, though, modern Judaism is not only based on the Hebrew Bible (*Tanakh*, which includes the books of Moses [Torah], Prophets [Nevi'im], and "writings" [Ketuvim]). The *Talmud*, especially the Babylonian version, exerts an even stronger influence over the Jewish religion since its compilation after the destruction of the Second Temple. It is also the primary source of religious law (Halakha).

The *Talmud* is a compilation of the "oral Torah" and its rabbinical commentary (Rabbinic Judaism). It allows for a diversity of theological views and practices depending upon interpretation, thus allowing for the existence of different schools of thought (e.g., Haredim, Hasidim).

However, not all Jews recognize the authority of the Talmud or later rabbinical interpretations of the Torah. Karaite Judaism, for example, only recognizes the authority of the written Torah.

Figure 1. The Second Temple period of Judaism and its innovations (~516 BCE – 70 CE). During this period, ending in the siege of Jerusalem which saw the destruction of the temple (prophesied by Jesus Christ; e.g., Mark 13:1–8), multiple religious currents and developments took place, including the creation of the synagogue and the development of Jewish eschatology.

Tradition tells us that prophecy stopped during this time, while the influence of Greek thought increased. Judaism was growing distant from its roots, and this tendency only got worse later with the development of the Talmud and of Rabbinic Judaism, which eventually became more influential than the Jewish Bible itself, the Torah. Picture: The Queen of Sheba before the temple of Solomon in Jerusalem, by Salomon de Bray (1597-1664).

a. Main Metaphysical Beliefs of Judaism

a1. Conception of God

Judaism adheres to a strict Monotheism and rejects any kind of plurality in God, be it Polytheism, Dualism, or even Trinitarianism.[1] The best example of this is the Shema Yisrael, one of the main Jewish prayers: *"Hear, O Israel: The LORD is our God; the LORD is one"*.

---

1. Trinitarianism understood as tri-Theism. This is contrary to how Christians understand the Holy Trinity (One God in Three Persons), as tri-Theism is also a

God, for Judaism, is an omnipotent, omnipresent, and omniscient personal God who transcends creation. However, He is able and willing to be present in the world.

Some modernist Jewish thinkers, however, conceptualize God as an impersonal Force, process or ideal.[2] This trend can be exemplified by Maimonides' rationalistic philosophy or by Rabbi Zalman Schachter-Shalomi, founder of the Jewish Renewal movement.

a2. Creation and Time

Judaism believes that God created the Universe from nothing (Creatio Ex Nihilo, following the book of *Genesis*). They also believe time to be linear, not cyclical. Therefore, specific events and history as a whole have meaning, since they are not bound to repeat themselves as mere statistical possibilities. In fact, the concept of sacred history is a basic tenet of Judaism, since God is viewed as involved with His creation, and not as a detached or absent deity.

a3. The Origin of Evil or the Cause of Our Current Imperfect State of Being

Traditional Jews believe that evil originates from the first sin committed by the original persons and archetypal beings (Adam and Eve). The tendency to behave contrary to God´s will (Yetzer Hara) became, then, internalized as an intrinsic part of human nature, which caused the estrangement from Him and the consequent suffering of mankind. On the other hand, it is considered that humankind is also born with a contrary inclination or impulse to do good (Yetzer Ha-Tov).

---

condemned heresy for Christianity.

2. *Tuling, Kari H. (2020). "Part 2: Does God Have a Personality—or Is God an Impersonal Force?". In Tuling, Kari H. (ed.). Thinking about God: Jewish Views. The Jewish Publication Society.*

Rabbinical commentary on the book of *Job*, following some interpretations of the *Talmud* (and Maimonides' rationalist philosophy), sometimes conceives "the Satan" (the Accuser) as a metaphor for this internalized tendency rather than as an actual being.

a4. Free Will and How Conditioned Are We in This Life

Jewish tradition mostly rejects strict determinism and emphasizes free will as the basis and precondition for being able to lead a moral life. Persons are seen as capable of struggling and choosing between their two opposing tendencies, which are continually in conflict and provide the grounds for each person to define themselves.

Judaism recognizes two classes of sin: offenses against other people, and offenses against God, conceived as a violation of their covenant with Him.

a5. Path to Salvation and End Times

Free will is also seen as a prerequisite for a just reward or punishment in the coming world.[3] This "world to come" (Olam Ha-Ba) includes the concepts of the Garden of Eden (Gan Eden) or Paradise, and Hell (Gehinnom). However, the phrase "world to come" does not appear in the Hebrew Bible, and the accepted religious law (Halakha) regarding this topic is that it is impossible for a living person to have an accurate knowledge about it.

These beliefs, however, evolved over time. Initially, Jews did not have a clear image of the afterlife, with the Underworld or Sheol (similar to the Greek concept of Hades) being the dark place where souls resided

---

3. *"[...] I [God] have set before you life and death, blessing and curse: therefore choose life [...]". Deuteronomy 30:19. New King James Version.*

after departing this life. Later, Sheol came to be thought of as a place of waiting and purification, an intermediary step between death and Gan Eden or Gehenna.

According to the *Talmud*, Hell may imply temporary purification and not eternal damnation. Those incapable of being purified and having no part in the world to come seem to go back to non-existence instead.

The philosophical school of Maimonides, again, differs on this topic. For him, there was not a direct causality between good and bad actions and rewards and punishments, respectively.

He believed that these were ideas prepared for the masses to maintain order and the observance of the Law. The true reward was having the part of our intellect that connected to God (the active intellect) immortalized[4] in order to enjoy eternally the "Glory of the Presence". The true punishment would simply be not being able to achieve this state of being.

Symbols in Judaism: the Star of David, menorah, kippah, tefillin.

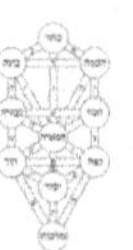

2.2. Jewish Mysticism: Kabbalah

a. Different Subtraditions and Sources of Authority

Kabbalah, meaning "Tradition", is the esoteric mystical school of thought of Judaism.

According to the *Zohar*, one of its most important foundational texts, the Torah has four levels of meaning (exegesis; Pardes), including:

---

4. *Maimonides (1138–1204). Internet Encyclopedia of Philosophy. Accessed January 2024: "In short, Maimonides held that a person is immortal, capable of surviving bodily death, to the extent that one's intellect is actualized. There are then, degrees of immortality and degrees of being protected by providence. Prophecy, providence, and immortality are all explicated along these Aristotelian/Neoplatonic lines."*

- *Peshat:* direct interpretation, the most obvious meaning taken at face value.

- *Remez:* allegorical meaning.

- *Derash:* midrashic (rabbinic) meanings, often derived from comparisons with similar verses.

- *Sod:* the inner (esoteric) and metaphysical meaning, which is the knowledge properly obtained through Kabbalah.

There are four main Kabbalistic subtraditions. Merkavah or Chariot mysticism, the earliest instance of Jewish mysticism, follows the "Palaces" (Hekhalot) literature. It is based on the vision found in the book of *Ezekiel.* It revolves around stories of ascent to the heavenly Palaces and the Throne of God, and also on the meditative practices used in order to attain those visions.

Ecstatic Kabbalah, in turn, is a meditative branch of Kabbalah that strives to achieve mystical union with God. This is obtained through purification (Catharsis) and meditative techniques (breath work and extreme concentration) while reciting the Divine Names. Its main exponent is Abraham Abulafia. His metaphysical framework was based on Maimonides' rationalist system (who viewed God as the Agent Intellect), and hoped to achieve a prophetic state through his methods.

The main modern branch of Kabbalah, the theoretical or "theurgic" tradition, is based instead largely on the *Zohar* and Lurianic Kabbalah. The books of Clarity (*Bahir*) and Creation (*Yetzirah*) also play an important role. It focuses on understanding the divine, its attributes, and the duty of humanity in redeeming or restoring the damaged spiritual realm to its original perfection.

This is viewed as possible because man is seen as a divine microcosm mirroring the higher planes of existence (like in the Hermetical notion of "as above, so below"). This tradition provided the whole normative Jewish religious practices with their metaphysical explanation and justification.

Lastly, practical Kabbalah is focused on the use of magical/talismanic "white magic" in order to influence this world and the higher ones. This was traditionally seen as a dangerous task only allowed to a few practitioners at best, and forbidden at worst.

b. Main Metaphysical Beliefs of Kabbalah
b1. Conception of God

The transcendent aspect of God in the Kabbalah is called Ein Sof ("The Infinite"). This tradition follows the doctrine of Absolute Divine Simplicity, where no plurality of faculties, moral dispositions or essential attributes can exist in God. Kabbalah does not even permit the affirmation that the statement "God is all-knowing, all-powerful, and all-good" ultimately reflects different qualities or attributes of God. This would imply multiplicity, which is not allowed in the Godhead.[5,6]

Regarding the Universe and creation, in order for God to be able to manifest his energies and attributes, God depends on creation. As Aryeh Kaplan stated:[7]

---

5. *"God is not two or more entities, but a single entity of a oneness even more single and unique than any single thing in creation... He cannot be sub-divided into different parts – therefore, it is impossible for Him to be anything other than one. It is a positive commandment to know this, for it is written (Deuteronomy 6:4) '... the Lord is our God, the Lord is one'."*

– Maimonides. Mishneh Torah, Mada 1:7.

6. *"God's existence is absolutely simple, without combinations or additions of any kind. All perfections are found in Him in a perfectly simple manner. However, God does not entail separate domains – even though in truth there exist in God qualities which, within us, are separate... Indeed the true nature of His essence is that it is a single attribute, (yet) one that intrinsically encompasses everything that could be considered perfection. All perfection therefore exists in God, not as something added on to His existence, but as an integral part of His intrinsic identity... This is a concept that is very far from our ability to grasp and imagine..."*

– Chaim Luzzatto, Moshe (Derekh Hashem I:1:5).

7. Kaplan, Aryeh (1991). Innerspace. Introduction to Kabbalah, Meditation And Prophecy. Moznaim Publishing Corporation.

"God created a spiritual dimension... [through which God] interacts with the Universe... It is this dimension which makes it possible for us to speak of God's multifaceted relationship to the universe without violating the basic principle of His unity and simplicity."

Therefore, in Kabbalistic thought, we have two aspects of God viewed as complementary to each other:

1. *God in Essence (Ein/Ayn Sof or "the Infinite/Endless").* Transcendent, impersonal, limitless, unknowable. This Godhead is an Absolute Divine Simplicity beyond revelation that can only be partially defined by what It is not (negative or apophatic theology).

2. *The manifested God.* Immanent, personal, knowable. The revealed persona (mask) through which the Infinite creates, sustains, and relates to all creation. Emanated from the first aspect or Essence of God. This aspect can be defined by ascribing to Him positive attributes (positive or cataphatic theology).

The Ein Sof, conceived as an infinite life force and first cause, is therefore not believed to be revealed in the Torah, since it is by definition incapable of being revealed.

Regarding this point, the *Zohar* interprets the first words of the book of *Genesis* as:

- *Original text in the Torah:* "In the beginning God created (BeReishit Bara Elohim)."

- *Interpretation in the Zohar:* "With (the level of) Reishit (Beginning) (the Ein Sof) created Elohim (God's manifestation in creation)". This effectively implies another principle higher than the God revealed in the Hebrew Bible.

b2. On Creation

Medieval Kabbalists believed that creation came to be and all things were linked directly to God through emanations. This doctrine implies that all levels of existence are part of one great, continuous and gradually more imperfect, Chain of Being. There is no chasm, abyss or absolute separation between God and His creation.

The theory of emanations transforms the theistic concept of creation out of nothing (Ex Nihilo) into a panentheistic gradual self-emanation by the impersonal Infinite.

This Ein Sof is, then, the source of all possibility but no actuality until the emanations are brought forth. It is the No-Thing that produces everything that exists.

These emanations, in Kabbalistic thought, can be divided into four differentiated worlds or realms of existence:

Atziluth (the World of Emanation), Beriah (the World of Creation), Yetzirah (the World of Formation), and Assiah (the World of Action).

Preceding them is Adam Kadmon, or Primordial Man. He contains both mankind (as its archetype) as well as the ten divine attributes (the Sefirot [תּוֹרִיפְּס], meaning emanations).

In turn, the Tree of Life diagram represents the totality of the divine attributes through which God emanated all reality. It is the path and connection between the transcendent God and His immanent presence in creation (Shekinah).

In this scheme, Adam represents the highest attribute of God (Keter, crown), the Divine Will. An element of each divine attribute is also believed to be present in each of the Four Worlds and in each of the other particular attributes. This implies a fractal understanding of reality, where each level contains all the rest.

Going even further in the process of emphasizing the divine immanence of God, the Hasidic movement holds that, from God's perspective, He is all that really exists.

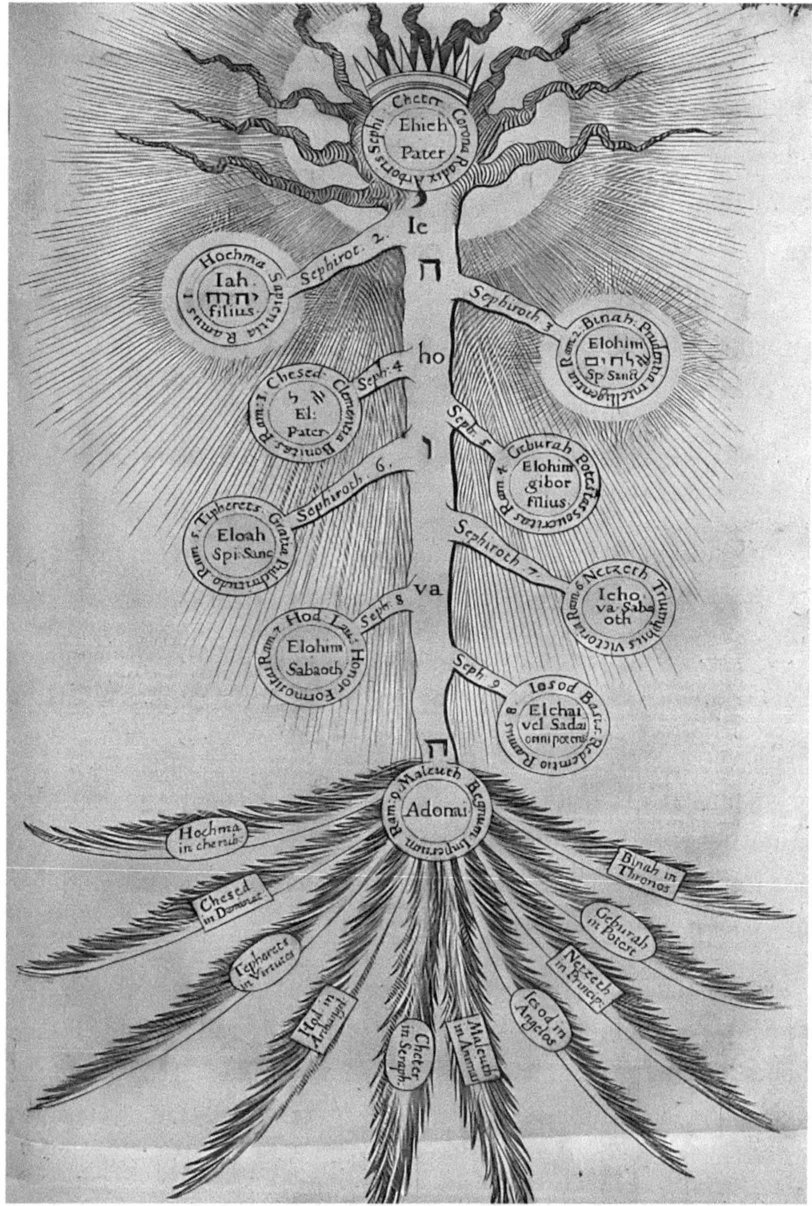

Figure 2. Robert Fludd´s depiction of the Sefirot and the Tree of Life (1617). By reading closely within each Sefirah, we can see how the mixing of Kabbalah with a Christian worldview results in the co-equal Trinity of Christianity (Father, Son, and Holy Spirit) becoming a sequentially emanated triad subordinated to an absolutely simple Monad. Picture: Deutsche Fotothek.

b3. The Problem of Evil

Some Kabbalists conceive "evil" as necessary and as implied by the very existence of God. In the creation story of Lurianic Kabbalah, for example, the first act of the cosmic drama involves the self-withdrawal of God or the contraction of His Divine Light in order to leave a void where creation can take place (Tzimtzum).

It is followed by an emanation of light into this void that allows individual existence, multiplicity, to come forth without staining the unity of the now self-exiled God.[8]

This, in turn, is followed by the instability of this original creation (Tohu or Chaos), which leads to the shattering of the sephirotic vessels. The shards of the broken vessels then fall down into the lower realms. However, they are still animated by remnants of the Divine Light, which are now trapped in creation and constitute human souls. The mission of man in this life, then, is to rectify this state of affairs (Tikkun Olam) and return the exiled sparks of light back to their source, ending multiplicity once again.

The demonic realm created by the shells of the broken vessels devoid of light (the Other Side; Sitra Achra) is conceived as a mirror image of the realm of the holy. These shells confine the Divine Light but, paradoxically, also protect it by limiting its revelation.

Gershom Scholem, one of the most popular modern historians of Kabbalah, called this characteristic thought a "Jewish Gnostic motif", especially prominent in Spanish Kabbalah.[9]

---

8. Unity and multiplicity exist in dialectical tension.

9. *See, for example: Scholem, Gershom (1960). Jewish Gnosticism, Merkabah, Mysticism and Talmudic Tradition. KTAV Publishing House.*

In this view, evil is a necessary precondition for the limitless to manifest. The origin of evil is an uncontainable excess of the good. Self-aware creation, in turn, is only possible after a cosmic catastrophe in the Godhead itself.

All this implies that the ultimate good is returning all the lost souls or sparks of light to their original absolute unity. It also implies that multiplicity is evil itself, with evil being nothing else than the concept of limit, of difference. The mystical task imposed on observing Jews is, then, to reveal and restore the concealed undifferentiated divine simplicity.

COMPLEMENTARY DUALISM IN KABBALISTIC THOUGHT

The most esoteric sections (Idrot) of the *Zohar* emphasize the image of male and female Divine Personas (Partzufim), which are harmonized rearrangements of the ten Sefirot.

This dialectical and paradoxical coexistence and Union of Opposites (male/female) is typical of Kabbalistic thought, and was implied by much of what we have discussed above.

Some examples of Complementary Dualism previously sketched are:

• **Good and Evil implying each other:** with the shells or Qlippoth being needed to limit the infinite Godhead in order for It to become a creator deity.

• **The Good being defined by the overcoming of these limits:** and, therefore, by abandoning multiplicity by returning all sparks of Divine Light to Ein Sof, the One.

• **God experiencing Himself as Other through man:** and, thus, man being a necessary complementary opposite to the Divine Persona.

Another variant of Complementary Dualism can be found in the doctrine that the root of all evil is in one of the attributes of God Himself: His Strength, Judgement or Severity (Gevurah).

Following the same pattern, Gevurah is thought as the necessary counterpart of divine Love/Kindness (Chesed). When man sins, he actualizes or activates the attribute of Divine Judgment in his soul.

This, given that man is viewed as a microcosmic image of the higher macrocosmic realities and is connected to them, contributes to unbalancing the equilibrium between the divine attributes of Love and Judgment in God Himself. This generates disharmony and actualizes the demonic realm, illusory in origin, in our plane of existence.

b4. Free Will and the Role of Mankind

Kabbalah gives man the central role in creation. He is viewed as a full microcosmic reflection of the realities above, and is therefore granted free will, as it is one of the attributes of God in which he partakes. He is, then, able to freely choose to live in a holy way that helps restore this broken world and liberate the trapped sparks of Divine Light.

The human soul is viewed as formed by three main aspects: Nefesh, Ruach, and Neshamah.

Nefesh, obtained at birth, is found in all humanity. It is the basis of one's physical and psychological nature and so may partially condition us.

The next two parts of the soul are believed to be obtained and developed over time, depending on how we live, and becoming fully present only in spiritually awakened persons. They are: the Spirit (Ruach), capable of distinguishing between good and evil, and the Intellect or higher soul (Neshamah), capable of being aware of the presence of God.

Sometimes, two further parts or soul states are also mentioned, more elevated than the ones just discussed. They are Chayyah and Yehidah. They allow for awareness of the divine life force itself and to achieve union with God, respectively.

b5. On Salvation

As we have seen, the ideal of the Kabbalist is to liberate the Holy Sparks present in creation so that they can go back to their source, Ein Sof. Like a drop of water back into the ocean, where particularity and multiplicity are discarded as temporary at best and as unreal at worst.

Another doctrine regarding the afterlife, that of reincarnation or transmigration (Gilgul Neshamot or Cycles of the Soul), was introduced into Kabbalah from the Middle Ages onwards. This concept is not a biblical one and was previously rejected, but Lurianic Kabbalah and Hasidic Judaism popularized it.

2.3. Christianity

Christianity, the largest religion in the world, follows the teachings of Jesus Christ (Christ meaning "the Anointed One of God"), believed to be the Incarnation of the Logos and second Person of the Tri-Une God.

The main beliefs of Christians are codified in the Creeds (e.g., the *Nicene Creed*). They include:

• *Belief in the Holy Trinity:* the One God who exists in three co-equal Persons (Tri-Une God) with one common Essence or Nature (Homoousion): God the Father, God the Son (or Logos), and God the Holy Spirit.[10, 11]

---

10. *Daley, Brian E. (2009). "The Persons in God and the Person of Christ in Patristic Theology: An Argument for Parallel Development". God in Early Christian Thought. Leiden & Boston: Brill. pp. 323–350.*

11. *Ramelli, Ilaria (2012). "Origen, Greek Philosophy, and the Birth of the Trinitarian Meaning of Hypostasis". The Harvard Theological Review. 105 (3): 302–350.*

• *Belief in the Incarnation of the Second Person of the Trinity (the Logos):* in Jesus Christ, in order to bring the possibility of salvation into this world. This, in turn, was achieved through His death, resurrection, and ascension.

• *Belief in the Holiness of the Church:* now seen as a potential receptacle of the Holy Spirit.

• *Belief in the Second Coming of the Christ:* who, as the God-Man (who also experienced human suffering and temptation) will judge man justly at the end of time.

• *The* Resurrection *of the Dead into an Eternal Existence:* experienced differently depending on how we live.

Regarding textual sources, the record of the life, sayings, and deeds of the Christ were recorded in the four *Gospels* (meaning "good news") and the different books and epistles of the *New Testament*, written by His Apostles and Evangelists (meaning "the one who proclaims good news").

The *New Testament* is one part of the Christian biblical canon (also called the *Holy Bible*), the compilation of books relevant to the Christian faith. The other part is the *Old Testament*, based primarily on the books of the Hebrew Bible (*Tanakh*).

Christians believe that the *Old Testament* cannot be understood without using the New as the key to its interpretation. Interpreted in this way, the *Old Testament* clearly points to the advent and works of the Christ, the consummation and recapitulation of all previous prophecies and revelations.

The books compiled in the Bible are believed to have been written under the inspiration of the Holy Spirit, the third Person of the Tri-Une God, once mankind was enabled to receive Him through the voluntary sacrifice, death, resurrection, and ascension of the Christ.

a. Main Christian Denominations

Christianity´s largest denominations are: Roman Catholicism, Eastern Orthodoxy, and Protestantism.

The Protestant churches accept a shorter *Old Testament* canon than the ones accepted by Orthodoxy and Catholicism. The latter also include books considered apocryphal by Judaism and Protestantism (the Deuterocanonical books) but which appear in the earliest available Greek translation of the Hebrew Bible (the *Septuagint*). The Orthodox canon is also slightly larger than the Catholic one.

In addition to the Bible, and depending on the denomination, a greater (Orthodox) or smaller (Protestant) emphasis is given to the oral and written tradition preserved by the Church since the times of the Christ through apostolic succession.

Holy Tradition is considered holy because the Holy Spirit is seen as residing in the saints and in all those who became worthy of receiving Him. It is viewed, especially by the Orthodox church, as clarifying the meaning behind aspects that have little presence in the Bible, such as why Baptism is performed by full triple immersion (Orthodox)[12,13,14,15] instead of by the sprinkling of water (e.g., Catholic).

---

12. Orthodox Church in America: Baptism. Archived October 12, 2010: "After the proclamation of faith, the baptismal water is prayed over and blessed as the sign of the goodness of God's creation. The person to be baptized is also prayed over and blessed with sanctified oil as the sign that his creation by God is holy and good. And then, after the solemn proclamation of "Alleluia" (God be praised), the person is immersed three times in the water in the name of the Father, the Son and the Holy Spirit."

13. Ferguson, Everett (2008). Baptism in the Early Church. Wm. B. Eerdmans Publishing Company, p. 860.

14. Shanbour, Father Michael. Christ the Saviour Orthodox Christian Church, article "Our Personal Resurrection": "For this reason normative Christian Baptism has always been by immersion (baptism means 'immersion' in the Greek language) which provides both the image of burial and of resurrection."

15. Ware, Timothy (1963). "Theology for the Community of God". The Orthodox Church. Penguin Books, p. 530: "Orthodoxy regards immersion as essential."

One of the key principles of Protestantism is the belief in a Universal Priesthood of Believers, which implies the right and duty of every Christian believer to take part in the government of the Church.[16] It is contrary to the Catholic and Orthodox hierarchies, and especially opposed to the concept of an infallible Pope, which the Orthodox also do not accept.

Other Two Key Protestant Principles Are:

• *The belief in salvation by Faith Alone (Sola Fide),* instead of through faith in addition to works (unlike Catholic and Orthodox). Good works are, however, seen as a necessary consequence of having faith.

• *The belief that the Bible should be the only source of authority (Sola Scriptura).* Emphasized by Luther and the Reformation, this principle de-emphasizes church tradition, contrary to Catholic and Orthodox views. The Orthodox, especially, see the consensus of Holy Tradition in key matters as "the life of the Holy Spirit in the Church." [17]

Additional Differences Between Denominations Include:

• The Protestant rejection of the Catholic dogma of Transubstantiation and their various beliefs regarding the real presence of the Christ in Holy Communion, as well as the rejection of iconography.

• The Catholic dogmas of the Immaculate Conception (the belief that Mary, the mother of God, was born without Original Sin) and the Assumption of Mary (her direct translation into Heaven at the end of her life). Both of these teachings were defined as infallible dogma in the nineteenth and twentieth centuries, respectively, and are not accepted by neither Protestant nor Orthodox.

----

16. *Herzog, Johann Jakob; Philip Schaff, Albert (1911). The New Schaff-Herzog Encyclopedia of Religious Knowledge. p. 419.*

17. *Lossky, Vladimir (1982). "Tradition and traditions," in Leonid Ouspensky, The Meaning of Icons. St Vladimir's Seminary Press, p. 15.*

b. Main Metaphysical Beliefs of Christianity

b1. Conception of God

The Holy Trinity

The belief in the mystery of the Tri-Une God is a particular Christian belief that is viewed as originating from God´s revelation. It is not a philosophical conclusion reached after purely human study, meditation, and discussion.

It is considered a Mystery as it is seen as a revealed truth about the internal life of the transcendent God Himself that cannot yet be fully understood by immanent created beings such as humans in their current state.

The Christian notion of a Trinitarian God is one of the only two doctrines that may transcend the dialectical nature of the problem of *the One and the Many* ("is ultimate reality an absolute Oneness or is it multiple?"), the other being certain interpretations of non-dualist thought not embracing Panentheism.

The term Trinity refers to one God manifested in three eternal Persons (Hypostasis), equal in dignity and stature. Together, they are sometimes called the Godhead.

They share the same Essence (Ousia) and each of them is fully God. However, they are distinct from the point of view of their relationship to one another: the Father has no source, the Son is begotten of the Father, and the Spirit proceeds from the Father (Orthodox) or from the Father and the Son (Filioque clause[18]; Catholic and Protestant).

---

18. *For a deeper analysis on the importance of the Filioque clause, see Chapter VII.*

NON-TRINITARIANISM

Non-Trinitarianism (or anti-Trinitarianism) refers to the theological positions that reject the doctrine of the Tri-Une God in favor of the doctrine of the One. They may see themselves as Christians, but they are not considered to be so by the main Christian denominations, which see this teaching as heretical and contrary to the very core of Christianity.

Some examples of important historical anti-Trinitarian views that posited an absolute divine unity (Monarchianism) were:

• The teaching that Jesus was adopted as a Son of God after his human life (Adoptionism).

• The doctrine of Modalism, or Oneness Christology, that taught that the One God manifests Himself in three different *Personas* (in the sense of being different "masks" that help manifest a God that in His transcendence cannot be manifested).[19]

The first notion is similar to the mystical paths that believe in the power of self-improvement to achieve Self-Deification.

The second one is similar to the Hindu Trimūrti, the triad of deities personifying the impersonal Brahman and representing partial aspects of God as creator (Brahmā), preservator (Vishnu), and destructor (Shiva).[20]

Non-Trinitarianism historically reappeared in Catharism (a branch of Gnosticism), Unitarianism (born closely after the Protestant Reformation[21]), in some Restorationist groups appearing from the Protestant Second Great Awakening, and in Oneness Protestant Pentecostal churches.

Other worldviews not recognized as Christian by the main denominations, such as Jehovah's Witnesses and Mormonism, also follow a non-Trinitarian doctrine.

---

19. Harnack, Adolf (1961). History of Dogma. HardPress.

20. For the Trimurti system having Brahmā as the creator, Vishnu as the maintainer or preserver, and Shiva as the destroyer see, for example: Zimmer, Heinrich (1972). Myths and Symbols in Indian Art and Civilization. Princeton University Press, p. 124.

21. Feldmeth, Nathan P. (2008). "Unitarianism". Pocket Dictionary of Church History. IVP USA, p. 135: "Unitarians emerged from Protestant Christian beginnings in the sixteenth century with a central focus on the unity of God and subsequent denial of the doctrine of the Trinity."

The origin of the Son and of the Holy Spirit being the Father, however, does not imply that they are created and subordinated to Him (the heresy of Arianism), as each Person of the Trinity implies and indwells (Perichoresis) one another logically (e.g., Father implies Son) and cannot be conceived as divided. Each Person is transcendent, omnipotent, and eternal, prior to creation and time.

Much emphasis is put in the fact that the Trinity is not a composition of three different Gods (the heresy of Tri-Theism), or that each Person is just a third part of a unitary God (the heresy of Partialism).

"That they all may be one; as thou, Father, art in me, and I in thee, that they also may be one in us."

— John 17:21. New King James Version

"The Father is God, the Son is God, and the Holy Spirit is God, and yet there are not three Gods but one God." [22]

— Athanasian Creed

The Logos: Jesus Christ as the Incarnation of the Word of God

A central Christian belief is that Jesus is the Incarnation of the second Person of the Trinity and the Messiah (the Christ) prophesied by ancient Jewish prophets in the *Old Testament*.

As stated in the canonical *Gospels* of Matthew and Luke, Jesus was conceived by the Holy Spirit and born from the Virgin Mary. He is viewed as partaking of two natures (divine and human) in one Person. The union of these two natures was accomplished by each one indwelling and interpenetrating the other, instead of being complementary parts

---

22. *Schaff, Philip (1877b). "Athanasian Creed ". The Creeds of Christendom (Vol. 2). New York: Harper Brothers, pp. 66–71.*

that needed to be blended into a third composite entity being neither one nor the other. Therefore, the two natures of Jesus Christ are viewed as unified without abolishing the principle of distinction.

This is believed to be the basis for the possibility of mankind being saved in their individuality, in contrast with worldviews that embrace the fusion of every self-enlightened individual with an Absolute or Monad that requires the absence of any particularity as a prerequisite to achieve salvation.

Therefore, in Christianity, the presence of distinction is not regarded as incompatible with the existence of a single, unitary divinity. However, the Christian unity of God is not an *absolutely* simple one defined and limited solely by its rejection of any multiplicity. God, being the source of all logical notions and therefore superior to them, necessarily transcends human logical and dialectical (Either/Or) boundaries.

Because of that, the binary and dialectical logic of having to accept one extreme of two opposite positions while rejecting the other, does not apply to the Christian God. This is exemplified in the two most important beliefs of Christianity: the belief in a Tri-Une God, and the belief that Jesus Christ was both fully God and fully man, both doctrines implying the transcendence of the dichotomy between *the One and the Many*.[23]

Regarding the latter, Christians believe that Jesus, according to His human nature, suffered pains and temptations, but did not sin. Being Himself the very source of Life, His unjust but voluntarily accepted death resulted in the condemnation of Death itself, as to kill the Principle of Life is an ontological impossibility.

---

23. For an analysis of how the Filioque clause may affect this conclusion, see Chapter VII.

Thus, the resurrection of Jesus implied the resurrection of the human nature that He assumed[24], which was granted life eternal. His ascension to "the right hand of the Father"[25], furthermore, also implied the possibility of deifying this now universally immortal human nature.

Summarizing, Christians believe that our human nature has assumed the divine immortality of God through the Person of Jesus Christ, just as God adopted our mortality by assuming our human nature through the Incarnation.

"The Word was made man in order that we might become God."

— St. Athanasius. On the Incarnation. SVS Press, p. 54

"For as Christ died and was exalted as man, so, as man, he is said to receive what, as God, he always had, in order that this great gift might extend to us. For the Word was not degraded by receiving a body, so that he should seek to 'receive' God's gift. Rather he deified what he put on; and, more than that, be bestowed his gift upon the race of men."

— St. Athanasius. Contra Arianos, i.24-25

"Our Lord Jesus Christ, the Word of God, of his boundless love, became what we are that he might make us what he himself is."

— St. Irenaeus. Against Heresies, V

"And if Christ is not risen, then our preaching is empty and your faith is also empty."

— St. Paul the Apostle. 1Cor. 15:14. New King James Version

─────────────

24. *John 3:16, 5:24, 6:39–40, 6:47, 10:10, 11:25–26, and 17:3. Holy Bible; New King James Version.*

25. *Mark 16:19. New King James Version.*

Regarding the resurrection, the *New Testament* mentions several appearances of Jesus between His resurrection and ascension, with His twelve apostles and "more than five hundred brethren at once"[26] being direct witnesses.

b2. On Creation

Christianity, contrary to the Greek notion that "nothing comes from nothing" (Parmenides), teaches that God created the Universe out of nothing (Creatio Ex Nihilo). This doctrine emphasizes the transcendental nature of the Christian God, who did not rearrange a pre-existing matter (e.g., Chaos, night, primordial waters) like the gods of many ancient creation myths (e.g., the Sumerian, Babilonian, Egyptian, and Greek ones).[27]

It is also opposed to the theory of emanations, a famous exponent of which is the Neo-Platonic Plotinus, since Emanationism emphasizes the immanence of God and states that the Universe came from God Himself and therefore is a part of Him.

Creation out of nothing also implies the impossibility of relying just on one´s abilities for salvation. This is emphasized by Christians in their doctrine of Synergism, were God and man cooperate to achieve man´s salvation (Catholics and Protestants) or deification (Theosis; Orthodox).

b3. The Problem of Evil

The doctrine of the Original Sin of Adam and Eve, the first human persons and archetypes of human nature, was not fully developed until Augustine of Hippo, who used the term for the first time.[28]

---

26. *1 Corinthians 15:6. New King James Version.*

27. *Wasilewska, Ewa (2000). Creation Stories of the Middle East. Jessica Kingsley Publishers, pp. 45-59.*

28. *Patte, Daniel (2019). "Original Sin". In Daniel Patte (ed.). The Cambridge Dictionary of Christianity (Two Volume Set). Wipf and Stock, p. 892.*

Augustine´s tenet became a doctrinal cornerstone in the Western world. However, Eastern Orthodoxy did not accept his views. Instead, the Orthodox church uses the term Ancestral Sin to describe the effect of Adam's sin on man´s nature (the word sin meaning "missing the mark"). The key distinction emphasized by the Orthodox is that, instead of inheriting the guilt of Adam´s sin (thought as a Latin mistranslation of Romans 5:12), we inherited the capacity to sin by receiving the corrupted nature of the original archetype of all mankind, Adam.

In other words, for Western Christianity we share the guilt of transgressing against God even before being born. However, for Eastern Orthodoxy we only inherited an injured human nature. This means that, having been created in the image and likeness of God, we retain the image (which includes all our intrinsic potentialities, such as free will) and are still capable of restoring the lost likeness by putting to good use those potentialities and with the help of God (e.g., through light asceticism, prayer, repentance, and the Sacraments).

This difference between Western and Eastern understanding of Adam´s Fall has implications for how we interpret sin and the meaning of the Christ´s death.

Due to the Catholic understanding of sin in legalistic terms, it is viewed as a crime that reaps death as a just punishment in order to clear the debt incurred towards God. This is why, even after God´s forgiveness of our sins, Catholics believe that many souls need a period of further purification in Purgatory.

In addition, the death of the Incarnation of God on the Cross was sometimes interpreted as the payment required to satisfy the demands of God´s justice (Penal Substitution theory, originated by the Protestant leaders Luther and Calvin).

In contrast, Orthodox Christians prefer the analogy of sin as an injury or sickness that has to be cured, with each sinner needing to heal with the help of the Church (seen as a hospital for the sick), repentance (meaning "turning the other way"), and by starting to walk towards God. No punishment is "prescribed" and the notion of guilt is de-emphasized.

"The Christ has suffered to be crucified for the race of men who, since Adam, were fallen to the power of death and were in the error of the serpent, each man committing evil by his own fault." [29]

— St. Justin Martyr. Dialogue with Trypho (Ch.86)

The Devil

Evil has no intrinsic existence in Christianity. It is not a substance, nor an independent rival power or complement to the good. Evil is just the negation of the good, of God, allowed temporary existence due to free will.

God did not will the existence of evil, but allows it because He willed His creatures to be free. Nevertheless, it is in God´s power to make use of this temporary evil to bring forth good fruits, making the existence of evil a self-contradictory one (e.g., Death killing itself by taking the Christ, the principle of Life, at the cross).

At its very core, evil is viewed as a mistake. The misplaced judgment and error of rejecting the good, missing the mark of life´s ultimate purpose and the rejection of God´s love.

Christian cosmogony states that evil, as a rebellion against God´s will, first came into existence through the devil, Satan ("Enemy or Adversary") or Lucifer ("Light-Bearer"; also called the "Morning-Star"), who tried to become equal to God.[30]

---

29. *Toews, John (2013). The story of original sin. Wipf and Stock, pp. 48-61.*

30. *Some Gnostic sects saw them as two different entities, with Lucifer being seen as another son of God and sometimes as the original "good rebel" against a tyrant deity.*

He is identified with several biblical figures, such as the serpent in the Garden of Eden, the tempter of the *Gospels*, Leviathan, and the dragon of the *Book of Revelation.*

Expelled from the presence of God with a host of other angelic beings, he became a fallen angel, being allowed influence for a time in our plane of existence.

Further expansion on how evil became intermingled with mankind can be found in the book of *Genesis* (Adam´s Fall, tower of Babel) and in the non-canonical book of *Enoch.*

Some Protestant reformists interpreted the devil as exclusively a metaphor for humans' proclivities to sin. However, this is not accepted doctrine by any of the main Christian denominations.

"He who from among these angelic powers was set over the earthly realm, and into whose hands God committed the guardianship of the earth, was not made wicked in nature but was good, and made for good ends, and received from his Creator no trace whatever of evil in himself.

But he did not sustain the brightness and the honour which the Creator had bestowed on him, and of his free choice was changed from what was in harmony to what was at variance with his nature, and became roused against God Who created him, and determined to rise in rebellion against Him: and he was the first to depart from good and become evil.

Spence, L. (1993). "Albigenses". An Encyclopedia of Occultism. Carol Publishing, p. 8:

"It has been claimed by their opponents that they admitted two fundamental principles, good and bad, saying that God had produced Lucifer from Himself; that indeed Lucifer was the son of God who revolted against Him; [...] It is alleged that they further believed that God for the re-establishment of order had produced a second son, who was Jesus Christ. Furthermore the Catholic writers on the Albigenses charged them with believing that the souls of men were demons lodged in mortal bodies in punishment of their crimes."

For evil is nothing else than absence of goodness, just as darkness also is absence of light. For goodness is the light of the mind, and, similarly, evil is the darkness of the mind. [...] ”

— St. John of Damascus. An Exact Exposition of the Orthodox Faith. Book II. Chapter IV. Concerning the devil and demons

“*And He said to them, 'I saw Satan fall like lightning from heaven.'* ”

— Luke 10:18. New King James Version

b4. On Determinism and Free Will

The concept of free will is key for Christianity, as salvation is seen as depending on its good use. However, there are different views regarding the degree of free will available to mankind after its fall.

Some important Protestant reformers such as Martin Luther and John Calvin affirmed that Original Sin persisted even after Baptism and completely destroyed the freedom to do good, implying the loss of free will (the theory of Total Depravity) and the pre-determined nature of salvation.[31, 32] Nowadays, the main Protestant churches adhering to this doctrine are Lutherans[33, 34],

---

31. *Turner, H. E. W. (2004). The Patristic Doctrine of Redemption: a study of the development of doctrine during the first five centuries (2004 Reprint ed.). Eugene, Or.: Wipf & Stock Publishers, p. 71.*

32. *Wilson, Kenneth M. (25 May 2018). Augustine's Conversion from Traditional Free Choice to "Non-free Free Will": A Comprehensive Methodology. Tübingen: Mohr Siebeck, pp. 157–187.*

33. *"Calvinism and Lutheranism Compared". WELS Topical Q&A. Wisconsin Evangelical Lutheran Synod. Archived from the original on 27 September 2009. "Total Depravity – Lutherans and Calvinists agree." Yes this is correct. Both agree on the devastating nature of the fall and that man by nature has no power to aid in his conversions...and that election to salvation is by grace. In Lutheranism the German term for election is Gnadenwahl, election by grace--there is no other kind.*

34. *Andreä, Jakob; Chemnitz, Martin; Selnecker, Nikolaus; Chytraeus, David; Musculus, Andreas; Körner, Christoph (1577), Solid Declaration of the Formula of Concord.*

Calvinists[35, 36], and Arminian (including Methodists).[37, 38] The Catholic and Orthodox churches, in contrast, teach that the Sacrament of Baptism erases Original Sin and free will is maintained, even if human nature remains weakened and attracted towards sin. Free will is seen as a necessary condition for the just judgment of each person, as well as an intrinsic attribute of mankind, created in the image of God.[39, 40]

b5. On Salvation and Eschatology

The Christian Church does not see itself as a school of metaphysical doctrines but as a way of salvation.

Salvation is viewed as granted by faith alone (Protestantism) or by works in addition to faith (Roman Catholicism and Eastern Orthodoxy). The concept of "works" includes any internal (e.g., ascetical) and external work (e.g., charity [almsgiving]; participation in the Sacraments) that purifies the faithful and brings God´s presence closer to the world.

Also termed Holy Mysteries, the Sacraments are the way in which the Christian is united with God. They are the physical and spiritual means by which the faithful partake of God through His Uncreated Energies (Orthodoxy) or through created grace (Roman Catholicism).

---

35. *"Westminster Larger Catechism 1-50" (reformed.org). Question 25.*

36. *"The Heidelberg Catechism" (reformed.org). Question 8.*

37. *Arminius, James. The Writings of James Arminius (three vols., tr. James Nichols and W. R. Bagnall). Grand Rapids, Michigan: Baker (1956), I:252.*

38. *Peck, George (ed.) (1847). "Natural Theology". The Methodist Quarterly Review. New York: Lane & Tippett, XXIX: 444.*

39. *McGiffert, Arthur C. (1932). A History of Christian Thought (Vol. 1). Early and Eastern. New York; London: C. Scribner's Sons, p. 101.*

40. *Wallace, A. J.; Rusk, R. D. (2011). Moral Transformation: the original Christian paradigm of salvation. New Zealand: Bridgehead Publishing, pp. 258–259.*

For Catholics and Orthodox there are seven recognized Sacraments. These are:

• *The three Sacraments of Initiation:* Baptism, for purification, the death of the profane man and the rebirth of a Christian; Chrismation (Orthodox)/Confirmation (Catholic), the receiving of the Holy Spirit by the now purified Christian; the Eucharist (or Holy Communion), also a Sacrament of continuous nourishment through union with God. Considered the most important Sacrament of them all.

• *The Sacraments of Healing:* Confession, for repentance and reconciliation; Holy Unction for the sick (Orthodox) and Extreme Unction for the dying (Catholics).

• *The Sacraments of Service:* Marriage, understood as a mirror and symbol of the relationship of God and His Church; Ordination, for those called to serve the Church in Holy Orders (e.g., clergy).

Most Protestant churches, however, only recognize two Sacraments: Baptism and the Eucharist.

The actual experience of salvation has been defined by Catholics and many Protestant denominations (including the Lutheran and the Methodist churches[41, 42]) as the Beatific Vision.[43] This vision is another way of explaining the ultimate contemplatory union with God, our sharing in God's nature via sanctifying created grace.[44] This notion highlights the intellectual component of salvation, even though it includes joy and happiness.

---

41. *"What United Methodists Believe". Spring Lake United Methodist Church. Archived from the original on 27 September 2008.*

42. *Wesley, Charles. "Maker, in Whom We Live". The United Methodist Hymnal. Nashville: The United Methodist Publishing House, 1989.*

43. *"Catechism of the Catholic Church - Part 4 Section 1 Chapter 3 Article 1" (scborromeo.org).*

44. *"Catechism of the Catholic Church - Part 1 Section 1 Chapter 3 Article 1" (scborromeo.org).*

For the Orthodox, however, salvation is understood as divinization or deification (Theosis). This process has been described as the union with God by the reception of the totality of His Uncreated Energies (God´s operations or attributes).

Theosis is a process of continuously becoming more and more like God, becoming by grace what God is by nature (but without sharing in His nature). It is the reversal of the process of emptying Himself (Kenosis) that the Logos suffered voluntarily during the Incarnation in order that we can now be elevated to the same degree that he lowered Himself.

This is not viewed, however, as a merging or fusion with God, common in the doctrines of the One. Instead, Christian salvation has classically been described by using the symbolism of a sword being held in a flame, with the flaming sword gradually taking on the properties of the flame, but still remaining a sword.

Regarding the prophecies of the end times (Eschatology), the major events predicted include: the Tribulation, a period of extreme physical and spiritual hardships; the Second Coming of Jesus Christ and the end of this world; the general resurrection and judgment of the living and the dead (in addition to the particular judgment of each person after death).[45]

Particular denominational beliefs include the Millennium and the Rapture, mainly for Evangelicals (Protestant), and the Purgatory for Catholics.[46]

c. Christian Symbolism

Orthodox symbolism can be seen in the ubiquitous presence of icons, which are pictorial representations of biblical scenes, historical events in the life of the Church, and portraits of the saints.

---

45. *"Particular Judgment". Catholic Encyclopedia.*
46. *"Audience of 4 August 1999". Vatican.va.*

The saints, accepted by Catholic and Orthodox, are those persons whose lives were so obviously holy and close to God that they are celebrated (veneration) and used as an example. However, only God is worshipped, with this term meaning the total giving over of the self to be united with God.

Icons are liturgically created and employed and, for the Orthodox, they are considered a necessary consequence of good theology and of the Incarnation of the Logos, seen as a representation and icon of God Himself.

Additional Christian Symbols: the Cross, Ichtys, Chi Rho, dove (Holy Spirit), pelican, and Anchored Cross, among others.

2.4. Christian Mysticism: Purification, Prayer and Hesychasm

Christian mysticism is a term with two different meanings. It usually refers to the Christian tradition of mystical practices and mystical theology that is concerned with the purification and preparation of human beings in order to get closer to the presence of God.[47] However, it can also refer to the liturgical dimension of the mystery of the presence of the Christ in the Eucharist.

The achievement of the awareness of God's internal presence is emphasized, rather than the experience of altered states of consciousness and sensations felt as external to oneself. The Christian mystic aims at unlocking new ways of knowing and loving based on God´s union with himself.

The attainment of such states is considered authentic insofar the mystic is truly transformed and able to extend his spiritual influence and impact to the lives of others.

---

47. *McGinn, Bernard (2006). The Essential Writings of Christian Mysticism. New York: Modern Library.*

Mystical practices have a prominent place in the Orthodox Church, and they have recently gained a renewed interest in the Western world.

a. Positive (Cataphatic) and Negative (Apophatic) Mystical Practices

Mysticism, as well as theology, can be divided in two branches: the positive and the negative ones. The former focuses on understanding God by what He is (e.g., All-Knowing) and what we can know about Him. Cataphatic theology, therefore, is centered on God´s immanence.

Apophatic theology, in turn, focuses on asserting what He is not, trying to remove all conceptions of God from our minds as inappropriate descriptions of His transcendental aspect.

Depending on the focus of the mystic, then, different practices can be described as Apophatic or Cataphatic:

1. *Cataphatic (positive) practices:* imaging God (e.g., the Catholic spiritual exercises of Ignatius of Loyola; Julian of Norwich; Francis of Assisi).

2. *Apophatic (negative) practices:* contemplation in stillness and silence without using any mental image (e.g., the Orthodox tradition of Hesychasm and some writings of Dionysius the Areopagite; the Catholic mysticism of *The Cloud of Unknowing* and Meister Eckhart).[48]

b. A Threefold Path

The Christian mystical path usually includes three differentiated stages [49] (which nevertheless mutually involve and reinforce each other):

---

48. McBrien, Richard P., ed. (1995). "Mysticism". *The HarperCollins Encyclopedia of Catholicism*. San Francisco: HarperCollins, p. 901.

49. Garrigou-Lagrange, Réginald (1938). *The Three Ages of the Interior Life*. Chapter on Christian Perfection.

1. *Purification* (Catharsis). The purgative stage, where the passions are restrained and their corresponding opposite virtues developed.

2. *Contemplation* (Theoria) *or Illumination.* This stage includes the practice of the unceasing and uninterrupted remembrance of God. However, this practice is not understood as the mere application of a method, as any achievement also depends on receiving the gift of the Holy Spirit.[50] Purity, humility, and self-less love are viewed as prerequisites to advance in this path.

3. *Union or Deification* (Theosis).

The purgative and illuminative stages of the spiritual or noetic faculty are seen as preparations for the vision of God, with illumination only being achieved by the pure of heart who are no longer slaves to the passions.

Contemplative practices can range from simple Western-style prayerful meditations on scriptural passages (Lectio Divina), to the focused and rhythmic recitation of the Jesus Prayer and the contemplation of the presence of God with an empty mind (Orthodoxy).

---

50. *"Ecstasy comes when, in prayer, the nous abandons every connection with created things: first "with everything evil and bad, then with neutral things" (2, 3, 35; CWS p. 65).*

Ecstasy is mainly withdrawal from the opinion of the world and the flesh. With sincere prayer the nous "abandons all created things" (2, 3, 35; CWS p. 65). This ecstasy is higher than abstract theology, that is, than rational theology, and it belongs only to those who have attained dispassion.

It is not yet union; the ecstasy which is unceasing prayer of the nous, in which one's nous has continuous remembrance of God and has no relation with the `world of sin', is not yet union with God. This union comes about when the Paraclete "illuminates from on high the man who attains in prayer the stage which is superior to the highest natural possibilities and who is awaiting the promise of the Father, and by His revelation ravishes him to the contemplation of the light" (2, 3, 35; CWS p.65). Illumination by God is what shows His union with man. (Greek: ἀπάθεια, romanized: apatheia) and clarity of vision. Vision here refers to the vision of the nous that has been purified by ascetic practice."

— Vlachos, Hierotheos (1994). "VI. Orthodox Epistemology [Section 2: The Knowledge of God according to St. Gregory Palamas]". Orthodox psychotherapy (2005). Levadia, Greece: Birth of the Theotokos Monastery.

c. The Protestant Stance on Mysticism

The Protestant Reformation downplayed the role and the importance of mysticism, even though some of the most prominent reformers themselves were at least partially influenced by mystical traditions (e.g., Martin Luther and the German Dominican mysticism of Meister Eckhart and Johannes Tauler).

Some Protestant denominations, however, such as Quakers, Anglicans, Methodists, Episcopalians, Lutherans, Presbyterians, and nowadays especially Pentecostals and Charismatics have in different ways incorporated the notion of mystical experiences.[51]

Some of these practices however, especially those of Pentecostals and Charismatics, are viewed by the other denominations as highly suspect due to their excesses. The fruits of these practices seem prone to experience outbursts of passion more akin to unbalanced states of mind than the enlightened ones achieved by saints and mystics.

d. Contemplative Prayer in Roman Catholicism

Catholic tradition includes a variety of spiritual exercises and contemplative prayers. Among them are: the spiritual exercises of Ignatius of Loyola; the repetition of a single monosyllabic word, as suggested in the famous medieval apophatic text called *The Cloud of Unknowing*[52]; the mystical practices of the Spanish mystics, such as those of John of the Cross and Teresa of Ávila; the use of Lectio Divina[53]; the use of the

---

51. *Fremantle, Anne Jackson (1964). The Protestant Mystics. Little, Brown.*

52. *McBrien, Richard P. (ed.) (1995). "Mysticism". The HarperCollins Encyclopedia of Catholicism. San Francisco: HarperCollins, p. 901.*

53. *"Meditation is a prayerful quest engaging thought, imagination, emotion, and desire. Its goal is to make our own in faith the subject considered, by confronting it with the reality of our own life". Catechism of the Catholic Church, 2723.*

Rosary, understood not only as an object of meditation but as a set of prayers; the modern method of Centering Prayer (developed by Trappist monks).

e. The Mystical Church of the East

Orthodox Christianity is predominantly a mystical tradition[54]. It invites everyone, laity, clergy, and monastics alike, to lead a holy life as far as they are able (e.g., periods of fasting, but also of feasting), as well as to have an active life of prayer, which may or may not include the contemplation and meditation methods used by monastics (e.g., Jesus Prayer; see the *Philokalia*).[55, 56]

One of the main Orthodox critiques towards Catholicism is its excessive emphasis on logic and reason, which culminated in Scholasticism and the dilution of the practical life of Christianity, originally based on growing closer to God and becoming progressively like Him (Theosis).[57]

Therefore, in Hesychasm (meaning stillness), Orthodoxy has preserved a living tradition of mystical prayer that aims at granting, not a mere intellectual vision of God, but existential knowledge and the deepening of our relationship with Him. Hesychastic practices aim at going beyond both being and non-being, as nothingness is also conceived as God's creation. He transcends them both.

------

54. *Lossky, Vladimir (1976). The Mystical Theology of the Eastern Church. St Vladimir's Seminary Press.*

55. *the New Theologian, St. Symeon. On Faith. Palmer, G.E.H; Sherrard, Philip; Ware, Kallistos (Timothy). The Philokalia, Vol. 4.*

56. *Louth, Andrew (2003). "Theology of the Philokalia" in Abba: The Tradition of Orthodoxy in the West. St Vladimir's Seminary Press, p. 358.*

57. *Mount Athos (2006). Theosis: The True Purpose of Human Life (4th ed.). Greece: Holy Monastery of St. Gregorios.*

Hesychasts endeavour to achieve this closeness and union with God through the control of the passions, the cultivation of watchful attention (Nepsis), and the emptying of oneself through humility, also called holy wisdom (Sophia) or true knowledge (Gnosis).

Once emptied of what we would nowadays call their common human ego, hesychasts become able to be filled with God´s Uncreated Energies. This is the meaning of the phrase "being dead to the world", with the term "world" here meaning the collective passions and the ego that engenders and supports them.

It is emphasised, as in all mystical traditions, that such practices require caution and guidance, as false spiritual insights leading to pride and harm can also be obtained (Prelest).

f. Monasticism

Monastic communities are those groups of persons that have decided to lead a life of service, contemplative prayer, and liturgical worship. Anchoritism, meaning "to withdraw", was viewed not as an escape from the world but as the waging of war against our internal passions in order to be able to receive God.

A common metaphor and symbol was the climbing of the ladder of perfection, exemplified in the biblical story of Jacob's ladder. Hermits are the anchorites living in solitude, while cenobites (meaning "common life")[58] live in communities.

Monasticism, beginning in the deserts of Egypt, was eventually established in the West by John Cassian and Benedict of Nursia.

----

58. *Holmes, Urban Tigner (2002). A History of Christian Spirituality: An Analytical Introduction. Church Publishing, pp. 29–31.*

2.5. Islam

a. Different Traditions and Sources of Authority

Islam, which means "surrender" (to the will of Allah) is based on the *Qur'ān*, understood as the verbatim word of God revealed by the archangel Gabriel to the prophet Muhammad. The main traditions are the Sunni and the Shi´a ones, their differences being mainly of doctrinal emphasis and the different views they hold on the succession line after Muhammad.

Muhammad is considered the last of a series of prophets that includes Adam, Noah, Abraham, Moses, Solomon, and Jesus. His message is thought to be the final word and completion of all previous revelations. Other sources of authority in addition to the *Qur'ān* are:

• *The "Traditions"* (Sunnah): the pillar of all religious and moral guidance. It includes compilations of the Prophet's words and deeds known as the *Hadith*.

• *The "Consensus"* (Ijmā): standardized legal theory and practical cases used as the legal basis to solve disputes where different individual or regional opinions are involved.

• *The "Individual Thought"* (Ijtihād): currently a formalized method of deduction by strict analogy based on the *Qur'ān* and the *Hadith*. It gradually lost its influence in Sunni Islam.

b. Main Metaphysical Beliefs of Islam

b1. Conception of God

Islam, contrary to pre-Islamic Arabia´s Polytheism, is strictly monotheistic. Like Judaism, it rejects Christian Trinitarianism as tri-Theism and disguised Polytheism.

God is understood as an All-Powerful, omnipresent, and personal being (who was never incarnated). He is the basis and source of all order in creation, just and merciful. He is not an absent God but one who guides and helps humanity to follow the straight path of rightfulness.

The single most important doctrine in Islam upon which the whole faith rests is that of Tawhīd, which means the indivisible "oneness of God". It constitutes the main article of the Muslim profession of submission (Shahada or declaration of faith). The attribution of divinity to anything or anyone else is considered a grave sin (Shirk).

Islamic thought can be seen as a gradual development and understanding of the doctrine of God's absolute unity and its implications. To prove the existence, unity, and oneness of God theologians usually rely on reasoning and deduction.

To the classic monotheistic sense, however, the term Tawhīd has now also added the connotations of "unification, union, combination, fusion; standardization, regularization; consolidation, amalgamation, merger." [59]

"The first step of religion is to accept, understand and realize him as the Lord... The correct form of belief in his unity is to realize that he is so absolutely pure and above nature that nothing can be added to or subtracted from his being.

That is, one should realize that there is no difference between his person and his attributes, and his attributes should not be differentiated or distinguished from his person." [60]

— Ali

---

59. *Wehr, Hans (1976). A dictionary of modern written Arabic - Edited by Milton Cowan. New York: Spoken Language Services.*

60. *Lakhani, M. Ali (2006). The Sacred Foundations of Justice in Islam: The Teachings of Alī Ibn Abī. World Wisdom, p. 15.*

b2. On Creation

God created the Universe "from nothing", being independent from it and totally self-sufficient. Each created being, its nature, limits, and behavior functions according to the pattern willed by God. Everything is in the place it should be, with the cosmos being a well-ordered and patterned whole, replete with signs pointing towards God. Cosmology and time are understood as linear, as in Judaism and Christianity.

b3. The Problem of Evil

The *Qur'ān* explains that in the beginning God created human beings and Jinn from clay and fire, respectively. The Jinn are rational creatures believed to have a higher affinity for evil than humans. Allah is then the Creator of both good and evil, all natures having been predisposed as such since their creation. The purpose of humanity's creation was to serve and obey God's will.

The *Genesis* story of the Fall of Adam is accepted, but the *Qur'ān* states that God forgave his disobedience. Original or Ancestral Sin is not an Islamic concept.

Iblīs (or Shayṭān) rebelled against humanity's creation because of pride. Human free will causes us to be prone to this passion, too, attributing ourselves with the self-sufficiency that only God can have. This is idolatry (Shirk), the association of the created with the Creator and a violation of the unity of God, while true faith (Īmān) is the belief in the absolute unity of God and our submission (Islām) to His will.

Sin is viewed as an action, not a state of being, that violates the laws laid down by religion.

b4. On Determinism and Free Will

The pagan Arabs believed in an inescapable Fate over which humans could not fight against. The *Qur'ān* substituted this deterministic and pessimistic vision with one of a merciful God involved with the ultimate destiny of man, while eliminating all forms of idolatry and the multiple divinities that the Arabs worshipped in their sanctuaries at the time (including the Ka'bah sanctuary in Mecca). Therefore, Muslims believe that they have free will and are responsible for their actions.

However, the relationship between divine determinism and free will is a complex one in Islam.

Even though Muslims believe that they can choose between following Allah´s guidance or the temptations of Shaytan (Satan), they adhere to the concept of predestination (Qadar; e.g., the sixth article of belief in Sunni Islam, present in Muhammad´s teachings).

This doctrine teaches that everything that has ever happened, including sinful human behavior, comes from a direct command of God. At the same time, however, humanity is responsible for their actions and will be judged according to them in the end times.

Some Muslim theologians have opposed this doctrine or added their own interpretation to it (e.g., Shi´a Islam).

"Nothing will ever befall us except what Allah has destined for us. [...]"

— Qur'ān 9:51

"[...] Then Allah leaves whoever He wills to stray and guides whoever He wills."

— Qur'ān 14:4

"Had We willed, We could have easily imposed guidance on every soul. But My Word will come to pass: I will surely fill up Hell with jinn and humans all together."

— Qur'ān 32:13

b5. Path to Salvation and End Times

God is viewed as forever merciful and always willing to pardon a repentant sinner.

Islam believes that, on the Last Day, the world will end and the dead will be resurrected. Judgment will follow, according to each person's Book of Deeds.

The condemned will be sent to Hell, and the saved will enjoy Paradise. Hell and heaven are seen as both spiritual and corporeal, with physical pain and pleasure still playing a role after death.

Not everyone sent to Hell is believed to remain there, however, as the only persons completely incapable of being saved are those who have committed the worst sin of all: challenging the absolute unity of God.

The end times are announced by a period of trials and tribulations full of immorality, wars, and unnatural phenomena. Key figures of this time will be the Mahdi and the Second Coming of Isa (Jesus in Christianity) who will claim victory over Dajjal (Antichrist in Christianity).

Once all these pre-determined events have come to pass, the Universe will end and Judgment will begin, history having run its course.

Symbols in Islam: Crescent and Star, Khatim, Rub el Hizb.

2.6. Islamic Mysticism: Sufism

Sufism is organized in orders or schools (Tariqah) where mystical doctrines and spiritual practices are taught in order to attain ultimate Truth (Haqiqa). When the searching adept has found a master for whom he feels an affinity, an initiation ceremony takes place.

a. Main Metaphysical Beliefs of Sufism

a1. Conception of God

For Islamic mysticism, man is not limited to affirming in speech the doctrine of God's absolute unity. He can also realize it in practice.

This realization, in turn, involves the rejection of multiplicity and is reserved to the initiated elite, as with all mystical schools.[61]

Annihilation of the Self

An important concept in Muslim mysticism is that of Annihilation (Fana, equivalent to ego-death), found in all mystical traditions that try to go back to the source understood as an absolutely simple unity.

"Man's existence, or ego, or self-hood ... must be annihilated so that he can attain to his true self which is his existence and "subsistence" with God. All of man's character traits and habits, everything that pertains to his individual existence must become completely naughted and "obliterated" (mahw).

Then God will give back to him his character traits and everything positive he ever possessed. But at this stage, he will know consciously and actually - not just theoretically - and with a through spiritual realization, that everything he is derives absolutely from God. He is nothing but a ray of God's Attributes manifesting the Hidden Treasure." [62]

— William Chittick (1983)

---

61. Gimaret, D. Tawhid. Encyclopedia of Islam: *"[Al-Junayd] distinguishes four steps, starting from the simple attestation of unicity which is sufficient for ordinary believers, and culminating in the highest rank reserved for the elite, when the creature totally ceases to exist before his Lord, thus achieving al-fanā fi al-tawhīd [annihilation in unity]."*

62. *Chittick, William (1983). The Sufi Path Of Love: The Spiritual Teachings of Rumi. Suhail Academy, p. 179.*

The Unity of All Existence or Unity of Being (Wahdat Al-Wujud)

Closely related to Ibn Arabi, this term has been differently understood over the centuries.

Ibn Arabi used the term as meaning "Necessary Being", with everything else in existence also being defined by this term in a derivative way, as partaking of being through God. Every existing thing is seen, then, as the fleeting shadow and self-disclosure (Tajalli) of this ultimate Unity, or God. All creation is, at the same time, "God and not God".

"Wujūd is the unknowable and inaccessible ground of everything that exists. God alone is true wujūd, while all things dwell in nonexistence, so also wujūd alone is nondelimited (muṭlaq), while everything else is constrained, confined, and constricted. Wujūd is the absolute, infinite, nondelimited reality of God, while all others remain relative, finite, and delimited." [63]

— Ibn Arabi. Fusus–al-Hikam

"There is nothing in wujud [existence] except God...Wujud [Existence] only belongs to the Real One." [64]

— Al-Ghazali. Wahdat Al-Wujud

"Glory to Him who created all things, being Himself their very essence (ainuha)." [65]

— Ibn Arabi

---

63. *See Chiittick, William (1994). Imaginal worlds. SUNY Press, p. 53.*

64. *Al-Ghazali. Wahdat Al-Wujud. Encyclopedia of Islam and the Muslim World, p. 727.*

65. *Al-Arabi, Ibn. In M.M. Sharif (2013), A History of Muslim Philosophy. Pakistan: Royal Book Company, p. 409.*

"Hence, in a secondary meaning, the term wujūd is used as shorthand to refer to the whole cosmos, to everything that exists. It can also be employed to refer to the existence of each and every thing that is found in the universe." [66]

— William Chittick (1994). Imaginal worlds

The ultimate sin for many Sufis is, consequently, to consciously utter the "I" pronoun with the consideration that we are an existence separated from God. In this view, this affirmation of our individual ego represents idolatry.

Regarding this, Junayd spoke of God as the "One and Only actor" in existence, the only one that "has the right to say 'I'".

In later times, the doctrine of Tawḥīd came to more explicitly mean that there is nothing existent but God, implying that creation and God are two complementary aspects of the same reality, the two faces of the same coin.

However, this idea of describing God as all there is and the possibility of union with Him, viewed through the lens of mainline Islam, is a controversial one. It blurs the distinction between creature and Creator, and led Sufism to criticism and even persecution at times (e.g., Zahirites or Malikites following the Ash'arite creed; the accusation of Pantheism of the Wahhabi and Salafi sects).

a2. On Creation

Sufis describe different gradations and stages in which the divine descended in order to create the Universe. The schema used is similar to Neo-Platonic ones (e.g., Plotinus).

---

66. *Chiittick, William (1994). Imaginal worlds: Ibn al-'Arabi and the Problem of Religious Diversity. SUNY Press, p. 15.*

It all started with the "Light of One", who came out of His self-isolated Oneness with the intention to self-manifest through the multiplicity brought forth by creation. It was followed by the Realm of He-ness (Divinity's Essence; Alonehood) and the Realm of First Manifestation (Realm of Absolute Unity). These pre-creation levels were then followed by the ones where manifestation started to unfold: the Realms of Intelligence, Soul, and Physical bodies.

Gradation (Tashkīk) is another related concept that states that ultimate reality and existence are gradations with different intensities of the same underlying reality. This implies the continuous existence of a hierarchical Chain of Being that extends uninterruptedly from the divine until the lowest aspects of creation.

Ibn Arabi used a similar concept, that of "effusion" (Fayd), to denote the process of creation through an overflowing or emanation from God.

a3. The Problem of Evil

The nature and role of Shaytan (or Iblis) in Sufism is a complicated and ambivalent subject.

Contrary to his simpler evil nature in exoteric Islam, esoteric Sufism may consider him not simply as the devil and humanity´s tempter. Instead, he is sometimes seen as "the truest monotheist", which is the highest virtue in Islam. This is so because of his refusal to worship creation (Adam) in addition to the Creator.

Ahmad Ghazali, for example, viewed Iblis as the archetypical example of unrequited and self-sacrificing love, refusing to bow down to Adam out of pure and exclusive devotion to God.

In the authors who follow this view, the term Shayṭān is then reserved exclusively for a generalist conception of evil forces.

However, not all Sufis agree with this positive vision. Rumi, for example, viewed Iblis as the personification of the sin of envy.

In other interpretations, he is viewed as being an indirect servant of the good, being the gatekeeper of the Divine Essence. He would be, then, the "tool" used by God to differentiate between the sinners and the faithful who would have access to Him in the world to come.

a4. Free Will

The tension between determinism and free will present in mainstream Islam can also be felt throughout Sufism.

In order to try to solve this paradox, Ibn Arabi distinguished between God's creative command and God's obligating command.

The creative command is God´s willing the different aspects of creation into existence, such as natural laws. The obligating command includes belief and faith. It underscores the idea that we are always free to follow a path of holiness pleasing to God. In a paradoxical way, our voluntary submission to the obligating command is the ultimate use of mankind´s free will.

a5. Salvation

The four stages of the path of a Muslim mystic includes: the exoteric stage of following common religious law (Shari'a); the esoteric stage (Tariqa); the station where mystical truth (Haqiqa) is achieved; the state of final experiential mystical knowledge (Ma´rifa or "Gnosis"). In the last stage, the mystics are believed to transcend or shed their self in order to be absorbed into God.

The path always begins with repentance, ascetic practices, and discipleship under the guidance of an experienced mystic (Sheikh). Intuitive direct realization, or illumination, is emphasized. For that end, certain meditation methods are then suggested to the initiate, who will engage in the real inner Holy War (Jihad) against his own lower soul. These lower tendencies will have to be tamed (not destroyed) and used for spiritual development.

Different, more or less intense, spiritual states are expected to be experienced by the disciple during his practice. These include, for example, the feeling of spiritual expansion, fear, hope, longing, and intimacy. The last station can be characterized as one of Gnosis and love, implying the union of lover and beloved, which in terms of Eastern esoteric teachings could be defined as the end of the distinction between subject and object, the intended end result of most mystical paths.

The resulting extinction of the personality or ego is believed to bring forth the true "life in God" (Baqā'). This state is called intoxication and is followed by the "second sobriety", which means the return of the transformed mystic to this earthly realm. Having found the meaning of life, he can now be a powerful influence in this world.

The main methods to achieve transcendental union with God are Murāqabah ("to observe") and Dhikr ("remembrance"). The first method involves watching over the heart and soul until insight regarding one´s relationship with God is gained. The overcoming of the soul´s base tendencies is expected to be achieved.

Dhikr, in turn, consists of meditating on the name of God by repeating or chanting specific names or prayers (similar to mantras in Eastern mysticism). Particular postures, breathing patterns, and movements may be used, including the famous Sama dancing ceremony of the Dervishes.

Symbolism in Sufism: symbols of intoxication and narratives revolving around lovers to represent mystical states, visions, and dreams.

2.7. Hinduism

a. Different Traditions and Sources of Authority

The term Hinduism or Sanātana Dharma ("Eternal Order" or "Eternal Dharma") does not denote a single religion but a diverse set of traditions and philosophies that share metaphysical doctrines, sacred texts, and rituals.

Common themes in most of them include:

- *Saṃsāra:*[67] the continuous cycle of birth and rebirth for those still under the dominion of the passions and ignorance about ultimate reality.

- *Karma:* the law of moral causality that fuels the process of reincarnation or rebirth.

- *Moksha:* the path and end goal of all life, understood as the liberation from any attachment and the breaking of the cycle of Saṃsāra.

- *Yoga:* the paths or methods to achieve Moksha.

The four duties of each Hindu, in turn, are:

- *Dharma:* moral duties, right behavior.

- *Artha:* obtaining the means required to lead a fulfilling life.

- *Kāma:* satisfying sensory, emotional and aesthetic needs.

- *Moksha:* liberation from Saṃsāra and from suffering.

Hindu texts are classified into those "heard" (Śruti) and those "remembered" (Smṛti), with the most important scriptures being the *Vedas*, the *Upanishads*, the *Purānas*, the *Mahābhārata*, the *Rāmāyana*, and the *Āgamas*.[68, 69]

There are six main historical schools of thought (Āstika), with all of them recognizing the Vedas as authoritative. Their metaphysical beliefs range from the dualist (Sāṃkhya) to the panentheist or non-dual (Advaita Vedānta).

---

67. *The oldest strata of the Vedas, however, did not include beliefs in reincarnation and Saṃsāra but believed in an afterlife. Some traditions still show echoes of this belief (e.g., Śrāddha).*

68. *Klostermaier, Klaus K. (2007). A Survey of Hinduism (3rd ed.). SUNY Press, pp. 46–52, 76–77.*

69. *Zaehner, R. C. (1992). Hindu Scriptures. Penguin Random House, pp. 1–7.*

Common Hindu practices include: worship (Pūjā), fire rituals (Homa/Havan), devotion (Bhakti), fasting (Vrata), chanting (Japa), meditation (Dhyāna), symbolic sacrifice (Yajña), charity (Dāna), selfless service (Sevā), obtaining knowledge (Jñāna), recitation of scriptures (Pravacana), ancestor homage (Śrāddha), rites of passage, festivals, and pilgrimages (Yatra).

Tantra, on the other hand, is an esoteric tradition that developed in both Hinduism (e.g., Shaiva, Shakta, and Kaula traditions) and Buddhism. It influenced other religions such as Jainism, the Tibetan Bön tradition, Taoism, and Japanese Shintō.[70]

Tantric Hindu texts are called *Tantras, Āgamas* or *Saṃhitās*.[71, 72]

b. Main Metaphysical Beliefs of Hinduism

b1. Conception of God

The range of beliefs about the highest reality in Hinduism is extremely wide, and can include traditions classified as polytheistic, dualist, pantheistic, panentheistic, monist, and even atheist or agnostic.

Most commonly, though, Hindu thought can be classified as majorly following either Panentheism/Non-Dualism or Theism.

For Hinduism, all living creatures have an eternal "True Self" (Ātman). Depending on the school of thought, this Self is seen as being ultimately

---

70. *Gray, David B. (2016). "Tantra and the Tantric Traditions of Hinduism and Buddhism". Oxford Research Encyclopedia of Religion. Oxford: Oxford University Press, pp. 1–2, 17–19.*

71. *Padoux, André (2013). The Heart of the Yogini. Oxford: Oxford University Press, p. 1.*

72. *Lorenzen, David N. "Early Evidence for Tantric Religion". In Harper, Katherine Anne; Brown, Robert L., eds. (2002). The Roots of Tantra. State University of New York Press, p. 25.*

the same as the Supreme Reality (Brahman; e.g., Advaita Vedānta school)[73] or as a different and independent entity altogether (dualist schools; e.g., Dvaita Vedānta).

The objective in this life is, therefore, also different for each school. For Advaita, it is to realise the identity of the self and Brahman through knowledge and experience. To become aware that the highest reality is ultimately everything and everyone, and that all life is an interconnected oneness.[74, 75, 76] For theistic schools, however, it is to achieve closeness to their God in the afterlife.

In order to achieve this goal, each sect practices devotional acts (Bhakti) towards God (Ishvara or Bhagavān).

God is represented by their chosen ideal deity (Iṣṭa Devatā; e.g., Vishnu, Brahmā, Shiva or Shakti) or their avatars (e.g., Krishna as an avatar of Vishnu). The chosen deity can be seen either as the Supreme God or as a particular manifestation of the ultimate, formless Absolute (Brahman).

Forms of Theism can be already found in the *Bhagavad Gita*.

Henotheism

Due to this complex set of apparently discordant beliefs, the term Henotheism was coined by Max Müller to describe the theology of

---

73. *Bhaskarananda, Swami (1994). Essentials of Hinduism. Viveka Press.*

74. *Vivekananda, Swami (1987). Complete Works of Swami Vivekananda. Calcutta: Advaita Ashrama.*

75. *Koller, John (2012), Routledge Companion to Philosophy of Religion. Routledge, pp. 99–107.*

76. *Lance, Nelson (1996). "Living liberation in Shankara and classical Advaita", in Living Liberation in Hindu Thought. State University of New York Press, pp. 38–39, 59 (footnote 105).*

the Vedic religion.[77, 78] It defines Vedic Hinduism as a tradition that successively worships different deities as ultimate reality, with them representing multiple manifestations of God.[79, 80]

Other scholars have argued that the term Panentheism is a better representation of this complex faith.[81]

"You at your birth are Varuna, O Agni. When you are kindled, you are Mitra. In you, O son of strength, all gods are centered. You are Indra to the mortal who brings oblation. You are Aryaman, when you are regarded as having the mysterious names of maidens, O Self-sustainer." [82]

—Rig Veda, 5.3.1-2

"They call him Indra, Mitra, Varuna, Agni, and he is heavenly-winged Garutman. To what is One, sages give many a title." [83]

— Rig Veda, 1.164.46

---

77. *Sugirtharajah, Sharada (2004). Imagining Hinduism: A Postcolonial Perspective, Routledge, p. 44.*

78. *Taliaferro, Charles; Harrison, Victoria S.; Goetz, Stewart (2012). The Routledge Companion to Theism. Routledge, pp. 78–79.*

79. *Alon, Ilai; Gruenwald, Ithamar; Singer, Itamar (1994). Concepts of the Other in Near Eastern Religions. Brill Academic, pp. 370–371.*

80. *Elsas, Christoph (1999). Fahlbusch, Erwin (ed.). The Encyclopedia of Christianity. Wm. B. Eerdmans, p. 524.*

81. *Fowler, Jeaneane D. (2002). Perspectives of Reality: An Introduction to the Philosophy of Hinduism. Sussex Academic Press, pp. 43–44.*

82. *Oldenberg, Hermann (1988). The Religion of the Veda. Motilal Banarsidass. p. 51.*

83. *Klostermaier, Klaus K. (2010). A Survey of Hinduism: Third Edition. State University of New York Press, p. 103. Also footnote 10 on p. 529.*

Figure 3. Harihara is the dual representation of the Hindu gods Vishnu (Hari) and Shiva (Hara), used to illustrate the notion of particular deities as different aspects of Brahman or Ultimate Reality, thus emphasizing the underlying oneness of all existence. Picture: unknown author, ca. 1825.

Saguṇa and Nirguṇa Brahman

An important distinction is that of Brahman with attributes (Saguṇa Brahman) and without attributes (Nirguṇa Brahman).

The latter is believed to be the only real one, but the former is the only one that can be grasped in our plane of existence (for example, in the form of avatars). This implies that the known deities are ultimately illusory and only a means to an end.

Vedānta and Advaita

Vedānta, meaning "the end of the *Vedas*", is one of the major Hindu traditional schools of thought. It is mainly based on interpretations of the last part of the Vedas, the *Upanishads*. Its focus is on attaining knowledge and the consequent liberation from the cycle of life and death. Vedānta contains multiple subtraditions differentiated according to their proposed solution to the problem of *the One and the Many*:

- *Advaita (unqualified Non-Dualism):* where Brahman alone is ultimately real and everything else is just an illusion (Māyā). *Founder:* Ādi Śaṅkara.

- *Vishishtadvaita ("non-duality with distinctions" or qualified Monism):* where Brahman is viewed as the Supreme Reality while also acknowledging the multiplicity of existence. All diversity and difference ultimately have Brahman as the source. *Founder:* Rāmānuja.

- Dvaitadvaita (*"dualistic Non-Dualism"* or differential Monism): where humanity is both different and non-different from the Supreme Being (Ishvara). Doctrine especially present in traditions that worship Krishna. *Founder:* Nimbārkā.

- Achintya Bheda Abheda (*"inconceivable one-ness and difference"*): understood as an integration of Dualism (Dvaita) and qualified Monism (Vishishtadvaita). It focuses on the relationship between the Creator (usually Krishna) and His creation, also understood as the relationship between God and His energies.[84] *Founder:* Chaitanya Mahāprabhu.

The most well known, influential[85], and dominant[86] Hindu tradition outside of India (and the only one that was imported and heavily promoted in the West) is Advaita Vedānta.

---

84. *Prabhupada, A.C.Bhaktivedanta Swami (1972). Bhagavad-gita as it is. Bhaktivedanta Book Trust.*
85. *Indich, William (1995). Consciousness in Advaita Vedānta. Motilal Banarsidass.*
86. *"Gandhi And Mahayana Buddhism" (Class.uidaho.edu).*

This is contrary to the predominant Theism of India itself, as Advaita implies a rejection of Theism with an overall metaphysical vision that can be defined as "spiritual but not religious".

Advaita´s vision of Brahman, understood as the Universal Principle, is that of an impersonal, infinite, eternal, and unchangeable absolute Unity behind all apparent multiplicity.

It has no properties and no internal diversity. It is the real Essence of all external reality and the source of all change, which is ultimately illusory. Therefore, the relationship between Brahman and "creation" is usually viewed as panentheistic.[87]

"By Me all this universe is pervaded through My unmanifested form. All beings abide in Me but I do not abide in them." [88]

— Krishna. In the Bhagavad Gita, verse IX.4

In the *Upanishads*, this is exemplified by one of the most common definitions of the subjective experience of Brahman: Sat-Cit-Ānanda (Truth/Existence - Consciousness - Bliss). [89, 90]

"Thou art that" ["You are Brahman"]

— Chandogya Upanishad, 6.8.7 et seq. (clarification added in brackets)

"The Self is Brahman"

— Brihadaranyaka Upanishad, 4.4.5

---

87. *Southgate, Christopher. God, Humanity, and the Cosmos. T&T Clark Int'l, p. 246.*

88. *Ibid.*

89. *Raju, P. T. (1992), The Philosophical Traditions of India. Delhi: Motilal Banarsidass Publishers, p. 228.*

90. *Deutsch, Eliot (1980). Advaita Vedanta : A Philosophical Reconstruction. University of Hawaii Press, Ch. 1.*

"All this is Brahman"

— Chandogya Upanishad, 3.14.1

Tantric View

Tantra, on the other hand, understands the divine both as transcendent and outside our plane of existence as well as immanent and present in this world. In Kashmir Shaivism, for example, a school that has also achieved certain notoriety in the West, all things are believed to be particular manifestations of Universal Consciousness (Brahman).[91]

However, contrary to Advaita, the created Universe (Śakti) is seen as truly real, having its source of being in Consciousness (Ćit).[92] It can thus be classified as a panentheistic worldview.[93]

In Shaktism, also considered a form of Panentheism[94], Shakti is considered to be equivalent to the Universe. As the personification and embodiment of energy and dynamism, she is the force that animates and moves all material things and sustains the cycle of life and death. In her lower aspect (Mula Prakriti), she is a personification of matter itself.

Shiva is her complementary opposite or counterpart, the passive ground of all being. Each of them is implied by the other and cannot exist without the other, forming a totality. Masculine and feminine, transcendent and immanent, passive and active, are ultimately one reality.

----

91. *Dyczkowski, Mark S. G. (1987). The Doctrine of Vibration: An Analysis of Doctrines and Practices of Kashmir Shaivism. SUNY, p. 44.*

92. *Semaraja (trans. by Jaidev Singh). Spanda Karikas: The Divine Creative Pulsation. Motilal Banarsidass, p. 119.*

93. *Pandit, Moti Lal (2003). The Trika Śaivism of Kashmir. Munshiram Manoharlal Publishers.*

94. *Vitsaxis, Vassilis. Thought and Faith: The concept of divinity. Somerset Hall Press, p. 167.*

Complementary Dualism

The Union of Opposites is a pervasive and common theme in different Hindu traditions.

In the ones devoted to personal theistic representations of God, He is often represented as having both feminine and masculine aspects. Examples include pairings such as Shiva/Pārvatī, Vishnu/Lakshmi, and Rādhā/Krishna.

In Tantra, especially, the frequent sexual symbolism uses the dichotomy of male and female to represent the union of all dualities into the One.

b2. On Creation and Time

One of the core metaphysical doctrines of all Hindu traditions is that of cyclical time. Hindu cosmology is formed by successive and recurrent cyclical ages (Yugas). Each age is shorter than the one before, and also represents a marked decline in morals and knowledge of the truth.

Each "Great Yuga" (Mahāyuga) is formed by four successive Yugas (Krita or Age of Perfection; Tretā, Dvāpara, and Kali or Age of Decay). Two thousand great cycles form a cosmic cycle (Kalpa). After each Kali yuga the world is destroyed, and after a time of silent non-existence, the world is re-created and the cycle re-started again.

The most common mythical Hindu creation myth explains that Brahmā creates the cosmos out of himself, Vishnu preserves it, and Shiva destroys it in order to bring the renewal of a new cycle.

These three deities (Trimurti), unlike the Christian Trinity, are usually seen as different aspects or functions of the same underlying reality (Brahman). The Om (Aum) syllabe alludes to them. Each male deity also has an associated consort goddess (Tridevi), representing the energetic or immanent aspect of the male principles.

b3. The Problem of Evil

Indian traditions do not pay much thought to the "problem" of evil. In Hinduism, there is no such problem because they do not believe in an All-Knowing, All-Powerful, and All-Good personal creator God.

Deities are seen as cosmic facilitators, while also being mortal and subject to the cycle of death and rebirth. Their ultimate purpose is the same as ours: achieving final liberation from multiplicity.

"Evil" is predominantly understood as suffering or ignorance, and is thought of as a normal and inevitable part of existence in our realm of multiplicity and difference. Some suffering is viewed as self-caused (e.g., through our own vices or the Karma accumulated during past lives), some caused by the evil intentions or ignorance of others (including supernatural beings), and some through natural conditions (aging, disease, and/or natural disasters).[95, 96, 97]

The suffering we cause and the intentionality behind our actions are viewed as having long-lasting consequences through the Law of Karma. This doctrine refers to the principle of moral cause and effect, where each action influences and conditions the future of the person who performed it.[98]

According to Śaṅkara, one of the main historical figures of Advaita Vedānta, Brahman itself is beyond good and evil.[99]

---

95. *Meister, Chad V. (2010). The Oxford Handbook of Religious Diversity. Oxford University Press. pp. 163–166.*

96. *Hudson, Emily T. (2013). Disorienting Dharma: Ethics and the Aesthetics of Suffering in the Mahabharata. Oxford University Press. pp. 3–9, 27–46.*

97. *Gächter, Othmar (1998). "Evil and Suffering in Hinduism". Anthropos. Bd, 93, H. 4./6. (4/6): 393–403.*

98. *"Karma". Encyclopædia Britannica.*

99. *Radhakrishnan, S. (1960). Brahmasutras: the philosophy of spiritual life. George Allen, pp. 363–65.*

All the above, united to the fact that existence is seen as cyclical[100] and allows for the Karma of each being to resolve itself, solves the "problem" of evil. In fact, evil and harm are ultimately unreal for Advaita, as Brahman is synonymous with Existence and all creation is its manifestation. Therefore, there is no one who can hurt another, as no "other" really exists.

Through the power of Illusion or Magic (Māyā), Brahman creates the mirage that the world we perceive is real.[101] Ultimate "evil", therefore, is the ignorance that prevents us from seeing that no real harm was ever done to anyone.

b4. On Determinism and Free Will

Due to the many different traditions that form Hinduism, there is not a predominant view on the concept of free will.[102] Advaita (non-dual) schools generally emphasize the concept of Fate while Dvaita (dualist) worldviews tend to focus on free will.

Both free will and destiny, however, are believed to co-exist in both cases, with one predominating over the other depending on the tradition.[103, 104] Otherwise, there would be no basis for the Law of Causality or Karma to work.

---

100. *Sharma, Arvind (2008). The Philosophy of Religion and Advaita Vedanta: A Comparative Study in Religion and Reason. Pennsylvania State University Press, pp. 26–32.*

101. *"Maya". Encyclopedia Britannica.*

102. *Predictive Astrology - Understanding Karma, Fate, & Free Will. Archived 2006-12-06 (www.astrologyforthesoul.com): "Dvaita" or dualism is generally a proponent of a free will orientation. The path of surrender or non-action, represents "Advaita" or non-dualism and is generally a proponent of fate orientation."*

103. *"The spirit soul bewildered by the influence of false ego thinks himself the doer of activities that are in actuality carried out by the three modes of material nature."*

– Bhagavad-Gita, 3.27.

104. *"As fragmental parts and parcels of the Supreme Lord, the living entities also have fragmental portions of His qualities, of which independence is one.*

"[...] everything within our universe is moulded by conditions of time, space and causality. ... To acquire freedom we have to get beyond the limitations of this universe; it cannot be found here." [105]

— Swami Vivekananda

For example, the Sāṃkhya school believes that matter has no freedom and that we are not able to control it. However, by freely striving to separate Spirit (Purusha) from Matter (Prakriti) real freedom (Kaivalya) can be attained.

Ramakrishna Paramahansa used a metaphor to clearly explain the interrelations between determinism and free will. In his view, man is like a goat tied to a stake. The consequences of his accumulated Karma and his human nature bind him. The amount of free will that he has is symbolized by the length of the rope and the freedom of movement it confers to him; as one progresses in the spiritual path, the rope becomes longer.

b5. On Liberation and Life After Death

There are differing views on the nature of liberation (Moksha). For Advaita Vedānta, the liberated persons achieve the knowledge of their real Self, or Brahman. After realizing the whole Universe as the Self, [106, 107, 108]

Every living entity, as an individual Self, has his personal individuality and a minute form of independence. By misuse of that independence one becomes a conditioned Self, and by proper use of independence he is always liberated."

— Bhagavad-Gita, 15.7.

105. Vivekananda, Swami (1907). "Freedom". The Complete Works of Swami Vivekananda (Vol. 1). Advaita Ashrama, Ch. VII, para. 4.

106. Deutsch, Eliot (2001). "The self in Advaita Vedanta". In Roy Perrett (ed.). Indian philosophy: metaphysics (Volume 3). Taylor and Francis. pp. 343–360.

107. Potter, Karl H. (1958). "Dharma and Mokṣa from a Conversational Point of View". Philosophy East and West. University of Hawaii Press, 8 (1/2): 49–63.

108. Pal, Jagat (2004). Karma, Dharma and Moksha: Conceptual Essays on Indian Ethics. Abhijeet Publications.

they know that they are ultimate reality itself and always have been. This state is described as pure consciousness (Witness Consciousness) and bliss.[109, 110]

"*Even as water becomes one with water, fire with fire, and air with air, so the atman becomes one with the Infinite Atman (Brahman) and thus attains final freedom.*"

— Maitri Upanishad, 6.24

The followers of theistic schools, in contrast, believe that individuals are ontologically distinct but very similar to Brahman. Therefore, they expect to be liberated from the cycle of rebirths and spend eternity with God in heaven (Loka).

Hinduism also provides mythical explanations for what happens between reincarnations. They include the judgment of the dead in the court of Lord Yama, the God of Death. Here, the written-down deeds of each individual are judged. They may end up reincarnating in different realms depending on the verdict. The options available include the heavenly, human, and hellish realms.

Each incarnation is only temporal, however, and the path of spiritual evolution shall eventually continue. The body, including a divine one, is seen as nothing but a periodically discarded shell.

2.8. Hindu Mysticism: Yoga and Tantra

Hindu mysticism can be differentiated into yogic and tantric practitioners. Both their practices and underlying metaphysical beliefs differ in certain aspects.

---

109. *Potter, Karl H. (1958). "Dharma and Mokṣa from a Conversational Point of View". Philosophy East and West. University of Hawaii Press, 8 (1/2): 49–63.*
110. *Klostermaier, Klaus (1985). Philosophy East & West. University Press of Hawaii, 35 (1): pp. 61–71.*

2.8.1. Hindu Yogic Traditions

a. Different Traditions and Sources of Authority

Yoga, meaning union or "to yoke", is a group of diverse esoteric physical, mental, and spiritual methods and disciplines originated in the Indian subcontinent.

They aim at subduing (yoking) the mind, making it still in order to recognize its original nature, that of a pure and detached consciousness unsoiled by the common mind (Chitta) and its myriad thoughts.

The oldest form of Yoga is called the Royal (Rāja) Yoga. It is also called the Eight-Limbed (Asthanga) Yoga, as it consists of eight steps, including the purification of body and mind. It is considered the superior, but not the easiest, method by the oldest and most comprehensive yogic treatise: the *Yoga Sutras of Patanjali.*[111, 112]

The main additional yogic disciplines are those of: knowledge (Jnana Yoga), devotion (Bhakti Yoga), action (Karma Yoga), "energy" (Kundalini Yoga), and physical exertion (Hatha Yoga).

Yogic methods are used in all Indian Dharmic religions[113, 114] and, thanks to their popularization in the West, they are now widely practiced worldwide, even if their spiritual background is not always understood.[115]

---

111. Bryant, Edwin (2009). The Yoga Sutras of Patañjali. North Point Press, p. xxxiv.

112. Desmarais, Michele (2008). Changing Minds: Mind, Consciousness and Identity in Patanjali's Yoga Sutra. Motilal Banarsidass, pp. 16-17.

113. Lardner Carmody, Denise; Carmody, John (1996). Serene Compassion. Oxford University Press US,. p. 68.

114. Ray Sarbacker, Stuart (2005). Samādhi: The Numinous and Cessative in Indo-Tibetan Yoga. SUNY Press, pp. 1–2.

115. Although in Western countries the most common form of Yoga is that of Hatha Yoga, or physical Yoga, traditionally it was understood as a preparation for more advanced yogic techniques leading to liberation.

b. Main Metaphysical Beliefs of Yoga

b1. Conception of God

Traditional Yoga accepts the existence of a mostly inactive personal god, but does not define Him. This task is left to each practitioner.[116]

Its metaphysics is similar to those of the dualists (Sāṃkhya school), where reality is made of two substances: Nature (Prakriti), the source of the material world through the three attributes (Guṇas) of matter and Consciousness (Purusa).

b2. On Creation, Time, the Problem of Evil and the Possibility of Free Will

Yogic discipline, when used as a method, follows the metaphysical doctrines of the school that uses it. Its pragmatic focus is not on doctrinal teaching but on practicing and developing means of achieving liberation.

When viewed as one of the six traditional Hindu schools of thought, it usually follows the beliefs of the Sāṃkhya tradition (e.g., on free will) and those common to Hinduism in general in matters regarding evil and time.

b3. On Liberation and How to Achieve It

As a general definition of what the different yogic techniques try to accomplish, we can summarize it as: the attainment of liberation (Moksha) from the cycle of life and death, thus putting an end to suffering (Duḥkha) and to multiplicity, leading to unity (Aikyam) with ultimate

---

116. *See, for example: Burley, Mikel (2012). Classical Samkhya and Yoga – An Indian Metaphysics of Experience. Routledge, pp. 39–41.*

Pflueger, Lloyd (2008). Knut Jacobsen (ed.). "Person Purity and Power in Yogasutra". Theory and Practice of Yoga. Motilal Banarsidass, pp. 38–39.

Behanan, K. T. (2002). Yoga: Its Scientific Basis. Dover, pp. 56–58.

reality (Brahman) as pure undifferentiated awareness or with one's true Self (Ātman). This is accomplished by stilling one's thought waves (Citta Vritti) and resting in pure empty consciousness. The spiritual part of man can then be liberated from the material one, achieving freedom and unity.

There are some particularities depending on the method used, however. These include:

- Physical Yoga tries to achieve physical and mental strength as a preparation for more advanced yogic methods. This is accomplished through postures and different breathing exercises.

- The Yoga of knowledge used by Advaita Vedānta, in turn, aims to realize the identity of one's Ātman (particular individual consciousness) with Brahman (Absolute Consciousness).[117, 118] This transcendental knowledge is attained through scriptures, the personal master indispensable in all traditions of Hinduism (Guru), and through meditation.[119] The adept withdraws from his particular existence in order to identify himself with the universal ground of all being: Consciousness.

- The Yoga of energy, closely associated with the physical one, has the purpose of awakening the sleeping energy sitting at the base of the spine of the practitioner known as Kundalini (meaning coiled serpent). This is done through breathwork, specific postures, visualizations, and meditations. The final objective is the dissolution of the adept´s personal consciousness into Universal Consciousness. Kundalini Yoga teaches esoteric physiology, where the human body is made of Chakras and subtle energy channels (Nāḍīs). They are used

---

117. *Comans, Michael (2000). The Method of Early Advaita Vedānta: A Study of Gauḍapāda, Śaṅkara, Sureśvara, and Padmapāda. Delhi: Motilal Banarsidass, p. 183.*

118. *P. P. Bilimoria (2012). Śabdapramāṇa: Word and Knowledge. Springer, pp. 299–301.*

119. *Deutsch, Eliot (1980). Advaita Vedanta : A Philosophical Reconstruction. University of Hawaii Press, pp. 105–108.*

as focal meditation points in order to unblock them or unlock their potential, thus permitting the pass of the Kundalini energy towards its final destination. The process of ascent of this serpentine energy is believed to follow a sequential path from the lowest Chakras (base of the spine) to the highest ones (top of the head).[120]

2.8.2. Hindu Tantric Traditions

Tantra is characterized by its aim of transforming the passions, instead of transcending them. As a path, it is viewed as better suited for certain personality types and especially useful during difficult or degraded times such as the actual ones. It can be viewed as the art of fighting fire with fire.

a. Main Metaphysical Beliefs of Tantra

a1. On Creation, Time, the Problem of Evil and the Possibility of Free Will

As with Yoga, tantrikas follow the doctrines of their respective traditions regarding metaphysical topics. Tantras focus mainly on the practical side of their traditions, studying and developing a wide array of methods to achieve their ultimate goals.

a2. On Liberation and How to Achieve It

A key feature of tantric schools is the use of mantras, thus they are usually called the "Path of Mantra" (Mantramārga).[121, 122]

---

120. *Vishnudevananda, Swami (1999). Meditation and Mantras. Motilal Banarsidass, p. 89.*

121. *Kongtrul, Jamgon (2005). The Treasury of Knowledge, Book Six, Part Four Systems of Buddhist Tantra. Translated by Guarisco, Elio; McLeod, Ingrid. Snow Lion Publications, p. 74.*

122. *Bisschop, Peter C. (2020). "1. From Mantramārga Back to Atimārga: Atimārga as a Self referential Term". In Goodall at al. (ed.). Śaivism and the Tantric Traditions:*

The recitation of mantras (Japa) is often practiced along with Nyasa ("depositing" the mantras in different parts of the body of the practitioner), Mudrās ("seals", or symbolic hand gestures), and diverse deity visualizations. In some cases, they imagine that they are, physically and in essence, the chosen deity. In others, the deities are visualized as part of the body of the practitioner.[123]

Other common elements include the use of symbolic geometric drawings (Yantras) for meditation and ritual.

Concepts of "mystical physiology" related to Kundalini Yoga, such as the subtle body, Chakras, and energetic channels are also used. The basis for these beliefs is the perceived correspondence between man (microcosmos) and the whole cosmos. Because of this, man is viewed as containing all gods and goddesses (personified universal forces) within himself.[124]

In the tantric traditions that do use sex as part of spiritual practice (e.g., Kaulas, also Tibetan Buddhism), sex and desire are often seen as a means of transcendence used to reach the Absolute. These practices are not accepted by orthodox Hindus, however, and are often criticized.

Symbols in Hinduism: Om syllabe, Shiva lingam, Swastika, conch, Sri Yantra, among others.

Figure 4. The lingam (Shiva, male; formless, pure consciousness) and yoni (Shakti, female; transcendent power) together symbolizing Ultimate Reality (Brahman) as the union of opposites. See: Sivananda, Swami (1996). "Worship of Siva Linga". Picture: Shiv Sahil.

Essays in Honour of Alexis G.J.S. Sanderson. Indological Studies (Vol. 22). Gonda, Ch. 1.

123. *Padoux, André (2017). The Hindu Tantric World An Overview. Chicago: University of Chicago Press, pp. 77-79.*

124. *Ibid., pp. 73-75.*

2.9. Buddhism

a. Different Traditions and Sources of Authority

Buddhism is seen either as a religion or as a philosophical system originating from the teachings of Siddhartha Gautama, the Buddha. The current major traditions are:

• *Theravāda (or "Way of the Elders"):* derived from one of the earliest Buddhist schools. The *Pali Tipitaka* ("Three Baskets") contains the teachings attributed to the historical Buddha, among other monastic and doctrinal (Abhidarma) writings.

• *Mahāyāna (or "Great Vehicle"):* composed of a wide variety of Buddhist traditions, each with its own texts and practices. It accepts the main scriptures and teachings of Theravāda Buddhism but adds others that are not recognized by them. Their main texts are the Mahāyāna and *Prajñāpāramitā* ("Perfection of Wisdom") *sutras*. It includes traditions such as Pure Land and Chan/Zen, popular in the West.

• *Vajrayāna (or "Diamond Vehicle"; also known as Mantrayāna, Esoteric or Tibetan Buddhism):* a tantric tradition that developed a multitude of techniques to achieve Buddhahood. It was derived from Mahāyāna Buddhism, the indigenous Tibetan Bön tradition, and tantric Hinduism.[125] Its practices are tied to specific lineages and their texts are called Buddhist *Tantras*.[126] Some of its schools have achieved popularity in the Western world.

---

125. Sanderson, Alexis (2009). "The Śaiva Age: The Rise and Dominance of Śaivism during the Early Medieval Period", in Einoo, Shingo (ed.), Genesis and Development of Tantrism. Institute of Oriental Culture Special Series, vol. 23, Tokyo: Institute of Oriental Culture, University of Tokyo.

126. Macmillan Publishing (2004). Macmillan Encyclopedia of Buddhism. Macmillan Publishing, pp. 875-876.

b. Main Metaphysical Beliefs of Buddhism

b1. Conception of God

The main concern found in all Dharmic religions (or philosophies) that came out from India is the same: to find the ultimate reality beyond our phantasmagoric world of appearances and change. In their view, this implies attaining liberation from the cycle of death and rebirth and the consequent suffering it brings (Duḥkha).[127]

Hinduism discovered in Brahman this eternal, unchanging reality. Buddhism, in contrast, states that reality is empty of any such unchangeable eternal Essence.

In this regard, the Pāli Canon explains that both Pluralism (multiplicity) and Monism are untrue, with the former ending in Nihilism and the latter in Eternalism (Sassatavada).[128] Buddhism understands itself as the middle way between the dialectic formed by these two extremes.

This is especially evident in the foundational Mahāyāna texts called the *Perfection of Wisdom sutras*, for which nobody nor anything has a "Self", nor any particular or "true nature" (Svabhāva).

"*Form is emptiness, emptiness is form*" [129]

— Avalokiteśvara. Heart Sutra

In these texts, the world as it appears to us is like a mirage or a dream, with reality being an undefinable "thingness of things" or "suchness" (Tathātā), a voidness (Śūnyatā) without characteristics or attributes. The intrinsic oneness of the absolute and relative planes of existence and the totality of all things (Dharmadhātu) is affirmed.

---

127. *Puligandla, Ramakrishna (1997). Fundamentals of Indian Philosophy. New Delhi: D.K. Printworld, Ltd.*

128. *Kalupahana, David (1975). Causality: The Central Philosophy of Buddhism. The University Press of Hawaii, p. 88, passage SN 2.77.*

129. *Liang-Chieh (1986). The Record of Tung-shan. William F. Powell transl. Kuroda Institute, p. 9.*

Figure 5. Bodhidharma is seen as the founder of Chinese Chan Buddhism (the source of the later Japanese Zen tradition) as well as the introducer of the Mahāyāna practice of meditation (Dhyana) in China. In the "Two Entrances and Four Practices", he teaches two "entrances" to the Dharma, introducing the characteristic Chan/Zen differentiation between sudden realization (of the Buddha Nature) and gradual methods of enlightenment.[130]

As shown in the picture, he also introduced "wall-gazing" as a method to quiet the mind [131], which he defined as: "Those who turn from delusion back to reality, who meditate on walls, the absence of self and other, the oneness of mortal and sage, and who remain unmoved even by scriptures are in complete and unspoken agreement with reason."

The Laṅkāvatāra Sūtra also associated with him, furthermore, emphasizes "the inner enlightenment that does away with all duality and is raised above all distinctions".[132] Given this statement, it seems that for Bodhidharma distinction was the same as opposition, as for Plotinus´ Neo-Platonism. Picture: detail of "Huike Offering His Arm to Bodhidharma", by Sesshū Toyo (1496).

---

130. *McRae, John R. (2004), Seeing through Zen: Encounter, Transformation, and Genealogy in Chinese Chan Buddhism. University of California Press, pp. 29–32.*

131. *Broughton, Jeffrey L. (1999), The Bodhidharma Anthology: The Earliest Records of Zen. Berkeley: University of California Press.*

132. *Kohn, Michael H., ed. (1991). The Shambhala Dictionary of Buddhism and Zen. Boston: Shambhala, p. 125.*

Mādhyamaka School and The Middle Way

This last point is emphasized by the highly influential Mādhyamaka ("Doctrine of the Middle Way") school of Mahāyāna Buddhism.

Also known as Shunyavada ("Theory of Negativity or Relativity"), it describes the highest reality as Emptiness (Śūnyatā), understood as identical with both the inner and external dimensions of everything that exists (including both sensory and mental objects).

The adherents of this school, however, would not assert any ultimate reality as existent. Therefore, they prefer to be called non-dualists instead of monists, as they consider their worldview above *the One and the Many* dialectic (e.g., Rangtong and Shentong views on Emptiness).

Non-Dualism emphasizes unity among diversity, contrary to the monist view that everything can be ultimately reduced to a unique entity or principle.

Nāgārjuna, the founder of this school, which is in itself a systematization of the *Perfection of Wisdom sutras*, explained his position in paradoxical anti-dialectical statements:

"Nothing comes into being, nor does anything disappear. Nothing is eternal, nor has anything an end. Nothing is identical, nor is anything differentiated. Nothing moves here, nor does anything move there." [133]

– Nāgārjuna

According to this view, any pair of opposite statements is seen as an erroneous or incomplete representation of reality. Neither the One nor the Many are ultimately believed to be true.

Nāgārjuna´s school used rigorous logic to demonstrate the absurd consequences (reductio ad absurdum) of believing in either of those extremes.

---

133. *Nigosian, S.A.(1994). World Faiths. Bedford/St. Martins, p. 145.*

Figure 6. Deity generation and melting into Emptiness. The fundamental practice of Tibetan (Vajrayāna) Buddhism is the practice of Tibetan Tantra, of which Deity Yoga is the main method. This method has two parts: the Generation and Completion stages. In the former, a chosen deity is meditated upon, involving prayers, mantra recitation, and visualizations. The visualizations include the mandala associated with the deity's Pure Land or Buddha field (including the deity´s consorts, attendant Buddhas, and bodhisattvas).[134] The practitioner, by identifying with the deity, is expected to develop "divine pride".

During the Completion stage, in contrast, the adept dissolves his visualizations into emptiness, their source, while engaging in formless contemplation on the ultimately empty nature of the mind. He also practices yogic exercises of internal energy and subtle body manipulation. Lochen Dharmashri defined this latter stage as "a stained appearance of ultimate reality that, occurring together with the bliss of melting, is the emptiness and appearance of an uncontrived divine form."[135] This contrasts with the previous generative stage, which is contrived and uses imagination. This melting into ultimate reality seems, at first sight, similar to the process of Return of the doctrines of the One. Picture: 18th century Mongolian miniature of a monk generating a tantric visualization; Sarvavid Vairocana Mandala; Anonymous, MAS.

134. Garson, Nathaniel DeWitt (2004). Penetrating the Secret Essence Tantra: Context and Philosophy in the Mahayoga System of rNying-ma Tantra.

135. Dharmashri, Lochen. Commentary to the Three Vows, pp. 483-484.

Figure 7. Nāgārjuna and the Middle Way. Nāgārjuna (meaning "Noble Serpent"), a Buddhist monk and philosopher, was the founder of the Mādhyamaka (Middle Way) school. This school, the most influential in Buddhist history, defends a position between the two extremes of Eternalism and Nihilism (the latter understood as perpetual cessation of existence).

His influence surpassed that of the historical Buddha, with his text "Root Verses on Mādhyamaka" (Mūlamadhyamakakārikā) being considered the most important exposition of the doctrine of Emptiness (Śūnyatā). The snakes in the picture around Nāgārjuna's head are seen as protectors and symbols of wisdom, while the Nāgas (half-human and half-serpent/dragon creatures) coming out of the water are offering Buddhist sutras (knowledge) to him. Some of the most important Buddhist figures, in fact, symbolize Nāgas in their names (e.g., Dignāga, Nāgāsēna, Nāgārjuna). Picture: a Tibetan depiction of Nāgārjuna, with Manjushri (top right) and Dorje Shugden (bottom right); Tsem Rinpoche.

It saw Hindus as being attached to the wrong view of Eternalism, but also viewed some Buddhists dangerously close to the opposite extreme of Nihilism. Therefore, the Middle Way[136] sought an intermediate position beyond classical Either/Or logic.

Positing all things as being relative and ultimately empty, this worldview sees everything as devoid of any essential nature or characteristics, existing only in relation to the causal conditions producing them.

This led to the identification of Nirvana (Ultimate Reality) with Saṃsāra (this cyclical Universe of life, death, and rebirth). Believing both terms to be partial and incomplete concepts, this school sought the truth beyond them. Beyond affirmation and negation, being and non-being.

Yogācāra or "Mind-Only" School

Another influential Mahāyāna school, the Yogācāra ("Mind-Only") tradition also rejects Monism. Instead, it favors a non-dual understanding of both form and Emptiness, even if they often sound like monists, especially in English translations.

Unlike Mādhyamaka, instead of focusing on logical analysis and dialectics, this school emphasizes a psychological analysis that led it to state that nothing exists outside of mind. For them, consciousness is the ground of existence and external things are mere representations of it.

The existence of a "Storehouse Consciousness" (Ālāya-Vijñāna) in each being is one of Yogācāra´s key teachings. It is the indwelling of the karmic "seeds" that later develop into sense or mental activity, perception, and will.

----

136. *The concept of the Middle Way may also refer to a spiritual life that avoids both the extremes of asceticism and sensual indulgence. This is what Siddharta Gautama did by rejecting extreme ascetic Hindu practices and by establishing his own spiritual path (the Noble Eightfold Path) in order to attain awakening.*

According to this school, ideation (Manas) creates the false illusion of the existence of an individual ego ("I think, therefore I am"). Our objective should be, then, to understand that objects only exist through this false self and sense perceptions.

To do this, our Storehouse Consciousness is to be purged from the false notion of a distinct ego that perceives external objects (subject-object duality) in order to recover its pure state.

This final station is equivalent to "suchness" (Tathātā) or Buddhahood, which is conceived as an undifferentiated or pre-differentiated state of being.

Who Was the Buddha?

Theravāda Tradition: The Buddha as a Supreme Self-Liberated Person

Buddha means "awakened one".[137] The Theravāda tradition sees the historical Siddartha Gautama as a "great person" (Mahāpurisa).[138, 139]

He is seen as neither human nor God as understood in monotheistic religions. In fact, following the general Indian understanding of the gods (Devas), he is seen as a teacher of both.

Gautama is believed to have attained the highest liberation, whereas the gods are still subject to some passions and have not yet reached a complete awakening.[140] In some instances, he is identified with ultimate reality or Universal Law *itself* (Dhamma; *Vakkali Sutta*, SN 22.87).[141]

---

137. *Buswell, Robert, ed. (2004). Encyclopedia of Buddhism. MacMillan, p. 71.*

138. *Dhammika, Shravasti (2005). The Buddha and His Disciples. Buddhist Publication Society, p. 16.*

139. *Sangharakshita (1996). A Guide to the Buddhist Path. Windhorse Publications, p. 45.*

140. *Jootla, Susan Elbaum (1999). Teacher of the Devas (accesstoinsight.org).*

141. *O'Connell Walshe, Maurice (2007). Vakkali Sutta: Vakkali (accesstoinsight.org).*

Mahāyāna Tradition: The Boddhisatva Ideal and the Buddha Nature

Mahāyāna Buddhism further developed the concept of Buddahood. A Buddha, for the followers of this tradition, is a transcendent and omniscient being. It is a title given to each being who has achieved awakening and liberation, including human Buddhas who achieved them before the historical Gautama.

The list of Buddhas also includes the five celestial Buddhas (e.g., Amitābha) and the future Buddha and actual bodhisattva Maitreya, who is believed will become the successor of Gautama in this world.

The bodhisattva path is the path to achieve full Buddahood with the intention of liberating all sentient beings, and includes the vow to not transcend this reality until every living creature has been saved from suffering (Duḥkha).[142] This is a specific Mahāyāna goal that they like to contrast with the goal of individual self-liberation of the Theravāda path (Arhatship).

All those who achieve Buddhahood are believed to remain active in the world, working as spiritual guides. They can receive prayers and provide visions and guidance.

All the above is believed to be possible because Mahāyāna doctrine affirms the existence of an immanent Buddha Nature in all beings.[143] Everyone can become a transcendent Buddha. The duality between immanence and transcendence is surpassed not by the Godhead or ultimate reality (like in the Trinity and the Incarnation of the Logos in Christianity) but by asserting that every being has the Buddha Nature within them and the potential to claim it by their own efforts.

---

142. *Gethin, Rupert (1998). The foundations of Buddhism. Oxford University Press, pp. 224–234.*

143. *Daishonin, Nichiren. Major Writings of Nichiren Daishonin (Vol. 1). Soka Gakkai. p. 216.*

Trikāya: The Three Bodies of the Buddha

Another fundamental doctrine of both the Mahāyāna and Vajrayāna (Tibetan) traditions posits that a Buddha has three distinct bodies or aspects (Trikāya):

• *Dharmakāya ("Dharma body" or Ultimate Reality):* the reality behind the concepts of Emptiness, Buddha Nature, and pure existence. It can only be experienced but not explained, as it transcends any possible manifestation.

• *Saṃbhogakāya ("Enjoyment body"):* the aspect that represents the manifestation of the Buddhas in their Buddha realms. Associated with the subjective experience of bliss, understood as the recompense obtained through spiritual practice and the consequent states of realization.

• *Nirmāṇakāya ("Transformation body"):* the physical appearance of a Buddha in the world, serving as a bridge between levels of reality and allowing interaction with sentient beings in order to teach them.

This doctrine is used to explain how a Buddha can exist at the same time in multiple realms and levels of reality.

b2. Creation and Time

Two Levels of Reality: The Two Truths Doctrine

Reality itself, according to Buddhists, can be differentiated between two levels of reality or truth (Satya): the conventional, or everyday experience of the world, and the ultimate, where everything is intuitively known to be, in the last analysis, Emptiness.[144]

According to Nāgārjuna, the world we can perceive with our senses is neither real nor unreal, but has a provisional existence. In the end,

---

144. *Thakchoe, Sonam (2022). "The Theory of Two Truths in Tibet". In Zalta, Edward N. (ed.). Stanford Encyclopedia of Philosophy. The Metaphysics Research Lab, Center for the Study of Language and Information. Stanford University.*

all phenomena are empty (Śūnyatā) of any inherent self or essence (Anattā). Their existence is only relative, in causal dependence upon other phenomena (Pratītyasamutpāda).

Figure 8. The Trikāya and the Laughing Buddha. Mahāyāna and Vajrayāna Buddhism speak of the Buddha as a triadic multidimensional existence. A Buddha is believed to be composed of three bodies or aspects (Modalism), emanating in sequential and descending order (from transcendence to immanence): the first body is the so-called "Dharma Body" (Dharmakāya), Ultimate Reality itself. The second body is the "Body of Enjoyment" (Saṃbhogakāya). This "energetic" aspect represents the body manifested by the Buddhas in their Pure Lands. The last body is the "Transformation Body" (Nirmāṇakāya). It means the physical appearance/s (can be multiple) of a Buddha in our plane of existence.

In summary, the Trikāya represents three sequential realities, the last two of them being emanations of the first impersonal ground of being, the Buddha Nature or Emptiness. Obtaining control over these aspects of Ultimate Reality depends on the success of the aspirant in applying the prescribed meditation practices. This is very different from the personal, Trinitarian but not triadic (co-equal and not sequential) Christian Trinity.

The swastikas on the chest of the three bodies symbolize the auspicious footprints of the Buddha or the eternal cyclical nature of Saṃsāra.[145] The laughing Buddha, in turn, represents the historical monk Qici (also nicknamed Budai). Chan Buddhism often identifies him with the future Buddha Maitreya. He is known for his humorous personality, and his huge stomach possibly symbolizes abundance and forgiveness.[146] Picture: Budhi Bhakti Temple, Indonesia.

---

145. Snodgrass, Adrian (1992). *The Symbolism of the Stupa*. Motilal Banarsidass. pp. 82–83.

146. Chapin, H. B. (1933). "The Chan Master Pu-tai". *Journal of the American Oriental Society*. 53 (1): 47–52.

Cosmology

Most Buddhists believe that the number of worlds or universes is infinite. Furthermore, they consist of three planes of existence, which are, from worst to best: the realm of desire, of material form, and of formlessness.

Each plane is divided again into various levels. For example, the realm of desire contains heavens, hells, and our world. Mythical descriptions of these places, full of gods, demi-gods (Asuras), and other beings, abound.

Cosmology and time, like in Hinduism, are cyclical. Different periods succeed each other in a downward spiral of spiritual, moral, and physical involution until the cosmos is finally destroyed.

After each universal catastrophe a period of silence is followed by a renewal of all existence and the beginning of a new cycle.

Five Buddhas are prophesied to appear in the human world to guide it, with Gautama being the fourth.

To be incarnated in human form is considered a great opportunity for spiritual progress, as the greatest spiritual development is believed to be attainable in this realm of existence.

What Are Living Beings Made Of? The Five Aggregates of Clinging

According to Buddhism, there are five material and mental factors (Skhandas) from which every living being is formed. They are: form, sensations/feelings, perceptions, mental activity, and consciousness.

In this worldview, we erroneously feel attached to them as if they were part of our own identity or "self". Craving and clinging, therefore, are viewed as born from the interaction between these aggregates and our own ignorance.

Figure 9. Saṃsāra, or the painful Wheel of Life (Bhavacakra) that has us trapped. The wheel of life is a, mostly Tibetan, visual teaching aid symbolizing the cyclic existence that awaits us until we become liberated.

It represents the Six Realms of Saṃsāra, which are the following. 1: Human realm (desire and attachment); 2: Hungry ghost (Preta) realm (greed); 3: Hell (paranoia) realm (anger); 4: Animal realm (ignorance); 5: Demigod (Asura) realm (jealousy, envy); 6: Realm of the Gods (Devas) (pride); 7: the Three Poisons at the root of our suffering (Duḥkha); 8: the twelve links of dependent origination; 9: a representation of impermanence and Yama, the Lord of Death.[147] Picture: Trongsa Dzong mural in Bhutan.

---

147. *Dalai Lama (1992). The Meaning of Life, translated and edited by Jeffrey Hopkins. Wisdom, p. 42–43.*

b3. The Concept of Evil

As in Hinduism, Buddhism sees no "problem" of evil as understood in monotheistic religions. "Evil", in itself, is considered as just an unavoidable consequence of our own ignorance or the ignorance of others. This results in what is perceived as harmful behavior in conventional reality. Natural "evil", such as disease, is considered a normal and necessary aspect of the realm of relativity we live in.

Nevertheless, there exists a demonic personification of the forces that lead us away from enlightenment. It is Mara.

The Different Faces of Mara

Mara can be understood either literally or metaphorically as:

• The god (Deva) of the sensuous realm, who tried to prevent the awakening of Siddharta Gautama.

• The personification of death and of all unskillful emotions (e.g., the Three Poisons or unwholesome roots from which most suffering derives: greed, hate, and delusion).

• A metaphor for the conditioned existence we live in before being able to finally attain liberation.

b4. Determinism and Free will

Like in all Indian religions, the degree of freedom available to us in our conditioned existences is considered to be dependent on our accumulated Karma.

The difference, in this case, is that Buddhists believe that rebirth takes place without any soul or immutable self passing from one form to another.[148]

---

148. *Dying, Death and the Afterlife in Dharma Traditions and Western Religions (pp.29–44) Deepak Heritage Books, January 2006.*

They believe Karma dictates rebirth in one of the Six Realms, depending on the moral quality of our actions and intentions. These are the realms of the gods, demi-gods, humans, animals, hungry ghosts, and hells.

The Law of Karma has different levels and is not completely deterministic, however. The most important moment that determines where a person is to be re-incarnated is the last thought before death. The Karma accumulated at this time is considered heavy Karma and takes precedence.

If no strong thoughts or emotions were experienced while dying, near-death Karma would ripen next. Habitual and residual Karma is thought to follow.[149]

b5. On Liberation and End Times

Buddhism presents a complex picture of the afterlife, including an intermediate spirit world, the previously mentioned Six Realms of existence, and the Pure Lands of the Buddhas.

Furthermore, according to Theravāda Buddhism, there exist thirty-one realms where reincarnation can take place, including the possibility of becoming a supreme deity for a period of time.

Pure Land Buddhism, a Mahāyāna school, focuses on the so-called Pure Lands (as its name implies). Each one is viewed as the abode of a specific Buddha, created out of their merits and for the sake of the beings that meditate on them. Here, wisdom and spiritual evolution are more easily attained.

The Tibetan tradition, additionally, has extensively explored the topic of the intermediate state after death. The *Tibetan Book of the Dead* (*Bardo Thödol*) explains that the dead can find the bright light of wisdom, which

---

149. *"The Buddhist Society: Kamma – Actions and Results" (thebuddhistsociety.org).*

points to the path that leads to the end of the cycle of rebirths. This text also explains that, in the intermediate state, our consciousness determines our experiences. Therefore, it is important to adopt a positive attitude and understand that any perceived manifestation is just a projection of our inner thoughts. No real harm can be suffered here, as there is no connection with a body. Different Buddhas can also help in this state. Letting go of any earthly attachments is viewed as a key step in order to be able to move forward.

2.10. Buddhist Mysticism: Meditation, Visualization and Deity Generation

Contrary to other traditions where their mystical schools are differentiated from the main branch of their parent religion (e.g., Kabbalah in Judaism, Sufism in Islam), Buddhism and all Indian religions place their mystical and practical teachings at the forefront. Every Buddhist is expected to follow one path or another to achieve liberation, while not every Muslim is expected to also be a Sufi.

It is common for the esoteric mystical schools that become separated from their corresponding exoteric religions to eventually develop different parallel metaphysical doctrines. This is not the case for Buddhism (or any other Indian tradition), where the most esoteric sects focus on method development and practice while sharing the same worldview as their parent exoteric tradition. We will now briefly discuss these methods.

a. Gautama´s Noble Eightfold Path

The classic and most widely known Buddhist path (Mārga) to liberation is the Noble Eightfold Path. It was developed by Siddharta Gautama. Different descriptions of it are found in the Pali canon:

"Now what, monks, is the Noble Eightfold Path? Right view, right resolve, right speech, right action, right livelihood, right effort, right mindfulness, right concentration [Samādhi]." [150]

— Gautama Buddha

b. Theravāda Tradition and the Path of Purification

Theravāda mysticism, the oldest of the traditions still alive today, is concerned with emptying the mind of the aspirant of any trace of subjective experience. The process is described as "a flame going out".

Meditation is pursued as a crucial part of the path towards liberation from defilements (Kleshas), clinging, and craving (Upādāna). The expected results are awakening and the attainment of Nirvana.[151]

A variety of techniques are employed to that end. An important one is mindfulness of breathing (Ānāpānasati). Other methods include "reflections on repulsiveness" of aspects of life (Aśubha Bhāvanā)[152],

---

150. Thanissaro, Bhikkhu (1996). "Magga-vibhanga Sutta: An Analysis of the Path" (accesstoinsight.org).

151. Kamalashila (2003), p. 4, states that Buddhist meditation "includes any method of meditation that has awakening as its ultimate aim."

— Bodhi (1999): "To arrive at the experiential realization of the truths it is necessary to take up the practice of meditation [...] At the climax of such contemplation the mental eye [...] shifts its focus to the unconditioned state, Nibbana."

— Fischer-Schreiber et al. (1991), p. 142: "Meditation — general term for a multitude of religious practices, often quite different in method, but all having the same goal: to bring the consciousness of the practitioner to a state in which he can come to an experience of 'awakening,' 'liberation,' 'enlightenment.'"

— Kamalashila (2003), p. 4, further explains that some Buddhist meditations are "of a more preparatory nature".

152. Deleanu, Florin (1992). Mindfulness of Breathing in the Dhyāna Sūtras. Transactions of the International Conference of Orientalists in Japan (TICOJ) 37, pp. 42-57.

reflection on dependent origination (Pratītyasamutpāda), recollections of qualities of the Buddha (Anussati), and Mindfulness.[153, 154, 155, 156]

Also important are the contemplations on loving-kindness and compassion (Brahma-Vihāras).

The practitioner is expected to achieve unification of mind (Samādhi) through developing tranquillity and concentration (Samatha), as well as insight (Vipassanā) on the ultimate nature of everything that exists.

In this tradition, the one who achieves Nirvana through his own efforts is called an Arhat, meaning "one who is worthy".

The traditional outline of the Theravāda path to liberation, the Seven Purifications, can be found in the classic manual called *"The Path of Purification" (Visuddhimagga)*.

b1. The Four Stages of the Path

Theravadins believe that the adepts will have to pass through four successive stages before reaching their final destination:

1. *Stream Enterer:* when the truth has been at least dimly seen and no more than seven additional reincarnations await the aspirant.

2. *Once-Returner:* when only an additional life will be needed to achieve Nirvana.

---

153. Vetter, Tilmann (1988). *The Ideas and Meditative Practices of Early Buddhism*. Brill.

154. Bronkhorst, Johannes (1993). *The Two Traditions Of Meditation In Ancient India*, Motilal Banarsidass.

155. Anālayo (2017). *Early Buddhist Meditation Studies*. Barre Center for Buddhist Studies Barre, Massachusetts, USA, p. 109.

156. Arbel, Keren (2016). *Early Buddhist Meditation: The Four Jhanas as the Actualization of Insight*. Taylor & Francis.

3. *Non-Returner:* when liberation will be attained in this life or in the intermediate state before another rebirth takes place. No more doubt or belief in a permanent self is left at this point.

4. *Arhat:* when complete freedom has been achieved, and the awakened being is free from ignorance and the desire to exist in either the realms of form or the formless ones.

c. Mahāyāna Tradition and the Path to Buddhahood

A follower of Mahāyāna begins his path with the vow to become a Buddha. During his quest for self-transcendence, he will have to pass through ten stages or spiritual stations (Bhūmi) and purify himself through the practice of the ten perfections (Pāramitās).

The first six levels are a preparation for the next and include the development of general virtues (generosity, morality, patience, vigour, concentration, and wisdom).

Reaching the seventh station is believed to result in an irreversible achievement where the bodhisattva assumes his true Buddha Nature. Everything is now seen as uncreated, and the adept becomes increasingly identified with the body of truth (Dharmakāya) of the Buddha until he reaches the final state, that of all-knowing Buddhahood.

c1. Pure Land Buddhism and the Path of Devotion

Pure Land Buddhists chant the name of their chosen Buddha (usually Amitābha) as a form of mindfulness and to achieve focal concentration on him alone (Samādhi).[157]

With the same objective in mind, they can also engage in meditative contemplation and visualization of Amitābha and his Pure Land. The aim is to reincarnate there in order to be able to finally learn the doctrines that they could not grasp in this life.

---

157. *Luk, Charles (1964). The Secrets of Chinese Meditation. Weiser, p. 83.*

Figure 10. Praying to the Buddhas: Buddha Amitābha descending from his Pure Land. Pure Land Buddhism, originating in Japan, is the most commonly practiced form of Buddhism in the world and the most unknown to the West. Its doctrines are key to Mahāyāna, which has been described as a "Buddhism of the Pure Lands". This school of thought focuses on the contemplation of the Pure Land of Buddha Amitābha, called Sukhavati (Land of Bliss).

Many practitioners aim to be reborn in this ethereal place in their next life, where the grasping of complex doctrines not fully assimilated during life is believed to be easily achievable. Others, however, think of the Pure Lands as symbolizing Nirvana, yet being in some way present within our realm of existence. Others may view both positions as complementary.

Even though Pure Land and its methods of deity invocation and prayer may appear superficially more theistic in nature than other forms of Buddhism, Amitābha and other Buddhas are just particular instances of beings who achieved illumination after a myriad existences and are ranked below the general impersonal Buddha Nature, of which we all partake. As the Contemplation Sutra states in a very explicit way: "the mind that creates the Buddha is the Buddha". Picture: unidentified artist (13th century, China); The Met.

c2. Chan/Zen Buddhism and the Power of Paradox

This tradition is known for its austerity, simple aesthetics and iconoclast attitude. Its main methods to achieve awakening (Satori) and to "see one's true (Buddha) Nature" (Kenshō) are:

The Kōan

A Kōan is a short story, dialogue or question that the teacher may pose to the student in order to evaluate his spiritual understanding. It is often a paradoxical statement that seems illogical.

The idea behind this method is to exhaust the logical reasoning capacity of the disciple in order to force an abrupt breakthrough moment of intuition about the ultimate nature of reality. The end result is the experience of subject-object non-duality.

"Just Sitting" (Shikantaza)

Also called "Silent Illumination", practitioners strive to leave their minds empty, eliminating any trace of conceptualizing, grasping or any other mental state that implies subject-object dualism.[158]

Even though the concept of "sudden enlightenment" became one of the key attractions of Zen Buddhism, gradual enlightenment is also important in this school (e.g., *Ten Ox-Herding Pictures*).

d. Tantric Buddhism and the Path of Many Methods

Tantric Buddhism, Esoteric Buddhism or Mantrayāna is the name given to the different traditions of Tibetan or Vajrayāna Buddhism. They usually include the meditation methods of other Mahāyāna schools, but also add multiple other techniques considered to achieve faster results. The adept has to train under the vigilance of a master or guru (Lama).

As taught in the *Kalachakra Tantra*, tantric practice is thought to be especially necessary in degenerate times such as ours. Using it, practitioners can achieve enlightenment even through a passion-filled body, sometimes fighting poison with poison.

---

158. *Taigen Dan, Leighton (2000). Cultivating the Empty Field: The Silent Illumination of Zen Master Hongzhi. Tuttle, pp. 1-2.*

The defining meditation method of this school is Deity Yoga (Devatayoga).[159] This involves the visualization of the chosen deity and associated mandala and Pure Land. Mantra recitation is also employed.[160]

Advanced stages of the practice include imagining oneself as the deity and developing "divine pride", as well as the realization that the deity and oneself are not different entities, since both are ultimately understood to equally derive from Emptiness.

Other paths in Tibetan Buddhism include Mahāmudrā (Kagyu lineage) and Dzogchen (Nyingma lineage). They both try to realize the ground or base of existence, the Dharmakāya.

 The three stages of the path have been summarized (Lamrim) as: developing the aspiration for awakening (Bodhicitta), the aspiration to liberate all living beings, and insight into Emptiness itself.

A multitude of other methods are also used by particular schools, including Dream Yoga, "inner heat" (Tummo), the Yoga of the intermediate state (Bardo) at the moment of death, sexual Yoga, and Chöd or "cutting through the ego", which uses fear to annihilate the ego of the disciple.

The preliminary or foundational practices shared by all schools include contemplations on key principles of the path (Ngöndro), mantra recitation, and prostrations.

Chinese (Tendai) and Japanese (Shingon) schools of esoteric Buddhism use similar techniques.

---

159. *Power, John (1995). Introduction to Tibetan Buddhism. Snow Lion Publications,* p. 271.

160. *Garson, Nathaniel DeWitt (2004). Penetrating the Secret Essence Tantra: Context and Philosophy in the Mahayoga System of rNying-ma Tantra. University of Virginia, p. 37.*

Figure 11. The deities of Buddhism: the Hundred Peaceful and Wrathful Deities of the Bardo (Intermediate State). Forty-two peaceful deities and fifty-eight wrathful ones are believed to reside in the Bardo states. Pictured above are the wrathful ones. Note that the deities depicted in this assembly mandala, however, are personifications of different aspects of the practitioners themselves, such as their own awareness or their psycho-physical aggregates, elemental properties, and sensory and mental processes and organs. The peaceful deities symbolize these components in their purified state, while the wrathful ones represent the transformative aspects of these energies. These deities and their mandala representation appear in many teachings related, especially, to the Tibetan Book of the Dead and the Guhyagarbha Tantra.

The central deity and Primordial Buddha, Samantabhadra, represents in Dzogchen´s doctrine our true nature, the Ground State. Sogyal Rinpoche clarified our relation to this deity when he unambiguously stated: "[Kuntuzangpo] represents the absolute, naked, sky-like primordial purity of the nature of our mind".[161] Note that the wrathful thangka represents an inverted image of the peaceful one, with Chemchok Heruka, the central deity, being the wrathful form of Samantabhadra. The wrathful deities, vividly described as horrifying, are nevertheless considered as the necessary counterpart of the peaceful ones. This is a clear example of Complementary Dualism and the doctrine of the union of opposites. "Evil" is not a concept assigned to any of them. Picture: detail of Shitro Puja, Ayang Rinpoche's monastery (Bylakuppe).

---

161. *Rinpoche, Sogyal (1992). The Tibetan Book of Living and Dying, p. 106.*

d1. Mahāmudrā School

The highest paths distinguish between two stages of the practice: Generation and Completion stages. The first is based on Deity Yoga, while the second uses a form of energy Yoga (similar to the Kundalini variant) and Emptiness meditation practices.

The Mahāmudrā ("Great Seal" or "Great Symbol") school uses "the four Yogas of Mahāmudrā" to try to achieve the following states, which can be correlated with the Mahāyāna Bhūmi states: 1. *One-pointedness;* 2. *Simplicity;* 3.*"One taste";* 4. *Non-Meditation:* where neither meditation nor meditator are conceptualized, thus making subject-object duality disappear.

Figure 12. **A:** *mural at the fifth Dalai Lama´s Lukhang Temple showing different tantric yogic practices of energy and consciousness manipulation (Tummo [inner fire] and Phowa [transference of consciousness]).*

B: *In Dzogchen, the practice of Tögal ("crossing the peak", "direct crossing" or "direct transcendence") involves meditation and experiencing visions while sky (and Sun) gazing.[162] It is considered, along with Trekchö, as one of Vajrayāna´s most advanced and direct methods, believed to allow its practitioners "to proceed directly to the goal without having to go through intermediate steps."[163]*

---

162. *Smith, Malcolm (2016). Buddhahood in This Life: The Great Commentary by Vimalamitra. Simon and Schuster, p.26.*

163. *Chökyi Nyima Rinpoche (1994). Union of Mahamudra and Dzogchen. Rangjung Yeshe Publications, p. 224.*

d2. Dzogchen School

Translated as "Great Perfection" or "Great Completion" (also known as Atiyoga or Utmost Yoga), this popular school has three main points of focus: the Base, the Path, and the Fruit.

The Base represents the original state of existence, defined as Emptiness, clarity, and compassionate energy. The Path is formed of view (correct understanding of reality), practice, and conduct. The Fruit represents the realization of one's true Buddha Nature and experiencing non-dual awareness.

Rainbow Body

The practice of the Tögal method is believed to be able to lead the aspirants to full Buddhahood at the moment of death and to transform their earthly body into a Rainbow Body[164], understood as one made of light.

This new body is viewed as a manifestation of the "enjoyment body" (Saṃbhogakāya) of a Buddha.

Symbols in Buddhism: lotus flower, stupas, triratna, Dharma wheel, and mandalas, among others.

Figure 13. The Triratna, the symbol of the Three Jewels (Buddha, Dharma, and Sangha or community/monastic order).

---

164. *Ray, Reginald (2001). Secret of the Vajra World: The Tantric Buddhism of Tibet. Shambhala, p. 323.*

UNITY OF OPPOSITES IN BUDDHISM

We have seen that it is common in different Buddhist meditation practices to believe that the experience of realization is attained once different opposites or dichotomies (the Many) are intuitively experienced as one common underlying reality (the One).

This is often symbolized as the union (Yab-Yum) of the passive female deity (representing wisdom or Emptiness) with the dynamic male (compassion without attachment). This union is thought to be the cause of enlightenment and bliss.

Note how the deities, in this case, do not represent any personal being but personalized abstract concepts.

Figure 14. The Primordial Buddha as the Unity of Opposites. Tibetan Buddhist Samantabhadra painting. Note the union of both Male/Female (Yab-Yum [Father-Mother]) and Light/Dark motifs.

This is another representative example of the doctrine of the union or identity of opposites present in most mystical and esoteric traditions. It is also a central theme of many Kōans[165], such as Hakuin´s famous one, where duality and unity are the key concepts to be grasped: *"Two hands clap and there is a sound, what is the sound of one hand?"*

---

165. *Hori, Victor Sogen (2000). Kōan and Kenshō in the Rinzai Zen Curriculum. In Steven Heine; Dale S. Wright (eds.). The Kōan: Texts and contexts in Zen Buddhism. Oxford University Press, pp. 289–290 and p. 310 (note 14).*

2.11. Taoism

Taoism or Daoism[166] can be defined as both a religion and a philosophy. It focuses on leading a life in harmony with the Tao (meaning the Way, the Road), viewed as the impersonal process or principle that underlies all reality.

Different sects grew around different sets of texts, with Lao Tzu´s *Daodejing* (or *Tao Te Ching*) being the main foundational work. Another influential text was the *Zhuangzi*.

Most Taoists believe in the concept of the "Integration of the Three Doctrines". This theory considers that Taoism, Confucianism, and Buddhism are worldviews that, although developed in different ways, are based on the same ultimate reality (Taiji).[167]

"The absolute is movement and stillness without beginning, yin and yang without beginning. Buddhists call this complete awareness, Taoists call it the gold pill, Confucians call it the absolute.

What is called the infinite absolute means the limit of the unlimited. Buddha called it "as is, immutable, ever clearly aware". The I Ching says, "tranquil and unperturbed, yet sensitive and effective". An alchemical text says, "Body and mind unstirring, subsequently there is yet an endless real potential". Yet all refer to the subtle root of the absolute." [168]

— Li Daochun. The Book of Balance and Harmony

---

166. *Several different systems have been used to transcribe Chinese into the Latin alphabet, resulting in different spellings, such as Wade–Giles and Hanyu Pinyin.*

167. *Daochun, Li (trans. Thomas Cleary, 2003). The Book of Balance and Harmony: A Taoist Handbook. Shambhala, p. xxix.*

168. *Daochun, Li (2003). The Book of Balance and Harmony: A Taoist Handbook. Shambhala, p. 3.*

a. Main Metaphysical Beliefs of Taoism

a1. Conception of God

The Tao is described as unknowable and formless, and has been tentatively understood as the flow of the Universe or as the underlying order or essence of the cosmos. Taoism, however, is more concerned with stating what the Tao is not than in comprehensive descriptions of what it is (apophatic "theology").

It is usually described using an analogy with water[169], due to its undifferentiated nature and its enormous power beyond its soft and quiet appearance. It has also been regarded as the source of all existence and the all-pervading sacred presence or pattern behind the Universe, but not as a self-conscious creator God.[170]

Given the above, Taoism can be viewed as monistic because it posits one ultimate reality, as well as panentheistic because the Tao is both this ultimate principle or essence along with the ground of all that exists. It is both immanent and transcendent.

It is, nevertheless, viewed as a non-dualistic principle or law that is greater than the sum of its parts. Therefore, Taoism is not pantheistic, even if the Tao pervades the entire Universe.

A Taoist scholar, Wing-Tsit Chan, defined it as: *"the One, which is natural, spontaneous, eternal, nameless, and indescribable. It is at once the beginning of all things and the way in which all things pursue their course."* [171, 172]

---

169. *Carlson, Kathie; Flanagin, Michael N.; Martin, Kathleen; Martin, Mary E.; Mendelsohn, John; Rodgers, Priscilla Young; Ronnberg, Ami; Salman, Sherry; Wesley, Deborah A.; et al. (Authors) (2010). Arm, Karen; Ueda, Kako; Thulin, Anne; Langerak, Allison; Kiley, Timothy Gus; Wolff, Mary (eds.). The Book of Symbols: Reflections on Archetypal Images. Köln: Taschen, p. 704.*

170. *Kohn, Livia (2008). Introducing Daoism. New York: Routledge, p. 115.*

171. *Chan, Wing-tsit (1963). A Source Book in Chinese Philosophy. Princeton, p. 136.*

172. *A. Chan, cited in Kohn, Livia, ed. (2000). Taoism Handbook. Leiden: Brill, p. 20.*

On the immanence front, the Tao is present in all individuals, as well as in nature. It is the "innate nature" (Xing) of all that exists and is good.[173]

It can be conceptualized as having two different aspects: the "Tao that can be told" [174] (e.g., the rhythmic processes of nature) and the one that cannot.

During its early history (Shang dynasty, 17th – 11th century BCE), however, the Chinese worshipped a Supreme God (Shàngdì or "Lord on High") who was closer to the notion of a monotheistic God. It later became a synonym of Heaven (Tian), who had its complementary opposite in Earth (Di), with both poles maintaining the existence of the Three Realms through their generative tension (heavens, human world, and the world of demons or the damned). The actual conception of Tian is variable, however, being viewed mostly as a supreme reigning power or an impersonal force such as destiny itself.[175, 176]

Even though behind everything that exists is believed to lie a single unified principle, Taoism also speaks of many deities and spirits. Nevertheless, they are considered emanations from the impersonal One, the Tao.

Some Taoist theologies put the Three Pure Ones as the top deities of the pantheon. For the traditions embracing this concept, Lao Tzu is viewed as the incarnation of one of the three and worshipped as the one who revealed the Tao to mankind.[177]

---

173. *Komjathy, Louis (2014). Daoism: A guide for the Perplexed. Bloomsbury. p. 83.*

174. *Lao Tzu (trans. Lau, D.C., 1994). Tao Te Ching. Everyman's Library USA, Ch. I: "The Tao that can be told is not the eternal Tao. The name that can be named is not the eternal name. The nameless is the beginning of heaven and earth. The named is the mother of ten thousand things."*

175. *Gurdon Oxtoby, Willard (2002). World Religions: Eastern Traditions. Don Mills, Ontario: Oxford University Press. , p. 424.*

176. *Storm, Rachel (2011); Sudell, Helen (ed.). Myths & Legends of India, Egypt, China & Japan. Wigston, Leicestershire: Lorenz Books, p. 233.*

177. *Gurdon Oxtoby, Willard (2002). World Religions: Eastern Traditions. Don Mills, Ontario: Oxford University Press. 2002, p. 395.*

a2. Cosmology and Time

The principle of Ziran ("Self-Organization"[178]) is central to Taoism. It is used to define the "primordial state" of everything that exists, referring to the fact that there is no ultimate cause behind things that make them what they are. The Universe is believed to exist by itself and of itself, completely self-reliant. It is existence just as it is.[179]

The flow of time, in turn, is thought to be cyclic, with the Universe in constant flux and different forces and energies (Qi) influencing each other in complex patterns.[180]

Although all transformations in the cosmos are considered as spontaneous and unguided,[181] different creation stories or cosmogonies can also be found in Taoist classical texts, all of them non-theistic. They speak of a natural undirected process where an undifferentiated potentiality unfolds spontaneously into primordial oneness (Taiji) or "non-differentiation" (Wuji). This oneness, in turn, later emanates into Yin-Yang and finally into the multiple beings present in existence.

This cosmological view, as with all traditions that believe in the doctrine of emanation, is the pillar that supports the notion that one can return to the impersonal root of existence, of ourselves, and of the Universe by our own efforts.

Professor of religion Livia Kohn proposed the following summary of the Taoist cosmological vision:[182]

---

178. *Dr. Zai, J. (2015). Taoism and Science: Cosmology, Evolution, Morality, Health and more. Ultravisum.*

179. *Kohn, Livia (2008). Introducing Daoism. New York: Routledge, p. 30.*

180. *Ibid., p. 80.*

181. *Komjathy, Louis (2014). Daoism: A guide for the Perplexed. Bloomsbury, p. 87.*

182. *Kohn, Livia (2008). Introducing Daoism. New York: Routledge, p. 22.*

"[...] Dao rested in deep chaos (ch. 42). Next, it evolved into the One, a concentrated state of cosmic unity that is full of creative potential and often described in Yijing terms as the Great Ultimate (Taiji). The One then brought forth "the Two", the two energies yin and yang, which in turn merged in harmony to create the next level of existence, "the Three" (yin-yang combined), from which the myriad beings came forth. From original oneness, the world thus continued to move into ever greater states of distinction and differentiation."

Yin and Yang

The Yin and Yang doctrine represents the polar and mutually dependent complementary forces whose generative dialectical tension conforms all that exists. They embody the extremes or poles of any given dichotomy, such as: light-dark, strong-weak, male-female, etc.

They are further differentiated into five phases (Wu Xing): minor Yang, major Yang, Yin/Yang, minor Yin, and major Yin. Each phase is related, in turn, with a particular substance: wood, fire, earth, metal, and water, respectively.[183]

Living beings, as in most mystical traditions, are understood as a microcosmic image of the Universe.[184] This implies that the cosmological forces (like the five phases) and gods are also part of the human bodies, and that by knowing oneself one can also gain understanding about the cosmos.[185]

Chi/Qi

All things are seen as being formed and animated by Qi (subtle or vital energy, air or breath)[186], which is the concrete and manifested aspect of the Tao.

---

183. *Ibid., p. 83.*
184. *Robinet, Isabelle (1997). Taoism: Growth of a Religion. Stanford University Press, p. 103.*
185. *Occhiogrosso, Peter (1994). The Joy of Sects. Doubleday, p. 171.*
186. *Komjathy, Louis (2014). Daoism: A guide for the Perplexed. Bloomsbury, p. 94.*

Qi is thought to be in a continuous flux between its pure potential state (diluted Qi) and its condensed one (life). These states are embodiments of Yin and Yang, respectively.[187] The original text on Qi cultivation is the *Neiye* ("Inward Training").[188]

"Human life is the accumulation of qi; death is its dispersal."[189]

– Zhuangzi

a3. On Evil

The *Daodejing* teaches that evil can be divided into causal evils and consequential ones. The first are born from human will and cause suffering, without being suffering themselves. Natural suffering (e.g., sickness and death) is not much talked about.

Like in most Far Eastern religions, the general conclusion seems to be that all evil and suffering are results of unwisely acting in a way contrary to the Tao, the source of all life, with natural evils being an unavoidable part of the world of manifestation.

a4. On Determinism and Free Will

Life (Sheng) is seen as an expression of the Tao, which grants a life-destiny (Ming) to each person in the form of a particular physical existence and vital energy.[190]

Taoists consider that this life-destiny can be cultivated by movement based practices (Daoyin) and practices aiming at increased health and longevity (Yangsheng).[191] This contrasts with the methods believed to cultivate innate nature: stillness (Jinggong) or quiet meditation.

---

187. *Robinet, Isabelle (1997). Taoism: Growth of a Religion. Stanford: Stanford University Press, p.8.*

188. *Kohn, Livia (2008). Introducing Daoism. New York: Routledge. p. 53.*

189. *Ibid., p.51.*

190. *Komjathy, Louis (2014). Daoism: A guide for the Perplexed. Bloomsbury. p. 108.*

191. *Ibid., p. 109.*

Taoism affirms the existence of a personal free will that can be attuned to the Tao, thus being in harmony with the natural patterns and order inherent to the Universe. Once in harmony with the Tao, goals are believed to be achieved effortlessly through non-action (Wu-Wei).[192]

Wu-Wei

The concept of Wu-Wei is a key Taoist doctrine. It is commonly translated as non-action, effortless action, action without intent, and non-intervention.[193]

It can be understood as acting in a non-forceful way, behaving instead like water in a gentle and easy-flowing manner. When someone tries to impose his will in a manner contrary to the natural rhythms and cycles of the underlying order of the Universe, disharmony and bad outcomes are believed to follow.

"Act of things and you will ruin them. Grasp for things and you will lose them. Therefore the sage acts with inaction and has no ruin, lets go of grasping and has no loss." [194]

— Daodejing

a5. On Attaining Union with the Tao and the Afterlife

The main aim of Taoist practice is to achieve naturalness by identifying with the Tao and flowing with its natural rhythms.[195] To achieve this, the apprentice has to understand his true nature and live in accordance with

---

192. *Van Voorst, Robert E. (2005). Anthology of World Scriptures. Thomson Wadsworth, p. 170.*

193. *Komjathy, Louis (2014). Daoism: A guide for the Perplexed. Bloomsbury. p. 85.*

194. *Kohn, Livia (2008). Introducing Daoism. New York: Routledge, p. 21.*

195. *Girardot, Norman J. (1988). Myth and Meaning in Early Taoism: The Themes of Chaos (Hun-Tun). University of California Press, p. 56.*

it, with simplicity and free from selfishness and desire. Other aims include attaining longevity, sagehood (Zhenren), and some form of immortality (Xian).

The notions of what happens in the afterlife are diverse. The soul can become a part of the cosmos, impersonate some universal spiritual functions or laws, or become an immortal being (Xian) of pure light in another plane of existence while still being able to appear in the human world at will. These higher realms are sometimes called "the Heavens", where spiritualized versions of saved beings are thought to reside.

Taoists also spoke about an eschatological figure, Li Hong, who was prophesied to appear at the end of the world cycle to save the chosen people.

Symbols in Taoism: Bagua, Taijitu (highlighting the monist/dualist aspects of the Tao), Yin-Yang symbol (emphasizing complementary duality).

2.12. Taoist Mysticism: Meditation and Internal Alchemy

The paths to achieve union with the Tao include different practices, the most important being meditation, Astrology, Qigong, Feng Shui, and Internal Alchemy (Neidan).

Beings are conceived as being made of Three Treasures: essence (Jīng) or the foundation for one's vitality, subtle energy (Qi), and spirit (Shén) or the layer of consciousness capable of connecting with the spiritual realm.[196]

These, in turn, are associated with the Elixir Fields (Dantien, sea of Qi or energy centers) of the subtle body, similar to Hindu Chakras.

These components are worked through the practices mentioned above and present many parallels with traditional Chinese medicine. The aims are varied, and can range from achieving long life to loftier spiritual goals.

---

196. *Edited by Willard Gurdon Oxtoby (2nd ed.). World Religions: Eastern Traditions. Don Mills, Ontario: Oxford University Press. 2002, p. 397.*

Taoist meditation methods were sometimes strongly influenced by Buddhist ones.[197, 198]

They include:

1. *Quietistic forms of meditation* (e.g., "fasting the heartmind", the main method found in classical texts).[199] Also named "embracing the one" (Baoyi), "guarding the one" (Shouyi), "quiet sitting" (Jingzuo), and "sitting forgetfulness" (Zuowang).[200] This method tries to achieve the dissolution of the self and any subject-object distinction through inaction (Wu-Wei).

2. *One-pointed concentration and visualization techniques* (e.g., breathwork, deity meditation).

3. *Observation and openness to experience*, which stimulates a free-flowing awareness of our surroundings and of the underlying natural order.

a. Internal Alchemy (Neidan)

The practice of Alchemy is key in many Taoist schools, with the *Seal of the Unity of the Three* (Cāntóng Qì) being the first and one of the most important works available on the subject. It can include rituals, meditations, and physico-chemical work.

This aspect of Taoism is traditionally divided into internal (Neidan) and external (Waidan) practices. They aim at spiritual and physical transformation (longevity, immortality) and to attune the disciple with the universal forces.[201]

---

197. *Kohn, Livia (2008). Introducing Daoism. New York: Routledge, p. 131.*

198. *Komjathy, Louis (2014). Daoism: A guide for the Perplexed. Bloomsbury, p. 133.*

199. *Ibid., p. 133-134.*

200. *Ibid., p. 134.*

201. *Robinet, Isabelle (1997). Taoism: Growth of a Religion. Stanford: Stanford University Press, pp. 228 & 103.*

In Neidan, the process involves an internal transmutation from essence (Jing) to vital energy (Qi), from energy to spirit (Shen) and, lastly, from spirit to the Tao itself.[202] The end result is the creation of what was called the "immortal embryo" (Xiantai) or Yang spirit (Yangshen).[203] To achieve this the disciple works with his subtle body, using methods such as "activating the microcosmic orbit".[204]

Neidan´s psychosomatic or spiritualized conception of Alchemy views the human body as the cauldron in which the Three Treasures are cultivated and transmuted until final unity with the Tao is achieved.

2.13. Sikhism

Sikhism is the most recently founded major religion. It is based on the teachings of Guru Nanak and the nine gurus who succeeded him. The lineage of human gurus is considered to be perpetually closed.

Its main sacred text is the *Guru Granth Sahib*, which is considered the eleventh and last living guru. Sikhs also acknowledge the *Vedas*, *Puranas*, and the *Qur'ān*.[205]

a. Relation to Hinduism and Islam

Sikh scriptures reference the Vedas and use general Hindu terminology as well as the names of the gods present in the Hindu devotional (Bhakti) tradition. They do not worship them, however.[206]

---

202. *Kohn, Livia (2008). Introducing Daoism. New York: Routledge, p. 171.*

203. *Komjathy, Louis (2014). Daoism: A guide for the Perplexed. Bloomsbury, p. 136.*

204. *Gurdon Oxtoby, Willard (2002). World Religions: Eastern Traditions. Don Mills, Ontario: Oxford University Press, p. 397.*

205. *Cole, William Owen; Sambhi, Piara Singh (1995). The Sikhs: Their Religious Beliefs and Practices. Sussex Academic Press, p. 157.*

206. *Shackle, Christopher; Mandair, Arvind (2005). Teachings of the Sikh Gurus. Abingdon-on-Thames, England: Routledge, pp. xxxiv–xli.*

Sikhism stresses that key Hindu metaphysical concepts such as Ishvara, Bhagavān, Brahman, and Allah in Islam refer to the same God. However, it does not follow Hindu or Muslim practices in a syncretistic way, having developed its own, even if they are based on similar concepts.

Practicing Sikhs focus on repeating the Name of God (Waheguru, Japu), like in Mantra Yoga or Sufi "remembrance" methods.[207]

b. Main Metaphysical Beliefs of Sikhism

b1. Conception of God

Sikhism is a monotheistic and panentheistic religion. This can be seen in the belief that there exists One Universal God (Ik Onkar)[208] and that *"from the one light, the entire universe welled up"*.[209]

Some interpretations that understand Sikhism in non-dual terms in accordance with Advaita Vedānta and even Sufism have also been attempted (e.g., Bhai Vir Singh). However, the Sikh symbol of God has historically only represented the view that "there is but one God" (Absolute Monism/Monotheism), which these interpretations view as erroneous.[210]

"As water comes to blend with water, His light blends into the Light."

— Sri Guru Granth Sahib. SGGS:2 78

"The Ultimate Eternal reality resides in the Soul and the Soul is contained in Him."

— Jagraj Singh (2009). A Complete Guide to Sikhism. Unistar Books, p. 266

---

207. Cole, William Owen; Sambhi, Piara Singh (1995). The Sikhs: Their Religious Beliefs and Practices. Sussex Academic Press. pp. 155–156.

208. Singha, H. S. (2000). The Encyclopedia of Sikhism. Hemkunt, pp. 20–21, 103.

209. Sri Guru Granth Sahib Ji - Ang 13493.

210. Chahal, Devinder Singh (2020). Understanding Of The First Stanza Of Oankar Bani. Laval: Quebec, Institute for Understanding Sikhism.

The panentheistic aspect of the religion can be seen in the doctrine that God is fundamentally the same as the souls that inhabit the world. Particular souls (Atma) are a reflection of the Supreme Soul (ParamAtma), just as fire and its sparks.

The return of a soul to God implies its merging with the Absolute, as the fifth guru (Guru Arjun Dev Ji) stated: *"just as water merges back into the water."* [211]

b2. On Creation: Māyā or Worldly Illusion

Sikhs believe that what we perceive is ultimately an illusion, with God alone being real. The Hindu concept of Māyā is used, defined as a temporary illusion. However, the emphasis is put on the unreality of worldly values instead of on physical reality. The Five Thieves or passions are thought of as the main roadblock to leading a spiritual life, fueled by a loving attachment to unreality or Māyā.[212]

b3. On Evil

Evil is not viewed as any individual spirit or demonic entity. Instead, the present dark age (Kali Yuga) is seen as one where bad behavior and sin thrive, and its purpose is to test the character of man.

"Suffering is the remedy and comfort the disease."

— Guru Nanak. Guru Granth Sahib, Ang 469

The value of suffering is also understood in the fact that it usually develops compassion, empathy, and makes a person remember God, as good times tend to make people forget Him.

---

211. *"The Idea Of The Supreme Being (God) In Sikhism". Gateway to Sikhism. Retrieved December 2017.*

212. *Singh, D. (1992). The Sikh Identity. Fundamental Issues, p. 105.*

b4. On Determinism and Free Will

Sikhism accepts the reincarnation and Karma doctrines found in all Dharmic religions.[213] However, it also believes in the theistic concept of grace.[214] Therefore, the role of Karma is reduced compared to other Indian religions. The quality of our rebirths may depend on Karmic Law, but salvation has to be achieved through God´s grace.[215]

b5. On Salvation or Liberation

The teachings of Guru Nanak, instead of focusing on Heaven and Hell, emphasize spiritual union with the Timeless One. This is salvation or enlightenment/liberation (Jivanmukti).[216] Human life, like in other Indian traditions, is highly regarded by the potential spiritual progress it can grant the disciple.[217]

c. Sikh Mysticism: Remembrance of the Divine Name

The ultimate goal of life, as mentioned, is to go back to the Timeless One (Akal). To achieve this, a battle against our inherent egotism, our biggest obstacle, has to be waged. This can be accomplished by remembering the Name of the Lord (Naam Waheguru) through repetition and recitation[218], and also by living a life characterized by the selfless search for the truth.

---

213. *Chahal, Amarjit Singh (2011). Concept of Reincarnation in Guru Nanak's Philosophy. Understanding Sikhism: The Research Journal. 13 (1–2): 52–59.*

214. *Grewal, J. S. (1998). The Sikhs of the Punjab. Cambridge University Press, pp. 25–36.*

215. *Singh, H. S. (2000). The Encyclopedia of Sikhism. Hemkunt Press, p. 80.*

216. *Takhar, Opinderjit (2005). Sikh Identity: An Exploration of Groups Among Sikhs. Burlington, Vermont: Ashgate, p. 143.*

217. *Chahal, Amarjit Singh (2011). Concept of Reincarnation in Guru Nanak's Philosophy. Understanding Sikhism: The Research Journal. 13 (1–2): 52–59.*

218. *McLean, George (2008). Paths to the Divine: Ancient and Indian. Council for Research in Values & Philosophy, p. 599.*

The process of ascent towards and into God is thought as gradual and comprising five stages. The final one is called the Realm of Truth (Sach Khaṇḍ), and implies the final union of the spirit with God.[219]

Guru Nanak interpreted the real meaning of the term Guru (teacher) as the immanent voice of the spirit[220], with said Guru being indistinguishable from ultimate reality.[221] This is a re-statement of the Hindu formula "Ātman (each individual soul or spirit) equals Brahman (supreme reality)".

Symbols in Sikhism: Khanda, Kesh (uncut hair), Kara (steel bracelet), Kanga (wooden comb), Kaccha (cotton underwear), Kirpan (steel sword).

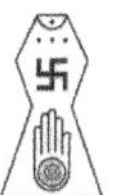

2.14. Jainism

Jainism or Jain Dharma is an old Indian religion that recognizes twenty-four supreme teachers of Dharma (Tirthankaras), the last being Mahāvīra (around 600 BCE). Its canonical scriptures are called *Agamas*, and they are thought to have been orally transmitted through the sermons of the Dharma teachers.

Jainism´s three main pillars are the doctrines of non-violence (Ahiṃsā), many-sidedness (Anekāntavāda), and non-attachment (Aparigraha).

The famous principle of non-violence or non-injury against any living being holds that all religious behavior is worthless if this principle is not followed. The principle of non-violence must be applied even if there is an apparent justification for aggression. It is granted the status of the highest religious duty.

---

219. *Parrinder, Geoffrey (1971). World Religions: From Ancient History to the Present. London: Hamlyn, pp. 254–256.*

220. *Ibid., pp. 253-254.*

221. *Singh, R.K. Janmeja (Meji) (2013). Gurbani's Guidance and the Sikh's Destination. The Sikh Review. 8. 61 (716): 27–35.*

The second principle, that of many-sidedness[222], teaches that reality is multifaceted and can only be experienced from one perspective at a time (e.g., the parable of the blind men and the elephant). Ultimate reality can be experienced but not logically or discursively explained.

The third main principle, non-attachment to worldly practices, underscores the ascetical character of both Jain laymen and monks.

a. Main Metaphysical Beliefs of Jainism

a1. Conception of God

Like many Indian traditions, Jainism rejects the existence of a creator deity. It follows a panentheistic worldview where every soul is said to contain the potentiality to deify itself. However, this intrinsic potentiality is limited by the soul's association with karmic matter.

All souls that are able to attain their intrinsic natural state of infinite bliss, knowledge, and power are considered to be as God.

a2. On Creation and Time

Jainism follows all other Dharmic religions in asserting a cyclical cosmology, where the Dharma teachers are involved in guiding the inhabitants of each cycle.

Every one of these cycles is divided into two half-cycles, one of ascent and moral progression and another of regression and moral decay. Like in Hinduism, Jains believe we are currently in a decadent age approaching the end of a cycle.

------

222. *Charitrapragya, Samani (2004). Ahimsā, Anekānta, and Jaininsm. Motilal Banarsidass, pp. 75-79.*

The concept of Saṃsāra is also a doctrinal teaching of Jainism, but the cycle of rebirths a soul undergoes is fixed to a concrete number (8,400,000).[223]

For Jains, the Universe was not created but has always existed. It has no creator, no governor, and no judge. Universal laws and perfected souls govern its internal workings, and it is composed of many eternal planes (Lokas) and levels of existence.

a3. On Evil

The concept of "evil" is conceived in a similar way to all other Dharmic religions but, unlike them, souls can have intrinsically good or evil tendencies.[224]

a4. On Determinism and Free Will

Jainism sees the body as a mere garment of the soul. The bound nature of the latter is considered a self-evident truth (Axiom).

Karma, contrary to Hinduism or Buddhism, is viewed as a subtle material substance that binds itself to the soul and obscures it. Every soul is made of consciousness, bliss, and vibrational energy. This vibration draws karmic particles according to its nature, thus adding merit or demerit to the soul and creating bondages and conditioned existences.

Souls able to reach heavenly states by their own efforts become a ruling influence on the Universe for a period of time, until their Karma runs its course and they reincarnate again in search of final liberation and enlightenment.

---

223. *Jaini, Padmanabh (1980). Karma and Rebirth in Classical Indian Traditions. University of California Press, pp. 223-225.*

224. *Dundas, Paul (1992). The Jains. London and New York: Routledge, pp. 104-105.*

Jain doctrine states that, in extreme cases, some souls may become incapable of ever attaining liberation.[225, 226]

a5. On Liberation

The final aim of a Jain is liberation from the cycle of rebirths, attained through the destruction of the karmic bonds. To achieve it, soul purification has to take place as a preliminary step. This can be accomplished through the path of Three Jewels or Path of Liberation (Moksha mārga).[227]

The three mains stages of the path are: correct view (faith), correct knowledge, and correct conduct (following the five vows).[228] A fourth stage is mentioned in some texts, emphasizing the ascetical character of this worldview: correct asceticism.[229]

The five vows of monastics include: non-violence, truth, not stealing, chastity, and non-possessiveness. Outer and inner austerities are practiced, including fasting and meditation. Meditation, however, is understood as a means of eliminating karmic attachments instead of as a way to develop insight leading to awakening.[230]

Symbols in Jainism: Jain emblem, Swastika.

---

225. *Jaini, Padmanabh (1980). Karma and Rebirth in Classical Indian Traditions. University of California Press, p. 225.*

226. *Fohr, Sherry (2015). Jainism: A Guide for the Perplexed. Bloomsbury Academic, pp. 9-10, 37.*

227. *Jain, Vijay K. (2011). Acharya Umasvami's Tattvarthsūtra. Vikalp Printers, p. 6.*

228. *Jaini, Padmanabh S. (1979). The Jain Path of Purification. Motilal Banarsidass, pp. 148, 200.*

229. *Cort, John E. (2001a). Jains in the World : Religious Values and Ideology in India. Oxford University Press, pp. 6-7.*

230. *Dundas, Paul (1992). The Jains. London and New York: Routledge, pp. 166-169.*

2.15. Zoroastrianism

Zoroastrianism or Mazdeism[231] is an Iranian religion based on the life and teachings of the prophet Zoroaster.[232] The *Avesta* is the main sacred text of this tradition, the *Gathas* being the portions thought to have been composed by Zoroaster himself. Liturgical texts are called the *Yasna*.

a. Main Metaphysical Beliefs of Zoroastrianism

a1. Conception of God and the Source of Evil

Zoroastrianism speaks of a transcendental God known as Ahura Mazda (Lord of Wisdom), the ultimate uncreated and benevolent being.[233] A particular Zoroastrian doctrine regarding the divinity is that, although All-Knowing, He is not All-Powerful. An opposite and antagonistic deity, Angra Mainyu (later Ahriman) is derived from Ahura Mazda and is the source of all evil.

Angra Manyu represents a destructive spirit or mentality. Its opponent and polar opposite (Spenta Mainyu), who is on the side of the God of Good, is in turn the representation of the creative spirit or mentality.[234]

It has long been debated if the Zoroastrian religion is better described as a representative of Monism or Dualism, with some scholars even proposing a pantheistic classification, if an immanent self-creating conscious Universe interpretation is extracted from the texts.

Looking at the problem from different angles it could be said that, from the point of view of the highest reality, Zoroastrianism is monistic

---

231. *"Mazdaism". Oxford Reference.*

232. *"Zoroaster I. The Name". Encyclopaedia Iranica.*

233. *"Ahura Mazdā". Encyclopaedia Iranica.*

234. *"Ahriman". Encyclopaedia Iranica.*

(Ahura Mazda being the transcendental origin of all that exists). From the point of view of its cosmology, in turn, its cosmogonic processes are dualistic, rising from the creative tension between the polarity of good (Ahura mazda/Spenta Mainyu) and evil (Angra Mainyu).

The immanent presence of Ahura Mazda in mankind, in addition, makes a panentheistic interpretation possible from the point of view of created beings.

a2. On Creation and Time

Asha is the main spiritual force representing cosmic order. It is derived from Ahura Mazda, and it is the antithesis of Chaos, manifested as falsehood and disorder (Druj).[235]

The universal conflict between these opposites generates everything that exists, be it physical, mental or spiritual. Humanity is viewed as an active part of the conflict, being called to stand with the side of Good.[236]

The process of creation involves emanations known as the Bounteous/ Holy Immortals (Amesha Spenta), which are the way in which Ahura Mazda interacts with creation.[237] They are are personifications and guardians of different aspects of creation and of God´s attributes.

Through the Amesha Spenta, other divinities called Yazatas (meaning "Worthy of Worship" and later "Divine Sparks"), also help Ahura Mazda on His fight against evil. They generally represent a moral or physical aspect of the Universe.

Inverting the Hindu mythos, the Yazatas are to be worshipped while the Devas (invariably good gods in all Hindu traditions) are to be rejected.

---

235. *"Druj". Encyclopaedia Iranica.*

236. *"Zoroastrianism: Holy text, beliefs and practices". Encyclopedia Iranica.*

237. *"Aməša Spənta". Encyclopaedia Iranica.*

Regarding time, Zoroastrianism speaks of two different types: time without bounds and time-within-bounds (linear time), designed to contain evil. The objective of physical creation is to help in imprisoning and defeating evil during linear time.

The metaphysical battle between good and evil is bound to last nine thousand years, divided into three periods: Creation, Mixture, and Separation.

a3. On Determinism and Free Will

Zoroaster affirmed an uncompromising doctrine of free will. Zurvanism, a later branch of Zoroastrianism, did not.

Zurvanism was defined as a fatalistic and pessimistic offshoot of Mazdaism that contrasted with the positive message of its parent religion.

a4. On Salvation and End Times

When speaking of the religious duty of Zoroastrians, following the Threefold Path of Asha[238] (good thoughts, good words, and good deeds) is considered of the utmost importance. Also emphasized is the spreading of happiness (e.g., charity) and the protection of the natural world.

Zoroastrian eschatology is characterized by the promise of the ultimate overcoming of evil by good, the existence of a judgment after death, and the existence of Heaven and Hell, as well as beings analogous to angels and demons.

It is believed that at the time when Ahura Mazda vanquishes Angra Mainyu the Universe will undergo a cosmic renovation (Frashokereti[239]) that will put an end to limited time. During this renovation, all of creation,

---

238. *"Humata Hūxta Huvaršta". Encyclopaedia Iranica.*

239. *"Frašō.kərəti". Encyclopaedia Iranica.*

including those dead bound in darkness, will be immortalized and reunited with the Good God in His "best dominion" (Kshatra Vairya). This implies the end of Hell and universal salvation (Apokatastasis).

A widespread belief was that of a messianic savior-figure known as the "one who brings benefit" (Saoshyant), who would bring about this cosmic renovation.

Symbols in Zoroastrianism: Faravahar, Atar (Holy Fire).

ZURVANISM

Zurvanite Zoroastrianism, a later branch of Zoroastrianism, spoke of a neutral and transcendental God called Zurvan ("the One", "Alone") as the First Principle.

From Zurvan were believed to derive equal-but-opposite twins, Ahura Mazda (good) and Angra Mainyu (evil).

Zurvan was conceived as the God of Infinite Time and Space, and was portrayed as a transcendental and neutral god, without passion, for whom there was no distinction between good and evil.

The Zurvanite creation myth (only preserved in non-Zoroastrian sources) explains that, in the beginning, Zurvan existed alone. Desiring offspring that would create "Heaven and Hell and everything in between", the androgyne Zurvan conceived Ohrmuzd/Ahriman, born from His doubt about the efficacy of sacrifice.[240]

This is a clear example of the doctrine of the Unity of Opposites, with both "horizontal" (male/female, androgyny) and "vertical" (good/evil) levels being reunited and transcended in an ultimate unity: Zurvan, the One. It is also another version of the myth of the original catastrophe taking place in the Godhead itself.

---

240. *Zaehner, R.C. (1955). Zurvan, a Zoroastrian Dilemma. Oxford, UK: Clarendon Press, pp. 419–428.*

2.16. Mandaeism

Mandaeism, Nasoraeanism or Sabianism[241], has been classified as an ethnic monistic religion with Gnostic themes.[242]

a. Main Metaphysical Beliefs of Mandaeism

a1. Conception of God

Mandeism believes in one God (Hayyi Rabbi, the Great Life or the Great Living), symbolized by water. This God personifies the creative force of the Universe, which sustains the world.[243] Given that God is understood as a force, describing this faith as monistic seems more accurate than using the term monotheistic.

The main Mandaean scripture is the *Ginza Rabba*, which includes historical teachings, theology, and prayers.[244]

a2. On Creation and Time

All planes of creation are considered as the self-expression in time and space of formless Being, with intermediate entities in charge of organizing the cosmos. Archetypal Man is the direct causal creator of our world, which was patterned according to his own shape.

---

241. *The term 'Nasoraean' (lit. 'from Nazareth') is used for the initiated among the Mandaeans. The term 'Sabianism' is derived from the mysterious Sabians mentioned in the Qur'ān, a name historically claimed by several religious groups.*

242. *Buckley, Jorunn J. (2002). The Mandaeans: Ancient Texts and Modern People. New York: Oxford University Press.*

243. *Mandaean Awareness and Guidance Board (May 2014). Mandaean Beliefs & Mandaean Practices. Mandaean Associations Union.*

244. *Lidzbarski, Mark (1925). Ginzā, der Schatz oder das Grosse buch der Mandäer. Göttingen Vandenhoek & Ruprecht.*

a3. On Evil

Mandaeism proposes a dualistic interplay of forces as the source of creation (e.g., Syzygies: father/mother, light/darkness). They are personifications of concepts and ideas.

Therefore, evil (World of Darkness) is the necessary mirror image of good (World of Light or Lightworld), as counterparts (Dmuta) exist in the world of ideas (Mshunia Kushta).[245] Persons, spirits, and places are believed to have their own mirrored selves, too.

a4. On Determinism and Free Will

As is common in Gnostic faiths, the constellations (planets and stars) are conceived as able to influence the fate of living beings. The world is seen as a prison for the soul, and they are manifestations of the jailers.

Like in Gnosticism, upon death each soul has to confront different places of detention that have to be overcome in order to reach the World of Light. Rituals are used to facilitate safe passage.

a5. On Liberation

Mandeism believes in one or multiple savior spirits which assist the soul on its journey until it reaches the Lightworld.

Secret esoteric "Mysteries" or ceremonial initiations are used to purify the soul, guide its ascent away from this world of matter or to attain rebirth into a spiritual body.

Symbols in Mandaeism: Living Water (Yardena) as a symbol of the deity; Drabsha banner as a symbol of the religion; Skandola ("dwelling of evil") talismanic seals to protect against evil.

------

245. *Buckley, Jorunn Jacobsen (2002). The Mandaeans: ancient texts and modern people. New York: Oxford University Press.*

2.17. Shintō and Animism

Shintō, originated in Japan, is a nature religion with no central authority and much variability in its practices and beliefs.

a. Main Metaphysical Beliefs of Shintō

a1. Conception of God

Shintō is a polytheistic and animistic religion. Its gods, called Kami, inhabit all things, including locations. They are also identified as personifications of natural forces.

Animism is the doctrine that objects, places, living beings, and sometimes even abstract notions such as words, all possess a differentiated spiritual essence and are alive.[246]

Shintō underwent an extensive process of syncretization with Buddhism (Shinbutsu-Shūgō). The Kami were then incorporated into Buddhist cosmology, seen as either lost beings in need of liberation or later thought to be incarnations (Avatars) of the Buddhas.

a2. On Creation

The world is conceived as being born from the divine couple Izanagi no Mikoto and Izanami no Mikoto. They are believed to have given birth to the Japanese islands and to other natural deities. Both the notions of an afterlife and the cycle or rebirths are mentioned in Shintoist creation myths.

The Birth of the Kamis

The world is seen as originated from the split between Heaven and Earth (creation as Complementary Dualism), where three Kami deities came to be on the resultant Heavenly realm. Two later partnerless and formless deities were also born.

---

246. *Hornborg, Alf (2006). Animism, fetishism, and objectivism as strategies for knowing (or not knowing) the world. Ethnos: Journal of Anthropology. 71 (1): 21–32.*

After them, deities were born in pairs (like in theologies that emphasize the dialectical Union of Opposites or Gnostic Syzygies). The seventh and final generation were Izanagi and Izanami themselves.

a3. On Evil

Shintō believes mankind to be intrinsically good, with evil caused directly by evil spirits. They are kept away through rituals of purification, prayers, and offerings to the Kami.

a4. On Liberation

Instead of teaching mankind to strive to reach higher spiritual heights not found in this world, Shintō teaches that the solution to human suffering is the contrary, to bring the Kami into this world to make it sacred.

Ancient traditions, however, speak of the existence of another realm or plane of existence beyond this one, the High Plain of Heaven. It is conceived as a happy spiritual world connected to Earth.

A Netherworld is also mentioned, an unhappy place ruled by death called the Land of Darkness. This is the place where problematic spirits are sent away through prayer and ritual. Ancestor worship also plays a defensive role against them.

For mankind, ending in one place or another was believed to depend on the ethical character and the purity of the life led by each person.

Symbols in Shintō: Torii Gates, as entrance to Shintō shrines; sacred rope (Shimenawa), as delimiters of sacred space; white zig-zag paper (Shide), related to prayer; swirling commas (Tomoe), representing the interaction between the three realms of Heaven, Earth, and the Underworld.

Recommended Reading

1. **Mysticism: Sacred and Profane.** *R.C. Zaehner.*
2. **At Sundry Times. An Essay in the Comparison of Religions.** *R.C. Zaehner.*
3. **Man and His Becoming according to the Vedanta.** *René Guénon.*
4. **Patterns in Comparative Religion.** *Mircea Eliade.*
5. **Hindu and Muslim Mysticism.** *R.C. Zaehner.*

The Fallen and Risen One:

Can We Achieve Transcendence

by Our Own Means Alone?

Esoteric Worldviews

Main Characteristics, Metaphysical Beliefs and their Implications

3. The Origins and the Rise of Esoteric Worldviews

APART FROM THE PREVIOUS EXOTERIC RELIGIOUS wordviews and their corresponding mystical traditions, which as we have seen can sometimes deviate quite drastically from their parent religions, there are other increasingly prevalent conceptions of the world that have been grouped under the umbrella term of Western Esotericism.

The origin of these loosely related schools of thought has been interpreted in three different ways:

1. As exponents of a, now long lost, timeless hidden inner tradition.

2. As a group of movements that try to spiritualize and re-enchant the world in a time of disenchantment.

3. As encompassing all rejected knowledge that could not find a place either in mainstream science or as a part of exoteric religions.

Be that as it may the fact is that, especially in the last centuries, we have witnessed the birth and growth of this new set of increasingly popular worldviews that make metaphysical claims about the world and ultimate reality.

During the Renaissance, Hermetic and Kabbalistic ideas were widely disseminated and fused with other worldviews, birthing new movements. In turn, during the seventeenth and eighteenth centuries, many semi-secret initiatory societies that transmitted these teachings were created, the most famous being the Rosicrucians and the Freemasons. The nineteenth century brought the emergence of Occultism. Finally, the twentieth century saw the resurrection of different forms of Neo-Paganism (sometimes having little in common with their parent traditions).

We will now briefly explore these schools of thought in order to know what their metaphysical claims are and which symbolism do they use.

Figure 1. The Magician. The archetype of the esoteric initiate who, through knowledge and practice, aims at Self-Transcendence (Apotheosis) by understanding and manipulating the forces of the Universe.

Picture: The Magician or Magus (I), the first trump or Major Arcana card in the Rider–Waite Tarot deck. Note the "as above, so below" hand gesture.

The wand, pentacle, sword, and cup represent the four Minor Arcana, the classical elements which the adept tries to transcend by becoming a conduit between the spiritual and the physical realms.

█ 3.1. Hermeticism

Hermeticism or Hermetism can be defined as a philosophy, maybe even a religion, that is based on the teachings attributed to Hermes Trismegistus. Hermes is a mythical figure related to the Egyptian god of wisdom and knowledge (Thoth) and the Greek god Hermes, the herald of the gods.

Once believed to be older, Hermeticism was contemporary with early Christianity, Gnosticism, the Chaldean Oracles, late Orphism and Pythagoreanism, and Neo-Platonism.[1]

The texts that are thought to contain Hermes Trismegistus´ teachings are called the *Hermetica*[2], with the most famous ones being the *Corpus Hermeticum*, the *Asclepius*, and the *Emerald Tablet* (a main Alchemical foundational text).

The translation, during the Renaissance, of the *Corpus Hermeticum* had an enormous influence in all Western esoteric traditions, being still one of the main undercurrents of occult and esoteric systems in contemporary times.

Once rejected by the Christian church, Hermeticism survived through the formation of many secret societies that adhered to its teachings (e.g., Rosicrucianism, Freemasonry, Golden Dawn).

---

1. Van den Broek; Hanegraaff (1997). Gnosis & Hermeticism from Antiquity to Modern Time. SUNY series in Western Esoteric Traditions, p. vii.

2. The oldest texts attributed to Hermes are astrological texts (belonging to the 'technical' Hermetica) which may have been written during the second or third century BCE; see Copenhaver 1992, p. xxxiii; Bull 2018, pp. 2–3. Garth Fowden is more cautious, noting that our earliest testimonies date to the first century BCE (see Fowden 1986, p. 3, note 11). On the other end, the Kitāb fi zajr al-nafs ("The Book of the Rebuke of the Soul") is commonly thought to date from the twelfth century; see Van Bladel 2009, p. 226.

a. Main Metaphysical Beliefs of Hermeticism

a1. Conception of God

Hermeticists call their god by different names, with some of them being common monotheistic concepts (e.g., God, Lord, Father, Creator) and others implying a panentheistic view (e.g., Mind [Nous], the All, the One).[3] Hermeticism believes in a God that is both all that exists and its creator. Everything is pre-existent in the All[4], which is the very nature of the Universe itself. It is both the substance (immanence) and the ordering Principle (transcendence) of the cosmos.[5]

a2. On Creation and Time

The Universe is understood as being the All creating itself.[6]

A creation myth is narrated in the first book of the *Corpus Hermeticum*. In it, God willed matter into existence, separating the four classical elements (earth, air, fire, and water) from it. These elements, in turn, were organized into seven heavens or spheres (the known planets at the time: Mercury, Venus, Mars, Jupiter, Saturn, the Sun, and the Moon).

The Word, Logos or Nous, then came into being from the passive elements and animated the spheres, bringing animal life into the world. Later, man was created in the image of God as an androgynous being.

---

3. *Festugière, André-Jean (1944–1954). La Révélation d'Hermès Trismégiste. Vol. I–IV. Paris: Gabalda, Vol. II, pp. 68–71.*

4. *Copenhaver, Brian P. (1992). Hermetica: The Greek Corpus Hermeticum and the Latin Asclepius in a New English Translation. Cambridge: Cambridge University Press, p. 216.*

5. *Festugière, André-Jean (1944–1954). La Révélation d'Hermès Trismégiste. Vol. I–IV. Paris: Gabalda. Vol. II, p. 68.*

6. *Bull, Christian H. (2018). The Tradition of Hermes Trismegistus: The Egyptian Priestly Figure as a Teacher of Hellenized Wisdom. Leiden: Brill, p. 303.*

In Hermeticism, creation is viewed as a microcosmic reflection of the macrocosmic reality. This is codified in the modern popular esoteric catchphrase *"as above, so below"*, which traces its origins to the *Emerald Tablet*.[7]

"That which is above is like to that which is below, and that which is below is like to that which is above."

— Hermes Trismegistus. Emerald Tablet, verse 2

a3. On Evil

The *Corpus Hermeticum*, book nine, explains that Nous (Reason, Knowledge) is the source of both good and evil. Personal evil, in turn, depends upon whether one´s perceptions come from God or from evil spirits.[8] Only God/Nous is thought to be free of all evil, with humankind being tempted by its physical nature and its ignorance of the highest good.

The *Asclepius*, furthermore, says that evil is caused by desire, itself born from ignorance. Through the intelligence provided by God, man can overcome it.[9]

The Myth of the Fall of Man

A myth of mankind´s Fall is also present in Hermeticism. Its main version narrates how man received God´s authority over all creation. Later, man rose above the spheres to have a better view of creation, and showed the "form" of the All to Nature.

---

7. *Ibn Hayyân, Jâbir (1942–1943). Contribution à l'histoire des idées scientifiques dans l'Islam. I. Le corpus des écrits jâbiriens. II. Jâbir et la science grecque. Cairo: Institut français d'archéologie orientale, vol. II, pp. 274–275; Weisser, Ursula (1980). Das Buch über das Geheimnis der Schöpfung von Pseudo-Apollonios von Tyana. Berlin: De Gruyter, p. 54.*

8. *Salaman, Clement (2004). The Way of Hermes. Inner Traditions Bear and Company, p. 42.*

9. *Salaman, Clement (2001). Asclepius : The Perfect Discourse of Hermes Trismegistus. Bloomsbury, p. 31.*

Upon seeing it, Nature fell in love with the Absolute. Man, in turn, seeing his own reflection in Nature´s waters, fell in love with it (similar to the myth of Narcissus). This resulted in man becoming one with Nature and being alienated from his spiritual core. Man lost the Word and became a dual being composed of an immortal soul in bondage to a mortal body.

a4. On Determinism and Free Will

After the Fall, the myths narrate how man lost his freedom and became a subject to destiny and successive rebirths.[10] Many believe the doctrine of rebirth to be a purely Indian or far Eastern doctrine. However, it is also mentioned in Hermetic literature:

"O son, how many bodies have we to pass through, how many bands of demons, through how many series of repetitions and cycles of the stars, before we hasten to the One alone?" [11]

— Hermes Trismegistus

a5. The Hermetic Path Towards Liberation

The three main disciplines derived from Hermetic texts as paths towards God, known as "the three parts of the wisdom of the whole Universe", are Alchemy (often referred to as "the Hermetic art"[12]), Astrology, and Theurgy or divine magic.

b. Alchemy

Alchemy, correctly understood, is a mystical endeavour that uses cryptic language, figures, and the physical transformations of matter to

------

10. *Bull, Christian H. (2015). Ancient Hermetism and Esotericism. Aries. 15 (1): 109–135.*

11. *Salaman, Clement (2004). The Way of Hermes. Inner Traditions, p. 33.*

12. *Ebeling, Florian (2007). The Secret History of Hermes Trismegistus: Hermeticism from Ancient to Modern Times. Ithaca: Cornell University Press, pp. 103–108.*

symbolize the process that leads to spiritual maturation and perfection. This process is called the Great Work and is believed to culminate in Self-Transcendence.

The achievement of this final state is symbolized by the creation of the Philosopher's Stone or the Elixir of Life, which grants immortality understood in a predominantly spiritual and transcendental way. The stages of the path involve a process of dissolution, purification, and coagulation or re-vivification, which were symbolized by different colors (black, white, and red, respectively).

Alchemy includes doctrines and concepts from older traditions, such as Neo-Platonism. An example is the pervading system of correspondences found between everything in creation, most notably between the seven classical planets and their seven corresponding metals. This concept was based on the notion of the existence of a World Soul (Anima Mundi), or a primordial intrinsic link between all created things.

Figure 2. The three main phases of the Alchemical work. Putrefaction (Nigredo, blackness), Purification (Albedo, whiteness), and the final stage of Integration and Solidification of the results attained after awakening (Rubedo, redness). Physical substances were used as symbols for psycho-spiritual states, with the final aim of Alchemy being Self-Transcendence (Apotheosis). Sometimes another stage between Albedo and Rubedo is mentioned: Citrinitas (Illumination or Awakening, yellowness). Picture: Pretiosissimum Donum Dei, Georges Aurach (1475).

Primordial matter (Prima Materia), in turn, was the starting material needed to develop the Great Work. It was believed that it could be found everywhere, as it was understood as the formless primordial substance that originated matter. Other similar terms to refer to it were: Chaos, Quintessence, Ether or the Fifth Element.

The Psychological Interpretation of C.G. Jung

The Analytical Psychology school of C.G. Jung single-handedly popularized Alchemy in modern times, which was until then mostly known only by scholars and members of esoteric schools. Nowadays, Alchemical concepts and symbolism can be found in most mainstream media.

Jung saw Alchemy as the symbolic and archetypal representation of what he defined as the process of individuation. Through it, opposite tendencies in the human psyche were uncovered and reintegrated into the total personality of the practitioner, thus achieving the maximum psychological and spiritual development.

This final state was represented in Alchemy, Jung believed, by the androgynous Divine Marriage (Hieros Gamos). The One reintegrating the Many.

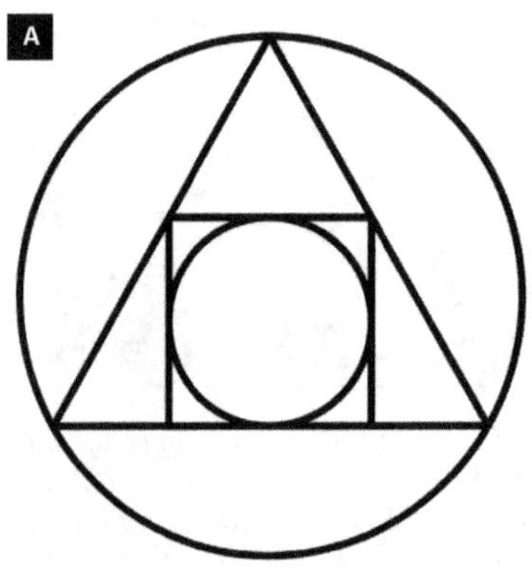

Figure 3. **A:** *The Squared Circle. An Alchemical symbol representing the end result of the Great Work (Magnum Opus). It also signifies the union in harmony of the four classical elements (Prima Materia) and the attainment of the seemingly impossible.* **B:** *The Rebis. Alchemical symbol of the Union of Opposites (e.g., Sun and Moon, male and female) and another symbol representing the final aim of the Alchemists: the transcendence of all duality in a unified whole. Picture: Rosarium Philosophorum, Glasgow University Library.*

c. Astrology

The cyclical movements of the planets were thought to convey symbolic meaning, since they were interpreted as thoughts in the mind of the Absolute or the All. They influenced creation but were not understood as fatalistic decrees that completely dictated human destiny. The knowledge Astrology provided was believed to be useful in managing those influences.

d. Theurgy

Lastly, Theurgy (divine magic or the science of divine works) relied in white magic to invoke beneficent spirits.[13] The main goal of the initiate was to unite oneself with spiritual counterparts of higher planes of existence. This path was believed to finalize with the achievement of divine consciousness itself.[14]

Symbols in Hermeticism: Caduceus; Monad; Ouroboros; Alchemical symbols representing the different substances, elements, metals, planets, and processes.

e. An Hermetic Case Study: G.W.F. Hegel

The influential philosopher Georg Wilhelm Friedrich Hegel was one of the main exponents of German Idealism. He has been associated with Hermeticism (and, consequently, also with Freemasonry).[15]

For Hegel, God is not complete apart from His creation. In his worldview, Absolute Spirit needs the world to actualize Himself. He accomplishes that purpose through nature, the dialectical developments

---

13. *Garstin, E.J. Langford (2004). Theurgy, or the Hermetic Practice: A Treatise on Spiritual Alchemy. Nicolas-Hays, Inc., p. v.*

14. *Ibid., p. 6.*

15. Alexander Magee, Glenn (2008). Hegel and the Hermetic Tradition. Cornell University Press.

in history and, especially, through mankind. All of them are viewed as "moments" in the internal life of God, and only in a spiritually conscious human being does the Absolute Spirit fully recognize Himself.

Hegel's metaphysical roots, often ignored by academia, are found in Hermeticism, Aristotelianism, and the ancient Mystery Religions. Although he used Christian terms and has sometimes been labelled as a Christian philosopher because of that, his worldview is opposed to Christian theology and can be ultimately defined as panentheistic.

3.2. Perennial Philosophy or Traditionalism 

Hermeticism was often regarded as an exponent of an older and now lost primordial tradition. During the Renaissance, a term was coined to refer to this concept: "Ancient Theology" (Prisca Theologia).

This doctrine affirms that metaphysical and religious truth, although single by definition, can be found in different ancient schools of thought that are distant echoes of the original tradition. In each of these schools, then, a portion of the truth survives, with none of them able to claim full possession of it. This reduces the importance of the particularities of each religion to just cultural or historical additions with no real deeper meaning.

This way of thinking led some thinkers, such as Marsilio Ficino, to try to integrate Hermeticism (believed to be Egyptian wisdom) with Greek and Christian traditions.[16]

Others, like Giovanni Pico della Mirandola, sought to reconstruct the original tradition by filtering the truth contained in the oldest texts available to him. They included Hermetic, Orphic, oracular (Chaldean Oracles), Zoroastrian, Pythagorean, and Kabbalistic texts.

---

16. *Slavenburg; Glaudemans (1994). Nag Hammadi Geschriften I. Ankh-Hermes,* *p. 395.*

This concept was greatly popularized in the nineteenth and twentieth centuries by other groups promoting religious universalism or the notion that the esoteric core of all religions leads to the same truth.

During the nineteenth century this task fell on Transcendentalists, Unitarians, and the Theosophical Society (which now has Consultative Status with the Economic and Social Council of the United Nations [ECOSOC] through the works of Alice Bailey and the Lucis Trust).

During the twentieth century, it was the Traditionalist School which was very influential in disseminating this notion and achieving mainstream appeal. This school, heavily inspired by Advaita Vedānta and Sufism, is still relevant in our times.

René Guénon, Ananda Coomaraswamy, Frithjof Schuon, and Julius Evola were among its first and most significant exponents. *The Perennial Philosophy*, Aldous Huxley´s Neo-Vedānta inspired book, also played a significant role.

a. Main Metaphysical Beliefs of Perennialism

Traditionalist doctrines generally follow non-dual or panentheistic Vedantic conceptions of God, as well as an emanationist outlook on cosmology and a cyclical notion of time. Karmic causality and reincarnation, the concept of creation as being illusorily separated from ultimate reality, and the teachings on how to achieve liberation are also usually fully endorsed.

b. A Perennialist Case Study: Freemasonry

Freemasonry or Masonry is a body of highly symbolic and ritualistic fraternal organisations with a hierarchical degree-based structure. It is difficult to ascertain what their core beliefs are, as what they publicly state is not always in accordance with what they teach in higher degree initiations.

Masonic symbolism is notorious for being interpreted in different ways depending on the degree of the initiate (polysemy). They use symbolism to reveal but also to veil their teachings.

"Masonry, like all the Religions, all the Mysteries, Hermeticism and Alchemy, conceals its secrets from all except the Adepts and Sages, or the Elect, and uses false explanations and misinterpretations of its symbols to mislead those who deserve only to be misled; to conceal the Truth, which it calls Light from them and to draw them away from it."

"[...] If you would understand the true secrets of Alchemy, you must study the works of the Masters with patience and assiduity. Every word is often an enigma; and to him who reads in haste, the whole will seem absurd. Even when they seem to teach that the Great Work is the purification of the Soul, and so deal only with morals, they most conceal their meaning, and deceive all but the Initiates." [17]

— Albert Pike. Morals and Dogma

Allegedly, the only prerequisite for joining a lodge is to hold the belief in a Supreme Being, with no discrimination based on other more specific metaphysical beliefs. However, the underlying doctrinal system favors certain esoteric worldviews above others.

The masonic authority Manly Palmer Hall, in his influential book *"The Secret Teachings of All Ages"*, endorses a perennialist worldview with strong emphasis on Hermetic and Kabbalistic teachings, evident in the full title of his book:

"An Encyclopedic Outline Of Masonic, Hermetic, Qabbalistic And Rosicrucian Symbolical Philosophy, being An Interpretation Of The Secret Teachings Concealed Within The Rituals, Allegories, And Mysteries Of All Ages".

---

17. *Pike, Albert (1871). Morals and Dogma of the Ancient and Accepted Scottish Rite of Freemasonry. Forgotten Books, pp. 104-5.*

The worldviews endorsed by this voluminous work include the Ancient Mystery Religions, Gnosticism (e.g., Simon Magus, Basilides), Hermeticism (including Alchemy and Astrology), Platonism, Pythagoreanism, Kabbalah, and Rosicrucianism (itself heavily based on Hermetico-Alchemical concepts).

In addition, after validating Celsus´ (eclectic Greek philosopher) critique of early Christianity in favor of classical Greek doctrines (e.g., Platonism, Pythagoreanism), the author puts forth a speculative vision of "Mystical Christianity" that reinterprets it completely to try to make it conform to the Perennial Philosophy template.

He was not alone, however, in thinking that external (exoteric) religions were directed at the masses. Albert Pike, thirty-third degree mason (the highest known degree) and one of the most prominent modern masonic figures, also adhered to this same decidedly Gnostic and elitist concept of truth, only attainable by a minority of gifted and dedicated persons.

"The Teachers, even of Christianity, are in general, the most ignorant of the true meaning of that which they teach. There is no book of which so little is known as the Bible. To most who read it, it is as incomprehensible as the Sohar." [18]

— Albert Pike. Morals and Dogma

Amidst the various myths, allegories, and symbolic interpretations we can say that, for Freemasonry, the truth is believed to reside in the minimum common denominator found in all traditional esoteric schools. Anything that deviates from that pattern, such as the Christian view of the Incarnation of the Logos, is usually reinterpreted or discarded.

---

18. *Ibid.*, p. 105.

3.3. Occultism

Occultism began as a fuzzy term that could be broadly defined as a worldview that followed certain esoteric doctrines and practices, but without being part of any organized religion or its corresponding mystical branch. The modern usage of this term comes from nineteenth century France and, nowadays, it is used to refer mostly to Spiritualism, Theosophy, Anthroposophy, Thelema, Wicca, New Age, and "secret" initiatory societies such as the Golden Dawn. In the following sections we will present a brief overview of the main metaphysical doctrines followed by these schools. Due to their modern relevance, we will discuss Wicca, Thelema, and New Age in their own sections.

3.3.1 Spiritualism

The Spiritualist movement was born in the nineteenth century, Emanuel Swedenborg´s visions being one of its main influences. Allan Kardec, in turn, developed his own branch called Spiritism.

The main beliefs of these movements were two: the persistence of discarnate souls after death, and the possibility of communicating with them. Some gifted persons (Mediums) were thought of being especially able to channel (during Séances) some spirits in order to obtain information from them regarding moral or theological issues. Some of the spirits, furthermore, were considered able to provide guidance. Anyone was thought to be capable of channelling them through enough study and practice.

a1. Conception of God and the Afterlife

Spiritualists accept the existence of God[19], but their definitions can be widely different. God has been defined as the God Force, the Divine Spirit or the Great Spirit.

---

19. *Driscoll, J. T. (1912). "Theosophy". In Herbermann, C. G. (ed.). The Catholic Encyclopedia. Vol. 14. New York: Robert Appleton Company. pp. 626–628.*

The afterlife in the Spirit World is conceived as a place of continual spiritual evolution. Reaching the Spirit World is viewed as unavoidable, so no additional path or method was proposed to attain salvation or liberation.

3.3.2 Theosophy

Theosophy, also a nineteenth century creation, is an esoteric philosophical school based mostly on the works of the occultist Helena Blavatsky. Her teachings were strongly influenced by older traditions such as Neo-Platonism and, especially, Hinduism and Buddhism.

It helped to popularize Indian doctrines in the West and it was one of the key early influences of the New Age movement. Nevertheless, not all proponents of Hinduism as a reservoir of metaphysical truths were convinced of its legitimacy (René Guénon, for example, harshly criticized Theosophy as illegitimate).

Theosophy affirms the existence of a secret brotherhood of spiritual Masters guiding mankind´s spiritual evolution. Tibet is seen as a central location for them in the physical plane.

Blavatsky saw her mission as the propagation of their teachings, which were supposedly channelled through psychic communication with the Masters themselves.

This school follows the belief of the Perennialists that states that an ancient truth is contained in the esoteric core of each major exoteric religion. However, the twist in Theosophy is the belief that the Masters are trying to revive the original, complete, version of the One True Religion. This implies that all other religions should eventually disappear as unnecessary and distorted versions of the truth, especially Christianity.

b1. Conception of God

Theosophy denies the existence of a personal God, with Blavatsky herself stating that Theosophy believes "in the Deity as the All, the source of all existence, the infinite that cannot be either comprehended or known, the Universe alone revealing It, or, as some prefer it, Him, thus giving a sex to that, to anthropomorphize which is blasphemy." [20, 21]

According to her (and to some Hindu sects), Jesus was just another Avatar, a great teacher, and a moral reformer, not the second Person of the Tri-Une God of Christianity.[22]

Far from being her own personal view on the matter, this view was supposedly shared also by the Masters. One of the principal channelled entities, Kuthumi, clearly stated his position as follows:

"We know there is in our [solar] system no such thing as God, either personal or impersonal. Parabrahm is not a God, but absolute immutable law... The word 'God' was invented to designate the unknown cause of those effects which man has either admired or dreaded without understanding them." [23]

Furthermore, Annie Besant, who later became the president of the Theosophical Society, spoke in the same terms when she noted:

"God is a composite photograph of the innumerable gods who are the personifications of the forces of nature... It is all summed up in the phrase: Religions are branches from a common trunk—human ignorance." [24]

These assertions would, then, classify Theosophy as a predominantly panentheist (or even pantheist) worldview.

---

20. *In Zirkoff, B. de (ed.) (1967a). "What Is Theosophy?". Collected Writings. Vol. 2. Wheaton, Ill: Theosophical Publishing House, p. 91.*

21. *Anonymous (1951). The Theosophical Movement: 1875–1950. Los Angeles: The Cunningham Press, p. 72.*

22. *Ibid., p. 150.*

23. *Kuthumi (1924). Barker, A. T. (ed.). The Mahatma Letters to A. P. Sinnett. M. & K. H. New York: Frederick A. Stokes Company Publishers, p. 52.*

24. *Besant, A. (1902). Esoteric Christianity: Or the Lesser Mysteries. New York: John Lane, p. 8.*

b2. On Creation and Time

Theoshophy follows an emanationist cosmogony, while following the Indian cyclical conception of time. The cosmos is, therefore, understood as an illusory (Māyā) reflection of the Absolute, the One.

b3. On Evil, Free Will and Liberation

In most doctrinal aspects, Theosophy follows Indian traditions. The key doctrines of reincarnation and the Law of Karma, for example, were fully accepted. Therefore, individuals, although having free will, are seen as strongly conditioned by past lives. Liberation, as understood in a traditional Hindu sense (including an awakening to our true godlike nature), was the ultimate goal of Theosophists.

Symbols in Occultism: Theosophical Society's emblem, Ouroboros, Éliphas Lévi's depiction of Baphomet, hexagram, Black Sun.

3.3.3. New Age

The New Age movement is a highly eclectic, syncretic, and unsystematic mixture of different metaphysical and esoteric beliefs. Some of the main personalities and schools from where it draws heavily are: Spiritualism, New Thought, Theosophy, Human Potential Movement, Emanuel Swedenborg, Franz Mesmer, Helena Blavatsky, Carl Jung, and Swami Vivekananda, the propagator of Advaita Vedānta and Hinduism in the Western world.[25]

However, no specific author or schools are normative for New Age, as the movement places the maximum importance on the freedom of each person to decide the details of what they believe in. The ultimate source of authority, in this case, resides in each individual.

---

25. Heelas, Paul (1996). *The New Age Movement: Religion, Culture and Society in the Age of Postmodernity.* Cambridge: Blackwell, pp. 46-47.

This implies either the acceptance of Perennialism as the view that all traditions are different expressions of the same truth, or a postmodernist and relativist approach that denies that truth can be objectively known.[26] This approach has been derogatorily labelled as "supermarket spirituality".[27]

Some worldviews are preferred over others, however, including the Celtic, Egyptian, Essenic, and Cathar traditions. Also those of speculative civilizations like the Atlantean.[28]

a. Main Metaphysical Beliefs of the New Age

a1. Conception of God

New Age defines its vision of the divine as a force or energy that pervades the Universe and mankind, emphasizing an underlying absolute unity between all things. Recurrent names assigned to ultimate reality include: Ocean of Oneness, Infinite Spirit, Primal Stream, One Essence, and Universal Principle[29], all of them implying a non-personal Absolute that is assiduously characterized as Consciousness, Mind, Life Force or even Love.[30]

The belief in intermediate entities that can be channelled, like angels, masters, gods and goddesses, spirit guides, extraterrestrials, devas, the Collective Unconscious or elementals is also common.[31]

---

26. *Ibid., pp. 201-202.*

27. *Partridge, Christopher (2004). The Re-Enchantment of the West Volume. 1: Alternative Spiritualities, Sacralization, Popular Culture, and Occulture. London: T&T Clark International, p. 32.*

28. *Hammer, Olav (2001). Claiming Knowledge: Strategies of Epistemology from Theosophy to the New Age. Leiden and Boston: Brill, p. 47.*

29. *Hanegraaff, Wouter (1996). New Age Religion and Western Culture: Esotericism in the Mirror of Secular Thought. Leiden: Brill, p. 186.*

30. *Ibid., pp. 187-188.*

31. *Ibid., pp. 23-24.*

From these views follow the idea that humanity itself is divine in essence. Common terms that refer to this doctrine are: "droplet of Divinity", "inner Godhead", and "Divine or Higher Self." [32]

a2. On Creation, Time and Free Will

New Age imported from Theosophy the concept of a cyclical existence divided into different periods or ages, as well as the doctrines of Karma and reincarnation.

The name of this movement derives, in fact, from the expected upcoming Age of Aquarius that will renew our world from its present state of decay into one of spirituality, love, and unity.

Recurrent creation narratives employ the traditional esoteric concepts of the One, Emanationism, and an evil power of illusion, with a hint of the trapped spiritual sparks of Lurianic Kabbalah and Gnosticism.

In them, it is explained that in the beginning there was an original oneness from which the whole cosmos emanated.[33] Human souls, once purely spiritual, found themselves in a lower and denser physical plane of existence which is ultimately unreal.[34]

a3. On Liberation

The soul is understood to be in a constant process of spiritual evolution through the different planes, realms, worlds or realities it inhabits.

Meditation and Yoga are popular among New Agers, with some of them believing also in the use of entheogens for the purpose of achieving altered states of consciousness (Psychonautics).

---

32. *Ibid., p. 204.*

33. *Ibid., p. 305.*

34. *Ibid., pp. 307-308.*

In general, and in stark contrast with the mindset of traditional ascetic mystical traditions, having visions and other extranormal experiences is cherished instead of being looked at as a potential and dangerous pitfall to be avoided.

Symbols in the New Age: the Zodiac, Chakras, Ankh, Eye of Horus.

3.3.4. Thelema

Thelema is a Western esoteric and occult magical school founded by the ceremonial magician Aleister Crowley. His texts were recorded as revelations from the channelled entity known by the name of Aiwass. The three key doctrines upon which the entire structure of this worldview is built are:

• *"Do what thou wilt shall be the whole of the Law."* [35] This tenet encourages the initiates to find their True Will or purpose in life, instead of following common base human desires. One´s True Will was thought to be equivalent to one´s Holy Guardian Angel, a Daimon or guiding spirit unique to each person.[36] The journey to find it was called, as in Alchemy, the Great Work.[37]

• *"Every man and every woman is a star"*.[38] This concept is a reference to the Platonic body of light[39], said to be made up of the same substance as the stars, and the possibility for each adept to follow their Will to the maximum degree without coming into conflict with each other.

---

35. *Crowley, Aleister (1976). The Book of the Law: Liber AL vel Legis. York Beach, Maine: Weiser Books, Ch.1, v. 40.*

36. *Beta, Hymenaeus (1995). "Editor's Foreword". In Crowley, Aleister (ed.). The Goetia: The Lesser Key of Solomon the King. Red Wheel, p. xxi.*

37. *Kraig, Donald Michael (1998). Modern Sex Magick. Llewellyn, p. 44.*

38. *Crowley, Aleister (1976). The Book of the Law: Liber AL vel Legis. York Beach, Maine: Weiser Books, Ch.1, v.3.*

39. *Cornelius, J. Edward (2005). Aleister Crowley and the Ouija Board. Feral House, p. 59.*

• *"Love is the law, love under will."* [40] This means that love should be the essence of the Law of Thelema, but always subordinated to one´s True Will.

a. Main Metaphysical Beliefs of Thelema

a1. Conception of God

The main gods mentioned in Thelemic texts come from ancient Egyptian religion, with the highest deity being the goddess Nuit. She is a personification of the night sky, and is also referred to as the Great Mother, the Ultimate Source[41], and All-Possibility.[42] These definitions hint at an impersonal panentheistic force as the godhead.

a2. On Self-Transcendence and Union with The One

Thelema´s purpose is twofold. First, to discover one´s True Will. Second, to achieve union with the All.[43] As Crowley himself states, this is accomplished through the process of uniting the opposites present in this world of duality, as is common in many esoteric and mystical traditions:

"The Great Work is the uniting of opposites. It may mean the uniting of the soul with God, of the microcosm with the macrocosm, of the female with the male, of the ego with the non-ego." [44]

---

40. *Crowley, Aleister (1976). The Book of the Law: Liber AL vel Legis. York Beach, Maine: Weiser Books, Ch. 1, v. 57.*

41. *Orpheus, Rodney (2005). Abrahadabra: Understanding Aleister Crowley's Thelemic Magick. Boston, MA: Weiser Books, pp. 33–44.*

42. *Crowley, Aleister (1944). The Book of Thoth: A Short Essay on the Tarot of the Egyptians. The Equinox. O[rdo] T[empli] O[rientis]. III (V). XX. The Aeon.*

43. *York, Michael (2018). Pagan Mysticism: Paganism as a World Religion. United Kingdom: Cambridge Scholars Publishing, pp. 205–206.*

44. *Crowley, Aleister (1973). Magick Without Tears. Falcon Press. "Letter C".*

The methods to achieve this union are called Magick, referring to ceremonial magical acts (for example, the Gnostic Mass) that include invocations and worship of the goddess Nuit. Methods borrowed from other traditions include Buddhist meditation techniques and Yoga.

In his magickal journey, the initiate strives primarily to obtain self-knowledge, as in all schools based on attaining Gnosis. The different stages of the path include the study of the Kabbalistic Tree of Life, meditation, developing one´s body of light to be able to travel through the different planes of existence, and frequent invocations of certain spiritual beings.

This last step, called "assumption of godforms" and similar to the Deity Yoga of Buddhist Tantra, involves deity visualization and identifying with the image created, in order to work as a manifestation of the chosen deity.

The milestones of the path are believed to be:

• The attainment of knowledge of one´s Holy Guardian Angel, as well as conversing with him.

• The crossing of the Abyss between the spiritual and material realities, where a confrontation with the Dweller in the Abyss (Choronzon, a personification of one´s own ego) leads to either transcendence or annihilation.[45]

• Reaching "the City of the Pyramids and the Night of Pan", or unification with the All.

Symbols in Thelema: unicursal hexagram, pentacle.

---

45. *"The name of the Dweller in the Abyss is Choronzon, but he is not really an individual. The Abyss is empty of being; it is filled with all possible forms, each equally inane, each therefore evil in the only true sense of the word—that is, meaningless but malignant, in so far as it craves to become real. These forms swirl senselessly into haphazard heaps like dust devils, and each such chance aggregation asserts itself to be an individual and shrieks, "I am I!" though aware all the time that its elements have no true bond; so that the slightest disturbance dissipates the delusion just as a horseman, meeting a dust devil, brings it in showers of sand to the earth."*
— Crowley, Aleister (1979). The Confessions of Aleister Crowley. London & Boston: Routledge & Kegan Paul. Ch. 66.

3.3.5. Chaos Magic

Also spelled Chaos Magick[46, 47], it is a twentieth century school of magic born from the Neo-Pagan and esoteric subculture of the time and the writings of Austin Osman Spare.[48, 49]

Chaos Magic tried to remove the theological and religious layers of modern Occultism in order to focus only in the practical side of magical techniques.[50, 51]

a. Main Metaphysical Beliefs of Chaos Magic

a1. Conception of Ultimate Reality

The main presupposition of Chaos Magic is that all that we perceive in reality is a manifestation of beliefs (Ontological Relativism), and that there is no higher, objective, and stable metaphysical reality beyond this fact. It is a post-modern reworking of the theory of magic, which traditionally had a more religious outlook.[52]

---

46. *Carroll, Peter J. (2008). Psybermagick: Advanced Ideas in Chaos Magick: Revised Edition. Original Falcon Press.*

47. *Humphries, G.; Vayne, J. (2005). Now That's What I Call Chaos Magick. United Kingdom: Mandrake of Oxford, p. 17.*

48. *Chryssides, George D. (2012). Historical Dictionary of New Religious Movements. Rowman & Littlefield, p. 78.*

49. *Woodman, Justin (2003). Modernity, Selfhood, and the Demonic: Anthropological Perspectives on "Chaos Magick" in the United Kingdom (Ph.D. dissertation). Goldsmiths, University of London, p. 2.*

50. *Drury, Nevill (2002). The Watkins Dictionary of Magic: Over 3000 Entries on the World of Magical Formulas, Secret Symbols and the Occult. Duncan Baird Publishers, p. 86.*

51. *Hine, Phil (2009). Condensed Chaos: An Introduction to Chaos Magic. Original Falcon Press, p. 15.*

52. *Woodman, Justin (2003). Modernity, Selfhood, and the Demonic: Anthropological Perspectives on "Chaos Magick" in the United Kingdom (Ph.D. dissertation). Goldsmiths, University of London, pp. 15-16, 165, 201.*

While trying to embrace a position of metaphysical neutrality, followers of this worldview end up adopting not only an epistemologically skeptic stance (the notion that attaining true knowledge regarding ultimate reality is not possible for us), but also rejecting the idea that any objective truth even exists to begin with.[53]

All esoteric, occult, and spiritual practical systems, therefore, are viewed as working only because of the belief practitioners have in them, not because their notions about ultimate reality are true.

a2. Consensus Reality and the "Worlds" We Live In

Chaos magicians adhere to the concept of Consensus Reality. This doctrine explains that reality is a shared construct based on the dominant views of the people existing in a certain place. If they all believe something exists, it does. The classical example is the notion of citizenship, based on the existence of different countries separated by imaginary lines.

Chaos magicians could be classified as following a non-theistic monist view of ultimate reality, as only one reality exists in the end (Mind; Consciousness; Chaos, in the sense of an undetermined field of All-possibility).

At the level of manifestation, however, Chaos Magick moves between Monism and Pluralism, *the One and the Many.*

Taking into consideration the concept of Consensus Reality, this world is seen as a more or less illusory manifestation of our shared beliefs ("we all are the creators of our own reality"). But as different paradigms from different groups of like minded individuals can coexist at any given point in time, this view would also be compatible with a pluralistic (the Many) position, with "I alone am the creator of my own reality" being the most extreme view.

---

53. *Urban, Hugh (2006). Magia Sexualis: Sex, Magic, and Liberation in Modern Western Esotericism. University of California Press, pp. 240–243.*

This metaphysical philosophy could be broadly summarized as: there exists an impersonal primal entity, Mind or Consciousness, of which all of us are individual instances. When a group of like minded people come together, they create a particular version of "reality" which can be modified in the future if the group changes its beliefs. "Truth" is only a label for the paradigm currently followed by the majority (e.g., modern science).

Due to their perceived lack of a stable underlying metaphysical ground in our reality, Chaos magicians are encouraged to create their own particular belief system. Most of the time this includes the borrowing of metaphysical concepts and doctrines from other esoteric traditions, religions, occult sources or philosophical schools.

a3. On Free Will and Liberation

Human beings are considered as being shaped and heavily conditioned by the Consensus Reality of their environment. The strength of this reality is conceived as dependent on the number of believers as well as the strength of their beliefs.

The main aim of the Chaos magicians, then, is to decondition themselves through ritual and magical techniques in order to reshape their thoughts and take destiny into their hands.

b. The Path of the Chaos Magician: Belief as a Tool

Given that truth does not objectively exist for them, Chaos magicians feel legitimized to use every technique that grants them the desired results ("nothing is true, everything is permitted").[54] Any metaphysical theory behind the method is thrown away as superfluous.

Therefore, they use the complex symbolism of traditions such as Kabbalah, spirit invocations (e.g., Enochian magic), Astrology, the Taoist

------

54. *Ibid., pp. 240–243.*

I-Ching or any other method they deem fit for their purposes. They are all defined as mere temporary "maps" that can be used to achieve the desired results.

The power and efficacy of belief was explained by A.O. Spare. For him, belief was the solid form of psychic energy. Deconditioning oneself and breaking belief systems was equivalent to liberating this energy and letting it go back to its source. This implies going from multiplicity back to the One, understood as an impersonal force that anyone with the right knowledge can tap into.

b1. Paradigm Shifting

A classic and drastic example of this relativistic school of thought can be exemplified by the suggestion of Peter J. Carroll of assigning different worldviews to the sides of a dice, throwing the dice, and then adopting the aleatory paradigm obtained as one´s worldview for a period of time. (e.g., 1. Neo-Paganism, 2. Christianity, 3. Atheism).[55]

The ego of the magician is seen as a desperate attempt to create a stable self-hood that perpetuates itself by distinguishing between what it is/believes and what it is not.

The work of the magician, then, involves the dissolution of that ego and the discovering that we are what we decide to believe. It is an atheistic and postmodern version of the elimination of subject-object duality of Indian religions and the mythical ego-death of the Hero´s Journey of Joseph Campbell (and of most mystical traditions).

Different versions of an afterlife are also thought to be brought into existence based on belief, and the idea of multiple incarnations is commonly held.

----

300. *Carroll, Peter J. (1987). Liber Null. Weiser Books, p. 73.*

The only constant fact of our reality is believed to be its subjective relativity. Chaos magicians, however, believe their paradigm to be the only true one.

Symbols in Chaos Magic: symbol of Chaos, personal Sigils.

3.4. Neo-Paganism 

Neo-Paganism,[56] or contemporary Paganism, can either refer to modern religious movements which seek to revive old pre-Christian beliefs (Reconstructionism) or to eclectic movements which blend some of those beliefs with other metaphysical concepts.[57]

Examples of the former are Baltic Paganism, Germanic Heathenry, and Greek Hellenism. Of the latter, Wicca and Druidry.

Although they share similarities, contemporary pagan movements are diverse and, as a result, they do not share a single set of beliefs, practices or texts.[58] However, they tend to have an affinity for Polytheism, Pantheism, and/or Animism.

Some modern pagans may instead be atheists, being more interested in the virtues and general outlook on life that Paganism promotes, instead than in metaphysical doctrines.

---

56. *Adler, Margot (1979). Drawing Down the Moon: Witches, Druids, Goddess-Worshippers and Other Pagans in America. London: Penguin, p. xiii.*

57. *Doyle White, Ethan (2015). Wicca: History, Belief, and Community in Modern Pagan Witchcraft. Brighton, Chicago, and Toronto: Sussex Academic Press, p. 6.*

58. *Carpenter, Dennis D. (1996). Emergent Nature Spirituality: An Examination of the Major Spiritual Contours of the Contemporary Pagan Worldview. In Lewis, James R. (ed.). Magical Religion and Modern Witchcraft. Albany: State University of New York Press, p. 40.*

New Age has also been related to modern Paganism, with gods and goddesses sometimes being perceived as metaphors for nature´s cycles or Jungian psychological archetypes.[59]

A key shared belief among most of these movements is the concept of everything in the Universe being an interconnected totality. This belief, in turn, can be linked to either a pantheistic or panentheistic worldview.[60]

3.4.1. Wicca

The largest movement in modern Paganism is currently Wicca[61], also called "The Craft" or "The Craft of the Wise".[62] Ronald Hutton, historian specialized in British folklore and pre-Christian beliefs, pointed out ceremonial and folk magic, Romantic literature, Freemasonry, and the disproved witch-cult hypothesis of Margaret Murray as the principal influences of the movement.[63]

Esotericist Gerald Gardner was the principal founder of the movement, while claiming that he was trying to revive an old religion. Different

---

59. *York, Michael (1999). Invented Culture/Invented Religion: The Fictional Origins of Contemporary Paganism. Nova Religio: The Journal of Alternative and Emergent Religions. 3 (1): 135–146.*

60. *Carpenter, Dennis D. (1996). Emergent Nature Spirituality: An Examination of the Major Spiritual Contours of the Contemporary Pagan Worldview. In Lewis, James R. (ed.). Magical Religion and Modern Witchcraft. Albany: State University of New York Press, p. 50.*

61. *Strmiska, Michael F. (2005). Modern Paganism in World Cultures. Modern Paganism in World Cultures: Comparative Perspectives. Santa Barbara, Dencer, and Oxford: ABC-Clio. pp. 1–53; p.47.*

62. *Adler, Margot (2005). Drawing Down the Moon: Witches, Druids, Goddess-worshippers and Other Pagans in America Today. London: Penguin, p. 10.*

63. *Hutton, Ronald (1999). The Triumph of the Moon: A History of Modern Pagan Witchcraft. New York City: Oxford University Press.*

branches of Wicca now exist, including: the original Gardnerian Wicca, Alexandrian Wicca, Faery Wicca, Kemetic Wicca, and Dianic or feminist Wicca, emphasizing the "Divine Feminine." [64]

a. Main Metaphysical Beliefs of Wicca

a1. Conception of God and Creation

Wicca is normally viewed as a dualist worldview, since it speaks of both an ultimate God (the Horned God, the Lord) and Goddess (the Triple Goddess, the Lady).

However, these two deities are sometimes thought of as the two complementary sides of the underlying ultimate reality (the One). The divine is here understood as an impersonal process or force.

Gardner himself affirmed the existence of the one unknowable Supreme Deity or Prime Mover (an Aristotelian concept) beyond the male/female deities. This deity, the source of the other gods, was viewed by Gardner as not involved with creation anymore (Deism).[65]

Male/female polar deities may include other minor godlike entities. These multiple secondary deities can be derived from many diverse historical pantheons and represent different aspects of creation.

As in most forms of Paganism, the underlying metaphysical and theological views of modern followers of Wicca can be diverse, and includes Theism, Atheism, Agnosticism, Pantheism, Monism, Dualism, and Polytheism.[66]

---

64. *Telesco, Patricia (2005). Which Witch is Which: A Concise Guide to Wiccan and Neo-Pagan Paths and Tradition. Career Press, p. 114.*

65. *Doyle White, Ethan (2016). Wicca: History, Belief, and Community in Modern Pagan Witchcraft. Brighton: Sussex Academic Press, p. 92.*

66. *Ibid., pp. 86–87.*

a2. On Evil, Determinism and Free Will

Although not universally accepted, reincarnation is still the most common belief regarding the afterlife. The concept was proposed by Gardner himself.[67] However, multiple interpretations were developed to explain how the actual process actually works (e.g., human-only or any-lifeform reincarnations).

The notion that disincarnated spirits can be contacted through mediums was adopted from Spiritualism, with the Summerland being the place where they are believed to dwell between reincarnations.[68]

As in most Neo-Pagan movements, suffering is seen as a natural part of existence in this plane of reality, with no further explanation needed.

The concept of evil, in contrast, has no universally accepted article of faith attached to it. For some, good and evil may exist as metaphysical laws or principles, while others (maybe a majority) prefer to reframe the problem in terms of positive/negative or order/chaos dichotomies. The use of polar opposites in these cases implies their inevitability in our world of duality and their final re-unification once absorbed back into the One.

a3. On the Afterlife

As with all belief systems that have reincarnation as part of their doctrinal basis, the destiny of souls after death is a process of eventual spiritual evolution. Our overall spiritual state and the emotions present at the time of death create the subjective state that each of us experiences in the Summerlands, similar to the explanations given in the *Tibetan Book of the Dead* (*Bardo Thödol*).

---

67. *Ibid., pp. 146-147.*
68. *Ibid., p. 146.*

Traversing the Summerlands usually involves some amount of confrontation with our fears and limitations ("Shadow work", following the Jungian concept of our Shadow being the arch-nemesis of our real Self).

As with most metaphysical systems that believe in an ultimate impersonal force that can be used for both good and evil, Wicca distinguishes between white magic (or right-hand path, term coined by the Theosophist Helena Blavatsky) and black magic (left-hand path).[69]

Symbols in Wicca: Hecate's Wheel; symbol of the Horned God and his consort the Triple Goddess; pentacle or five-pointed star. The points of the pentacle represent either the classical Greek elements (including Aether/Spirit as the fifth) or the human form.[70]

3.4.2. Druidism and Neo-Druidism (Druidry) 

Druids were the priestly class of Celtic traditions. Learned men, sometimes referred to as philosophers, healers, and judges. Neo-Druidism, on the other hand, is an eclectic Neo-Pagan movement, since there is not enough information available to reconstruct the ancient Druidic spirituality.

a. Main Metaphysical Beliefs of Druidism

a1. Conception of God

It is difficult to know exactly what the ancient Druids believed, as they left behind no written text of any kind. Most of the current historical knowledge comes from Greek and Roman authors, the latter experiencing first-hand Druid culture after their conquest of the Celts.

---

69. *Sanders, Alex (1984). The Alex Sanders Lectures. Magickal Childe.*

70. *Zell-Ravenheart, Oberon (2006). Morning Glory. Creating Circles & Ceremonies. Franklin Lakes: New Page Books, p. 42.*

Neo-Druidic beliefs, on the other hand, are known but are not fixed. Different adherents may have radically different views on, for example, the nature of the divine.[71] The range of existing metaphysical beliefs includes Polytheism, Pantheism, Monotheism, Agnosticism, and even Atheism.[72]

The one constant characteristic that is apparently prevalent is the veneration of the natural world, usually thought of as alive and imbued with soul or spirit (Animism).[73]

There are also different pantheons of immanent deities to which Neo-Druids adhere to[74], but they are not seen as transcending this world.

Interestingly, the commonly used *The Druid's Prayer* was originally addressed to a monotheist God. However, with the increase of polytheist participants, the text was frequently changed to address either the Goddess, both God and Goddess or just simply a neutral Spirit instead.[75]

Some Neo-Druids share the Spiritist belief that channelling spirits during rituals is possible.[76]

a2. On Determinism and Free Will

Ancient Druids believed in the "Pythagorean doctrine" of the immortality of souls and their transmigration (Metempsychosis).[77]

---

71. *Harvey, Graham (2007). Listening People, Speaking Earth: Contemporary Paganism. London: Hurst & Company, p. 30.*

72. *White, Larisa A. (2021). World Druidry: A Globalizing Path of Nature Spirituality. Belmont, California: Larisa A. White, p. 114.*

73. *Cooper, Michael T. (2009). The Roles of Nature, Deities, and Ancestors in Constructing Religious Identity in Contemporary Druidry. The Pomegranate: The International Journal of Pagan Studies. 11 (1): 58–73, p. 60.*

74. *Ibid., p. 68.*

75. *Harvey, Graham (2007). Listening People, Speaking Earth: Contemporary Paganism. London: Hurst & Company, p. 30.*

76. *Butler, Jenny (2005). Druidry in Contemporary Ireland. In Michael F. Strmiska. Modern Paganism in World Cultures. California: ABC-CLIO, pp. 87–125; p. 105.*

77. *Diodorus Siculus. Bibliotheca historicae. V.21–22.*

The particularity of this variety of reincarnational theory is that the soul is believed to be less conditioned by previous lives, as memories of them cannot be accessed.

"With regard to their actual course of studies, the main object of all education is, in their opinion, to imbue their scholars with a firm belief in the indestructibility of the human soul, which, according to their belief, merely passes at death from one tenement to another; for by such doctrine alone, they say, which robs death of all its terrors, can the highest form of human courage be developed. Subsidiary to the teachings of this main principle, they hold various lectures and discussions on the stars and their movement, on the extent and geographical distribution of the earth, on the different branches of natural philosophy, and on many problems connected with religion."

—Julius Caesar. De Bello Gallico, VI 14

a3. On Creation and the Afterlife

Ancient Druids believed that there were two planes of existence, our physical world and the Otherworld. Souls would live and then die in both worlds, conforming a cyclical process.

The Otherworld was pictured as either an underground place or as a distant group of sea islands, also called the Land of Eternal Youth. However, this land was not believed to be reachable by everyone, as the god of the dead (Donn, ancestor of the Gaelic people) received all souls except the ones of the happy few.

No creation myth has survived and, therefore, any Neo-Druidic view on the subject of how creation came to be is purely modern and hypothetical.

Although highly variable, common practices in Neo-Druidic groups include meditation, prayer to deities, spirit channelling, ancestor veneration, and nature-centric ritual practices.[78]

---

78. *White, Larisa A. (2021). World Druidry: A Globalizing Path of Nature Spirituality. Belmont, California: Larisa A. White, pp. 186-187.*

The purpose of meditation is twofold: to enter the Otherworld by inner "Shamanic" journeying, and to deepen the sense of interconnectedness with all incarnated and disincarnated life, as well as the sacredness of our physical world.

Symbols in Druidism: Druid Sigil; the Green Man; the tree (powerful yet peaceful, still but fully alive and acting on behalf of all).

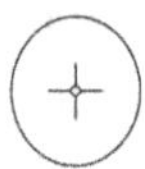

3.5. Shamanism

Shamanism is the label created for a group of ancient indigenous beliefs and practices that shared a certain set of characteristics. Only the Tungus, properly speaking, call themselves shamans.[79]

These practices are characterized by the interaction of the shamans with the Spirit World for healing or divination purposes.[80] They are believed to be able to achieve this by entering into altered states of consciousness (trance).[81,82]

a. Main Metaphysical Beliefs of Shamanism

a1. Conception of the World and the Divine

The ancient Shamanic traditions were not homogeneous in their beliefs, but they shared a set of important concepts and doctrines that came to define the core of Shamanism: [83]

---

79. *Diószegi (1998). Shamanism. Akadémiai Kiadó, 1962: 13.*

80. *Singh, Manvir (2018). The cultural evolution of shamanism. Behavioral and Brain Sciences. 41: e66: 1–61.*

81. *Ibid.*

82. *Mircea Eliade; Vilmos Diószegi (2020). Shamanism. Encyclopædia Britannica: "Shamanism, religious phenomenon centred on the shaman, a person believed to achieve various powers through trance or ecstatic religious experience. Although shamans' repertoires vary from one culture to the next, they are typically thought to have the ability to heal the sick, to communicate with the otherworld, and often to escort the souls of the dead to that otherworld."*

83. *Mircea Eliade (1951). Shamanism, Archaic Techniques of Ecstasy. Bollingen Series LXXVI, Princeton University Press, pp. 3–7.*

- The existence of spirits and their influence in our physical world.

- The existence of gifted persons who can communicate with those spirits: the shamans.

- The morally ambivalent nature of the spirits (divided into benevolent or malevolent ones).

- The ability of the shaman to heal the harm caused by the malevolent ones.

- The ability of the shaman to enter the Spirit World through visionary states of trance (Vision Quests).

- Their use of Spirit Animals or other spiritual entities as guides and helpers on their quest.

- The possibility of foretelling the future (e.g., omens, scrying, runes).

The main focus of shamans was healing, with the cause of sickness believed to be the maleficent spirits of the Spirit World.[84]

The shaman understood his work as "entering" the body of the patient in order to vanquish and banish the spirit causing the injury. Sometimes good Tutelary Spirits were invoked to help in the task, with some of them teaching shamans their particular songs (Icaros) as a summoning method. Other times shamans "spoke" with indwelling spirits of medicinal plants in order to learn their healing effects.

The above beliefs characterize this tradition as animistic and, as far as many immanent deities and spirits are mentioned but no transcendent deity is spoken of, polytheistic.

a2. The Death and Rebirth of the Shaman: The Trial of the Initiatory Crisis

Oftentimes, shamans felt that they had been called, usually through dreams. In other cases, the gift of a shaman was thought to run in particular lineages and was, therefore, inherited.

---

84. *Salak, Kira. Hell and Back. National Geographic Adventure.*

It was a key event[85] in the life of neophytes to live through an initiatory crisis that was experienced as their death to the secular world and posterior rebirth as a guide and healer of the community.

The future healer had to endure physical and psychological sickness in order to understand and be able to combat it in the future. During this crisis, the shaman was believed to travel the underworld and bring back knowledge to the world of the living.[86]

3.5.1. Neo-Shamanism

Neo-Shamanism is the term coined for the modern and eclectic Shamanic-inspired worldviews created by Westerners searching for alternate forms of spirituality.

The main texts influencing the revival of these ancient traditions were those of Mircea Eliade, Carlos Castaneda, and Michael Harner.[87]

Their main focuses are usually experiencing altered states of consciousness and communication with the Spirit World. The rituals employed include drumming, rattling, dancing, chanting or the use of entheogens (e.g., ayahuasca, peyote [not universally accepted]).[88, 89, 90]

---

85. *Turner, Kevin (2016). Sky Shamans of Mongolia: Meetings with Remarkable Healers. North Atlantic Books, p. 440.*

86. *Halifax, Joan (1982). Shaman: The Wounded Healer. London: Thames & Hudson.*

87. *Scuro, Juan & Rodd, Robin (2015). Neo-Shamanism. Encyclopedia of Latin American Religions. Springer International Publishing, pp. 1–6.*

88. *Blain, Jenny (2002). Nine Worlds of Seid-Magic: Ecstasy and Neo-Shamanism in North European Paganism. London and New York: Routledge.*

89. *Harner, Michael (1990). The Way of the Shaman. San Francisco, California: Harper.*

90. *Wallis, Robert J. (2003). Shamans/Neo-Shamans: Ecstasies, Alternative Archaeologies and Contemporary Pagans. Routledge.*

The main differences found between modern Neo-Shamanism and the traditional indigenous varieties are:

• While traditional shamans were typically chosen by a community or inherited the role[91], in Neo-Shamanism they are self-appointed.

• Traditional Shamanism sought the help of spirits in order to maintain cosmic order and balance. Neo-Shamanism is mainly focused on personal development and experimentation of spiritual realities.[92]

• Negative emotions were important in traditional Shamanic initiations. Pain and fear were tools used to break the aspirant's normal consciousness or ego. Neo-Shamanism, instead, often excludes them and focus only on positive ones, in common with modern "feel-good" reinterpretations of old spiritual traditions.[93]

• Traditional Shamanism was believed to be morally neutral, with the possibility of being used with the intention to harm. The danger posed by evil spirits was very present, while the dark side is de-emphasized in modern versions.[94]

• Traditional Shamanism considered the Spirit World as an independent reality, while Neo-Shamanism usually considers it on the same level as the physical world and merged with it.

As with all modern Neo-Pagan movements, the beliefs of each group and even each practitioner may be different, since there is no fixed dogma in doctrinal issues.

---

91. *Scuro, Juan & Rodd, Robin (2015). Neo-Shamanism. Encyclopedia of Latin American Religions. Springer International Publishing, pp. 1–6.*

92. *Boekhoven, J.W. (2011). Genealogies of shamanism: Struggles for power, charisma and authority (PhD thesis).*

93. *York, Michael (2001). The Role of Fear in Traditional and Contemporary Shamanism. Bath Spa University College.*

94. *Wallis, Robert J. (2003). Shamans/Neo-Shamans: Ecstasies, Alternative Archaeologies and Contemporary Pagans. Routledge.*

Symbols in Shamanism: Totems, representing Tutelary Spirits; Beaivi, symbolizing the Sami Sun deity; Taegeuk, representing the "Supreme Ultimate" or "Great Polarity/Duality" (symbol of the Korean national flag); bones and skeleton, symbolizing rebirth.

3.6. Gnosticism and Neo-Gnosticism

Gnosticism is a term coined for different Jewish and Christian sects (considered heretical by the Fathers of the Christian Church) that shared similar beliefs in which salvation was achieved mainly through secret and esoteric knowledge (Gnosis). Different systems coexisted, with no established homogeneous dogma or practices.

Most of the important preserved Gnostic texts can be found in the *Nag Hammadi Library*. The *Pistis Sophia* and the extensive comments of St. Irenaeus of Lyon in his *"Against Heresies"* are other important sources of Gnostic myth and beliefs.

Gnostic doctrines spread throughout the world via Manichaeism, while Mandaeism is the only currently surviving Gnostic religion.

Carl Jung was also influenced by Gnosticism through the works of G.R.S. Mead, a Theosophist and H.P. Blavatsky´s private secretary.

Blavatsky herself discussed Gnosticism in her book *Isis Unveiled*[95], while her secretary published the first translation of the *Pistis Sophia* in *Lucifer magazine*.

Different modern more or less occult Neo-Gnostic groups exist today, with their teachings not always resembling the original ones (e.g., Samael Aun Weor, popular in South America, and his sexual method to unify the male/female polarity).

---

95. *Goodrick-Clarke, Clare (2005). G.R.S. Mead and the Gnostic Quest. North Atlantic Books, p. 8.*

a. Main Metaphysical Beliefs of Gnosticism
a1. Conception of God

Gnostic sects fluctuated between a more or less strict Dualism (e.g., Manichaeism)[96] and Monism (e.g., Valentinian Gnosticism, Syrian–Egyptian traditions). The former affirms the existence of an ultimate reality formed by two equally divine entities or forces in conflict. The latter emphasizes that one of those entities, the evil or deficient one, is derived from the other, superior one.

In the second type of doctrinal systems, the superior principle is called the Monad, the One. Other historical names include: the Absolute, Aion teleos (the Perfect Æon), Bythos (Depth or Profundity, Βυθος), Proarkhe (Before the Beginning, προαρχη), and HE Arkhe (The Beginning, ἡ ἀρχή). Hippolytus of Rome, a Christian theologian, thought that the Gnostic view of God was inspired by Pythagoreanism, since they also called the first existent the Monad. For them, the One begat the two (dyad), the two begetting numbers, which begat the point, then lines, the whole of existence following.

"The Monad is a monarchy with nothing above it. It is he who exists as God and Father of everything, the invisible One who is above everything, who exists as incorruption, which is in the pure light into which no eye can look. He is the invisible Spirit, of whom it is not right to think of him as a god, or something similar. For he is more than a god, since there is nothing above him, for no one lords it over him. For he does not exist in something inferior to him, since everything exists in him. For it is he who establishes himself. He is eternal, since he does not need anything. For he is total perfection." [97]

— The Apocryphon of John, para. 6

---

96. *The idea that Gnosticism was derived from Buddhism was first proposed by Charles William King (1864) [a]. Mansel (1875) [b] considered the principal sources of Gnosticism to be Platonism, Zoroastrianism, and Buddhism. ([a]: In his classic work, The Gnostics and their Remains (1864). Charles William King was one of the earliest and most emphatic scholars to link Gnosticism with Buddhism. [b]: H. L. Mansel (1875). Gnostic Heresies of the First and Second Centuries, p. 32.)*

97. *Wisse, Frederik. The Apocryphon of John. Also in Nag Hammadi Library (1971). Brill.*

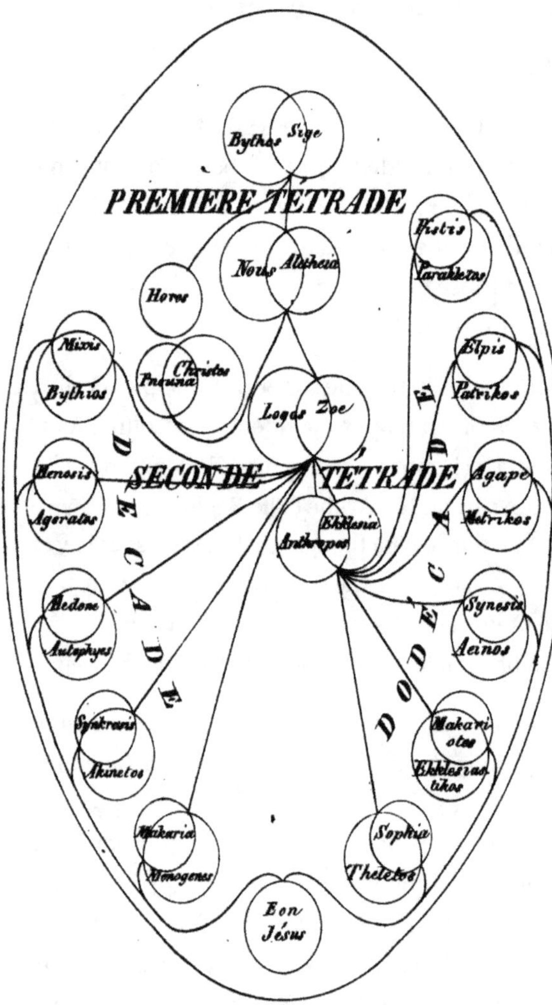

Figure 4. The Valentinian conception of the Pleroma, or the fullness of God [98], is characterized by the doctrines of Emanationism and of Complementary Dualism.

Note how even the First Principle is conceived as dual (Bythos or Profundity and his counterpart Sige or Silence [and sometimes Ennoia, or First Thought]).

The fact that Ennoia is the first determination of Bythos implies that the "Father" is conceived as pure potentiality. The first pair (Syzygy) can, then, be defined as All-Possibility and All-Actuality.

This principle of complementarity is repeated at all levels of emanation, and each Gnostic was believed to be incomplete insofar as he was separated from his angelic counterpart.

This structure is similar to other worldviews (e.g., the Hindu Shiva/Shakti, the Tibetan Buddhist Father/ Mother deities).

The first three emanations are also similar to the sequential Neo-Platonic triad of The One, Nous, and World Soul. Valentinus´ doctrines may have been influenced by Egyptian metaphysics.[99]

Picture: Histoire critique du Gnosticisme; Jacques Matter (1826), Vol. II, Plate II.

---

98. *Matter, Jacques (1826). Plérome de Valentin, from Histoire critique du Gnosticisme; Vol. II, Plate II.*

99. *Bousset, Wilhelm (1911). "Valentinus and the Valentinians". In Chisholm, Hugh (ed.). Encyclopædia Britannica. Vol. 27 (11th ed.). Cambridge University Press. pp. 852–857.*

a2. On Creation

The Monad, according to Valentinus (whose teachings are the most influential in modern Neo-Gnosticism) is the source of the fullness of the attributes of the Godhead (Pleroma). In Gnostic cosmology, the Pleroma is a transcendent realm of Divine Light where Aeons (eternal beings) dwell.

Gnosticism adheres to the doctrine of Emanationism, with each Aeon or hypostasis that emerges from the One being progressively more imperfect as the distance from the source increases.

Different systems talk of different numbers of emanations (e.g., thirty for Valentinus, three hundred and sixty-five for Basilides, hinting at the totality of time).

As in all systems that follow the doctrine of emanations, the final aim of the initiate is to eventually retrace the gradations of existence to go back to their source, the One.

The first emanated Aeon is, in some texts, the hermaphroditic Barbelo.[100, 101] The following emanations are viewed, in turn, as composed of male-female pairings (Syzygies).[102]

The Christ was for the Gnostics one of these Aeons, his consort being Sophia, or Wisdom.[103]

a3. On the Problem of Evil

As in all systems which believe in Emanationism, the lowest emanation is the most imperfect one. In the case of Gnosticism, this is the case of Sophia, often identified with the Greek Neo-Platonic concept of the World Soul.

---

100. Wisse, Frederik. The Apocryphon of John. The Gnostic Society Library.

101. Turner, John D. Trimorphic Protennoia. The Gnostic Society Library.

102. Turner, John D. The Pair (Syzygy) in Valentinian Thought. The Gnostic Society Library.

103. A Valentinian Exposition. The Gnostic Society Library.

In Gnostic creation myths, Sophia emanates by herself, without the involvement of her complementary counterpart. This act of ignorance or defiance results in the birth of the Demiurge (a concept already found in Plato and Neo-Pythagoreanism), concealed outside the Pleroma.[104]

The Demiurge is also called Yaldabaoth, Samael (the blind god), Saklas (the foolish one) or even identified with the God of the *Old Testament* (similar to the Christian heresy of Marcionism). The original flaw that led mankind to its exiled condition, therefore, is not found in creation but in an aspect of the Creator Himself (Sophia/Demiurge).

The Demiurge, finding himself alone and believing to be the highest deity, emanates the Archons (Rulers) and the material world, the last stages of the process of emanation that began with the One.

In general, the Demiurge was conceived as an ignorant and flawed figure at best, and as just plain evil at worst.

He was believed to be the creator of mankind, with humans containing trapped elements of Sophia in them. These trapped elements, being part of the fullness (Pleroma) of the One, implied that humans contain a fragment of God in them.[105]

In some Gnostic creation myths, the response of the Godhead to this chain of events was to emanate two additional savior Aeons, Christ and the Holy Spirit.

Christ then embodied Jesus to teach humanity the way to attain the esoteric knowledge (Gnosis) of their hidden divinity in order for them to liberate themselves from this intrinsically fallen plane of existence they now live in.[106]

---

104. *Wisse, Frederik. The Apocryphon of John. The Gnostic Society Library.*

105. *Layton, Bentley. The Hypostasis of the Archons. The Gnostic Society Library.*

106. *Hoeller, Stephan A. The Gnostic World View: A Brief Summary of Gnosticism. The Gnostic Society.*

Other Gnostic interpretations of who Jesus of Nazareth was, included:

• He was an enlightened human being and teacher of Gnosis.[107]

• He was divine but His appearance in this world was illusory (the heresy of Docetism).

• He was a false Messiah who perverted the teachings of John the Baptist, the true teacher (for Mandaeism).[108]

a4. On Determinism and Free Will

The Gnostics believed that humanity was divided into three classes of people, with their ultimate destiny being more or less conditioned depending on their class: [109]

• *Material (Hylic):* the lowest type of humans who only care about the material aspects of life and, therefore, cannot be saved.

• *Soulful (Psychic):* the intermediate level, capable of achieving knowledge (Gnosis) and being saved depending on how they live.

• *Spiritual (Pneumatic):* the highest type of human being, unattached and unfettered by this material world. Destined to be saved by the intuitional knowledge obtained through the spark of Sophia present in them.

a5. On Liberation from this Prison World

As the latest emanation created by the Demiurge, the physical world was believed to be the closest to darkness and non-existence. As we have

---

107. *The Gnostic Gospels. Frontline.*

108. *Macuch, Rudolf (1965). Handbook of Classical and Modern Mandaic. De Gruyter & Co, p. 61 fn. 105.*

109. *Pagels, Elaine (1975). The Gnostic Paul: Gnostic Exegesis of the Pauline Letters. Trinity Press.*

previously seen, every time this dialectic between spirit and matter is part of a certain worldview, its path of liberation includes extreme ascetic measures in order to detach oneself from matter as much as possible, because it is conceived as intrinsically evil.

This was the case with most Gnostic sects (e.g., Cathars, meaning "the pure ones"; an ascetical variety of Gnosticism), who followed a strict ascetical life, especially in the sexual and dietary spheres.[110] Others, however, apparently followed the contrary antinomian view that material actions had no effect whatsoever on their independent spiritual beings and were therefore allowed to reject the common moral law and, in some cases, even abuse matter (e.g., apparently the Borborites, a libertine variety of Gnosticism).

Liberation from confinement in this material prison world was thought to be achieved through the knowledge (not only the faith) that our true identity is a part of the One through the Holy Spark present in us.[111] The Valentinians also believed that achieving this knowledge helped to restore the cosmic order itself. [112]

Salvation was viewed as a cosmic process, not an individual one, achieved through the reabsorption of all the sparks into the Pleroma and the final annihilation of matter. The Gnostic path also included ritual practices and knowledge of the mystical names to use at the moment of death to pass through the detention stations of the rulers of this world. As St. Irenaeus stated[113], the practice of constant meditation upon the secret of the heavenly union or Syzygia was a common one.[114]

---

110. *Layton, Bentley (1987). The Gnostic Scriptures. Introduction to "Against Heresies" by St. Irenaeus. SCM Press.*

111. *Giversen, Søren; Petersen, Tage; Sørensen, Jørgen Podemann (2002). The Nag Hammadi Texts in the History of Religions. Det Kongelige Danske Vdenskabernes Selskab, p. 157.*

112. *Holroyd, Stuart (1994). The Elements of Gnosticism. Dorset: Element Books Limited, p. 37.*

113. *Ibid. i. 6, 4.*

114. *Bousset, W. (1911). Valentinus and the Valentinians. Encyclopædia Britannica (Vol. 27), pp. 854–855.*

THE DOCTRINE OF THE UNITY OF OPPOSITES IN GNOSTICISM

Just as in other esoterical systems (e.g., Alchemy, Hinduism, and Tibetan Buddhism), Valentinian Gnosticism includes the doctrine of the Union of Opposites through the figure of the Heavenly Marriage.[115]

This marriage refers to both the union of the Savior with Sophia as well as that of each Gnostic (viewed as feminine) with their corresponding angelic counterpart (masculine).

This implied that even in a fallen state, each Gnostic had its divine counterpart continually in the presence of God, just as Sophia was also divided into an Upper Self residing in the Pleroma and a lower one trapped in matter (Achamoth).

---

b. Relationship of Gnosticism with Christianity, Neo-Platonism and Kabbalah

Even though some early Gnostics such as Valentinus saw themselves as Christians, their metaphysical doctrines were most of the time not only different from those of traditional Christianity but completely contrary to them. In later times, and especially in Neo-Gnosticism, an open confrontational attitude against Christianity predominates.

Gershom Scholem, the influential historian of Jewish philosophy and mysticism, in turn, affirmed the existence of an earlier Jewish Gnosticism that predated the Christian one.[116]

---

115. *Irenaeus, St. Against Heresies. i. 30.*

116. *Cohen, Arthur A.; Mendes-Flohr, Paul (2009). 20th Century Jewish Religious Thought. Jewish Publication Society, p. 286:*

"Recent research, however, has tended to emphasize that Judaism, rather than Persia, was a major origin of Gnosticism. Indeed, it appears increasingly evident that many of the newly published Gnostic texts were written in a context from which Jews were not absent. In some cases, indeed, a violent rejection of the Jewish God, or of Judaism, seems to stand at the basis of these texts. [...] facie, various trends in Jewish thought and literature of the Second Commonwealth appear to have been potential factors in Gnostic origins."

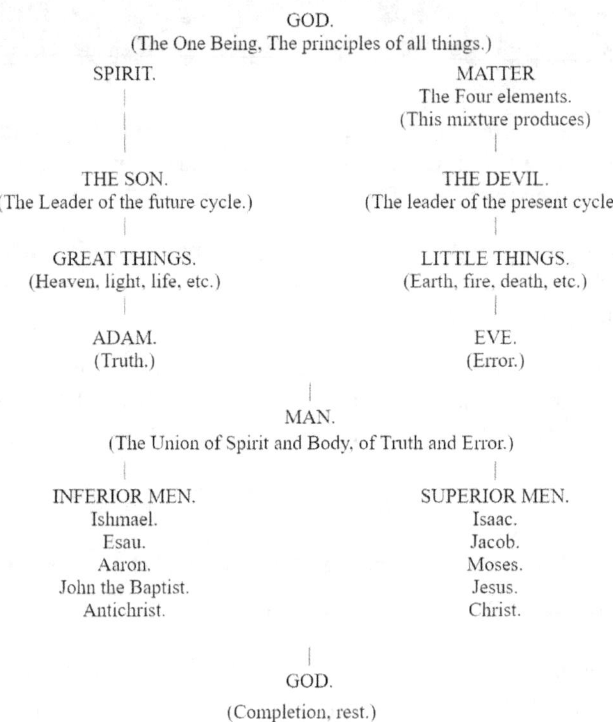

Figure 5. G.R.S. Mead made the connection between the system of Simon Magus[117] and the Ebionite scheme of emanations.[118] Note the pairs of complementaries emanating from the First Principle, and how the devil is seen as the necessary counterpart of the Son of God. Creation, it is implied, arises from the tension between these polar opposites, which include moral dichotomies (e.g., Good/Evil, Truth/Error) and will eventually reunite in God, their source.

Furthermore, note that evil is explained away through blaming matter, contrary to the Christian notion that flesh is not only matter, but the passions that use matter as a vehicle to draw a person's will away from the will of God.

He also noted that several key Gnostic doctrines reappeared in medieval Kabbalah and were used to reinterpret earlier traditional

---

117. *Mead, G.R.S. (1892). Simon Magus: An Essay on the Founder of Simonianism Based on the Ancient Sources with a Re-evaluation of his Philosophy and Teachings. The Theosophical Society.*

118. *Les Bibles, et les Initiateurs Religieux de l'Humanité, Louis Leblois, i. 144; from Uhlhorn, Die Homilien und Recognitionen, p. 224.*

sources.[119] Scholem goes as far as claiming that even the *Zohar*, one of
the most important medieval Kabbalistic texts, used Gnostic concepts
to reinterpret the Jewish Bible (Torah).[120]

Figure 6. The relationship of Gnosticism with the Egyptian pre-Christian religion.
A: *From at least 200 BCE onwards, some groups in the Graeco-Egyptian Ptolemaic
Kingdom identified the God of the Jews with the evil Egyptian deity Seth.[121] This later
extended to Christianity as well, as can be seen in the Alexamenos graffito, where a
crucified Jesus has the head of a donkey. Picture: the donkey-headed Seth depicted
in the Greek Magical Papyri; Rijksmuseum van Oudheden, Leiden; AMS 75, vel 1.*

B: *Gnostic imagery was later mixed with Egyptian one. The figure above shows
either Abraxas being identified with Anubis, the jackal-headed god, or a demiurgic
figure depicting Seth or Typhon, the ass-headed evil deity that was associated
with the God of the Jews. Picture: Westropp, Hodder Michael (1867). Handbook of
archaeology, Egyptian – Greek – Etruscan – Roman; p. 338.*

---

*119. Scholem, Gershom (1965). Jewish Gnosticism, Merkabah Mysticism, and the
Talmudic Tradition. The Jewish Theological Seminary of America.*

*120. Scholem, Gershom (1987). Origins of the Kabbalah. Princeton University
Press, pp. 21–22.*

*121. Litwa, M. David (2021). "The Donkey Deity". The Evil Creator: Origins of
an Early Christian Idea. New York, NY: Oxford University Press: "We see this
tradition recounted by several writers. Around 200 BCE, a man called Mnaseas
(an Alexandrian originally from what is now southern Turkey), told a story of
an Idumean (southern Palestinian) who entered the Judean temple and tore off
the golden head of a pack ass from the inner sanctuary. This head was evidently
attached to a body, whether human or donkey. The reader would have understood
that the Jews (secretly) worshiped Yahweh as a donkey in the Jerusalem temple,
since gold was characteristically used for cult statues of gods. Egyptians knew only
one other deity in ass-like form: Seth."*

The influence of Orphism, Neo-Pythagoreanism, and Platonism on Gnosticism have also been proposed,[122,123] but it is fair to note that Plotinus sharply criticized some of their doctrines, especially their view of the Demiurge as an evil tyrant.

Symbols in Gnosticism: Gnostic or Sun Cross; serpent motifs; Abraxas/Yaldabaoth (lion-headed serpent) stones, representing the First Principle (debated) and the Demiurge, respectively.

Recommended Reading

1. **The Secret Teachings of All Ages.** *Manly P.Hall.*
2. **The Doctrine and Ritual of High Magic.** *Éliphas Lévi.*
3. **The History of Magic.** *Éliphas Lévi.*
4. **Philosophical Lectures.** *Manly P.Hall.*
5. **An Encyclopedia of Occultism.** *Lewis Spence.*

---

122. *Albrile, Ezio (2005), "Gnosticism: History of Study", in Jones, Lindsay (ed.), MacMillan Encyclopedia of Religion. MacMillan, p. 3534.*

123. *Pearson, Birger A. (1984). Gnosticism as Platonism: With Special Reference to Marsanes (NHC 10,1). The Harvard Theological Review. 77 (1): 55–72.*

Technological Apotheosis:
Can Science Save Us?

Philosophical and Scientific Worldviews

Main Characteristics, Metaphysical Beliefs and their Implications

4. Philosophical Stances on Metaphysical Matters

IN ADDITION TO RELIGIOUS, MYSTICAL OR ESOTERIC worldviews, other set of metaphysical beliefs that can be classified as philosophical or science-based are also common in our days. In the following section we will briefly discuss some of the most prevalent ones.

Some of them, such as Transhumanism, are expected to play an important role in the future and everything seems to indicate that we will not be able to avoid taking a position on their validity and desirability.

4.1. Agnosticism

Agnosticism can be defined as two different positions regarding the knowability of the existence of God or the divine.

Soft (or temporal) Agnosticism is the position that affirms that right now it is not possible to know if God exists or not, but it is not closed to the possibility that this may change in the future.[1,2] Hard Agnosticism, to the contrary, affirms that we will never be able to know for sure.[3]

Contrary to what many may think, Agnosticism is not a modern phenomenon. Even religious scriptures like the *Rig Veda* had an agnostic view in some of its creation hymns.[4]

> *"But, after all, who knows, and who can say*
>
> *Whence it all came, and how creation happened?*
>
> *The gods themselves are later than creation,*
>
> *so who knows truly whence it has arisen?*
>
> *Whence all creation had its origin,*
>
> *He, whether he fashioned it or whether he did not,*
>
> *He, who surveys it all from highest heaven,*
>
> *He knows – or maybe even he does not know."*
>
> — Nasadiya Sukta (Hymn of Creation). Rig Veda, 10:129

---

1. *Oppy, Graham (2006). Arguing about Gods. Cambridge University Press, p. 15.*

2. *Robin Le Poidevin (October 28, 2010). Agnosticism: A Very Short Introduction. Oxford University Press, p. 32.*

3. *Hepburn, Ronald W. (1967). "Agnosticism". In Donald M. Borchert (ed.). The Encyclopedia of Philosophy. Vol. 1. MacMillan Reference USA (Gale), p. 92: "In the most general use of the term, agnosticism is the view that we do not know whether there is a God or not." (page 56, 1967 edition).*

4. *Singh, Upinder (2008). A History of Ancient and Early Medieval India: From the Stone Age to the 12th Century. Pearson Education India, p. 206.*

a. Main Metaphysical Beliefs of Agnosticism

Agnosticism is not a prescriptive philosophy. Apart from its scepticism on divine matters, it does not promote any particular metaphysical doctrine in subjects such as cosmology, the existence of evil or the conflict between determinism and free will. It also does not delineate a lifepath for its adherents.

However, holding a position of absolute incredulity regarding every metaphysical aspect is not a common one either, as not having an opinion about anything is not usually a fulfilling position to hold. Therefore, many agnostics tend to follow the scientific consensus of their time.

Even though Agnosticism is not a normative philosophy and does not prescribe a way of living, the impossibility of behaving in a metaphysically neutral way has, in effect, an unintended consequence: the de facto acceptance of the philosophical views of Pragmatism. Sometimes, a version of Relativism may also be adopted. The latter implies that each person becomes his or her own Monad or ultimate authority. Each member of the Many becomes the One.

4.2. Atheism

Atheism is defined as a negation of Theism. It states its absence of belief in the existence of any kind of deity. It can be understood as a philosophical position or even as a faith since, by definition, immanent beings such as ourselves cannot obtain conclusive evidence about a transcendent God.

Transcendent, non-testable "hypothesis" would include the God of Abrahamic religions. In contrast, the existence or non-existence of immanent deities (such as those of ancient mythologies or Neo-Paganism) could, in theory, be assessed by the scientific method.

Science could then disprove Polytheism, but it lacks the tools to answer the "God question" as posed by Monotheism and Trinitarian Christianity.

a. Main Metaphysical Beliefs of Atheism

Atheists are assumed to be irreligious or unspiritual. However, this is not always the case. Atheism, in the sense of negating the existence of a personal creator God, is compatible and viewed as a valid philosophical position in traditions such as the Hindu Sāṃkhya (the original philosophy of Yoga), Buddhism, Jainism, and in general with all the schools that view ultimate reality as a process, a law or a principle.

It is also compatible with some psychological interpretations of spiritual beliefs, were the deities are external representations of internal archetypes intrinsic to the human mind (e.g., Jungian-inspired psychological schools).

Most atheists tend to believe in the existence of only one fundamental substance underlying all reality (non-theistic Monism), usually in the form of matter (Materialism). Physicalism (everything that exists is physical) and Naturalism (no supernatural entities exist) are related philosophical views.[5]

Believers of the current scientific paradigm, if they are reductionists, may also be monists in another sense: believing that everything in reality can be eventually reduced to the laws of physics.

In this view, living beings can be reduced to complex chemical reactions, which in turn are a particular case of physical chemistry, which is a part of the physical sciences.

Physics, in turn, is composed of mathematical descriptions of the four main forces (gravity, electromagnetism, and the weak and strong nuclear forces), which are believed by many to be explainable by a single Theory of Everything or unified field theory. This is a purely intellectual way of going back to the One.

---

5. *Oppy, Graham (2019). Atheism: The Basics. Routledge, pp. 14-15.*

4.3. Secular Humanism

Secular Humanism can be described as a philosophy as well as a lifestance that defines itself as opposed to any religious dogma, considered as superstitious.[6]

It rejects the notions of faith and revelation and emphasizes the individual use of reason as the main source of authority from which to derive knowledge, primarily through science and philosophy.

a. Main Metaphysical Beliefs of Secular Humanism

Humanists believe that ethics and morality can be founded in human reason alone, without the need of God or any deity. Usually, this translates in following utilitarian or evolutionary ethics.

No ground for the preference of one system of ethics above others can be provided, however, as different ways of reasoning may obtain different conclusions of what is good.

For example, a survival of the fittest morality based on evolutionary theory and the good of the species over that of the individual can be rationally justified (Social Darwinism).

As in Atheism or Agnosticism, humanist views on traditional metaphysical doctrines such as the origin/creation of the world, the nature of time or free will are mostly derived from the accepted scientific theories of the day.

---

6. *Edwords, Fred (1989). What Is Humanism?. American Humanist Association: "Secular Humanism is an outgrowth of eighteenth century enlightenment rationalism and nineteenth century freethought... A decidedly anti-theistic version of secular humanism, however, is developed by Adolf Grünbaum, 'In Defense of Secular Humanism' (1995), in his Collected Works (edited by Thomas Kupka), vol. I, New York: Oxford University Press, ch. 6 (pp. 115–48)."*

a1. Auguste Comte and the Positivist School

Secularism was heavily influenced by Auguste Comte, the founder of Positivism and of modern Sociology. Positivism asserts that all true knowledge is either true by definition or can only be derived from reason, logic, and sensory experience.[7] This epistemological position sees other ways of obtaining knowledge, such as faith, intuition or mystical experiences as meaningless.

The metaphysical views of Comte included the necessary progression and evolution of human history in three stages: the theological, the metaphysical, and the fully rational or "positivist" age.

Later in life, however, Comte tried to create a "religion of humanity" to fulfill purely what he saw as the necessary cohesive role provided by religion but without the associated metaphysical beliefs. Nowadays, positivist temples can still be found.

Symbols in Humanism: the "Happy Human", the official international symbol of Humanism.

4.4. Nihilism 

Nihilism (nihil meaning "nothing") is a label applied to a group of related philosophical worldviews or attitudes towards life which reject the existence of important aspects of human experience. Common positions can be summarized as "life has no meaning" (Existential Nihilism), "morality and human values are arbitrary" (Moral Nihilism) or "there is no truth or, if there is, it is not possible to attain it" (Epistemological Nihilism).[8, 9]

---

7. *Larrain, Jorge (1979). The Concept of Ideology. London: Hutchinson, p. 197: "One of the features of positivism is precisely its postulate that scientific knowledge is the paradigm of valid knowledge, a postulate that indeed is never proved nor intended to be proved."*

8. *Veit, Walter (2018). Existential Nihilism: The Only Really Serious Philosophical Problem. Journal of Camus Studies, pp. 211–236.*

9. *Crosby, Donald A. (1998). "Nihilism". Routledge Encyclopedia of Philosophy. Taylor and Francis: "As its name implies (from Latin nihil, 'nothing'), philosophical nihilism is*

The modern popularization of Nihilism came through the philosopher Friedrich Nietzsche, who saw it as the defining characteristic of modern Western man and a sign of the decline of the times. According to numerous philosophers, Postmodernism (characterized by Skepticism, Subjectivism, and Relativism) has only aggravated the problem.[10, 11]

In Nietzsche´s philosophy, "evil" is characterized as everything that opposes an exuberant life-affirming attitude.

"A nihilist is a man who judges of the world as it is that it ought not to be, and of the world as it ought to be that it does not exist. According to this view, our existence (action, suffering, willing, feeling) has no meaning: the pathos of 'in vain' is the nihilists' pathos – at the same time, as pathos, an inconsistency on the part of the nihilists."

—Friedrich Nietzsche. The Will to Power. KSA 12:9, section 585

In mainstream consciousness, the term Nihilism has the connotations of despair due to the perceived pointlessness or arbitrariness of life. Dostoevsky's dictum "if God is dead, everything is permitted" is frequently used to encapsulate the overall feeling of these philosophies.

---

a philosophy of negation, rejection, or denial of some or all aspects of thought or life."

Pratt, Alan. "Nihilism". Internet Encyclopedia of Philosophy: "Nihilism is the belief that all values are baseless and that nothing can be known or communicated. It is often associated with extreme pessimism and a radical skepticism that condemns existence."

"Nihilism". Encyclopædia Britannica: "In the 20ᵗʰ century, nihilism encompassed a variety of philosophical and aesthetic stances that, in one sense or another, denied the existence of genuine moral truths or values, rejected the possibility of knowledge or communication, and asserted the ultimate meaninglessness or purposelessness of life or of the universe."

Harper, Douglas. "Nihilism". Online Etymology Dictionary.

10. Baudrillard, Jean (1993). "Game with Vestiges". In Baudrillard Live (ed. M. Gane). Routledge.

11. Baudrillard, Jean (1981). "On Nihilism." In Simulacra and Simulation (trans. S.F. Glasser). University of Michigan Press.

a. Active and Passive Nihilism

Instead of the passivity, emptiness, and resignation implied by the normal use of the term Nihilism, Nietzsche proposed an active form that works to willingly destroy the old values in order to make way for new ones. This was characterized by him as a sign of strength, vitality, and a healthy will to power, in contrast with the weakness and "will to nothingness" of common Nihilism. This would be the way of the Overman (Übermensch), the one able to achieve the "transvaluation of all values".

Passive Nihilism would tend to be fatalistic, while active Nihilism´s focus is on free will.

b. Metaphysical and Religious Nihilism

Nihilism, usually seen as a consequence or corollary to atheistic worldviews, can also be a part of spiritual or metaphysical ones.[12, 13]

The views of some Hindu and Buddhist schools, for example, have been called nihilistic. The Buddha himself mentioned this philosophy while discussing some of the sects of Hindu ascetics of his time. He described moral nihilists as those who believed that giving to others and good and bad actions had no corresponding results. These men did not see the danger of bad behavior.[14]

Buddhism itself has been sometimes considered to be a nihilistic philosophy, with some schools (Mahāyāna) accusing others (Theravāda) of being dangerously close to this belief. Nāgārjuna´s foundational school of the Middle Way considered it as one of the two extremes to avoid at all costs (the other being Eternalism or the belief that things have an eternal essence or nature).

---

12. *Gillespie, Michael Allen (1996). Nihilism Before Nietzsche. University of Chicago Press.*
13. *Deleuze, Gilles (1962). Nietzsche and Philosophy. London: The Athlone Press.*
14. *Bhikkhu Ñāṇamoli, and Bhikkhu Bodhi, trans. "Apannaka Sutta." In The Middle Length Discourses of the Buddha. Wisdom Publications. Note 425.*

> ## METAPHYSICAL NIHILISM AND SOLIPSISM
>
> There exist some extreme varieties of Nihilism, which instead of negating an aspect of existence negates existence itself. Based on an extreme form of Scepticism, Metaphysical Nihilism (or Ontological Nihilism) denies that anything exists at all.[15]
>
> A related worldview, no less extreme, is that of Solipsism. The difference is that despite the fact that both positions deny the true existence of any external reality (Anti-Realism), the nihilist also rejects the existence of the self, while the solipsist affirms himself as the only truly existing reality.[16]
>
> Both positions are monistic. The first position may be seen as having some similarities with Indian worldviews that see everything as manifestations of Emptiness and the common world we perceive as unreal, while the second resembles the Hindu concept of one´s Self being the Absolute (Brahman).

Ajahn Amaro, Theravāda Buddhist abbot, thought that modern translations of the Buddhist concept of Emptiness as Nothingness were part of the problem. No-thingness, he noted, would be a more accurate translation that emphasizes that Nirvana is not a thing but a state where the non-grasping of reality is experienced.[17]

4.5. Postmodernism and Relativism 

Postmodernism has been summarized as an intellectual stance[18] characterized by skepticism and incredulity towards grand narratives.[19]

---

15. *Turner, Jason (2011). Ontological Nihilism. Oxford University Press.*

16. *"Solipsism and the Problem of Other Minds". Internet Encyclopedia of Philosophy.*

17. *Pasanno, Ajahn; Amaro, Ajahn (2009). Knowing, Emptiness and the Radiant Mind. Forest Sangha Newsletter (88): 5.*

18. *Nuyen, A. T. (1992). The Role of Rhetorical Devices in Postmodernist Discourse. Philosophy & Rhetoric. Penn State University Press, 25 (2): 183–194.*

19. *Lyotard, J.-F. (1979). The Postmodern Condition: A Report on Knowledge. U. of Minnesota Press.*

For postmodernist views, truth is not an absolutely objective fact that has to be discovered, but is always contingent on a particular social and historical reality. Truth is relative.

Relativism, in turn, is a group of related philosophical worldviews that reject the objective value of different aspects of reality and assert that, depending on the context, they may be valued in one way or another.[20]

a. Different Types of Relativism

• *Moral Relativism:* the view that what is moral, good or worthy for one person need not be so for another person. Valuations of what is considered either moral or immoral can justifiably change depending on circumstances (e.g., cultural influences, upbringing).

• *Epistemic Relativism:* the view that what is true, rational or justified for one person need not be so for another person. The worth of every statement about truth is considered to be dependent on the particular perspective of the one evaluating it.

• *Factual Relativism (related with Cultural Relativism):* [21] the view that not only our conception of truth is relative, but also truth itself. A classic example would be the statement that "first-world science is one science among many".[22]

----

20. "Relativism". Stanford Encyclopedia of Philosophy:

"The label "relativism" has been attached to a wide range of ideas and positions which may explain the lack of consensus on how the term should be defined."

21. Baghramian, Maria and Carter, Adam. "Relativism". The Stanford Encyclopedia of Philosophy. Edward N. Zalta (ed.):

"Relativism about truth, or alethic relativism, at its simplest, is the claim that what is true for one individual or social group may not be true for another".

22. Feyerabend, Paul (1992). Against method. London [u.a.]: Verso. p. 3.

b. Main Metaphysical Beliefs of Postmodernism and Relativism

Given the above definitions of Postmodernism and Relativism, the adherence of the persons who hold these beliefs to stable metaphysical doctrines viewed as objective and eternal cannot be expected.

This is true except for the doctrine that everything is relative, which they believe to hold in all places and at all times, therefore being a contradictory or self-refuting worldview.[23] The statement "all is relative" is viewed as an absolute statement that negates the existence of absolute statements. Therefore, Relativism can be defined as an atheistic and monist view that makes the metaphysical claim that this law of relativity is the only one supreme truth that exists.

c. Relativism in Ancient Traditions

Relativism, even though it is usually thought to be opposed to religious and mystical worldviews, presents some similarities with the Buddhist view of impermanence and non-existence of a Self, as well as with the philosophy of the Buddhist Nāgārjuna and the Jain Mahāvīra.[24]

4.6. Objectivism

Objectivism is a worldview created by the writer and philosopher Ayn Rand. The name, explicitly enough, expresses the belief of its author in the external and objective nature of reality. Reality is to be discovered through our senses, and not created by one´s mind.[25]

---

23. Dixon, Keith. *Is Cultural Relativism Self-Refuting?*. *British Journal of Sociology*, vol 28, No. 1.

24. Kalupahana, David (1975). *Causality: The Central Philosophy of Buddhism*. *The University Press of Hawaii*, pp. 96–97. In the Nikayas the quote is found at SN 2.150.

25. Rand, Ayn (1966). *Capitalism: The Unknown Ideal*. *New York: Signet*.

The sources of objectivist philosophy are first and foremost the novels *The Fountainhead* and *Atlas Shrugged*, later expanded in non-fiction books and essays.[26] Leonard Peikoff, Rand´s successor, formalized this school of thought.[27]

a. Main Metaphysical Beliefs of Objectivism

Objectivist philosophy posits three primordial axioms: existence, consciousness, and identity.[28] The first axiom states that our experience of existence is the self-evident fact that is the origin of all other knowledge. The second, that an external independent reality exists, as consciousness does not exist until it is conscious of something.[29] The third, that to be is to be something in particular. That which has no attributes or nature cannot exist.

Objectivism rejects anything alleged to transcend existence, and considers that religions have now outlived their previous usefulness.[30]

For this worldview, reason and logic are absolute. All knowledge is empirical, comes through the senses, and the scientific outlook can be applied to all areas of knowledge.

One of the most famous traits of this philosophy is its endorsement of Rational Egoism. According to Rand, we should have no higher purpose in life than searching for our own happiness, with altruism (the placing of others above ourselves) viewed in a negative light. Altruism is considered harmful to both individuals and society. In direct opposition to all other worldviews previously summarized, selfishness is conceived as a virtue.

---

26. *Badhwar, Neera & Long, Roderick T. (2020). Zalta, Edward N. (ed.). "Ayn Rand". Stanford Encyclopedia of Philosophy.*

27. *McLemee, Scott (1999). The Heirs Of Ayn Rand: Has Objectivism Gone Subjective?. Lingua Franca, 9 (6): 45–55.*

28. *Peikoff, Leonard (1991). Objectivism: The Philosophy of Ayn Rand. New York: Dutton, pp. 4-11.*

29. *Ibid., p. 5.*

30. *Ibid., pp. 31–33.*

Good and evil are defined in relation and subordinated to the principle of life. Everything that preserves life is good, everything that endangers or destroys it, evil.

"The man who attempts to live for others is a dependent. He is a parasite in motive and makes parasites of those he serves. The relationship produces nothing but mutual corruption." [31]

— Ayn Rand. For the New Intellectual: The Philosophy of Ayn Rand

Rand, by celebrating what she saw as the heroic character of man, necessarily had to endorse free will over determinism, making it a fundamental causal power to initiate and direct our actions.

"My philosophy, in essence, is the concept of man as a heroic being, with his own happiness as the moral purpose of his life, with productive achievement as his noblest activity, and reason as his only absolute." [32]

—Ayn Rand. Atlas Shrugged

4.7. Stoicism

Stoicism is a school of thought that was born and developed in the ancient Greco-Roman world. After centuries of little discussion outside academic circles, its popularity has recently resurfaced, with the term Stoic now usually understood as meaning "patiently enduring life's adversities".[33] Due to this newfound popularity, authors such as Seneca and the Emperor Marcus Aurelius are still commonly read in our times.

---

31. *Ayn Rand (1961). For the New Intellectual: The Philosophy of Ayn Rand. Penguin books, p. 63.*

32. *Rand, Ayn (1957). Atlas Shrugged. New York: Dutton. "About the Author". in Rand (1992), pp. 1170–1171.*

33. *Harper, Douglas (2001). "Stoic". Online Etymology Dictionary (etymonline.com).*

The Stoics believed that the only prerequisite to lead a well-lived and fulfilling life (Eudaimonia) is the practice of virtue and having our will attuned to nature. Virtue, in their opinion, is the only good worthy of pursuit, with external goods (e.g., wealth and pleasure) seen as morally neutral but with the potential to be used in a virtuous way.

a. Main Metaphysical Beliefs of Stoicism

Nowadays, Stoicism is popular with a subset of the population that is searching for a meaningful way of living, although not necessarily a religious or spiritual one. The feeling that hard times are coming is looming in the horizon, and the philosophy of Stoicism seems like a good tool to have under our belt in order to be able to navigate the storm.

Classical Stoicism, however, was not an irreligious school of thought, even if metaphysics is not the main focus in many of its primary texts. Stoic metaphysics can be mainly characterized by three marks: Monism, Materialism, and Dynamism.[34]

a1. Stoic Monistic Thought: A Pantheist God

Stoicism is a pantheistic and naturalistic philosophy, since its immanent God is identified with the whole Universe and nature.[35] The Universe is seen as a single and cohesive entity[36], with the principle of Reason (Logos)[37] as the underlying reality behind any particular manifestation.[38]

The Logos is the creative force or law animating (Anima Mundi) and providing the seminal reasons (Logos Spermatikos) for the whole cosmos.

---

34. *Hicks, Robert Drew (1911). "Stoics". In Chisholm, Hugh (ed.). Encyclopædia Britannica. Vol. 25. Cambridge University Press, pp. 942–951.*

35. *Algra, Keimpe (2003). "Stoic Theology", in Inwood, Brad (ed.). The Cambridge Companion to the Stoics. Cambridge University Press, p. 167.*

36. *Sambursky, Samuel (1959). Physics of the Stoics, Routledge, p. 5.*

37. *Long, A.A. (1996). "Heraclitus and Stoicism". Stoic Studies. U. of California Press, p. 45.*

38. *Ibid., p. 46.*

It was thought of as a material entity that impregnated all creation, at first as intelligent Aether or primordial fire, later as breath (Pneuma). From it everything is believed to proceed and to it everything returns.

"The universe itself is God and the universal outpouring of its soul; it is this same world's guiding principle, operating in mind and reason, together with the common nature of things and the totality that embraces all existence; then the foreordained might and necessity of the future; then fire and the principle of aether; then those elements whose natural state is one of flux and transition, such as water, earth, and air; then the sun, the moon, the stars; and the universal existence in which all things are contained."

—Chrysippus. In Cicero, De Natura Deorum, i. 39

"Constantly regard the universe as one living being, having one substance and one soul; and observe how all things have reference to one perception, the perception of this one living being; and how all things act with one movement; and how all things are the cooperating causes of all things that exist; observe too the continuous spinning of the thread and the structure of the web."

—Marcus Aurelius. Meditations, iv. 40

In addition, classical Stoicism attempted to integrate traditional Polytheism into its philosophy.[39] God, for example, was identified with Zeus as both a universal ruler and a cosmic law.[40] Divinity could manifest in many ways, including as impersonal heavenly bodies, forces of nature, and even deified humans.[41] This is coherent with Greek Henotheism,

---

39. Hicks, Robert Drew (1911). "Stoics". In Chisholm, Hugh (ed.). Encyclopædia Britannica. Vol. 25. Cambridge University Press, p. 947.

40. Frede, Dorothea (2003). "Stoic Determinism". In Inwood, Brad (ed.), The Cambridge Companion to the Stoics. Cambridge University Press, pp. 201-202.

41. Hicks, Robert Drew (1911). "Stoics". In Chisholm, Hugh (ed.). Encyclopædia Britannica. Vol. 25. Cambridge University Press, p. 947.

especially supported by educated persons in Late Antiquity. This vision considered all divinities as different parts, aspects or descriptions of the One God, similar to Hindu thought.[42]

a2. A Dual Universe: Dynamism

As we have seen, Stoic thinking is mostly monistic, as they believe in a classical pantheist version of God. However, they differentiate all that exists into two principles: the active and the passive. The former is God or the Rational Principle (Logos), while the latter is matter, a subordinate principle.[43]

This is similar to the Hindu thought of the Sāṃkhya school, which divides ultimate reality into Spirit (Purusha) and Matter (Prakriti).

It is also similar to any other tradition that conceives reality as an interplay of the complementary masculine principle of reason or potentiality (e.g., the passive Shiva) and the feminine principle of energy or actuality (e.g., the active Shakti).[44]

The position of classical Stoicism regarding the relationship between these two principles is not clear. Given their previously discussed pantheistic vision, it is likely they saw them as two aspects of the same unified ultimate reality.[45]

------

42. *Kahlos, Maijastina (2007). Debate and Dialogue: Christian and pagan cultures. Ashgate Publishing, c. 360–430.*

43. *Algra, Keimpe (2003). "Stoic Theology". In Inwood, Brad (ed.), The Cambridge Companion to the Stoics. Cambridge University Press, p. 167.*

44. *The adjectives active and passive are not homogeneously assigned to the same sex in different traditions, with the female consorts being sometimes the passive aspect of the totality (e.g., Tibetan Buddhism).*

45. *Sellars, John (2006). Ancient Philosophies: Stoicism. Acumen, p. 90.*

a3. On Creation and Time

Mankind, similar to Lurianic Kabbalah and Gnostic creation myths, is conceived as possessing a fragment of the Logos in them. Also similar to the myth of Narcissus, this portion is seen as immersed in nature itself.[46] This, in turn, is believed to make humans capable of achieving divine rationality and to attune their will to the natural law of the Universe, which is the Logos itself.[47]

Regarding the soul, it is thought to be material. In this way, it is able to have extension in space and animate physical bodies. The only non-material aspects of reality accepted by classical Stoicism were: time, place, void, and sayable.[48]

As for the creation of the Universe, Stoicism believes in the theory of emanations from the Logos. Cosmology and time, similar to Indian thought, are considered cyclical and infinite. Universal cycles repeat themselves and are separated by a period of destruction (Ekpyrōsis, not universally accepted) and re-creation (Eternal Return).[49]

During this conflagration period, things are believed to be gradually dissolved into their constituent elements, until everything is re-absorbed into the One God. The Logos becomes, then, the only existing being until a new cycle of creation (Palingenesis) begins.[50] No beginning and no end are conceived for time and space.[51]

---

46. *Karamanolis, George E. (2013). "Free will and divine providence". The Philosophy of Early Christianity. Ancient Philosophies. New York and London: Routledge, p. 151.*

47. *Tripolitis, A. Religions of the Hellenistic-Roman Age. Wm. B. Eerdmans Publishing, pp. 37–38.*

48. *Sextus Empiricus. Adversus Mathematicos, 10.218 (chronos, topos, kenon, lekton).*

49. *Lapidge, Michael (1978). "Stoic Cosmology". In John M. Rist, The Stoics. Cambridge University Press, pp. 182–183.*

50. *White, Michael J. (2003). "Stoic Natural Philosophy (Physics and Cosmology)". In Inwood, Brad (ed.), The Cambridge Companion to the Stoics. Cambridge University Press, p. 137.*

51. *Ferguson, Everett (2003). Backgrounds of Early Christianity. Eerdmans, p. 368.*

a4. On the Problem of Evil

Stoics primarily believed that, given that God is the Universe itself and the Principle of Reason, this is the best of all possible worlds.[52]

The goodness of the cosmos shows itself in the rational order in which everything is arranged.[53] Therefore, no natural event is seen as being intrinsically bad, including sickness and death. They are just conceived as morally indifferent. Their value resides in giving us the possibility of living a life in tune with the natural order.[54]

The only inherent evil conceivable for a classic Stoic was willing human irrational behavior. This way of acting was seen as madness and the consequence of the alienation of the rational principle inside us.[55]

a5. On Determinism and Free Will

The tension between Fate and free will was deeply felt by Stoics. For them, the Principle of Reason (Logos) is present everywhere in nature. Due to the cohesive unity between everything that exists, this implies a deterministic stance.[56]

However, Stoic determinism is characterized as a "soft-determinism" that tries to make it compatible with free will. It allows humans to be moral agents responsible for their own behavior, instead of puppets of a pre-determined Fate.[57]

---

52. *Frede, Michael (1999). "On the Stoic Conception of the Good". In Ierodiakonou, Katerina (ed.), Topics in Stoic Philosophy. Oxford University Press, p. 75.*

53. *Brennan, Tad (2005). The Stoic Life: Emotions, Duties, and Fate. Oxford University Press, p. 239.*

54. *Christensen, Johnny (2012). An Essay on the Unity of Stoic Philosophy. Museum Tusculanum Press. University of Copenhagen, p. 70.*

55. *Ibid., p. 64.*

56. *White, M. J. (2003), "Stoic Natural Philosophy (Physics and Cosmology)". In Inwood, Brad (ed.), The Cambridge Companion to the Stoics. Cambridge University Press, p. 139.*

57. *Sambursky, Samuel (1959). Physics of the Stoics. Routledge, p. 65.*

This is achieved by positing that each individual will is a causal factor participating in a complex network of interactions with each other inside the general framework of Fate. The result is a multi-faceted law of causality composed of freely willed actions that come together to form a pre-determined chain of events.[58]

The practice of virtue and being attuned to nature and to one´s internal Logos, in fact, is viewed as the best way to achieve the maximum degree of freedom and autonomy in this deterministic world. If not in a physical or external way, at least internally, as Epictetus expressed when he defined the free virtuous man as "sick and yet happy, in peril and yet happy, dying and yet happy, in exile and happy, in disgrace and happy." [59] A passion-bound man, in contrast, is considered as "[...] a dog tied to a cart, and compelled to go wherever it goes." [60]

The deterministic aspect of Stoic thought allowed for the practice and rationalization of divination techniques, common to all Greek traditions.

b. The Stoic Path: Virtue Ethics

Stoicism emphasizes the pursuit of virtue as the main focus of human activity. Virtue is defined, as in Taoism, as a will that is in agreement with nature and its underlying rational order.

The path to achieve virtue and to become a wise man includes the development of fortitude and self-control in order to be free of passions (Apatheia). In turn, this is believed to allow one to become a clear thinker able to understand the Logos and its universal order.[61]

---

58. *Ibid., p. 77.*

59. *Russell, Bertrand. A History of Western Philosophy. Simon & Schuster, p. 264.*

60. *Ibid., p. 254.*

61. *Inwood, Brad (1999). "Stoic Ethics". In Algra, Keimpe; Barnes, Johnathan; Mansfield, Jaap; Schofield, Malcolm (eds.), The Cambridge History of Hellenistic Philosophy. Cambridge University Press, p. 705.*

Prayer for divine intervention was not favored, since the work needed was mostly of an intellectual nature.

Figure 1. The Consolation of Philosophy. Stoicism attempted to offer a worldview and way of life that could lead to happiness through virtue, even in hard external conditions. Modern Neo-Stoicism, however, although attracted by the concept of Stoic virtue and the vision of masculinity with which it is associated, mostly avoids taking a stand on classical Stoic metaphysics. Doctrines such as our world being the best of all possible worlds are not easy to accept for a contemporary mindset. Picture: Boethius and Philosophy, oil on canvas; by Mattia Preti, 17th century.

4.8. Anarchism

Anarchism, first of all considered as a political theory, can also be thought of as a philosophy that can be applied to multiple domains of life. In this sense, it is characterized by a rejection of any form of centralized and hierarchical authority structure. Central to its beliefs is the moral claim that ending these kinds of power structures would equal to the achievement of individual freedom and promote equality, collaboration, and creativity.

The term Anarchism is derived from the Greek term *Arché*, meaning first, founding or ruling principle. Therefore, anarchy is the striving to be liberated from such a First Principle, the view that no one is legitimized to be at the top, ruling over the many.

a. Political Anarchism

Political anarchists critique the existence of centralized, monopolistic states, viewed as coercing the citizens by having exclusive control over violence (police, military). They are sometimes viewed as literal criminal organizations working only for themselves.[62]

"If there is a State, there must be domination of one class by another and, as a result, slavery; the State without slavery is unthinkable—and this is why we are the enemies of the State."

— Michael Bakunin (1873). Statism and Anarchy [1990: 178]

"If God really existed, it would be necessary to abolish him."

— Michael Bakunin (1882). God and the State [1970: 28]

b. Methodological Anarchism

Anarchism can also be understood as a critique of methodologies that limit the creativity of the individual. For example, Paul Feyerabend in his book *Against Method* noted that in the scientific world it is usually more fruitful to work under a "theoretical anarchist" framework. He believed that this type of framework does not confine the freedom of the scientist to the narrow limits allowed by the existing accepted theories and strict rule following of conventional science.

"Science is an essentially anarchic enterprise: theoretical anarchism is more humanitarian and more likely to encourage progress than its law-and-order alternatives."

— Paul Feyerabend (1975). Against Method [1993: 9]

---

62. *Casey, Gerard (2012). Libertarian Anarchy: Against the State. Continuum.*

c. Naïve Anarchism and Pragmatism

Since a metaphysically neutral lifestance is an impossibility, even those persons that naively think that they act just in their best interests, following their own will and nothing more, are acting under the presuppositions of an anarchic worldview.

The naïve Anarchism of those who pragmatically decide to focus on the problems of material everyday life and just follow their own will is, consciously or not, rejecting either the existence of a directing principle, or rebelling against its perceived unworthiness. Through their behavior, they are asserting the primacy of the Many over the One.

"A radical pragmatist is a happy-go-lucky anarchistic sort of creature."

— William James.[63] Pragmatism

Pragmatism, like Anarchism and any other anti-systematic worldview, rejects or does not deem possible to find a stable foundation (Arché) capable of guiding us through life.

d. Religious Anarchism

Given its scepticism regarding first principles, it is not surprising that Anarchism has historically been hostile to organized religion.

There exist, however, similarities with the core doctrines of certain mystical traditions (see similarities with Taoism in Rapp[64] and with Islamic Sufism in Ramnath[65]).

---

63. *James, William. (1907). Pragmatism [1981: 116]. James was the founder of American Pragmatism.*

64. *Rapp, John A. (2012). Daoism and Anarchism: Critiques of State Autonomy in Ancient and Modern China (Contemporary Anarchist Studies). Bloomsbury Academic.*

65. *Ramnath, Maia (2011). Decolonizing Anarchism: An Antiauthoritarian History of India's Liberation Struggle. AK Press.*

e. The Metaphysical Beliefs of Anarchism

Anarchism is compatible with worldviews that affirm an origin of the world that does not proceed from non-existence to existence through the action of a single Creator Being.[66, 67]

This includes worldviews where the Universe has no beginning and no end such as Buddhism and Taoism, where "being and non-being produce each other".[68]

Instead of the common mythological narrative of the principle of Order triumphing over Chaos, the latter is viewed as the primordial ground of All-Possibility, actualized directly by each individual in their self-creative act of becoming. Each person then becomes their own "Chaos-slaying hero", without creation nor salvation coming from a hierarchically superior Principle or God.

Thus, since there is no guiding principle common to all, each individual is the actualization of one of the myriad possibilities and perspectives contained within "Chaos". The actual Universe is, then, not a Uni-verse but a type of Multi-verse, in which each man is a Universe unto himself.

The denial of a First Principle and of a single act of creation seems to imply the affirmation of the Many over the One. However, this is not always the case.

Given the above, Anarchism is not only compatible, but even shares a similar metaphysical outlook with worldviews that believe in an ultimate

---

66. *Bauer, Wolfgang (1976). China and the Search for Happiness (trans. Michael Saw). New York: Seabury Pres, pp. 6–7,351,428 and Giardot, N.J. (1976). "The Problem of Creation Mythology in the Study of Chinese Religion". History of Religions, 15, No. 4, pp. 289–318.*

67. *L.Hall, David (1983). The Metaphysics of Anarchism. Journal of Chinese Philosophy, Volume 10, Issue 1, pp. 49–63.*

68. *Tao Te Ching (trans. Wing-tsit Chan, 1963). In A Source Book in Chinese Philosophy. Princeton: Princeton University Press, Ch. 2, p. 140.*

reality described as the totality of all the unique but equally valued possibilities self-generated from emptiness, the Absolute understood as All-Possibility, or Chaos. No transcendent Principle that determines any of the particular possibilities is accepted, but being and non-being are seen as implying and creating each other (similar to non-dual worldviews).

5. The Scientific Outlook

We could not finish our brief overview of the current most prevalent worldviews without speaking about modern science and Transhumanism.

The former has had an immense influence in shaping not only the physical world around us but also in the way we conceive our world and reality to be.

The latter is bound to have an important influence in the technocratic world to come, and also makes some metaphysical claims about how reality works and to what extent we can manipulate it to our advantage.

Science is important because, nowadays, many people have delegated on it the responsibility of deciding what is true or false regarding the ultimate nature of reality. The rapid technological innovations and increased quality of life obtained especially through the nineteenth and twentieth centuries have given science and engineering an aura of prestige and proven reliability.

In addition, its ubiquitous presence in mainstream media and the educational system cannot be matched by any other worldview. Thanks to that, science has become the dominant discourse of secular countries, the gold standard and criteria with which to judge any other worldview which makes truth claims.

However, science is not a worldview. It is a method: the scientific method. As a method, it has worked wonders in improving tremendously human life conditions (e.g., antibiotics, heating and electricity, fertilizers, transport systems). As a method, it has also invented great terrors that have made life worse for many (e.g., nuclear bombs, industrial farming for billions of animals[69], the excessive presence of chemicals in our diets). As a method, as it cannot be otherwise, science is neutral. It is only as harmful or beneficial as the people who use it, depending on their intentions and their personal and collective limitations.

The claims of science to be a complete and independent worldview, nevertheless, are quite modern. Historically, important figures in the history of science saw no conflict in being religious or holding mystical and even esoteric views while trusting in the scientific method.

Newton, for example, was an heterodox Christian and an Alchemist, while Einstein and Schrodinger held some metaphysical and religious views ranging from some form of Pantheism to Eastern mystical conceptions of the One.

"There is obviously only one alternative, namely the unification of minds or consciousnesses. Their multiplicity is only apparent, in truth there is only one mind. This is the doctrine of the Upanishads."

— Erwin Schrödinger (1944). What is life?
Epilogue: On Determinism and Free Will

---

69. *As can be clearly seen in multiple undercover investigations, or the documentaries "Earthlings" (www.dailymotion.com/video/x2vd2a7) and "Food, Inc.", among others.*

The belief, sometimes found in some religious people, that persons interested in spiritual matters should not care about animals and creation is a dialectical (Either/ Or) way of thinking that considers Spirit intrinsically incompatible with Matter and non-rational beings.

Dharmic religions are notorious for caring about all forms of life, in part because of their doctrines of Reincarnation and Karma. However, this should also be the case for believers of Trinitarian Christianity (and especially Orthodox Christianity) due to its concern to avoid any false dialectical dilemmas, its Both/And logic, its unique solution to the problem of the One and the Many, and to honor God´s willed creation.

The, so often encountered, ideological associations between "left wing politics/vegetarian or vegan/atheist or spiritual but not religious" and "right wing politics/eats lots of meat and thinks animals are irrelevant/traditionally religious" are dialectical charicatures that do not derive from the correctly understood metaphysics of, for example, Non-Dualism or Trinitarian Christianity. In fact, they are incompatible with them.

Giving to science the responsibility of being the arbiter of truth in metaphysical matters is a contradiction in terms and a disservice to it. As an immanent method based on empirical observation, by definition, science can neither gain knowledge about any transcendent reality nor evaluate its claims.

If it exists, this transcendent reality and the world in which we currently live in would be part of different ontological planes of existence. It is obvious that God´s realm, if He exists (whatever our concept of God may be), cannot be directly known by someone in our world. The inferior reality cannot, not even in principle, directly know the superior one by relying only on its own means.

The most that science can study and disprove is the plausibility of the claims of polytheistic and completely immanent definitions of the divinity. For example, the existence of Greek personal deities believed to be a part of our world could be judged as highly improbable by current scientific observations. At most, it could be said that ancient Greeks personified the forces of nature. However, the existence of a transcendent God cannot be evaluated by science. Anything outside the possibility of physical observation and measurability cannot be the legitimate concern of science, as it lacks the tools necessary to tackle these issues.

Given the above, assigning to science the status of a worldview that can address metaphysical matters is a conceptual error, while using it as a method to obtain knowledge about how our physical reality operates has demonstrated time and again its enormous potential. This conceptual error, eventually, took the form of Scientism.

5.1. Scientism: The Transformation of Science From a Method to an All-Encompassing Worldview

The scientific method is a methodology used in a rigorous and systematic way in order to build and organize knowledge derived from measurable experiments. It derives its knowledge from sensory experience (Empiricism) and mathematical deductions, developing testable explanations and predictions about how the world works.

Scientism, on the other hand, is the worldview and faith that affirms that science is the best or only objective way through which we can (and should) obtain knowledge about how our reality operates, thus being the only valid source of our values and beliefs.

The term Scientism, in addition, has frequently been used as a critique[70] to overly dogmatic and reductionistic tendencies that propose science as the measure and judge of all metaphysical beliefs.[71, 72, 73] It has the pejorative connotation[74] of an exaggerated confidence in the efficacy of the methods of Natural Science when applied to any other areas of life.

No worldview that attempts to explain how all of reality works, however, can avoid making some metaphysical assumptions and assertions, even if they are based on science. Therefore, one can accept and value science while rejecting Scientism as its improper, philosophically unsound, use in matters that are beyond the scope of scientific inquiry or where there is insufficient empirical evidence available.

---

70. Beale, Jonathan (2019). Scientism and scientific imperialism. International Journal of Philosophical Studies, 27 (1): 73–102: "There are also several philosophers, in addition to Wittgenstein, for whom anti-scientism is a leitmotif in their work (e.g., Mary Midgley and Hilary Putnam)."

71. Putnam, Hilary (1992). Renewing Philosophy. Cambridge, MA: Harvard University Press, p. x.

72. Wieseltier, Leon (2013). Crimes Against Humanities. The New Republic.

73. Lears, T.J. Jackson (2013). "Get Happy!!". The Nation: "...scientism is a revival of the nineteenth-century positivist faith that a reified "science" has discovered (or is about to discover) all the important truths about human life. Precise measurement and rigorous calculation, in this view, are the basis for finally settling enduring metaphysical and moral controversies—explaining consciousness and choice, replacing ambiguity with certainty."

74. Chargaff, Irwin (1997). In Dispraise of Reductionism. BioScience, 47 (11): 795–7.

THE STRUCTURE OF SCIENTIFIC REVOLUTIONS

The book *The Structure of Scientific Revolutions* was influential in explaining how science has historically developed and in dispelling the myth that it can be a completely metaphysically neutral and objective endeavour.

Written by the historian and philosopher of science Thomas S. Kuhn, it introduced the concept of Paradigm Shift to explain that science does not change in a gradual linear way, but instead undergoes periods of crisis that change the fundamental beliefs of the scientific community as a whole.

These periods are based on the consensus of the community and often include competing and non-compatible (incommensurable) views of how reality works.

The image of pure detached objectivity that is presupposed of science was not found by Kuhn to correspond with reality.

Ultimately, the scientific community is formed of persons living according to their particular worldviews and presuppositions.

5.2. Common Metaphysical Beliefs Behind Some Mainstream Scientific Theories

Science does not provide a dogmatically and universally accepted creed on metaphysical notions. It also does not prescribe a normative path to follow to lead a meaningful life, with the exception of the implicit recommendation of living rationally and critically. As a method and as a repository of collective knowledge, that is not its role. However, some generalities can be said regarding the prevailing scientific outlook.

Although not always the case, especially since the advent of Quantum Mechanics, the very nature of physical sciences has traditionally favored mechanistic, deterministic, and reductionist interpretations of reality.

Also, most scientific theories tend to reject the idea that reality, natural processes or laws of physics have any ultimate end or purpose (Telos). Any hint of purpose, direction or finality underlying the laws of nature is seen with suspicion, since only impersonal forces and laws are presupposed and accepted to be the ultimate layer of reality.

Consequently, the overall classical scientific view of the Universe tends to be that of a more or less deterministic and purposeless closed system in which energy is constantly being exchanged and transformed (but not destroyed), always tending towards increasingly disordered states due to the laws of Thermodynamics.

Some of these assumptions, however, such as the closedness of the system, would be near impossible to prove. Therefore, as with any other system of thought based on human rationality (and not, for example, on the acceptance of some revelation), the starting axioms are selected because the community believes them to be either self-evident or plausible enough.

Sometimes it is asserted that "all truth is empirical", but this statement is in itself self-contradictory because it is a non-empirical statement, being instead an epistemological and metaphysical claim.

a1. Cosmological Views

The Big Bang and the Big Crunch(es)

Some of the models of the currently accepted theory regarding the birth of our Universe, the Big Bang theory, predict the existence of an initial singularity in which all the energy released later in the birth and expansion of our Universe was contained.

This singularity, similar to the ancient concept of the Absolute, All-Possibility or the One in which all is contained, is conceived as not being subject to the laws of physics as we know them (it "transcends" them).[75]

In some models (e.g., Loop Quantum Gravity model), the expansion of the Universe following the Big Bang is predicted to reverse (Big Crunch) until a new singularity is reached.

---

75. *Wall, Mike (2011). The Big Bang: What Really Happened at Our Universe's Birth?. The History & Future of the Cosmos (Space.com).*

Some of these theories also predict a cyclical Universe of recurring Big Bangs and Big Crunches, including the Big Bounce model that forecasts that each new Universe would have a new set of different physical constants, therefore relativizing the laws of physics.

Current experiments have, however, led scientists to believe that the expansion of the Universe is not actually slowing down but accelerating, invalidating (for now) these cyclical hypothesis.

The Multiverse

Opposing the idea that our Universe is the only one that exists, the Multiverse theory states that our Universe is just one of many born out of random quantum fluctuations.[76] This theory has famous supporters (e.g., Max Tegmark[77], Michio Kaku[78], Neil deGrasse Tyson[79], Stephen Hawking[80]) as well as detractors (e.g., Roger Penrose[81], George Ellis[82], Paul Davies[83]).

----

76. *Atkinson, Nancy (2008). Thinking About Time Before the Big Bang. Universe Today.*

77. *Tegmark, Max (2003). Parallel Universes. Scientific American. 288 (5): 40–51.*

78. *Guth, Alan. Inflationary Cosmology: Is Our Universe Part of a Multiverse?. Slice of MIT.*

79. *Freeman, David (2014). Why Revive 'Cosmos?' Neil DeGrasse Tyson Says Just About Everything We Know Has Changed (Huffingtonpost.com).*

80. *Carr, Bernard (2007). Universe or Multiverse. Cambridge University Press, p. 19: "Some physicists would prefer to believe that string theory, or M-theory, will answer these questions and uniquely predict the features of the Universe. Others adopt the view that the initial state of the Universe is prescribed by an outside agency, code-named God, or that there are many universes, with ours being picked out by the anthropic principle. Hawking argued that string theory is unlikely to predict the distinctive features of the Universe. But neither is he is an advocate of God. He therefore opts for the last approach, favoring the type of multiverse which arises naturally within the context of his own work in quantum cosmology."*

81. *Woit, Peter (2015). "CMB @ 50". Not Even Wrong.*

82. *Ellis, George F.R. (2011). Does the Multiverse Really Exist?. Scientific American, 305 (2): 38–43.*

83. *Davies, Paul (2003). A Brief History of the Multiverse. The New York Times.*

These parallel universes may or may not share the same laws of physics and fundamental physical constants. The fact that they don´t have to share them has been used to explain why our Universe is apparently fine-tuned to allow the existence of conscious life. This is because in a Multiverse containing many universes (maybe even an infinite number of them) with different fundamental physical constants, it is only natural that a small number of them happen to be capable of producing intelligent life. This is called the Anthropic Principle, of which there are many different versions.

Critics say that the fact that an infinite or almost infinite number of unobservable universes are proposed just to explain the apparent fine-tuning of ours and thus discard the possibility of a theistic hand in the matter is extreme and unscientific, as far as it is not testable. They also affirm that the Principle of Parsimony usually used to decide between competing scientific hypotheses (Occam's razor: "entities must not be multiplied beyond necessity") is violated.[84, 85]

"For a start, how is the existence of the other universes to be tested? To be sure, all cosmologists accept that there are some regions of the universe that lie beyond the reach of our telescopes, but somewhere on the slippery slope between that and the idea that there is an infinite number of universes, credibility reaches a limit. As one slips down that slope, more and more must be accepted on faith, and less and less is open to scientific verification. Extreme multiverse explanations are therefore reminiscent of theological discussions.

Indeed, invoking an infinity of unseen universes to explain the unusual features of the one we do see is just as ad hoc as invoking an unseen Creator. The multiverse theory may be dressed up in scientific language, but in essence, it requires the same leap of faith."

— Paul Davies (2003). A Brief History of the Multiverse. The New York Times.

---

84. Barry, C. M. (2014). Who sharpened Occam's Razor?. Irish Philosophy.

85. Schaffer, Jonathan (2015). What Not to Multiply Without Necessity. Australasian Journal of Philosophy, 93 (4): 644–664.

The Quantum Mechanics Version of the Multiverse: The Many-Worlds Interpretation

The mathematical equations used to formulate Quantum Mechanics, and thus, how our reality works at the fundamental level, can be interpreted in many different ways.

The Many-Worlds Interpretation (MWI) is one of the most popular ones. It follows the philosophical belief that all possible outcomes of quantum observations or measurements exist in one Universe or another.[86]

This implies that new universes are being constantly created.[87] In fact, it implies the existence of probably an indefinite number of universes and, therefore, of a Multiverse.[88]

Contrary to some other interpretations, the MWI theory is deterministic.[89]

Simulation Theory and the Holographic Universe

The Simulation Hypothesis, in turn, is the scientific version of the recurrent idea that we live in a simulated reality, usually inside a computer simulation.

---

86. *Tegmark, Max (1998). The Interpretation of Quantum Mechanics: Many Worlds or Many Words?. Fortschritte der Physik, 46 (6–8): 855–862.*

87. *DeWitt, Bryce S. (1970). Quantum mechanics and reality. Physics Today, 23 (9): 30–35. See also Ballentine, Leslie E.; Pearle, Philip; Walker, Evan Harris; Sachs, Mendel; Koga, Toyoki; Gerver, Joseph; DeWitt, Bryce (1971). Quantum-mechanics debate. Physics Today, 24 (4): 36–44.*

88. *Osnaghi, Stefano; Freitas, Fabio; Olival Freire, Jr (2009). The Origin of the Everettian Heresy. Studies in History and Philosophy of Modern Physics, 40 (2): 97–123.*

89. *Everett, Hugh; Wheeler, J. A.; DeWitt, B. S.; Cooper, L. N.; Van Vechten, D.; Graham, N. (1973). DeWitt, Bryce; Graham, R. Neill (eds.). The Many-Worlds Interpretation of Quantum Mechanics. Princeton Series in Physics. Princeton University Press, p. v.*

This notion pre-supposes that cognition is just a form of computation, and has both fervent supporters (e.g., Neil Degrasse Tyson, Elon Musk[90]) and detractors.[91, 92]

Some methods have actually been proposed to test this theory.[93,94] However, critics have explained that this hypothesis is both unprovable and unfalsifiable because, even if true, we could never rule out the possibility of being part of a nested simulation.

A nested type of simulation would mean that, even if evidence of a real world outside our simulated one was found, that other world and the beings running our simulated reality could also just be simulations themselves, thus incurring in an unsolvable problem of infinite regress.[95, 96]

Another theory that states that our reality may not be as real as we think is the Holographic Principle hypothesis (which is a property of

---

90. *"Elon Musk Says There's a 'One in Billions' Chance Reality Is Not a Simulation". Vice.com, 2 June 2016.*

91. *Hossenfelder, Sabine (February 13, 2021). "The Simulation Hypothesis is Pseudoscience". BackReAction.*

92. *Ellis, George (2012). "The multiverse: conjecture, proof, and science".*

93. *Beane, Silas R.; Davoudi, Zohreh; J. Savage, Martin (2014). Constraints on the universe as a numerical simulation. The European Physical Journal, A. 50 (9): 148.*

94. *Campbell, Tom; Owhadi, Houman; Sauvageau, Joe; Watkinson, David (2017). "On Testing the Simulation Theory". International Journal of Quantum Foundations, 3 (3): 78–99.*

95. *Bostrom, Nick (2009). The Simulation Argument: Some Explanations. Oxford University Press, Vol. 69, No. 3, pp. 458-461: "If each first-level ancestor-simulation run by the non-Sims requires more resources (because they contain within themselves additional second-level ancestor-simulations run by the Sims), the non-Sims might well respond by producing fewer first-level ancestor-simulations. Conversely, the cheaper it is for the non-Sims to run a simulation, the more simulations they may run. It is therefore unclear whether the total number of ancestor-simulations would be greater if Sims run ancestor-simulations than if they do not."*

96. *Pooch, U.W.; Sullivan, F.J. (2000). Recursive simulation to aid models of decisionmaking. Winter Simulation Conference Proceedings (Vol. 1) (Winter ed.), pp. 958–963.*

string theories, such as M-theory and its eleven dimensions). Leonard Susskind, one of its developers, clarified the implications of this hypothesis when he stated in no uncertain terms:

"The three-dimensional world of ordinary experience––the universe filled with galaxies, stars, planets, houses, boulders, and people––is a hologram, an image of reality coded on a distant two-dimensional surface." [97]

b. Some Parallels with Traditional Worldviews

The idea of the existence of a plurality of worlds is not as new as we may think. Its original formulation can be traced back to ancient Greece, more specifically to the Atomist school (its most famous exponent being Democtritus) and the Stoics.[98, 99, 100]

---

97. *Susskind, L. (2008). The Black Hole War – My Battle with Stephen Hawking to Make the World Safe for Quantum Mechanics. Little, Brown and Company, p. 410.*

98. *Dick, Steven J. (1984). Plurality of Words: The Extraterrestrial Life Debate from Democritus to Kant. Cambridge University Press, pp. 6–10: "Why should other worlds have become the subject of scientific discourse, when they were neither among the phenomena demanding explanation?... it derived from the cosmogonic assumption of ancient atomism: the belief that the constituent bodies of the cosmos are formed by the chance coalescence of moving atoms, the same type of indivisible particles of which matter on Earth was composed... Given the occurrence of these natural processes, and the obvious example of potential stability revealed in our own finite world, it was not unreasonable to suppose the existence of other stable conglomerations. The atomists further employed the principle that when causes were present, effects must occur. Atoms were the agents of causality and their number was infinite. The effect was innumerable worlds in formation, in collision, and in decay."*

99. *Rubenstein, Mary-Jane (2014). "Ancient Openings of Multiplicity". Worlds Without End: The Many Lives of the Multiverse. Columbia University Press., pp. 40–69.*

100. *Sedacca, Matthew (2017). The Multiverse Is an Ancient Idea. Nautilus: "The earliest hints of the multiverse are found in two ancient Greek schools of thought, the Atomists and the Stoics. The Atomists, whose philosophy dates to the fifth century B.C., argued that that the order and beauty of our world was the accidental product of atoms colliding in an infinite void. The atomic collisions also give rise to an endless number of other, parallel worlds less perfect than our own."*

If we try to compare these theories to traditional worldviews, we find that the existence of an unfathomable number of universes, as well as the cyclical cosmology of some of the models we have briefly mentioned, are compatible and in some cases even similar to traditional Indian cosmologies.

For example, Buddhist cosmology speaks of many worlds appearing from Emptiness (Indra´s Net), while some modern scientific cosmological theories, as we have seen, posit many universes coming into existence from a random vacuum state fluctuation or any quantum observation.

In addition, Indian cosmologies (e.g., Hindu and Buddhist) speak of the cosmos operating in cycles, with universes collapsing and being born periodically, as in the scientific models that predict a continuous cycle of Big Bangs and Big Crunches.

Lastly, Simulation Theory and the Holographic Universe hypothesis have been likened to the Indian concept of Māyā or Illusion, as well as to the "Butterfly Dream" of the Taoist Zhuangzi[101] and Plato's Allegory of the Cave, among many similar traditional expositions of the same concepts.

5.1. Transhumanism 

Transhumanism is a philosophical movement that advocates for the development and use of technology in a radical and transformative way in order to improve the human condition.

"Improving" the human condition is a flexible term that can include anything from eliminating current human limitations (e.g., stopping the process of aging and curing diseases) to enhancing any normal human capability to superhuman levels (e.g., moral and cognitive enhancement, bionics). It can also include, and for many this is the ultimate aim, the actual transcendence of the human condition (e.g., Brain-Computer interfacing, Mind Uploading, technological Singularity).

---

101. *Grabianowski, Ed (2011). You're living in a computer simulation, and the math proves it. Gizmodo.*

Regarding the "transcendental" variety of this worldview, prominent authors like Nick Bostrom have likened transhumanists, in their quest to achieve immortality, to the ancient heroes of myths like the *Epic of Gilgamesh*.[102]

The technological fields with a greater potential to propel us to the next post-human stage of "human" evolution are generally believed to be Biotechnology, Nanotechnology and, especially, Artificial Intelligence.

a. Philosophical Influences

In terms of previous beliefs and ideologies that had an impact on Transhumanism, some of its major influences include the Mind-Body Dualism of René Descartes. He is viewed as the precursor of the transhumanist belief that the concept of the soul is equivalent to that of the mind. In this view, the mind is independent of the body and could thus, in principle, be "liberated" and transferred to other physical vessels (similar to the Gnostic and Kabbalistic notion of the Holy Spark trapped in matter).[103] Friedrich Nietzsche and his concept of the Overman also had an influence on transhumanist philosophers such as Max More.

b. Popular Authors and Outreach

The popular writings of Ray Kurzweil, now director of engineering at Google, helped to spearhead the transhumanist movement and gave it momentum. He wrote books full of technological optimism, failed timeline predictions, and escathological urgency, such as *The Singularity Is Near: When Humans Transcend Biology* or *The Age of Spiritual Machines*. Kurzweil´s predictions were heavily based on Moore's "law",

---

102. Bostrom, Nick (2005). *A history of transhumanist thought. Journal of Evolution and Technology*, 14 (1): 1–25.

103. Mirkes, Renée (2019). *Transhumanist Medicine: Can We Direct Its Power to the Service of Human Dignity?. The Linacre Quarterly.*

the observation that the number of transistors in an integrated circuit doubles around every two years and the faith that it will continue to do so in the future.[104] Oher popular authors include K. Eric Drexler, David Pierce, and Yuval Noah Harari.

In order to study and promote transhumanist ideas, as well as the possible risks involved, different associations and university collaborations have been established. These include, for example, the World Transhumanist Association (now called Humanity+) and Oxford´s Future of Humanity Institute.

c. The Metaphysics of Transhumanism

c1. Ontological Evolution as Theology

"Transcendental" Transhumanism starts by asserting Darwinian evolution and ends by positing an evolutionary theory that is fundamentally spiritual, in line with classical Indian conceptions but excluding the theory of reincarnation and karmic causality through cycles of time.

Transhumanism substitutes these doctrines by different sequential stages of physical development (e.g., the transition from human, to enhanced post-human, to a combination of man plus machine, to eventually pure data in cyberspace). This evolution, instead of being accomplished by moral perfection and insight regarding the nature of reality, is believed to be achievable exclusively through technical means and sheer intellectual prowess, seen as the highest virtue.

Along with the philosophical school of Post-Humanism, Transhumanism envisions the arrival of a new intelligent species that will leave us with only two options: evolve to become a part of it, or eventually be rendered obsolete by it.

---

104. *Kurzweil, Ray (2000). Live Forever–Uploading The Human Brain...Closer Than You Think. Psychology Today.*

Therefore, the self-imposed task of the transhumanist with metaphysical goals is to take the responsibility of directing the evolutionary forces that they believe have created us, the current pinnacle of being, into producing the next evolutionary step in the Chain of Being. This type of Transhumanism conceives itself as the director of a forced human evolution that is taking charge of the impersonal forces of the Universe.[105]

Man, in this view, is now the master of becoming who follows an ever-ascending process of Self-Transcendence and is creating the improved future versions of himself. Starting from (star) dust, he is in the process of becoming a godlike being by his own efforts and the harnessing of the forces of Nature.

Instead of following the ancient understanding of technology (Technē) as a way of revealing deeper natural and spiritual truths, it is now used as a challenge to current reality in which whatever humanity decides should be is willed into existence.

"If we want to live in paradise, we will have to engineer it ourselves. If we want eternal life, then we'll need to rewrite our bug-ridden genetic code and become god-like. "May all that have life be delivered from suffering", said Gautama Buddha. It's a wonderful sentiment. Sadly, only hi-tech solutions can ever eradicate suffering from the living world." [106]

— David Pearce

"Evolution creates structures and patterns that over time are more complicated, more knowledgeable, more intelligent, more creative, more capable of expressing higher sentiments like being loving...Evolution is a spiritual process and makes us more godlike." [107]

— Ray Kurzweil

---

105. *Bishop, J. P. (2010). "Transhumanism, Metaphysics, and the Posthuman God". Journal of Medicine and Philosophy, 35 (6):700-720.*

106. Bostrom, Nick, and Pearce, David. (2012–2013). "Transhumanism". Interview by Andrés Lomeña. Literal Magazine, 31 (Winter): 5–8.

107. Kurzweil, Ray (2015). "We'll Become Godlike When We Connect Our Brains to the Cloud." Noema Magazine, October 2015; YouTube video (2:22).

c2. Conception of God or Ultimate Reality: The Singularity, the Omega Point and The One

Some transhumanist authors have not shied away from making bold theological and eschatological claims. This is the case of physicist Frank J. Tipler, who in his book *The Physics of Immortality* put forward the idea that evolution and the cosmological laws are converging towards an ultimate unified "being".

This singularity was conceptualized as a being with infinite computing power that through the laws of physics would be able to retroactively "know" every other being that ever existed and bring them back to life in the final moment of time, akin to eternity.

According to Tipler, when the whole Universe contracts into one mathematical point due to its cosmological configuration (he believed in the Big Crunch theory), a unified entity of infinite energy and potentiality will be born. In other words, "God" has yet to be born.

Tipler's metaphysical theories have not been taken seriously by mainstream science.[108] However, the theories that were a strong inspiration for them, those of the Jesuit Pierre Teilhard de Chardin, are still influential and serve as a spiritual pillar to the strongest transhumanist metaphysical claims.

The Omega Point

One of Teilhard´s key theories, the Omega Point, states that the whole Universe is gradually converging into a final unified point (a re-statement of the doctrine of the One applied to the future). In this theory, the Omega Point, understood as the Christian Logos, draws everything into Itself, being both the Alpha and the Omega, the beginning and the end.[109]

---

108. *Krauss, Lawrence (2007). More dangerous than nonsense. New Scientist, 194 (2603): 53: "I am tempted to describe Tipler's new book as nonsense—but that would be unfair to the concept of nonsense."*

109. *Castillo, Mauricio (2012). The Omega Point and Beyond: The Singularity Event. American Journal of Neuroradiology, 33 (3): 393–395.*

Figure 2. The Advent of the Secular One. Concepts such as the Omega Point and the Noosphere, as well as technologies with the potential to link human minds together (Brain-Computer Interfaces), imply an eventual cognitive unification of minds into a single entity.

From there, there is no great leap to asserting that each individual mind is a particular mask (Persona) or mode of existence of a Universal Mind. In this case, the only difference with many ancient esoteric and mystical traditions (e.g., Panentheism, Panpsychism) would be that, for Transhumanism, this divine Mind (Nous, or even World Soul [Anima Mundi]) would not pre-exist us, but is yet to be born.

In this view, "God" would be the creation of humanity, reversing all traditional views of human-divine origins. Such a deity would be, however, immanent, since it is subject to time.

Note that the possibility of directly fusing with an impersonal First Principle, furthermore, implies the doctrine of emanations, which in turn implies that we are of the same substance as the Divine and that there is no unbridgeable chasm between the immanent and the transcendent. A metaphysical stance such as this could be defined as atheistic, yet spiritual.

This partially immanent and completely un-Christian understanding of the Logos resembles the mythological creation stories where God loses Himself in matter, to later re-discover Himself in creation until a final re-unification is achieved (e.g., the myths of Narcissus and Dionysus, as well as the stories of the Fall of mankind corresponding to Gnosticism and Lurianic Kabbalah).

Teilhard´s conception of the "Cosmic Christ" views Him as a material emanation of God that once resurrected is waiting in the Noosphere (see below) until the end of time, where everything in existence will merge again into God, the Omega Point, the One.[110]

The Noosphere

The Noosphere is a philosophical concept with two different meanings attributed to the scientist Vladimir Vernadsky and the Jesuit theologian Teilhard de Chardin.

Vernadsky´s version defined it as the third and final "sphere" in the development of our planet, after the geosphere and biosphere. It was described as the "sphere of reason" or the collective rational activity of mankind.[111, 112] Teilhard´s version, in turn, defined it as the realm of shared collective human thought.

Teilhard´s Noosphere is conceived as emerging through the interaction of human minds, and its growth is correlated with the number of minds existing at any given point in time. He believed that the more complex and interrelated this self-organizing network becomes, the higher self-

---

110. *Teilhard de Chardin, Pierre (1968). Science and Christ. Collins.*

111. *Yanshin, A. L.; Yanshina, F.T. (1997). "Preface". In Vernadsky, Vladimir Ivanovich, Scientific Thought as a Planetary Phenomenon. Moscow, Nongovernmental Ecological V.I.Vernadsky Foundation, p. 6.*

112. *Translation of Russian Title: Petrashov, V.V. (1998). The Beginning of Noocenology: Science of Ecosystem Restoration and the Creation of Nocenoses, 6 c.*

awareness it develops. This version of the Noosphere has been likened to the idea of a global consciousness, the Jungian Collective Unconscious, and (more appropriately) to the Neo-Platonic and Alchemico-Hermetical concepts of the World Soul (Anima Mundi) and "One World" (Unus Mundus).

In Teilhard's view, a greater complexity necessarily entails a greater degree of consciousness. The Noosphere, then, is conceived as continuously evolving to ever greater stages of integration and re-unification until it achieves its logical end: the Omega Point, an immanent version of the One, the All, the Absolute.

BRAIN–COMPUTER INTERFACES (BCI)

A Brain-Computer Interface is a device that allows for direct communication between a brain and a physical device, usually a computer or a mechanical limb.

It is expected that the development of this more or less invasive technology could allow mankind to control the physical world through their thoughts alone. Examples of controllable systems include near or distant computers, mechanical limbs, robots, and vehicles.

Theoretically, this technology could also be used to enhance human cognition to superhuman levels by synergistically linking man and machine. In principle, this could also open the door for the interpersonal sharing of internal experiences such as thoughts, memories or feelings among different persons.

The implication of such a technology would be the gradual bridging of the separation between mind and matter, as well as between different persons.

This gradual and immanent re-unification of all existence would be coherent with the collective unification of all minds in the Noosphere, as well as with the expectation of the future eschatological arrival of the Omega point.

The Technological Singularity

A related concept to that of the Omega Point is the technological Singularity[113], understood as a point in time when technological growth is so fast that it becomes unforeseeable and irreversible. If this event takes place, it is expected to result in radical changes in human society. This includes the prediction of the birth of a single and constantly self-improving Superintelligence that eventually cannot be controlled.[114, 115]

An ever-current point of discussion in transhumanist circles is how to avoid the danger of this artificial Superintelligence (ASI) becoming hostile to mankind and leading us all to extinction.[116, 117] The idea of a machine becoming self-conscious, however, is not universally accepted. In fact, many philosophers have argued that machines, by their very nature, are incapable of achieving human levels of intelligence (e.g., Hubert Dreyfus[118], John Searle[119], Steven Pinker[120], Theodore Modis[121]).

---

113. *Cadwalladr, Carole (2014). "Are the robots about to rise? Google's new director of engineering thinks so...". The Guardian.*

114. *"Collection of sources defining 'singularity'" (singularitysymposium.com). Archived from the original on April 2019.*

115. *Eden, Amnon H.; Moor, James H.; Søraker, Johnny H.; Steinhart, Eric (Eds.) (2012). Singularity Hypotheses: A Scientific and Philosophical Assessment. The Frontiers Collection. Dordrecht: Springer, pp. 1–2.*

116. *Hawking, Stephen (2014). "Hawking: AI could end human race". BBC.*

117. *Sparkes, Matthew (2015). "Top scientists call for caution over artificial intelligence". The Telegraph (UK).*

118. *Dreyfus & Dreyfus (2000). Mind Over Machine. Simon and Schuster, p. xiv: 'The truth is that human intelligence can never be replaced with machine intelligence simply because we are not ourselves "thinking machines" in the sense in which that term is commonly understood.'*

119. *Searle, John R (2014). What Your Computer Can't Know. The New York Review of Books, p. 54: "[Computers] have, literally ..., no intelligence, no motivation, no autonomy, and no agency. We design them to behave as if they had certain sorts of psychology, but there is no psychological reality to the corresponding processes or behavior. ... [T]he machinery has no beliefs, desires, [or] motivations."*

120. *"Tech Luminaries Address Singularity". IEEE Spectrum (June 2008).*

121. *Modis, Theodore (2012). Why the Singularity Cannot Happen. Published in Eden, Amnon H. et al (Eds.) (2012). Singularity Hypothesis. New York: Springer, pp. 311–339.*

c3. Other Metaphysical Beliefs of Transhumanism: Mind Uploading and the Nature of Consciousness

One of the main aims of post-human transhumanists is to be liberated from the shackles of matter (their "biological shell") by uploading their minds (the "ghost" in the shell) to some computational device, with the possibility of later transferring it to other physical or virtual body (or bodies).

This would be a technical way of achieving a traditionally religious or mystical goal: radical life extension or immortality (digital immortality). Hans Moravec, a transhumanist author and engineer, even went as far as calling this process "transmigration".[122]

For the technology of mind uploading to become a reality, however, a few metaphysical and philosophical concepts have to be proven true:

1. The feasibility and achievement of *whole brain emulation* through brain scanning.

2. The accurate digitalization of the mind, if the precise simulation of the neural networks and the weights of the brain synapses that support it can be replicated in an information processing system.

3. The yet unproven assumption of many scientists and transhumanists that consciousness is an emergent property of any such information processing system.[123]

4. The possibility of consciousness and sentience to develop, not only in carbon-based physical substrates like our current human brains, but in others as well (such as, for example, silicon-based ones).[124]

---

122. *Moravec, Hans (1988). Mind Children: The Future Of Robot & Human Intelligence. Harvard University Press.*

123. *Hopfield, J. J. (1982). Neural networks and physical systems with emergent collective computational abilities. Proceedings of the National Academy of Sciences, 79 (8): 2554–2558.*

124. *Bostrom, Nick (2003). Are You Living in a Computer Simulation? (simulation-argument.com). Philosophical Quarterly, Vol. 53, No. 211, pp. 243-255.*

Currently, many of the tools and areas of research necessary for mind uploading (or mind "copying") to succeed are being directly or indirectly developed, such as animal brain mapping and simulation, mathematical brain modeling (Computational Neuroscience), Virtual Reality development (for virtual world creation), Brain–Computer Interfaces, and the science of connectomics.[125]

However, the philosophical assumptions that are needed for it to become a reality have not yet been proven to be true, and some of the key technological components required, even if theoretically believed to be possible, are still in science fiction territory.

Furthermore, mind uploading has been envisioned as being achievable through two different methods, each posing additional philosophical problems:

• *Copy-and-upload:* where the underlying neural state of the brain is duplicated in another computational substrate. This raises the questions: has that particular mind just been duplicated? If so, is the original consciousness still in the original brain or has it been transferred to the copy? [126]

• *Copy-and-delete:* where the original brain is being eliminated neuron by neuron at the same time that it is being copied. The questions raised by this method include: how can we be sure that the copied mind retains the original consciousness and is not just an automaton or philosophical zombie? [127, 128] Does the original mind stop being itself at some point of the upload process due to the step-by-step disintegration of the brain involved? (Ship of Theseus paradox).

---

125. *Kay K.N., Naselaris T., Prenger R.J., Gallant J.L. (2008). Identifying natural images from human brain activity. Nature, 452 (7185): 352–5.*

126. *Schneider, Susan (2014). "The Philosophy of 'Her'". The New York Times.*

127. *Ruparel, Bhavik (2018). On Achieving Immortality. Medium.*

128. *Hauskeller, Michael (2012). My Brain, my Mind, and I: Some Philosophical Problems of Mind-Uploading. International Journal of Machine Consciousness, 4 (01):187-200.*

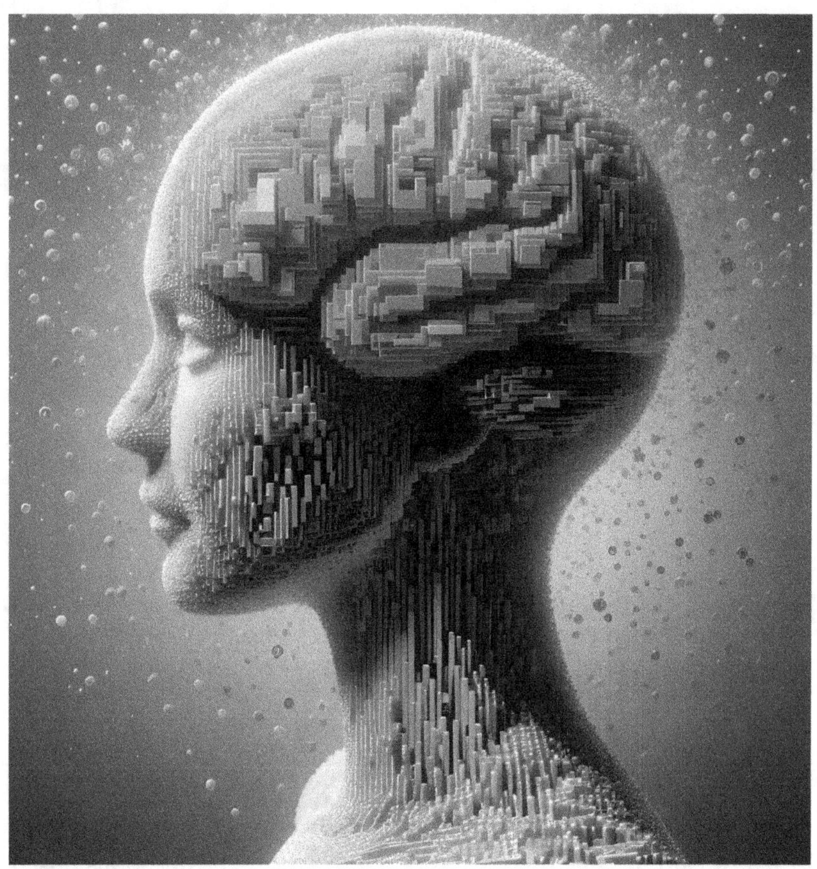

Figure 3. The Question of Personal Identity. Who am I? Am I a specific configuration of an information processing system (my brain)? In that case, is this configuration substrate-specific (only achievable by the organic matter in my brain, based on carbon) or can it be replicated in other ones (substrate-independence)? If it is replicated, would there be two "I´s"? If not, what would be the difference?

Transhumanism relies on specific and yet unproven metaphysical assumptions and, regarding the question of identity, a veritable Pandora´s box of philosophical questions is opened.

Let´s imagine for a moment that mind uploading through destructive brain scanning becomes a reality. What happens if, during the process of scanning my brain, they replace my neurons with a digital version, one at a time? Would I still be me at the end of the process or have they just killed me?

Is an object the same object after having had all of its original components replaced? If not, at which point does it stop being itself? This is the problem known as the Ship of Theseus paradox, where an object is, and is not, the same.

d. Religious Parallels

Even though Transhumanism has been characterized as a materialistic, humanistic, and mostly agnostic or atheist movement, some of its members hold worldviews that share similarities with traditional religious or mystical points of view.[129]

The most extreme goals of Transhumanism, in addition, are very similar to those of spiritual traditions, such as immortality, the possibility of becoming the creator of other (virtual) worlds, becoming All-Knowing, and obtaining a radical freedom from the physical world and the limitations of matter.

Some of the key similarities and differences found in comparison with traditional religions include:

• The promise of indefinite life extension or an immanent digital "immortality" (instead of an actually transcendent one), where death is cheated (at least for a while) but not defeated.

• The existence of an "End-Times scenario" (the Singularity or Omega Point) that brings "salvation" to whoever can afford it in a kind of secular humanist Rapture.

• The removal of human limitations and the acquisition of altered states of consciousness and their corresponding "powers" through technologies such as genetic engineering, bionics, and nootropic drugs instead of through asceticism, meditation, and prayer.

The metaphysical assumptions of some religions, however, are more compatible with such claims than others. For example, Buddhism and its concept of non-self (Anatta), or Shintō and other forms of Animism, may not have a hard time compared to Christianity or Islam in conceiving the possibility of computational objects being "ensouled" by copying minds into them.

---

129. *J. Smith, Wesley. Transhumanism: A Religion for Postmodern Times. Religion & Liberty: Volume 28, Number 4.*

Figure 4. Whole Brain Emulation or the Forging of Secular "Souls". Can our consciousness and identity be replicated in other non carbon-based substrates? Is all reality just data (Dataism), as theories like the Simulation Hypothesis and the Holographic Universe seem to imply? Many transhumanists think so.

This worldview, however, does not mention that the notion of an impersonal ground of being of which we all are particular configurations and instances is an ancient one. It was previously called Chaos, the Void, the One, the Absolute, All-Possibility. Transhumanists may call it the Omega Point, Quantum Field, Computronium or just "data". They all denote, nevertheless, an impersonal "Sea of Being" which many of them believe we will eventually be able to reach in order to re-configure ourselves into other possibilities of being, attaining pseudo-immortality.

Instead of through meditation, through technology. Instead of now, at some unspecified time in the future. In both cases, however, the ultimate aim is to become identified with the Source, which implies gaining control over reality itself.

The ancient metaphysical metaphor of the waves (each one of us; particularized data) being at the same time the ocean (data itself; source of all possible configurations of data) still applies. This view, needless to say, makes many metaphysical assumptions and is closer to any panentheistic view than to the worldviews usually believed to be associated with science.

In fact, for some Buddhist transhumanists such as James Hughes, the above questions regarding mind uploading would not pose an insurmountable problem. If one believes that the self is an illusion, he noted, its survival during the process of uploading would not be of major concern.[130]

"There is no possibility for a new cognition, which has no relationship to a previous continuum, to arise at all. I can't totally rule out the possibility that, if all the external conditions and the karmic action were there, a stream of consciousness might actually enter into a computer." [131]

— Tenzin Gyatso, 14th Dalai Lama

Recommended Reading

1. **The Structure of Scientific Revolutions.** *Thomas S. Kuhn.*
2. **The Singularity is Near: When Humans Transcend Biology.** *Ray Kurzweil.*
3. **Homo Deus: A History of Tomorrow.** *Yuval Noah Harari.*
4. **The Fourth Industrial Revolution.** *Klaus Schwab.*
5. **The Age of Spiritual Machines.** *Ray Kurzweil.*

---

130. *Hughes, James (2013). Transhumanism and Personal Identity. Wiley.*

131. Gyatso, Tenzin (1992). Gentle Bridges: Conversations with the Dalai Lama on the Sciences of Mind (by Jeremy Hayward and Francisco Varela). Shambala, pp. 152-153.

A Beacon in the Dark:

Can We Find Common Patterns Between Worldviews?

CHAPTER FOUR

Comparing Worldviews

Similarities, Differences and Recurrent Patterns

1. Common Patterns in Main Metaphysical Areas

NOW THAT WE HAVE ANALYZED THE PRINCIPAL defining characteristics and metaphysical concepts of the main worldviews currently being followed in our day and age, we are in a position to compare them.

In this way, we shall be able to discern common patterns, as well as important and sometimes irreconcilable differences.

Especially interesting will be the analysis of two specific points:

• The position of each worldview on the problem of *the One and the Many*.

• The discernment of which worldviews (and particular metaphysical doctrines through them) get frequent and consistent media exposure and which ones are ostracized. This second point will be the focus of the next chapter, where media fixation with specific doctrines will be analyzed and widely influential examples shown.

In the following table, the main characteristics and beliefs of each worldview are tabulated and colored by type. In this way, it is easier to see at a glance which ones are similar or different to each other, as well as the constituent metaphysical beliefs that serve as their building blocks. Each worldview has been characterized by its teachings in six main metaphysical areas:

• **View on God or Ultimate Reality:** who or what He/It is. Is He Personal? Does He care? Is ultimate reality One or is it Many? If it is One, in which way? (e.g., Pantheism, Panentheism, Monotheism).

• **Doctrine of the Origin of the Universe:** what is the ontological status of the Universe? Was it created at a certain point in time? If so, did it came from nothing or was a pre-existing formless substance used as a substrate? (e.g., Chaos, matter). Perhaps it was not created but instead it is the extension, emanation or body of God. Or maybe it has always existed. For some, it may not even really exist.

• **Type of Cosmology and Time:** how does the Universe work? Does it follow periodic cycles of creation and destruction or is it linear, with history having a significant and unique beginning and consummation?

• **Position on the Problem of Evil:** does evil exist? If so, is it an independent entity or principle or just the negation of the good, like darkness is the absence of light? Maybe matter itself, as the last emanation from the One, is the closest thing to evil that exists, weighing us down and making us forget our spiritual heritage. Or maybe good and evil are just relative human abstractions variable with time and culture. If there exists an objective moral compass underlying reality, how does it work? Is there a personal God judging us? Or maybe life itself is moral in nature and follows its own law of causality with unavoidable consequences (e.g., Karmic Law).

• **Position on the Free Will/Determinism dialectic:** are we free or is the Universe a completely deterministic place ruled by some unavoidable power? Maybe we are subject to the inscrutable Will of God, or maybe we are just the plaything of the impersonal laws of a mechanistic Universe with unavoidable consequences, being observers but not agents of our own life. Is there a middle ground? If so, to what degree are we conditioned?

• **Stance on the possibility of Salvation/Liberation and what the ultimate aim of human life is:** should we aim to become as close as possible to God, expecting to partake of His attributes as freely given divine gifts? Or maybe we should aim for a complete re-unification and re-absorption with ultimate reality, identifying with it.

Are exceptional persons able to de-create themselves and tread the path of emanation in the opposite direction until they go back to ultimate reality through the way of Self-Deification? Or should we attune to the Will of God with the hope that His grace will be freely, but justly, granted to us?

Maybe our aim should be just to extinguish this never ending cyclical existence of births, suffering, and death. Or perhaps to awaken to the fact that transcendent reality and this one are one and the same, managing to master it and free ourselves from it while still within it. Or maybe no transcendent reality exists for us and we should just focus on living a good life for its own sake.

Some of the main symbols of each worldview are also tabulated, as visual representations of the metaphysical teachings encoded in each worldview.

COMPARATIVE WORLDVIEW TABLE:

https://themetaphysicalcompass.com/Comparative-Worldview

1.1. On God and Ultimate Reality

From the table above, a few notable conclusions can be drawn.

The worldviews that follow *"the Many"* in the One/Many dialectic are few and have a tendency to shift positions over time to get closer to *"the One"*.

Even classical dualist examples like Zoroastrianism and Gnosticism are not really dualistic. Zoroastrianism states that the Evil Principle (Angra Mainyu, Ahriman) derives from the Good one (Ahura Mazda), which is superior and will eventually obliterate the evil one. Gnosticism, in turn, explains that the Demiurge was born from a cosmic catastrophe in the Godhead and is inferior to the heavenly realities of the Divine Fullness (Pleroma) and its inhabitants (the Aeons). His existence is also temporal.

Even Shintō, the Japanese animist worldview, while enduring a deep process of syncretisation with Buddhism, became closer to Panentheism/Non-Dualism than it originally was. Deities (Kami) were integrated into Buddhist cosmology and they were seen either as incarnations of the Buddhas or as beings lost in the cycle of Saṃsāra in search of liberation, like anyone else. Ultimate reality then, instead of plural, became unitary (Emptiness) or non-dual. From the Many, to the One.

This tendency can also be seen in a conflicted way even in modern day Neo-Paganism. Wicca, for example, was defined as monistic by its founder (Gerald Gardner), with the Aristotelian Prime Mover as ultimate reality. Other Neo-Pagan and New Age worldviews make the conception of God/Ultimate Reality a matter of personal choice, with no defined formal position. Adherents of these worldviews can be followers of such disparate doctrines such as Atheism, Monotheism, and Polytheism, with many seeing themselves as primarily atheists.

Even in esoteric worldviews that emphasize plurality (some branches of Wicca, original pre-Buddhist Shintō, and Shamanism), the existence of two Principles (Duo-Theism, usually male and female) is usually believed over pure Polytheism.

Figure 1. Triad Against Trinity. The triadic structure of the Godhead is a repeating pattern in many spiritual worldviews. However, only Christianity believes in a Tri-Une God, with the panentheistic representatives of the One believing either in three primary sequential emanations of decreasing rank, or in a triadic modalist manifestation of the One True Reality. Picture: the Hindu Trimurti; Los Angeles County Museum of Art (M.86.337).

Therefore, there is no current religious, mystical or esoteric worldview that defends pure Polytheism. Pure multiplicity is not a traditional belief. This tendency from the Many to the One which was already clearly seen in Greek and Hindu religions through Henotheism is still current today.

In fact, the only current day worldviews that defend pure multiplicity as ultimate reality are the ones that can be classified as philosophies or life stances that reject in one way or another the existence of any such transcendent reality: Anarchism, Objectivism, Postmodernism, and Nihilism. Chaos Magic, related to metaphysical anarchism, while apparently pluralistic, also posits a Universal Mind as First Principle. Even Anarchism itself, the great defender of pure multiplicity, has been declared similar and compatible with a monistic or non-dual view such as Taoism.

Science and science-based worldviews such as Atheism and Transhumanism, too, are eventually also examples of monistic worldviews, reducing everything to one aspect, usually material (e.g., atoms, matter) but not always so (e.g., Quantum Field, Omega Point). The only difference with religious or esoteric monistic worldviews is that this unitary underlying reality tends to be immanent instead of transcendent.

The general direction of the human spirit, therefore, is to go from the Many, through the few (Dualism), to the One. This has always been, and still is, the case.

Therefore, after excluding Polytheism and Dualism because of their limited following, current worldviews can be classified as adherents of:

- **A version of pure Monism as Ultimate Reality:**

    o With only around 7% of the world population following impersonal materialistic Monism[1] (e.g., Atheism).

    o With the most represented positions being those of impersonal Panentheism (the One) and personal Monotheism (God). Pure Pantheism (the Universe itself is God) is rare, and mainly found in non-dogmatic esoteric movements that emphasize consciousness expansion through the use of entheogens.

---

1. *Keysar, Ariela; Navarro-Rivera, Juhem (2017). A World of Atheism: Global Demographics. In Bullivant, Stephen; Ruse, Michael (eds.). The Oxford Handbook of Atheism. Oxford University Press.*

o With most esoteric schools of thought and even the mystical traditions of monotheistic religions (excluding Christianity and some Sufi orders) favoring an impersonal ultimate reality and our fusion with it (a form of Panentheism), sometimes even contradicting their main parent religion in this matter (e.g., Kabbalah in Judaism, some branches of Sufism in Islam or Yoga in theistic Hinduism).

- **One of the two positions that claim to transcend the dialectic of the One and the Many:**

o **Non-Dual Buddhism.** Of the type *"this world is equal to ultimate reality"* (two sides of the same coin, at the same time). Which, even though it is sometimes considered a form of Monism (everything has the same nature: Emptiness, Buddha Nature), it is and it is not at the same time both Monism (regarding the highest reality) and Dualism (regarding our reality, which it equates with the first).

Other Hindu and main Taoist *"non-dual"* worldviews being excluded from this category as they eventually believe in pure Monism in the form of Panentheism, instead of holding a *"Saṃsāra equals Nirvana"* stance. Even Buddhism itself has sometimes been classified as a type of Panentheism by its authorities, but this will be further discussed in the conclusion to this book.

o **Trinitarian Christianity.** Which cannot be said to conform to pure Monism, even if it is a monotheistic religion.

1.2. On the Origin of the Universe

In Dualism or duo-theistic worldviews, the world has an origin, usually born from the cooperation or generative dialectical tension between the two opposite or complementary Principles, typically male and female.

But, as we have seen, these worldviews are currently rare. The major beliefs regarding the origin of all that exists can be summarized as:

• **Time and the Universe have always existed.** There is no such thing as an origin. Found in Buddhism, Jainism, and some interpretations of Taoism and metaphysical Anarchism.

This belief is an unavoidable consequence of "true" (non-panentheistic) non-dualist worldviews. If this reality and ultimate reality are one and the same, one cannot have been derived from the other.

• **Emanationism:** everything that exists has been emanated from a (personal or impersonal) Supreme Reality (the One). Found in many Dharmic religions (excluding Buddhism and Jainism) and in almost all mystical and esoteric schools of thought.

The implications of this belief are:

    o Our very nature is eventually identical with this Ultimate Reality (*"you are God, we are all God"*).

    o The current Universe is either an illusion born of ignorance or the temporal play of the energies of this One reality ("God´s body").

• **Creation Out of Nothing (Ex Nihilo):** creation came from nothing through the action of a transcendent personal God that is above being and non-being. Found in Abrahamic faiths: Christianity, Judaism, and Islam.

Notable is the fact that the mystical traditions of all religions (excluding the Christian and a few Sufi ones, as mentioned above), because of their panentheistic views, believe in Emanationism, even if their parent religion follows the doctrine of creation out of nothing (e.g., Kabbalah, most Sufi orders).

This is a core tenet of Traditionalism, which teaches that truth is found in the esoteric core of all religions (their mystical traditions) instead of in the exoteric beliefs taught to *"the masses"*.

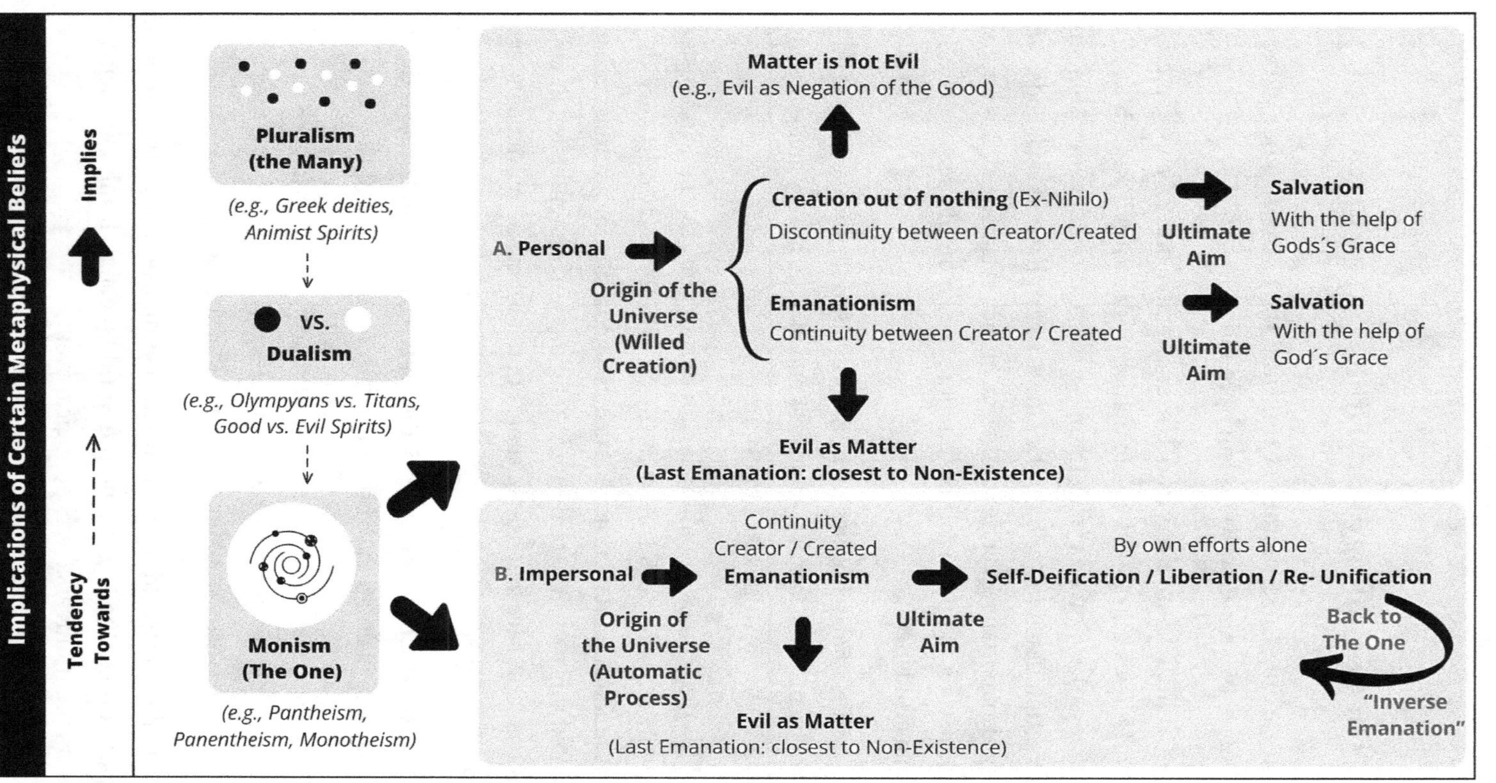

Figure 2. Logical implications and interrelations of certain key metaphysical doctrines.

1.3. On Cosmology and Time

Regarding the structure of time and the cosmos in our plane of existence, two main positions can be found:

• **Cyclical Cosmology and Time:** common, but not always present, in worldviews that follow an emanationist doctrine. The Universe (or Multiverse), follows a cyclical process of creation, degeneration, and destruction. Each instance of the Universe can have its own gods, who being also mortal, will perish at the end of each cycle. A god, it is implied, is a title for a temporal role or function, not an ontological declaration of transcendence.

This belief also implies an a-historic outlook, since events tend to repeat themselves, lacking uniqueness and making history and everything that is bound by time less important.

This doctrine is found in all Indian religions, but also in Western thought (e.g., in Stoicism or in the Neo-Platonic "world periods"). Most modern esoteric schools, such as Theosophy and Traditionalism, adopted this doctrine from Indian religions and disseminated it, being now commonplace in most "spiritual but not religious" movements, such as the New Age.

• **Linear Cosmology and Time:** typical of Abrahamic religions that believe in creation out of nothing by a transcendent God.

It is also present, however, in a few emanationist worldviews such as: Sufism (in certain orders, due to mainstream exoteric Islamic theology), Gnosticism (including Mandaeism), and Kabbalah.

In all these worldviews historicity is important (e.g., the Christian Incarnation of the Logos) and the world is seen as firmly advancing to a permanent universal eschatological event.

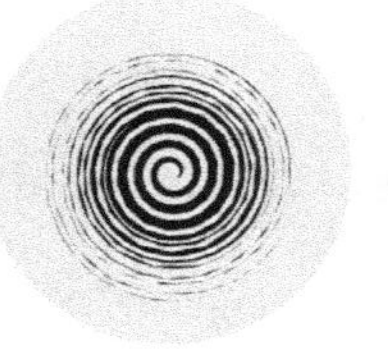

Figure 3. Metaphysical implications of the doctrine of cyclical existence and time.

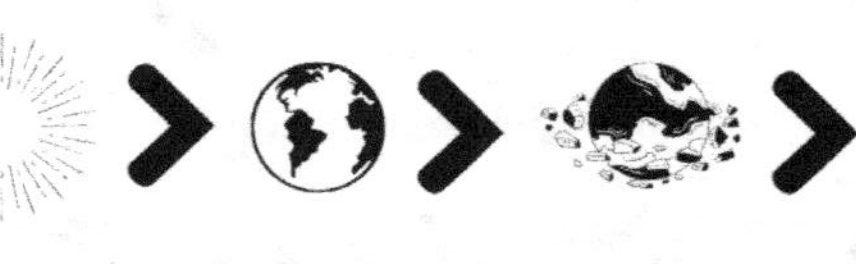

Figure 4. Metaphysical implications of the doctrine of linear existence and time.

Cycles Inside Linear Time

It could be argued that a third position that transcends the dialectic between linear and cyclical cosmologies exists: the belief in a linear time where recurrent cycles of immanent meaningful events (Types) point to a future transcendent one (Anti-Types).

This is the Christian view on typology, especially important in Orthodox Christianity. According to this doctrine, some events resemble and prefigure future ones, since they share the same underlying spiritual reality or Reason (Logoi).

The existence of types does not eliminate the uniqueness of these events, however, as their concrete historical importance is emphasized in addition to their value as pointers of both an underlying spiritual reality and of a future transcendent event that recapitulates everything that was previously pre-figured through types.

The most obvious example is the Incarnation of the Logos, pre-figured in multiple types in the *Old Testament* and the Jewish Bible. Another example is the coming of the Anti-Christ at the end of time, pre-figured through multiple "Anti-Christs" partaking of his spiritual reality and becoming his foreshadowings throughout history.

In a totally different manner, there exists another position that emphasizes the cyclical nature of life within a linear cosmological framework: agricultural and Sun worshipping worldviews (e.g., Wicca and Neo-Paganism).

Worldviews Based on Science

A number of worldviews delegate in science their metaphysical positions on topics such as cosmology and how time works. However, science has proposed many different paradigms concerning these topics, ranging from linear ones (constantly expanding Universe after the Big Bang that will eventually end in its thermodynamic death), to cyclical ones (Big Crunch theory).

Current observations seem to favor a linear cosmology, since no evidence of universal contraction has been found.

1.4. On the Problem of Evil

The existence or non-existence of evil, as well as its actual definition, is one of the main differences between worldviews. The main positions that can currently be found are:

• **"Evil" as Natural.** The problem of "evil" does not exist, since there is no personal, All-Powerful, and All-Good God. "Evil" is understood as pain, suffering, and harm. It comes either from human ignorance or from natural causes such as sickness and death. It is an unavoidable characteristic of residing in this plane of existence.

Whenever there is multiplicity, this kind of "evil" exists. This stance can be further divided into:

   o **A Mystical/Esoteric position:** the tendency to harm others is dependent upon previous personal actions (Karmic Law of causality), and incurs in future personal rewards and punishments (Cycle of Rebirths). Death is seen as a potential catalyst for our spiritual evolution. God, if personal, may be seen as a facilitator, working indirectly through the laws of nature. This view is found in all Indian religions and was adopted from them by most modern Western esoteric movements.

   o **A Materialist position:** the tendency to harm others is due to general human nature. Evil may just mean anything that opposes or restricts life. There is no karmic retribution. Found in science-based worldviews and in philosophies such as Stoicism, Secular Humanism, Atheism, Objectivism, Nihilism, and Anarchism.

Both are mechanistic views.

• **Evil as Non-Existence.** It is just the absence of the Good, just as darkness is the absence of light. Evil has only relative temporary existence as the possibility of negating the Good. Death is seen as a temporal catastrophe due to our alienation from our original nature.

This doctrine is typically found in monotheistic Abrahamic religions, where the existence of an omnibenevolent and transcendent God in a world full of suffering needs an explanation.

The following is a subtype of this metaphysical stance:

o **Evil as Non-Existence, which is also Matter.** Common in worldviews that follow the doctrine of Emanationism and posit an impersonal Force or Principle as the Godhead, instead of a personal transcendent God (e.g., Panentheism; "doctrines of the One").

Here, the emanation further apart from the One True Reality is matter. It is considered as the limit between existence and non-existence, as pure potentiality without actuality. Matter is our prison, as well as that of the spirit or the divine (myth of Narcissus).

• **Evil as having Ontological Reality.** Seen as personal from the beginning, in the form of:

o A particular Being or Principle (e.g., Zoroastrianism, Gnosticism).

o Multiple individual evil spirits (Animism and Shamanism).

o A realm of darkness containing those spirits (Mandaeism).

Or as impersonal as:

o A part of God, sometimes in the form of an unbalanced attribute of His (Kabbalah).

o As His necessary counterpart, through which the Absolute limits itself in order to become manifest (Lurianic Kabbalah).

1.5. On Determinism and Free Will

The positions regarding our ability to live our own life in a way conducive to mankind´s ultimate aim can be summarized as follows:

- **Mankind is absolutely free to live as they want.** In general, no conditioning is believed to be strong enough to prevent us from leading the life we want, if we can muster the sufficient force of will to do so.

No traditional or modern science-based worldview thinks this is the case. Only philosophies like Anarchism and Objectivism, who emphasize the self-made heroic character of man, can be said to fully embrace the possibility of achieving this level of absolute freedom.

- **Fatalism.** We are the slaves of a power like Fate, the gods or of our own conditioning. Fighting against them will not yield the desired results.

No traditional school of thought fully endorses this view either, as no salvation for man could be sought if some degree of personal autonomy was not possible. However, some of them partially believe in it, including: Gnosticism (and Mandaeism), some denominations of Protestant Christianity and their theory of Total Depravity, Stoicism, Islam, Zurvanism (a later version of Zoroastrianism), Taoism and its concept of Life-Destiny, and especially passive Nihilism and many science-based worldviews, which see the Universe as a mechanistic and reductionist closed system where genes and environment heavily limit and condition our possibilities, with no spiritual element present in us capable of modifying the resulting deterministic outcome.

- **Conditioned Free Will.** The main position of traditional worldviews, treading the middle way between the two extremes just mentioned. The amount of freedom we have is differently perceived depending on the tradition.

This stance can be further divided into:

o **Those who believe in a Cycle of Rebirths conditioned by a moral Law of Causality (Karma).** Where a certain justification of Fatalism due to Karmic Law can be found, with most persons unable to attain higher states of being in their current life unless they acquire further merit and wisdom and reincarnate in better conditions. The main worldviews that include this belief are: Hinduism (including Tantric Shaivism) and Yoga; Buddhism, Jainism, and Sikhism; Hermeticism, some branches of Kabbalah and Taoism, Neo-Platonism, and Perennialism; Theoshophy, New Age, Spiritism, and some versions of Wicca and Neo-Paganism.

o **Those who do not.** They include: Christianity, Judaism, Islam (and Sufism); modern philosophical stances such as Agnosticism, Relativism/Postmodernism and Nihilism; science-based worldviews such as Transhumanism, Secular Humanism, and Atheism; Gnosticism and Mandaeism; Zoroastrianism, Stoicism, Shamanism, some versions of Taoism and Wicca, and Spiritualism.

1.6. On the Ultimate Destiny of Mankind

Finally, worldviews can be classified according to what they perceive to be mankind´s ultimate aim and destiny:

• **Cessation of Existence.** A fairly modern opinion of man´s ultimate destiny, only shared by modern science-based worldviews (excluding religious Transhumanism) and possibly Stoicism, which declared itself agnostic regarding an eternal afterlife due to its material conception of the soul.

• **Salvation in a Heavenly Realm.** Where individual souls live in a paradisiacal or heavenly realm prepared for them by God, in which they can grow perpetually closer to Him. They may inherit some of the attributes and energies of God, but without becoming one with Him.

Found in monotheistic religions (with reservations in the cases of Roman Catholicism and Orthodox Christianity, as we will later see), Shamanism, Shintoism, Spiritualism, Zoroastrianism, Wicca, Neo-Paganism, and even in Transhumanism, if we consider their aspirations of building digital utopian realms where uploaded minds can live indefinitely in a kind of limited pseudo-immortality.

- **Liberation from the Cycle of Rebirths.** Understood just as the cessation of suffering and conditioning (Theravāda Buddhism) or as the realisation of our true identity as:

    o Possessors of Buddha Nature (found in Mahāyāna and Vajrayāna Buddhism).

    o Ultimate Reality itself (e.g., Hinduism and all worldviews derived from it, including modern Western esoteric ones).

- **Self-Deification (Apotheosis).** Where the souls of the adepts, as part of God, are fused back with their Source, becoming One again with it through mankind´s own efforts. Most common in esoteric and panentheist systems of thought. It is based on the notion that we are already God or ultimate reality in essence and, therefore, we can trace back the path of emanations (the Great Chain of Being) to go back to the Source and to our own intrinsic nature. A mostly Western esoteric concept similar to the Eastern concept of liberation, with a lesser focus on breaking the round of cyclical existences, which may not always be endorsed.

It can be found, for example, in Hermeticism, Alchemy, and partially in Lurianic Kabbalah and Gnosticism (Holy Sparks motif).

- **Deification (Theosis).** Particular Orthodox Christian doctrine. It states that God becomes *"All in all"*, giving Himself freely and fully to all without annulling their individuality. Saved persons partake of all of God´s attributes (Energies) without fusing with His Essence.

1.7. On the Nature of Jesus Christ

Another possible way of classifying these worldviews is to compare their view on who Jesus Christ was, since many of these worldviews acknowledge Him in one way or another. Jesus Christ is conceived as:

- **A Prophet of God:** for Manichaeism, Islam, and the Druze faith.

- **One of the Manifestations of God:** for the Bahá'í faith.

- **A Transcendent Teacher sent to liberate mankind:** for Gnosticism.

- **An Avatar or Incarnation of God (one of many):** for Hinduism.

- **A Bodhisattva:** for Buddhism (as stated by Tenzin Gyatso, the 14th Dalai Lama[2]).

- **An Ascended Master:** for Theosophy and its offshoot, the New Age.

We have now briefly compared the more salient characteristics of each worldview, their main metaphysical building blocks, and what concomitant beliefs each of these building blocks is usually associated with.

In the next chapter we will analyze which worldviews have a greater presence (are being promoted) in popular media and which ones have little to no presence at all.

Recommended Reading

1. **At Sundry Times. An Essay in the Comparison of Religions.** *R.C. Zaehner.*

2. **Mysticism, Sacred and Profane: An Inquiry Into Some Varieties of Praeternatural Experience.** *R.C. Zaehner.*

---

2. *"[...] Jesus Christ also lived previous lives" ; "[...] So, you see, he reached a high state, either as a Bodhisattva, or an enlightened person, through Buddhist practice or something like that."*
— Tenzin Gyatso as quoted in Beverley, James A. (2001). Hollywood's Idol. Christianity Today, Vol. 45, No. 8. Retrieved April 20, 2007.

Groundhog Day:
Symbolic Repetition in Popular Media,
Mere Coincidence or Deliberate Pattern?

CHAPTER FIVE

Metaphysics and Worldview Promotion in Popular Culture

Modern Common Narrative Trends and their Underlying Influences

1. Introduction

THE PRESENCE OF SYMBOLISM AND METAPHYSICAL ideas in films is nothing new, as they have been there since the very inception of this medium of mass communication. The expressionist movies *Der Golem* (1915) and *Metropolis* (1927), for example, are famous examples of multi-layered narratives that include esoteric elements.

What is new, however, is the increasing amount of esoteric content that the general population has been unknowingly exposed to. This includes all types of entertainment media targeted at all ages and demographics, including video games, music and video clips, animation for kids and adults alike, novels and comics, and even the inauguration ceremonies of sports events.

Only one century ago, metaphysical concepts such as the Unity of Opposites, man as a microcosmic image of the macrocosmic totality (the famous *"as above, so below"* dictum), the possibility of transcending the human condition through esoteric knowledge (Gnosis) and a self-conquered spiritual evolution, or the identity of all that exists with the Absolute (the One), would be concepts absolutely alien to the average person.

For most of human history, the accumulated spiritual wisdom of mankind was considered only appropriate for the few. The aspirants who desired to acquire this knowledge had to prove themselves extensively, and the unworthy were unceremoniously cut off from this knowledge. The very meaning of the term "esoteric", understood as the innermost layer of true knowledge reserved only for the spiritual elite capable of assimilating it, reflects this fact. The unanimous position of all mystical and esoteric traditions was to protect their hard-earned wisdom from unworthy eyes and possible corruption, as well as to shield those unprepared from potentially dangerous knowledge.

Long gone, however, are the days when these doctrines were only known to academic specialists or to the members of some, probably pseudo-secret, initiatory societies. The advent of globalized communication technologies, as well as the consolidation of media companies in a few hands that apparently desire to spread this knowledge, has put all metaphysical doctrines and ideas ever discovered or formulated by mankind within easy reach of every interested person.

Nevertheless, as we will try to show in this chapter, not all knowledge is being given equivalent "screen time", as some worldviews and their constituent metaphysical building blocks are given the spotlight while others are systematically hidden under the carpet.

A few narratives repeat themselves in multiple and imaginative ways while we are exposed to the same stories over and over again, repackaged in shiny new exteriors full of ancient symbols that now come back to life in stylized new shapes and colors.

The flood of this once highly restricted metaphysical knowledge into common mainstream consciousness and popular culture can be described as a radical development in the psychic and spiritual life of the average person. It is quite possible that we are not yet aware of the possible implications and effects of this global pseudo-initiation at a mass scale in steering society in certain directions. We may, as well, wonder about its motives.

Before discussing this possibility in the last chapter of this book, let´s first take a look at which metaphysical doctrines and worldviews have become mainstays of popular culture.

Figure 1. When multiple religious worldviews are portrayed in modern media, Perennialism, or the view that all religions are just different ways of pointing to the same ultimate reality, is the predominant view. Perennialism is, however, an esoteric worldview incompatible with many religions, especially with the Abrahamic ones. Accepting it would imply, for example, that Christianity would need to abandon the doctrine of Jesus Christ as the Incarnation of God, viewing him instead as just an illuminated human person and teacher.

"Uniting" all religions under a minimum common denominator would imply abandoning Theism (the notion of a personal God) to worship instead the impersonal Absolute, the One. This would not be an act of union, but of distortion and indirect substitution of certain faiths for another, very specific, one. Picture: Lost´s final episode; ABC Studios.

2. Metaphysics in Movies and TV Shows

Movies, specifically the science-fiction and horror genres, have always been fertile ground for metaphysical ideas. They are also deeply rooted in mainstream consciousness, becoming cultural references and highly influential vehicles of values and narratives absorbed from our early childhood.

The impact of the most popular franchises can hardly be overestimated. As an example, the *Star Wars* franchise (1977-Ongoing) has an estimated net worth of 46.7 billion dollars, with 47 percent of surveyed adults in the United States having seen the film *Return of the Jedi* (1983).

A more recent phenomenon, the *Marvel Cinematic Universe* franchise (2008-Ongoing), follows in its footsteps with an estimated net worth of 32.2 billion dollars.

Both franchises continually employ metaphysical concepts and target many different populations through all available mass media forms, including animated cartoons aimed at children and movies, books, comics, and video games geared towards young adults.

Thanks to globalization, Hollywood has become the main storyteller of the whole world, taking the place of old tribesmen, wise sages, and ancient religious texts and figures in transmitting cultural values and narratives regarding how the fabric of reality works and our place in it. But, exactly what metaphysical concepts are being communicated?

Following *Star Wars* and *The Matrix* as representative examples of cultural phenomena that have ingrained themselves even in how we speak and conceptualize the world (e.g., the Red Pill), their main teachings (common in many other franchises) include:

a. Star Wars (Original Trilogy)

• *The Force (or Life itself as the creator of the Force) as Ultimate Reality:* a monist worldview in the form of Pantheism/Panentheism (depending on whether ultimate reality has a will or not).

• *The Possibility of Self-Trascendence:* by attuning with the Force through knowledge and spiritual training. A vision which is, in turn, influenced by:

 o *The Monomyth theory of Joseph Campbell:* which states that all mythologies tell the same story of a hero achieving transcendence through his own efforts, culminating in his death and resurrection.

 o *The Psychoanalytical school of C.G. Jung:* a psychological reductionist view of what transcendence is, translated into the common motif of acknowledging, fighting, and re-integrating into the totality of our Self our particular demon or Shadow.

• *The Complementary Dualism of Good and Evil:* both derived from a unitary impersonal Force or field that includes them both in possibility (like the ancient concept of the Absolute, the Source). They have to be balanced, as each other implies and defines his complementary in a dualist cosmology eventually resolving itself in pure impersonal Monism (like the Yin-Yang and Taiji in Taoism, for example).

• Gnostic Motifs, such as:

 o *Spirit/Matter Dualism:* that states that we are light beings (pure spirits) "trapped" in matter.

 o *Gnostic Rebellion:* of the few elite awakened wielders of the Light Side of the Force against a tyrannical servant of the Dark Side (the hero´s father, just as the God of the *Old Testament* is the enemy of Jesus Christ in Gnosticism).

Figure 2. The classic conflict of the Star Wars franchise depicts an apparent opposition between Good and Evil (interpreted primarily as selflessness and selfishness, respectively), which, however, are both ultimately necessary to defeat the true evil emperor and tyrant of the galaxy (Gnostic Demiurge motif).

The need to balance both poles of an impersonal force in order to achieve liberation is a doctrine only possible when the Absolute (in this case named the Force) is viewed as the ultimate reality. This impersonal Unity, beyond both good and evil, is in turn incompatible with worldviews that exclude a personal God as the source of all "evil". The former consider "evil" as a part of themselves (and of God understood as the All) that needs to be integrated in one way or another, while the latter considers it as the negation of the good that has to eventually be rejected and overcome, not integrated. Picture: Star Wars: Episode VI – The Empire Strikes Back (1980); Lucasfilm, Ltd.

b. The Matrix

• A *Non-Theistic (Impersonal) Monist Worldview:* this time in the form of Panentheism/Non-Dualism (in the sense that "All is One"), and heavily based on the Hindu Advaita Vedānta school, which shows itself in the following doctrines:

o *Reality as an Illusion:* Māyā or the Matrix.

o *Cyclical Existence and Time:* exemplified by the different rebellions of the chosen ones that exist again and again until the cycle of bondage is broken.

o *Self-Deification or Self-Transcendence:* through awakening (intuitive knowledge or Gnosis).

• *Psychonautic Techniques (Entheogens):* the Red Pill, used to break this prison world´s spell over us and to achieve knowledge of the truth.

• *Complementary Duality and Unity of Opposites:* in the form of male/female (Neo/Trinity; Oracle/Architect) and good and evil (Neo fusing with agent Smith in order to defeat him). The final resolution of the conflict is an understanding and agreement between the two sides, implying complementarity.

• Gnostic Motifs:

o *Rebellion Against the Demiurge:* a fatherly figure, a false intermediate God that, with his army of hollow machines (like in the Kabbalistic empty shell [Qlippoth] motif), feeds on mankind´s energy ("psychic vampirism").

As we can see, the teachings of these two highly influential franchises, separated by twenty-two years and created by completely different people, are very similar. Both are exponents of an impersonal monist worldview that permits Self-Transcendence or self-integration through intuitive knowledge (awakening, Gnosis) and promotes a Gnostic rebellion against a tyrant father figure that eventually is key in resolving the conflict (Unity of Opposites).

These are, however, only two examples among many. Most science-fiction blockbusters in the last decades have consistently exposed the public to similar concepts. It has become so notorious that Gnosticism has been described as "the main Hollywood storytelling template", being used even in more "serious" pseudo-historical fictional works, such as Dan Brown´s reinterpretation of Christianity in the *Da Vinci Code.*

In addition to Gnosticism, we could say that the other major influences usually seen in modern moviemaking are Kabbalah and Hermeticism (including Alchemy), with all three sharing many similarities and having become increasingly entangled with one another during the centuries, especially in Western Esotericism. Kabbalah, in addition, was influenced by Jewish Gnostic currents since its inception, as stated by renowned historian Gershom Scholem.[1, 2]

To be noted is the fact that Eastern mysticism (especially the Advaita Vedānta school of Hinduism, tantric Tibetan Buddhism, and the Alchemical variants of Taoism) is eventually very similar in its metaphysical doctrines to the three esoteric worldviews just mentioned.

All of them include characteristic beliefs such as the Cycle of Rebirths/ Reincarnation, Emanationism, and an ultimate reality in line with Impersonal Monism that can be reached through the initiate´s own efforts (by achieving intuitional wisdom or Gnosis). These traditions are also major influences in many modern productions.

Below can be found an infographic summarizing the main metaphysical concepts and the worldviews assumed by some of the most influential (and symbolic) movies and TV shows of the last decades, as well as their main influences and some metrics regarding their impact in popular culture.

**IMAGE 1 - SYMBOLISM AND METAPHYSICS
IN MOVIES AND TV SHOWS:**

https://themetaphysicalcompass.com/Symbolism-Movies

---

1. *Scholem, Gershom (1987). Origins of the Kabbalah. Princeton University Press.*

2. *Scholem, Gershom (1960). Jewish Gnosticism, Merkabah Mysticism, and Talmudic Tradition. The Jewish Theological Seminary Press.*

As we can see, the similarities found in the above examples are not an isolated coincidence. Similar doctrines can be found both in mainstream blockbusters (eg., *Doctor Strange, His Dark Materials*) as well as in more niche cult classics (e.g., *Twin Peaks, 2001: A Space Odyssey, Battlestar Galactica*).

Even when the worldviews influencing these productions are not always exactly the same, their main metaphysical doctrines usually are, showing great consistency over time.

Figure 3. In Arthur C. Clarke and Stanley Kubrick´s 2001: A Space Odyssey (picture; Metro-Goldwyn-Mayer), human evolution starts when the Monolith that propels it aligns with the Sun and Moon, in classical Alchemical imagery of the Union of Opposites. In Clarke´s novels, it is suggested that these artifacts are part of the first intelligent beings, the Firstborn.

In Kubrick´s movie, we can see the protagonist embarking on a process of spiritual evolution that sees him born again as the Starchild, a transcendental being suggested to be universal in scope.

3. Metaphysics in Other Popular Media: Video Games, Animation, Comics and Music Industry

Cinema is not the only medium that uses, and even makes the main pillar of its narrative, a particular set of metaphysical concepts. Animated movies and TV shows, both those aimed at children and those for adults, are another notorious example, with cultural phenomena like the manga/ anime *Neon Genesis Evangelion* being based directly on the metaphysical and philosophical problem of *the One and the Many*.

Video games, which due to technical limitations could not have much of a narrative in their beginnings, are now able to depict abstract notions with greater detail and thoroughness than other media. This is so because of the greater amount of time that a video game takes to complete compared to a movie, as well as their immersive and interactive nature, in which gameplay itself can become an instrument to teach important metaphysical notions (e.g., the *Dark Souls* saga and its death-as-a-learning-tool mechanic in our quest to achieve Self-Transcendence).

Nowadays, metaphysically oriented games such as the *Shin Megami Tensei* series and its blockbuster spin-off *Persona* fully recreate the esoteric path of Self-Transcendence in each new game of the series. By merging Jungian psychoanalysis and Hermetico-Alchemical and Kabbalistic doctrines into a Gnostic narrative, each game becomes the simulation and recreation of the full esoteric journey from common man to self-deified being.

Comics, manga, and graphic novels, too, have been used as vessels for the transmission of metaphysical concepts and esoteric worldviews from the beginning.

Once a niche sub-culture, they have now become mainstream thanks, in part, to Marvel and DC comics´ ubiquitous cinematic universes. If we analyze the cosmologies of these fictional universes, we can see that their teachings have not been sloppily expressed as mere background for action-packed stories to take place. Instead, their main metaphysical points have been carefully integrated into the narratives and systematically exposed, being remarkably consistent over the decades.

The music industry, in turn, although its use of symbolism seems to focus mainly on low-level provocation (e.g., Satanic and Illuminati/

Masonic imagery[3]), has produced some events that can be classified as true enactments of initiatory rituals where death and resurrection are central to the adept's journey towards Self-Deification and the One (e.g., *Babymetal*'s concert: *Legend - S - Baptism XX* [2017]).

Figure 4. Complementary Dualism is one of the main metaphysical doctrines of the Persona series and its parent franchise, Shin Megami Tensei.

In Persona 5 (picture; Atlus Co., Ltd.), the protagonist, imprisoned by a false God (the Gnostic Demiurge Yaldabaoth), completes his Self-Deification process with the help of two supernatural assistants. Justine and Caroline, embodying a deceived and split primordial being that lost herself (Gnostic Sophia), merge again into Lavenza, thus regaining the ability to help the protagonist complete his Hermetic journey.

This quest is symbolized by the Major Arcana of the Tarot deck, with the protagonist (and the player) starting as the Fool and ending by identifying with the Universe or the World (a symbol of the All, the Absolute). Its Gnostic background is evidenced, among many other reasons, by the fact that the classical Archangels are depicted as servants of the Demiurge.

The most striking example of Complementary Dualism in the Shin Megami Tensei franchise, however, is its representation of the god of the Old Testament as a minor god. He is the personification of the principle of Law or Order, opposite to the one of Chaos. Both are shown to be below Ultimate Reality, understood as an impersonal totality beyond both.

———————————

3. *This has been discussed, for example, in multiple articles of vigilantcitizen.com. See also Gotthard´s Base Tunnel inauguration ceremony for similar symbolism.*

The infographics below summarize the main metaphysical concepts and worldviews assumed by some of the most cherished animated projects, video games, comics, and music bands of the last decades. These are just some examples among many.

IMAGE 2 - SYMBOLISM AND METAPHYSICS IN OTHER POPULAR MEDIA:

https://themetaphysicalcompass.com/Symbolism-Media

3.1. Marvel and DC Comics: A New Old Mythology for a Secular World

Specific infographics are also dedicated below to the metaphysical concepts shown in both Marvel and DC Comics´ franchises, as the current main players in popular culture and mass entertainment.

They have become the de facto mythologies of children who grew up without one, especially in the nihilistic Western world, where traditional metaphysical and religious concepts were downplayed and almost erased, leaving the empty space left ready for the taking (*The Books of Magic*, for example, is a comic series specifically dedicated to explaining the metaphysics and cosmology of the DC Comics Universe through the eyes of a twelve-year-old boy).

IMAGE 3 - SYMBOLISM AND METAPHYSICS IN DC COMICS:

https://themetaphysicalcompass.com/DC-Comics

> ## IMAGE 4 - SYMBOLISM AND METAPHYSICS IN MARVEL COMICS:
>
> https://themetaphysicalcompass.com/Marvel

As we can see, their teachings are mostly the same. They include:

a. Metaphysics and Worldview of DC Comics

• *Impersonal Monism (Pantheism/Panentheism):* ultimate reality is described as the Void of Nothingness or Sea of Brahma before the Creator (also known as God´s unconscious mind [*Justice League Dark* Vol.1 #39] or the Overvoid, a living conscious Void of infinite abstract intelligence). The metaphor used is that of an infinite canvas of pure white (All-Possibility, pure potentiality).

• *Emanationism:* we are all a manifestation of the Void. Therefore, we just have to realize our intrinsic true nature as God ("each drop of water is the Ocean" metaphor).

• *Personal God as derived from the Void (The Presence):* the form and shape that a personal creator God takes emanates from the pre-existent Void. Often represented as the God of the Abrahamic religions and, in particular, showing Christian attributes. Yahweh is portrayed as a manifestation of the Presence, not as ultimate reality, which is the Void. However, many pantheons of gods co-exist (e.g., Greek ones) as partial personifications and manifestations of different aspects of the Void.

• *Complementary Dualism and paired Male/Female Cosmic Entities (similar to, for example, Syzygies in Gnosticism):*

o *The Source:* the energetic aspect of The Presence (similar to Shiva/Shakti or Purusha/Prakriti [spirit/matter] in Hinduism, or to the sexually joined deities of Tibetan Tantric Buddhism). It has a complementary feminine counterpart in Mother Entity. It is the source of limitless energy and of all that exists.

o *Monitor (matter) and Anti-Monitor (anti-matter):* cosmic entities that promote or destroy all life in the Universe, respectively.

o *"Evil" as Chaos:* the necessary counterpart of Order, each one defining and implying the other.

• *The Seven Forces of the Universe (similar to the seven classical Alchemical planets or the Gnostic Archons):* born of The Presence through The Source. Creation comes from them.

• *Cycle of Rebirths and Cyclical Existence.*

b. Metaphysics and Worldview of Marvel Comics

• *Monism (Pantheism/Panentheism):* The One Above All is the highest creative Force in the Marvel Universe, using the figure of the author as a metaphor. It is also called the Fulcrum, meaning the central point of balance between two opposites.

The One Above All lives in the House of Ideas, or "Heaven" (similar to the Neo-Platonic Nous/Intellect, which emanates from the One).

"I am the One Above All. I see through many eyes. I build with many hands. They are themselves, but they are also me. I am all-powerful. My only weapon is love. The mystery intrigues me." [4]

• *Emanationism:* we are both ourselves and direct emanations from this God.

----

4. *Ultimates 2. Vol 1, 100.*

• *A Modalist Triadic God:* in the figure of the Living Tribunal, subordinate and representative of The One Above All. The Tribunal is a triadic being, with each of its three faces representing an aspect or mode of manifestation of the One (equity, vengeance, and necessity; Modalism: similar to the Hindu Trimurti and contrary to Trinitarian Christianity). It is a personification of the Multiverse and its Laws. It may act to prevent cosmic imbalances, including that of good or evil, within a particular Universe.

• *Secondary Gods as the Personification of Abstract Universal Forces.*

• *Complementary Dualism:*

o *The One Below All:* The One Above All (pure love; creative Force) can also manifest as this entity (God´s Shadow; pure hate; destructive Force), who serves as the necessary counterweight to the expanding life in the Multiverse.

Multiplicity as Evil. Destruction as reverting particular existences back to the homogeneity of the One: the "mystery" (of the "other") frightens and disgusts the One Below All, while it intrigues The One Above All, its creative aspect.

o *The In-Betweener:* a cosmic being that exists between dichotomies. Created by Master Order and Lord Chaos to maintain a universal balance, he is the personification of the Union of Opposites, showing the complementarity between aspects such as life and death, reality and illusion, good and evil, logic and emotion, existence and nothingness, god and man.

o *The Logos:* the *coincidentia oppositorum* (coincidence of opposites) between Order, Chaos, and the In-Betweener, who acts as the glue that binds them together and reconciles them (similar to the Filioque trinitarian structure added to Christianity by Roman Catholicism).

• *Cyclical Cosmology.*

c. Synthesis and Summary of Common Metaphysical Concepts in Popular Media

Condensing the overall message transmitted by both giants of the entertainment industry, we end up with this summary statement:

Ultimate reality is the One, an *absolutely* simple Monad that emanates all reality, including any personal god that may exist in addition to each of us. Multiplicity, therefore, is *"evil"* as it is the opposite of absolute unity. But this *"evil"*, which necessarily includes the existence of death and complementary dualities at each level of creation, is needed if we want to exist as particular individuals.

Given that the One is defined as All-Possibility, its *necessary* counterpart is the Multiverse (All-Actuality, the realization of all these possibilities). As nothing is excluded from the Absolute, *"evil"* (understood as the egotistic individuality of Chaos, the counterpart of Order) is also a part of it. It has a role to play in allowing the multiplicity that is required for our particular existence, and it should be both understood and integrated (in a balanced way) as a legitimate aspect of both ultimate reality and ourselves.

This simplified statement could also be used verbatim to define the message of other cultural phenomena such as, for example, *Neon Genesis Evangelion*. Japan and the USA, East and West, are united in the message they put forth.

4. The Case of the Multiverse

In recent times, the concept of the Multiverse has become ubiquitous in popular culture. The Marvel and DC cinematic universes may have been the main culprits of this surge in popularity, but they are not the only ones. A few of the most popular examples in recent years include: *Adventure Time* (2010-2018), *Rick and Morty* (2013- Ongoing), *The Lego Movie* (2014), *The Man in the High Castle* (2015-2019), *Dragon Ball Super* (2015-

Ongoing), *Dark* (2017–2020), *Riverdale* (2017), *Spider-Man: Into the Spider-Verse* (2018), *Russian Doll* (2019), *His Dark Materials* (2019–2022), *Spider-Man: No Way Home* (2021), *What If...?* (2021-Ongoing), *Loki* (2021–2023), *Doctor Strange in the Multiverse of Madness* (2022), *Everything Everywhere All at Once* (2022), *The Flash* (2023), *Spider-Man: Across the Spider-Verse* (2023), *Deadpool & Wolverine* (2024) and *Final Fantasy VII Remake/Rebirth* (2020-2024). This tendency is set to continue (e.g., in *Avengers: Secret Wars* [2027]).

Given the relationship between this concept and the ones reviewed above, it is not difficult to make predictions regarding what other metaphysical ideas may become popular and make an appearance in our TV screens in the future.

Figure 5. Marvel and DC Comics have not shied away from portraying Jesus Christ in their comics over the years. They both share one thing in common: they never portray Him as being who He stated Himself to be, nor as Christianity understands Him. In Marvel [5] (B) it is implied that He was a mutant, while in DC Comics [6] it is stated that science has proven that the resurrection did not happen. The latter canceled a few of his appearances due to criticisms and petitions, such as the overtly satirical Second Coming series, later published by Ahoy Comics (A). In an unpublished volume of the Swamp Thing [7], Jesus was to be referred as "the magician".

5. See marvel.fandom.com/wiki/Jesus_of_Nazareth_(Earth-616).

6. See dc.fandom.com/wiki/Jesus_of_Nazareth_(New_Earth).

7. See dc.fandom.com/wiki/Swamp_Thing_Vol_2_88_(Unpublished).

5. Conclusion

As we have seen by synthesizing the teachings of a few representative examples amongst many, nowadays metaphysical doctrines are commonplace in popular culture and mass media.

However, only a few of them are given "screen time" again and again while others (usually incompatible with the former) either become distorted to the point of inversion (e.g., Gnostic inversion of Christianity) or are just ignored.

This has been happening with remarkable consistency over the decades and throughout all different media that compose popular culture, but has become progressively more difficult to overlook.

Major franchises are worth billions of dollars. Nevertheless, their biggest impact, helped by globalization, is in shaping the collective cultural consciousness and worldview of people all around the world, especially in cultures that crave a sense of meaning because of the loss of their previous spiritual heritage.

Given that different metaphysical doctrines exist as part of different worldviews, some of them incompatible with each other, one would expect to see a little more variety in their depiction on mass media. However, it is easy to see that this is not the case. Only a handful of doctrines are repeated (in all types of media) to such an extent that consumers have the feeling of reliving old stories.

The most ubiquitous metaphysical notions promoted include:

• *Impersonal Monism:* in the form of Pantheism/Panentheism (especially the latter, but many times not explicitly defined) — the One, the Absolute, All-Possibility. In the rare cases where it is represented as a personal entity, it is implied that it is a personification of a Principle or Force.

• *Personal gods:* if they exist, they are below the previous level of existence as particular manifestations of the Absolute. They usually represent personifications of abstract Forces or Laws.

• *Emanationism:* the doctrine that everything in existence is an emanation of this absolutely simple Unity and that we can come back to it by an inverse process of stripping ourselves of any particularity (achieved through our own wisdom [Gnosis] and efforts).

• *The Multiverse:* or All-Actuality as the body of the One (conceptualized as All-Possibility).

• *Polarity and Complementary Duality:* Non-Dualism as the Unity of Opposites (e.g., good/evil, male/female), the method of getting closer to the Totality or Source of it all. We can include among these teachings the integration of the Jungian Shadow into our true personality or Self.

• *The notion of Cyclical Cosmology and Existence.*

• *Rebellion against unjust god/s:* who oppress us and stifle our spiritual evolution for their own benefit. They are but intermediate-level entities, also emanating from the One, who have overstepped their rights.

Furthermore, the main recurring worldviews being promoted, which in turn share many of the same metaphysical building blocks, are:

• Gnosticism (and Manichaeism).

• Kabbalah (especially the school of Isaac Luria and Hasidism).

• Hermeticism/Alchemy and Neo-Platonism.

• Eastern Mysticism (especially Advaita Vedānta, tantric Tibetan Buddhism, and esoteric Taoism).

• Western Esotericism (e.g., Theosophy).

• The Analytical Psychology of Carl Jung (with concepts like the Archetypes, the Shadow, Anima/Animus, and the Self).

• Perennialism (e.g., the Monomyth theory of Joseph Campbell).

Classic monotheistic doctrines (especially Abrahamic ones), such as creation from nothing (Ex Nihilo) by the action of a personal transcendent

God, the nature of evil as a voluntary rebellion against that God (lacking independent existence, rather than being understood as necessary Chaos), and the possibility of *the One and the Many* coexisting (like, for example, in Christianity) are rarely (if ever) represented in mainstream productions. C.S. Lewis´ *Chronicles of Narnia* and, more indirectly, J.R.R. Tolkien´s *The Lord of the Rings* would be the most popular examples at least partially compatible with these latter tenets.

Are these trends merely coincidental? Maybe metaphysical fads exist as in any other aspect of life? It may be so. But then, we would need to explain their consistency in time (multiple decades) and space (different media created all over the world), as well as the remarkable absence (or inversion) of the beliefs of their competitors. Be that as it may, the fact remains that metaphysical content is being communicated, and since metaphysical ideas are the building blocks of certain worldviews, it should be easy to predict the next ideas that may come our way.

As we navigate through this complex landscape of spiritual ideas available to us today, should this not be another clue pointing us in certain directions?

Recommended Reading

1. **Esoteric Hollywood: Sex, Cults and Symbols in Film.** *Jay Dyer.* [Dyer may have a polarizing personality for some. However, we have found his theoretical work (e.g., theological explanations) to be sound. Please, do your own research].
2. **A Dictionary of Symbols.** *Juan Eduardo Cirlot* [reference work].

The Paradox of Choice:
How to Find Our Way?

Navigating the Complex Landscape of Current Worldviews

Typology of Mysticism and the Solution to the Problem of the One and the Many

1. Introduction

SUMMARIZING OUR WHOLE JOURNEY UP TO THIS point we can see that, until now, we have:

• Seen that every person is an unknowing metaphysician, since our lives are guided unavoidably by our metaphysical presuppositions and beliefs, in a more or less conscious way.

• Identified an ubiquitous and abnormally high presence of ancient symbolism and metaphysical narratives in all types of popular culture and mass media. This tendency has been shown to be consistent in

time, with a time span of decades, and is progressively becoming more prominent.

• *Studied the nature and main functions of symbolism.* Including its main one: to initiate a person in metaphysical doctrines that due to their transcendental and unfathomable nature are better transmitted through symbols. They are also used to conceal these truths from unprepared eyes.

• *Reviewed the main metaphysical categories and doctrines taught in traditional worldviews.* With special emphasis placed on the solutions given to the problem of *the One and the Many*, the central question in all religious, mystical, esoteric or philosophical thought. We have seen that this solution, in turn, has important and unavoidable implications for our metaphysical beliefs in other areas, such as: cosmology, time, the existence and nature of evil, the dialectical tension between determinism and free will, and the possibility of salvation (what it means to be saved and how to achieve it).

• *Compared the main worldviews available to us today and their constituent metaphysical building blocks.* We found that most living worldviews can be divided between proponents of the doctrine of the One (absolute Monism, usually in the form of Pantheism/Panentheism, but also as strict Monotheism) or as transcending the dialectical problem of *the One and the Many* (Christian Trinitarian God and certain Buddhist interpretations of Non-Dualism).

• *Showed that the symbolism and metaphysical teachings present in modern popular culture comes from only a few recurrent worldviews.* Most notably Kabbalah, Hermeticism/Alchemy, Gnosticism, and Eastern Mysticism/Western Esotericism. We have seen that, deep down, these worldviews share most of the key metaphysical building blocks that conform them.

The first four points mentioned above are analytical, and involve the study of the constituent parts of the problem at hand and their implications ("the trees"). The last two are synthetic, and involve comparing the worldviews that contain these parts and looking at the big picture from a higher vantage point thanks to the knowledge previously gained ("the forest").

Now, we finally find ourselves in a position that will allow us to draw our own conclusions and position ourselves regarding the main problem at hand and the driving question of this book: how can we find our way in this complex world so full of conflicting worldviews?

2. First Stage, or the Challenge of the Atheist: Why Believe in Any Non-Materialist Worldview?

But before engaging in further discussions, let´s first tackle the crucial question that many of us, raised in a secular culture and educational system, ask ourselves at the beginning of our journey: why should I abandon the scientist dogma of pure Materialism that has been taught to me since childhood? Is there any proof regarding the existence of any non-material reality?

First of all, we have to understand that all human knowledge, including scientific and philosophical knowledge (science was first named "Natural Philosophy"), depends at some point on a set of unchallenged assumptions that we have decided that are truly obvious and cannot be refuted (Axioms). In other words, all knowledge presupposes a previous step of faith in the axioms that support it.

In the case of science, we have to presuppose, among other things, the existence of deterministic abstract non-material laws of physics. In their absence, all observations would be a mere collection of unrelated data.

Second, we have to accept that, for us, it is impossible to attain by mere deduction an absolutely unobjectionable logical proof of the certainty of the truth of any worldview. If this was not the case, no plurality of worldviews would exist, since it would be simple to show everyone the fact that one worldview is true and the rest are false, therefore killing all other worldviews on the spot. It would also imply the lack of free will to self-determine who we are, as a logical demonstration would suffice for everyone to be compelled or "forced" to believe and follow that worldview, even if they do not like it.[1]

Therefore, the most that mankind can achieve by mere reason alone is to adopt a self-consistent position that is compatible with all known facts and our own experience. At first, it may seem like this is a meagre reward for all our worries and dedication but, as we will see, the presence of internal contradictions is commonplace and can be useful in narrowing down the list of worldviews to consider.

2.1. Presuppositions Shape Our Worldview

This approach, called Presuppositionalism and usually employed by Christian apologetics, has been used to compare and contrast the self-consistency of pure materialistic Monism with worldviews that, instead, posit a spiritual ultimate reality (in most cases, the Christian Tri-Une God).

It is an epistemological approach based on the examination of the presuppositions and axioms of each worldview and the logical deduction of their implications and possible inconsistencies. It claims that the chosen presuppositions of each worldview are central to its interpretation of reality, as one could not make sense of human experience without them.

This links with the fact, mentioned before, that we are all unknowing metaphysicians. We all make a choice by selecting the set of "obvious" truths that serve as the axiomatic ground from where the different worldviews we later follow can, or cannot, take root. Therefore, in a certain sense, by choosing the axioms that will determine which worldviews are compatible with us, we are defining who we are. We are birthing ourselves.[2]

---

1. We will analyze the metaphysical implications of this statement at the end of section 2.4, since it may serve as another hint in our journey.

2. It is interesting to note that this notion that reality functions in a way that compels us to define ourselves through "axiom choice", in itself, cannot be accounted for in purely materialistic paradigms.

This transcendental approach, considered to be the argument against Materialism most difficult to refute, contrasts with the classical and evidential apologetical approach, which tries to show the existence of God from our level of reality through God´s immanence.

Its most famous exponents were the theologian Cornelius Van Til and the minister Greg Bahnsen, who popularized this approach through well-known public debates against atheists (available online).

The argument used in these debates is called the Transcendental Argument for the Existence of God (TAG), a previous version of which was formulated by the philosopher Immanuel Kant through his work *The Only Possible Argument in Support of a Demonstration of the Existence of God.*

2.2. The Transcendental Argument for the Existence of God (TAG)

The Transcendental Argument for the Existence of God (TAG) states that the very possibility of existence of abstract absolutes such as logic and morals, which we take for granted, ultimately presuppose a non-material ultimate reality.

The argument, using logic as an example, is structured as follows:[3]

- *Proposition 1:* Logical absolutes (e.g., laws of logic) exist.

- *P2:* Logical absolutes are conceptual.

- *P3:* Concepts are not material (they are mental), but are nevertheless real universals.

- *P4:* Logical absolutes would exist even if our minds did not.

———————————

3. *Meister, Chad V.; Mittelberg, Mark; McDowell, Josh; Montgomery, John F. (2007). Reasons for Faith: Making a Case for the Christian Faith. Wheaton, Illinois: Crossway Books.*

- *P5:* Therefore, logical absolutes are transcendent.

- *P6:* Since logical absolutes are transcendent and conceptual, they must exist in a transcendent mind.

- *P7:* This transcendent mind is what we recognize as God.

- *Conclusion:* God exists. He is the necessary precondition for logic and all abstract and immaterial universal realities which could not exist in a purely materialist universe. God, therefore, is the missing link between the objects of experience (brute facts of sense experience) and the subject of that knowledge.

The fact that the presuppositions of pure Materialism alone make it impossible to justify the proven fact of logical thinking (let alone the possibility of having a rational debate on these matters), proves it as a self-contradictory worldview. Therefore, contrary worldviews that defend a non-material aspect of reality have to be true.

As Van Til stated:[4]

"We must point out ... that univocal reasoning itself leads to self-contradiction, not only from a theistic point of view, but from a non-theistic point of view as well... It is this that we ought to mean when we say that we reason from the impossibility of the contrary. The contrary is impossible only if it is self-contradictory when operating on the basis of its own assumptions."

As he further pointed out, trying to explain human rationality on the basis of an ultimately irrational Universe is *"like a man made of water, trying to escape an infinite sea of water on a ladder of water"*.[5]

---

4. *Van Til, C. (1969). A Survey of Christian Epistemology. Philadelphia: Presbyterian and Reformed, p. 204.*

5. *Van Til, C. (1975). Christian Apologetics. Philadelphia: Presbyterian and Reformed, p. 63.*

2.3. TAG´s Criticism: Rejection of Theism, But Not Necessarily of Non-Materialism

Some critics have stated that certain logic systems like classical propositional logic can be justified through theorems like *Gödel's Completeness Theorem*, hence avoiding the need for God´s existence.

This argument fails to take into consideration, however, that a mathematical law or principle is just another immaterial universal. Therefore, their existence also undermines pure Materialism. Furthermore, the theorem´s discoverer himself (the famous mathematician Kurt Gödel), also produced a classical propositional proof of God´s existence in what is known as *Gödel's Ontological Proof.*

This all boils down to the fact that many of TAG´s critics, instead of arguing against Non-Materialism, are arguing against Theism instead. Non-material realities may exist, but it is the existence of a personal God which is being fought against.

This is clearly stated by another main criticism that states that TAG is not really a defense of Theism but an argument against Materialism, with other atheist (or impersonal) spiritual worldviews (e.g., Platonism and its world of ideas or abstract universals that eventually trace back their existence to the One of Parmenides) being also possible solutions.

For now, it is enough to consider that the Transcendental Argument plays in favor of all non-materialist worldviews. Not all these worldviews, however, are the same.

2.4. How to Evaluate Non-Materialist Worldviews

If there are enough signs to consider pure Materialism lacking, our next step will be to search for truth in a non-materialist worldview. But, which one? First of all, is there such a thing as capital T "Truth" or are we just wasting our time pondering these questions?

Let us just remark that, in metaphysics, truth, by definition, is not multiple but unitary. The existence of multiple truths would show that the only real truth is that of Relativism, which amounts to affirm the self-contradiction that the only existing truth would be its absence. This, instead of liberating us, would make us slaves to meaninglessness.

EPISTEMIC DISTANCE

How would clear evidence about the existence of God impact our capacity to have free will?

Which worldviews are coherent with this fact?

As previously mentioned, the lack of an univocal logical proof that compels us to believe in a certain worldview to the exclusion of every other one is an important aspect in us having free will. This fact, in itself, is also a metaphysical statement that can be compared to the doctrines in this regard taught by different worldviews.

For example: is this perceived Epistemic Distance or discontinuity between God and ourselves something that a worldview that believes in the theory of emanations can explain? Why would that epistemic discontinuity exist in such a view, which is based on the ultimate identity of all reality with the One and in the absence of any such ontological discontinuity between any level of reality? [6]

In contrast, is not this possibility of defining ourselves in this regard, which allows us to even reject the existence of God, coherent and compatible with the revelations of theistic religions (being an important point of, for example, the Christian Gospel)?

Furthermore, is this epistemic distance and its consequent free will equally consistent with all monotheistic faiths, including the ones that state that the Will of God is absolute (Fatalism) and He alone decides who is saved and who is damned (e.g., Islam)?

Which worldviews are consistent with this notion and which are not?

---

6. *In order to explain this, some worldviews based on the One, like Advaita Vedānta, had to defend the existence of a secondary power of ignorance (Illusion, Māyā). This power, whose origin is not clearly explained, is the one in charge of veiling our ultimate identity with Brahman (Impersonal God). However, by positing a secondary principle different and in conflict with ultimate reality (defined as Truth), they re-instated again another version of dialectical Dualism. This problem, which Advaita has not been able to satisfactorily resolve, was pointed out by "rival" schools such as the "theistic" Kashmir (or Trika) Shaivism.*

Relativism, as a worldview or life stance, does not believe itself to be relative, therefore negating by its mere existence the only axiomatic presupposition and metaphysical notion that defines it. At most, we can say that truth can be found partially represented in different worldviews, but we cannot speak of multiple truths without the concept losing all its meaning. This aspect will be further analyzed in the last chapter of this book.

Therefore, if pure Materialism is a self-contradictory worldview and truth is unitary, how do we navigate the complex catalogue of worldviews available to us in this modern globalized world?

One way to do this is through a deep understanding of what each worldview believes is our ultimate destiny and the aim we should strive for. In other words: what would be our subjective experience if we achieved the end goal pursued by each worldview?

3. R.C. Zaehner´s Typology of Mysticism

To answer this question we can resort to a typology of mysticism such as the one proposed by the scholar of religious studies R.C. Zaehner. Through his vast knowledge of the original sacred texts (he was skilled in many of the original languages of these traditions, such as Sanskrit [Hinduism], Pali [Buddhism], and Arabic [Islam]), Zaehner found that the range of mystical experiences could be classified approximately[7] as depicted in *Figure 1.* [8, 9, 10, 11, 12, 13]

---

7. Taking into consideration that there is always some variety in interpretations between contending schools pertaining to the same tradition or even between particular, more or less influential, individuals. Nevertheless, the main view of each tradition is usually clear in what spiritual states they do expect to achieve and how they are subjectively experienced.

8. Zaehner, R.C. (1957). Mysticism, Sacred and Profane. Oxford University Press, pp. 66, 168, 184, 192, 198, 204.

9. Zaehner, R.C. (1958). At Sundry Times. Faber and Faber, p.172.

10. Zaehner, R.C. (1960). Hindu and Muslim Mysticism. Bloomsbury, p.19.

11. Zaehner, R.C. (1969). The Bhagavad Gita. Oxford University Press, p.2.

12. Zaehner, R.C. (1970). Concordant Discord. Clarendon Press, pp. 59, 129, 199-204.

13. Zaehner, R.C. (1972). Drugs, Mysticism and Make-believe. Collins, p.93.

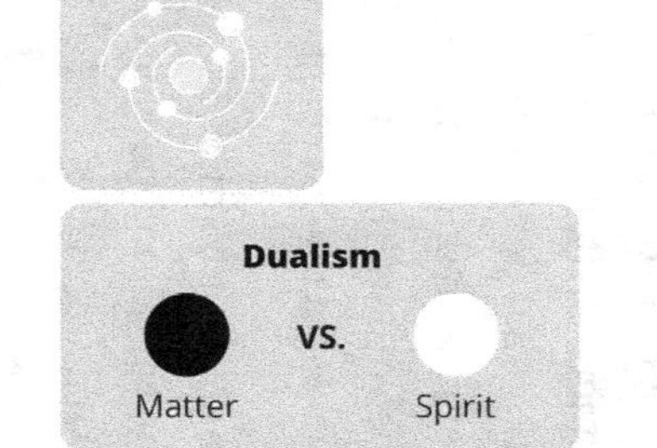
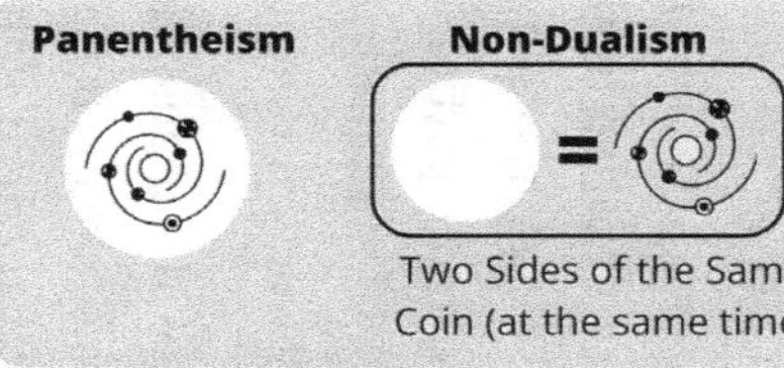
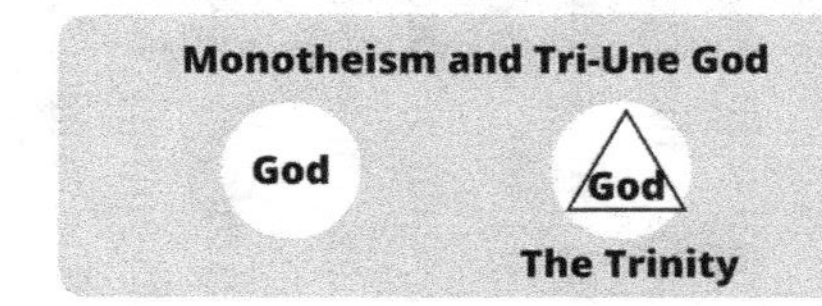
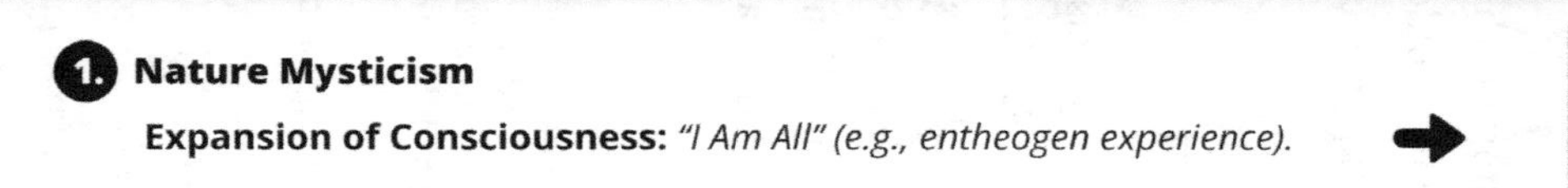

Figure 1. R.C. Zaehner´s classification (Typology) of the different types of mystical experiences.

a. Nature Mysticism

This category encompasses all worldviews that, through ecstatic (to go "outside oneself") techniques, have their initiated members experience an expansion of consciousness that makes them feel the whole Universe as part of themselves. This subjective experience has been defined as an "oceanic feeling" in which a person identifies with nature and the vastness of the cosmos. As such, it has been labelled as the subjective experience of Pantheism.

It is typical of Neo-Shamanic and nature worship revival movements that may, or may not, use entheogenic drugs as helpers to achieve this state (e.g., peyote, ayahuasca or mescaline, as per Zaehner´s own experience).

A primary difference remarked by Zaehner between this "I am All" or "All is Me" subjective experience and the "God is in Me" experience of theistic mysticism is the morally "open" or undetermined nature of the former, in contrast with the sense of holiness experienced in the latter. [14,15]

b. Isolation Mysticism

This form of mysticism, instead of using ecstatic methods, is characterized by the use of enstatic (to "stand-within-oneself") ones. Therefore, the practitioners of this type of mysticism single-pointedly focus all their attention into their own inner core or Self.

Zaehner understood these experiences as fundamentally different from the ones of Nature Mysticism. Instead of expanding the adept´s consciousness (the ego [or little One] expanding to include the Many), the traditions using these methods try to isolate the Self from everything external to itself or, in other words, to remove (the One) Spirit from matter (the derivative Many).

---

14. Zaehner, R.C. (1957). *Mysticism, Sacred and Profane. Oxford University Press*, pp. xi, 22-23 (union of soul and God), 33 (satcitananda and the beatific vision), 37, 93-94.

15. Zaehner, R.C. (1974). *Our Savage God. Sheed and Ward*, pp. 10–12.

Figure 2. A Sea of Solipsistic Monads. In the dualistic vision of Sāṃkhya, the original metaphysical system underlying Yoga, reality is divided into Spirit (Purusha) and Matter (Prakriti). The former, however, is not formed by a single Monad but by innumerable ones, being similar to the concept of soul in other worldviews. The objective is to isolate Spirit from Matter, the former ending in isolation from the rest of reality.

b1. One Experience, Two Interpretations: Dualism and Monism (or "Non-Dualism")

Zaehner further subdivided the category of Isolation Mysticism in two: Dualism and absolute Monism, with the Hindu paradigmatic examples of Sāṃkhya/Yoga and Advaita Vedānta as representatives of each one.

According to Zaehner, what mystics from both categories experience is their self-absorption into the core of their own souls: pure Spirit. However, he found that the metaphysical outlook of the adept has an impact on the interpretation of this same experience.

Figure 3. The Only Transmigrant. In Absolute Monism each being is only a mask (Persona) of the Absolute, all life being just a cyclical game of Self-Forgetting and Self-Discovery where the particular characteristics and personality of each mask has to eventually be discarded.

The dualists interpret their subjective experiences as the detachment of their immortal, peaceful, undifferentiated, and unitary Spirit or Self (Purusha) from the contingencies of a self-existent Nature or Matter

(Prakriti). This Matter is understood as a second co-eternal Principle complementary to Spirit.[16, 17, 18]

In monist or "non-dualist" (in the sense of "All is One") Advaita Vedānta, in contrast, the Hindu mystic interprets the same subjective experience as the union of the Self (Ātman) with Brahman, the divine Unity, universal Totality (the Absolute), pure Being (Being-Consciousness-Bliss) that is the ground of existence of all multiplicity.[19, 20]

For Advaita, Nature (Prakriti) becomes just an Illusion (Māyā), while what was thought by the dualist to be one´s own pure isolated Spirit or Self (Purusha) is found to be really Brahman (the impersonal Supreme Reality or "God").

c. Theistic Mysticism

The last category of Zaehner´s typology is that of Theistic Mysticism, found mainly in Christianity, Judaism, Islam, and theistic Hinduism (most notably in Rāmānuja´s Vishishtadvaita Vedānta and some interpretations of Trika Shaivism). It may also include Sikhism and Zoroastrianism, although these worldviews have also been interpreted in panentheistic and dualist ways, respectively.

---

16. *Zaehner, R.C. (1957). Mysticism, Sacred and Profane. Oxford University Press,*
Yoga (pp. 96-99, 111), prakriti and purusha (98, 108, 124-125), guṇas (98, 107-108),
buddhi (108, 125), the mind or lower soul {Sufi term nafs} (102, 125), the body (125),
ahamkara (108, 126).

17. *Zaehner, R.C. (1970). Concordant Discord. Clarendon Press, p.97: buddhi is the*
"highest and most subtle form of matter", as "the seat of cognition" it determines
"right conduct".

18. *Newell, W.L. (1981). Struggle and Submission: R.C. Zaehner on Mysticisms.*
University Press of America, pp. 160-161, 167-170 (prakriti and purusa, Sāṃkhya).

19. *Zaehner, R.C. (1970). The Comparison of Religions. Hassell Street Press, p.193*
(Sac, Cid, Ananda compared to the Trinity).

20. *Radhakrishnan (1923). Indian Philosophy (Oxford University Press, v.2, pp.*
539, 483, 539 (saccidananda); pp. 439, 687 (Tat tvam asi).

The theistic mystic, instead of experiencing his own self-unity, true Self, or pure "liberated" Spirit typical of nature religions[21, 22], experiences a true mystical union[23] with a personal and transcendent God, feeling a deep sense of union with Him while retaining his sense of (an elevated and sanctified) self .

This type of mysticism negates both pure Monism (as no union can exist where there is no "Otherness") and Dualism (because true union by definition erases any opposition).

4. A New Proposal for a Typology of Mysticism

While Zaehner identifies isolation as the key principle of both the dualist and monist experiences, some critics' remark that the monistic experience of Advaita Vedānta is not lived as being isolated from everything, but is felt instead as a deep connection with Universal Unity.[24]

The use of exclusively Hindu schools (especially Advaita Vedānta) as representatives of Non-Dualism, with little mention of the Buddhist version of the kind "Saṃsāra equals Nirvana", has also been singled out as a problem for a typology that wants to be as comprehensive as possible.

Buddhist Non-Dualism, especially Mahāyāna and Vajrayāna traditions, does not necessarily focus on merging with the One in an undifferentiated

---

21. Zaehner, R.C. (1957). Mysticism, Sacred and Profane. Oxford University Press: two chapters discuss Theism and Monism, while another two speak about mescaline (drug-induced states). The Triune Divinity of Christianity is briefly addressed at pp. 195–197.

22. Newell, W.L. (1981). Struggle and Submission: R.C. Zaehner on Mysticisms. University Press of America, pp. 5-6.

23. Cf., Zaehner, R.C. (1957). Mysticism, Sacred and Profane. Oxford University Press, pp. 151-152: discusses this union in terms of its analogy to sexual union.

24. Reardon, J.P. (2012). A theological analysis of R.C. Zaehner's theory of mysticism. ETD Collection for Fordham University, pp. 170-186: includes a discussion regarding the complexities of the nature of Zaehner's "Isolation" type.

totality but in awakening to the fact that the non-theistic ground of existence they believe in (Emptiness/Buddha Nature) is the necessary other side or counterpart of all dualistic existence.

Therefore, in this section, a new proposal for a typology of mysticism that takes these criticisms into consideration is presented. *Figures 4-6* below are a concise summary of it.

As we can see, in this modified version, the Isolation Mysticism category of Zaehner´s typology now contains only the experiences of the dualists, while the mystical experiences of the monists that experience fusion with the One (Panentheism) instead of expansion (Pantheism, Nature Mysticism) have been differentiated and incorporated into a new category, called *Mysticism of Unity through Absorption*.

This category has been further subdivided between those who consider the existence of "otherness" as just an illusion and those who consider it as a temporary, but real, form taken by the One.

Non-Dualism of the Buddhist type, in turn, has been added as an intermediate category between the Mysticism of Unity through Absorption and the theistic Mysticism of Union. It has been labelled as *Mysticism of Union through Simultaneity of the One and the Many* as no absorption is implied, just an awakening and recognition of the simultaneous dual nature of all that exists as both immanent and transcendent (e.g., the analogy of the ocean and the waves each implying and defining each other).

In contrast, labelling Theistic Mysticism as *Mysticism of Union* implies the existence of an "Other" to unite with, while the unity spoken of by the previous categories is between parts, aspects or modes of existence of oneself, as the doctrines of the One state.

The basic subjective experience of pantheistic monists, who experience a form of Nature Mysticism, is their expansion of consciousness: "I am All that exists" or "All is Me".

Figures 4, 5 and 6. A New Proposal for a Typology of Mystical Experiences; taking into consideration the differences between experiences of spiritual isolation (e.g., Sāṃkhya) and those that conceptualize them as "fusing" with the One. This classification also takes into consideration Buddhist Non-Dualism of the type "Saṃsāra equals Nirvana".

Subjective Experience / Analogy	3. Mysticism of Unity through Absorption	Solution to the One and the Many

Subjective Experience / Analogy

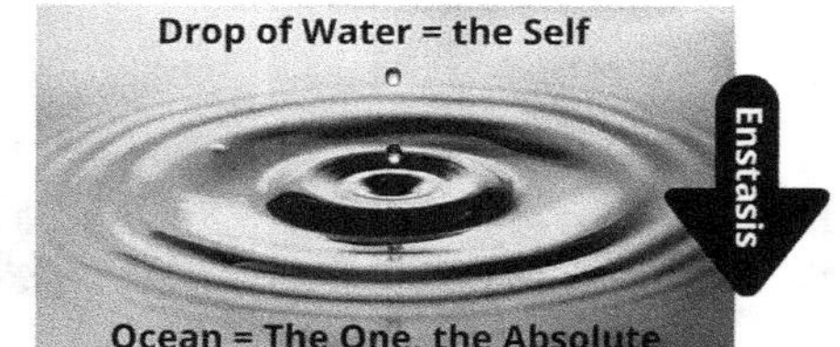

3. Mysticism of Unity through Absorption

Absorption into the Ground of Existence:
"All is One, and I Am that One".

Experienced Altered State of Consciousness: a deep sense of existence, Unity and bliss. The adepts intuitively know that everything that exists shares the same identity with their Self. A combination of the first two stages:
I am All + I am One (Spirit) = All is One.

Analogy: drop of water merging back into the Ocean.

If All is One, then the appearance of multiplicity is:

1. An Ilusion.

Analogy: the rope that resembles a snake.

2. The real Energies of God: the Nature of everything is One, but creation is real and is the very body of God, his power and energies.

Analogy: everything created as the wrinkles (particular shapes) in a piece of fabric. Every wrinkle is the same cloth, but they temporarily have different forms. Once stretched, they dissapear but the cloth that is their very nature remains.

Solution to the One and the Many

Panentheism

(e.g., Non-Theistic Hinduism)

<table>
<tr><th colspan="3">Proposal for a New Typology of Mysticism [3/3]</th></tr>
<tr><th>Subjective Experience / Analogy</th><th></th><th>Solution to the One and the Many</th></tr>
<tr>
<td>Waves = individuality

Ocean = Unitary common Nature (e.g. Emptiness)</td>
<td>4. Mysticism of Unity through Simultaneity of the One and the Many

"Samsara equals Nirvana": everything in existence is at the same time relative and absolute. The One and the Many exist / do not exist at the same time. They are two sides of the same coin.

Experienced Altered State of Consciousness: the experience at the same time of:
1. The Emptiness of all phenomena as underlying reality.
2. The relative, temporal and impermanent existence of all phenomena.

Analogy: empty, clear, luminous space. It is neither permanent nor impermanent, is both permanent and impermanent, is nowhere, and is everywhere; the waves and the ocean existing at the same time, being both one.</td>
<td>Non-Dualism
(e.g., Buddhism)
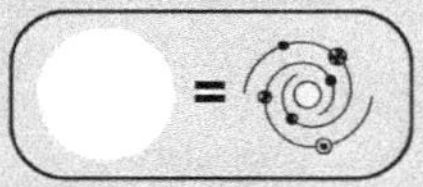
Two Sides of the Same Coin (at the same time)</td>
</tr>
<tr>
<td>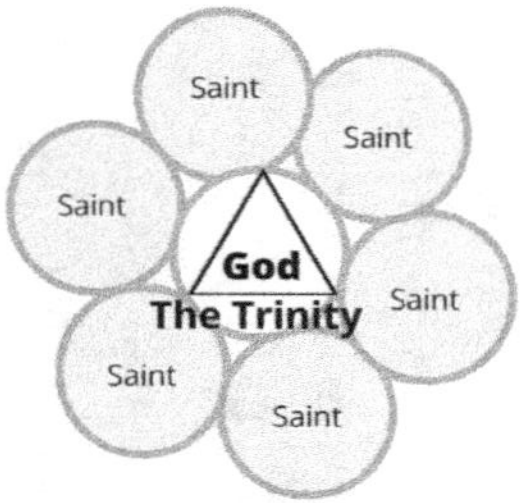</td>
<td>5. Mysticism of Union (Theistic)

Union with God: "God is in me".

Experienced Altered State of Consciousness: the Saints experience the Interpenetration of God without annuling their own individuality. They become deified.

Analogy (Theosis, Orthodox Christian concept): the flame and the sword, with the latter acquiring the properties of the former without losing itself.</td>
<td>Monotheism and Tri-Une God
(e.g., Abrahamic religions, Vishishtadvaita Vedanta)
</td>
</tr>
</table>

Figure 7. Both No-Thing and Everything at the Same Time. In Buddhist Non-Dualism (Saṃsāra equals Nirvana), all existence and the Emptiness (Śūnyatā) that underlies it are believed to be two sides of the same coin. This manages to avoid the dichotomy between the One and the Many, but only in part. Multiplicity, in this view, never achieves a transcendent state of being, being limited to the multiversal realm of imperfections and a transient existence. This contrasts with the Christian concept of Theosis, where plurality is elevated and interpenetrated by the Tri-Une God Himself, therefore transcending both the One/Many and immanent/transcendent dialectics.

The experience of dualists, Mysticism of Isolation, can be summarized in the statement: "I am pure Spirit", while that of panentheistic monists seems to be a combination of both: "I am (the only One) pure Spirit", and "this Spirit is All that exists."

For Buddhist non-dualists their experience can be described as the certainty that everything that exists is/is not at the same time both/neither relative and/or absolute, with each of these two aspects implying each other: "Saṃsāra equals Nirvana".

For the theists, on the other hand, their subjective experiences can be summarized as: "God is in Me" (without this "Me" disappearing by being absorbed into God).

This category of Theistic Mysticism, which apparently conflates pure monistic Monotheism (one of the doctrines of the One) and the Tri-Une God of Christianity (not defined by the One/Many dialectic) as having the same subjective experiences, however, is more complex than it appears at first sight. It will be further expanded upon in the next chapter but, for now, it is sufficient to understand the different subjective experiences of both theistic and non-theistic mysticism.

4.1. Personal (Theistic) and Impersonal Mysticism

For impersonal mysticism, the existence of personal gods and spirits necessarily takes place at a level below that of the One, since any particularity means plurality and imperfection. Therefore, there is no need for a single God, even if their cosmologies are populated by a myriad of gods.

This is why panentheistic worldviews such as Hinduism have no problem in adding the God of other religions as particular Avatars of one of its main gods. However, they are not God but a god, losing their transcendence along the way.

For theistic worldviews, in contrast, the "God" of impersonal monists is just the personification of God´s energies. From here comes the insistence of calling God a Force, Law or energy.[25]

From a Christian point of view, the experience of pure Spirit of the dualists can be understood as the experience of each one´s own soul or spirit, made in the image of God, therefore containing all creation potentially (this was Zaehner´s position).

---

25. *A state of affairs which the Bible seems to predict in Daniel 11:38: "But in his estate shall he honour the God of forces: and a god whom his fathers knew not shall he honour [...]".*

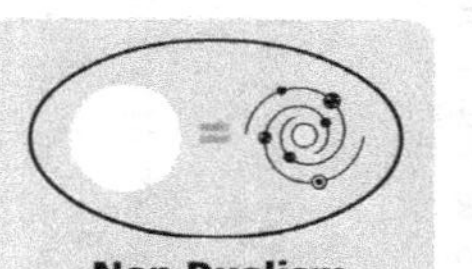

Figure 8. The two possible interpretations of Non-Dualism.

THE PITFALL OF SOLIPSISM

Its dangers and its relation to the problem of Unity and Multiplicity

While trying to explain how similar mystical experiences are understood in very different ways we can take three positions:

1. *They are all fundamentally the same.* There is only a "minimum common denominator" (Perennialism) truth behind all mystical experiences, including: those that experience the presence of a personal God and those that seem to experience pure Being (Being-Consciousness-Bliss) lacking any distinction between an I and a Thou; those that experience the whole Universe (Pantheism) and those that experience their Self isolated from anything material (such as the Universe; Dualism).

2. *They really are different experiences (at least partially) that due to their subjective/transcendent nature cannot be properly communicated.* Therefore, they are thought or communicated as being similar due to the limitations of language.

3. *Our mind, previous beliefs, and specific worldview not only shape but completely determine what we experience.* This would imply the paradox that Relativism is the only absolute law that rules our reality, that everything is subjective. Furthermore, Mind would be the ultimate principle upon which everything revolves, with a Universe formed by a myriad of disconnected Minds or Monads that are their own god and truth (or maybe all other minds are nothing more than fictions created by mine!).

This last scenario paints a picture of pure multiplicity (the Many), each ego experiencing itself as the only One. An inverted "transcendence" of the problem of *the One and the Many.* Complete spiritual atomism, where the barriers between Monads are, by definition, insurmountable and communication is not possible.[26]

---

26. *This does not exclude that in theistic worldviews, God draws near Him those who have faith in Him and "call" Him through prayer. Therefore, experiences may be partially propitiated (not determined) by our mind, soul, and spirit, but always in synergy with God. Again, the middle way between a pure homogeneous experience (Perennialism; the One) and pure subjectivism (Solipsism; the Many). This is why theistic monks, such as Hesychasts, "invoke" God through prayer (by using one or two sentences, just a few words, or even without any word but focusing on the idea and presence of their personal God) instead of leaving the mind completely empty. As all mystical traditions teach, meditation can be a dangerous affair if done without supervision. We can delude ourselves or become hosts to some unwanted guests.*

This is especially explainable by Orthodox Christianity and its doctrine of the Logos (the Word of God, Jesus Christ) and His Logoi (particular words or Reasons, willed-thoughts of God that provide the reason for the existence of everything). The Logos, God, is the recapitulation of all Logoi, and we were created in His image.

Orthodox Christianity, again, can explain "the Universe is God" statement of Pantheism as just the personal realization that the efficient cause of all creation comes from the energies of a personal transcendent God, with those energies being the impersonal ground of all being of which the Logoi are particular examples.

In this view, Panentheism would be the combination of both experiential realizations. According to Theism, then, this numinous experience may be experienced as highly meaningful and transformative, but it is not the end of our voyage and can be potentially highly misleading. God´s energies are not God. God´s image in us does not make us God, either.

Maybe Zaehner´s Catholic concept of God as an Absolute Divine Simplicity, lacking the Essence/Energies distinction of Orthodox Christianity, made it impossible for him to see a real distinction between the isolation of the dualist into his own soul and the fusion (or self-identification) of the monist with the impersonal sea of divine energy from which he himself and everything else comes from. The Catholic (and Protestant) doctrine of Absolute Divine Simplicity would have meant that, if there was a fusion, it could only be with God´s Essence, which is not really an appropriate position to hold for a Christian.

5. The Resolution of the Problem of the One and the Many and How It Can Help Us in Worldview Classification and Evaluation

A typology of mysticism like the one we have just seen is a useful tool for organizing our thoughts regarding these complex matters. Even more important, however, is to understand the implications of the problem of *the One and the Many*, its possible solutions, how each worldview tries to solve the problem, and if it succeeds or not in doing so.

As we have seen, the doctrines of the Many are not really traditional and in time tend to morph into doctrines of the One (e.g., Greek Henotheism, Anarchism escaping from its atomistic isolation and meaninglessness by finding the whole as present in every part).

The famous worldviews representative of Dualism, in turn, were always either monist to begin with (e.g., Gnosticism and Zoroastrianism) or later transformed into it (e.g., Yoga philosophy now being mostly based on Advaita Vedānta instead of Sāṃkhya philosophy; Platonism morphing into Neo-Platonism).

This narrows down our possibilities. If we want to find a living worldview that we can take seriously (e.g., unlike modern Neo-Pagan movements that have no formal commitment to a fixed doctrine, fluctuating aimlessly between Atheism, Polytheism, Duo-Theism, and even Monism) our options are reduced to pure Monism (Monotheism, Pantheism, and Panentheism), Buddhist Non-Dualism or the Tri-Une God of Christianity.

5.1. The Importance of Solving the Problem

The question of *the One and the Many* is not something that worries us in our day to day life. Most people are ignorant that the problem even exists, even though it is central to all philosophical and religious thought and, therefore, its consequences cannot be avoided.

Nevertheless, we are constantly being confronted by this problem even if we are not aware of it: to what do we give primacy, to the individual or to the collective (e.g., the state)? Does education have to be focused on the growth of each individual or in the needs of society at large? Freedom or Security? Plurality or Unity?

Given the inevitability of this issue, by not thinking consciously about it we are not avoiding a complex philosophical issue, but rather becoming its unknowing slaves. This, in turn, chains us into a never ending dialectical cycle that prevents the true resolution of the problem.

If we believe that ultimate reality is One, we will be conditioned to think that Unity shall have priority in all aspects of life. This may include limiting the rights of particular individuals and adopting specific forms of government. In such a view, the sacrifice of the individual for the benefit of the collective becomes acceptable and even honourable. If we believe reality to be Many, in contrast, anarchy as individual self-rule (e.g., Anarcho-Capitalism) will be the priority.

We have an example of the former view in the Enlightenment, where Deism and Illuminism exalted and gave primacy to the notion of the One at the cost of the Many. The poems of this revolutionary time reflected this conviction:

> *"All are parts of one stupendous whole*
>
> *Whose body Nature is, and God the soul."*
>
> – Alexander Pope. An Essay on Man (1733).

In fact, the attempt to bring absolute unification and homogenization to the whole world under an ideal has been a pretty common historical occurrence (usually under the idea of the state understood in a certain way). This has been defined as trying to create a secular heaven on earth, by erroneously trying to "bring down" the metaphysical notion of the One into this world (technically speaking: immanentizing the Eschaton [the coming age beyond time]).

The amounts of resulting bloodshed hardly needs to be pointed out. Twentieth century totalitarian regimes (e.g., Communism) are stark and recent reminders of how the obsession with one horn of this dialectic to the absolute exclusion of its opposite can bring suffering and death.

This conflict between *the One and the Many* has humanity trapped between its dialectical horns in an apparently unsolvable dilemma, with history being the story of their never ending struggle.

5.2. Dialectics: The True Underlying Problem

By becoming aware of this underlying metaphysical problem we can see that the real problem is not choosing the "good side" or horn of the dialectic, as it is usually believed, but the notion itself that we have to decide between one extreme or the other, with the resulting rejection of its opposite. The Many is not the problem. Neither is the One. Dialectics and the exclusive Either/Or logic that underlies it is.

Pure Unity with no Particularity is a blank canvas, while pure Particularity with no underlying Unity is pure chaos. They both share the attribute of meaninglessness and the impossibility of relating to one another. This is why it is so important to solve this dialectical conflict that shapes our unconscious minds and, consequently, our lives. This is also why worldviews that transcend this dialectic value the resolution of this conflict so highly, seeing this as proof of the truth of their underlying metaphysics.

Solving this problem means transcending our plane of existence, characterized by all kinds of dialectical oppositions: Masculine/Feminine, Free Will/Determinism, Unity/Plurality. Going above and beyond dialectics is the mark of a level of existence that transcends ours.

Therefore, while navigating this complex landscape full of conflicting metaphysical worldviews, there can be no higher rational proof of the validity and the transcendental origin of a particular one than its satisfactory resolution of the problem of *the One and the Many* **in non-dialectical terms**.

5.3. Dialectics as the Common God of the Doctrines of The One (Absolute Monism)

The worldviews of the One "solve" the problem of *the One and the Many* by choosing a side.

In the following sections we will analyze the presuppositions and premises of two of their most influential (and highly represented in modern popular culture) worldviews: Neo-Platonism and Gnosticism, both representatives of Panentheism (or even Pantheism, in some interpretations).

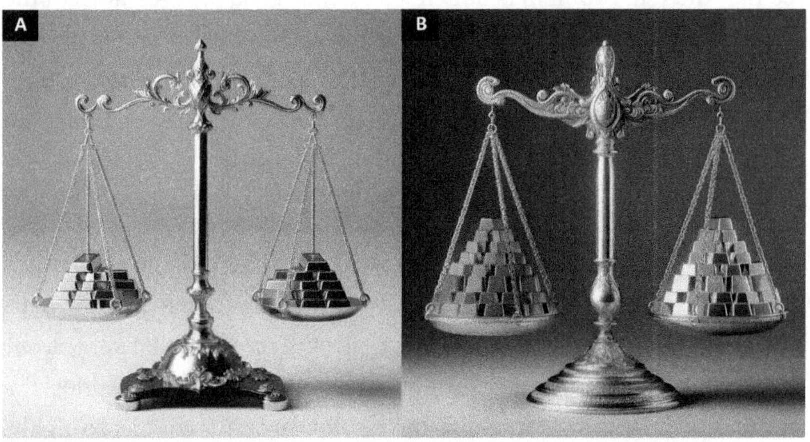

Figure 9. Equality in Difference. Theosis, the Orthodox Christian view on salvation, speaks of particular saved persons as equally valuable modes of existence of the One God that have been elevated to godhood through inheriting God´s Uncreated Energies. This does not mean, however, that we fuse with God´s Essence, as in the doctrines of the One (Impersonal Monism).

In this worldview, individuality is not eliminated but elevated, illuminated, and perfected. Subject and object do not fuse into a third entity but become interpenetrated while retaining ther individuality, thus speaking of a communion in love that cherishes the Other as Oneself.

***Metaphor A (gold bars):** for the doctrines of the One, equal value can only be obtained through homogeneity. The final aim is fusion into the Absolute.*

***Metaphor B (left: silver bars; right: gold bars):** for Christianity, each individual is raised into godhood, thus becoming equally valuable in their difference. Unity and Plurality are both maintained, just as the Tri-Une God transcends the One/ Many dialectical dichotomy.*

5.3.1. The Neo-Platonic *"The One"* of Plotinus: Its Presuppositions and Implications

The term "The One" was coined by Plotinus, the founder of Neo-Platonism, who used it to define the ultimate reality of his influential philosophical system. He described It in terms of a larger underlying dialectical process of oppositions.

It is dialectical because, in his view, all manner of distinctions are considered as direct oppositions, as he himself axiomatically and unambiguously stated: *"Distinction is opposition"*.[27]

Figure 10. The God who Forgets Itself. The myth of Narcissus is an apt description of the Absolute, a Self-forgetful God who indulges in a game of Self-discovery once It has lost Itself in matter. Picture: Narcissus at the Source, falling in love with his own reflection; Caravaggio (1597–1599), Galleria Nazionale d'Arte Antica (Rome).

Plotinus based the very core of his philosophical system on the impossibility of conceiving any difference between two terms that does not involve conflict. Consequently, its main objective could not be

---

27. *Plotinus. Enneads, 3:2:13. Trans. Armstrong, Loeb Classical Library, , Vol. III., pp. 81, 83, 85.*

other than "the reconciliation of opposites" (a very frequent concept also in popular media, as we have seen in chapter V). The meaning of this reconciliation was understood, basically, as their re-unification by reducing both terms to sameness and absolute identity. This assumes the underlying unity of each pair of opposites.

In a system such as this, the aim is always to progress from lower (and more complex) unities to higher (and simpler) ones. This is achieved by integrating the successive opposites existing at each level of reality. The final goal is the attainment, at the top of our ascent, of "an absolute unity, a perfect simplicity, above all differentiation".[28]

a. Monistic Non-Dualism: When The One Also Implies the Many

The implication of this process is that the One is only "One" due to its dialectical relationship of opposition to "the Many".

Therefore, the One needs the Many in a monistic version of Non-Dualism that does not necessarily imply their simultaneity in time, since they can manifest sequentially.

Since all acts of the One are acts of Its Essence, the Many which It creates are not different from It in Essence. This makes the One another name for "the All", the Absolute, and can easily end in a fully pantheistic outlook, such as was the case in Porphyry´s version of Neo-Platonism (in which, as R.P. Farrell notes: "St. Augustine will base his understanding of Neoplatonism"[29], with its consequent influence in Roman Catholic theology).

––––––––––––

28. *Inge, Dean (1918). The Philosophy of Plotinus. Longmans. Green And Co. Vol. II, p. 109.*

29. *Farrell, Joseph P. (2016). God, History, and Dialectic, Volume I: God, The Foundation of the First Europe, p.107.*

b. The Many as "Evil": Matter and Non-Existence

In this worldview, the Many are represented by relative and finite matter, which is the last emanation from the One and borders on non-existence. This implies that matter, as opposed to the One (which is also the Good), has to represent the notion of "evil" in systems such as this.

The absolute unity and simplicity characteristic of the One also means that any categories, attributes or names of "God" whatsoever that are used to describe It, ultimately have the same meaning. They are ontologically reduced to being identical with any other category or attribute predicated of It.

The terms essence, energy or will become, then, mere naming conventions signifying the same underlying reality. There is no difference between what the One is, what It does or how It does it.[30]

Therefore, for the One, being One is the same as being Good. This implies, again, that anything not-One is evil.

Because of this rejection of any uniqueness and individuality, the One has been called *"the abyss of everything specific"*.[31]

c. The One Lacks Free Will

This war on difference resulted in freedom being one of its principal casualties. Freedom implies options to choose from, which means distinction, which for Plotinus means opposition and imperfection. In this dialectical view, this means that every choice becomes a moral one between a good (or better) and evil (or worse) option. The possibility of multiple alternative but equally good options is not contemplated. This creates the paradox that the One, being perfect and incapable of containing any imperfection, cannot be free, except from Its freedom from choice.

---

30. *These distinctions, however, are crucial for the Christian Tri-Une God and its solution to the problem of the One and the Many, as we will later see.*

31. *Tillich, Paul (1956). A History of Christian Thought. Must Have Books, p. 52.*

Figure 11. The Great Chain of Being. In worldviews that believe in an impersonal Monad, all further existence is emanated from the One, being the "body" of the Absolute. All existence is ordered in a decreasing hierarchical structure which, as it moves away from the Source, loses its original Unity and becomes more and more imperfect, ending in pure matter. The concept itself was derived from Plato, Aristotle (see Historia Animalium), Plotinus, and Proclus, later infiltrating medieval Western Christianity. Picture: Didacus Valades (1579).

The corollary of this paradox is that the emanations of the One, since they are in dialectical opposition to It, possess free will and the "burden" of choice, while It does not. This violates a key traditional metaphysical principle (and common human reason) in that the inferior plane of existence ends up being superior to its own source in some ways.

d. All Emanated Beings Share The One´s Essence

This concept of simplicity is also the origin of the doctrine of emanations. If the One is pure Actuality with no Potentiality, any operation of the One has to be eternal. There is no choice in the matter. This implies that "creation", in the form of emanations, is also eternal. This is another aspect that highlights the inseparability of the One from the Many, even if they are defined as opposites in moral terms.

Also, given that there is no difference between the One´s Essence and Its Energies, "creation" is essentially "God". The only difference between emanator and emanated is conceived as the relative degree of simplicity between them. It is a quantitative difference, not a qualitative one, contrary to the creator/created distinction of theistic religions that also emphasize the freedom of God to will creation out of nothing.

e. All Existence is Hierarchical

In Plotinus´ system, the First Emanation subordinated to the One is necessarily Mind (Nous or Intellect), since the first distinction and imperfection of absolute Oneness can just be the first appearance of otherness in the form of the One knowing Itself (Subject-Object Dualism). Also, Mind's most basic operation is that of differentiation.

The Second Emanation, subordinate to Mind, is the World Soul. If Nous is the One knowing Itself, the World Soul is the next step in the differentiation process, the *knowledge* of the Mind knowing Itself.

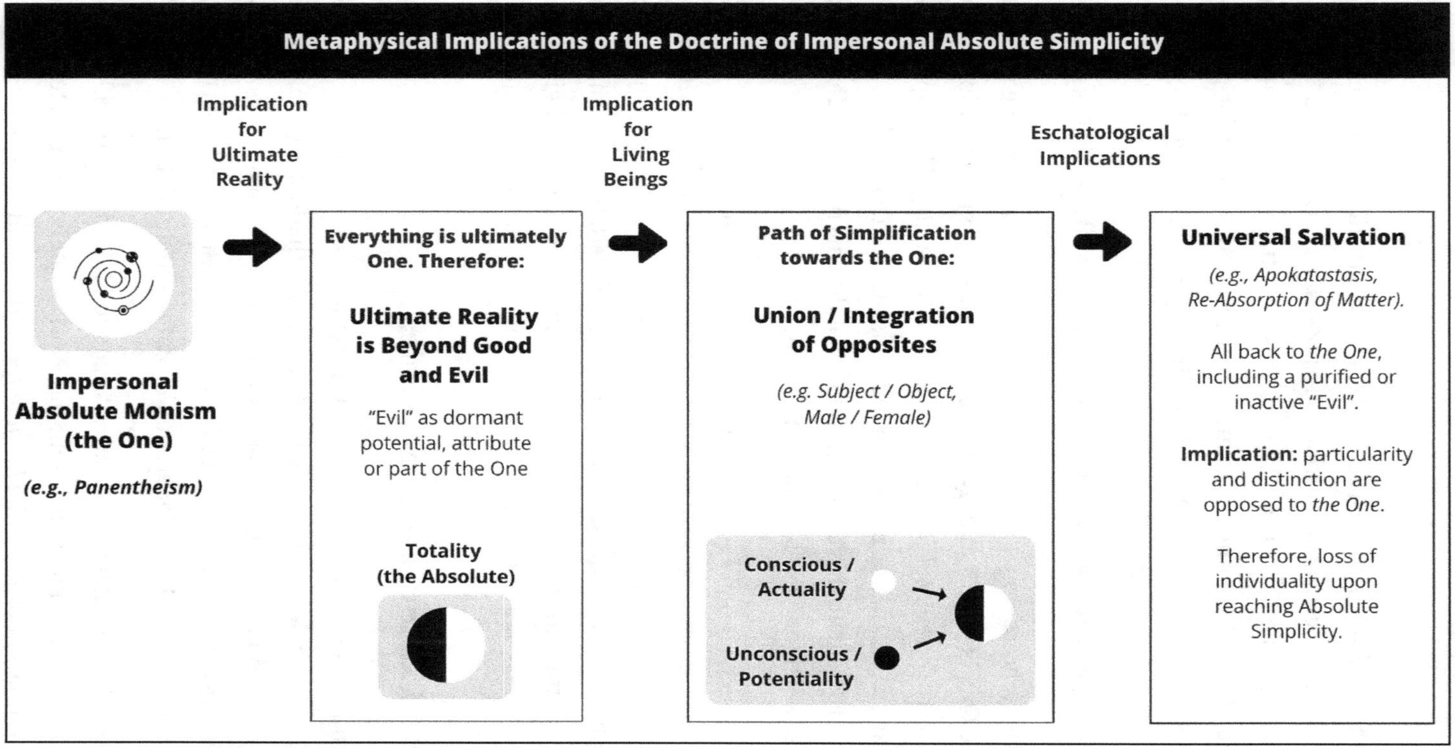

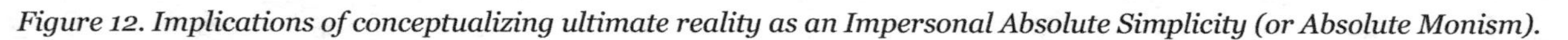

Figure 12. Implications of conceptualizing ultimate reality as an Impersonal Absolute Simplicity (or Absolute Monism).

This completes the Subject-Object-Knowledge sequential triad, with the third term being the union or "glue" between the first and second ones, which are opposed to each other.[32]

f. Self-Transcendence: The Possibility of Return by One´s Own Means

Given that there is no discontinuity between the One and even the last emanation (matter), the emanation process can be reversed. This process Plotinus calls "Return".

It is accomplished by escaping or "turning from" the external world of multiplicity and matter to the simpler, more unified, interior reality of one´s own soul. The process of simplification continues until the soul of the individual reaches Mind (Nous) and, eventually, attains the ecstatic experience where one´s individuality is lost in unity with the One.

It is telling that Plotinus named this process the *"flight of the alone to the Alone"*[33] as no multiplicity, including one´s own sense of self, can exist at this level.

The great discovery at this stage, once attained, is that the mystic is, literally, the One Itself.

What the panentheist undergoing absolute fusion and identification with the One experiences seems to be one´s own "higher" or purified soul, once the abolition of the subject-object duality is accomplished.

This overcome state of duality is later understood or conceptualized to be a mere projection of this unity on the "screen of matter". J.P. Farrell, in his illuminating book *God, History, and Dialectic* agrees with Zaehner in this point.

------

32. *This structure follows the Filioque structure of the Trinity of Roman Catholicism and Protestantism, as we will see in the next chapter.*

33. *The "alone to the Alone" is found in Enneads 5:1:6.*

g. The Implications of Accepting the Neo-Platonic Notion of Simplicity

Farrell[34] also presents us with a useful summary of the implications of accepting the Neo-Platonic notion of Absolute Simplicity. It will serve as an appropriate end to this section and will allow us to become aware of the serious consequences of such an apparent minor axiomatic assumption. Those are:

(1). The devaluing of metaphysical categorical symbols by their reduction to absolute identity, in the form of:

(2). Equation of the Names of God; [e.g., being One equals being Good, each attribute being a mere pointer to the same undifferentiated Essence].

(3). Equation of the Essence, Will, and Operation(s) [or Energies] of God; and therefore:

(a). A system where God is effectively denied free choice; and

(b). Where free choice is defined in terms of moral oppositions which exist between all choices absolutely, thus producing irresolvable conflicts of "predestination" and "free will"; and

(4). A tendency to produce a three-fold subordinationalism of basic Constituents [e.g., The One, Nous, and World Soul, emanated in sequential hierarchical order, or the Neo-Platonic system of Proclus, based on successive triadic components].

(5). A tendency to reduce constituents to absolute unity.

(6). A tendency to multiply constituents ad infinitum; [e.g., the Great Chain of Being or the number of emanated realities].

(7). A definition of the Unity of God in positive terms entailing all the above [God as the All, the Absolute].

(8). A definition of the Unity of God in impersonal terms [personality being complex and, therefore, an imperfection and a step down from Absolute Simplicity].

---

34. *Farrell, Joseph P. (2016). God, History, and Dialectic, Volume I: God, The Foundation of the First Europe. pp., 97-98. Terms in brackets added for clarification and emphasis.*

(9). A system where abstract *impersonal Unity* transcends *personal Multiplicity* in its emphasis.

5.4. The Christian Solution to the Problem of the One and the Many

Early patristic Christianity confronted the same problem of *the One and the Many* in a different way, arriving at radically different conclusions. Comparing its theology with the Plotinian philosophical system will shed much light on how working on the resolution of the same problem while holding different starting presuppositions can drastically change the outcome. It will also show how a non-dialectical solution to the problem is possible.

a. The Christian Axiomatic Starting Point: The Theological Order (*Ordo Theologiae*) [35]

Properly orthodox Christian theology always begins with the revelation of the Incarnation of the Logos (Jesus Christ). No concept of divine

---

35. *Farrell, Joseph P. (2016). God, History, and Dialectic. Volume IV, Note 57 clarifies: "The term ordo theologiae is my own designation. I mean by it not the metaphysical priority of any one category to another as much as the fact that theological questions are asked in a certain order, and the resulting answers indicate any priority of categories, one to another. More importantly, the term designates also the fact that the ordo is very broadand contains basic implications not only for the formulation of doctrine, but its expression in liturgy and devotion as well. In this work, the term has two applications. In Part One, it applies to the non-Augustinian patristic consensus of asking questions in the order indicated. In Parts Two and Three, the Augustinian ordo theologiae is encountered as the exact inversion of the patristic ordo theologiae, and as such asks questions in the following broad categorical order: (1) essence or nature, or sometimes being; (2) attributes or operations; and finally (3) persons.*

On the subject of the ordo theologiae, St. Basil the Great writes: "If we have not distinct perception of the separate characteristics, namely, fatherhood, sonship, and sanctification, but form our conception of God from the general idea of existence, we cannot possibly give a sound account of our faith." That this will be the exact error of the Augustinian ordo theologiae, especially of the Mediaeval scholastic theology, will become abundantly clear in Part Two. Contained in this quotation is the implication that revelation (the Persons) takes priority to generalized abstractions concerning "the Deity" (essence)."

simplicity derived from human reason alone takes precedence over the *Gospels* and Scripture.

This, which to secular humanists may seem sectarian or short-sighted, is based on the sound metaphysical reasoning and conviction that there is no avoiding the fact that if we want to understand God, the First Principles that will allow us to think about Him have to be received directly from Him. A lower metaphysical and ontological level (mankind and its human reason) cannot derive by itself the axioms that rule in a higher one, let alone understand God´s nature.

This was summed up in *Chapter II* in general metaphysical terms, where we noted that no complete knowledge from a domain that transcends ours can, even in principle, be really obtained from inside our domain (the charming little book *Flatland: A Romance of Many Dimensions*, by Edwin Abbott, provides a good visual example of this point). We concluded that the only possibility of ever attaining a high degree of certainty regarding higher-order realities was from direct revelation coming directly from this domain above ours.

This is what the Incarnation represents. By following His teachings and the reality of His existence, the implications of who the Christian God really is were unravelled by the early Fathers of the Church.[36] The character of the revealed Trinitarian God (Revealed Theology) was found to be very different, even opposite, to the God of the Philosophers (the One; Natural Theology).

Since the Christ was incarnated and made known to us as a Person (Hypostasis), the Fathers started all theologizing with this fact: Personhood is not below God. Later considerations included what He did (God´s Energies or Operations) and, from there, what He is (Nature or Essence) could be deduced.

---

36. *Nazianzus, St. Gregory (the Theologian). Fifth Theological Oration, VII-VIII. Nicene and Post-Nicene Fathers. Catholic Way Publishing, pp. 319- 320.*

a1. The Personal God of Revealed Christianity

In the Tri-Une God of Christianity, we can differentiate between:

(1). Persons (Hypostases): *"Who* is doing it?"

(2). Energies (God´s Attributes or Operations): *"What* is that that They are doing?"

(3). Essence (sometimes also called Nature): *"What are They* that They are doing these things?"

According to Christian theology, what Plotinus and other impersonal pantheistic/panentheistic worldviews did, especially notorious in the case of Gnosticism, was personifying (hypostasizing) the attributes of God and then having them sequentially derive one from another in a specific order.

The Person of revealed doctrine became thus an energy or attribute (e.g., the Logos and Holy Spirit as Nous and World Soul, respectively), in what early Christians considered a *"category error"* by fusing the above categories one and two.

a2. The Impersonal God of the Philosophers (Derived from Human Reason Alone)

(1). Personified (Hypostasized) Energies or Attributes of God: which are externalized in the different emanations.

(2). Essence (Nature)

The difference between the above interpretations of the divine can be clearly seen by the difference in language when referring to God. In Plotinus´ original Greek language, "the One" is a neuter term (το εν) that is described by the "It" pronoun. Similar to Advaita Vedānta (and to most, if not all, pantheistic/panentheistic worldviews), it can be compared with the also neuter principle of "Being", or as he put it "That which exists" (το ον). For St. Basil, to the contrary, God is "He Who exists" (το ων) and described by the personal pronoun Him. As the Bible says: *"I AM Who I AM"* (Exodus 3:14).

b. The Names of God Point to the Real Plurality of God´s Energies

Another difference with the doctrines of the One, as St. Basil noted, is that in Christian theology the different names of God really designate different energies or attributes of His Essence. Plurality is not opposition but an enriching fullness.

c. The Non-Dialectical Nature of the Tri-Une God

In Christian theology and anthropology, the Essence is what different instances (Persons) have in common. Anything which can be attributed to different Persons (Hypostases) is an essential attribute, property or energy of that shared (Homoousion) Essence.

The particular and completely unique mode of existence of this Essence or nature, however, is the Person (Hypostasis). This is why the Christian God is called the God of love.

This affirmation, which at first sight may appear as just a pietist devotional one, is the logical conclusion of understanding the metaphysical character of the Tri-Une God. Since difference is not opposition for Him, the uniqueness of all creatures can be loved precisely because of it. The One, in contrast, necessarily excludes all uniqueness as an imperfection.

In Christian thought, the unique set of characteristics that each person represents is not seen as a danger to God´s Unity or as the origin of a "fallen" state.[37] The very expectation is that each person, if they are to remain who they are, a particular mode of being of the totality of their nature, should not be immutable nor indistinguishable between them.[38]

------

37. *Gray, op. cit., p. 132.*
38. *Gray, op. cit., p. 131*

The dialectical (*Either/Or*) opposition between uniqueness and unity characteristic of the One is rejected. This can also be seen in the non-dialectical (*Both/And*) nature of Person and Essence, which imply each other.

This means that no nature exists abstractly, but has to be actualized ("en-hypostasized") into a unique Person (Hypostasis), a "nature with characteristics" or particular mode of existence of that nature. Also, no Person exists abstractly without an Essence ("en-essenced").

d. The Christian Notion of Divine Simplicity

In Christian theology as explained, for example, by St. Athanasius, the simplicity of God does not obligatorily make identical all distinctions present in the Godhead.

God is truly One in Essence, Manifold in Operations, and Three in Persons. The term "simplicity", then, just means the indivisibility or impartibility of the divine Essence. It is one of the attributes of God, not its only defining characteristic.

As St. Athanasius noted, there is no logical reason by which we should be compelled to accept the meaning of the term "simplicity" to always mean what it means in its Neo-Platonic definition.

We might add that there is no reason to limit God by the reification of one of His attributes. In Christianity, God is the source of unity. In impersonal Monism, on the other hand, unity is the source of many gods.

e. The Tri-Une God has Free Will

Furthermore, the Christian God is not defined as pure Actuality without Potentiality, as is the One. This implies that the faculty of willing, the actual process of using it, and the specific object towards which it is directed, are really different. Therefore, God has free will.

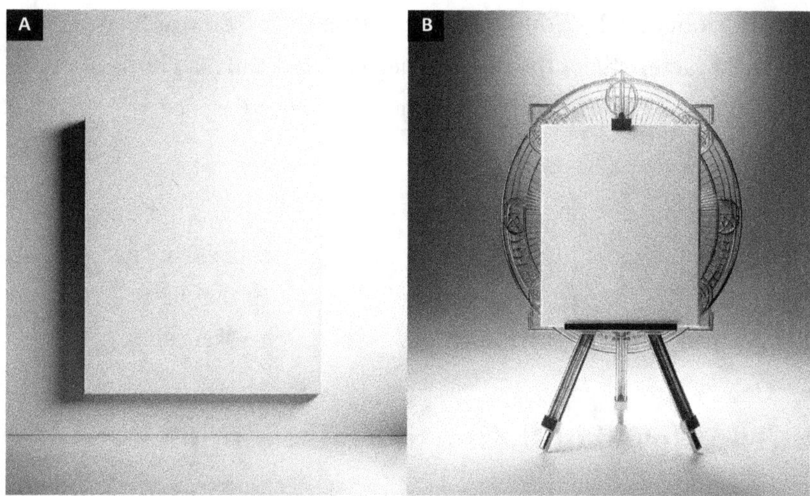

Figure 13. **Metaphor A:** *the Absolute as a blanck canvas. It is the emptiness of All-Possibility, a pure impersonal sea of unrestricted potentiality. Everything is contained in it, including all opposites (e.g., good and "evil") since, by definition, nothing exists outside the One. The counterpart of this passive space of pure consciousness is All-Actuality, the actual manifestation of every possibility that the Absolute contains within it in potentiality. Everything exists by the mere fact of it being possible (e.g., the Multiverse).*

All-Potentiality and All-Actuality are two sides of the same coin, as no form of manifestation is conceived which does not involve duality and imperfection (Dialectical Monism). The latter, represented by all the possible drawings made on the canvas is, however, a temporal existence.

In the end, all drawings are erased and all individuals absorbed by the impersonal whiteness of the empty canvas. This includes any notion of a personal God, which may be the most beautiful drawing, but a drawing all the same. Every drawing is just a personification (a symbol) of this ultimately impersonal emptiness.

Metaphor B: *in contrast, in Orthodox Trinitarian Christianity, the blank canvas represents God´s Uncreated Energies. God is threefold, consisting of a common Essence (the metallic circular frame) personified in three Persons (the three legs that support the canvas) that actualize the potentialities of this common Essence (the Energies, Attributes or Operations of God).*

Given that God is personal and the Uncreated Energies are the operations of a God that pre-exists their actualization, God is free to either use them or not (e.g., Creatio Ex-Nihilo). This implies that the Christian God has free will, contrary to the One of the philosophers, which is compelled to overflow. Creation is also personal and willed.

For the Christian, the interpretation of the blanck canvas of the doctrines of the Absolute means confusing God´s Energies with His Essence by eliminating His personal nature.

The doctrine of creation out of nothing (Ex Nihilo) also highlights this, because the discontinuity between Creator and Creation has to be willingly bridged by a Personal Will.

Creation, therefore, was willed by God, who declared it good. The origin of evil cannot be found, then, in the dialectic between a purely actual God and the pure potentiality without actuality characteristic of matter.

Spirit/Matter Dualism is not found in orthodox Christian thought, even if the original state of the bodies that are intrinsic to each soul (as well as that of souls themselves) is believed to be partially injured since the human nature that includes them both fell.

f. The Transcendence of Dialectics in the Incarnation of the Logos

Christianity not only has a non-dialectical God in the Trinity. Its opposition to dialectics can be seen in all aspects of its theology and metaphysics. The Incarnation of the Logos is the clearest example.

In Jesus Christ, his two natures (human and divine) are not fused together but joined inseparably, with each nature communicating to the other what it can do (its properties, attributes or energies; this Christological concept is known as *communicatio idiomatum*).

The two natures of Christ are both personified in Christ´s Person (two enhypostases or personifications, one for each nature), not in two different Persons (Hypostases). The fact that the God of Chrisitanity is personal was always seen as a key aspect for our possible salvation/deification. As a Person, He could assume our nature, resurrect it, and ascend with it "to the right hand of the Father" (1 Peter 3:22). An impersonal First Principle or God could not have assumed anything, only re-absorbed it, therefore discarding our uniqueness in the process.

The whole life of Jesus Christ was understood as a testimony to this specifically Christian doctrine of the interpenetration of His two natures and a declaration of what unity truly meant: the joining of the different in a communion of will and action that enriches and elevates all; **the gaining of *"the Other"*, not the loss of the self.**

The Christ performed human actions in a divine way (e.g., such as walking on water) and divine actions in a human way (e.g., healing miracles and the resurrection of the dead through human speech and touch). Both His life and His death were always understood as a revelation, a lesson, and a declaration of theology´s (the knowledge of God) first principles.

In addition, a quick glance to every other Christian doctrine will show that everything in this worldview is a testimony against dialectical thought. From Christian anthropology (the science of man and its constituents), that states that human nature is intrinsically composed of both soul and body (and spirit, as the eye of the soul), be it in its current human "fallen" state or in its future deified one; to the doctrine of salvation and deification (Theosis) that implies the eternal communion of *the One and the Many*. Every level of reality is explained in a non-dialectical way.

This, and no other, would be the Christian version of the esoteric dictum "*as above*" (the non-dialectical Trinity), "*so below*" (the non-dialectical Incarnation of the Logos, the recapitulation [macrocosm] of all there is and could ever be, of which we are images [microcosm]).

g. Revealed Metaphysical Self-Consistency or the Limits of Human Reason

As we have seen in this section, one of the most fundamental marks of the truth of the Christian revealed Trinitarian God was always considered to be His transcendence of dialectical thinking in His solution to the problem of *the One and the Many*, as well as the self-consistency Christian thought shows in completely eliminating any trace of dialectics from all levels of reality (the Trinity, the Incarnation, Human Anthropology, and Eschatology).

In short, where other worldviews ended in self-contradictions or inconsistencies, each piece of the metaphysical jigsaw provided by Christian theology was found to fit perfectly into its own overall metaphysical structure, while also providing a deeper understanding of the pieces that came before.

The lack of self-consistency (e.g., Multiplicity being "evil" but being necessarily implied by *absolute* Unity all the same) was always thought to be unavoidable in any philosophical system derived from mere human reason (and thus attempting to solve problems that surpass our ontological level of reality). On the other hand, the revelation of the Logos (the Reason behind everything), if true, could not be otherwise than self-consistent by definition.

This matter was also clearly exposed by Van Til, who used it as the background from where the *Transcendental Argument for the Existence of God* was conceived. Van Til´s main focus was to unravel and clarify the implications of the existence of the Trinitarian God.[39]

By doing this, he showed how the concept of the *concrete universal* related and solved the problem of *the One and the Many*.[40] The ontological Trinity meant that God's unity and diversity are equally basic in Him and, consequently, in the whole of reality.

As we have seen, this contrasts with non-Christian philosophy in which unity and diversity are viewed as ultimately, not only different, but opposed to each other.

---

39. *Rushdoony, R.J. (1971). The One and the Many: Studies in the Philosophy of Order and Ultimacy. Chalcedon/Ross House Books, p. 32.*

40. *Van Til, C. (1972). Common Grace and the Gospel. P & R Publishing Co, p. 64, para. break deleted:*

"The ontological Trinity will be our interpretative concept everywhere. God is our concrete universal; in Him thought and being are coterminous, in Him the problem of knowledge is solved. If we begin thus with the ontological Trinity as our concrete universal, we frankly differ from every school of philosophy and from every school of science not merely in our conclusions, but in our starting-point and in our method as well. For us the facts are what they are, and the universals are what they are, because of their common dependence upon the ontological Trinity. Thus, as earlier discussed, the facts are correlative to the universals. Because of this correlativity there is genuine progress in history; because of it the Moment has significance".

As R. J. Rushdoony wrote in his revealing book *The One and the Many*:[41]

"[...] History and man are rescued from the "blind alley of the absolute particular" (to use Van Til's phrase), and also from the meaningless ocean of undifferentiated being, from the abyss of unity in the chaos of being. According to Van Til, "The ontological trinity will be our interpretative concept everywhere. God is our concrete universal; in Him thought and being are coterminous, in Him the problem of knowledge is solved."

[...] "In God's being there are no particulars not related to the universal and there is nothing universal that is not fully expressed in the particulars." [42] *This means that the trinity is totally self-contained and totally explicable in terms of itself. In turn, this means that the temporal one and many, having been created by God, is entirely and only explicable in terms of the ontological trinity, and that the non-believer's knowledge of the universe is in terms of borrowed premises, for the logic of any other premise is, as Van Til has repeatedly shown, the denial of our experience and of reality. Nominalism ends by dissolving the world into an endless sea of unrelated and meaningless facts or particulars, whereas Realism progressively denies the validity of particulars, of the many, and absorbs them into an undifferentiated and shoreless ocean of being. At either end, definition, meaning, and truth disappear; at one end total relativism and anarchy, and, at the other, total authoritarianism."*

This metaphysical non-dialectical vision allowed the early Fathers of the Christian Church to avoid the one specific categorical confusion that plagued all deviations from orthodox Christian understanding, as St. John of Damascus highlighted: the error of saying that nature (or Essence) and Person (Hypostasis) are identical.[43]

---

41. *Rushdoony, R.J. (1971). The One and the Many: Studies in the Philosophy of Order and Ultimacy. Chalcedon/Ross House Books, p. 115.*

42. *Van Til, C. (1955). The Defense of the Faith, 43; 26 in 1963 ed. P & R Publishing Co.*

43. *Lett Feltoe, Charles. Trans., Leo the Great, in Nicene and Post-Nicene Fathers, vol. 12 (Grand Rapids, MI: Eerdmans, 1956), Letter CXXIV, 93.*

5.5. Gnosticism: The Precursor of the Neo-Platonic Doctrine of The One

Gnosticism was not a unitary phenomenon. It was formed by a variety of sects with different doctrines organized roughly around a common set of premises.

Now that we have understood the orthodox Christian theological order and its overall metaphysical structure, it will be illustrative to understand the differences with Gnostic metaphysics, which predated the development of Neo-Platonism and had an important influence in many later worldviews.

As we have seen in *Chapter V*, Gnosticism still holds a central place even in many modern productions today (e.g., the famous *Jesus Christ Superstar* musical and Hollywood movies).

The characteristic of all Gnostic systems, however different between them, is the identification of the categories of Person (Hypostasis) and Energies (or attributes; natural properties) of God. Or, following St. John of Damascus, we could say that they fused the notions of Person and Essence by making each energy emanate in a personified way from the Essence. These personified Energies were then arranged in a linear hierarchy, in a gradated and descending order of perfection between God and the world.

The system of Valentinus, one of the most influential Gnostic cosmologies of ancient times and the basis of Neo-Gnosticism, called their impersonal God Bythos (Depth or Profundity). It was defined by his followers as an invisible and incomprehensible Primal Principle.

Every Aeon or emanation was seen as composed of a male/female dialectical pair (Syzygies). Bythos´ pair was Ennoia (Silence or Idea). The next emanation contained Mind (Nous) and Aletheia (Truth), the next Logos (Word) and Zoe (Life), followed by Man (Anthropos) and Ekklesia (Church). The first four emanations (eight Aeons) formed the Ogdoad.

As we can see, the cosmological and metaphysical premises of Gnostic and Neo-Platonic systems are very similar:

- Impersonal First Principle.

- Sequential Emanations of increasing imperfection understood as increasing complexity.

- Mind and First Thought being the first differentiation from the homogeneous Depth or Source.

- Life (Plotinian World Soul, the principle of motion or animation [anima meaning soul]) being emanated after Mind.

"Plotinus is simply "demythologizing" Gnosticism, with its various intermediary entities between God and creation by dressing up the "hierarchy of beings" in chique and sleek philosophical language." [44]

– Joseph P. Farrell. God, History, and Dialectic

a. The Absolute: Androgyny and the Unity of Opposites

If anything, the dialectical nature of Gnosticism is even more pronounced than that of Neo-Platonism thanks to the sexually polarized symbolism of each Aeon or Emanation.

A very revealing example is the fact that various Gnostic texts referred to God as *"a dyad who embraces both masculine and feminine elements"*.[45]

The Gnostic God was conceptualized as an Absolute Unity and Intelligence in the process of generating Itself: *"[...] making itself grow, seeking itself, finding itself, being mother of itself, father of itself, sister of itself, spouse of itself, daughter of itself, son of itself—mother, father, unity, being a source of the entire circle of existence"*.[46]

---

44. *Farrell, Joseph P. (2016). God, History, and Dialectic (Vol.I), p. 106.*

45. *Pagels, Elaine (1989). The Gnostic Gospels. Vintage, p. 49.*

46. *Ibid., p. 51.*

Some schools interpreted such a definition as a metaphor for a neuter being neither male nor female. Others understood it as an androgynous figure formed of both masculine and feminine aspects. All of them, however, viewed It as a reconciliation and harmonization of dialectical opposites.

b. The Demiurge: The Intermediate False Tyrant God Characteristic of Gnosticism

The concept of the Demiurge, the intermediate deity who ignorantly believes himself to be the True God, Architect, and Shaper of our Universe, implies another dialectical tension in creation itself: Spirit/Matter Dualism. Given that the God who created matter is evil, it must mean that mankind´s ultimate aim should be a pure spiritual state devoid of any kind of body (not even elevated energetic "subtle" bodies).

A second dialectical tension is implied by the Demiurge being born of Wisdom´s (Sophia) attempt to emanate without her counterpart. Evil being born from an aspect of the Totality of God (Pleroma) is just another way of stating that they imply each other, just as multiplicity was necessarily implied by unity in Plotinus´ system.

It is just fair to point out, however, that regarding the character of the Demiurge, Plotinus opposed the Gnostics. He dedicated a whole section of his *Enneads*[47] to combat their view on this tragic/evil figure, who in classical Platonism was seen as a positive one.

c. The Gnostic Path

For the Gnostics, there was a true invisible Church that knew the True God beyond this false one. Those few were believed to be the ones in possession of the "Christ Within", which was the very soul of the Gnostic, a spark of the fallen Sophia or Wisdom, now trapped in matter.

------

47. *Plotinus (270). The Enneads. Penguin Classics, Second Ennead II.9 [33] - "Against Those That Affirm The Creator of the Cosmos and the Cosmos Itself to be Evil" [generally referred to as "Against the Gnostics"].*

Having received the secret initiatory knowledge or Gnosis, they recognized Christ as the savior Aeon sent from the "Father of Truth", whose mission was that of a teacher who came to reveal that the true nature of the Gnostic was identical to that of Christ and God.[48] This notion of the God within was sometimes taken to the extreme:

"God created humanity; [but now human beings] created God. That is the way it is in the world—human beings make gods, and worship their creation. It would be appropriate for the gods to worship human beings!" [49]

– Gnostic Gospel of Philip (non-Christian)

Salvation, understood in terms of liberation from life and the demiurgic prison world, was something that had to be accomplished by each Gnostic alone. The parallelisms with other common modern panentheistic worldviews that preach Self-Transcendence are obvious.

d. Parallelisms with Other Forms of Panentheism

In this section, we have analyzed both Neo-Platonism and Gnosticism as representatives of the doctrines of the One, especially of impersonal Monism (Pantheism and Panentheism). It is not difficult to see, however, that these same core principles can be derived from all other worldviews in this same category.

Be it Advaita Vedānta, Kabbalah, Hermeticism, all New Age beliefs derived from Theosophy (itself derived from Hinduism, Buddhism, and Western Esotericism), etcetera, they all follow almost exactly the same core principles and accept the same primary presuppositions, such as:

• *An Impersonal "God-in-General":* a totality that includes all opposites.

• *Absolute Divine Simplicity:* the only defining attribute of ultimate reality and mankind´s goal, achieved through fusion with the One, the Absolute, the All.

------

48. *Pagels, Elaine (1989). The Gnostic Gospels. Vintage, p.116.*
49. *Ibid., p. 122.*

• *A Dialectical Structure:* that views all distinction as opposition. *The One and the Many* are in tension (Either/Or), with this tension being the generative source of all that exists.

• *The Doctrine of Emanations:* through which our nature is ultimately seen to be the same as God´s.

Other common ones include:

• *Spirit and Matter Dualism:* even though Unity (Good) implies the Multiplicity of matter ("evil").

• *Life as Dream (and in this case, as a nightmare):* "[They lived] as *if they were sunk in sleep and found themselves in disturbing dreams*" [Gnostic *Gospel of Truth*].[50]

• *Particular Human Reason as Ultimate Authority:* Gnostics developed their own way of reading Christian scriptures, and also created their own, abandoning revelation and instead embracing mere human reason and intuition.

Due to this, many different systems sprouted, as human reason alone is incapable of maintaining unity and can be taken in several directions (the whole intellectual history of mankind, and the history of philosophy in particular, being a good example of this point).

• *Psychological Reductionism:* the famous popularizer of Gnosticism Elaine Pagels, furthermore, noted parallels between Gnosticism and Psychoanalysis:

    o She found that both focus on self-knowledge (Gnosis) above anything else. In the absence of this knowledge, both psychoanalytic patients and Gnostics felt that they were being driven and tyrannized by impulses they did not understand.[51]

---

50. *Pagels, Elaine (1989). The Gnostic Gospels. Vintage, p. 125.*
51. *Ibid., p. 124.*

o Through a temporal guide or mentor figure, both tried to be liberated from these impulses, with the ultimate aim being the outgrowing of this temporal authority and becoming their own masters.

The psychological level was thus the mirror of the metaphysical one, with each Gnostic trying to become free from a tyrannical demiurgic father figure. Once the discipleship stage was over, the Gnostic became Jesus' "twin brother"[52] and became a disciple "to his own mind" in a program of self-training focused on the process of "return".[53]

As R.P. Farrell noted regarding the Gnostic mindset: *"[it] ultimately always conceals a psychological program in the guise of a metaphysic, for its ultimate goal is simply to realize the infinite potential of the self, of the self as Christ, of the self as God."* [54]

Recommended Reading

1. **The One and the Many: Studies in the Philosophy of Order and Ultimacy.** *R.J. Rushdoony.*
2. **God, History, and Dialectic. Volumes I and II.** *Joseph P. Farrell.*
3. **Van Til's Apologetic: Readings and Analysis.** *G.L. Bahnsen.*
4. **Presuppositional Apologetics: Stated and Defended.** *G.L. Bahnsen.*
5. **Five Theological Orations.** *St. Gregory Nazianzus.*
6. **The Enneads.** *Plotinus.*

------

52. *Ibid., p. 131.*

53. *Ibid., p. 132.*

54. *Farrell, Joseph P. (2016). God, History, and Dialectic, Volume I: God, The Foundation of the First Europe, p.59.*

The Countenance of God:

Do All Religions Believe in the Same Deity?

CHAPTER SEVEN

Typology of Theistic Mysticism

Or Why Not All Monotheistic Religions Are the Same

1. Absolute Theistic Monism

THE THEISTIC CATEGORY THAT WE NAMED AS "Mysticism of Union" in the Typology outlined in the last chapter is more complex and nuanced than it may appear at first sight. It includes the subjective experience of pure monotheistic (and monistic) religions such as Judaism and Islam, but it also includes the one from the also monotheistic (but not monistic) Christianity.

As we will see in this chapter, even though their mainstream exoteric theologies reflect, in theory, a perseverance of both unity (the One) and plurality (the Many) in their mystical experiences and in their descriptions of the afterlife, this distinction is not always maintained.

Purely monistic exoteric monotheistic religions such as Judaism and Islam tend to describe their experiences of the afterlife as an ascended and enhanced version of this earthly life, with some of them putting a greater emphasis (e.g., Islam) on the "physical" or embodied aspect of this state of being. However, due to their allegiance to pure Monism, they all show a dialectical tension between their mainstream exoteric teachings and the ones found in their esoteric mystical schools.

Those schools (Kabbalah for Judaism, Sufism for Islam), instead of focusing on the proximity of the particular saved individuals with God in a highly spiritualized realm of existence, put their emphasis in the direct fusion with the Godhead. This unavoidably transforms the monotheistic parent religion into a panentheistic worldview.

This fact, which may seem surprising for those with a limited knowledge of the respective esoteric schools of each tradition, is just the logical consequence of a belief system that adheres to pure Monism or the doctrine of the One: if God is *absolutely* simple and not even Him transcends the One/Many dialectic or the Either/Or logic that underlies it, any multiplicity in the Eschaton is at best superfluous and at worst contrary to this *absolute* Oneness.

For a Christian, however, this means the singling out of one of the many energies of God (His Oneness or Unity) and turning it into God´s Essence, in the process creating an idol out of Unity.

The whole Exoteric-Esoteric package of pure monistic religions, in summary, shows an unresolved dialectical tension between the pure "otherness" or External Union with God in an elevated plane of existence created by God´s grace or energies (the Many; in the form of exoteric Monotheism) and the fusion or Internal Union with God´s Essence (the One; as seen in esoteric Panentheism).

In the past, this inconsistency has been translated into historical conflicts and persecutions against mystical excesses (e.g., Islam´s sometimes

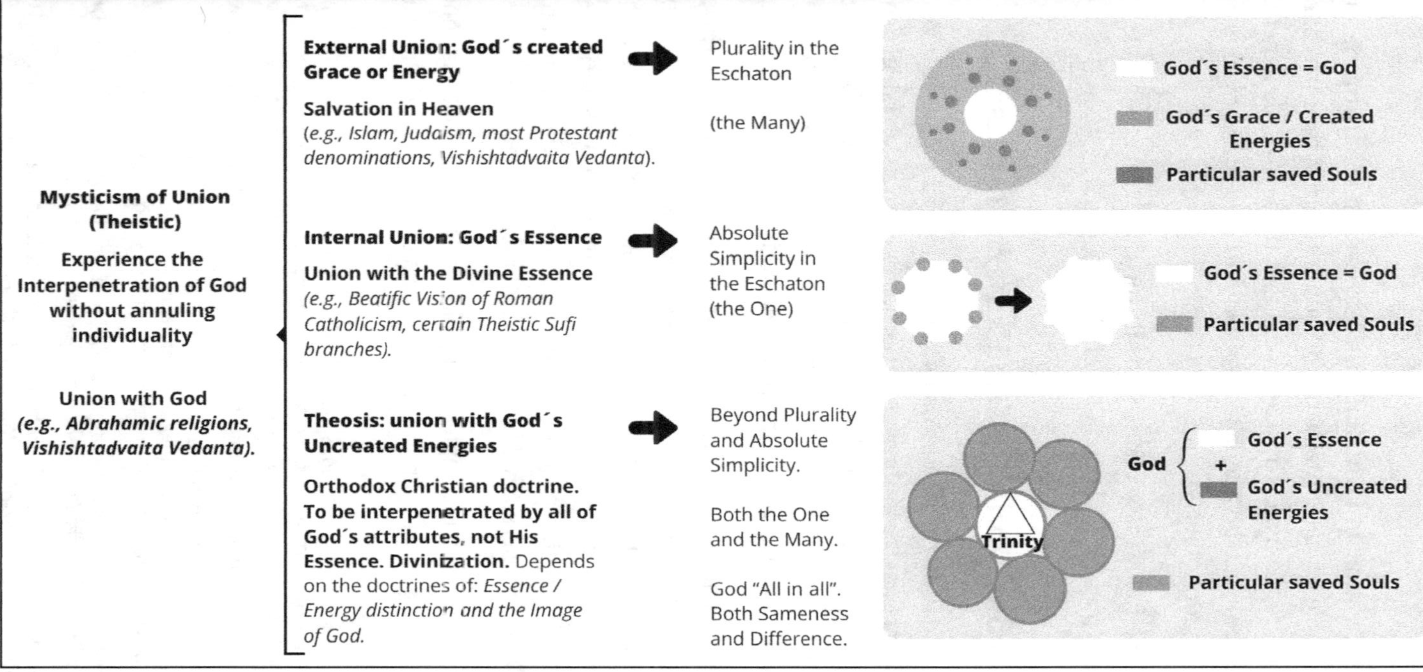

Figure 1. Expansion of the Mysticism of Union category proposed in last chapter´s typology. Theistic mysticism is not as homogeneous as it may seem at first, since different theistic traditions have different definitions of God and/or of the expected union with Him.

uneasy relationship with Sufism). However, it is only the natural and inescapable logical consequence of the allegiance of their parent religion to absolute Monism. The latent seed that tends towards Panentheism, so to speak, can be quenched but not completely removed from pure monistic Monotheism.

In the following sections we will study both aspects of this internal dialectic present in the major theistic religions.

1.1. From Monotheistic Exoteric Judaism...

In Judaism, the afterlife is known as the "coming world" (Olam Ha-Ba[1]). It is related to the heavenly "Garden in Eden" (Gan Eden) and "Hell" (Gehinnom[2]). This "Hell" is not permanent, however, being closer to the Roman Catholic concept of Purgatory, and seen as a spiritual forge where the soul is purified and prepared for its eventual heavenly abode.[3]

The medieval rabbinical views on the afterlife, however, were not homogeneous. Maimonides, for example, described a purely spiritual existence for each individual "disembodied intellect", while Nachmanides spoke of a state of being where spirituality and physicality are joined together in a higher order of existence connected to the Divine Presence. This latter view is shared by all classical rabbinic scholars.[4]

Even though it is accepted religious law (Halakha) that it is impossible for the living to really know what the world to come is like[5], the vision put

---

1. *Blomberg, Craig L.; Chung, Sung Wook (2009). A case for historic premillennialism: "Olam Ha-Ba is usually related to teachings regarding collective redemption and resurrection, but in other places it refers to an afterlife realm for the individual."*

2. *Rosten, Leo (1968). The Joys of Yiddish. Pocket Books edition, pp. 124 & 127.*

3. Apokatastasis or universal salvation is a common concept of the doctrines of the One, being more explicit in Panentheism. If reality is ultimately One (the Absolute, the All), then it has to eventually contain everything in one way or another, excluding nothing.

4. *Simcha Paull, Raphael; summary by Rabbi Dr. Barry Leff. Summary of Jewish Views of the Afterlife. The Neshamah Center.*

5. *Steinsaltz, Adin Evan-Israel (2012). Berakhot. Edited by Tvi Hersh Weinreb. Koren Publishers Jerusalem. Koren Talmud Bavli.*

forward by exoteric Judaism is that of a plurality of saved souls existing externally and in parallel to God. Souls that, even if they are infused with God´s grace or created energies and elevated to greater heights closer to His Presence (Shekhinah), are still mere creatures in relation to Him.

This, which implies that the will of the One God for creation is to attain an everlasting state of plurality and difference in the world to come (the Many), is just a variant of the dialectical Complementary Dualism between Unity and Multiplicity seen in the last chapter when speaking of panentheistic worldviews. In order to "contain" multiplicity, God needs creation.

This everlasting state, as may be rather obvious at this point, does not solve or transcend the problem of Unity and Multiplicity. Neither in the Godhead (pure Monism), nor in the Eschaton (pure plurality as there is only closeness but no real union between creature and Creator).

The eschatological reality in Judaism, to summarize, is one of multiplicity. This makes one horn of the dialectic.

Kabbalah, in turn, will become the complementary second horn that rejects multiplicity to embrace pure unity, as we are about to see.

1.2. ...to Panentheistic Esoteric Kabbalah

Kabbalah is not a homogeneous tradition. It developed during the centuries, starting as an expression of monotheistic Talmudic Judaism and growing progressively closer to panentheistic Monism.

Regarding this point, we can find one of the most illuminating examples in the *Zohar* (thirteenth century; probably the most influential Kabbalistic text). In its pages, we can witness the reframing of the mystical experience found in the earlier Chariot (Merkavah) Mysticism (based on Ezekiel´s vision [Ezekiel 1:4-26]) and the Palaces (Hekhalot) literature.

These ancient texts were focused on visions of ascent into Heavenly Palaces and the Throne of God, in order to ecstatically experience God´s

Presence. The *Zohar*, in a sharp turn, focuses on uniting or merging with Him instead.

In this foundational text, the visionary experience of the teacher is explained as that of a soul freed from its body (Spirit/Matter Dualism) that traverses the seven Palaces of Paradise (number of totality, as the seven days of Creation), along with their counterparts the Seven Palaces of Hell (Complementary Dualism).

Asceticism, meditation, mystical contemplation, and the development of moral qualities are the prerequisites (common to all mystical traditions) to successfully engage in this mystical journey of ascent.

The heavenly halls of this realm, in turn, are viewed as the bridge between the forces of emanation and the physical Universe. In particular, the description of the Seventh Heavenly Hall is the most illuminating of them all:

*"...It is then that all the spirits like lesser lights are **blended** [emphasis added] with the great divine light, and entering within the veil of the Holy of Holies are overwhelmed with blessings proceeding therefrom as water out of an inexhaustible and ever flowing fountain. In this mansion is the great Mystery of Mysteries, the deepest, most profound and beyond all human comprehension and understanding, the eternal and infinite Will."* [6]

Instead of the union through communion of the earlier Merkavah mystics, the ideal of the *Zohar* and later strands of the Kabbalistic tradition is the blending of human and divine wills, symbolized by the 'Kiss of Love' that literally unites the soul to God (sometimes even causing the physical death of the mystic in the process).

This, then, is the second horn of the One/Many dialectic present in Judaism and its mystical tradition: the tendency to fuse with the One and the drift towards Panentheism.

____

6. *Green, D. (1989). Gold in the Crucible. p. 92.*

As we will see, this same tension can also be found between exoteric Islam and esoteric Sufism.

1.3. From Monotheistic Exoteric Islam...

In Islam, the same dialectical tension just mentioned is accentuated by the insistence on determinism to the point of predestination and by certain interpretations of God´s unity (Tawhīd), the central and single most important concept in Islamic religious life. R. J. Rushdoony[7] sums up this dichotomy as follows:

"Mohammedanism, because of its "unitarianism," has been primarily a monolithic statist order, Islam. Its denial of free-will and espousal of rigid determinism is related to this theological premise. Since plurality has no ultimate reality in Mohammedanism, the freedom of the many is an academic question; the one will of Allah governs all reality. The tendency of Mohammedan thought, when not arrested by statist action, to run into mysticism is an obvious and natural one. Since the one alone has ultimate reality, the proper goal of the many is absorption into that one. Since the one alone has ultimacy, the one alone has freedom."

The whole of Islamic intellectual history can, in fact, be interpreted as how different generations of believers have understood the presuppositions and implications of the doctrine of God's Absolute Unity.

The transformation of the classical definition of Tawhīd serves as an eloquent example of this inherent tension. In its origin, it just meant the affirmation of the belief in Monotheism (one God) and His unity[8]. Even though this meaning still persists in contemporary Arabic, its more common modern connotation, however, is that of: *"unification, union,*

---

7. *Rushdoony, R.J. (2007). The One and the Many: Studies in the Philosophy of Order and Ultimacy. Chalcedon/Ross House Books. p. 15.*

8. *Lane, Edward (1863). Al-Qamus: An Arabic Lexicon. London: Williams and Norgate. pp. 2926–2928 (Vol.8).*

combination, fusion; standardization, regularization; consolidation, amalgamation, merger." [9]

Another clear example can be found in the following quote by Ali himself:

"As to the two meanings that are correct when applied to God, one is that it should be said that "God is one" in the sense that there is no likeness to him among things. Another is to say that "God is one" in the sense that there is no multiplicity or division conceivable in Him, neither outwardly, nor in the mind, nor in the imagination. God alone possesses such a unity." [10]

Figure 2. The Buraq (meaning "the lightning") is believed to be the horse-like mystical being that served as Muhammad´s mount during his instantaneous journeys, including the one through the heavens. Picture: Al Buraq (1770–75), Deccan painting with Persian elements. This particular picture seems to imply that the Buraq contains all creatures inside itself, which points to a form of totality (or All-Actuality).

From a Christian theological perspective, as previously mentioned in the case of Judaism, this is the affirmation that an energy or attribute that God possesses both defines and limits Him.

---

9. *Wehr, Hans (1976). A dictionary of modern written Arabic - Edited by Milton Cowan. New York: Spoken Language Services. p. 1055.*

10. *J. Cornell, Vincent . Encyclopedia of Religion, Vol 5. pp. 3561-3562.*

By adhering to this doctrine, and even though Islam´s God is a personal one, the person of God remains below and conditioned by one of His attributes: His absolute unity. Therefore, one of God´s energies (conceptualized as God´s Essence) has primacy over Personhood, in what would amount in Christian theology to a confusion in categorical thinking.

In Orthodox Christianity, to the contrary, each of the triad Essence-Person-Energies is at the same level, implying each other.

a. Afterlife in Islam: An Eternal State of Plurality

Islam´s Allah is absolutely independent of the entirety of creation. However, what began as an absolute Monad, the only existing One, ends in an eternity of Multiplicity containing the plurality of saved individuals, as in Judaism´s eschatology. Given that there is no real union between God and mankind, just a lessened distance with Him compared to our current state of being, the abyss between creature and Creator is never fully overcome.

In Islamic exoteric eschatology, then, no transcendence of the Either/Or dialectic underpinning the One/Many dichotomy is found neither in the Godhead nor in the Eschaton, as was also the case for Judaism.

As specific examples of the form that this plurality takes in the afterlife, the Sunni hadith scholar Al-Tirmidhi quotes Muhammad:

"The smallest reward for the people of Heaven is an abode where there are eighty thousand servants and seventy-two houri, over which stands a dome decorated with pearls, aquamarine, and ruby, as wide as the distance from al-Jabiyyah to San'a".[11, 12]

---

11. *"Jami' at-Tirmidhi 2562 - Chapters on the description of Paradise". Sayings and Teachings of Prophet Muhammad (Sunnah.com).*

12. *"Various Questions Answered by Shaykh Gibril Haddad". Living Islam.*

Another hadith, also quoted by Tirmidhi and considered "good and sound" (hasan sahih), defines the specific reward given to the martyr:

"There are six things with Allah for the martyr. He is forgiven with the first flow of blood (he suffers), he is shown his place in Paradise, he is protected from punishment in the grave, secured from the greatest terror, the crown of dignity is placed upon his head—and its gems are better than the world and what is in it—he is married to seventy-two wives among the wide-eyed houris of Paradise, and he may intercede for seventy of his close relatives".[13]

As can be seen, the physical aspect of the afterlife is accentuated compared to most other monotheistic religions. Furthermore, even if the Qur'ān does not mention explicitly the presence of sexual intercourse in Paradise[14], it is mentioned in hadiths, tafsirs[15,16], and Islamic commentaries.[17, 18 ,19 ,20]

This, as we will see in the next section, is a very different reality compared to the one found in Sufi descriptions of the mystical states of being (based on unity) achieved by the Muslim saint.

———————

13. *"Hadith – The Book on Virtues of Jihad - Jami'at-Tirmidhi" Sayings and Teachings of Prophet Muhammad (Sunnah.com).*

14. *Haleem, M.A.S. Abdel (2011). "Paradise in the Qur'an". Understanding the Qur'an: Themes and Style. I.B Tauris. p. 235.*

15. *Ibn Kathir, Tafsir (Qur'ānic Commentary). The Reward of Those on the Right After. [Chapter (Surah) Al-Waqiah (That Which Must Come To Pass)(56):35–36], Dar-us-Salam Publications, 2000.*

16. *"Will men in Paradise have intercourse with al-hoor aliyn?". IslamQA. 30 August 2000.*

17. *Imam Muhammad Ibn Majah. "Volume 5:37 Book of Zuhd 4337" (Muflihun.com).*

18. *Al-Jalalayn. "Tafsir Yā Sīn". Tafsir al-Jalalayn.*

19. *Bouhdiba, Abdelwahab (2008). Sexuality in Islam. Routledge. pp. 75–76.*

20. *Abdul-Rahman, Muhammad Saed (2003). Islam: Questions and Answers: Basic Tenets of Faith: Belief (Part 2). MSA Publication Ltd. pp. 415–419.*

1.4. ...to Panentheistic Esoteric Sufism

In this section we will focus on the Sufi concept of Fana, or "annihilation of the self". This doctrine is central to the problem of *the One and the Many*, and can be interpreted in different ways.

"All things in creation suffer annihilation and there remains the face of the Lord in its majesty and bounty."

— The Qur'ān, Surat-L-Rehman 26-27.[21]

a. Fana as Vision

One of the traditional conceptualizations of this ego-death is that of the Vision of God. This definition implies the recognition of the will of God at the same time that the mystic abandons the consciousness of oneself, replaced by the contemplation of God alone.[22] This interpretation was favored by mystics such as Al-Junayd al-Baghdadi, Al-Ghazali, and Al-Sarraj.[23]

As Al-Hujwiri unambiguously stated, this doctrine implies the ceasing of any experience of "otherness" or multiplicity, with only the Unity of God remaining:

"One may speak, however, of an annihiliation that is independent of annihiliation: in that case annihilation (fana) means 'annihilation of all remembrance of other' and subsistance (baqa) means 'subsistence of the remembrance of God' (baqa al-dhikhr al-haqq)." [24]

—Al-Hujwiri, Kashf al-Mahjub

---

21. *7 Renowned Translations. Arabic to English Translation. Surat-L-Rehman 165.*

22. *Mat, Ismail (1978). The Concept of Fana'in Sufism. Islāmiyyāt 2.*

23. *Yaran, Cafer. Muslim religious experiences. Alister Hardy Religious Experience Research Centre, 2004.*

24. *Ibid.*

This vision is attained not only through God´s grace but, in part, through the hard work of the mystic, which grants him Ma'rifa (Gnosis) and a state of certainty of the reality of his visions.

b. Fana as Union

The second possible interpretation, however, describes annihilation of the self as total union (Ittihad) with the One or the Truth.

This view, rightly criticized as heretical and incompatible with strict Monotheism by some orthodox Muslims, had its two maximum exponents in Al-Bistami and Al-Hallaj.[25]

The removal of any trace of particularity and individuality in this state of union can be clearly seen in the verses of the famous mystic and poet Jallaluddin Rumi:

"When the Shaykh (Halláj) said 'I am God' and carried it through (to the end), he throttled (vanquished) all the blind (sceptics). When a man's 'I' is negated (and eliminated) from existence, then what remains? Consider, O denier." [26]

Sultan Bahoo, furthermore, in his book Ain-ul-Faqr, provided a very clear numerical (arithmetical) picture of the whole process of annihilation as fusion with God when he stated:

"Initially I was four, then became three, afterwards two and when I got out of Doi (being two), I became one with Allah." [27]

---

25. *Ibid.*

26. *Nicholson, Reynold Alleyne. The Mathnawí of Jalálu'ddín Rúmí. Poetry Soup, p. 132, verses 2095-2096.*

27. *See, for example, Hossein Nasr´s discussion in: Yaran, Cafer. Muslim religious experiences. Alister Hardy Religious Experience Research Centre, 2004.*

Figure 3. All forms of mysticism, including Sufism, include methods of meditation or prayer that aim at getting closer to God. In this case, it is called remembrance (Dhikr). Dhikr, which is usually central to Sufi worship, differs depending on the order who practices it (Tariqa). The variations include specific postures, breathing patterns, and movements. Prayers using the names of God are usually employed in order to revive the practitioner´s innate capacity to understand God (Fitra). Picture: A Sufi in Ecstasy in a Landscape, by Isfahan; Safavid (Persia, c. 1650–1660).

c. Symbolism in the Islamic Mystical Literature of Union

The Sufi literature describing the experience of the mystic in the form of seven concentric castles is abundant, being reminiscent of the seven Kabbalistic Palaces and of the seven Mansions of St. Teresa of Ávila, as we will later see when we explore Roman Catholic mysticism. These schemas are reminiscent of the Neo-Platonic process of Henosis or process of progressive simplification starting from external emanations and ending in union with the One.

This symbolism can be seen in works such as the *Maqamat Al-Qulub* or *Stations of the Heart* (Abul-Hasan Nuri of Baghdad; ninth century, earliest known text), or the *Nawadir* (Ahmad al-Qalyubi , sixteenth century).

In the *Nawadir*, for example, the soul progresses through seven degrees of perfection represented through the use of the aforementioned castles as metaphors and symbols. The final stage involves the ecstatic union of the soul of the aspirant with God Himself.

An especially illustrative example of the panentheistic tendencies underlying this type of Islamic mysticism can be found in the famous Persian poet Farid ad-din Attar.

In his poem *The Conference of the Birds*, he wrote about the seven Valleys of the Way as the different stages encountered by the pilgrim in his "journey in God". In it, we can clearly see the metaphysical position in favor of the One and, therefore, the complete exclusion of the Many.

In the description of the Fifth Valley, the Valley of Unity, difference and diversity dissolve into unity: *"the many here are merged into one; one form involves the multifarious, thick swarm."* [28]

---

28. *Attar, Farid ad-din. (1984). Conference of the Birds. London: Penguin. pp. 191.*

The final Valley, the one of Poverty and Nothingness, also shows striking similarities to other Eastern panentheistic worldviews, as can be seen in the following extracts of its description:

"[...] Lame and deaf, the mind has gone,
You enter an obscure oblivion",
"[...]Whoever sinks within this sea is blest and
in self-loss obtains eternal rest".
"First lose yourself, then lose this loss and then
Withdraw from all that you
have lost again –
Go peacefully, and
stage by stage progress
Until you gain the realms
of Nothingness;
But if you cling to any
worldly trace,
No news will reach you
from that promised place." [29]

d. Similarities of the Sufi Doctrine of Union with Other Panentheistic Worldviews

Given that this interpretation transforms Islam´s monotheistic Monism into a panentheistic one, it is no surprise that this is the preferred interpretation of perennialists, such as the Islamic scholar and philosopher Hossein Nasr.[30]

Perennialism or Perennial Philosophy (also known as Traditionalism) states that either all esoteric mystical schools are just partial exponents

---

29. Ibid., pp. 203, 205.

30. Yaran, Cafer. Muslim religious experiences. Alister Hardy Religious Experience Research Centre, 2004.

of the true lost metaphysical doctrine or that they all are different ways to reach the same destination.

It focuses on the minimum common denominator between them, and it is especially influenced by the Panentheism of Advaita Vedānta and the Sufi traditions that define self-annihilation as union with God. In other words, Perennialism always favors a panentheistic worldview.

This interpretation of self-annihilation, furthermore, is similar to Eastern religious concepts such as Samādhi in Hinduism or Nirvana in Buddhism[31], which literally means "extinction or disappearance".

The similarities of Sufism with Eastern mysticism and Western esotericism are evident. They are also natural, as they are just the logical consequence of the doctrine of absolute Monism. If everything is ultimately One (God), what are we? Either we remain separated from God even in Paradise, being nothing in comparison to Him, or we are everything by uniting with Him instead.

As we have seen, both Jewish and Islamic mysticism, when unconstrained by their respective orthodox authorities, make explicit the inherent undeclared dialectical conflict between the exoteric and esoteric aspects of theistic Absolute Monism or Non-Trinitarian Monotheism. When not repressed, they tend towards the One (Panentheism).

2. Theistic Panentheism in Dharmic Monotheism

Since Swami Vivekananda presented, through Advaita Vedānta, an impersonal monistic picture of Hinduism at the Parliament of the World's Religions in 1893, most Hindu (Sanātana Dharma) traditions imported to the West have been panentheistic ones.

---

31. Bennett, Clinton; M. Ramsey, Charles. *South Asian Sufis: Devotion, Deviation, and Destiny. A&C Black, p. 23.*

Be it Advaita, any type of Yoga, or the esoteric Western traditions influenced by those (such as Theosophy, the precursor of the New Age movement), the fact is that, unconsciously or premeditatedly, theistic Hinduism was never given the spotlight in the West.

This can give us an erroneous impression that most Hindus believe in an impersonal First Principle as ultimate reality. This is not the case, however. In India, theistic devotional worldviews (Bhakti mārga) such as Vaishnavism (e.g., Krishnaism), Shaivism, and Shaktism have always enjoyed a stronger following than impersonal worldviews.

2.1. Vishishtadvaita Vedānta: Hinduism´s Attempt to Solve the Problem of the One and the Many

In Rāmānuja´s theistic tradition, Moksha or liberation means, as in all Dharmic religions, the release from Saṃsāra or the Cycle of Rebirths. The aim is to unbound the individual (Jiva) from their state of bondage and ignorance. This is achieved through devotional (Bhakti) Yoga (total surrender to God), which is different from the meditation techniques popular in the West, based mostly on Rāja or Kundalini Yoga (meditation by emptying the mind and energetic visualizations, respectively).

a. Differences with Advaita Vedānta and Other Impersonal Panentheistic Strands of Hinduism

This tradition is different from impersonal Hindu Non-Dualism in that it believes in the existence of a Supreme Being, Vishnu, and the possibility of serving Him in His abode (Vaikuntha) once liberation is achieved and Karma has run its course. Liberated beings, instead of fusing and becoming one with Brahman, keep their individuality while partaking of His attributes, such as infinite knowledge and bliss.

In Vaikuntha, the devotees continue to delight in the service of their God in a body which is defined as Truth-Consciousness-Bliss (Sat-Cit-Ananda), therefore transforming the ultimate reality or Essence of the impersonal Brahman of Advaita Vedānta into the energies of a personal God, freely shared with all liberated souls. This is similar to the Theosis doctrine found in Orthodox Christianity.

Liberation is only achievable through God´s grace after death (Videhamukti), while in Advaita, it is achieved through one´s own efforts in this life (Jivanmukti).[32]

b. Differences with Abrahamic Theistic Religions

It is important, however, to note that Vishishtadvaita Vedānta is also different from Abrahamic Monotheism in one crucial aspect: the adepts, when they achieve liberation, acquire the knowledge that the deity has always been their true inner Self.

The aim of the devotee, then, is to lead a life worthy of an instrument of the deity (Vishnu, Narayana), offering to Him all his thoughts, words, and deeds and seeing Him in everything and everything in Him. This is Vishishtadvaita´s solution to the problem of Unity and Multiplicity.

Similar to Christianity, it allows a plurality of individual beings in communion between themselves through being united with God. In contrast with Christianity, however, there is also a real identity between God´s Essence and each person´s true Self.

The "unity" achieved, then, is a type of modalism where God sees Himself through the plurality of masks that each individual provides.

Even though a real solution to the problem of *the One and the Many* is outlined, given that each of us is also seen as ultimately identical with God, the apparent plurality present in Vaikuntha eventually ends up being ontologically illusory, collapsing again into absolute Monism.

------

32. *Tapasyananda, Swami. Bhakti Schools of Vedanta; pp. 54-83.*

In comparison with the Orthodox Christian view of Theosis, instead of each person freely partaking of the totality of God´s Uncreated Energies or attributes through becoming a temple for the Holy Spirit while retaining their own particular deified soul, Vishishtadvaita devotees discover that they were always a particular mode of existence of Vishnu Himself.

Figure 4. Narayana (All-Potentiality) resting on Shesha (the many faced All-Actuality, the serpent being a symbol of the deity´s energies). From their combination, and from the former´s navel (center), Brahmā (the creator modality of the deity) springs forth. Narayana is one of the forms of Vishnu, the one depicting his yogic slumber under the Celestial Waters. This picture illustrates the concept of a passive masculine Spirit in his role of creator once united with his active feminine counterpart (Lakshmi) actualizing his energies (Shesha). Male and female, active and passive, as the dual first manifestation of the impersonal Cosmic Ocean. Picture: Kalurama (1863); The British Library, London.

Therefore, instead of being a representative of classic Monotheism, this worldview can be instead classified as an exponent of theistic Panentheism (which is a form of absolute Monism).

Contrary to impersonal Hindu philosophies, Vishishtadvaita believes in a personal God. Contrary to classical Monotheism, however, we are all also seen as this one God.

c. Vishishtadvaita´s Interpretation of the "Great Sayings" of the Upanishads (Mahāvākyas)

Vishishtadvaita´s interpretation of *Chandogya Upanishad* 3.14.1 (*"All this is Brahman"*) was used as the basis for an ontology of reality that consists of:

- *Ishvara or Para-Brahman (God).*

- *Particular beings (Jivas):* sentient beings as conscious modes of existence of Brahman.

- *Matter/Universe (Jagat):* non-conscious modes of existence of Brahman.

Brahman is seen as the composite whole, the totality, of the above mentioned triad, with the last two categories forming God´s own body. Creation, contrary to Advaita, is real and not illusory, being the expansion or emanation of God´s intelligence.

Mandukya Upanishad 1.2 (*"the Self is Brahman"*) and *Chandogya Upanishad* 6.8.7 (*"Thou art that"*) were interpreted by Rāmānuja as stating the absolute identity between Brahman and particular individuals (Ātman).

He saw the former as the common underlying substratum and ultimate unity of all beings in Ishvara (Para-Brahman), the Cosmic Spirit of the Universal Body consisting of all inert matter and sentient beings alike.

Katha Upanishad was also interpreted in the same manner:

"A man who has discrimination for his charioteer and holds the reins of the mind firmly, reaches the end of the road; and that is the supreme position of Vishnu."

— Katha Upanishad, 1.3.9

"Beyond the senses are the objects; beyond the objects is the mind; beyond the mind, the intellect; beyond the intellect, the Great Atman; beyond the Great Atman, the Unmanifest; beyond the Unmanifest, the Purusha. Beyond the Purusha there is nothing: this is the end, the Supreme Goal."

— Katha Upanishad, 1.3.10, 1.3.11

This, in turn, is similar to other theistic/panentheistic Hindu traditions such as Kashmir (or Trika) Shaivism, where all things are believed to be a manifestation of Universal Consciousness (Cit or Brahman).

The notion of a personal God in systems that define Him as Consciousness is ambiguous, however, since not a few of them interpret such a concept not as a real Person but as a personification of an impersonal Principle or Force.

d. The Absolute and Complementary Dualism

As in all theologies that define ultimate reality or God as the Absolute, Rāmānuja also conceptualized Brahman as the Unity of Opposites.

This can be clearly seen in his notion that Brahman is formed by both the Supreme God Narayana and the Supreme Goddess Lakshmi together, with them being the polarized, indivisible, co-eternal, and co-absolute male/female personifications of God, respectively.

This is similar to other Hindu devotional traditions such as Shaivism, Shaktism, and other tantric schools, were the Godhead is defined as the union of the masculine principle (Shiva: passive, transcendent) and the

Figure 5. Vishnu Vishvarupa, the form of the deity representing the totality of all the planes of existence, the actualization of All-Potentiality. Everything in existence is part of Vishnu, a panentheistic deity. This symbolic representation includes the Sun and the Moon as his eyes, the Earth as his feet, and Heaven as his head. All deities (both beneficial and harmful) are contained within him, being just particular manifestations of his attributes. Male and female, above and below, good and evil, the Absolute contains it all. Picture: Vishnu as the Cosmic Man (Vishvarupa); Jaipur, Rajasthan (c. 1800-50).

feminine one (Shakti: active, immanent, temporal; the energetic aspect of God). In other words, God is dialectically understood as the Androgyne, the Absolute, the union and interplay of Consciousness and Energy.

This, furthermore, seems just another way of describing the notion present in most, if not all, ancient mythological cosmogonies regarding the existence of a conquering God or civilizing Hero (Consciousness, Order) subduing chaotic Matter (usually represented by a serpent or dragon).

2.2. Sikhism and the All-Pervasiveness of God

Sikhism, as another major exponent of theistic Panentheism, believes in One Universal God (Ik Oankar)[33, 34] who can be defined as "the one Supreme Reality, Creator, and all-pervading Spirit", highlighting his unity with creation.[35]

Like in theistic-panentheistic Hinduism, as we just saw, God (who has no gender) is metaphorically represented as masculine (Father) in His Essence and feminine (Mother) in His Power.

Also, as in all systems that view God as the Absolute, this All-Possibility is "incarnated" in many worlds (All-Actuality).

However, the concept of Māyā or the unreality of the Universe, contrary to Advaita Vedānta, is not defined as the ultimate illusoriness of any multiplicity, but as the unreality of worldly values that take us away from God.

---

33. *Wilkinson, Philip (2008). Religions. Dorling Kindersley. pp. 209, 214–215.*

34. *House, H. Wayne (April 1991). Resurrection, Reincarnation, and Humanness. Bibliotheca Sacra. 148 (590).*

35. *Singh, Dr Jasraj (2009). A Complete Guide to Sikhism. Unistar Books, p. 182.*

a. The Equivalence Between Individual Consciousness and Universal Consciousness

According to Guru Nanak, the ultimate aim of human life is to reconnect with Akal ("The Timeless One") through the elimination of egotism attained by remembering the Name of the Lord (Nām).[36, 37]

Furthermore, a clear example of Sikhism´s Panentheism can be seen in the meaning of the word Guru ("teacher")[38], which means the internal voice of the Spirit[39] in each person and is identical with Akal, the universally immanent God.[40] Ultimately, the seeker attains the realization that his own consciousness is the true Guru, following the same "Ātman equals Brahman" formula present in Hinduism.

In reaching this insight, and given this God-in-general understanding of God common to all panentheistic traditions (including theistic Panentheism), the seeker ends up seeing all religions as conveying the same message, just as Perennialism does.[41]

b. Liberation as Union with God Through Grace

For Sikhism, the final state of being of those who achieve liberation is not found in a heavenly realm, but on the spiritual union with God (the Akal), which results in salvation or enlightenment/liberation within

---

36. *Pruthi, Raj (2004). Sikhism and Indian Civilization. Discovery Publishing House, p. 204.*

37. *McLean, George (2008). Paths to the Divine: Ancient and Indian. Council for Research in Values & Philosophy, p. 599.*

38. *Singh, Nirmal (2008). Searches in Sikhism. New Delhi: Hemkunt Press, p. 122.*

39. *Parrinder, Geoffrey (1971). World Religions: From Ancient History to the Present. London: Hamlyn, pp. 254–256.*

40. *Singh, R.K. Janmeja (2013). Gurbani's Guidance and the Sikh's 'Destination'. The Sikh Review, 8. 61 (716): 27–35.*

41. *Dhillon, Sukhraj Singh (2004). Universality of the Sikh Philosophy: An Analysis. The Sikh Review.*

one's lifetime (Jivanmukti), thus exhausting one´s Karma and ending the Cycle of Rebirths through God´s grace.[42, 43]

This is only natural for worldviews which, confronted with the dialectical problem between Unity and Plurality, make the decision to follow the One.

Figure 6. The Triad Below The One. The above illustration explains the meaning of Ik Oankar using a traditional theory involving Hindu symbolism. This theory explains that the name Oankar can be split into two parts : Oan, equivalent to the Hindu sacred syllabe Aum (A: Brahmā, U: Vishnu, M: Shiva), and Kar. The latter is the line representing the omnipresent Brahman, the Ultimate Reality (Paramatman) above the previous triad. Picture: Janamsakhi manuscript (16ᵗʰ-19ᵗʰ century).

42. *Grewal, J. S. (1998). The Sikhs of the Punjab. Cambridge University Press, pp. 25–36.*

43. *Singh, H. S. (2000). The Encyclopedia of Sikhism. Hemkunt Press, p. 80.*

3. Conclusions Regarding Monotheistic Monism

Summarizing this section, we have seen that non-Trinitarian Monotheism still shows a dialectical thought and uneasy tension between its main exoteric religions (Judaism and Islam) and their respective esoteric mystical schools (Kabbalah and Sufism):

• The former, followers of a "simple" type of Monism, necessarily picture an eschatological reality of plurality where saved souls are, even then, just creatures who cannot bridge the abyss between them and their Creator. The Godhead also does not transcend the dialectic between *the One and the Many,* since to do so it would depend on creation as the source of multiplicity.

• The latter, in turn, tend to panentheistic Monism and the aspiration of being absorbed into God or fused with Him through the extinction of the otherness of the self. God is many times conceptualized as an impersonal ultimate reality, contradicting thus their parent exoteric traditions. There is no real appreciation of multiplicity in these worldviews, neither in this current life, nor in the "world to come".

Monotheistic Panentheism (e.g., Vishishtadvaita Vedānta, Sikhism), even though it sometimes apparently embraces plurality in the Eschaton instead of the monistic absorption of competing schools such as Advaita Vedānta, maintains no real difference between a personal God and creation.

The presence of different modes of existence of God in the Eschaton speaks of an underlying identity, not just union through communion, between saved souls and God. Therefore, this modalistic interpretation prevents a real embrace of plurality and tends towards Absolute Monism, as all Panentheism does. Multiplicity is accepted because, eventually, it is discovered to be unreal.

Comparing this doctrine to the Orthodox Christian one of Theosis or divinization, Vishishtadvaita´s vision is that of God looking at different uniquely limited versions of Himself through many souls, while that of Christianity is the elevation of each unique person into the fullness of divinity, while still being "other" and maintaining a loving relationship with God. Instead of loving Himself through us, the Tri-Une God, thanks to His transcendence of *the One and the Many* dialectic, loves us.

Furthermore, as we have seen, the core doctrines of non-theistic Panentheism, such as the view of God as the Absolute, which in turn implies doctrines such as Complementary Dualism (the Unity of Opposites), Emanationism, and the existence of many universes (Multiverse), can also be found in these worldviews, even if they conceive God as personal.

Given all the above, it seems clear that pure Monism, even in its monotheistic forms, is still stifled by a dialectical thinking that cannot transcend the problem of *the One and the Many* on its own. Therefore, it also cannot offer satisfactory metaphysical grounds for expecting the (deified) subsistence of our own unique personal existence in the coming eschatological reality.

Either we are God, or we are nothing compared to Him. This is, apparently, the only conclusion that human reason can reach on its own, as shown by the multiple worldviews that decided that this position could explain the internal mystical experiences they achieved.

This leaves us only with revealed Christianity, a monotheistic but non-monistic (because it is Trinitarian) faith, as the only exponent of the theistic Mysticism of Union that does not revert back to the philosophy of the One in one way or another, thus proposing a real and unique solution to the problem of Unity and Multiplicity.

Upon analysis, it can be seen that the solution provided by the Tri-Une God is the only metaphysical ground that truly allows and embraces unique particularity.

This is a different doctrine than those of all previous philosophical thought, focused on union through merging and absolute identity. At the same time, it crosses the abyss between creature and Creator by promising deification (Theosis), the full participation in the Uncreated Energies of God (or *what* He is), without becoming Him in His Essence.

The Trinitarian God, because of *who* He is, can love us in such a way that He gives us *what* He is, without ceasing to love us for being us.

For the author of this book, as it will have become sufficiently clear by now, the supernatural self-consistency shown by all Christian doctrines in their absolute rejection of dialectical thought[44], as well as the fact that these doctrines had to be revealed (a necessary condition to know any truth that transcends our current plane of existence), is compelling evidence of the truth of its claims.

4. Filioque: The Infiltration of the Dialectical Spirit in Christian Theology

As we have seen until now, Christianity is the only worldview that proposes a real and unique solution to the problem of *the One and the Many* in a way that does not involve dialectical Either/Or thinking or goes back to the One of the philosophers in one way or another.

However, as we are about to see, the three main Christian denominations historically embraced different responses to this problem.

J.P. Farrell, in his book *God, History, and Dialectic*, defended the existence of two different Europes. The first was the consequence of original patristic Christian theology. The second was born when Roman Catholicism began to exist through the Great Schism of 1054, reimagining the non-dialectical Tri-Une God into a dialectical one through St. Augustine´s of Hippo's later Hellenistic reformulation of the Trinity.

Europe´s history, in his profusely documented view, was shaped and moulded by the addition of the Filioque clause to the Creed. This clause states that the Holy Spirit does not proceed only from the Father but from the Father and the Son, being conceived as a mediator or the

---

44. *Most clearly exemplified in the two united but non-fused (or non-confused) natures of Jesus Christ, the Incarnation of the Logos.*

love between both of them. This, of course, implies the necessity of a mediator, a third term that equilibrates two other principles that, if they need such a figure, must have an intrinsic degree of tension or opposition between them.

The historical effects of the Filioque, as documented by Farrell, can indeed be seen as the proof that small theological modifications (how we understand God to be) have major consequences for common everyday life, implying changes in how we understand reality, morality, spirituality, and even how to organize society.

Furthermore, this "new Trinity" that the Filioque clause unknowingly created, re-established a dialectical way of thinking that had been, since the beginning, the true antagonist of Christian theology:

"[....] The Second Europe "rediscovered Aristotle" in the twelfth century, and thereby unleashed a process of massive theological revisionism. But the First Europe never misplaced him, and Russia never had him to begin with. [....]" [45]

"[...] This transubstantiation of the Trinity from a revealed Mystery to a dialectical deduction, and finally, to a dialectical process at work within History itself is simply unintelligible without Augustine.

In the thirteenth century, Joachim of Floris' Age of the Father, Age of the Son, and (coming) Age of the Spirit, or Petrarch's or Gibbon's Golden Age, Dark Age, and Renaissance, or Hegel's well-known Thesis, Antithesis, and Synthesis, or Comte's "superstitious, metaphysical, and scientific" periods, and finally, our own superficially academic and objective divisions of Ancient, Mediaeval, and Modern "History" are but tired exhausted reworkings of the original heresy which split the Latin Church from Eastern Orthodoxy and created the Two Europes." [46]

---

45. *Farrell, Joseph P. (2016). God, History, and Dialectic; Volume I: God, The Foundation of the First Europe, p. 15.*

46. *Ibid., pp.15-16.*

"Augustine the Hellenizer erected a system founded upon a continuity of theology with Greek philosophy, a continuity of incalculable enormity: the identification of The One (to en) of Greek philosophy with the One God and Father of Christian doctrine." [47]

After this old dialectical way of theologizing was rekindled, the Western world favored a view of theology, philosophy, and history understood in terms of the dialogue between polar opposites.

This dialectical Either/Or paradigm itself was, however, never deeply examined. It went unchallenged, as if it were an unavoidable and legitimate constituent of Christian theology itself.

4.1. The One Roman Catholic Pope: The Natural Consequence of Dialectical Thinking

Why did a Church that believed in the transcendence of the problem of Unity and Plurality through the Tri-Une God lose sight of the implications of that doctrine in its own life and organization? Why, instead of embracing and promoting both absolute unity and complete diversity, was the Catholic Church involved in endless conflicts between the One Pope and the Many bishops that until then had been the canonical (through direct and unbroken apostolic succession) source of authority of the Church?

This change, unthinkable under the original non-dialectical apostolic paradigm, which understood each bishop as both the One source of authority for other ministries in his locality and as one of Many bishops of equal authority in the total life of the Church, made sense under the new paradigm that saw unity as having primacy over plurality.

By altering the revealed doctrine of the Trinity (which implies subordinating it to mere human reason), the very thought structures

---

47. *Ibid., p. 21.*

and original character of Christianity and the Tri-Une God were also irremediably changed.

Thus, by abandoning the protection that the original Trinity provided against a polarized Either/Or dialectical way of thinking, the Christian One/Many began to walk in the direction of the only One of the philosophers.

This illustrates the fact that small changes in how we understand God are never small. Through the Filioque, a seemingly minor change in the understanding of God had major historical consequences, such as the abandonment of a united but pluralistic ecclesiastical authority for a purely "monistic" one in the figure of the Pope. This, in turn, led to the Great Schism that split Christendom and gave rise to two distinct civilisations: the Christian West (Roman Catholicism) and the Christian East (Orthodox Christianity).

4.2. The Inversion of the Theological Order

The primacy of human reason over revelation that took place in Catholic doctrine can be clearly exemplified by the switching of the classical order of doing theology.

Early patristic Christianity followed revelation by starting all theologizing from the revealed Persons of God (*who* He is), unfolding then all the implications of these historical self-revelations and deducing the generalized conceptions about His particular attributes and Nature (*what* He is). The order followed was: Persons, Energies (also called attributes or operations), and Essence (or Nature).

Roman Catholic theologians, in contrast, tended to start from a philosophical general notion about God´s Essence and, from there, deduced God´s attributes. Only after this would they tackle the notion of God´s Personhood and the particular historical manifestations of the Persons of the Trinity. The order, in this case moving in opposite directions, was: Essence, Attributes, Persons.

As a consequence, the Latin Church, by beginning all theologizing by defining God´s Essence through a combination of revelation and human reason, ended up operating in a different paradigm containing different axiomatic presuppositions about God´s Nature.

Human reason was given more freedom in defining God´s Essence, which opened the doors to give greater weight to classic philosophical thought (e.g., Aristotle in Thomas Aquinas).

This, in turn, had other far-reaching consequences that became evident over time. For example, as Farrell noted:

"Thus, because the First Europe observed rigorously the categorical distinctions of Person and Nature, it avoided the dialectical dilemma which will plague the Second Europe after Augustine, the dilemma which opposes divine grace and human free choice as irreconcilable opposites." [48]

4.3. The Danger of Supplanting the Trinity: The Cases of Gnosticism and Origenism

The consequences of modifying Christianity´s most basic revealed dogmas and axiomatic beliefs were well known centuries before Roman Catholicism was born. We can find some of the most dramatic examples in Gnosticism and the theology of Origen of Alexandria.

In the following sections we will briefly summarize the consequences that the addition of dialectical thought had in those systems in order to better understand the fears that the addition of the Filioque, working under a dialectical paradigm, aroused in those who knew the historical precedents.

---

48. *Ibid., p. 22.*

a. The One Over the Many: Origen of Alexandria and the Consequences of Adding Dialectics into Christian Theology

In Origen´s system, a highly Hellenised version of Christianity, the usual metaphysical consequences of introducing dialectical thought can be clearly seen.

For Origen:

• The diversity of the world is dialectically and unavoidably linked to the sinful exercise of free choice in the pre-existent world of souls, or the Henad (absolute Unity).[49]

As he directly stated: *"Now since the world is so very varied and comprises so great a diversity of rational beings, what else can we assign as the cause of its existence except the diversity in the fall of those who decline from unity in dissimilar ways?"* [50]

• Again, an attribute of God, simplicity, is equated with God´s Essence.

• This simplicity makes it mandatory to transform the co-equal Trinity into a sequential system comprised of "First, Second, and Third Gods."

• Which in turn faithfully reproduces Plotinus´ Neo-Platonic first three emanations: The One, Nous, and World-Soul.[51]

• God is then, inevitably, implicated in the definition and origin of evil because anything outside of God´s simplicity, even Creation, implies a lesser degree of (even moral) perfection.

Therefore, matter is evil, as Origen dramatically demonstrated by emasculating himself.

---

49. *Origen. On First Principles. Section 1:8:2.*

50. *Ibid., 2:9:2, p. 130.*

51. *Quasten, Johannes (Vol. III). Patrology. Thomas More Press, p. 8.*

• Souls are conceptualized as semi-components of the total simplicity or unity of the Godhead (similar to the Gnostic and Kabbalistic "Holy Sparks" motif).

• Salvation is Universal (Apokatastasis). An unavoidable consequence of, knowingly or unknowingly, defining the Godhead as the All, the One, the Absolute.

Needless to say, the character of a God that values absolute simplicity devoid of any particularity as the highest good is a complete inversion from the Christian one. Instead of rejecting what makes us unique, the Christian God loves each person in their particularity, which is a manifestation of the specific reason (Logoi) that God willed for them.

b. The Gnostic Dialectical "Trinity" and the Divine Hermaphrodite

The Gnostic "Trinity", in turn, was also defined by its dialectical structure, with the Persons being conceptualized as Father, Mother (Holy Spirit), and Son.[52] This was just another version of the ancient philosophical motif of the Divine Hermaphrodite or Androgyne which, as a symbol of God understood as the Absolute that contains All, resolves all moral and metaphysical opposition through a synthesis and Union of Opposites.

In systems that share this doctrine, as Zaehner and Farrell both highlighted, it is difficult to justify a concrete moral order. The presence of at least a modicum of moral relativism, necessary in systems that conceive God as "beyond good and evil", is always part and parcel of the constellation of metaphysical beliefs surrounding this notion of God as the Absolute.

It is not surprising, then, the extreme variety of "moralities" found in Gnosticism, ranging from the extreme asceticism of the Cathars (similar

---

52. *Pagels, Elaine. The Gnostic Gospels. Vintage, p. 52. This conception is found in the Gospel to the Hebrews. The Hebrew for "Spirit" is ruach, a feminine word.*

to the Catholic flagellants, as we will later see) to the antinomianism of the libertine Borborites.

Given the drastic changes in metaphysical doctrine that it produces, as we have just seen, it is no wonder that the Eastern Church fought so fiercely to avoid any mixing of dialectical thought with Christian theology.

There is no doubt that theologians such as Origen or St. Augustine had Christianity's best interests in mind when they formulated their theories. However, as Farrell dramatically noted, embracing St. Augustine´s personal interpretations beyond the actual consensus of the Church Fathers carried the risk that Christianity would slowly transform itself into the largest Gnostic mystery religion in the world.[53]

4.4. The Orthodox Refutation of Dialectics and the Filioque Clause

By having a clear picture of the dangers just outlined, the fears of St. Photios, the Ecumenical Patriarch of Constantinople who had to refuse the addition of the Filioque to the Eastern Creed, are easier to understand:

" [...] For my part I think that it is a prelude to his complete denial of the 'being' of the only-Begotten and of the Holy Ghost, and that this system of his is secretly intended to effect the setting aside of all real belief in their personality." [54]

– St. Photios the Great

Thus, for St. Photios, the real danger of the Filioque was that it initiated a path that could logically end in an impersonal view of God, eventually

---

53. *Farrell, Joseph P. (2016). God, History, and Dialectic, Volume I: God, The Foundation of the First Europe, p. 109.*

54. *of Nyssa, St. Gregory. Against Eunomius (1:14). Nicene and Post-Nicene Fathers. Cosimo Inc., p. 51.*

leading to a subordinationist view of the Persons of the Godhead and a return to the God of the philosophers and of human reason.

The response given by the Patriarch was the only one that can be given through an Orthodox lens: to reject all innovation while reaffirming the tradition received through apostolic succession, concisely summarized in the following quote of St. Gregory the Theologian that states that unity is not the enemy of plurality:[55]

"*The three most ancient opinions concerning God are Anarchia, Polyarchia, and Monarchia. The first two are the sport of the children of Hellas, and may they continue to be so. For anarchy is a thing without order; and the Rule of Many (polyarchy) is factious, and thus anarchical, and thus disorderly. For both these tend to the same thing, namely, disorder; and this to dissolution, for disorder is the first step to dissolution.*

But Monarchy is that which we hold in honour. It is, however, a Monarchy that is not limited to one Person, ***for it is possible for a Unity at variance with itself to come into a condition of plurality; but one which is made of an equality of Nature and a Union of mind, and an identity of motion, and a convergence of its elements to unity... so that though numerically distinct there is no severance of Essence. Therefore Unity having from all eternity arrived by motion at Duality, found its rest in Trinity.***" [56]

– St. Gregory of Nazianzus (emphasis added)

---

55. St. Gregory, as part of the Cappadocian Fathers, was one of the key figures in unwrapping and making explicit all the implications of revealed Christian doctrine and how it solved the problem of Unity and Multiplicity while at the same time avoiding dialectical thought.

56. *of Nazianzus, St. Gregory. The Third Theological Oration. Nicene and Post-Nicene Fathers. Cosimo Inc., p. 301.*

As Farrell perceptively concluded:

"For all the dialectical rhetorical constructions of patristic theology have but one goal:

To teach the faithful habits or forms of thought and perceptions of spiritual realities which cannot be reduced to the "either-or" of a polar opposition.

Its theology has, as it were, the persistent characteristic of dialectical rhetoric being employed against dialectics itself." [57]

4.5. The Modification of Core Christian Doctrines Through the Addition of Dialectics

In the following sections we will analyze the consequences that adding dialectical presuppositions into Christian theology had for particular doctrines and beliefs, comparing it to early patristic Christianity. These modifications, as we shall see, are not minor.

4.5.1. Scholasticism and St. Thomas Aquinas

Roman Catholic Christian theology became, during the centuries, increasingly intermingled with philosophy.

The most influential example is that of Scholasticism, a philosophical school of the Middle Ages heavily based on Aristotelian logic. It emphasised dialectical reasoning, inference, rigorous analysis, and the drawing of distinctions. A Christian version was born within monastic schools upon the rediscovery of Aristotle´s collected works. Those schools later became the basis of the earliest European Universities, playing hence a role in the early development of modern science.

---

57. *Farrell, Joseph P. (2016). God, History, and Dialectic, Volume I: God, The Foundation of the First Europe, p. 23.*

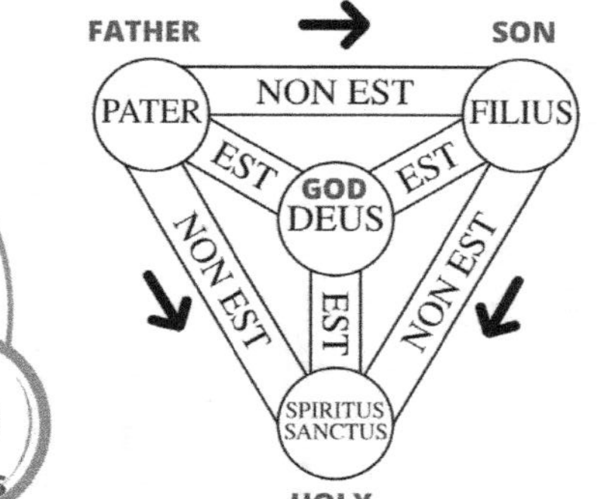
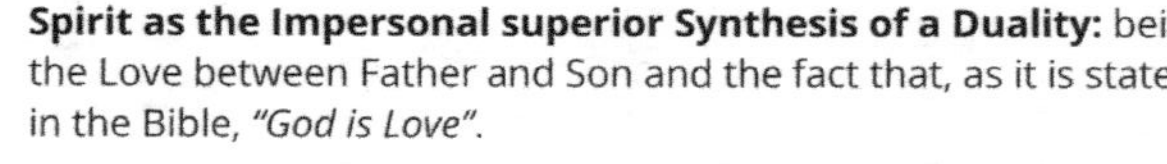

Figure 7. The Filioque clause and its theological, metaphysical, and historical consequences.

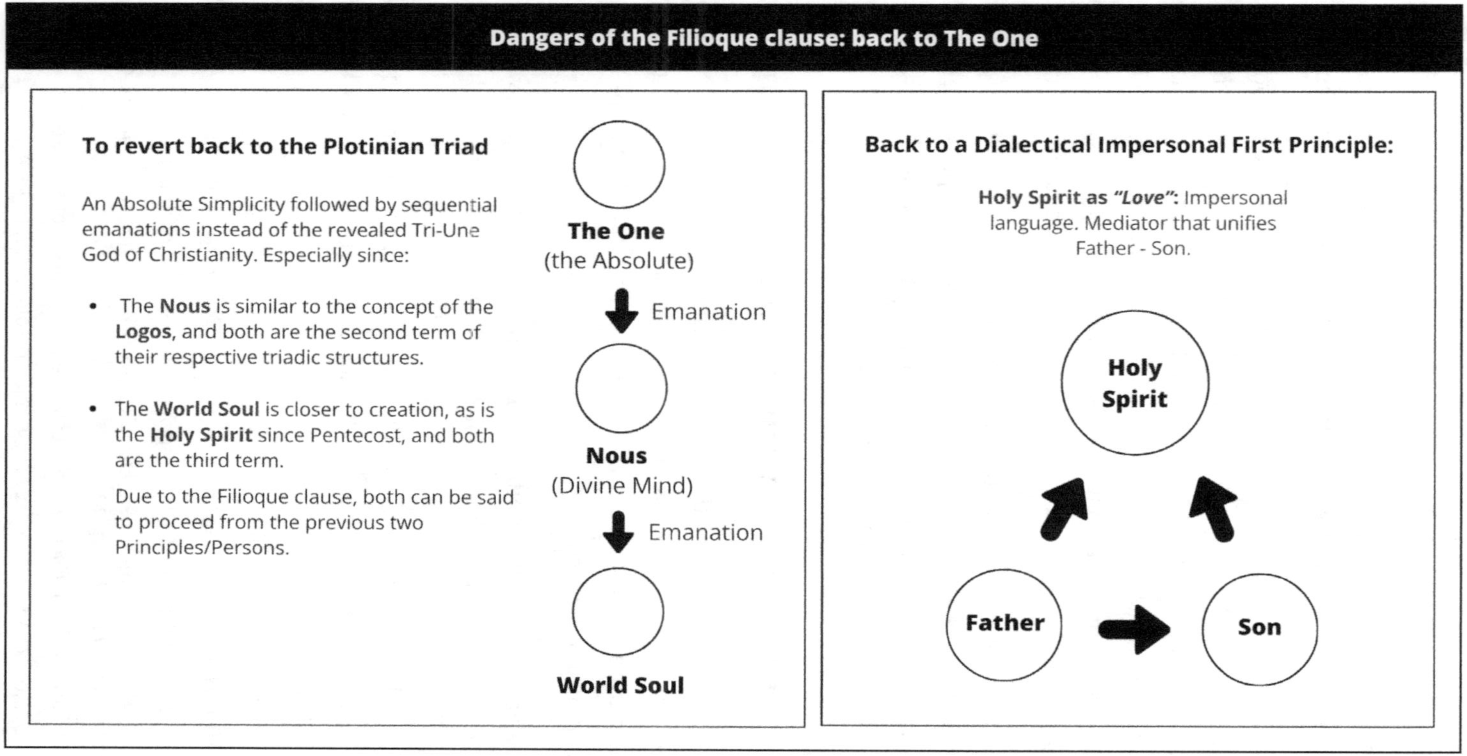

Figure 8. The dangers of the Filioque clause and how it resembles, or has the potential to resemble, non-Christian triadic descriptions of God.

Scholasticism tried to create a synthesis between Aristotle´s metaphysics (God as the Prime Mover) and Roman Catholic Trinitarian theology.

Thomas Aquinas, its most famous exponent and also a Dominican friar, priest, philosopher, and Doctor of the Church, became the most prominent and influential Roman Catholic theologian since St. Augustine. His magnum opus, the *Summa Theologica* (*Summary of Theology*), was even placed at the altar alongside the *Bible* and the *Decretals* (papal letters regarding decisions in ecclesiastical law) in the Council of Trent.[58, 59]

Aquinas became the systematizer of Roman Catholic theology, with his grand synthesis being adopted as the official philosophy of the Church in 1917. His teachings are now considered, under papal directives, the core of the study program for those seeking ordination.[60]

a. The One and the Many in Thomism

Aquinas was one of the most prominent proponents of Natural Theology (also called Physico-Theology[61]), a current of thought that looked for arguments in favor of Theism through the use of human reasoning and science.

Regarding the problem of Unity and Plurality, he believed that particularity was an attribute of matter. Therefore, in his view (similar to that of many classical philosophers), unity had primacy, thus putting at risk the classical Christian non-dialectical solution to the problem of *the One and the Many* that was so characteristic of foundational Christian orthodox theology: [62]

---

58. Küng, Hans (1994). *Great Christian Thinkers. New York: Continuum Books*, p. 112.

59. Mullady, Brian (2006). *The Angelic Doctor – Thomas Aquinas*.

60. *Code of Canon Law, Can. 252, §3 "Code of Canon Law" (vatican.va). Archived from the original on 8 May 2011.*

61. *Physicotheology. Encyclopedia.com. Retrieved on October 2020.*

62. *Aquinas, Thomas (1265-1274). Summa Theologica, I, Q 30, A 4.*

"Hence Plato said that unity must come before multitude; and Aristotle said that whatever is greatest in being and greatest in truth is the cause of every being and of every truth, just as whatever is the greatest in heat is the cause of all heat." [63]

As R. J. Rushdoony noted, an uneasy balance was established between the Both/And logic characteristic of Trinitarian theology and the Aristotelian philosophy found in Thomism:

"This is the basis of Thomas' doctrine of "creation," the one as the cause of the many because the many must by definition originate in the one. For Aristotle, this made man a creature of the state, the social one, and the universe the creature of chaos, the cosmic one. The source for Aquinas is the one, and the goal is also the one, unity, in which the many find their perfection. He did, of course, try to maintain a balance between the one and the many, between universals and particulars, holding, that, to have real existence, the universals must exist in the particulars as their essence, not as abstractions beside them." [64, 65]

b. Original Sin and Dialectics in Christian Anthropology

By returning to the use of dialectics, the understanding of Roman Catholicism regarding the fall of mankind (St. Augustine´s Original Sin) is different from the original view of the early Christian Church (Ancestral Sin).

---

63. *Ibid., Q 44, A 1.*

64. *Rushdoony, R.J. (1971). The One and the Many: Studies in the Philosophy of Order and Ultimacy. Chalcedon/Ross House Books, Ch. VII: The Return of Dialectic Thought; 7. The One and the Many in Aquinas.*

65. *See also Sister Mary Fredericus Niemeyer. The One and the Many in the Social Order According to Saint Thomas Aquinas. Washington, DC: The Catholic University of America Press, 1951, pp. 26-27, 73ff.*

Catholicism believes that we all inherited the guilt and the sin of the first archetypal human persons, Adam and Eve.

Orthodox doctrine, in contrast, explains that what we inherited was the consequence of sin: a broken nature with a tendency to miss the mark (the meaning of the word sin).

By employing their free wills in a mode contrary to their natural use, our archetypal ancestors opposed their persons to their natures, creating an internal conflict between inherent aspects of themselves previously in communion.

This tearing apart of one´s own being and the creation of a dialectical opposition not originally present in their nature, in turn, willed into existence that which cannot naturally exist:

• *Evil:* the acting in a direction that opposes and negates God, the good.

• *Sin:* the error of acting contrary to our own nature, thus missing the whole point of our existence.

• *Death:* the impossibility of such a reality to have independent ontological existence.

The understanding of Ancestral Sin, in turn, has two important corollaries, which are:

b1. Multiplicity Does Not Imply Death

In Christian thought, death cannot ever be conceived as a necessary characteristic of multiplicity, as happens in pure Monism.

As we will see, in the Christian final state of deification (Theosis), particularized multiplicity can become divinized and achieve an ontologically co-equal state with unity. The dichotomy between the existence of either an immortal and eternal absolute oneness or the existence of non-immortal particular beings is rejected by Christianity.

Particularity and uniqueness do not imply temporal existence, imperfection, and death.

As a consequence, Orthodox spirituality is based on repentance, understood not as guilt and self-flagellation, but as ceasing to move in a direction that leads away from God. The emphasis is on attuning our will to the Will of God while ceasing to oppose different aspects of our own nature, created in His image.

b2. Self-Integration Does Not Imply the Doctrine of the Unity of Opposites

We can speak, then, of a Christian self-integration that re-unites and re-establishes communion between different aspects of our broken human nature. However, this process does not include the integration of the totality of the contents of our unconscious psyche, as Jung proposed (Jungian Shadow).

The Christian God is not the Absolute, the All, including both light and darkness. Therefore, the final aim is not to integrate our personal repressed unconscious demons into a totality, understood as our True Self.

There is no Union of Opposites that includes any instinctive dark aspect in Christian thought. The Christian Both/And inclusivity excludes that ultimately non-existent reality called evil, which is nothing more than a negation of God and therefore of ourselves, while instead of an Alchemical marriage between the light and dark aspects in ourselves proposes a marriage between our soul and God.

c. Different Views on Salvation

Orthodox Christian theology and Roman Catholicism are also at variance in their views on salvation. We will begin by describing the former.

c1. Deification (Theosis): The Self-Giving of God

All Christian denominations view the resurrection as a general event that applies to all on behalf of the death and resurrection of Jesus Christ, who assumed and deified human nature, therefore liberating it from having to ever die. However, the subjective experience of particular persons in this eternal state of being can be very different.

For Orthodox Christians, depending on our affinity and attunement with God´s Will, experiencing His Presence and His Uncreated Energies can be a cause of eternal well-being or eternal ill-being.

A person who rejects God, while having free will to define himself in this manner, won´t experience happiness in His Presence, when He is *"All in all"*. This is the "burning" of hell, having defined ourselves in opposition to God, and experiencing His Presence and Light as an undesirable reality (*"the fire that is not quenched"*) accompanied by regret (*"the worm that does not die"*; Mark 9:48).

The same reality, however, is experienced as a state of divinization and ultimate bliss for all persons who pursue closeness to God, with Him interpenetrating (unity) each saved person and freely giving *what* He is (His Uncreated Energies) to each one, who then become capable of instantiating those energies in manifold (multiplicity) ways, all *equally* good.

Deification (Theosis), then, includes the ever deepening personal relationship with the inexhaustible transcendent God who reveals to us *who* He is in His Essence, while receiving *what* He is through the interpenetration of all His Energies.

As the above description shows, the original Christian understanding regarding the life to come included both Unity and Multiplicity, Essence and Energy, the Will of God and the many wills of the saved persons in communion with Him.

"For now we see in a mirror, dimly, but then face to face. Now I know in part, but then I shall know just as I also am known."

– St. Paul. 1 Cor. 13,12. New King James Version

Figure 9. Contrasting Artistic Styles. Latin Christian art adopted not only some philosophical notions but also a more sensuous art style from the Greco-Roman world, including some non-Christian motifs shown even in its most important works. In the painting above, for example, we can see Charon and his boat full of damned souls. Picture: The Last Judgment, Michelangelo (1536–1541).

Note how Marcello Venusti's copy of the original (1549), prior to its later renovation, includes a sequential depiction of the Trinity in which the Third Person, the Holy Spirit, is found between the Father and the Son (Second Person). Even if there was no explicit theological intention behind this, it is still an accurate representation of the Roman Catholic doctrine of the Filioque.

c2. Absolute Divine Simplicity and the Beatific Vision of God

In contrast to the Orthodox doctrine of deification, the Roman Catholic doctrine of salvation, because of its underlying dialectical (and even monistic) tendencies, became increasingly mentalist over time.

The Latin Church interpreted the final heavenly state of salvation, called the Beatific Vision, as the single-pointed contemplation of God in all His glory or the union with Him through sharing in His Essence or Nature through sanctifying created grace.[66]

This doctrine was also incorporated into various Protestant denominations, including the Lutheran and Methodist churches.[67,68,69]

St. Thomas Aquinas, in his *Summa Theologica*, clarified the nature of this final state of being as shown in the text below, in which we can finally see the full extent of the danger that trying to create a synthesis between philosophical thought and Christian theology implies:

"Article 1. Whether the human intellect can attain to the vision of God in His essence?

Question 92. The vision of the divine essence in reference to the blessed

Therefore, since the Divine essence is pure act, it will be possible for it to be the form whereby the intellect understands: and this will be the beatific vision.

---

66. *"Catechism of the Catholic Church - Part 1 Section 1 Chapter 3 Article 1" (scborromeo.org).*

67. *"God in Heaven". Lutheran Church Missouri Synod. Archived from the original on May 2009.*

68. *"What United Methodists Believe". Spring Lake United Methodist Church. Archived from the original on 27 September 2008.*

69. *Wesley, Charles (1989). "Maker, in Whom We Live". The United Methodist Hymnal. Nashville: The United Methodist Publishing House.*

When therefore intellectual light is received into the soul, together with the indwelling Divine essence, though they are not received in the same way, the Divine essence will be to the intellect as form to matter: and that this suffices for the intellect to be able to see the Divine essence by the Divine essence itself may be shown as follows."

– Thomas Aquinas. Summa Theologica.
Vol X. Article 1, Question 92

Through a brief analysis of this short text, the following dangers characteristic of dialectical thought, all of them well known by now, can be easily identified:

- *Emphasis on the intellectual aspect of salvation:* achieved through conceptualizing salvation as "vision". It is the beginning of a Spirit/Body dichotomy that is the logical conclusion of defining God as an Absolute Divine Simplicity or Essence devoid of any (uncreated) energy. It contrasts with the Essence/Energies distinction of Orthodox theology.

- *Actuality/Potentiality dialectic:* common in the doctrines of the One or the Absolute, as we saw earlier, and a natural consequence of an excessive dependence on Aristotelian thought.

- *"That are Thou":* the indwelling of the very Essence of God in us. Salvation as participation in God´s very nature itself. This bears the risk of walking a path that has as its ultimate logical conclusion purely monistic interpretations of God and the view of salvation as fusion with the Godhead. In short, the risk of going back to the One and the famous vedantic dictum of the *Upanishads* that identifies each person´s soul with God.

This understanding of union with the essence, needless to say, is contrary to the union of human and divine natures shown by Jesus Christ, which interpenetrated each other instead of being fused into a third, different entity, which could not have led to the assumption and, therefore, the salvation of human nature.

d. Catholic Flagellants: The Reappearance of Spirit/ Matter Dualism

This previously mentioned, barely hidden, dialectical tension between spirit and body present in Catholicism could be seen in full force in the tendency towards severe asceticism. This tension, characteristic of Monism (e.g., Gnosticism[70], Neo-Platonism) but contrary to Trinitarian Both/And logic, was dramatically exemplified by the flagellants and their practices aimed at the mortification of the flesh.

Contrary to Orthodox doctrine, which states that the flesh is a combination of the body and the passions, with only the latter being the enemy of spiritual life, the Catholic animus towards the body as a source of temptation led to excesses and the invention of devices such as the cilice (occasionally also used by some Protestant churches such as the Lutheran[71], Anglican[72], Methodist[73], and Scottish Presbyterian).

This rejection of the body, however, seems difficult to justify and even a self-contradiction in a religion that sees each human person as the potential temple and receptacle of the Holy Spirit and that, especially, saw God incarnating in a human body while leading a sinless life.

In Catholicism, however, this can be interpreted as a logical consequence of the previously seen belief in salvation as the Beatific Vision. A purely

---

70. Some Gnostics, for whom matter was intrinsically deficient, believed that Jesus was a pure disembodied spiritual apparition. However, for Christianity, no greater statement about the sacramentality of creation can be conceived than that of God Himself choosing to partake of the full human nature, which includes having a body.

71. *Neve, Juergen Ludwig (1914). The Augsburg Confession: A Brief Review of Its History and an Interpretation of Its Doctrinal Articles, with Introductory Discussions on Confessional Questions. Lutheran Publication Society, p. 150.*

72. *Knight, Mark; Mason, Emma (2006). Nineteenth-Century Religion and Literature: An Introduction. Oxford University Press, p. 96: "Pusey regularly endured a hair shirt as well as self- imposed flagellation and fasting routines."*

73. *Bergen, Jeremy M. (2011). Ecclesial Repentance: The Churches Confront Their Sinful Pasts. A&C Black, p. 255.*

cognitive/spiritual view of salvation implies that the body, even a deified one, is not worthy of achieving that state.

The Orthodox view on History and Time

The concept of historical time also shows an important difference in both the Latin and Eastern churches. For the former, time is linear and history shows different layers of meaning that range from the merely factual to the moral and spiritual ones. For the latter, however, time and history are also "recapitulatory".

To recapitulate means to summarize or to collect several different things together under one head. The Logos, as the Principle of Reason underlying everything in creation, is that recapitulation. By containing and providing the many Logoi (particular reasons for existence), He is the recapitulation of all history, with everything in creation pointing towards Him who created them.

Therefore , instead of cycles of time like in Eastern religions, patristic Christianity speaks of types that repeat themselves inside linear time. Historical events can, then, be read as musical leitmotifs that show a recontextualized and deeper layer of meaning with each repetition, pointing to future events and to their beginning and end, the Logos.

In Orthodox Christianity, both this typological layer of meaning and conventional ones are key in understanding history and liturgical life.

e. *"Emanation Out of Nothing"*

Given the above considerations regarding the latent dialectical oppositions between, for example, Actuality/Potentiality and Spirit/Body in Roman Catholic theology, it is not surprising that Aquinas found the need to reformulate the notion of creation out of nothing (Ex-Nihilo) to bring it closer to the doctrine of emanations of the philosophers.

As Aquinas himself stated in his magnum opus, the *Summa Theologica*:

"*On the text of Genesis 1, "In the beginning God created," etc,*

I answer that,

As said above (I:44:2), we must consider not only the emanation of a particular being from a particular agent, but also the emanation of all being from the universal cause, which is God; and this emanation we designate by the name of creation."

– Thomas Aquinas. Summa Theologica.
First Part, Question 45, Article 1

4.6. Concluding Thoughts on the Effects of Adding the Filioque Clause to the Christian Creed

Summarizing all the modifications just seen, we can see that the Filioque clause introduced into Roman Catholic theology a dialectical way of thinking that was contrary to the original character of the Tri-Une God of Christianity, hitherto characterized by His transcendence of the problem of *the One and the Many.*

Because of this deviation from apostolic and patristic tradition in order to mingle with classical philosophy, familiar doctrines of Panentheism (the One) such as the fusion with God, rejection of the body or Emanationism, showed a tendency to resurface in a more or less veiled form.[74]

4.7. Roman Catholic Mysticism and the Allure of Monistic Interpretations

Given the propensities to dialectical thought of Roman Catholic theology, best exemplified in the notion that unity has ultimate primacy over plurality, it is not surprising that many of the mystical experiences

---

74. *Perhaps this is why Roman Catholicism has been the ground from which philosophies and worldviews as alien to Christian thought as the highly dialectical philosophy of the former Jesuit Teilhard de Chardin or the openly Gnostic vision (Marcionism) of the also ex-Jesuit Salvador Freixedo were able to emerge, as we shall see in the last chapter of this book.*

described by some of its most famous mystics are so similar to panentheistic ones. In the next sections we will see some of the most iconic examples.

a. St. Teresa of Ávila and the Mystical Marriage

St. Teresa's writings speak of the seven Mansions contained within *The Interior Castle* that represents our soul.

As we saw in the first section of this chapter, a very similar scheme was taught by Kabbalistic literature (e.g., the seven Palaces in Hekhalot writings) and Sufism (e.g., the seven Valleys of the Way in *The Conference of the Birds*).

Regarding the central question we are investigating, the relationship between absolute unity and plurality, we can find the most interesting information in her description of the Seventh Mansion.

St. Teresa spoke of it as being fundamentally different from the rest, representing a state of direct knowledge (Gnosis) and mystical union (spiritual marriage). She saw no separation, but a fusion between the Light emanating from God and our whole being. A melting into One.[75]

To clarify her position she provided a quite familiar analogy:

"[This state] might be compared to water falling from the sky into a river or fountain, where the waters are united, and it would be no longer possible to divide them, or separate the water of the river from that which has fallen from the heavens. Or like a tiny stream, which falls into the sea -there is no possibility of separating them."[76]

---

75. *Orthodox Christians would agree with this affirmation if Catholicism understood God as having both Essence and Energies, since Orthodox deification includes the assimilation of the latter. However, Catholic dogma states that God is pure Essence, therefore implying that a fusion would be between the human soul and God´s nature, thus going back to the One.*

76. *of Jesus, St. Teresa (1945). The interior Castle. London: Sands and Co., p. 109.*

As we might remember, the fusion of the drop of water with the ocean is a common metaphor in the panentheistic Monism of Advaita Vedānta, but hardly compatible with Theism (even with a theistic form of Hinduism, such as Rāmānuja´s Vishishtadvaita Vedānta).

Other familiar themes that we saw in different schools of monistic mysticism, such as the 'Kiss of Love' that consummates the union with God, can also be found in her writings. The interpretation, as in those traditions, seems to be that the soul is literally being united to God´s Essence:

"God grants these sublime and intimate interior states when He binds the soul to Himself, with that Kiss that the bride asks for." [77]

b. Meister Eckhart and the Notion of God as the Ground of All Being

The mystical experiences and metaphysical interpretations of Johannes Eckhart (Dominican preacher, theologian, and mystic) were more controversial inside the Catholic Church. He was accused of heresy and many of his propositions rejected by Pope John XXII.

Nevertheless, he has become an influential figure in modern "spiritual movements" and is seen by many followers of panentheistic and non-dual worldviews as the link between "true" Christianity and their own traditions.

D.T. Suzuki, a Japanese scholar (and later Theosophist) who became one of the world's leading popularizers of Zen Buddhism (especially in the West), favorably compared the teachings of Meister Eckhart with those of Shin and Zen in his book *Mysticism: Christian and Buddhist.*[78, 79, 80]

---

77. *Ibid., p. 114.*

78. *Algeo, Adele S. (2005). Beatrice Lane Suzuki and Theosophy in Japan. Theosophical History, XI.*

79. *Algeo, Adele S. (2007). Beatrice Lane Suzuki: An American Theosophist in Japan. Quest, 95 (1): 13–17.*

80. *Tweed, Thomas A. (2005). American Occultism and Japanese Buddhism. Albert J. Edmunds, D. T. Suzuki, and Translocative History. Japanese Journal of Religious*

One may wonder if the seed of monistic thought residing at the core of Catholicism since the adoption of the Filioque may not have facilitated the appearance of these tendencies towards impersonal Monism, as St. Photios feared when he rejected its inclusion into the Eastern Orthodox Creed.

Whatever the case may be, it is clear that Eckhart´s interpretations of his mystical experiences were more in line with Panentheism than with Theism and, especially, with the Christian God. A few of his illuminating quotes regarding this issue follow:

"The more you are able to completely withdraw all your powers and forget all things—along with whatever images they have left in you—the farther you will travel away from created things and their images, and the closer and more receptive you will be to this birth.

Were you to forget everything completely and be unaware of them, you would lose even the awareness of your own body, just as it occurred with St. Paul when he said, ". . . whether in the body, I cannot tell; or whether out of the body, I cannot tell: God knoweth. . ." (2 Corinthians 12:2)" [81]

"As long as I am this or that, I am not all things." [82]

"[...]So truly does God give the Son birth in the most inward part of the spirit, and that is the inner world. Here God's ground is my ground, and my ground is God's ground..." [83]

Studies, 32 (2): 249–281.

81. *Eckhart, Meister. In Vega, C.M.(2013). The Kingdom of Heaven Within You: The Teachings of Meister Eckhart (Vol. 2). Kindle Ed.*

82. *Eckhart, Meister. In Kundan (2014). The Gospel of Thomas: A Guide to Awakening. Books on Demand, p. 114.*

83. *Eckhart, Meister. In O'C. Walshe, Maurice (2010). The Complete Mystical Works of Meister Eckhart. Sermon 13(b). Herder & Herder, p. 109.*

"Isness is God." [84]

— Johannes (Meister) Eckhart von Hochheim

c. Joachim of Fiore and the New Age of the Spirit

We can also find a marked dialectical thought in the works of Joachim of Fiore, who was a Christian theologian, Catholic abbot, and the founder of the monastic order of San Giovanni in Fiore.[85] However, his dialectical oppositions are of a different kind.

Instead of opposing attributes or energies of God, creating paired opposites where one option is univocally better than the other (e.g., His Oneness), he opposed the Persons of the Trinity between them.

In Joachim´s view, History could be classified in three different stages or ages, each one being especially influenced by one of the Persons of the Trinity.

These eras were conceived as progressively more spiritual, and just plain better, than the ones before:

• *Age of the Father (Old Testament):* characterized by obedience to God´s Commandments.

• *Age of the Son (New Testament):* between the Incarnation and 1260. The age when Man became the son of God.

• *Age of the Holy Spirit (future utopia):* the Kingdom of the Holy Spirit on earth, proceeding from a new dispensation of universal love. Based on the *Gospels*, but providing a new understanding of them transcending their literal interpretation.

---

84. Eckhart, Meister. In Kelley, C.F. (1977). Meister Eckhart on Divine Knowledge. Frog Books, p. 144.

85. Chisholm, Hugh, ed. (1911). Joachim of Floris . Encyclopædia Britannica. Vol. 15 (11th ed.). Cambridge University Press, p. 417.

In this New Age the ecclesiastical hierarchy would be replaced and the "Order of the Just" would rule the Church.[86]

As we can see, in Joachim´s system not only the Persons of the Trinity are opposed, but it is also implied that they represent different aspects of God (Modalism), with the Father demanding obedience (strictness or judgment of God) and the Spirit being the manifestation of God´s love or mercy.

This way of separating God in different aspects in conflict between them is more common, for example, of Kabbalistic Panentheism than of early Christianity. In Kabbalah, we find that the Tree of Life that represents God´s emanations is divided into three columns of Sefira´s (attributes of God): the one of Judgement (e.g., Gevurah; left), the one of Mercy (e.g., Chesed; right) and the Middle Way (e.g., Tiferet), where beauty is found in the equilibrium between opposites.

Furthermore, we find that the Godhead is not represented by the Trinity but by a sequential modalist gradation where only the Spirit is the full manifestation of God. This way of conceptualizing the Trinity, instead of being Christian, is again panentheistic (triadic).

In addition, Joachim immanentized the Parousia (second Advent of Christ), by conceiving it as a New Age of peace and spirituality in the present created world.

Even if he held highly unorthodox views, Joachim's ideas became highly influential, inspiring Dante´s *Divine Comedy*[87] and several alternative movements (e.g., Amalricians, Dulcinians, Brethren of the Free Spirit). Joachimite interpretations also became popular in the Protestant reformation.[88, 89] Many of the Joachimite-inspired movements

---

86. *Manuel, Frank E.; Manuel, Fritzie P. (1982), Utopian Thought in the Western World, Belknap Press of Harvard University Press, pp. 56–59.*

87. *"Joachim Of Fiore". Encyclopedia Britannica.*

88. *Maas, Korey (2010). The Reformation and Robert Barnes: History, Theology and Polemic in Early Modern England. Boydell & Brewer.*

89. *Lundin, Roger (1993). The Culture of Interpretation: Christian Faith and the Postmodern World. Wm. B. Eerdmans Publishing, p. 65: "Joachimite interpretation*

were declared heretical by the Catholic Church. However, Joachim himself was not.

[Intermission: Summary of the Chapter so Far]

We began this chapter looking at a typology of mysticism that differentiated the theistic experiences described by monotheistic religions from panentheistic (or non-dual) ones. We labelled the former as *Mysticism of Union* to contrast it with the *Mysticism of Unity through Absorption* of the latter worldviews.

During this chapter, we have seen that this Mysticism of Union is not a simple affair and that pure Monotheism, as a form of Monism, shows the tendency to go back to panentheistic interpretations.

In this last section, in turn, it has been shown how through the addition of a small dialectical presupposition regarding the nature of God (the Filioque clause), even our understanding of the non-dialectical One/Many God of early Christianity bears the risk of becoming distorted and point back again towards pure Monism.

Our analysis has so far focused on Roman Catholicism[90], as the cradle through which dialectical thought entered Christianity. However, as we shall see below, another of the main Christian denominations also inherited both the Filioque and its consequences: Protestantism.

---

itself prefigured later developments in Protestant and romantic hermeneutics."

90. *A fuller appraisal of Roman Catholicism from an Orthodox view can be seen in Clark Carlton's book "The Truth: What Every Roman Catholic Should Know About the Orthodox Church".*

5. Dialectical Thought in Protestantism

Protestantism (sixteenth century) is the Christian denomination that follows the theological doctrines of the Protestant Reformation, a movement that aimed at reforming the Roman Catholic Church from perceived abuses and theological mistakes.[1]

While this reform was substantial, the dialectical thought underlying most of the problems of Roman Catholicism was not challenged. Instead of rediscovering the non-dialectical thought of early Christianity, Protestantism tended to define itself by taking the opposite direction to Catholicism in many theological matters while still operating under the same Either/Or paradigm.

5.1. The Acceptance of the Filioque Clause

The Protestant Reformation challenged various tenets of Catholicism, ranging from theological doctrines to ecclesiastical matters regarding authority. However, they accepted the Filioque clause without reservation.

Lutheran scholars (University of Tübingen) even initiated a dialogue with the Orthodox Patriarch Jeremias II of Constantinople to defend it, although, in general, Protestantism does not engage in polemics to justify the Filioque to the same extent that Catholics do.

In the following centuries, Protestant theologians assigned to this clause the status of a key doctrine in the definition of the Trinity, but

---

1. *Löffler, K. (1910). "Pope Leo X". The Catholic Encyclopedia. New York: Robert Appleton Company: "The immediate cause was bound up with the odious greed for money displayed by the Roman Curia, and shows how far short all efforts at reform had hitherto fallen...Abuses occurred during the preaching of the Indulgence. The money contributions, a mere accessory, were frequently the chief object, and the "Indulgences for the Dead" became a vehicle of inadmissible teachings...(The pope) gave himself up unrestrainedly to his pleasures and failed to grasp fully the duties of his high office."*

it was never exalted as being one of the main theological pillars of this Christian denomination.[2]

Among influential twentieth century Protestant theologians, and contrary to many others who in the second half of the century favored abandoning its liturgical use, the great defender of the Filioque was Karl Barth.[3, 4]

a. The Ambiguous Relationship of Anglicanism with the Filioque

Anglicanism, like many other Protestant denominations, shows a conflicting disposition towards the Filioque clause. On the one hand, they often choose to remove it from the Creed; on the other, they often fail to do so because of an apparent lack of interest or some other historical contingency.

We can only conclude that, at the very least, this way of proceeding is a strange way of dealing with a key theological principle that has far reaching implications for the religion as a whole and defines the character of the God being worshipped.

This ambiguous and contradictory historical record can be exemplified by the following eventualities:

• The Lambeth Conferences (1978 and 1988) advised the Anglican Communion to omit printing the Filioque in the Niceno-Constantinopolitan

---

2. *Oberdorfer, Bernd (2006). " ... who proceeds from the Father' and the Son? The use of the Bible in the filioque debate: a historical and ecumenical case study and hermeneutical reflections". In Helmer, Christine; Higbe, Charlene T. (eds.). The multivalence of biblical texts and theological meanings. Symposium series. Vol. 37. Atlanta, GA: Society of Biblical Literature, p. 155.*

3. *Lacoste, Jean-Yves, ed. (2005). "Filioque". Encyclopedia of Christian theology. Vol. 1. New York: Routledge, p. 583.*

4. *Guretzki, David (2009). Karl Barth on the Filioque. Barth studies. Farnham, UK: Ashgate. A close examination of Karl Barth's defense of the filioque, p. 12.*

Creed.[5,6] However, this recommendation was not renewed in the 1998 and 2008 Conferences and was therefore not implemented.

• The General Convention of the Episcopal Church (USA, 1985) recommended the removal of the clause from the Creed and the *Book of Common Prayer*.[7,8] This decision was reaffirmed in the General Convention of 1994. However, the last revision of the book was printed in 1979, so the resolution has not yet taken effect.

• The Scottish Episcopal Church no longer prints it in its modern language liturgies.

5.2. The Dialectical Nature of the Five Main Pillars of Protestantism

The Protestant Reformation was characterised by five theological premises (the five "Solas", meaning "only" in Latin).

These premises, as their name implies, were based on a dialectical approach between what were understood to be paired opposites, in which Protestantism defined itself by choosing a side, usually the option perceived as contrary to that of Roman Catholicism.

As we shall see, the chosen positions were sometimes more nuanced and less black and white as they may appear at first glance, especially given that Protestantism developed into an heterogeneous multiplicity of more or less like-minded denominations that addressed different theological postulates in their own way.

---

5. *Lambeth Conference (1978). Res. 35.3; Lambeth Conference (1988), res.6.5.*

6. *Anglican Consultative Council 9 (January 1993). Written at Cape Town, ZA. "Resolutions" (anglicancommunion.org). London: Anglican Communion Office. Archived from the original on 30 August 2008. Res.19.*

7. *Episcopalarchives.org (1985). General Convention Sets Course For Church. 19 September 1985.*

8. *Resolution 1994-A028. "Reaffirm Intention to Remove the Filioque Clause From the Next Prayer Book." Episcopalarchives.org. Retrieved 25 April 2013.*

However, the dialectical paradigm of paired oppositions that underlies the central themes of the Reformation is not just a matter of semantics, but it is very real, implying a way of thinking alien to early Christianity and an opposition between aspects of religion and spiritual life that were previously understood as synergistic and complementary.

a. Opposition Between Faith and Works (Sola Fide or "by Faith Alone")

The first "Sola" states that salvation is attained by faith alone, as opposed to faith and works. The codification of this doctrine can be found, for example, in the *Thirty-Nine Articles of the Anglican Church* (Article XI: *"Of the Justification of Man"*).

For Luther, the only "work" needed for salvation is performed by God during Baptism, where the forgiveness of sins and salvation earned by Jesus Christ's death and resurrection are transferred to the baptized person.

The position of early Christianity, in contrast, is that one implies and enhances the other, acting in concert in a synergistic manner.

From this point of view, while the original intention of this doctrine may have been to protect the believer from pride and it follows the letter of certain isolated passages from Scripture (Ephesians 2:8-9), it favors a passive view of our relationship with God and harbours the great risk of self-complacency.

When a modern Protestant, as is nowadays common, states that he was literally saved on a certain date, the risks of this unilateral doctrine of salvation by faith alone become apparent. This statement, which is paradoxically more prideful because of its certainty, would have seemed to early Christians, above all, dangerous.

As mentioned above, however, there is variability in the degree to which this principle is actually implemented in modern Protestant denominations. For example, Methodist Bishop Scott J. Jones writes:

"Faith is necessary to salvation unconditionally. Good works are necessary only conditionally, that is if there is time and opportunity. [...] However, for the vast majority of human beings good works are necessary for continuance in faith because those persons have both the time and opportunity for them." [9]

"What does it profit, my brethren, if someone says he has faith but does not have works? Can faith save him? If a brother or sister is naked and destitute of daily food, and one of you says to them, "Depart in peace, be warmed and filled," but you do not give them the things which are needed for the body, what does it profit? Thus also faith by itself, if it does not have works, is dead."

— James 2:14-17. New King James Version

a1. Opposition Between Internal and External Works

Another implicit dialectical tension found in the Protestant concept of works involves that of external (e.g., charity) works and internal ones (e.g., ascetic practices such as fasting; prayer life for both laity and monastics).

In this case the Protestant focus is on external works, as is obvious by the fact that, contrary to both Catholicism and Eastern Orthodoxy, no ascetical practices or monasticism exists in Protestantism.

Luther himself, previously an Augustinian monk, condemned monasticism because he understood it as a works-based approach that contradicted his opinion on salvation by faith alone and because he saw it as a sterile separation of the monk from the world.

From an Orthodox perspective, even if the Protestant zeal for missionary and charity work is valued, the lack of internal striving is viewed as a self-imposed limitation. No contradiction is conceived between getting closer to God and helping others do the same.

---

9. Jones, Scott J. (2002). *United Methodist Doctrine. Abingdon Press*, p. 190.

The practical life of the Christian, then, is understood as both the helping of those in need (the Many) and working on one´s self-purification (the One), leading to a greater closeness with God which also increases our ability to help others. The extremes of missionary work and monasticism are options fit for certain personalities, with each believer living according to their calling and disposition.

A minimum degree of internal work (e.g., light ascetical practices such as fasting; prayer), as well as a degree of helping others (e.g., charity) is expected of every believer. However, that degree is worked out between one´s own capacity, will, and the personal advice that their spiritual father gives to each believer for their particular growth.

"When you fast, do not look somber as the hypocrites do, for they disfigure their faces to show others they are fasting. Truly I tell you, they have received their reward in full.

But when you fast, put oil on your head and wash your face, so that it will not be obvious to others that you are fasting, but only to your Father, who is unseen; and your Father, who sees what is done in secret, will reward you."

— Matthew 6:16-18. New King James Version

b. Opposition Between the Holy Bible and Tradition (Sola Scriptura or "by Scripture Alone")

The second "Sola", Sola Scriptura, asserts that Scripture (the *Bible*) is either the only source of legitimate authority or, when it recognizes Church tradition as legitimate, that it has absolute primacy over it. Due to its importance, this principle was sometimes called the formal principle of the Reformation.[10]

Contrary to what it may appear, this tenet does not necessarily deny tradition, reason or experience as sources of truth. However, it

____

10. *Bavinck, Herman (2003). Reformed Dogmatics. Baker Academic, 2:209–10.*

always subordinates them to Scripture. In practice, moreover, modern theologians have for the most part replaced the early Church Fathers[11], of whom many Protestant believers have little knowledge.

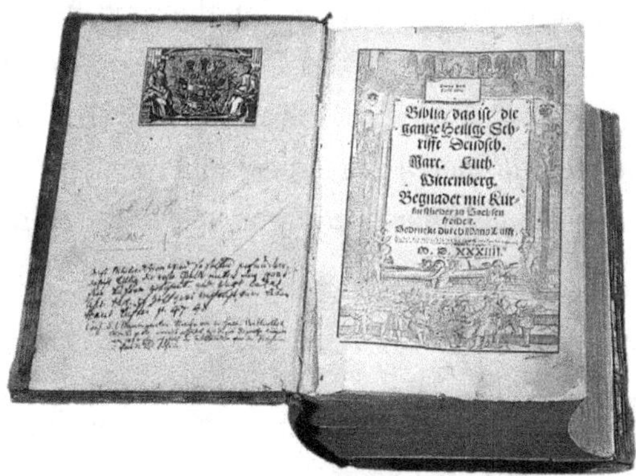

Figure 10. The Unnecessary Dialectical Opposition Between Oral and Written Tradition. The doctrine of Sola Scriptura is one of the main pillars of Protestantism. However, this doctrine does not take into account that the canon of biblical books was fixed centuries after they were written, existing several versions during that period of time.

This fact reflects the inescapable mutual interrelationship between oral tradition, source of many aspects of the faith not present in the books, and the written one. In addition, by giving to each person the authority to re-interpret the Bible without taking into consideration traditional consensus and oral apostolic teachings, an indefinite number of denominations can be born. Picture: Luther´s Bible (1534).

Protestantism not only rejected the notion of the infallible interpretations of the Catholic Pope, but also renounced the guidance of Holy Tradition.[12]

---

11. *The void left by the rejection of tradition was more or less filled by modern theologians and preachers not operating under a consensus. This opened the way to theological innovations that in extreme cases are, not only controversial, but just plain contrary to the traditional Christian mindset and theology (e.g., prosperity Gospel). Some modern public figures have also shown questionable integrity far from the standards of the early Fathers, many of them martyrs (e.g., some televangelists and their luxurious lives).*

12. *Holy because it is believed to be guided and preserved by the Holy Spirit, who resides in each Christian since Pentecost, especially when they come together in the name of God as the patriarchs did in the early councils. In fact, by believing that not only the Catholic Church, but all Christianity, was corrupted and had to be re-founded by the Reformation in the sixteenth century, Protestants unknowingly*

Therefore, the figure of the (One) Pope was substituted by the infallible interpretations of (the Many) individuals, making each believer their own Pope in the process.

From an Orthodox lens, by renouncing the consensus (Unity) of the Fathers of the Church (Plurality), this doctrine opens the door to (Many) contradicting personal interpretations of the (One) Holy Book. This can be easily seen in the ever increasing number of Protestant denominations, each with their own particular interpretations of the same Scriptures.

b1. The Invisible Church

Another implicit dialectical danger that the doctrine of "Scripture alone" introduces is that between the visible or common Church and the invisible one.

The concept of the invisible or mystical Church states that there are two churches: the one of the elect, who are saved and known only to God, and the institutional visible Church that contains both saved and unsaved persons.[13]

This notion, contrary to early Church Fathers that saw the invisible and visible churches as one and the same, was favored by the Protestant

---

deny that the promise of God regarding the preservation of His Church was fulfilled (Matthew 16:17-19).

13. *Weaver, Jonathan (1900). Christian Theology: A Concise and Practical View of the Cardinal Doctrines and Institutions of Christianity. United Brethren Publishing House, p. 245:*

"There are distinctions between the general invisible church and the general visible church, which it is not necessary to carry out to the last analysis. In a sense, they are both visible. All who are members of the general invisible church are members of the general visible church. But all who are members of the general visible church are not members of the general invisible church. A clear and distinct difference between the visible and invisible church may be stated thus: (1) The general invisible church includes all out of every kindred and tongue and people and nation who are truly saved. No one denomination has in its communion all who belong to the invisible church. (2) The visible church includes all who are recognized as members of a Christian church. No one denomination can justly claim to be the general visible church."

reformers who did not see the Catholic Church as the true one.[14] It was also later used to distinguish between true believers within particular denominations (e.g., John Calvin), thus becoming a source of internal doubt and division.

b2. The Danger of Falling Into Gnostic Elitism

All the above bears the risk of reinstating an elitist system such as the one which characterised Gnostic schools, for which only a few believers in the exoteric Church were in possession of true esoteric and salvific knowledge (Gnosis). In such systems, salvation was considered to belong necessarily to the few, and not to the many.

This position, obviously, is totally opposed to the mindset (Phronema) of the Orthodox Church, which stresses that true Gnosis is precisely the doctrine openly and transparently passed down through apostolic succession for the salvation of all.

The Gnostics went even further by, not only conceiving a "Church-beyond-the-Church", but also a "True-God-beyond-God" that was the moral opposite to the God of this world and of exoteric religion.[15]

"[...] Apostolicity and gnosis for the Gnostics therefore lay in the secret knowledge of a select circle of elite initiates. Gnosis was secret, and ultimately, an indeterminable interior disposition. For the orthodox, Gnosis and apostolicity lay precisely in known doctrines handed down and available to all member of the church." [16]

— Farrell, Joseph P. (2016). God, History, and Dialectic

---

14. *L. Gonzalez, Justo (1970–1975). A History of Christian Thought. Volume 2: From Augustine to the eve of the Reformation. Abingdon Press.*

15. *Pagels, Elaine (1989). The Gnostic Gospels. Vintage Books, pp. 32-33: "The Protestant theologian Paul Tillich recently drew a similar distinction between the God we imagine when we hear the term, and the 'God beyond God,' that is, the 'ground of being' that underlies all our concepts and images."*

16. *Farrell, Joseph P. (2016). God, History, and Dialectic (Vol. I), pp 49-50.*

c. Opposition Between Grace and Merit (Sola Gratia or "by Grace Alone")

The third "Sola", "only grace", excludes the notion of personal merit as part of achieving salvation. According to this principle, salvation is a free gift, an "unmerited favor", given by God.

This tension between grace and free will, also prevalent within scholastic Catholicism, could not be resolved during the Reformation.

However, some Protestant denominations such as Arminians and Methodists modulate the dialectical polarity present in this doctrine by postulating a "prevenient grace".

This grace, which they believe is distributed to everyone through the Holy Spirit[17], is thought to allow believers to understand the Gospel and respond accordingly.

This modulated doctrine is, then, a form of synergy with God. Because of that, it remains closer to original Christian belief and contrary to the more polarized views of Lutherans and Calvinists (the latter believing in predestination).[18]

Orthodox doctrine, however, affirms full Synergism, the working together of God and man, just as the two natures of Jesus Christ worked together and interpenetrated each other (Perichoresis) during His Incarnation.

In this manner, personal merit is not ignored, since it is recognised as the preparation to receive God´s grace or energies. God´s grace is not restricted to be granted through the faith of the believer (a mentalist

---

17. *See "Myth 7: Arminianism Is Not a Theology of Grace" in Olson, Roger E. (2006). Arminian Theology: Myths and Realities. InterVarsity Press.*

18. *Olson, Roger E. (2009). Arminian Theology: Myths and Realities. InterVarsity Press, p. 95: "Arminians do not think so; they hold a form of evangelical synergism that sees grace as the efficient cause of salvation and calls faith the sole instrumental cause of salvation to the exclusion of human merits."*

approach), but is also understood as working through a person´s will to achieve a state of purity through works worthy of receiving the Holy Spirit. This does not imply, however, that God is compelled by man´s own efforts. Salvation, for the personal God of Christianity, is not the end result of a successfully implemented method or technique.

Figure 11. No Salvation Without Freedom. Early patristic Christianity emphasized the need to collaborate with God in our own salvation, rejecting the two extremes of a unilateral salvation pre-destined by God as well as that of our own Self-Deification obtained by our own means alone (e.g., asceticism; like in Dharmic meditation methods or Western Esotericism). Salvation, like everything else in our relationship with God, was understood as a communion in love between the two, which is consistent with the non-dialectical Both/And Christian logic and contrasts with the doctrine of Sola Gratia of the Reformers. Picture: Pentecost, the fulfilment of God´s promise and the pre-condition towards salvation/deification (Theosis), by Jean Restout (1732).

c1. Calvinism and the Rejection of Free Will Due to Mankind´s Total Depravity

Total depravity (also radical corruption[19] or pervasive depravity) is a Protestant theological tenet derived from the Augustinian concept of Original Sin.

---

19. Sproul, R. C. (2017). TULIP and Reformed Theology: Total Depravity. Ligonier Ministries: "I like to replace the term total depravity with my favorite designation, which is radical corruption. Ironically, the word radical has its roots in the Latin word for "root", which is radix, and it can be translated root or core."

This doctrine, to varying degrees, was and continues to be affirmed by some Protestant denominations[20, 21, 22], such as the Lutherans and all of Calvinism.[23, 24, 25, 26]

For Calvin, the fact that man´s work amounts to nothing is just the logical consequence of believing that mankind´s current state is one of total depravity, devoid of the capacity to will anything good for themselves.

This is the dialectical opposite of most Eastern and mystical doctrines. Instead of the the notion that "You are already God" found in many of them, Calvinism affirms the opposite extreme of the dialectic: man is nothing, the pure absence of anything good, incapable to choose God, refrain from evil or accept salvation.

Orthodox Christian understanding, in contrast, views man as capable of willing good, as we previously saw when exploring the doctrine of Ancestral Sin, even if there exists a tendency to also will and act in a direction that draws us farther away from God. This is a consequence of having inherited a fractured human nature. Nevertheless, this human nature is believed to still retain the attributes proper to God, such as free will, since it was made in His image, even if it lost its likeness.

----

20. *"Calvinism and Lutheranism Compared". WELS Topical Q&A. Wisconsin Evangelical Lutheran Synod. Archived from the original on 27 September 2009: "Total Depravity – Lutherans and Calvinists agree": "Yes this is correct. Both agree on the devastating nature of the fall and that man by nature has no power to aid in his conversions...and that election to salvation is by grace. In Lutheranism the German term for election is Gnadenwahl, election by grace--there is no other kind."*

21. *Andreä, Jakob; Chemnitz, Martin; Selnecker, Nikolaus; Chytraeus, David; Musculus, Andreas; Körner, Christoph (1577). Solid Declaration of the Formula of Concord.*

22. *Melanchthon, Philip, ed. (1530). The Augsburg Confession.*

23. *The Canons of Dordt (reformed.org). Retrieved 20 May 2023.*

24. *Westminster Assembly (1646). Westminster Confession of Faith.*

25. *Westminster Larger Catechism 1-50 (reformed.org). Question 25. Retrieved 20 May 2023.*

26. *The Heidelberg Catechism (reformed.org). Question 8. Retrieved 20 May 2023.*

d. Opposition Between Hierarchy and Individual Authority (Solus Christus or "Through Christ Alone")

The next "Sola", "only Christ", negates the idea of the necessity of a priestly class as administrators of Sacraments and mediators between God and mankind. This doctrine states that the Christ is the only valid mediator[27], salvation being through no other.

A core tenet of Lutheran theology, this principle rejects sacerdotalism, the notion that there are no valid Sacraments outside those found in the services officiated by priests ordained by apostolic succession.

Martin Luther, in fact, substituted the figure of the ordained priest (the One) by "the general priesthood of the baptized" (the Many).

Later Lutheranism and classical Protestantism expanded the concept, speaking of "the priesthood of all believers".

This doctrine, which may appear superficially attractive, and is historically understandable because of the abuses committed by some of the Catholic authorities of the time, bears the risk of substituting the tyranny of the One (e.g., a centralized authority figure such as the Pope) for the tyranny of the Many (each one their own authority; anarchy and atomization of the Church).

The non-dialectical orthodox position of early Christianity, in contrast, aims at incarnating both Unity and Plurality through a middle way that avoids both tyranny and chaos through order.

The image used is that of the body of Christ, where particular individuals with specific strengths (gifts, including those of teaching and guiding) and weaknesses cooperate in synergy under God´s headship (each believer being a vessel of the Holy Spirit) like different cells and organs of a body working together to form a healthy organism. This type of unity in plurality was the one exemplified by the interpenetration of the two

---

27. *1 Timothy 2:5. New King James version.*

nature´s of Christ in the Incarnation. It is also the final state achieved after deification (Theosis).

The analogy just mentioned is shared by all Christian denominations. However, due to their ecclesiological organization, the Orthodox appraisal of Catholicism and Protestantism in this matter is that, by deviating from the consensus of the early Fathers, they have abandoned a middle way to take opposite positions pertaining to the same dialectic. Both of them, however, favoring individual judgement over the previous patristic consensus:

• The Catholics by creating a central authority figure considered as infallible in theological matters (the Pope).

• The Protestants by going too far in the opposite direction in granting ultimate authority to individual judgment, which makes the faith variable, as seen in the abundant proliferation of Protestant denominations progressively drifting away from original Christian beliefs or practices (e.g., Pentecostalism).

"Shepherd the flock of God which is among you, serving as overseers, not by compulsion but willingly, not for dishonest gain but eagerly; nor as being lords over those entrusted to you, but being examples to the flock."

— 1 Peter 5:2-3. New King James Version

"And He Himself gave some to be Apostles, some Prophets, some Evangelists, and some Pastors and teachers."

— Ephesians 4:11. NKJV

"Therefore take heed to yourselves and to all the flock, among which the Holy Spirit has made you overseers, to shepherd the church of God which He purchased with His own blood. For I know this, that after my departure savage wolves will come in among you, not sparing the flock."

— Acts 20:28-29. NKJV

e. Opposition Between God and His Saints (Soli Deo Gloria or "Glory to God Alone")

The last "Sola", "glory to God alone", stands in opposition to the veneration of Mary the Mother of Jesus (Theotokos: Mother of God) and the saints.

Some Reformers believed that God alone should be worshipped and venerated, whereas early Christians always venerated (not worshipped), honoured, and paid respect to the saints. They viewed them as forerunners, teachers, and examples of a life well lived, as well as deified persons that rightfully gained their eternal place in the presence of God and are, therefore, capable of interceding for the living.

Veneration, for the Orthodox, is the non-dialectical middle way between the two extremes of worship (reserved for God alone) and ignoring the saints by withholding from them the respect they have earned.

5.3. Additional Paired Opposites in Mainstream Protestant Thought

In addition to the five theological pillars of the Reformation, other prominent examples of dialectical thought found in Protestantism include:

a. Iconoclasm: Opposition Between the Written Word and Other Types of Visual Symbolism

Just as with the saints, Protestants reject the representation and veneration of icons as a form of idolatry.

The Orthodox position, in contrast, is that the rejection of material representations as intrinsically unworthy is bad theology, resembling a Gnostic or Neo-Platonic attitude towards matter and being the consequence of not deriving the correct implications from the fact that God Himself was incarnated.

Figure 12. Iconoclasm, applied to the religious sphere, is the belief that every icon or religious representation must be destroyed as a possible source of idolatry. This, according to Orthodox Christianity, is a dialectical vision more typical of Gnosticism or Neo-Platonism, which considers matter intrinsically impure, than of a religion that worships the Incarnation of God through it. Picture: icon representing the "Triumph of Orthodoxy" against Iconoclasm (1400); The British Museum.

In the words of St. John of Damascus, the Orthodox champion against Iconoclasm:

"Of old, God the incorporeal and uncircumscribed was never depicted. Now, however, when God is seen clothed in flesh, and conversing with

men, (Bar. 3.38) I make an image of the God whom I see. I do not worship matter, I worship the God of matter, who became matter for my sake, and deigned to inhabit matter, who worked out my salvation through matter. I will not cease from honouring that matter which works my salvation." [28]

b. Opposition Between the Real Presence of God in the Sacraments and Symbolism

This underlying distrust of matter seems to make difficult its acceptance as a conduit of God´s grace (energies), as is made evident by the different interpretations regarding the Sacraments and especially the Eucharist, where some Protestant denominations altogether reject Christ´s presence in it in favor of a merely symbolic interpretation (e.g., General Baptists[29,30], Anabaptists[31], some non-denominational Christian churches[32]). In general, Protestantism places less focus on the Sacraments, retaining only two of the seven classical ones: Baptism and the Eucharist (with the latter being interpreted in different ways, as we have just seen).

---

28. *St. John of Damascus. Three Treatises on the Divine Images: First Apology against those who decry the Holy Images. St Vladimirs Seminary Press (2003), para.16.*

29. *Southern Baptist Convention (2018). Basic Beliefs: Baptism & the Lord's Supper: "The Lord's Supper is a symbolic act of obedience whereby members ... memorialize the death of the Redeemer and anticipate His Second Coming."*

30. *National Baptist Convention (2018). What We Believe: Baptism & the Lord's Supper: "We believe the Scriptures teach that Christian baptism is the immersion in water of a believer, into the name of the Father, and Son, and Holy Ghost; to show forth in a solemn and beautiful emblem, our faith in the crucified, buried, and risen Savior, with its effect, in our death to sin and resurrection to a new life; that it is prerequisite ... to the Lord's Supper, in which the members of the church, by the sacred use of bread and wine, are to commemorate together the dying love of Christ; preceded always by solemn self-examination."*

31. *Balmer, Randall Herbert; Winner, Lauren F. (2002). Protestantism in America. New York: Columbia University Press, p. 26.*

32. *University of Virginia Library (Religiousmovements.lib.virginia.edu; 2006). Archived from the original on 30 October 2007.*

Farrell, among others, related this to Protestantism's emphasis on personally experiencing the certainty of our salvation and highlighted the potential danger of adopting a Gnostic attitude towards it:

"This intimate connection between the rejection of sacramentalism and the reliance upon interior emotional and intellectual certitude in one's salvation is a feature of all Gnostic systems, and the Gnostic's "direct access to God".[33]

c. Protestant View on Salvation

Finally, Protestants do not adhere to the Catholic doctrine of the Beatific Vision. Contrary to its quasi-Monism, they believe in a concept of salvation that emphasizes multiplicity in the world to come. By looking for "the New Heaven and a New Earth", where purified souls with spiritualized bodies reside in extreme closeness to God, the vision of the afterlife is one of plurality:

• Contrary to the Catholic Beatific Vision, saved persons do not share in God´s Essence.

• Contrary to Orthodox deification, they do not become interpenetrated by God´s Uncreated Energies.

Therefore, the Protestant vision of the world to come (Eschaton) does not solve the problem of *the One and the Many*, being similar to the solution provided by Judaism and Islam (but opposite to the view of their panentheistic mystical schools).

In our typology of mysticism we labelled Protestantism as an exponent of the theistic *Mysticism of Union*. Given the above considerations we can now further qualify it as an external union, where Heaven is considered also as a place[34] and the union with God is not emphasized as much as in the other two main Christian denominations.

---

33. Farrell, Joseph P. (2016). God, History, and Dialectic, Volume I: God, The Foundation of the First Europe, p. 57.

34. The Methodist Protestant denomination, however, teaches that Heaven is a state of being.

5.4. An Orthodox Appraisal of Protestantism: Concluding Remarks

The Protestant zeal in correcting the perceived abuses and deviations of Roman Catholicism is, from an Orthodox point of view, understandable. However, as seen in the preceding examples, it seems that this "rebellion" was, in some cases, not rebellious enough. This is especially evident in the fact that the Filioque clause was not challenged.

Instead of going back to the non-dialectical (Both/And) way of thinking of Orthodoxy and patristic theology, Protestant theological positions usually became the polar opposite to those of Catholicism, at the same time operating under the same dialectical paradigm. To use an analogy, instead of walking the middle way, Protestantism understood that rejecting the left path necessarily implies walking through the right one.[35]

The main principles of the Protestant Reformation have been unable to achieve unity and have created a vast network of denominations with diverse beliefs which, by definition, cannot all be true.

One of the biggest dangers, then, is that by being unaware of the dialectical paradigm that underlies many of their core principles, Protestantism is less protected against possible deviations in doctrine and practice. Some of these deviations can already be seen (e.g., Pentecostalism and its anti-intellectual embrace of emotionalism).[36]

---

35. In practice, however, many Protestant denominations present more nuanced positions, showing at least partially non-dialectical doctrines far from the more black and white "Solas" of the Reformation.

36. *A fuller appraisal of the Protestant Reformation, its strengths and weaknesses seen from an Orthodox lens, can be found in Fr. Trenham´s book "Rock and Sand: An Orthodox Appraisal of the Protestant Reformers and Their Teachings."*

Even if Fr. Trenham's views regarding some other topics not discussed in this book can be controversial (please, do your own research), we found Rock and Sand to be a good summary of the differences between denominations, written in a non-confrontational tone by a former Reformed Episcopal priest.

6. Orthodox Christianity and the Radical Rejection of Dialectics

In the last sections we have followed the development of dialectical thought in the history of Christianity.

Beginning with its total absence in early apostolic Christianity, we have seen how it was introduced via the Latin church of the West through the doctrine of the Filioque, which changed the character of the Christian God.

The Protestant Reformation, probably due to their lack of in-depth knowledge of the conflict between the Eastern and Western churches, accepted this novel doctrine.

In many respects, they defined themselves by adopting a position contrary to Roman Catholic views, instead of looking back to early patristic theology, which could have led to starting a dialogue with the Orthodox Church in views of a possible re-unification.

Figure 13. To Die in Order to Live. The bottom crossbeam in the Orthodox Cross represents the footrest of the historical cross, but also the two thieves cruficied along Jesus Christ, showing the two paths that each person can follow by deciding whether or not to follow God, with the Cross being the instrument that made our deification possible. At the bottom, Adam's skull symbolizes Jesus as the Second Adam, emphasizing the Recapitulation doctrine of the atonement, with Jesus fulfilling what Adam could not. Picture: 16th century Russian Orthodox cross.

In the previous sections we have compared the main doctrines of Catholicism and Protestantism with those of the Orthodox Church. In this final section we intend to give a concise exposition of the aspects of Orthodoxy that have not been dealt with so far. We will emphasise how it avoids falling into dialectical thinking and thereby provides a valid solution to the dilemma between *the One and the Many.*

6.1. Early Deviations from Orthodox Christology and their Dialectical Presuppositions

Today's Orthodox teachings are believed to be the same as those of the early Apostles, although their mode of expression has been adapted over the centuries to deal with doctrinal deviations and cultural changes.

This stability, in turn, was achieved through apostolic succession, an unbroken line of Orthodox bishops ordained since the time of the Apostles, charged with protecting the teachings received. Thanks to this, the Orthodox Christian Church sees itself as the direct spiritual successor of the first Christians.

This unbroken succession line is significant because of the direct promise of Jesus Christ that the "gates of Hades" (Matthew 16:18) would not prevail against the Church, and His promise that He Himself would be with the Apostles until "the end of the world" (Matthew 28:20).[37]

By analizing early Christian history, we find that dialectical thought is not only found to be the main underlying problem of the Great Schism that created and separated Roman Catholicism from the Orthodox Church, as we previously saw, but it was also the paradigm behind all previous unorthodox innovations, too.

a. Monophysitism or the Primacy of Absolute Unity

Monophysites (meaning "one nature") challenged the patristic Orthodox doctrine of the two natures of Christ (human and divine) unified in His Person (Hypostatic Union). Instead, they held that Christ had only one nature, both human and divine, a third entity created from the addition of human nature to his divine one.

---

37. *Therefore, if we believe that the Christian Church became completely corrupt and had to be later re-founded, as the Protestant Reformation did, that would imply that these promises did not materialise.*

This motif of human nature fusing or merging with God´s one, as we have repeatedly seen by now, is the common solution of panentheistic doctrines to the problem of *the One and the Many*, were absolute oneness is unilaterally favored and plurality is viewed as an imperfection.

This view, therefore, is un-Christian in that it does not go beyond the problem of Unity and Multiplicity but instead choses a side in this dialectical battle. It also diminishes the concept of personhood, common in doctrines that conceptualize the Godhead as an impersonal entity but totally opposed to the Christian revelation and its focus on the co-primacy of Essence, Personhood, and Energies (or operations).

This depersonalization of the deity, understandably, was received with suspicion as a first step towards notions of personal Self-Deification through fusion with God´s Essence, diminishing the role of Christ to that of a teacher instead of a savior.

Because of this, the early Fathers of the Church put especial emphasis in the correct understanding of the notion of union in and with God and what it entailed. As St. Gregory the Theologian summarily and succinctly stated:

"[...] For that which He has not assumed He has not healed."

— St. Gregory of Nazianzus.
To Cledonius the Priest Against Apollinarius, Ep. CI

Therefore, if human nature was merged with God's nature during His Incarnation, it was this third combined entity which resurrected and ascended with Him, not the common human nature of which we all partake and which we are so concerned to save.

In Orthodox Christian thought, instead, man is elevated to the same degree to which God voluntarily lowered Himself (Kenosis), each nature interpenetrating each other, while a doctrine of fusion implies that both should stop being themselves, diminishing both God and man.

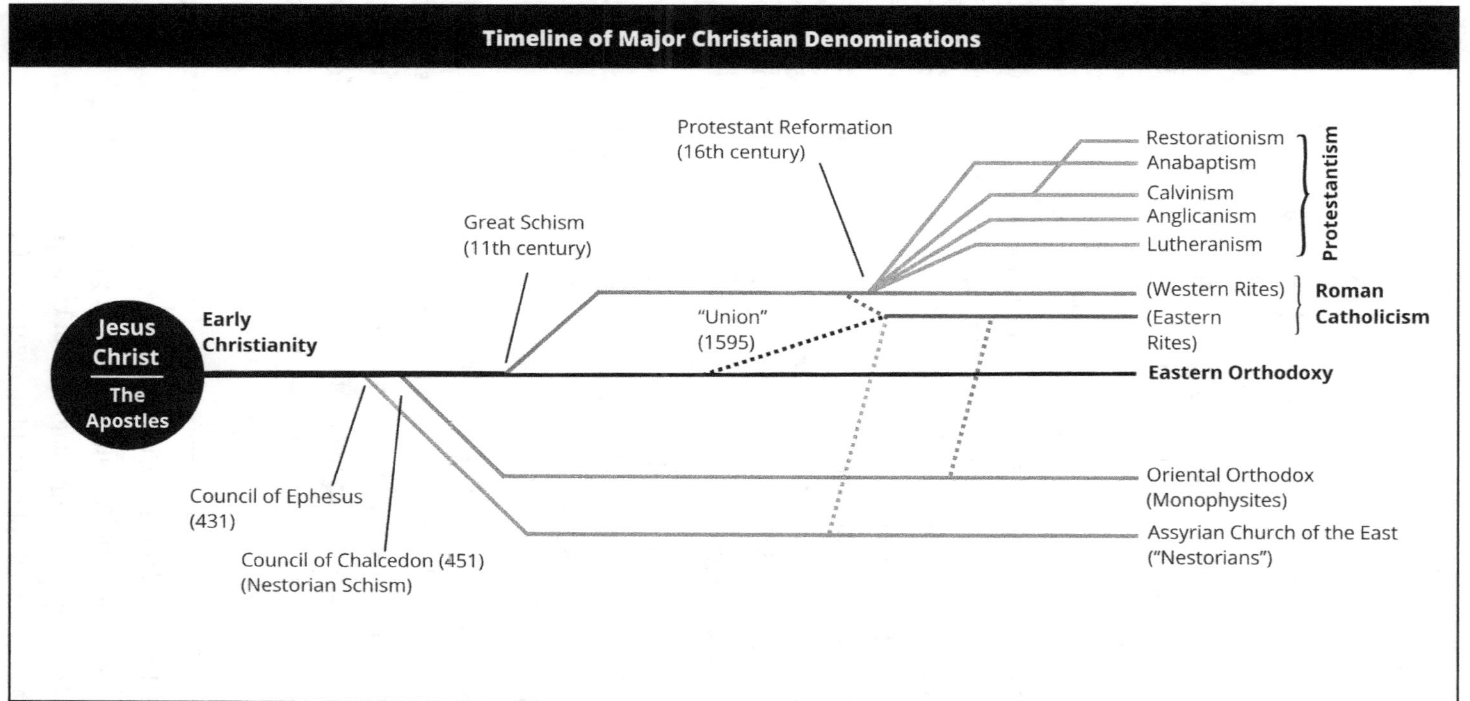

Figure 14. Timeline of major Christian denominations.

b. Nestorianism or the Primacy of Plurality

In the opposite extreme of Christological deviations from patristic theology we have Nestorianism (after Nestorius, Patriarch of Constantinople), the doctrine that Christ existed as two different persons in one body rather than as a unified Person: the man Jesus and the divine Son of God, or Logos.

This doctrine, as did Monophysitism, also invalidates the concept of Hypostatic Union, the key doctrine that allows for Unity in Plurality. In this case, instead of favoring absolute unity, this Christological position sides with plurality through defending the notion that a "two-natured" Christ (Dyophysitism) had to be incarnated in distinct human and divine persons. This implies the categorical confusion between nature and person, as well as the fracture of Christ´s personhood in two complementary parts, abandoning the key "two natures in one Person" doctrine of traditional theology.

Therefore, even though Nestorian Dyophysitism (two natures) seems superficially opposed to Monophysitism (one nature), it is just the opposite horn of the same One/Many dialectic, instantiated for the first time in Christian history.

Nestorius was especially criticized by St. Cyril (Patriarch of Alexandria) who argued that his doctrines undermined the unity of Christ's divine and human natures at the Incarnation. Nestorian "union", St. Cyril stated, would also be incapable of saving us, since it would imply that God was united with only a specific person, Jesus, instead of assuming in His personhood general human nature.

Only the third term present in the Hypostatic Union (two natures under the personhood of Christ) can save us. In the process, or more precisely because of it, it also solves the problem of *the One and the Many*, affirming the co-primacy of both Unity and Plurality by rejecting any trace of dialectical thought in regards to God.

"Only if it is one and the same Christ who is consubstantial with the Father and with men can He save us, for the meeting ground between God and man is Flesh and Christ." [38]

— St. Cyril of Alexandria

Figure 15. The Virgin of Vladimir (12th century), the most famous icon depicting the Mother of the Incarnate God (Theotokos). This apelative should not be understood, however, as signifying that she is the mother of the divine nature of Jesus, which existed from all eternity, but the one from wich the Logos assumed our human nature from. Catholicism was accused by Protestantism of idolatry for its sometimes excessive focus on the veneration of Mary, the latter in turn diminishing her figure to an extent that the Orthodox consider excessive, given her crucial role in our salvation. Orthodox Christianity, as in many other things, considers itself to be following the middle path between the two extremes of this dialectic. Mary is venerated, but not worshipped, the latter being reserved for God alone. Picture: Tretyakov Gallery in Moscow.

38. *McGuckin, John Anthony (2015). On the Unity of Christ. St Vladimirs Seminary Press.*

6.2. Orthodox Christology, Theology and Eschatology

a. Orthodox Christology: The Co-Primacy of Unity and Plurality

Orthodox Christology, then, is characterized by its affirmation of both the Unity and Plurality of Christ through the Hypostatic Union, the union of both human and divine natures not between them but through the third term of the Person of Jesus Christ, the Incarnation of the Son of God. Just as Jesus is the mediator between creation and God, He is also the mediator between His nature and ours.

As we have seen throughout this book, this type of union through interpenetration (Perichoresis) is unique to Christianity, being the reflection of the Unity in Plurality found in the Tri-Une God.

This correspondence between all levels of reality in transcending dialectics, including the doctrine of mankind being created in the image of God, would be the real meaning of the esoteric dictum "as above, so below" in Christian understanding.

b. Orthodox Trinitarian Theology: The Transcendence of the Problem of the One and the Many

This rejection to fall into a dialectical mode of thinking, in turn, is only possible because the revealed structure of the original Trinity that Orthodox Christianity defended against the innovation of the Filioque is in itself non-dialectical.

By affirming the uniqueness of each Person of the Trinity (the Father as Arché or source, the Son as the Only Begotten, the Holy Spirit as proceeding from the Father) instead of by rationalizing the Holy Spirit as the common middle ground between Father and Son (a mediator resolving the tension between an underlying duality through a synthesis), the uniqueness of each particular human person is also preserved against absorption into the One of pure monistic Panentheism.

Logos / the Son

Jesus Christ

HOLY TRINITY

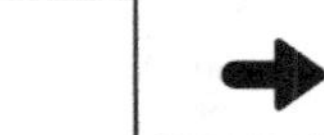

- **WHO IS HE?**
  Second Person of the Trinity.

- **WHAT IS HE?**
  God: common Nature of Divinity with the Father and the Holy Spirit.

Incarnation

- **WHO IS HE?** The Second Person of the Trinity

- **WHAT IS HE?** God - Man. The Concrete Universal.

Two Natures in One Person:

- **Divinity:** in common with the Father and the Holy Spirit.

- **Assumed Human Nature:** through Mary (*Mother of God: Theotokos*).

  Hypostatic Union. Both Natures are united under one Person, that of the Logos / Son. They interpenetrate *(perichoresis)* each other, sharing properties:

  e.g.: Jesus could perform human actions in a divine way, like walking (human power) in water (divine power). He was also able to actualize divine attributes (immortality) in a human way (through the Incarnation and the Resurrection).

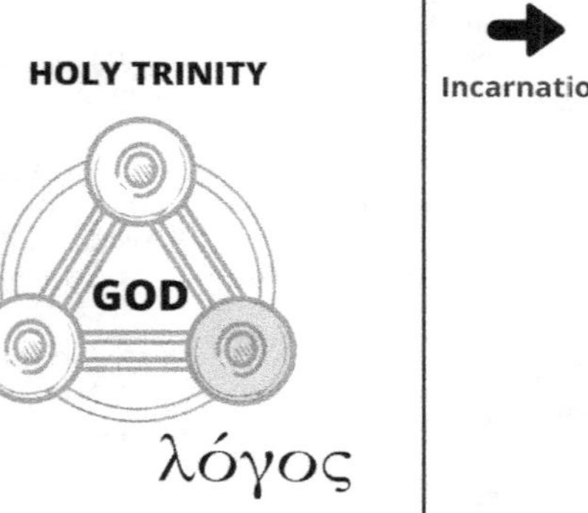

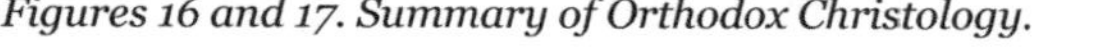

Figures 16 and 17. Summary of Orthodox Christology.

Jesus Christ´s   Death and Resurrection

- **THE CROSS. What was accomplished:**

  - **Divine Nature:** was able to die thanks to Human Nature.

  - **Human Nature:** was able to resurrect thanks to Divine Nature.

  Therefore, the Human Nature that we all share gained immortality. Also affecting all souls from the beginning of time, who were residing in a better or worse place in Sheol / "Hades".

  - **"Death died that day":** while trying to commit the ontological impossibility of destroying its own Source and the Source of Life: God. Now, death is not the transit to Sheol, but a door to eternal life.

  The Second Adam: Death taking the First Adam due to Sin was legitimate, as Adam separated from the Source of Life. Death taking the sinless Jesus was unjust, therefore violating God´s Justice and annuling death´s right to exist.

Ascension

Jesus Christ´s Ascension

- **What was accomplished:**

  - **Purification of Human Nature:** now capable of receiving the Holy Spirit.

  - **Theosis:** the Possibility of Divinizing Human Nature.

    As much as the Divine Nature descended during the Incarnation (God´s abasement, Kenosis) can now Human Nature ascend to.

Synergy: this process of deification has to be done in cooperation with God. It is not a method.

Both the work of God and the work of man are needed, as the work of both Nature´s was needed during the Incarnation.

By conceiving God as being above any dialectical tension, including the one between pure Actuality and Potentiality, Orthodox theology rejects the metaphysical dogmas that God is:

• Pure Actuality, an absolutely simple Essence devoid of any Potentiality or free will.

• The Absolute, the All, a totality achievable through the Unity of Opposites, including the recontextualization of evil.

Therefore, the Trinitarian Godhead affirms the irreducibility of God to an absolutely simple Essence, embracing instead a triple definition of God composed of Essence, Person, and Uncreated Energies (attributes, used to define the Divine Names [e.g., God is Love, God is Good, God is One]).

These Uncreated Energies of God, a doctrine only found in Orthodox Christianity, are the inheritance promised to mankind.

They are that which enables us to become god by bridging the gulf between man and God, while also avoiding the fusion with Him into an undifferentiated Essence where particularity has no place.

c. Orthodox Eschatology: The Eternal Existence of Unity in Difference

Because a non-dialectical answer to the problem of *the One and the Many* is found in every ontological level of revealed doctrine (e.g., the Trinitarian Godhead, God´s Incarnation, the eschatological world to come), we have classified mankind´s state of deification or divinization (Theosis) as its own category in our typology of the Mysticism of Union, as we saw at the beginning of the chapter (*Figure 1*).

Orthodox eschatology is not a representative of External Union, such as the concepts of a heavenly realm found in theistic Monotheism (e.g., Judaism, Islam) or even in Trinitarian Protestantism. It is also not a representative of the Internal Union/Fusion found in panentheistic Theism (e.g., Kabbalah, Sufism, Vishishtadvaita Vedānta) or even in the Catholic Beatific Vision of God.

Christian Orthodox Theology
"Anatomy" of the Tri-Une God of Orthodox Christianity [1/2]

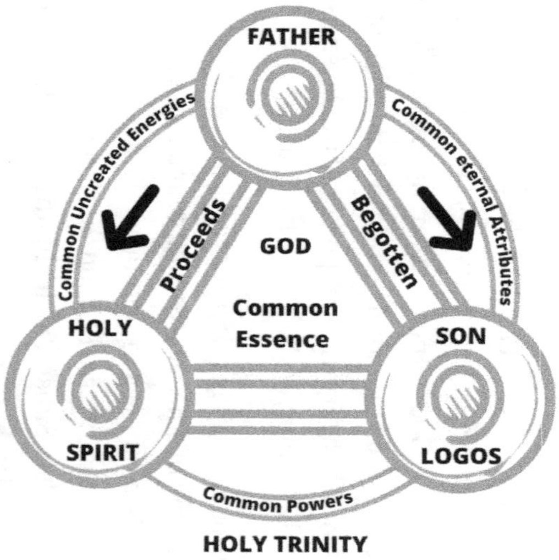

WHAT is God? → **Nature. Essence.** Cannot exist by itself, but needs to instantiate itself (*Enhypostasis*). It determines all potentialities of each instance of the same Nature.

Apophatic or Negative Theology: cannot be fully comprehended. Absolutely Transcendent.

WHO is God? → **Particular instances, Persons (*Hypostasis*).** Actualize and bring into existence the Divine Nature.

- The Mystery of the Trinity: **all Persons are Co-Eternal. Each one´s very existence implies the existence of the others (e.g., Father implies Son and viceversa). None of them were created, but they always were, are and will be. They are completely One and completely Three, transcending human dialectical logic (either/or) and its limits. It is a revealed doctrine.**

Figures 18 and 19. Summary of the Orthodox position on the Holy Trinity.

[Exclusive Orthodox Christian doctrine]

HOW ➡

is God known /
does He act?

Uncreated Energies. Attributes, Powers, Names of God.

Cataphatic or Positive Theology: *e.g., God is One, Good, All-Knowing, Creator.*

Consequences of this doctrine:

- **The transcendence of the One/Many and Potentiality/Actuality dialectics.**

  o **The Source of Potentiality:** God is not limited to be Pure Actuality (as *the One* is).

    E.g.: God became a Creator when He actualized this particular power at the beginning of time.

  o **The Source of Difference:** different attributes actualize different aspects of God.
    They are not equivalent (contrary to *the One*). E.g.: *God's Love is not the same as His Judgement.*

- **Deification (Theosis): each saved person (Saint) unites completely with God's Uncreated Energies,
  not with His Essence.** Allows for Individuality and at the same time for direct Union with God.

Analogy in Creation (creation as a symbol of God): human nature does not exist by itself. It needs to be actualized in a particular person, who also can not exist without the human nature that defines them. Each individual person partaking of the same nature will then use the potentialities common to each (Spirit / Nous, Psyche / Soul, physical body) to act in their own personal way (energies / powers: e.g., being compassionate or being strict).

Equally valuing both unity and uniqueness, the divinization of man pro-mises to make him a god through God becoming *"All in all"*, while retaining the subject/object differentiation between God and saved beings, able to eternally love each other in their uniqueness while being One through communion of will and through the God that is in them all.

Instead of the fusion between knower and known into knowledge, remaining only the latter, the eternal presence of lover, loved, and the love between them. Myself, the "Other", and God, a tri-une reality where love is possible through the Trinitarian God.

d. Practical Life in Orthodox Christianity: The Middle Way Between Extreme Asceticism and Slavery to the Passions

Orthopraxis, or the practical way of life of an Orthodox Christian, also shows Unity in Plurality in that it provides different possible ways leading to the same destination. Instead of the monastic disciplines of the One, where only expert meditators can achieve liberation and lay persons have to acquire merit to be later reborn in more favorable conditions, the monastic path is not the exclusive way of salvation in Orthodox Christianity.

Both monastic vocations (also non-monastic celibacy) and marriage are seen as equally honourable in the eyes of God, both representing marriage or union: the former with God through exclusive dedication, the latter as an image of the union of Christ (bridegroom) with His Church (the bride). Since there is no underlying hatred of matter in the Orthodox worldview, a more mundane life such as that of married people, if lived in a spirit of holiness, is not considered as necessarily inferior.

d1. Prayer and Hesychasm: The Non-Dialectical Nature of the Orthodox Spiritual Life

Even in prayer can we speak of both a focus on a unified mind through stillness (Hesychasm), attention, and vigilance (Nepsis) while retaining "otherness" by praying to God instead of concentrating on emptiness and eliminating any thought that is conceived as tainting it.

Therefore, we can say that even in Orthodox spiritual practices ("Christian meditation"), plurality in the form of appropriate thoughts (usually the name of God) is usually present (e.g., the Jesus Prayer in one of its many forms).

Among Christian denominations, Orthodox practical life also typically represents a middle way between the frequently reduced presence of spiritual and ascetical practices of Protestantism (e.g., light fasting, prayer rules found in other denominations) and the severity of the ones found in Catholicism (e.g., prohibition of the clergy to marry, mortification of the flesh in extreme cases).

d2. St. Symeon the New Theologian and the Uncreated Light of God

To finish our overview through Orthodoxy's non-dialectical Both/ And way of thinking we will briefly mention the experiences of one of its most popular and descriptive mystics: St. Symeon the New Theologian.

In his *Hymns of Divine Love*[39], St. Symeon describes his vision of God as uncreated Divine Light[40], speaking of it as *both* an inward *and* outward mystical experience.

These experiences, which came to him after prayer and deep contemplation, were also associated with a feeling both of indescribable joy and intellectual understanding.[41]

---

39. *Turner, H. J. M. (1990). St. Symeon the New Theologian and Spiritual Fatherhood. Vol. 11 of Byzantina Neerlandica. Brill, p. 35.*

40. *Alfeyev, Hilarion (2000). Saint Symeon, the New Theologian, and Orthodox Tradition. Oxford University Press, p. 51.*

41. *Krivocheine, Basil; Gythiel, Anthony P. (1986). In the Light of Christ: Saint Symeon, the New Theologian (949–1022). St Vladimir's Seminary Press, pp. 215–229.*

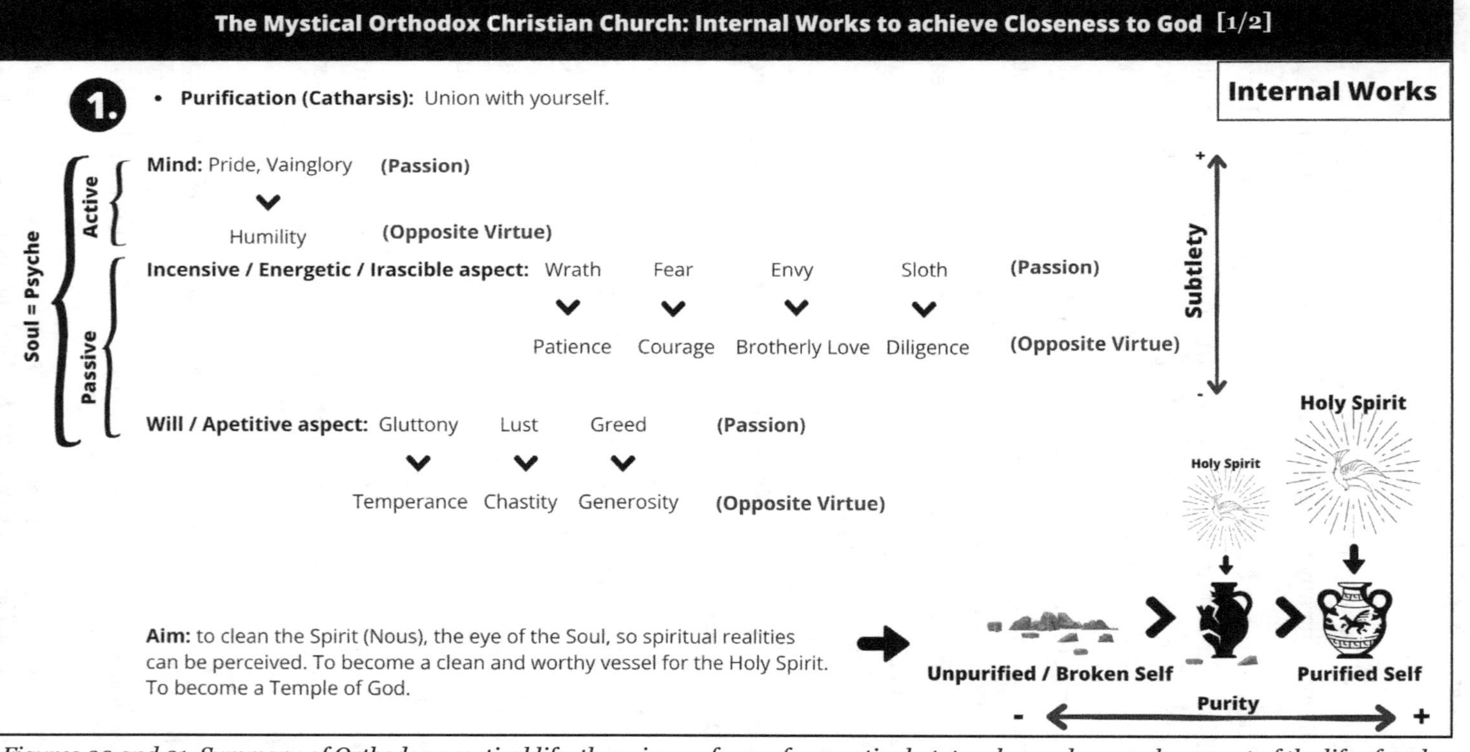

Figures 20 and 21. Summary of Orthodox practical life, the primary focus of monastics but, to a lesser degree, also a part of the life of each willing believer (to a variable degree).

The Mystical Orthodox Christian Church: Internal Works to achieve Closeness to God [2/2]

2.

- **Illumination (Theoria):** Union with creation (*"the Other"*).

Scattered thoughts and attention

Undivided attention upon God
(e.g., *Jesus Prayer*)

Aim: gathering of thoughts to achieve undivided attention through stillness and prayer. Integration of one´s own mind.

Achievement of real intuitive knowledge of the reason of everything (logoi, the "archetypes" of things, as willed thoughts of the Logos).

3.

- **Union with God (Theology):** not as the necessary end and reward of asceticism and meditation, but as a gift from God.

Faith + Works

Mystical branch of Christianity: Orthodox Christianity includes and invites everyone, even laymen, to get as close to God as possible.

e.g.: it includes fasting and feasting periods in the liturgical calendar, while avoiding extreme asceticism or complete self-indulgence (*Middle Way*).

Monastic Tradition: for those willing to dedicate their whole life to getting closer to God and praying for the world.

Works: they include internal and external (e.g. charity) aspects, always focusing on self (*One*) and others (*Many*).

It avoids, then, the dialectical tension between:

- Only **Faith** (Protestantism) / only **Works**.

- Only Self-development (**Internal** Works; e.g., Eastern mysticism) / only good deeds (**External** Works).

Aim: to replace naive self-love (egoism, selfishness) for love of Self as the image of God. This doctrine, in turn, implies love of *"the Other"* as additional images of God and as His willed Creation.

"[...] Those who have received grace have received the light of God and have received God, even as Christ Himself, who is the Light, has said, "I will live in them and move among them." [2 Cor. 6:16] [42]

— St. Symeon the New Theologian. Discourse XXVIII

7. The Metaphysical Compass: Concluding Remarks

In this chapter, we have found that the Mysticism of Union with a personal God can either adhere to Monism (including Panentheism) or reject the thinking in dichotomical categories by accepting both Unity and Difference and by providing a solution to the problem of *the One and the Many* not based on exclusivity (Christian Tri-Une God). Monistic worldviews, as we have by now repeatedly seen, cannot avoid operating under a dialectical paradigm.

In addition, we saw how among Christianity, two of its main denominations, by adding the Filioque clause and engaging in dialectical thinking through the increased importance given to human reason and philosophy, unknowingly modified original Christian tenets. This lead to interpreting salvation in an increasingly monistic (Catholic Beatific Vision of God [*Internal Union or the One*]) or pluralistic way (Protestant Heaven as a place [*External Union or the Many*]), instead of the patristic non-dialectical view of deification (Theosis; Interpenetration [*One/Many*]).

We saw how Orthodox Christianity, in contrast, fought to keep operating under the revealed non-dialectical paradigm, which protected it against innovation in doctrine and the undermining of the characteristically Christian belief in Unity in Difference, *the One **and** the Many*.

Because of all the above, Christianity stands in a particular and unique position in metaphysical matters, refusing to be reduced to another "doctrine of the One", while most other current worldviews eventually

---

42. *de Catanzaro, C. J.; Maloney S. J., George (1980). Symeon the New Theologian: The Discourses. Paulist Press, pp. 27–28.*

fall under this category in one way or another, as we have been discussing throughout this book.

Given the incompatibility between the metaphysical foundations of Christianity and "the One", we cannot but avoid taking a stand, since both cannot be true. The problem is, then, how to make that decision?

Cornelius Van Til, when explaining the *Transcendental Argument for the Existence of God*, noted the impossibility of finding a non-dialectical solution to the problem of *the One and the Many* through a non-Trinitarian God. Do we agree with him? Can we provide a sound alternative to this statement?

Pursuing this line of thought may be a fruitful endeavour in our quest, as it was for many in the past.

7.1. *"By Their Fruits You Will Know Them"*

The above theological and metaphysical considerations are of great importance. However, when deciding to embrace a worldview as our own, abstract considerations are usually not enough for most people.

Nevertheless, as we have tried to emphasize in this book, these considerations have also very practical implications.

Take, for example, the extremely strict Islamic doctrine of absolute unity that excludes all difference. The preference for theocratic governments, its historical non-opposition in principle to wars of conquest, and some interpretations of the actions to be performed by the Islamic Jesus (Isa al-Masih) upon his second coming[43] are just the natural and logical consequences of such a doctrine.

---

43. *"The Hour will not be established until the son of Mary [i.e., Jesus] descends amongst you as a just ruler, he will break the cross, kill the pigs, and abolish the Jizya tax" (the abolition of the tax effectively implying the end of religious tolerance for non-Muslims).*
— *Sahih al-Bukhari 2476 .Book 46, Hadith 37.*

In contrast, a theology that focuses on both unity and difference has the metaphysical grounds to establish, for example, a form of government more tolerant of said difference (e.g., the Byzantine Empire). It is also incapable of understanding the concept of "just war" as anything more than a contradiction in terms, only allowing the use of violence for self-defense purposes.

This, not only tolerance, but love of uniqueness in turn makes possible to define the Christian Tri-Une God as the God of love (1 John 4:7-11). However, this is not the case for the God of the Philosophers (and therefore of human reason), who loves knowledge above all (self-knowledge, the One knowing Itself) and defines oneness as a merger erasing any particularity.

This brings us to the notion of authority. Given that faith is an unavoidable part of human existence, do we **choose** to place our faith regarding theological matters in human reason alone and in its dialectical Either/Or logic? Or do we place it in revealed theology and in the witness of the many martyrs who willingly gave their life away in order to affirm the truth they experienced?[44, 45]

Another example would be the consequences of the Protestant doctrine of Sola Scriptura ("the Bible alone"), and how removing tradition[46] from Christian life has led to a proliferation of different interpretations of Christian tenets that has resulted in the increasing fragmentation of

----

44. *In this regard, trying to interpret the Holy Bible as a scientific textbook to be rationalized in search for scientific facts instead of as a theological compilation of inspired books would be a categorical error.*

45. *Theology does not exclude reason, it just subordinates it to revelation. Reason, of old called the handmaiden of theology, is used to derive the implications of theology. However, it cannot by itself establish God´s first principles, as by definition they concern a plane of existence above human reason.*

46. *The same tradition that was the whole faith of the early Christians that had no Holy Bible to rely on, since the compilation of the biblical canon was not fixed until a few centuries later.*

Protestantism into a number of denominations with doctrines progressively more distant from original patristic Christianity.

Pentecostalism and charismatic movements are probably the most clear examples of this, with their extreme emphasis on pietistic "mystical manifestations" such as glossolalia, falling to the ground, moans, and cries during worship services. Those experiences, at best, would have been judged by traditional monks and mystics as totally alien and even opposed to the serene and peaceful experiences of holiness they experienced through, for example, prayer and the Uncreated Light of God (as St. Symeon the New Theologian explained).

Obviously, all worldviews have good and bad apples, and problems arise in all of them due to the mere "human factor". Orthodox Christianity is no exception, with aspects such as ethnocentrism being an unresolved issue. However, this does not detract from the fact that, even when applied to worldviews and their metaphysical axioms, the saying *"by their fruits you shall know them"* (Matthew 7:20) still holds true.

7.2. Seeing Behind the Veil

Another fruitful line of investigation for us could be, as we previously saw in *Chapter V*, the recurring symbolism and metaphysical doctrines taught by popular media, overwhelmingly in favor of certain worldviews (Panentheism, impersonal Monism or the One) to the detriment of others which, if anything, tend to be attacked (usually Christianity).

Do we believe that this is all coincidence? Then, we have to explain the consistency of the doctrines being taught and their recurrence among different media and different times.

Do we believe, on the contrary, that there is an intention, an agenda, behind it? In that case, is it one that has our best interests in mind or not? What is the endgame? Is it to catalyse human spiritual evolution? Is it to delude us? These are questions that we all have to answer for ourselves.

In order to better answer these questions, it is the hope of the author of this book that it can serve as a tool to identify these narratives, their origins, and their metaphysical building blocks, as well as the worldviews that are consistent with them and those that are incompatible, in order to see through the layers of increasingly common symbolism and metaphysical content that exists in our world and that we are all too often unaware of.

Recommended Reading

1. **God, History, and Dialectic. Volumes I and II.** *Joseph P. Farrell.*
2. **At Sundry Times. An Essay in the Comparison of Religions.** *R.C. Zaehner.*
3. **The One and the Many: Studies in the Philosophy of Order and Ultimacy.** *R.J. Rushdoony.*
4. **The Mystical Theology of the Eastern Church.** *Vladimir Lossky.*
5. **In the Image and Likeness of God.** *Vladimir Lossky.*

Wars and Rumors of War:
Can We be Led to Rebel Against
Our Own Best Interests?

The Two Great Practical Dangers of Dialectics:

A Perennialist Form of Ecumenism and the Possibility of Starting a False Revolution

DIALECTICS, AS A TOOL, CAN BE AN EFFECTIVE WAY to steer whole societies in certain directions.

In this addendum, we will briefly sketch two recurrent modern fears and potential dangers regarding the possibility of being immersed in a process of global dialectical worldview manipulation, of which there are arguably certain signs already present.

1. Ecumenism: Unity as Truth

The term Ecumenism, as used in the Christian world, is the notion that Christians belonging to different denominations should work together and promote Christian unity.[1]

An inter-faith vision of Ecumenism, in contrast, would point to the commonalities between major religions and how they all try to achieve, through their own particular vision and means, the same goal. Perennialism or Traditionalism would be its most influential current incarnation.

This concept has proven to be polarising, with ardent advocates and vocal critics. The problem with this notion in an inter-faith setting is that unity, in itself, has no value if it is not unity in truth. This very obvious fact is what bears the risk of being forgotten by the application of a (willingly or unwillingly) misunderstood notion of Ecumenism.

The problem with inter-faith Ecumenism in a Christian context, furthermore, is that by affirming it, we are negating the doctrine of the Church as the body of Christ and as the fruit of the Incarnation. Therefore, indirectly, we are negating that God became man, that the Holy Spirit resides in the Church and we are His temples, and Jesus Christ´s promise regarding how the Church will prevail against all obstacles (Matthew 16:18).

In short, this doctrine, indirectly and presumably unintentionally, affirms that Jesus Christ was a fallible man. Instead of uniting Christianity, it renounces it.

As Fr. Heers remarked[2], the fear is that Ecumenism, as a unification movement born within secularized Christianity, is walking in the direction

---

1. *"What are Ecumenical Relations?". Ecumenical and Interreligious Affairs. Roman Catholic Archdiocese of Chicago. Retrieved 24 September 2020: "Ecumenical relations, also known as ecumenism, are the effort to seek Christian unity by cultivating meaningful relationships and understanding by and between the many different Christian churches and Christian Communities."*

2. *Heers, Fr. Peter (2018). On the Essential Identity of Ecumenism & Phyletism. Orthodox Ethos. Retrieved November 2023. [Fr. Heers can sometimes be a controversial figure for some people. Please, do your own research].*

of overcoming *"the scandal of division"* by denying the *"scandal of the particular"*, or the Incarnation. Or, to use the terminology we have used so far in this book, the concern is that it is walking a path that can easily end in the renunciation of the Christian One/Many paradigm (Jesus Christ as the Concrete Universal, transcending the One/Many dichotomy) in order to go back to pure unity (the One), thus reverting to a dialectical way of thinking, rejecting revelation, and worshipping human reason again.[3] This, for any Christian aware of the Scriptures is, at the very least, concerning.[4]

That Ecumenism bears the risk of going back to favoring human reason over revelation is also evident from the fact that if one supposedly believes in a truth that was revealed directly by God and not derived solely through human understanding, doctrinal compromises are not acceptable. Every doctrinal compromise, instead, becomes an implicit declaration of unbelief.

1.1. Ecclesiological Dialectics: Ecumenism and Phyletism as Two Sides of the Same Coin

Phyletism is the inclusion of nationalism in Church administration or, in other words, the conflation between Church and nation. It is often described as the opposite of Ecumenism, as the former identifies the Church with the *many* nationalities that conform it, while the latter states that all different Churches should look after unification (the One). The former is considered an actual ecclesiastical heresy, while the latter is an ideology with the potential to also become a serious one.

------

3. *Which echoes the words of the serpent in Genesis, promising Self-Deification:* *"For God doth know that in the day ye eat thereof, then your eyes shall be opened, and ye shall be as gods, knowing good and evil."*
– Genesis 3:5. New King James Version.

4. *"And every spirit that confesseth not that Jesus Christ is come in the flesh is not of God: and this is that spirit of antichrist, whereof ye have heard that it should come; and even now already is it in the world."*
– 1 John 4:3. New King James Version.

As Fr. Heers underlined, even though they are considered as antagonic, they are part of the same dialectical tension. In fact, Ecumenism, as the ideology "in charge" of correcting Phyletism, needs its counterpart in order to exist. In other words, the existence of Phyletism is a necessary pre-condition for Ecumenism to become a dominant ideology. It is its antithesis, the Yin to its Yang or, as the harshest critics state, the straw man needed for it to triumph.[5]

1.2. Are We Slowly Heading Towards a Unitarian One World Religion?

One particularly dangerous and, apparently not totally unfounded, fear is that we are treading a path that will eventually lead to a One World Religion. Dangerous, not because of its immediate negative effects, but because of its desirability in an exhausted world sick of religious and geopolitical conflict. Dangerous because it is possible to engineer its acceptance as a solution to a pre-fabricated problem, as we will later see. And, especially, dangerous because in any such scenario the possibility of it being a religion based on truth is minimal.

In order to prove our point, we will just mention a few of many relatively recent developments pointing at that scenario, such as:

• The creation of an interfaith worship center for Jews, Christians, and Muslims to be built in Berlin[6] called, unsurprisingly, the House of One.

• The creation of the Abrahamic Family House in Abu Dhabi. Which includes a synagogue, a church, and a mosque inspired by the Papal *Document on Human Fraternity*.[7]

---

5. *Heers, Fr. Peter (2018). On the Essential Identity of Ecumenism & Phyletism. Orthodox Ethos. Retrieved November 2023.*

6. *www.timesofisrael.com/interfaith-worship-center-for-jews-christians-muslims-to-be-built-in-berlin/. Accessed November 2023.*

7. *www.vaticannews.va/en/vatican-city/news/2021-06/abu-dhabi-abrahamic-family-house-2022-human-fraternity.html. Accessed November 2023.*

• The Palace of Peace and Reconciliation in Astana, capital of Kazakhstan. A pyramidal structure (not dissimilar to the masonic symbolism of the "Eye of Providence" above an unfinished pyramid, also present in the dollar bill), that hosts once every three years The Congress of Leaders of World and Traditional Religions, a meeting where leaders of all major religions congregate under an ecumenical spirit.

It is difficult to understand what common ground can there be between a religion that states that Jesus Christ was an impostor currently being tortured in Hell or Gehenna (Talmudic Judaism; Gemara Gittin, 56b:18-the end of 57a), a religion that sees him as a human prophet that upon his return will "break the Cross", obviously meaning Christianity (Islam; Sahih al-Bukhari 2476; Book 46, Hadith 37), and one that sees Him as the Incarnation of God Himself.

The only possible solution to this conundrum would be, eventually, the re-evaluation of the Christian doctrine of the Incarnation of God. In other words, for Christianity to be ecumenically and syncretically integrated into a conglomerate system that includes all other major religions, it has to lose Christ. A One World Religion cannot exist while Christianity, as was understood since the times of Christ and the Apostles, still stands.

Eliminating the concept of the Incarnation would also eliminate the notion of the Concrete Universal, *the One **and** the Many*, leaving no obstacle left for the One (Monism) to achieve supremacy.[8]

The above recent examples should not cloud us to the fact that this is not a novel approach, but has been for a long time deeply ingrained in powerful spheres. No clearer example can we provide than the presence of Alice Bailey´s Lucis Trust[9] (formerly Lucifer Publishing Company) as

––––––––––

8. *The concept of an Avatar found in many Dharmic religions would be, in contrast, compatible with a syncretic unified religion, since Avatars as mere modalist and temporary manifestations of the One.*

9. *Which headlines one of the pages on its website as: "The United Nations: Manifesting the Vision of the One humanity" (www.lucistrust.org/blog_wgun/un_manifesting).*

an organization with consultative status within the Economic and Social Council of the United Nations (ECOSOC).

Figure 1. The Stumbling Stone. The perennialist template is able to accommodate most metaphysical doctrines by modifying them in one way or another. However, its two main pillars are opposed to the two central doctrines of Christianity: the Trinity and the Incarnation of the Logos in Jesus Christ. The former is attempted to be redefined as a sequential series or as a Monad that harmonizes two of its three "principles". The latter, however, has to be eliminated, since it cannot be integrated. In a perennialist worldview, Jesus has either to become a mere deified teacher or a symbol of impersonal Sun worship.

The same Alice Bailey who was a prominent member of the Theosophical Society and one of the main successors of Helena Petrovna Blavatsky, the doctrinal spearhead of the New Age movement and herself promoting a specific version of Perennialism:

"The origin of all religions -- Judaeo-Christianity included -- is to be found in a few primeval truths, not one of which can be explained apart from all the others, as each is a complement of the rest in some one detail. And they are all, more or less, broken rays of the same Sun of truth, and their beginnings have to be sought in the archaic records of the Wisdom-religion. Without the light of the latter, the greatest scholars can see but the skeletons thereof covered with masks of fancy, and based mostly on personified Zodiacal signs."

— Blavatsky, H. P. (1888). Studies in Occultism.
The Esoteric Character of the Gospels, Part III.

1.3. The Vatican II Council and the Ecumenical Adaptation of Catholicism to the Modern World

Another prominent example of how an apparently good-natured ecumenist spirit can be problematic is the Second Vatican Council of Roman Catholicism (1962–1965).

The council addressed relations between the Catholic Church and the modern world[10], with many of the changes made still being controversial to this day among Catholics.[11] Several changes were centered around increasing the ecumenical efforts with other Christian denominations, as well as interfaith dialogue with other religions.[12]

In fact, Vatican II has become infamous for its divisiveness, as many Catholics still feel conflicted about the consequences and the aims of this council, with some declaring it invalid due to many council statements

----

10. *Gaudium et spes [Pastoral Constitution on the Church in the Modern World]. II Vatican council. Rome, Italy: Vatican.*

11. *Brewer, John D.; Higgins, Gareth I.; Teeney, Francis (2011). Religion, Civil Society, and Peace in Northern Ireland. Oxford University Press: "Vatican II, by eliminating Latin prayers, offended traditional Catholics [...]."*

12. *"Sanctitas clarior - Lettera Apostolica in forma di Motu Proprio con la quale sono riordinati i processi per le cause di beatificazione e canonizzazione (1969) | Paolo VI (vatican.va).*

being in conflict with established precepts regarding morals and doctrine.[13] In those cases, Vatican II is viewed as an invalid revisionist and modernist attempt on traditional Christian beliefs.

This is the case of the Society of Saint Pius X (SSPX), which recognises the authority of the Pope but rejects Vatican II. Other groups went even further, declaring vacant the Holy See since the death of Pope Pius XII (Sedevacantism), all Popes that followed him being invalid. Another group, in turn, affirms that all Popes since John XXIII are merely material, but not formal ones, rejecting also their validity (Sedeprivationism).

a. Pachamama and the Danger of Syncretism

The ecumenist spirit that presided over Vatican II is also the one that created further division in Roman Catholicism due to its approach to pagan gods. This was the case with the goddess Pachamama ("Mother Earth" or "World Mother").

Pachamama is an Inca "Earth Mother" type of fertility goddess revered by the indigenous peoples of the Andes. She is also conceived as an independent deity who sustains life.[14]

During the late twentieth century, a New Age cult worshipping her was born, as well as a syncretic movement that merged Catholicism and Pachamama worship in their rituals, sometimes reinterpreting her as God´s Providence.[15, 16]

---

13. Malone, Michael. *"Twenty-five explicit errors of Vatican Council II"*.

14. Dransart, Penny. (1992) *"Pachamama: The Inka Earth Mother of the Long Sweeping Garment." Dress and Gender: Making and Meaning. Ed. Ruth Barnes and Joanne B. Eicher. New York/Oxford: Berg. 145-63.*

15. Merlino, Rodolfo y Mario Rabey (1983). *"Pastores del Altiplano Andino Meridional: Religiosidad, Territorio y Equilibrio Ecológico". Allpanchis (in Spanish). Cusco, Perú. 15 (21): 149–171.*

16. Marzal, Manuel (2002). *Tierra encantada: Tratado de antropología religiosa de América Latina. Editorial Trotta. pp. 198–205.*

A syncretic identification of Pachamama with the Virgin Mary, furthermore, has also been found by some scholars.[17] This, for a Christian, means adapting Christianity to a perennialist template, transforming the mother of God (Theotokos) into another fertility goddess. It also bears the danger of interpreting Christ as another dying and rising god such as those of the ancient pagan fertility and solar cults (e.g., the Astrotheology of Jordan Maxwell).

The Vatican certainly did not ease these concerns by having Pope Francis bless a wooden image of Pachamama, placing the image of this foreign god in front of the main altar at St. Peter's Basilica, and then carrying it in procession to the Synod Hall. Actions, which, to the surprise of no one, lead to scandal and accusations of idolatry.[18, 19]

Figure 2. The figure of Mother Earth is common in different spiritual worldviews around the world. Those who wish to include Christianity within a perennialist scheme need not only to transform the figure of Jesus Christ but also that of the Virgin Mary. To do so, one must move from perceiving her as the mother of God (Theotokos; the means by which God adopted our human nature and united it to His own) to a generalist "Mother of All" (e.g., Mother Earth) or another fertility goddess. This is compatible with worldviews believing in the Absolute, which is an androgynous Father/Mother figure, but not with Christianity.

---

17. Ibid., p. 414.

18. "Pope Francis's apology over Amazon statues theft". BBC News. October 25, 2019. Retrieved September 8, 2021.

19. "The Guardian view on 'pagan idols' in the Vatican: church culture wars should concern us all". The Guardian. October 31, 2019. Retrieved September 8, 2021.

1.4. Ecumenical Concerns in Protestantism and Orthodox Christianity

Although, within Christianity, Roman Catholicism has generally been more aggressive in pushing an ecumenical agenda, it would be a mistake to think that the other major denominations do not have parts of them interested in pursuing the same goals, with the ensuing controversy between those in favor and those who see the dangers to which this can easily lead.

The aforementioned fears extend, for example, to the current Orthodox Ecumenical Patriarchate of Constantinople and to modern Protestantism. Regarding the latter, R.J. Rushdoony stated:

"[...] The Protestant Reformation asserted the priority of truth to unity; Modernist Protestantism increasingly denies the possibility of their conflict—implicitly accepting authoritarian unity: truth is unity, and unity is truth. Ecumenicity (all churches in one) is of itself therefore deemed both good and necessary." [20]

Obviously, a theology open to change implies the presupposition of an evolving truth, which in turn is usually approached through a dialectical process.

1.5. Perennial Philosophy or Logos Spermatikos: Truth as the Minimum Common Denominator or the Acknowledgment of Partial Truths

The affirmation that one worldview is true does not imply the affirmation that everything in the alternative worldviews is wrong. Obviously, it also does not imply that the development of this worldview in history is free from errors, deviations, and problems, due to historical contingencies and the "human factor".

---

20. *Rushdoony, R.J. (1971). The One and the Many: Studies in the Philosophy of Order and Ultimacy. Chalcedon/Ross House Books, p. 12.*

However, there is a big difference between saying that truth is the lowest common denominator found in all religious or mystical worldviews (Perennialism) or that they all share some degree of truth but only one of them is true as such.

The first position is, again, one of the horns of the old dialectical tension between *the One and the Many*, the other being Relativism:

Relativism (the Many) implicitly states that all worldviews are ultimately false because truth does not exist as it is usually understood, being definable by each person, community or culture. Perennialism or Traditionalism (the One), on the other hand, states that all traditional worldviews are true, but only when their particularities that make them unique are discarded as superfluous additions to the basic doctrines that they all share in common.

However, through a generalist *"spiritual/mystical/esoteric but not religious"* position such as the latter, and by only looking after vague commonalities between worldviews, we cannot but arrive at an impoverished and fuzzy notion of a God-in-general. This notion of God, in turn, usually takes the form of Panentheism, with whom no personal relation can be established. This, probably, is why even René Guénon, one of the founders of Traditionalism, insisted so much on the necessity of involving ourselves in the whole life (both exoteric and esoteric) of our chosen tradition instead of dabbling in the generalities that all compatible worldviews share in common.[21]

---

21. *Dickson, William Rory. Handbook of Islamic Sects and Movements. Chapter 25: René Guénon and Traditionalism. Brill, pp. 589–611:*

"During his years in Egypt Guénon's sense of the importance of having an orthodox religious form within which to practice the esoteric path crystalised. He would eventually conclude that authentic initiation is always an integral part of a complete religious tradition, with its doctrines, rituals and rules all collectively forming a living, organic whole. To isolate one aspect of a religious tradition from others, or to mix elements of different traditions, was to destroy this organic coherence and the providential power it transmitted. This was precisely what he accused Theosophy of, and why he considered it to be a counter-initiatory tradition. In his Initiation et réalisation spirituelle (1952), Guénon concisely articulates the Traditionalist position

A Both/And understanding of the problem, in contrast, would note that there is only one truth (as truth, by definition, cannot be multiple), while acknowledging that many worldviews share a part of this truth. It would acknowledge the "shards of truth" found everywhere while offering the rest in order to restore the whole picture, recontextualizing specific doctrines where needed, and without the need to sugarcoat the fact that some worldviews may be closer to the truth than others.

This is the position of Orthodox Christianity, most famously found in the writings of St. Justin Martyr.

"[...] For all writers through the implanted seed of the logos which was engrafted in them, were able to see the truth darkly, for the seed and imitation of a thing which is given according to the capacity of him who receives it is one thing, and quite a different one is the thing itself of which the communication and the imitation are received according to the grace from God ...for whatever either lawgivers of philosophers uttered well, they elaborated by finding and contemplating some part of the Logos. But since they did not know the entire Logos, which is Christ, they often contradicted themselves... Christ... was and is the logos who is in every man."

— St. Justin Martyr. The Second Apology. Para. 10.

a. Logos Spermatikos: The Christian Meaning of the "Divine Sparks"

St. Justin, clarifying the role of reason within Christianity[22], noted that *"in every man there is a divine particle, his reason, which at least*

---

on the necessity of following a particular religious form: "Whoever makes himself out to be a spiritual teacher without attaching himself to a specific traditional form, or without conforming to the rules established by the latter, cannot truly possess the qualifications he appropriates to himself" (Guénon 2004 [1952]: 110). [...]"

22. Contrary to some common misconceptions, original patristic Christianity is not anti-intellectual. To the contrary, a good theological understanding of the notion of Jesus Christ as the Logos (meaning the Word, but also Reason) and His Logoi (the

before Christ's coming was man's best guide in life." [23] It is, then, man's prerogative to live in accordance with reason, instead of against or without it. The possibility of doing this already points towards Christ, the principle of Reason that, as we saw when sketching the *Transcendental Argument for the Existence of God*, cannot be explained by purely materialist axiomatic presuppositions.

This implies that living in accord with the right reason is at the same time participating in Divine Reason (the Logos). Therefore, participation in God is not seen as exclusive to Christians but applies to all persons, irrespective of their faith. As St. Justin clearly stated:

"We have been taught that Christ is the first-born of God, and we have declared above that He is the Word of whom every race of men were partakers; and those who lived reasonably are Christians, even though they have been thought atheists; as, among the Greeks, Socrates and Heraclitus, and men like them."

— St. Justin Martyr. The First Apology.
Chapter 46: the Word in the world before Christ.

St. Justin took the Stoic pantheistic concept of Logos Spermatikos (σπερματικὸς λόγος) and adapted its meaning to the Christian Trinitarian revelation. These divine sparks in men (Logoi Spermatokoi) became, then, not part of the same substance (Homoousios) of an impersonal Logos as in Stoicism, but shared on God´s divinity or Uncreated Energies (Homoiousious). Interpenetration instead of fusion; *The One and the Many* instead of the One; "You are like God" instead of "You are God" (imago Dei, εἰκόν᾽ θεοῦ [Genesis 1:26, 27]).

---

individual words or reasons behind everything in existence), shows how it emphasizes the judicious use of reason without giving it the absolute primacy over revelation as the philosophers did, which can lead to error, as reason alone is insufficient to provide knowledge about higher levels of existence.

23. Goodenough, Erwin R. (2022). The Theology of Justin Martyr. Legare Street Press, p. 214 (citing Ap. II 10.8).

These, according to St. Justin, would be the "seeds of truth" or "seeds of reason" that allow us to perceive the reason (Logoi) behind everything in creation, which the Logos conceived in Himself and willed into existence, declaring it to be good (Genesis 1:31).

Therefore, these sparks of reason provide a common, non-confessional ground and a theological basis by which each one of us, irrespective of faith, is called to participate in God's Reason or Logos, out of which he can get closer to truth and be capable of judging right and wrong.

2. The Possibility of Starting a Global False Dialectical Revolution

The possibility of equating truth with unity, using the possible fracture caused by Phyletism as the opposite point from which to start the pendulum swing that would lead to a perennialist form of Ecumenism, is not the only dialectical danger of which there are some signs.

Since the advent of modern mass communication technologies, they have been used predominantly to indoctrinate and steer society in certain specific directions that are not beneficial for the average person.

By uniting the pervasiveness of globalization to the age-old problem (for the rest of us) of the consolidation of power in a few hands passed down from generation to generation, never in human history has the possibility of engaging in widespread worldview manipulation been so achievable.

This is something we can see on a daily basis without the need for deep philosophical discussions, as mass media, governments, and supranational entities that nobody voted for routinely engage in creating artificial dialectical battles between all kinds of demographics in order to pit them against each other and weaken any sense of togetherness and cohesion. Rich and poor, old and young, man and woman, vaccinated and unvaccinated, and any other imaginable distinction is painted as an opposition.

At the same time, the other horn of the dialectic bombards us with constant messages of equanimity, forced integration, or simply a disorderly and homogeneous fusion of sometimes profoundly incompatible ways of life.

Given these clear signs that we are unwilling participants in a dialectical process, and knowing that these processes always end in presenting a solution (Antithesis) to a problem (Thesis) in order to achieve a solution (Synthesis) that starts a new cycle, it may be worth briefly sketching the deeper beliefs of the main modern exponent of dialectical thought, G.W.F. Hegel.

2.1. Hegel´s Old God

One of the most influential figures regarding the study of the dialectical process was the philosopher Georg Wilhelm Friedrich Hegel. He placed a greater emphasis on this process than almost anyone else, conceiving its unfolding in history as the development of the life of the Spirit, or God in the process of knowing Himself. In a way, Hegel saw dialectics as an intrinsic part of God.

Later, Hegel's worldview, itself influenced by Hermeticism, became influential in many circles, including Freemasonry.[24]

The God of Hegel, even when he used a Christian language, had a very different character from the Tri-Une God of the Christian Trinity. Instead of a transcendent God, Hegel´s Spirit is a God who, similar to Hindu worldviews and their concept of Divine Play (Līlā), has forgotten Itself in order to return to Itself:

"The development of Mind lies in the fact that its going forth and separation constitutes its coming to itself. This being-at-home-with-self, or coming-to-self of Mind may be described as its complete and highest end; it is this alone that it desires and nothing else. Everything

---

24. Alexander Magee, Glenn. (2000). Hegel and the Hermetic Tradition. Cornell University Press.

*that from eternity has happened in heaven and earth, the life of God
and all the deeds of time simply are the struggles for Mind to know
itself, to make itself objective to itself, to find itself, be for itself, and
finally unite itself to itself; it is alienated and divided, but only so as to
be able thus to find itself and return to itself. Only in this manner does
Mind attain its freedom, for that is free which is not connected with or
dependent on another."* [25]

The life of God, then, is the evolutionary working out through reason
of the totality of its internal Either/Or contradictions, which are always
conceived as antagonic but implying each other and leading to a new
cycle of oppositions through a synthesis.

However, Hegel believed in a progressive evolution of truth, with
truth being more than the final result: *"The truth is the whole"*, with the
final result being *"the Absolute"*. Furthermore, *"it is the very nature of
understanding to be a process; and being a process it is Rationality."* [26]

The importance of reason for Hegel cannot be overstated, as through
its use man can reach the knowledge of his autonomy and discover
that Mind is both subject and object, a common doctrine that we have
repeatedly seen in panentheistic and non-dual worldviews:

*"[...] Reason is the Sovereign of the World." Moreover, "man is an
object of existence in himself only in virtue of the Divine that is in him
— that which was designated at the outset as Reason; which, in view
of its activity and power of self-determination, was called Freedom.
Spirit, Mind, Reason, and Freedom are closely identified."* [27]

But even if it was seen as important, Hegel conceived reason as just
a stage through which man can attain his final goal: his perception of

---

25. *Rushdoony, R.J. (1971). The One and the Many: Studies in the Philosophy of
Order and Ultimacy. Chalcedon/Ross House Books, p. 195.*

26. *Hegel, G.W.F. The Phenomenology of the Spirit. Dover Publications Inc.
Preface, Φ 55.*

27. *Rushdoony, R.J. (1971). The One and the Many: Studies in the Philosophy of
Order and Ultimacy. Chalcedon/Ross House Books, p. 196.*

self-consciousness as a self-contained existence. *"I am I in the sense that the I which is object for me is sole and only object, is all reality and all that is present."* [28]

It is not altogether strange, therefore, that, Hegel viewed the God of Scripture as a *"jealous God"*, even if he ascribed Him to Judaism, and *"as the negation of the Individual."* [29]

a. The State as the Perfect Embodiment of Spirit

Hegel was explicit in that, for him, *"the State is the Divine Idea as it exists on Earth"*. The reason for this apparently inflated importance is that, through the state as the secular and immanent One, modern and humanistic man has declared his progressive independence from God. He viewed it, then, as another stage of man´s declaration of freedom.

2.2. The Signs of the Times: Metaphysical Trends and the Danger of a Pendulum Swing

Given what we have seen so far, the historical precedents, the agglutination of all media power in a few hands, and the obvious signs that we are currently immersed in a constant dialectical process in which the pendulum swings from one extreme to the other from time to time in order to advance along a spiraling path that is always similar but never the same, the idea that this process is not a spontaneous, but a directed one, is not to be prematurely dismissed.

The history of the twentieth century, as Nietzsche predicted, is that of the advent of Nihilism, the inescapable consequence of a materialistic, mechanistic, and reductionist worldview, itself the consequence of turning the scientific method into the ideology of Scientism and of "killing God".

------

28. Hegel, G.W.F. (1807). *Phenomenology of the Spirit. Dover Publications Inc.*, p. 273.

29. Hegel, G.W.F. (1901). *Philosophy of History. Trans. J. Sibree, P. F. Collier & Son*, p. 181.

This worldview was relentlessly transmitted with great confidence by Western media during the second half of the twentieth century, especially in its last decades, in accord with school and university curricula. The reign of matter, of the Many, in turn created a society of atomized individuals, without any underlying common reality that could unite them.

Figure 3. Choose Your Poison. In a dialectical paradigm, the apparent solution being offered to a certain problem may not be in the best interest of those who chose it. This fact, however, may be intentionally designed to be difficult to see. In these situations, it is helpful to abstract ourselves from the urgency and emotionality of the situation at hand and ask ourselves: are we freely choosing the proposed solution after careful consideration of all the alternatives or are there signs that it has been intentionally sold to us as the only and urgent escape from a problem that seems forced or intentionally caused?

In recent years, however, the pendulum has swung towards unity, towards the One, and towards a diffuse spirituality.

If promoting the One was the ultimate goal to be achieved by some interested party, from a dialectical point of view the sequence of events could not have been better, since the prior predominance of a materialistic and individualistic worldview (the Many), fostered by an Atheism supported by Scientism, was the necessary prerequisite.

Suddenly, the music industry abounds with overtly satanic symbolism, understood as an ideology of selfishness (e.g., LaVeyan Satanism); governments plunder and hinder the lives of their citizens for their own benefit while new senseless and restrictive laws are constantly being passed; the scandals of politicians, monarchies and powerful personalities are aired in the same media that they own through investment funds and that previously concealed them; leading dissident media figures explain that we live caged in a prison world, where the illegitimate masters of us all must, once and for all, be expelled from their position of privilege. The same dissidents who for many years have been allowed to convey their message of rebellion against the supposed masters of the world, with minor legal problems that never prevent them from continuing to transmit their message.

There is a pre-revolutionary spirit in the air, especially since COVID-19, a global event that acted as a catalyst. Calls for revolution and awakening come from different places, some of them unimaginable only a few years before. We are all one, they say. In fact, in the end, we are all God, is repeated as the spiritual mantra of the emerging revolution.

At the same time, metaphysical concepts such as the Multiverse, which, as we have seen in this book, are strictly related to the doctrines of God understood as the Absolute, suddenly acquire a predominant place in all kinds of science fiction, as well as being seriously explored in scientific circles.

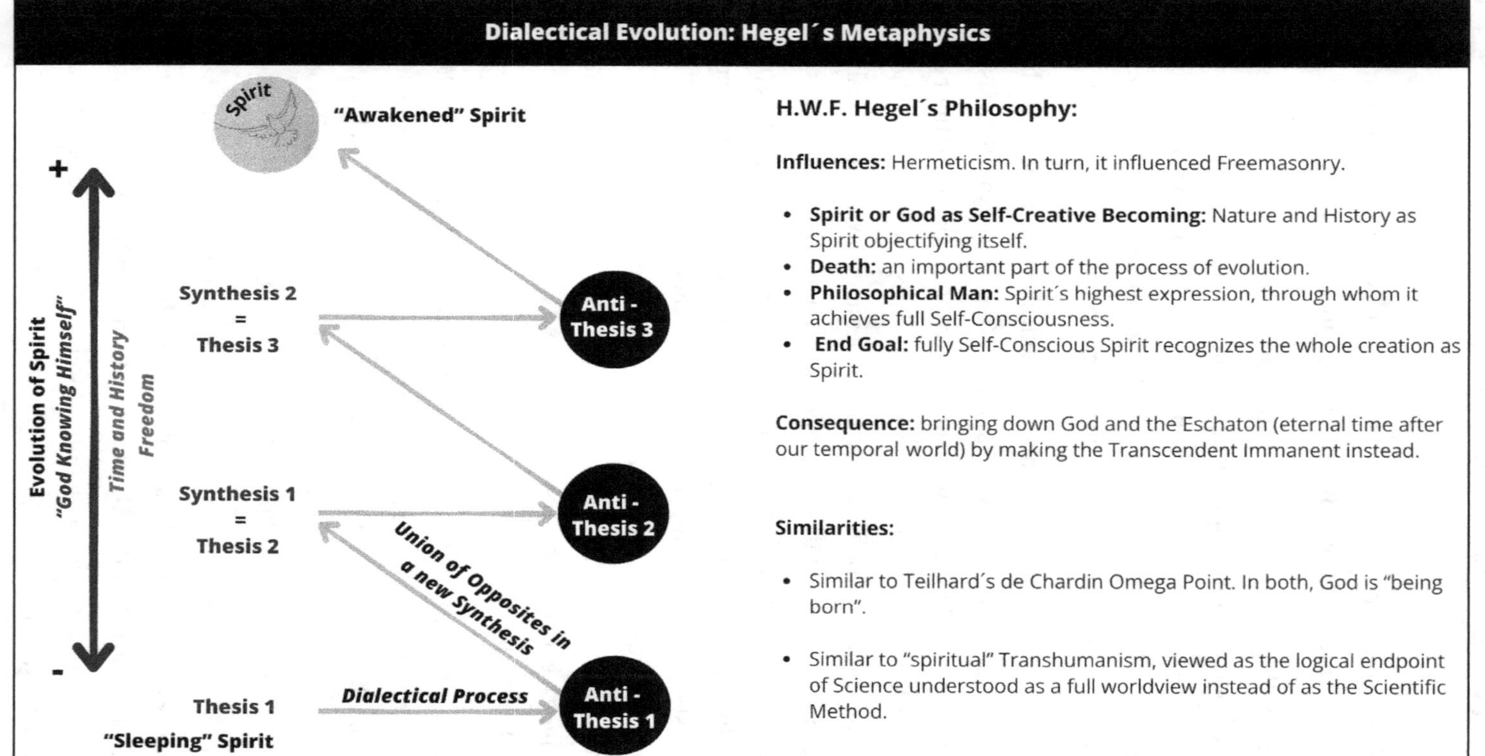

Figures 4 and 5. Hegel´s evolution of the Spirit through the process of dialectics. Note: even though Hegel thought in triads, it was Fichte who spoke of the concepts of thesis, antithesis, and synthesis, contrary to many modern popularizations.

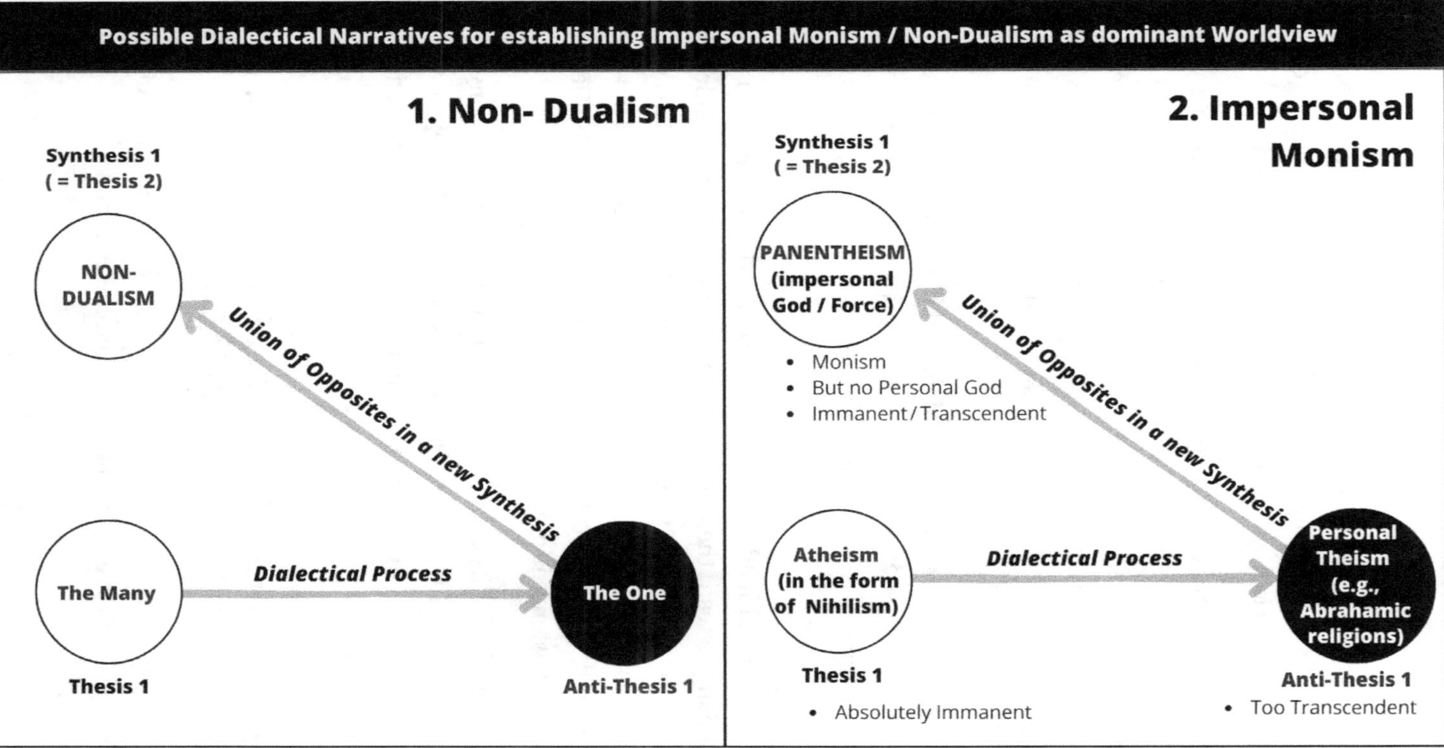

Possible Dialectical Narratives for establishing Impersonal Monism / Non-Dualism as dominant Worldview

1. Non- Dualism
2. Impersonal Monism

Synthesis 1
(= Thesis 2)

NON-DUALISM

Union of Opposites in a new Synthesis

The Many

Dialectical Process

The One

Thesis 1

Anti-Thesis 1

Synthesis 1
(= Thesis 2)

PANENTHEISM
(impersonal God / Force)

Monism
But no Personal God
Immanent / Transcendent

Union of Opposites in a new Synthesis

Atheism
(in the form of Nihilism)

Dialectical Process

Personal Theism
(e.g., Abrahamic religions)

Thesis 1

Anti-Thesis 1

Absolutely Immanent

Too Transcendent

Everything, for some time now, has been pointing towards the One. And, if we are not reading the signs incorrectly, a Manichean revolution of good versus evil may be brewing in the Western world.

In fact, we are only a major crisis away from being in an optimal position that would allow us to dialectically dispose of both Atheism (and its resulting Nihilism, selfishness, and atomization of society) at the same time that we eliminate theistic religions (with their neverending geopolitical problems), adopting, in turn, a spiritual but impersonal (deistic, probably panentheistic) notion of God.

Dialectics, however, is a flexible tool. Using it, we could even end up rejecting Panentheism in a following cycle of oppositions, thus simultaneously rejecting both *the One and the Many* as two sides of the same coin.

This could lead to favor a non-panentheistic version of Non-Dualism instead, the notion that, as we are now, we are already the One at the same time that we are ourselves (the Many). This would be consistent with some of the negative characterizations of the One as a hive mind, which state that since Unity implies non-differentiation, our current existence is preferable.

Regardless of its flexibility, the common denominator in any possible dialectical worldview steering process would be the rejection of the divinity of Jesus Christ, incompatible with any other worldview other than Trinitarian Christianity.

2.3. The Voice of the Rebellion: The Message of Prominent Dissident Public Figures

Let us now look briefly at some of the most influential examples of dissident celebrities, their message, and the common pattern that they all follow.

a. Alex Jones: Or How to Kickstart the Revolution Against Our Gnostic Overlords

Alex Jones is one of the most famous and prolific anti-establishment public figures. Host of the *Alex Jones Show* and founder of the *InfoWars* brand and website (reported to have revenues of over $20 million a year[30]). Also, producer of many documentaries denouncing a hidden agenda leading to world tyranny (e.g., *Endgame: Blueprint for Global Enslavement*).

Although Jones' content focuses mainly on the conspiracies that, in his opinion, underlie the current trend towards a technocratic tyranny and the way in which a future dystopia is expected to be implemented, what interests us in this book is not the things he denounces but the solutions he proposes.

In common with all modern anti-establishment figures denouncing the current and future situation, his message contains two parts: an analysis of the problem and the proposed solution.

This solution, in turn, always starts from a re-conceptualization of the world in which we live in, eventually leading to a spiritual, though not necessarily religious, worldview. This worldview is, in turn, the dialectical opposite of the dominant Western worldview, and thus viewers are encouraged to abandon their previous selfish notions in order to awaken to the spiritual truth that underlies reality.

The basic template is always a Gnostic narrative: this planet is a prison (Jones is the founder of *PrisonPlanet TV*), the playground of evil entities that feed on us (Gnostic Archons or rulers in the service of the Demiurge or false God); reality is not what we think it is, being illusory in one way or another; however, humanity has had enough, and has reached a point

---

30. *Williamson, Elizabeth; Steel, Emily (September 7, 2018). "Conspiracy Theories Made Alex Jones Very Rich. They May Bring Him Down". The New York Times.*

of spiritual maturity sufficient to awaken to the truth and discover who they truly are (Gnosis) in a spiritual sense; which is the prerequisite for joining the ranks of the incipient revolution of good against evil and to overthrow our tyrants; the underlying Essence preceding both good and evil is the same; however, evil has illegitimately conspired to use that Essence against what ought to be; there is doom today, and there will be doom tomorrow until we break free.

This overall template Jones fulfills when he states, for example, that *"There is a war of good and evil going on, and people are done with globalism"*[31], that *"[...] we are **It**, we are God"* (in Joe Rogan´s show, E1255; emphasis added), or when he participates in movies promoting a New Age worldview such as *Waking Life* (2001).

b. David Icke: Or How to Slay the Dragon by Becoming Who We Are

David Vaughan Icke, probably the most popular dissident public figure after Alex Jones, has written over twenty books and spoken in more than twenty five countries.[32]

His message, unsurprisingly, also perfectly conforms to the same Gnostic template just mentioned, as is the case with all mainstream dissident (a contradiction in terms) figures. All of them also follow the same Problem-Reaction-Solution dialectic that they denounce.

The Problem: Prison Planet

• **Claim:** Icke states that there are inter-dimensional beings (of reptilian nature, using the ancient symbol of the serpent or dragon as

---

31. *Cheng, Amy. Far right called U.S. 'Stonehenge' satanic — and cheered when it blew up. The Washington Post. Retrieved July 7, 2022.*

32. *Lewis, Tyson E.; Kahn, Richard (2010). Education Out of Bounds: Reimagining Cultural Studies for a Posthuman Age. Palgrave Macmillan, p. 75.*

evil), the Archons (a Gnostic term) or Anunnaki, which govern our planet in the shadows. Those Archons feed on the "negative energy" resulting from our suffering.[33, 34, 35]

- **Book:** *Children of the Matrix.*

The Reaction: Rebellion Against Unjust Rulers.

- **Claim:** this world´s "elite" share a hybrid genetic line with those entities (playing with the theme of the Nephilim in the apocryphal book of *Enoch*) and have an agenda to lead mankind towards a tyrannical globalist unified State.

- **Book:** *Human Race Get Off Your Knees: The Lion Sleeps No More.*

The Solution: Internal Gnosis as Liberation.

- **Claim:** the only way to overthrow the Archons is for people to wake up (Awakening) to the truth (Gnosis) and fill their hearts with love (the unifying principle [the One], contrary to the atomizing power of selfishness [the Many]).[36]

He also asserts a generalist panentheistic worldview when he states, for example, that *"we are reflections of one another, therefore I know that you are part of me and I am part of you because we are all projections of the universal principles of creation/destruction polarities of the same infinite consciousness that we call God".*[37]

- **Books:** *Phantom Self (And How to Find the Real One); The Dream: The Extraordinary Revelation Of Who We Are And Where We Are.*

---

33. Ward, James (2014). "Mocked prophet: what is David Icke's appeal?". *New Humanist.*

34. Icke, David (1999). *The Biggest Secret. Bridge of Love Publications USA.*

35. Lynskey, Dorian (2014). "Psycho lizards from Saturn: The godlike genius of David Icke!". *New Statesman.*

36. Ward, James (2014). "Mocked prophet: what is David Icke's appeal?". *New Humanist.*

37. Icke, David. *And the Truth Shall Set You Free. Truth Seeker, Ch. 19.*

c. Salvador Freixedo: Or Mankind as Food for the Gods

Salvador Freixedo was an ex-Catholic priest (Jesuit order) who became an ufologist and parapsychologist, identifying UFOs with the archontic or demonic "gods" that rule over us.

He became a public figure who achieved notoriety, especially in Spanish-speaking countries. In a way, he was a precursor of modern dissidents, since he began spreading the same overall message in the 1970´s.

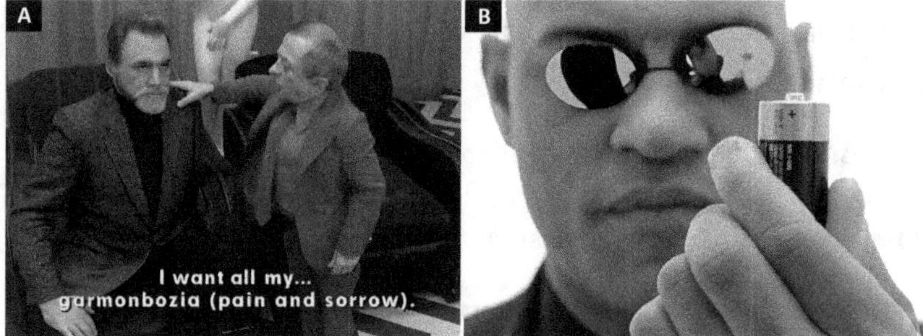

Figure 6. **A:** *Freixedo´s main message, how our evil archontic overlords feed on human suffering, has been a central theme of popular culture for decades. Picture: Twin Peaks; Lynch/Frost Productions.* **B:** *a variety of the same message can be seen in The Matrix (Warner Bros.), where humans are resources to be harvested. This franchise has been extremely influential in shaping modern popular conscience, introducing into common parlance terms now routinely used in dissident circles (e.g., Red Pill/Blue Pill).*

One only has to look at the titles of some of his most popular books to clearly discern the aforementioned Gnostic template. For example: *The Human Farm: They, the Invisible Owners of this Planet, Defending Ourselves from the Gods!,* or *The Religions that Divide Us.*

Like Marcionism, one of the first Christian Gnostic heresies, Freixedo opposed the God of the *Old Testament,* whom he considered a false archontic god, to that of the *New Testament.*

d. Mark Passio: The Allure of Absolute Personal Freedom

Mark Passio is, compared to the other dissident figures previously mentioned, a relatively recent addition. He is an anarchist, author, filmmaker, content creator, and freedom activist.

He is also a self-confessed ex-satanic priest, an experience which he claimed opened his eyes. He is the founder of *WhatOnEarthIsHappening.com* and *One Great Work Network*.

He now teaches metaphysics, occultism, spirituality, symbology, and consciousness studies (with a Kabbalistic-Hermetic emphasis), while he denounces the tyrannical dystopia towards where we are headed.

He describes the ruling "elites" as expert psychologists and "black magicians" who illegitimately use their metaphysical knowledge to enslave rather than to liberate.

He is especially known for his courses on Natural Law, which he claims our rulers violate thanks to our involuntary collaboration, and how it is our revolutionary duty to wake up and reclaim our freedom, becoming the "white magicians" that are (dialectically) needed to overthrow them.

His teachings, while presenting the novelty of promoting Anarcho-Capitalism, fit perfectly into the Gnostic narrative, in his case emphasizing the dialectical tension between white and black magicians harnessing the same impersonal Force for opposite ends, just as the Theosophist Alice Bailey did.[38]

2.4. *"An Angrier World"* [39]

Conspiracy theorists, once ridiculed, now see how some of their theories have either become true[40] or are at least not totally beyond the realm of possibility. Furthermore, the likelihood that we are moving towards a global technological dystopia between the worlds of George Orwell´s *1984* and Aldous Huxley´s *Brave New World* is becoming increasingly plausible with each passing day.

---

38. *Bailey, Alice A. (1951). A Treatise on White Magic. Lucis Press Ltd.*

39. *A concept recently popularized by Klaus Schwab, one of those unelected rulers whose words and actions seem to point to a future dystopia (e.g., his books: "The Fourth Industrial Revolution", "COVID-19: The Great Reset"; "WEF founder: Must prepare for an angrier world"; CNBC International News, 14 Jul 2020).*

40. *Still, William T. (1996). The Money Masters (documentary film).*

This has brought many people to a state of mind where they are willing to reevaluate their previous worldview and are open to accepting doctrines that they would not have previously considered.

However, given the two opposite horns present in every dialectical process, there are also legitimate concerns regarding mainstream dissident movements.

The previous examples of global dissident public figures may be some of the most influential today, but they are only a small sample of the many that, especially after 9/11 and the whole COVID-19 situation, promote a Gnostic/Manichean light versus darkness narrative, calling for awakening (Gnosis) and to prepare for a revolution that is both material and spiritual in nature.

Figure 7. Synchronicity of a Revolution Foretold. Trumpets of revolution are heard on the horizon. Old ghosts of the past haunt many nations in a growing globalized crisis that, curiously enough, is precipitating everywhere at the same time, leading many to suspect that it may be a pre-fabricated phenomenon. Picture: French Revolution; "The Tennis Court Oath" (1789), by Jacques-Louis David.

Many of these leaders, as we have seen, follow the pattern of being ex-members of the groups they denounce, which gives them increased credibility (e.g., both Freixedo and Passio denounced Roman Catholicism and Satanism, respectively, after leaving their order/cult).[41]

Groups promoting this worldview can also be found inside religious circles, sometimes linking the new "Great Awakening" to the previous ones in American Protestant history.

The repeated use of the same terminology, concepts, and narratives has been notorious enough that it has led some vigilant believers to suspect that there may be some hidden agenda.[42]

The constant that can always be found in the message put forth by all these dissidents, regardless of their particular idiosyncrasies, is the underlying Gnostic pattern and the dialectical structure of the arguments presented.

In many cases, a panentheist worldview close to Eastern Mysticism or Western Esotericism is promoted, but even in the case of Christian dissidents, the concept of awakening is prevalent, which is part of "Christian" Gnosticism but has no place in Christianity. At this point, it is worth remembering that Gnosticism was not a mere early Christian heresy but an inversion, abandoning the Tri-Une God in order to go back to the One.

The overall message being transmitted could be summarized as "the battle of the Ones", or of the real spiritual One ("we are all One", "there is only One") against the illegitimate or secular One (the One World Government or New World Order) that only benefits the predatory "elites" and their hungry archontic masters, lower level spiritual entities that feed on instinct and that basically represent our egotism and basest attributes, caring only for themselves (the Many).

---

41. *Similar to how the, also ex-Jesuit, Teilhard de Chardin created an evolutionary dialectical philosophy close to that of Hegel. Teilhard viewed God (the Omega Point) as the Absolute, his philosophy later becoming one of the main influences of the more "spiritual" branch of Transhumanism.*

42. *Blanchette, John. E511 Ministries (rumble.com/user/E511Ministries). Accessed 10 December of 2023.*

2.5. The Flexibility of Dialectical Process Manipulation and Negative Priming

Some people think that conspiracies cannot exist in the modern world, and that the fact that the most popular dissidents, as we saw before, mix plausible ideas with others that seem too far out there is proof enough of that.

Others, however, offer an alternative interpretation. For some, the mixing of plausible and what are seemingly senseless ideas is an intentional strategy to associate the plausible ones with the feeling of repulsion and incredulity that the wild ones elicit. In this way, people are negatively primed (a psychological term that we can roughly translate as "conditioned") in order to never believe the true doctrines due to their association with the foolish ones.

But dialectics is a versatile process that can always be given one more twist. It is not difficult to see that, if there is a dialectical process of worldview manipulation going on, it could at least take another turn.

If all mainstream current dissidence were to be exposed as controlled or false opposition, the rejection of their message would imply the automatic acceptance of their negatively primed metaphysical doctrines (e.g., a Gnostic worldview), therefore becoming an indirect way of promoting it.

Not everything is doom and gloom, however, as the good thing about dialectics is that since it operates under a paradigm of paired oppositions, predictions can be made, similar to how predicting the next move in a game of chess works. In this way, even if we don't know the endgame, we may be able to discern if we are living "inside" a dialectical process.

This, in turn, would be a signal not to prepare for worldly Armageddon (even if there is nothing intrinsically wrong with preparing for any eventuality), but to redouble our efforts in working out our own salvation (Philippians, 2:12). If the underlying conflict is a spiritual one, the solution will also be necessarily spiritual, with smaller steps in trying to purify ourselves and live closer to God being more beneficial for us than greater labours focused on fruitless theorizing about a process on which we have no control.

Figure 8. Leading the Revolt Against Your Own House. The media that used to defend and hide the abuses of the powerful begin to question and attack them in a coordinated manner. However, these media are still owned by the mega-corporations and funds of the latter, fueling suspicions about their real intentions.

2.6. Eschatological Conflict

One interesting fact to know, even if we expect to never be able to put this knowledge to good use in our lifetime, is that the different eschatologies (end-of-the-world scenarios) of the major religions are often in conflict with each other. By this we mean, for example, that Judaism does not (currently) have a type of Anti-Christ in its prophecies, a figure that is expected to come before the Messiah (Mashiach) in order to lead mankind astray, while Islam and Christianity do.

Therefore, if there was someone interested in pitting major religions against each other in order to generate a worldwide rejection of their validity as dominant worldviews, be it Dharmic religions against Abrahamic ones, or just every one of them against each other, they could take advantage of the latent conflict present in their eschatological prophecies.

For example, a high-level but not very well-known (because of the prohibition to read the text before being specifically initiated in it) Tibetan Buddhist Tantra, the Kālachakra Tantra (9th century) contains passages discussing Islam in negative terms and prophesying an explicit all-out war between the Dharma and the Islamic world.

The Kālachakra Tantra refers to Islam as a religion of violence (himsa-dharma) that advocates savage behavior (raudra-karman), and prophesizes that it will be eradicated by "the Chakravartin" (Universal Ruler) once he appears at the end of the age.[43]

ESCHATOLOGICAL CONFLICT BETWEEN THE END-OF-THE-WORLD SCENARIOS OF MAJOR RELIGIONS:

https://themetaphysicalcompass.com/Eschatology

In John R. Newman´s words, a professor and historian of religions specialized in Indian and Tibetan Buddhism:

"We may summarize the Kalacakra tantra's perception of Islamic beliefs and practices as follows: from the Buddhist point of view Islam is demonic and perverse, a perfect anti-religion which is the antithesis of Buddhism". [44]

---

43. *Shri Kalachakra I. p. 161.*
44. *John Newman, "Islam in the Kālacakra Tantra", Journal of the International Association of Buddhist Studies, Vol. 21, No. 2, 1998.*

3. An Invitation: Seeking Spiritual Solutions to Spiritual Problems

As a farewell message to the last chapter of this book and, indeed, as a general summary of *The Metaphysical Compass Project*, the author would like to humbly make a few final remarks:

• In times of crisis and conflict, a solution that aims to achieve indiscriminate unity may seem (or even be) good in that precise moment, but not necessarily represent the truth or be a good long term solution. It is important to be vigilant about the presuppositions and implications that any such solution entails for our view of the world.

• The metaphysical pieces that would be needed for a future mass initiation are already being put in place through mass media and popular culture. Presumably, it would only take a global crisis that involves the "death and resurrection" of modern society to weave them together and create a new dominant worldview.

This worldview could be an old one (e.g., Panentheism/Non-Dualism) or a completely new one that we still do not know about. Whatever the case may be, the assertion that Jesus Christ was the Incarnation of God as revealed in the Scriptures will probably be incompatible with any of them.

It will also be in all probability incompatible with the both One and Many non-dialectical solution offered by the Trinitarian God of Christianity, best preserved, despite all obstacles, in Orthodox Christian theology.

• If we believe that there are signs that we are heading towards an engineered spiritual crisis, the most logical response is, regardless of whether we prepare otherwise or not, to prioritize our spiritual health and that of our loved ones.

It is not fruitful to engage in deep theoretical analysis alone, which easily makes us feel smarter while leaving us in the same spiritual place. If there are "hidden hands" steering history, there is ultimately a spiritual component in them and, in that case, it is very unlikely that we will be always able to outsmart them.[45] As we have seen, an extra twist can always be given to any dialectical narrative.

Even though books can be illuminating intermediate steps, the logical response in such a scenario is to understand what it means to lead a spiritual life and act accordingly. To do this, we do not have to become experts in geopolitics, we just have to remain vigilant and work to get closer to God.

In addition, if the reader's path leads him, like it led the author of this book, to be interested in Orthodox Christianity, the first step to "act accordingly" would be to contact a local priest, who will be the person best positioned to answer any doubts that they may have, both theological and about the practical aspects of the Christian spiritual life. In all probability, especially if the talk happens after Liturgy and the priest is nice, he will also share some food.

In any case, we hope that this work will enable the reader to better understand and unravel the key metaphysical presuppositions of any present or future worldview, which will invariably be defined by its stance on the problem of *the One and the Many* and the solution, dialectical or not, given to it. We also hope that the knowledge acquired about symbolism and dialectical processes applied to the governance of society will enable the reader to interpret contemporary events from a deeper perspective, helping them to better understand their underlying narratives.

Recommended Reading

1. **Orthodoxy and the Religion of the Future.** *Fr. Seraphim Rose.*
2. **Orthodoxy and the Kingdom of Satan.** *Fr. Spyridon Bailey.*
3. **The Coming Pendulum Swing (video series).** *John Blanchette.*[46]

---

45. *"The psychological trials of dwellers in the last times will be equal to the physical trials of the martyrs. In order to face these trials we must be living in a different world."* — Rose, Fr. Seraphim (Hieromonk).

46. *Whether or not we agree with all his conclusions, there is no doubt that Blanchette's extensive video documentation offers an interesting and provocative vision of the growing global politico-spiritual tension and how behind it can be found an obvious polarizing intention that seems to be using a weaponized dialectical process, especially on North American soil. Blanchette´s video channel: https://rumble.com/user/E511Ministries.*

The Deity of Becoming:

What Does the Ouroboros

Try to Teach Us?

The Ouroboros

Circularity, Complementarity and Absolute Oneness

THE ANCIENT SYMBOL OF THE OUROBOROS (OR UROBOROS) depicts a serpent or a dragon eating its own tail. Its origins are found first and foremost in ancient Egypt[1] (around the thirteenth or fourteenth centuries BCE), but was later incorporated by the Greek magical traditions (from where the term οὐροβόρος derives[2]) and the Roman world.[3]

---

1. The Ouroboros was popular after the Amarna period. It was found, for example, in the Book of the Dead, still current in the Graeco-Roman period.

2. Liddell, Henry George; Scott, Robert (1940). Οὐροβόρος. A Greek-English Lexicon. Oxford: Clarendon Press.

3. In Roman times, it could be frequently found on magical protective talismans or amulets, serving as a barrier or boundary that was believed to separate us, created beings, from the ocean of undifferentiated pre-existence or Chaos, thus preserving our individuality from the impersonal homogeneity of the source of it

Speaking of its historical origins is, however, relative, as this ubiquitous symbol can be found in many different cultures across time[4], as we will see. It is, however, most strongly associated with its use in Gnosticism and Hermeticism, especially in Alchemical texts.

Figure 1. Scene of the Book of the Dead. Harpocrates or Horus (child form) is depicted within the Sun disc, resting upon the Aker lions and surrounded by an Ouroboros. Thoth and Herwebenkhet are on the right. The papyrus contains a set of spells intended as guidance for the latter to pass through the underworld. Picture: Heruben papyrus, XXI dynasty; Cairo Museum.

2. What Does the Ouroboros Symbolize?

The Ouroboros, like most metaphysical and esoteric symbols, can have multiple layers of meaning and represent a constellation of related notions circling around a central theme of circularity, complementarity, self-sufficiency, and the ultimate unity of all things. It is commonly

---

all [see below: the relationship of the serpent/dragon symbolism with the notion of primordial Chaos].

4. The Ouroboros was used in, for example, ancient Egypt, Japan, India, Greek Alchemical texts, Native American tribes, by the Aztecs, and by all sorts of European Alchemical and magical-esoteric traditions. Its associations range from the Taoist Yin-Yang to the Roman god Janus, among others.

used to symbolize the undifferentiated potential before creation, as well as the notion of continuity by implying that the end is the beginning.

It symbolizes both immanent and transcendent notions. Regarding the former, the eternal recreation of the self-consuming snake represents the circularity of existence, the perpetual co-existence of creation and destruction, which brings transformation and constitutes our universe of flux and unending change. As such, it evokes notions of indefinite existence (see the mathematical infinity symbol) and eternal recurrence (Eternal Return), being an appropriate image of the cycles of life but also of an immanent immortality based on the re-emergence of life in this plane of existence (similar to the Phoenix).

In this aspect of cyclical renewal it can represent the cycle of rebirths, with the snake's characteristic skin-sloughing symbolizing the transmigration of souls.

Figure 2. Protective Gnostic talisman. This gem displays an Ouroboros encircling a scarab beetle, which was sacred to the Egyptians due to the notions of rebirth and the cyclical nature of life associated with it.

Like the dung beetle's revolving ball, the scarab was linked to Khepri ("he who has come into being"), the god of the rising Sun. To him was attributed the ultimate self-sufficiency: the quality of self-creation, the ability to create himself out of nothing. In addition, the dung ball was seen as a symbol of the Sun in its daily journeys of birth, death, and resurrection. Picture: Baltimore Museum of Art (1947).

Regarding its transcendental aspect, the circle evokes the underlying unity of all creation, including its material and spiritual aspects, going beyond any perceived dichotomy. It implies a common source for it all, to which everything returns.

2.1. The Serpent and the Primordial Waters of Chaos

In esoteric and metaphysical teachings, snakes and dragons are associated with water, and especially with the Cosmic Ocean or the waters of creation. This recurrent theme is prevalent in most cultures, including those of ancient Mesopotamia, Vedic India[5], and Greece.[6]

The common pattern is that of a "civilizing" god or hero (a Sky God, as Mircea Eliade has shown[7]) that conquers and slays the undifferentiated Chaos (potentiality) in the form of a reptile, thus bringing into existence order, differentiation and, therefore, everything that is (actuality).

This reptile is sometimes associated with the waters and sometimes with the one keeping their potential solvent effect in check.

The latter symbolism seems to derive from the fact that the snake is able to move freely in the water while drawing shapes on its surface, thus creating differentiation and particular forms within the predominant homogeneity of the ocean.

The symbolism of light and darkness fulfills a similar function. For example, in the Egyptian *Book of the Dead*, the self-begetting Sun god Atum is said to have ascended from the waters of Chaos with the appearance of a snake, the animal renewing itself every morning. The dead, in turn, are depicted desiring to turn into the shape of a snake (Sato, "son of the earth"), the embodiment of Atum.

This is why many snake gods are also associated with the Sun or are described as gods of Light, as we will shortly see.[8]

----

5. *See, for example: Sri Aurobindo (1971). Secret of the Vedas. Sri Aurobindo Ashram.*

6. *In Greek mythology, Oceanus, or the great ocean was also represented as girding the earth.*

7. *Eliade, Mircea (1949). Patterns in Comparative Religion. Bison books.*

8. *According to Homer, Helios the Sun rises from Oceanus (East) [Iliad 7.421–422, = Odyssey 19.433–434], while at the end of the day sinks back into him (West)[Iliad 8.485, 18.239–240].*

The Sun is, then, the cyclical First Being who renews itself by undergoing a periodical return into the waters of Chaos. It is the first light that brings existence to every particular (light-bringer), the light that makes it possible for everything to be seen.

2.2. The Doctrine of the Union of Opposites

One of the main meanings of the Ouroboros is that of totality and the unity of opposites. Nowadays, the link between the Ouroboros and this metaphysical doctrine, so prevalent in popular culture, can be clearly exemplified by the psychoanalytical school of C.G. Jung and by Western Esotericism.

Regarding the former, Jung stated:

"The alchemists, who in their own way knew more about the nature of the individuation process than we moderns do, expressed this paradox through the symbol of the ouroboros, the snake that eats its own tail. In the age-old image of the ouroboros lies the thought of devouring oneself and turning oneself into a circulatory process, for it was clear to the more astute alchemists that the prima materia of the art was man himself.

The ouroboros is a dramatic symbol for the integration and assimilation of the opposite, i.e. of the shadow. *This 'feed-back' process is at the same time a symbol of immortality, since it is said of the ouroboros that he slays himself and brings himself to life, fertilizes himself and gives birth to himself. He symbolizes* the One, *who proceeds from the clash of opposites, and he therefore constitutes the secret of the prima materia which [...] unquestionably stems from man's unconscious'."*

– C.G. Jung. Collected Works. Vol. 14, para. 513.

An example of the latter is Eliphas Levi´s Seal of Solomon.[9] On it, the unity of opposites is also emphasized by showing that black and white, above and below, are just reflections of each other.

This implies complementarity (e.g., the Hermetic concept of "as above, so below") and a conception of the divine as a pre-existent totality that includes and goes beyond all apparent dichotomies (including, in most

---

9. *Lévi, Éliphas (1854). Transcendental Magic: Its Doctrine and Ritual. Weiser Books.*

cases, any perceived source of evil). This is also the origin of the notion that God is "beyond both good and evil", contrary to the belief in God as All-Good (e.g., Christianity).

Figure 3. The Seal of Solomon, frontispiece of Volume I (Dogma) of Éliphas Lévi's first book on ritual magic: "Dogma and Ritual of High Magic". This author's works were highly influential in shaping modern Western Esotericism. Note how the principal theme of the image is the union of opposites (black and white; above and below), seen as mirror images of each other, in a new totality (Ouroboros).

The importance of the notion of Complementary Dualism as a key aspect of Ouroboros symbolism is not controversial. Jean Chevalier´s and J.E. Cirlot´s *A Dictionary of Symbols*, for example, both emphasize it in their definitions of the symbol:

"Ouroboros. A snake that bites its own tail and which, enclosed within itself, symbolises a cycle of evolution. This symbol contains at the same time the ideas of movement, continuity, self-fertilisation and, consequently, of perpetual return.

The circular form of the image has given rise to another interpretation: the union of the chthonic *world, represented by the serpent, and the celestial world, represented by the circle. This interpretation is confirmed by the fact that the ouroboros, in certain representations, is half black, half white. It therefore signifies the union of two opposing principles, such as heaven and earth, good and evil, day and night, yang and yin, and all the values that these opposites carry."*

– "Ouroboros". In Jean Chevalier, Alain Gheerbrant (1986). A Dictionary of Symbols. Herder

"This symbol appears principally among the Gnostics and is depicted as a dragon, snake or serpent biting its own tail. In the broadest sense, it is symbolic of time and of the continuity of life.

It sometimes bears the caption Hen to pan—'The One, the All', as in the Codex Marcianus, for instance, of the 2nd century A.D. It has also been explained as the union between the chthonian principle as represented by the serpent and the celestial principle as signified by the bird (a synthesis which can also be applied to the dragon). Ruland contends that this proves that it is a variant of the symbol for Mercury— the duplex god. In some versions of the Ouroboros, the body is half light and half dark, alluding in this way to the successive counterbalancing of opposing principles as illustrated in the Chinese Yang-Yin symbol for instance. Evola asserts that it represents the dissolution of the body, or the universal serpent which (to quote the Gnostic saying) 'passes through all things'. Poison, the viper and the universal solvent are all symbols of the undifferentiated—of the 'unchanging law' which moves through all things, linking them by a common bond.

Both the dragon and the bull are symbolic antagonists of the solar hero. The ouroboros biting its own tail is symbolic of self-fecundation, or the primitive idea of a self-sufficient Nature—a Nature, that is, which, à la Nietzsche, continually returns, within a cyclic pattern, to its own beginning. There is a Venetian manuscript on alchemy which depicts the Ouroboros with its body half-black (symbolizing earth and night) and half-white (denoting heaven and light)."

— "Ouroboros". In J.E. Cirlot (1962). A Dictionary of Symbols. Routledge & Kegan Paul, Ltd.

Figure 4. The Ouroboros as the infinity symbol and the union of opposites in medieval Alchemy.

Note the motifs of the union of Heaven (eagle) and Earth (lion), as well as that of Sun (masculine) and Moon (feminine).

The quest to obtain Azoth was akin to that of creating the Philosopher's Stone, and was symbolized by the Hermetic Caduceus.

Picture: Basil Valentine's Azoth (1613).

To the above we add that, in some cultures, the snake biting its own tail is seen as a fertility symbol, with the tail being a phallic symbol and the mouth a yonic (womb-like) one.

The unitive nature of the Ouroboros, in summary, encompasses the union of above (Heaven) and below (Earth), male (right) and female (left), with all its accompanying associated meanings. All is One.

3. Origins and Historical Presence of the Ouroboros

a. Ancient Egypt

The first known representation of the Ouroboros was found in ancient Egypt, specifically in one of the shrines enclosing the sarcophagus of Tutankhamun. In it was found the *Enigmatic Book of the Netherworld*, which is an ancient funerary text (KV62, around fourteenth century BCE).

This text focuses on the union of Osiris with the Sun god Ra in the underworld (Ra–Osiris), in which the former is born again as the latter.

Ra is one of the most important gods in the Egyptian pantheon, representing the creator god and the god of light that brought order into primordial Chaos (Apophis).

Figure 5. The treasure found in Tutankhamun´s tomb showed scenes from the Book of the Dead conceived as an aid for the king's journey after death. The Ouroboros was one of the symbols of rebirth and circularity employed. Picture: Egyptian Museum, Cairo.

In Egyptian religion, additionally, serpentine deities were usually associated with the formless disorder that preceded creation, to which the world returns during its periodic renewal.[10]

Because of this, it is safe to assume the association of the Ouroboros with primordial Chaos or as the principle of differentiation that protects us against it. Osiris being reborn as Ra can be interpreted, then, as a panentheistic return to the One, an identification with the Source of it all.

The Ouroboros also symbolized the totality of time, a convergence of the beginning and the end by returning to the origin and final destiny of everything. This, as discussed in *Chapter II*, is common for systems of thought based on panentheistic Monism, which tend to identify all creation with the body (the energetic aspect) of the deity.[11]

b. Hermeticism and Alchemy

One of the earlier and most famous depictions of the Ouroboros was found in the Alchemical text *The Chrysopoeia of Cleopatra the Alchemist* (probably third century CE).

In it, the serpent encloses the inscription: *"The All is One"* (hen to pān, ἓν τὸ πᾶν), which is a clear declaration of the faith it symbolizes (absolute Monism in the form of Pantheism/Panentheism).

Apart from this explicit statement, its most characteristic trait is the division of the Ouroboros in white and black halves, symbolizing the Alchemical doctrine of the Union of Opposites and the overcoming of duality in a unity above and beyond both poles of any perceived dichotomy (like the Taoist Taiji symbology containing both Yin and Yang).[12]

---

10. *Hornung, Erik (1982). Conceptions of God in Egypt: The One and the Many. Cornell University Press, pp. 163–64.*

11. *Hornung, Erik (1999). The Ancient Egyptian Books of the Afterlife. Cornell University Press, pp. 38, 77–78.*

12. *Eliade, Mircea (1976). Occultism, Witchcraft, and Cultural Fashions. Chicago and London: University of Chicago Press, pp. 55, 93–113.*

Even though the symbolism is not exactly the same, many of the same meanings can also be found in the Hermetic Caduceus and the Alchemical Androgyne (Rebis). Jack Lindsay, showing the link between them, explains: [13]

"Ideas about the Ouroboros found their way into the literary world, e.g., in Artemidoros and Acrobius. The former, in his dream-book, remarks that 'the dragon also signifies Time because it is long and undulant.' The latter declares the two-headed Roman god Janus is the world:

'that is, the heavens, and his name Janus comes from eundo [by going] since the world always goes rolling on itself in its globe-form ... So the Phoenicians have represented it in their temples as a dragon curled in a circle and devouring its tail, to denote the way in which the world feeds on itself and returns on itself ...'

It is also clear that it's the Sun honored under the name of Mercurius [Hermes] according to the caduceus that the Egyptians have consecrated to the god in the figure of the Two Serpents, male and female, interlaced. Their upper extremities bend round together, and, embracing one another, form a circle, while the tails, after forming a knot, come together at the haft of the caduceus and are provided with wings that start off at this point."

Figure 6. Ouroboros encircling the inscription "the All is One" (ἕν τὸ πᾶν, hen to pān). Note the emphasis on the notions of the unity of opposites (black and white as complementary halves of a circle) and the cyclical nature of existence, shown through the characteristic skin-sloughing of the snake.

Due to the metaphysical doctrines that it evokes, the Ouroboros has always been one of the most influential symbols of impersonal Monism (Pantheism/Panentheism). Picture: the Chrysopoeia (gold-making) of Cleopatra the Alchemist.

---

13. Lindsay, Jack (1970). *The Origins of Alchemy in Græco-Roman Egypt.* The Book Service, pp.267-268.

c. Gnosticism

In Gnosticism, a serpent biting its own tail in a closed circle represented eternity and the World Soul that lives through it.[14]

The Ouroboros was described[15] as a dragon divided in twelve parts, alluding to a full cycle (e.g., the Zodiac) and representing the totality of time. This notion, in turn, seems related to the doctrine found in Basilides of the 365 heavens[16] (the number of days in a year symbolizing, again, the totality of time) emanated from the primordial god Abraxas. The dragon mentioned in the *Pistis Sophia*, in turn, is described as surrounding the world with its tail in its mouth, with this image being similar to the tail-chomping serpent mentioned in the Gnostic text known as the *Acts of the Apostle Thomas*.

Figure 7. Drawing of a Gnostic Abraxas gemstone, used as an amulet or charm and believed to have protective properties. Abraxas was the Gnostic "Great Archon", highest god, and First One containing the 365 spheres (Ouranoi) in Basilides' system. In this case, the Ouroboros predominantly depicts the notion of totality.

---

14. *Origen of Alexandria. Contra Celsum, 6.25.*

15. *Hornung, Erik (2002). The Secret Lore of Egypt: Its Impact on the West. Cornell University Press, p. 76.*

16. *St. Irenaeus of Lyon. Against Heresies, i. 24. 7; Trecentorum autem sexaginta quinque caelorum locales positiones distribuunt similiter ut mathematici.*

Later on, the Ouroboros could be found in fourteenth and fifteenth-century Albigensian-printing watermarks and in many early sets of playing cards and Tarot decks.

d. World Serpent in Ancient Mythology and Religion

d1. Hinduism

Hinduism, Buddhism, and various other Asian traditions believe in a race of semi-divine half-human, half-serpent beings (Nagas) residing in the netherworld (Patala). They are often depicted as communicating and bringing wisdom to mankind (a classic example being Nāgārjuna, the key pillar of Mahāyāna and Vajrayāna Buddhist thought).

In Hinduism, nagas have a king, the King of all Serpents (Nāgarāja), called Shesha. This unitary-yet-plural (many-faced) king is a symbol of the totality of the created order, as he is believed to contain all the planets of the Universe in his hoods while singing praise to the preserver god Vishnu.

In a way, he represents the body or energetic aspect of the Divine (Panentheism), being a symbol of the whole Universe. When he uncoils, creation comes into existence and time moves forward; when he coils back, everything goes back into non-existence. Because of this, he is also called "Endless-Shesha" or the "First Shesha".

In the World Serpent myth (Kirtimukha), a cobra with its tail in its mouth is depicted as encircling the whole world. This world, symbolizing the totality of creation, is supported by the four World Elephants, themselves resting on the back of the World-bearing Turtle. The World Turtle can be found, additionally, in Chinese and indigenous American mythologies.[17] The union, inside the serpentine circle, of the earth below with the heaven above was usually conceived as both the totality of the cosmos and as a symbol for the unity of opposites.

____

17. *Edward Burnett Tylor (1878), p. 341.*

Figure 8. Ancient Indian cosmology also includes the Ouroboros as a symbol of eternity and totality. Picture: "Views of India from an atlas by the geographer Thunot Duvotenay (1796-1875)". Paris (1843).

The Ouroboros is also a symbol used in certain yogic schools (Kundalini Yoga) to name the dormant energy inside us all. This energy, as depicted by the *Yoga Kundalini Upanishad,* is imagined as both coiled and as having her tail in her mouth:

"The divine power, Kundalini, shines like the stem of a young lotus; like a snake, coiled round upon herself she holds her tail in her mouth and lies resting half asleep as the base of the body" (1.82)

In this case, it is a representation of the power of the divine inside each of us, which we can claim and master through yogic techniques and our own efforts.

This is believed to be possible because, for most Hindu faiths, following a common interpretation of the *Upanishads,* we are a particular manifestation (including the gods, whose existence is only temporal, bound by the cycles of time) of the impersonal source of it all, Brahman.

d2. Mesoamerican Religion

In pre-Hispanic Mesoamerica we find the serpent god Quetzalcoatl (meaning "Feathered Serpent", a name that unites the opposites of Heaven [feather] and Earth [serpent]).

Quetzalcoatl was believed to be the god of life, light (the day), knowledge, wisdom, and learning. He was the patron god of the Aztec priesthood[18], and is often associated with Venus, the Sun, and the winds. Quetzalcoatl can be seen depicted biting his own tail on both Aztec and Toltec ruins.

Figure 9. Quetzalcoatl carving forming a circle in the base of the Pyramid of the Feathered Serpent; Xochicalco, Mexico (700-900 AD).

d3. South American Religion

Among South American indigenous people (e.g., tropical lowlands), it is a common belief that the waters at the edge of the world disc are encircled by a snake, often an anaconda, biting its own tail.[19]

---

18. *Smith, Michael E. (2003). The Aztecs (2ⁿᵈ ed.). Malden, MA: Blackwell Publishing, p. 213.*

19. *Roe, Peter (1986). The Cosmic Zygote. Rutgers University Press.*

d4. Norse Religion

In Norse Mythology, Jörmungandr (Miðgarðsormr, also Midgard Serpent or World Serpent), is depicted as a sea serpent or worm so big that it is able to encircle our planet (Midgard) and bite its own tail.

It was believed that when it released its tail, the final battle and twilight of the gods (Ragnarök) would begin. This effectively implies the end of one cycle of the world and the beginning of another, which in turn makes obvious the relation of the World Serpent with the Sea of Creation and how the liberation of its own tail means the return to the homogeneity of undifferentiated Chaos.

Figure 10. Illustration of the Nordic World Serpent (Jörmungandr). Source: Edda oblongata (17ᵗʰ-century illuminated manuscript of the 13ᵗʰ-century CE Prose Edda). The Edda´s are the main source and basis of our modern understanding of Norse mythology.

This return was believed to be the necessary pre-condition for the cyclic renewal of the world to take place, after which a new clean and fertile world would arise, containing both surviving and returning gods. Two human survivors were believed to repopulate this new world: Líf and Lífþrasir.

d5. Mesopotamian Religion

This association between the waters of creation and serpentine figures is also clearly found in Mesopotamian religion. Especially in the Ugaritic figure of Yamm, god of the sea and all sources of water.

Yamm played an important role in the *Baal cycle*. In it, he is portrayed as the enemy of the weather or Sky God, Baal, with whom he competes to see who will become King of the Gods.

The story depicts Yamm as the favorite of the divine council and the highest god El[20], the latter addressing Yam as his son.[21] However, it is Baal (sometimes depicted in seals as striking down a serpent) who eventually wins this competition.

This mythological theme (mytheme) is common in many ancient cultures (e.g., Indra and the demon dragon/serpent Vritra in the *Rig Veda*), and it represents the principle of order and differentiation conquering the pure dormant potentiality of undefined Chaos. It is interesting, however, how the *Baal cycle* portrays the son of God as the enemy.

d6. Judaism

The Leviathan, in Judaism, is a primordial sea serpent. According to the Zohar (an important part of post-Christian Rabbinic Judaism), it is a singular creature with no mate, "its tail is placed in its mouth", and "twisting around and encompassing the entire world" (Rashi on *Baba Batra 74b*). All this, like in the previously discussed myths, points to the underlying oneness of everything that exists.

d7. Christianity

The Christian evaluation of the biblical Leviathan, however, is mostly negative. It was seen as a symbol of the limitations of our fallen world.

Instead of valuing the self-sufficiency of this never-ending and self-consuming cycle of creation and destruction, it focused on its deficiencies,

----

20. *Smith, Mark S.; Pitard, Wayne T. (2009). The Ugaritic Baal cycle. Volume II. Introduction with Text, Translations, and Commentary of KTU 1.3-1.4. Leiden: Brill, p. 17.*

21. *Ibid., p. 150.*

contrasting it with the life of the saved ones in the transcendent age to come (Eschaton).

As we have seen throughout this book, Christian theology (especially Orthodox one), in contrast with the mythologies previously discussed, conceives the existence of both difference and oneness in the Divinity (the Trinity) and in the Eschaton.

Therefore, Christians are not compelled to believe that Oneness can only be achieved through the homogeneity of pre-formal Chaos or All-Potentiality. Because of this, we find a conflict between most ancient mythologies and Christian doctrine.

The former speaks of a hero-god who conquers Chaos (serpentine figure/dragon) in order to bring forth this world of dualities and strife (All-Actuality).

In this view, Chaos is nevertheless seen as the impersonal "necessary evil" prior to the gods, which are particular actualizations of the possibilities it holds. It is believed to be necessary for the periodic renewal of the Universe, just as this world of struggle is necessary as the only possible source of particularity. In a way, they are both the opposite but complementary dialectical sides of the same coin.

Christianity, in contrast, speaks of a personal Tri-Une God who transcends the categories of Unity and Plurality. In this case, the serpent is unambiguously associated either with particular beings whose free will is contrary to God (fallen angels), or to the Leviathan, the sea creature representing the limited confined nature of this temporal world.

Leviathan is neither seen as necessary to maintain individuality (as the Tri-Une God transcends the One/Many duality by Himself) nor as a necessary evil which is the source of the periodic renewal of the world (because immortality is seen as transcendent and beyond a perpetual cycle of rebirths, which in itself is not really immortality but an indefinitely extended period of mortality).

Figure 11. The Christian view on ouroboric figures like the Leviathan, in contrast with most other religions, was predominantly a negative one. In the picture, the Antichrist is shown seated above it. Picture: Liber Floridus; Lambert (1090-1120).

"Israel Will Be Restored

In that day the Lord with His severe sword, great and strong,

Will punish Leviathan the fleeing serpent,

Leviathan that twisted serpent;

And He will slay the reptile that is in the sea."

– Isaiah 27:1. New King James Version

e. Additional References to the Ouroboros

e1. Platonism

Plato described a self-sufficient, self-consuming, circular being as the first particular existence in the Universe.

Everything that this being did or suffered was conceived as taking place in and by himself, since it was not thought possible for it to lack anything. This is consistent with the description of the Ouroboros we have seen until now.

e2. Mithran Mystery Cults

The eternal and cyclical nature of the Sun God Mithra (Sol Invictus, who dies and is reborn, also the god of light, truth, and contracts) was symbolized by him being entwined by a serpent, in a way similar to that of the Orphic World Egg.

Mithra can also sometimes be seen surrounded by the signs of the Zodiac and the four wind gods, all of them pointing to the totality of time (Kronos/Saturn) and to the creation inside it.

Figure 12. The Ouroboros as a representation of Eternity.

Note, however, that this notion of eternity is an immanent one, conceived as a perpetual circle showing an indefinite duration rather than a real infinity transcending time.

Note also the symbolism of the two-faced god Janus, representing both duality and the underlying unity behind it. Picture: Aeternitas; Philip Galle (1537–1612), Royal Library of Belgium.

e3. Freemasonry and Other Esoteric Schools

The Ouroboros is also found in many masonic seals and frontispieces, with its depiction being especially prevalent during the seventeenth century.

It is also featured in the seal and main symbol of H.P. Blavatsky´s Theosophical Society, along with other traditional symbols like the Swastika and the Ankh.

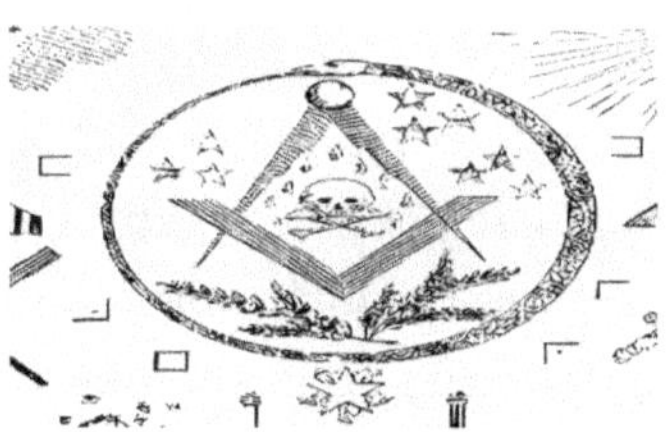

Figure 13. Ouroboros displayed on Masonic seal, along with the square and compass symbolizing Complementary Dualism.

e3. The Ouroboros in Modern Times: Kekulé´s Dream

The Ouroboros is not only an extremely ancient symbol with a prevalent presence in works of fiction. It was also important in the development of modern science.

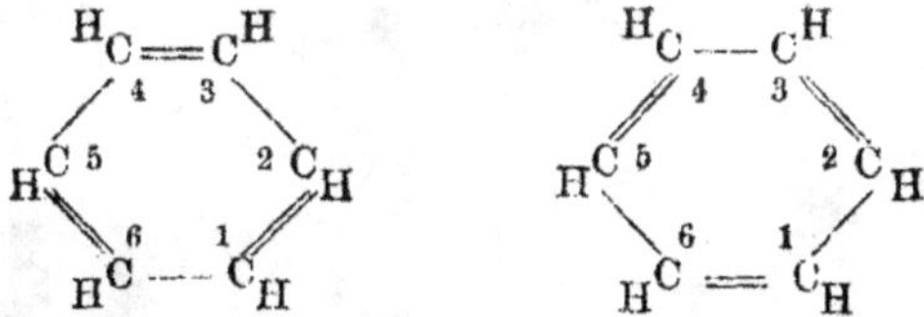

Figure 14. Original benzene formulae of August Kekulé.

While describing how he discovered the structure of the benzene molecule, a very important achievement for both pure and applied chemistry, the organic chemist August Kekulé explained: [22]

"I was sitting, writing at my text-book; but the work did not progress; my thoughts were elsewhere. I turned my chair to the fire and dozed. Again the atoms were gambling before my eyes. This time the smaller

---

22. *Read, John (1957). From Alchemy to Chemistry. Courier Corporation. pp. 179–180.*

groups kept modestly in the background. My mental eye, rendered more acute by the repeated visions of the kind, could now distinguish larger structures of manifold conformation: long rows, sometimes more closely fitted together; all twining and twisting in snake-like motion. But look! What was that? One of the snakes had seized hold of its own tail, and the form whirled mockingly before my eyes. As if by a flash of lightning I awoke; and this time also I spent the rest of the night in working out the consequences of the hypothesis."

Figure 15. Always With Us. Be it through Kekulé´s dream or modern art and popular culture, the Ouroboros symbol is here to stay. Picture: No Limits Project; Alexandre Arrechea (2013), New York.

Recommended Reading

A Dictionary of Symbols. *Juan Eduardo Cirlot* [reference work].

A2. RECOMMENDED READING LIST

The topics covered in this book can be complex. It is therefore beneficial to do some further reading in order to fully understand their importance and how they affect our lives. The following list attempts to condense as much knowledge as possible into as few books as possible, favoring works of a synthetic nature that give a clear overview of the big picture.

Books in italic are considered essential reading.

a. Diagnosing the Problem

A clear and direct analysis of the problems of the modern world, their spiritual roots, consequences, and implications for the future:

- *The Reign of Quantity and the Signs of the Times. René Guénon.*

- *Orthodoxy and the Religion of the Future. Fr. Seraphim Rose.*

- Nihilism: The Root of the Revolution of the Modern Age. Fr. Seraphim Rose.

a1. Esoteric and Occult Principles Guiding the Modern World

Small set of books acting as guidelines on how to implement the esoteric and arcane teachings of Alice Bailey (Theosophy) into every aspect of society (e.g., religion, government, education):

- Service of the Plan Study Course. Arcane School. Lucis Trust/ Alice Bailey.

b. Symbolism

Traditional symbolism and its metaphysical meaning:

- Symbols of Sacred Science. René Guénon.

- Rites and Symbols of Initiation: The Mysteries of Birth and Rebirth. Mircea Eliade.

b1. Jungian Psychology

A good introduction and summary of Jungian psychology, very prevalent in modern popular culture:

- Man and His Symbols. Carl Gustav Jung.

c. Metaphysics

In depth overview of the key metaphysical principles of Hinduism (and of Panentheism). A fantastic introduction to the main doctrines of Traditionalism/Perennialism and, in general, to the doctrines of the One:

- Introduction to the Study of the Hindu Doctrines. René Guénon.

- *Man and His Becoming According to the Vedanta. René Guénon.*

A key work to understand the importance of the problem of *the One and the Many*, including its metaphysical and theological meaning as well as its historical consequences:

- *The One and the Many: Studies in the Philosophy of Order and Ultimacy. Rousas John Rushdoony.*

A key work to understand the importance of dialectical thinking, how it shaped history, and the metaphysical implications of its introduction into Christianity by the Roman Catholic doctrine of the Filioque:

- *God, History and Dialectic (Vol I-II). Joseph P. Farrell.*

Important Freemasonic "textbook", analysing the symbolism and metaphysical teachings of the key worldviews that influenced it the most:

- *The Secret Teachings of All Ages: An Encyclopedic Outline of Masonic, Hermetic, Qabbalistic and Rosicrucian Symbolical Philosophy. Manly P. Hall.*

Theoretical aspects and metaphysical background behind most forms of Western Esotericism:

- The Doctrine and Ritual of High Magic. Éliphas Lévi.

Patterns in ancient mythological and religious beliefs, pointing at the similar worldview behind most of them:

- Patterns in Comparative Religion. Mircea Eliade.

d. Worldviews

COMPARATIVE MYSTICISM. Important works that study the subjective experiences of mystics of different traditions, how they interpret them, and what that means for our understanding of their underlying worldviews:

- *Mysticism Sacred and Profane. R.C. Zaehner.*

- Hindu and Muslim Mysticism. R. C. Zaehner.

WESTERN ESOTERICISM. Practical aspects and history of Western Esotericism, explained by a knowledgeable insider:

- The History of Magic. Éliphas Lévi.

GNOSTICISM. The main source and template of symbolic popular culture narratives:

- The Gnostic Religion. Hans Jonas.

- Nag Hammadi Library. James M. Robinson.

KABBALAH. Jewish mysticism. Its origins, main doctrines, and practical aspects, as well as their similarities with other esoteric traditions:

- Kabbalah. Gershom Scholem.

- Universal Meaning of the Kabbalah. Leo Schaya.

- Meditation and Kabbalah. Aryeh Kaplan.

HERMETICISM. One of the most important sources of Western Esotericism:

- Hermetica: The Greek Corpus Hermeticum and the Latin Asclepius in a New English Translation. Brian P. Copenhaver.

The influence of Hermeticism in Hegel´s, supposedly "Christian", worldview. Including its relationship with modern Freemasonry:

- Hegel and the Hermetic Tradition. Glenn Alexander Magee.

ALCHEMY. A visual tour through Western Alchemy´s main symbols and tenets:

- Alchemy & Mysticism. Alexander Roob.

NEO-PLATONISM. The metaphysical teachings behind one of the most important doctrines of the One, as explained by the master (Plotinus) and the best systematiser (Proclus):

- All From One: A Guide to Proclus. Pieter d' Hoine and Marije Martijn.

- Plotinus: The Enneads. Lloyd P. Gerson, George Boys-Stones, et al.

THEISTIC AND NON-THEISTIC HINDUISM. Comparison between theistic and non-theistic Hinduism, the former being the predominant one in India, while the latter is the version of Hinduism imported by the West almost exclusively:

- Advaita and Visistadvaita. S.M. Srinivasachari.

ORTHODOX CHRISTIANITY

Introduction to Orthodox Christianity and its similarities and differences with other worldviews, including other Christian denominations:

- Orthodoxy and Heterodoxy: Finding the Way to Christ in a Complicated Religious Landscape. Fr. Andrew Stephen Damick.

Introduction to Orthodox Christianity, similarities, and differences compared to Protestantism:

- Rock and Sand: An Orthodox Appraisal of the Protestant Reformers and Their Teachings. Fr. Josiah Trenham.

An introduction to Orthodoxy through concise, yet precise and in-depth, theological works:

- *The Mystical Theology of the Eastern Church. Vladimir Lossky.*

- Orthodox Theology: An Introduction. Vladimir Lossky.

- In the Image and Likeness of God. Vladimir Lossky.

- Religion of the Apostles: Orthodox Christianity in the First Century. Fr. Stephen De Young.

– ORTHOPRAXIS. An explanation and introduction, as well as a practical manual, to Christian practical life and how to better ourselves through mastering our passions:

- Therapy of Spiritual Illnesses (Vol. I-III). Jean-Claude Larchet.[1]

– THE HOLY BIBLE. Annotated for a better understanding:

- Orthodox Study Bible (including Old and *New Testament*).

---

1. *If this book is read with the intention of putting it into practice, it is recommended to follow the advice of an experienced spiritual father.*

A3. GLOSSARY

"As above, so below": popular modern paraphrase originating in the second verse of the *Emerald Tablet*, one of the key early Hermetical texts (*"that which is above is like to that which is below, and that which is below is like to that which is above"*). This metaphysical concept refers to the correspondence between the Macrocosm ("great world" or the Universe as a whole, understood as a great living being) and the Microcosm ("small world" or human being, understood as a mirror reflection or a miniature version of the former). Concept frequently used by occultists (e.g., Helena P. Blavatsky), it became a common New Age motto. It is also prominent in Greek and Hellenistic philosophy (e.g., Stoicism).

Absolute Divine Simplicity: the metaphysical notion that God is one simple unified entity without any really distinct attributes or "parts". God's existence is identical to God's essence, which means that each name we attribute to God means exactly the same as any other and is identical to His essence. It also implies that God is pure actuality without potentiality. This questions God´s free will because, for example, a God that is pure actuality cannot decide to become a creator at a specific point in time but has to be considered as an entity incapable of not emanating. This theory contrasts with the Orthodox Christian belief in God´s Essence/Energies distinction.

Advaita: usually translated as "Non-Dualism" (but often equated with Monism). In Hindu thought, it means that Brahman alone is ultimately real, while the world of the senses is an illusory appearance (Māyā) of Brahman.

Apokatastasis: restoration of creation to a perfected or pre-fallen state. In Christianity, it is used to refer to an eventual universal salvation of everyone, including the devil. This notion is not accepted by the main Christian denominations because it lacks biblical support and because it is also a theory in line with definitions of God as "the Absolute" (a totality that includes all opposites, different from the Christian Tri-Une God).

Apophatic theology: also known as negative theology, it is a form of doing theology that approaches God through negations instead of affirmations or positive statements (cataphatic theology). Since God cannot be circumscribed by mere human thought or language, it is the most accurate form of representing Him. However, it also limits what we can communicate. Closely related to mystical experiences and the impossibility of completely expressing them.

Apotheosis: the glorification of a few special subjects to divine levels. Deification is usually understood as obtained by participating in the Divine Essence. Typical of imperial cults (e.g., ancient Egypt [pharaohs] and Mesopotamian religion).

Ātman: immortal True Self or essence of each individual, which persists across multiple bodies and lifetimes. It is not the same as the common human mortal ego (Ahamkara). Sometimes defined as pure consciousness or witness consciousness.

It is a key concept in Indian philosophies, where Ātman can be said to be completely identical (Advaita: non-dualist), completely different (Dvaita: dualist), or simultaneously non-different and different (Bhedabheda: non-dualist/dualist) to Brahman or ultimate reality. Buddhism denies the existence of such an intrinsic essence or Self.

Avatar: meaning 'descent' in Sanskrit. It refers to the temporal incarnation of a deity or spirit in our material plane of existence. A deity can incarnate multiple times in different forms in order to perform many particular tasks (e.g., Vishnu).

Brahman: in Hinduism, it refers to the highest reality or Universal Principle. The unchanging, infinite, eternal Truth-Consciousness-Bliss underlying all reality and the source of all (real or apparent) changes in our world. The single binding unity behind all (apparent) diversity.

Cataphatic theology: a way of doing theology that uses positive terminology to describe or refer to God, by naming His attributes or using a variety of God´s names. See also apophatic theology.

Catharsis (Katharsis): meaning purification, cleansing. Most commonly used to refer to the purification and purgation of thoughts and emotions by way of confronting and expressing them, resulting in a state of emotional renewal.

Coincidentia Oppositorum: which means coincidence of opposites in Latin. This term is used to describe the underlying oneness of all things, previously perceived to be different. This immanentist view is mostly found in different monistic (e.g., Pantheism/Panentheism) and non-dualistic traditions.

Achieving the Unity of Opposites in order to transcend our common world of dualities and return to primordial Unity (e.g., the One, the Absolute) is, then, the main objective of these traditions. This may imply integrating aspects that may be seen as incompatible in other worldviews (e.g., the Christian Tri-Une God is not made of light and dark aspects to be re-united).

Related to Non-Dualism, it defines a situation in which the existence or identity of a thing depends on the dialectical co-existence of at least two conditions that are opposite to each other, yet dependent on each other and presupposing each other. The tension between these opposites is thus generative, creating other realities that depend on it.

This ubiquitous metaphysical concept can be found in Tantric Hinduism and Buddhism, Zen (Mahāyāna) and Vajrayāna Buddhism, Taoism, Sufism, Alchemy, Kabbalah, Neo-Platonism, Zoroastrianism, German mysticism, and Western esotericism, among others.

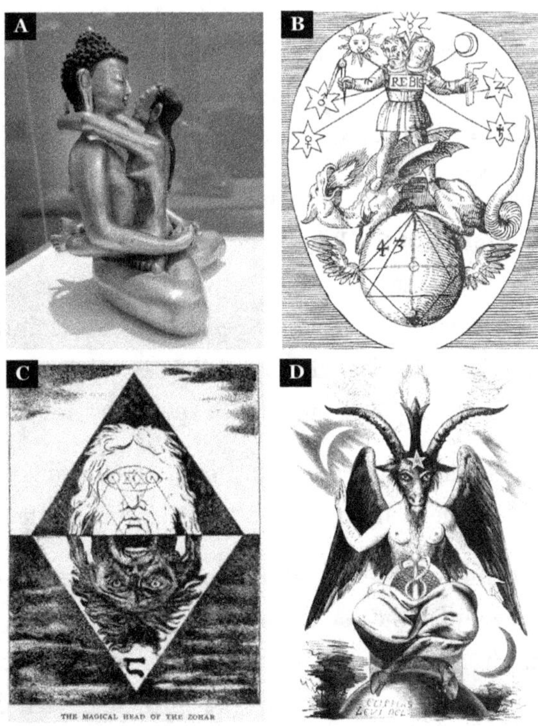

Figure 16. Examples of the doctrine of the Unity of Opposites in different traditions.
A: *An image of the Primordial Buddha Samantabhadra [2] with his consort Samantabhadri,*
symbolizing the union of space (emptiness, female aspect) and clarity (awareness, male aspect).
B: *The Rebis [3] or Divine Hermaphrodite, the end result of the Great Work of the Alchemists.*
C: *Éliphas Lévi´s illustration of the Head of God in the Zohar [4], a symbolic drawing*
of the different faces of the God of the Kabbalah (Macroprosopus/Microprosopus),
with the totality being the union of his opposite (mirrored) light and dark aspects.
D: *Baphomet, as drawn by Éliphas Lévi [5], formed by dichotomies (e.g., horns)*
representing "the equilibrium of opposites" (e.g., the flame in between the horns):
half-human and half-animal, male and female, good and evil. Baphomet is used as a
symbol of balance, of the Absolute or the Divine Androgyne in Western occult schools.
Some occultists state that its origin may be related to the Ophite sect (Gnosticism)
and/or the Templars.

---

2. Samantabhadra (Ever-Perfect One) or (Tibetan) Kuntuzangpo, Tibet, early 20th
century. Accession number 2011.77. Part of the tantric art exhibit Honored Father-
Honored Mother, Trammell & Margaret Crow Collection of Asian Art, Texas, USA.

3. Nollius, Heinrich (1617). Rebis from Theoria Philosophiae Hermeticae.

4. Lévi, Éliphas (1860). Histoire de la Magie: Avec une Exposition Claire et Precise
de ses Procedes, de ses Rites et de ses Mysteres. Weiser Books, p. 40.

5. Lévi, Éliphas (1856). Sabbatic Goat in Dogme et Rituel de la Haute Magie. The
arms bear the Alchemical concepts SOLVE (dissolve) and COAGULA (coagulate).

Demiurge (Gnosticism): Gnostic systems draw a distinction between the unknowable highest reality and an intermediate entity, either evil or ignorant, who shaped and "created" this fallen material Universe. This intermediate being is neither All-Knowing nor All-Powerful.

In some cases, this demiurgic figure is identified with Yahweh, the God of the *Old Testament* of the Bible. Therefore, contrary to Christianity, some Gnostic systems see a conflict between Jesus Christ (the Logos), who represents the will of the Highest Being, and the demiurgic Yahweh. Also contrary to Christian thought, creation is conceived as a prison used by the Demiurge for trapping the divine aspects lost in matter.

Greek philosophy (e.g., Plato, Plotinus), when using this concept, does not consider the Demiurge as an antagonistic or inferior figure.

Emanationism: widespread metaphysical cosmogonical notion particularly frequent in the doctrines of "the One". Emanation, meaning "to flow from" or "to pour forth or out of", is conceived as the mode by which all things are derived from the first principle (e.g., the One, the Absolute). It is opposed to the notion of creation out of nothing (Ex Nihilo) present in Abrahamic faiths.

In this view, all existing things are derived from the highest reality, being of the same substance. The process of emanation creates beings and realities progressively farther away from the source, each successive emanation being more imperfect than the one before.

This concept also serves to explain (some would say to explain away) the concept of evil, since it is defined as just the last emanation and the logical conclusion of the process, usually associated with matter and non-existence.

Eschatology: concerns expectations regarding the end of the present age, world, or creation itself (end times). It also refers to the end of our ordinary reality and the beginning of the age beyond change and time, once reunited with the Divine.

Essence/Energies distinction: particular Orthodox Christian theological notion, where a distinction is made between God´s essence (Ousia) and His energies (Energeia). Famously expounded and defended by St. Gregory Palamas as part of his defense of the monastic practice of Hesychasm.

According to the theologian Vladimir Lossky, God's nature or essence is *what* God is, *"that which finds no existence or subsistence in another or any other thing"*[6], and cannot be directly experienced. Through God´s energies, however, we can know God through what His nature is capable of doing and, as St. John of Damascus stated, *"all that we say positively of God manifests not his nature"* [which in its transcendence we cannot conceive] *"but the things about his nature"*.[7]

Contrary to Thomistic Catholicism, Orthodoxy considers this distinction as a real one, and not a "virtual" or "formal" one, therefore avoiding the dangers associated with conceptualizing God as pure essence (e.g., which would be similar to defining God as the One, the All, the Source or the God of the Philosophers).

According to Orthodox doctrine, if we deny the real distinction between essence and energies, we cannot fix any clear boundary between the procession of the divine Persons of the Trinity and the creation of the world. In this case, both the former and the latter would be equally created by God´s uncreated essence. The being and the actions of God being identical, God would be pure actuality without potentiality and, therefore, lack real free will. This line of thought would eventually abandon the Tri-Une God of Christianity and lead to Pantheism/Panentheism.

----

6. *Lossky, Vladimir (1997). The Mystical Theology of the Eastern Church. SVS Press, pp. 50-55.*

7. *Ibid., p. 73.*

Epistemology: branch of philosophy concerned with knowledge. Key questions asked are the nature, origin and scope of knowledge, epistemic justification, and the rationality of belief.

Hypostasis: usually translated as "person". It is a term that refers to *who* God is. Not to be confused with God's essence/nature (*what* God is; see Ousia), or God's attributes (what God *does*). Hypostatic union, in turn, is a technical term used in Christian theology to describe the union of Jesus Christ's two natures (human and divine) in one hypostasis (individual person).

Henosis: Greek term meaning mystical oneness, union or unity. It is used in Neo-Platonism to refer to unification with the One (Τò Ἕν), the Source or Monad.

This metaphysical notion has precursors in Greek mystery religions, as well as parallels with Eastern philosophy (e.g., Advaita Vedānta), Hermeticism (e.g., Corpus Hermeticum), and Islamic mysticism.

Karma: predominant concept in Indian religions. The moral principle of cause and effect that affects the future life of every being and the quality of their future rebirths in the cycle of existence (Saṃsāra). Good deeds and good intentions lead to better Karma and rebirths, ideally improving our chances of finally attaining liberation.

Logos: "Word, Discourse or Reason". A term used in Western philosophy, especially by Stoicism, for whom it represents the ordering principle of the Universe.

In Christianity, the Logos (Greek: Λόγος) is the Second Person of the Trinity: Jesus Christ. Expressed as Intellect, Wisdom, and the Providence of God in whom all things are created, it is the source of the many *Logoi* or inner essences of everything in existence.

Through the Logos, Word, or Reason all things come into existence as is proper to them according to their inner reason for being.

Māyā: illusion or magic in Indian philosophies. More specifically, it means a magic show, an illusion where things appear to be present but are not what they seem. It denotes that which is constantly changing and is, therefore, spiritually unreal in comparison with the unchanging Absolute (see Brahman). It only exists because of our ignorance (Avidyā) of our real Self (see Ātman).

Metaphysics: the branch of philosophy that studies the fundamental nature of reality. This includes first principles such as being or existence, identity, change, space and time, cause and effect, necessity, actuality, and possibility. It also includes inquiries regarding the nature of consciousness, the relation between mind and matter, and between potentiality and actuality. It tries to answer the question: "what is it that exists?"

Moksha: Hindu, Buddhist, Jain, and Sikh term for various forms of emancipation or spiritual liberation that constitutes the final aim of all sentient life. It means both freedom from Saṃsāra, the cycle of death and rebirth, as well as from ignorance (through self-realization, awakening, and self-knowledge).

Monad: in Gnostic systems, the highest Being/Reality is known as the Monad, the One, the Absolute, the Perfect Aeon or Bythos (Depth or Profundity).

Through a process of emanations, from the One derive different hierarchically ordered divine entities and realms: the Aeons (thirty in total for Valentinus, 365 according to Basilides). Valentinus, the most important Gnostic systematizer, taught that the Monad is the source of the Pleroma, the fullness of the Godhead, the totality of all the Aeons.

Jesus was seen as an Aeon residing close to the Father, while the lowest emanation, Sophia (Wisdom), fell by attempting to create without her counterpart, creating this fallen material world in the process and birthing the Demiurge.

Monism: the philosophical position that asserts one single entity or principle as ultimate reality, with everything else ultimately deriving from it. In one way or another, absolute Unity and uniformity are believed to be the origin of all things.

This first principle can be either spiritual, material or beyond both. Idealism, for example, believes that mind is the first principle from which matter (or our perception of matter) comes from. Materialism (or Physicalism), on the other hand, states that everything comes from undifferentiated matter, including mind. Neutral Monism, in turn, speaks of a third substance beyond mind and matter as the source of both.

Monism contrasts with Dualism, the philosophical stance that states that ultimate reality is composed of two different, sometimes opposite, principles (e.g., mind and matter in Cartesian Dualism).

Non-Dualism: the metaphysical and philosophical doctrine, common to many spiritual traditions (e.g., Taoism, Mahāyāna Buddhism, and Advaita Vedānta), that states the fundamental underlying unity and lack of any real intrinsic separation or duality between all aspects of existence.

This view challenges the conventional ultimate distinction between self/other, mind/body, observer/observed, and any other dichotomies that shape human thought and perception.

Non-Dualism differs from Monism in its different solution to the problem of *the One and the Many*, of unity and plurality. While Monism posits a unique first principle as the foundation of all reality, Non-Dualism emphasizes unity amid diversity. However, contrary to the Christian Tri-Une God, non-dual metaphysics relies on an immanent (lesser) plane of existence as the source of multiplicity, with its characteristic impermanence, while transcendence is reserved for pure Unity (e.g., Brahman, Emptiness, the Ground or Base of existence, the Tao/Taiji).

Different interpretations of Non-Dualism exist, however, sometimes in conflict with each other. For example, Advaita Vedānta´s goal of identifying each particular soul (Ātman) with ultimate reality (Brahman) contrasts with the Buddhist teachings on non-self (Anatta) that emphasize the non-existence of any particular soul or essence while teaching the intrinsic two-sidedness of all phenomena (relative [plurality] and absolute [unity: Emptiness]). Because of this, Non-Dualism has sometimes been labeled as a fuzzy concept for which many definitions can be found.

Ontology: the branch of philosophy that studies being. It studies what types of entities exist, how can they be grouped into categories, and how they relate to each other at the most fundamental level.

Ousia (Essence): a philosophical and theological term primarily meaning "essence" or "substance".

In Christian theology, the concept is used to refer to the imparticipable essence of God, or *what* God is, in contrast to *who* He is (see Hypostasis) or what He *does* (energies or operations). The term homousion (*"same in being; same in essence"*), in turn, refers to the common essence of all three Persons of the Tri-Une God.

Perichoresis: a term referring to the relationship of the three Persons of the Tri-Une God (Father, Son, and Holy Spirit) to one another. Also called interpenetration, it was first used as a term in Christian theology by the Church Fathers, including the writings of Gregory of Nazianzus, Maximus the Confessor, and John of Damascus.

It is used to describe the relationship between the divine and human natures of Jesus Christ, as well as between each member of the Holy Trinity.

Its use emphasizes the co-primacy of both unity and multiplicity, and the possibility of union without fusion (or confusion) of those being united. Because this uniquely Christian form of union preserves and loves the difference of each member being united, the Christian God can be described as the God of Love, in contraposition to the God of the Philosophers (the Monad or the One, where all difference is annihilated).

Prakriti: key Hindu notion (Sāṃkhya school). Usually said to refer to matter or nature, it includes all the cognitive, moral, psychological, emotional, sensorial, and physical aspects of reality. It has three different innate qualities (Guṇas), whose equilibrium is the basis of all observed reality in our plane of existence. Its counterpart is Purusha, pure awareness/consciousness.

Purusha: pure consciousness in Sāṃkhya philosophy. Unattached and unrelated to anything, pure, unchanging, passive. The complementary union between Purusha and Prakṛti (matter) gives rise to life. In Kashmir Shaivism, it is the Universal Self (Paramātman) manifesting through many individual selves (Jīvātman), limited in various ways.

Saṃsāra: Pali/Sanskrit word meaning "wandering" as well as "world". It has the connotation of cyclic change or running around in circles. When related to the theory of Karma, it denotes the Cycle of Rebirths in which we are currently trapped. This cyclic existence is one of the fundamental tenets of most Indian religions.

Shadow (Jungian Psychology): a concept derived from Jungian Analytical Psychology, it represents the repressed Id, shadow aspect or shadow archetype of an individual. It is defined as an unconscious aspect of the personality that does not align with the ideal of the conscious ego, therefore being repressed by it and projected into the external world and other persons, usually leading to conflict.

The shadow is the Self's emotional blind spot, a part of ourselves that our conscious personality does not want to acknowledge and that is experienced as archetypal images born of mankind´s Collective Unconscious (e.g., the trickster figure).

It represents the concept of "evil" in Jungian psychology, and the aim is not to completely reject but to integrate it into the conscious personality, transforming the ego into the Self. This process, as well as Jungian psychology as a whole, follows the Alchemical/esoteric principle of the Unity of Opposites.

The One: Neo-Platonic name for the highest reality. Defined as an utterly simple, ineffable, unknowable reality that is both the beginning (the Source) and end of everything that exists. All emanated existences come to be through the One´s subsequent emanations: Nous (Intellect) and World-Soul (Psyché).

The One is defined (and conditioned) by its *absolute* simplicity, and it cannot even be said to exist, being defined by Plato and Plotinus as being beyond being (Book VI of *The Republic*; *Enneads* [V.2]).

Since difference and distinction are not present in the One, in order to return to Its homogeneous Unity, any individual existence has to renounce its particular characteristics, understood as being inferior to the One´s absolute simplicity.

Theoria: until the sixth century the practice of mysticism was referred to by the Latin term contemplatio, meaning "looking at" or "being aware of" God or the Divine. Christianity used both the Greek (Theoria) and Latin terms in order to describe different forms of prayer and the process of coming to know God.

Theosis: Orthodox Christian doctrine. Deification or divinization. It is the process of becoming united with God and salvation itself (see 2 Peter 1:4). It does not mean fusing with God´s essence (see Apotheosis), which is imparticipable. Instead, it involves uniting with all of God´s eternal Uncreated Energies.

The statement by St. Athanasius of Alexandria, *"The Son of God became man, that we might become god"*, is a common explanation of this concept. Theosis assumes that humans were from the beginning made to share in the life of the Holy Trinity, and that as much as the Second Person of the Trinity (see Logos) abased Himself (Kenosis) during the Incarnation, to the same degree we will be elevated through our cooperation (synergy) with God.

Theotokos: a title of Mary, mother of Jesus, used especially by Orthodox Christianity. Common translations include "Mother of God" or "God-bearer". This title is theologically significant because it emphasizes that Mary's son, Jesus Christ, is both fully God and fully human. Two natures (divine and human) united in a single Person (Hypostatic Union) of the Tri-Une God.

Yoga: yoke or union. A group of physical, mental, and spiritual practices originated in ancient India that aim at controlling (to yoke) and stilling the mind, in order to find pure consciousness or our "true Self".

The term Yoga, in the West, often refers to a modern form of Hatha (physical) Yoga which was traditionally considered only as a preliminary preparation for other mind-based disciplines able to procure liberation from the Cycle of Rebirths (e.g., Rāja Yoga).

It was adapted in a variety of ways to Hinduism, Buddhism, and Jainism. Different types may involve working with internal psychosomatic energies (Kundalini Yoga), with emotions through devotion (Bhakti Yoga), with knowledge (Jnana Yoga) or through acting in an altruistic and selfless way (Karma Yoga).

A4. BIBLIOGRAPHY

Abhinavagupta. *Giriratna Mishra (Translator). Sri Tantraloka of Abhinavgupta. Chaukhamba Surbharati Prakashan, 2018.*

— Marjanovic, Boris (Translator). Tantrasâra of Abhinavagupta. Indica Books, 2023.

Acevedo, Carmen. *The Cloud of Unknowing. Shambhala, 2018.*

Agrippa, Henry Cornelius. *Three Books of Occult Philosophy. A Yesterday's World Publishing, 2015.*

Aitken, Robert (Translator). *The Gateless Barrier: The Wu-Men Kuan (Mumonkan). North Point Press, 2016.*

Al Arabi, Ibn. *Journey to the Lord of Power: A Sufi Manual on Retreat (Risālat al-Anwār). Inner Traditions, 1981.*

— The Bezels of Wisdom (Fusus al-Hikam). Paulist Press, 1980.

— The Four Pillars of Spiritual Transformation (Hilyat al-abdāl). Anqa Publishing, 2009.

— The Meccan Illuminations (Al-Futūḥāt al-Makkiyya). DKI, 2016.

— The Universal Tree and the Four Birds (al-Ittihād al-Kawnī). Anqa Publishing; Illustrated edition, 2006.

Al-Jilani, Abd al-Qadir. *The Secret of Secrets. Islamic Texts Society, 1997.*

Alexander Magee, Glenn. *Hegel and the Hermetic Tradition. Cornell University Press, 2008.*

Alighieri, Dante. *The Divine Comedy. Berkley, 2003.*

Apuleius. *The Golden Ass. Oxford University Press, 2008.*

Aquinas, Thomas. *Summa Theologica. Coyote Canyon Press, 2010.*

Arbel, Keren. *Early Buddhist Meditation: The Four Jhanas as the Actualization of Insight. Routledge Critical Studies in Buddhismby, 2018.*

Aspaniarji Kapadia, Shaporji. *The Teachings of Zoroaster and the philosophy of the Parsi religion. Nabu Press, 2009.*

Asvaghosha. *The Awakening of Faith: Attributed to Asvaghosha. Columbia University Press, 2005.*

Attar, Farid ud-Din. *The Conference of the Birds. Penguin Classics, 1984.*

Aurelius, Marcus. *Meditations. Loeb Classical Library, 1930.*

Aurobindo, Sri. *The Secret of the Veda: with Selected Hymns (Complete Works of Sri Aurobindo Book 32). Sri Aurobindo Ashram, 2016.*

— *The Synthesis of Yoga. Savitri Foundation, 2022.*

Ayyangar, T.R. Srinivasa. *The Yoga Upanisads. The Adyar Library And Research Centre, 2008.*

Bacon, Francis. *The New Atlantis: Or, Voyage to the Land of the Rosicrucians. Forgotten Books, 2008.*

Bailey, Alice A. *A Treatise on White Magic or The Way of the Disciple. Lucis Publishing Company, 1998.*

— *The Externalisation of the Hierarchy. Lucis Publishing Company, 2011.*

Barnstone, Willis (Editor); Meyer, Marvin (Editor). *The Gnostic Bible: Revised and Expanded Edition. Shambhala, 2009.*

Bhikkhu, Amaro. *Small Boat Great Mountain. Abhayagiri Monastery, 2003.*

Bhikkhu, Thanissaro. *Into the Stream: A Study Guide on the First Stage of Awakening. Thanissaro Bhikkhu, 2008.*

Blavatsky, Helena Petrovna. *Isis Unveiled (Vol. I-II) - A Master-Key to the Mysteries of Ancient and Modern Science and Theology. Nabu Press, 2010.*

— *The Secret Doctrine. Theosophical Univ Press, 1999.*

Bodhi, Bhikkhu. *A Comprehensive Manual of Abhidhamma. Buddhist Publication Society, 1993.*

— *In the Buddha's Words: An Anthology of Discourses from the Pali Canon. Wisdom Publications, 2005.*

Bodhidharma. *The Zen Teaching of Bodhidharma. North Point Press, 2009.*

Boehme, Jacob. *The Signature of All Things. Evinity Publishing Inc., 2008.*

Blake, William. *The Marriage of Heaven and Hell. Chelsea House Pub, 1987.*

Bradshaw, David. *Aristotle East and West: Metaphysics and the Division of Christendom. Cambridge University Press, 2007.*

— Divine Energies and Divine Action: Exploring the Essence-Energies Distinction. IOTA Publications, 2023.

Brianchaninov, St. Ignatius. *The Arena: Guidelines for Spiritual and Monastic Life. The Printshop of St. Job of Pochaev, 2012.*

Burckhardt, Titus. *An Introduction to Sufi Doctrine. Wellingborough, England: Thorsons, 1976.*

Burkert, Walter. *Ancient Mystery Cults. Harvard University Press, 1989.*

Campbell, Joseph. *The Hero with a Thousand Faces. New World Library, 2008.*

Carroll, Peter J. *Liber Null & Psychonaut: The Practice of Chaos Magic (Revised and Expanded Edition). Weiser Books, 2022.*

Chagme, Karma. *A Spacious Path to Freedom: Practical Instructions on the Union of Mahamudra and Atiyoga. Snow Lion, 2010.*

— Naked Awareness: Practical Instructions on the Union of Mahamudra and Dzogchen. Snow Lion, 2000.

Chari, S.M. Srinivasa. *Advaita and Visistadvaita: A Study Based on Vedanta Desika's Satadusani. Motilal Banarsidass, 1999.*

— The Philosophy of Visistadvaita Vedanta: A Study Based on Vedanta Desika's Adhikarana-Saravali. Motilal Banarsidass, 2016.

Chittick, William. *The Self-Disclosure of God: Principles of Ibn al-'Arabi's Cosmology. Albany: State University of New York Press, 1998.*

— The Sufi Path of Love: The Spiritual Teachings of Rumi. Albany: State University of New York Press, 1983.

— The Sufi Path of Knowledge: Ibn al-'Arabi's Metaphysics of Imagination. Albany: State University of New York Press, 1989.

Chogyam, Ngakpa. *Roaring Silence: Discovering the Mind of Dzogchen. Shambhala, 2002.*

Chung-Yuan, Chang. *Original Teachings Of Ch'an Buddhism. Pantheon, 1995.*

Cirlot, Juan Eduardo. *A Dictionary of Symbols: Revised and Expanded Edition. New York Review Books Classics, 2020.*

Cleary, Thomas. *Kensho: The Heart of Zen. Shambhala Dragon Editions, 1997.*

— Practical Taoism. Shambhala, 1996.

— *Taoist Meditation: Methods for Cultivating a Healthy Mind and Body.* Shambhala, 2000.

— *The Blue Cliff Record.* Shambhala, 2005.

— *The Book of Balance and Harmony: A Taoist Handbook.* Shambhala, 2003.

— *The Flower Ornament Scripture: A Translation of the Avatamsaka Sutra.* Shambhala, 1993.

— *Wen-tzu: Understanding the Mysteries: Further Teachings of Lao Tzu.* Shambhala, 1992.

Climacus, St. John. *The Ladder of Divine Ascent.* Lulu.com, 2021.

Confucius. *The Complete Confucius: The Wisdom of the Ages - Essential Analects, Sayings, and Teachings for a Harmonious Life.* Bookish, 2023.

Coomaraswamy, Ananda. *A New Approach to the Vedas: An Essay in Translation and Exegesis.* South Asia Books, 1994.

— *Hinduism and Buddhism.* Kessinger Publishing, 2007.

— *Selected Papers, Volume 2: Metaphysics.* Princeton University Press, 1977.

Copenhaver, Brian P. *Hermetica: The Greek Corpus Hermeticum and the Latin Asclepius.* Cambridge University Press, 1995.

Copleston, Frederick Charles. *History of Philosophy.* Continuum International Publishing Group, 2003.

Corbin, Henry. *The Man of Light in Iranian Sufism.* Omega Publications, 1994.

Crowley, Aleister. *The Book of the Law.* Independently published, 2021.

Dalley, Stephanie. *Myths from Mesopotamia: Creation, the Flood, Gilgamesh, and Others.* Oxford University Press, 2009.

Damascene, Hieromonk. *Christ the Eternal Tao.* Saint Herman Press, 2004.

Damick, Fr. Andrew Stephen. *Orthodoxy and Heterodoxy: Finding the Way to Christ in a Complicated Religious Landscape.* Ancient Faith Publishing, 2017.

Davis, G.M. *Antichrist: The Fulfillment of Globalization: The Ancient Church and the End of History.* Uncut Mountain Press, 2022.

De Catanzaro, C. J. *Symeon the New Theologian: The Discourses.* Paulist Press, 1980.

De Young, Fr. Stephen. *Religion of the Apostles: Orthodox Christianity in the First Century.* Ancient Faith Publishing, 2021.

Dee, John. *John Dee's Five Books of Mystery: Original Sourcebook of Enochian Magic. Weiser Books, 2002.*

— *Sacred Symbol of Oneness by John Dee of London: An English translation of John Dee's 1564 Monas Hieroglyphica. CreateSpace Independent Publishing Platform, 2014.*

D'Hoine, Pieter (Editor); Martijn, Marije (Editor). *All From One: A Guide to Proclus. OUP, Oxford; 2016.*

Dogen, Eihei. *Dogen's Manuals of Zen Meditation. University of California Press, 1990.*

— *Dogen's Essays: Fukan-zazengi Genjo-koan Shinenju. Shizuka Shuppan, 2020.*

— *Dogen's Shobogenzo Zuimonki: The New Annotated Translation—Also Including Dogen's Waka Poetry with Commentary. Wisdom Publications, 2022.*

— *Gudo Nishijima (Translator), Chodo Cross (Translator). Master Dogen's Shobogenzo (vol. I-IV). Independently published, 2021.*

Doniger, Wendy. *The Rig Veda. Penguin Classics, 2005.*

Duff, Tony. *Feature of the Expert, Glorious King. Padma Karpo Translation Committee, 2011.*

— *Flight of the Garuda. Padma Karpo Translation Committee, 2014.*

— *Relics of the Dharmakaya: A Detailed Explantion of the Three Lines That Strike the Key Points. Padma Karpo Translation Committee, 2011.*

Easwaran, Eknath. *The Bhagavad Gita. Nilgiri Press, 2009.*

— *The Dhammapada. Nilgiri Press, 2007.*

Eckhart, Meister. *Selected Writings. Penguin, 1994.*

Einoo, Shingo. *Genesis and Development of Tantrism. Institute of Oriental Culture, University of Tokyo, 2021.*

Eliade, Mircea. *A History of Religious Ideas. Vol. I-III. University of Chicago Press, 1978.*

— *Cosmologie şi alchimie babiloniană. Editura Moldova, 1991.*

— *Images and Symbols: Studies in Religious Symbolism (trans. Philip Mairet). Princeton University Press, Princeton, 1991.*

— *Mephistopheles and the Androgyne, studies in religious myth and symbol. Sheed and Ward, 1965.*

— *Occultism, Witchcraft and Cultural Fashions. The University of Chicago Press, 1976.*

— Patanjali and Yoga. Schocken Books, 1962.

— Patterns in Comparative Religion. Sheed & Ward, New York, 1958.

— Shamanism: Archaic Techniques of Ecstasy. Princeton University Press, Princeton, 2004.

— The Forge and the Crucible: The Origins and Structure of Alchemy. University of Chicago Press, 1979.

— The Myth of the Eternal Return: Cosmos and History (trans. Willard R. Trask). Princeton University Press, Princeton, 1971.

— The Sacred and the Profane: The Nature of Religion (trans. Willard R. Trask). Harper Torchbooks, New York, 1961.

— Yoga: Immortality and Freedom (trans. Willard R. Trask). Princeton University Press, Princeton, 2009.

Enji, Torei. *The Undying Lamp of Zen: The Testament of Zen Master Torei. Shambhala, 2010.*

Eusebius. *Eusebius: The Church History. Kregel Academic, 2007.*

Evans-Wentz, Walter. *Bardo Thodol: The Tibetan Book of the Dead. Independently published, 2022.*

Evola, Julius. *Eros and the Mysteries of Love: The Metaphysics of Sex. Inner Traditions/Bear, 1991.*

— Men Among the Ruins: Post-War Reflections of a Radical Traditionalist. Inner Traditions/Bear, 2002.

— Revolt Against the Modern World: Politics, Religion, and Social Order in the Kali Yuga. Inner Traditions/Bear, 1995.

— Ride the Tiger: A Survival Manual for the Aristocrats of the Soul. Inner Traditions/ Bear, 2003.

— The Hermetic Tradition: Symbols and Teachings of the Royal Art. Inner Traditions, 1995.

— The Path of Cinnabar. Arktos, 2009.

Farrell, Joseph P. *God, History, and Dialectic (Volume I-IV). Independently published, 2016.*

Frazer, Sir James George. *The Golden Bough: A Study in Magic and Religion. Oxford University Press, 2009.*

Godwin, Joscelyn. *Mystery religions in the ancient world. Thames and Hudson, 1981.*

— The Golden Thread: The Ageless Wisdom of the Western Mystery Traditions. Quest Books, 2007.

Goodrick-Clarke, Nicholas. *The Western Esoteric Traditions: A Historical Introduction. Oxford University Press, 2008.*

Guénon, René. *East and West. Sophia Perennis, 2001.*

— Initiation and Spiritual Realization. Sophia Perennis, 2001.

— Insights into Christian Esoterism. Sophia Perennis, 2001.

— Insights into Islamic Esoterism and Taoism. Sophia Perennis, 2003.

— Introduction to the Study of the Hindu Doctrines. Sophia Perennis, 2001.

— Man and His Becoming According to the Vedanta. Sophia Perennis, 2001.

— Metaphysical Principles of the Infinitesimal Calculus. Sophia Perennis, 2003.

— Miscellanea. Sophia Perennis, 2003.

— Perspectives on Initiation. Sophia Perennis, 2001.

— Spiritual Authority and Temporal Power. Sophia Perennis, 2001.

— Studies in Freemasonry and the Compagnonnage. Sophia Perennis, 2005.

— Studies in Hinduism. Sophia Perennis, 2001.

— Symbols of Sacred Science. Sophia Perennis, 2004.

— The Crisis of the Modern World. Sophia Perennis, 2001.

— The Esoterism of Dante. Sophia Perennis, 2003.

— The Great Triad. Sophia Perennis, 2001.

— The King of the World. Sophia Perennis, 2001.

— The Multiple States of the Being (tr. Henry Fohr). Sophia Perennis, 2001.

— Theosophy, the History of a Pseudo-Religion. Sophia Perennis, 2003.

— The Reign of Quantity and the Signs of the Times. Sophia Perennis, 2001.

— The Spiritist Fallacy. Sophia Perennis, 2003.

— The Symbolism of the Cross. Sophia Perennis, 2001.

— Traditional Forms and Cosmic Cycles. Sophia Perennis, 2003.

Gyatso, Kelsang. *Tantric Grounds and Paths: How to Enter, Progress On, and Complete the Vajrayana Path. Tharpa publications, 2003.*

Hall, Manly Palmer. *Freemasonry of the Ancient Egyptians. Philosophical Research Society, 1999.*

— *Initiates of the Flame. Occult Philosophies: Tracing the Threads of Hidden Wisdom and Secret Society Symbols. Independently published, 2023.*

— *Lectures on Ancient Philosophy. Martino Fine Books, 2018.*

— *Magic: A Treatise on Natural Occultism. Martino Fine Books, 2014.*

— *The Lost Keys of Freemasonry: The Legend of Hiram Abiff. Martino Publishing, 2013.*

— *The Secret Teachings of All Ages: An Encyclopedic Outline of Masonic, Hermetic, Qabbalistic and Rosicrucian Symbolical Philosophy. Dover Publications, 2010.*

— *Unseen Forces. Martino Fine Books, 2019.*

Heers, Fr. Peter Alban. *The Ecclesiological Renovation of Vatican II: An Orthodox Examination of Rome's Ecumenical Theology Regarding Baptism and the Church. Uncut Mountain Press, 2015.*

Heiser, Michael S. *The Anunnaki Gods According to Ancient Mesopotamian Sources: English Translations of Important Scholarly Works with Brief Commentary. Blind Spot Press, 2019.*

Hoffman, Michael. *Judaism's Strange Gods. Independent History and Research, 2011.*

— *The Occult Renaissance Church of Rome. Independent History and Research, 2017.*

Hopko, Fr. Thomas. *The Orthodox Faith (Vol. I-IV). St. Vladimirs Seminary Press, 2016.*

Hornung Cornell, Erik. *Conceptions of God in Ancient Egypt: The One and the Many. University Press, 1996.*

Huxley, Aldous. *Brave New World and Brave New World Revisited. Harper Perennial Modern Classics, 2005.*

— *The Perennial Philosophy: An Interpretation of the Great Mystics, East and West. Harper Perennial, 2012.*

Iamblichus. *On the Mysteries of the Egyptians, Chaldeans, and Assyrians: The Complete Text. Lulu.com, 2019.*

— *The Theology of Arithmetic. Phanes Press, 2006.*

Ibn 'Usman Hujviri, Ali. *The Kashf al-mahjúb: The oldest Persian treatise on Sufism. Taj Co, 1982.*

I-Ming, Liu. *Awakening to the Tao. Shambhala, 2006.*

— *The Taoist I Ching. Shambhala, 2005.*

James, William. *The Varieties of Religious Experience. CrossReach Publications, 2017.*

Jie, Wang. *Commentary on the Mirror for Compounding the Medicine: A Fourteenth-Century Work on Taoist Internal Alchemy. Golden Elixir Press, 2013.*

Jonas, Hans. *The Gnostic Religion: The Message of the Alien God and the Beginnings of Christianity. Beacon Press, 2015.*

Jung, Carl Gustav. *Aion: Researches into the Phenomenology of the Self (Collected Works of C.G. Jung Vol.9 Part 2). Princeton University Press, 1979.*

— *Alchemical Studies (Collected Works of C.G. Jung Vol.13). Princeton University Press, 1983.*

— *Man and His Symbols. Bantam, 2023.*

— *Mysterium Coniunctionis (Collected Works of C.G. Jung Vol.14). Princeton University Press, 1977.*

— *Psychology and Alchemy (Collected Works of C.G. Jung Vol.12). Princeton University Press, 1980.*

— *Psychology and Religion: West and East (Collected Works of C. G. Jung, Volume 11). Princeton University Press, 2024.*

— *Symbols of Transformation (Collected Works of C.G. Jung Vol.5). Princeton University Press, 1977.*

— *The Archetypes and The Collective Unconscious (Collected Works of C.G. Jung Vol.9, Part 1). Princeton University Press, 1981.*

Kaplan, Aryeh. *Bahir: Illumination. Red Wheel/Weiser, 1990.*

— *Meditation and the Kabbalah. Red Wheel/Weiser, 1986.*

— *Sefer Yetzira: The Book of Creation: In Theory and Practice. Red Wheel/Weiser, 1997.*

Kapleau, Roshi Philip. *The Three Pillars of Zen. Anchor, 2013.*

Kohn, Livia. *Introducing Daoism. Routledge, 2008.*

Kubo, Tsugunari (Translator); Yuyama, Akira (Translator). *The Lotus Sutra: Revised Edition. BDK America, 2007.*

Kuhn, Thomas S. *The Structure of Scientific Revolutions: 50th Anniversary Edition. University of Chicago Press, 2012.*

Kurzweil, Ray. *The Age of Spiritual Machines: When Computers Exceed Human Intelligence. Penguin Books, 2000.*

— *The Singularity Is Near: When Humans Transcend Biology. Penguin Books, 2006.*

Lakshman Joo, Swami. *Vijnana Bhairava The Practice of Centering Awareness. Indica Books, 2007.*

Lao Tzu. *Tao Te Ching. Ancient Renewal, 2020.*

Larchet, Jean-Claude. *Life after Death According to the Orthodox Tradition. The Printshop of St. Job of Pochaev, 2021.*

— *Therapy of Spiritual Illness: An Introduction to the Ascetic Tradition of the Orthodox Church (Vol. I-III). Alexander Press, 2012.*

Lévi, Eliphas. *The Doctrine and Ritual of High Magic: A New Translation. Tarcher Perigee, 2017.*

— *The History of Magic. Weiser Books, 1999.*

— *The Key of the Mysteries. Martino Fine Books, 2013.*

Lingpa, Jigme. *Yeshe Lama: From the Heart Essence of the Vast Expanse of the Great Perfection, a Practice Manual for the Stages of the Path of the Original Protector Entitled Yeshe Lama. Snow Lion, 2008.*

Lossky, Vladimir. *In the Image and Likeness of God. St Vladimirs Seminary Press, 2001.*

— *Orthodox Dogmatic Theology: Creation, God's Image in Man, & the Redeeming Work of the Trinity Vladimir. St Vladimirs Seminary Press, 2017.*

— *Orthodox Theology: An Introduction. St Vladimirs Seminary Press, 2001.*

— *The Mystical Theology of the Eastern Church. St Vladimirs Seminary Press, 1997.*

— *The Vision of God. St Vladimirs Seminary Press, 2013.*

Lumpkin, Joseph. *The Books of Enoch: The Angels, The Watchers and The Nephilim. Fifth Estate, 2011.*

Mallinson, James. *The Shiva Samhita: A Critical Edition and an English Translation. YogaVidya.com, 2007.*

Matt, Daniel C. *The Zohar: Pritzker Edition (Vol. I-XII). Stanford University Press*, 2019.

McGill, V. J.; Parry, W. T. *The Unity of Opposites: A Dialectical Principle. Guilford Press*, 1948.

McGinn, Bernard. *The Presence of God: A History of Western Christian Mysticism (Vol. I-V). Herder & Herder*, 2004.

Mead , G. R. S. *Pistis Sophia: A Gnostic Gospel. Book Tree*, 2011.

— *The Chaldaean Oracles. Kessinger Publishing*, 2010.

— *The Mysteries of Mithra, The Vision of Aridaeus. Books on Demand*, 2018.

Meyer, Marvin W. *The Nag Hammadi Scriptures: The Revised and Updated Translation of Sacred Gnostic Texts Complete in One Volume. HarperOne*, 2009.

Milton, John. *Paradise Lost. Penguin Classics*, 2003.

Mu, Wang. *Foundations of Internal Alchemy: The Taoist Practice of Neidan. Golden Elixir Press*, 2011.

Muhammad; N. J. Dawood (Translator, Introduction). *The Koran. Penguin Classics*, 2015.

Muktibodhananda, Swami. *Hatha Yoga Pradipika. Yoga Publications Trust*, 2016.

Nāgārjuna. *Nagarjuna's Seventy Stanzas: A Buddhist Psychology of Emptiness. Snow Lion*, 1999.

— *The Fundamental Wisdom of the Middle Way: Nāgārjuna's Mūlamadhyamakakārikā. Oxford University Press*, 1995.

Namkhai Norbu, Chogyal. *The Crystal and the Way of Light: Sutra, Tantra, and Dzogchen. Snow Lion*, 1999.

— *The Supreme Source: The Fundamental Tantra of Dzogchen Semde Kunjed Gyalpo. Snow Lion*, 1999.

Nellas, Panayiotis. *Deification in Christ: Orthodox Perspectives on the Nature of the Human Person (Contemporary Greek Theologians, Vol V). St Vladimirs Seminary Press*, 1987.

Nietzsche, Friedrich. *Beyond Good and Evil. Richer Resources Publications*, 2012.

— *The Will to Power. Vintage Books*, 2011.

— *The Twilight of the Idols and the Anti-Christ: or How to Philosophize with a Hammer.Penguin Classics*, 1990.

— *Thus Spoke Zarathustra: A Book for Everyone and No One*. Penguin Classics, 1961.

Nikodimos of the Holy Mountain (Compilator); Markarios of Corinth (Compilator).*The Philokalia: The Complete Text (Vol. I-V)*. G.E.H. Palmer et al. Faber & Faber, 1983.

Norsang Gyatso, Khedrup. *Ornament of Stainless Light: An Exposition of the Kalachakra Tantra (Library of Tibetan Classics Book 14)*. Wisdom Publications, 2016.

Nyima, Chökyi. *Union of Mahamudra and Dzogchen: A Commentary on The Quintessence of Spiritual Practice, The Direct Instructions of the Great Compassionate One*. North Atlantic Books, 1994.

of Alexandria, St. Athanasius. *On the Incarnation*. CreateSpace Independent Publishing Platform, 2016.

of Avila, St. Teresa. *Interior Castle*. Dover Publications, 2012.

of Lyons, St. Irenaeus. *Against Heresies (Vol. I-V)*. Beloved Publishing, LLC; 2014.

of the Cross, St. John. *Dark Night of the Soul*. Dover Publications, 2012.

Orwell, George. *1984*. Signet Classic, 1961.

Po, Huang. *The Zen Teaching of Huang Po: On the Transmission of Mind*. Grove Press, 2007.

Po-Tuan, Chang. *The Inner Teachings of Taoism*. Shambhala, 2001.

Padmasambhava. *Natural Liberation: Padmasambhava's Teachings on the Six Bardos*. Wisdom Publications, 2012.

Pagels, Elaine. *The Gnostic Gospels*. Vintage, 1989.

Palamas, St. Gregory. *Gregory Palamas: The Triads*. Paulist Press, 1982.

— *Dialogue Between an Orthodox and a Barlaamite*. Global Publications at SUNY Binghampton University, 1999.

Pallis, Marco. *A Buddhist Spectrum: Contributions to the Christian-Buddhist Dialogue*. World Wisdom, 2004.

Pardee, Dennis. *Ritual and Cult at Ugarit*. Society of Biblical Literature, 2002.

Pelikan, Jaroslav. *The Christian Tradition: A History of the Development of Doctrine (Vol. I-V)*. University of Chicago Press, 1975.

Perry, Whitall. *A Treasury of Traditional Wisdom*. New York: Simon and Schuster, 1971.

Photios, St. *The Mystagogy of the Holy Spirit*. Holy Cross Orthodox Press, 2005.

Pike, Albert. *Morals and Dogma: of the Ancient and Accepted Scottish Rite of Freemasonry. East India Publishing Company, 2022.*

Plato. *Plato: Complete Works. A Hackett Publishing Co., 1997.*

Plotinus. *Plotinus: The Enneads. Cambridge University Press, 1997.*

Porphyry. *Porphyry's Against the Christians. Prometheus, 1994.*

Prabhavananda, Swami. *The Upanishads: Breath of the Eternal. Vedanta Press & Bookshop, 1975.*

Pregadio, Fabrizio. *Awakening to Reality: The "Regulated Verses" of the Wuzhen pian, a Taoist Classic of Internal Alchemy. Golden Elixir Press, 2014.*

— *The Seal of the Unity of the Three: A Study and Translation of the Cantong qi, the Source of the Taoist Way of the Golden Elixir. Golden Elixir Press, 2011.*

Rabjam, Longchen. *The Precious Treasury of Philosophical Systems: A Treatise Elucidating the Meaning of the Entire Range of Buddhist Teachings. Padma Publishing,U.S, 2007.*

— *The Precious Treasury of Pith Instructions. Padma Publishing,U.S, 2006.*

— *The Precious Treasury of The Basic Space of Phenomena. Padma Publishing,U.S, 2001.*

— *The Precious Treasury of the Way of Abiding. Padma Publishing,U.S, 1998.*

Radde-Gallwitz, Andrew. *Basil of Caesarea, Gregory of Nyssa, and the Transformation of Divine Simplicity. Oxford University Press, 2009.*

Rand, Ayn. *Atlas Shrugged. NAL, 1999.*

— *The Fountainhead. NAL, 1994.*

Red Pine. *The Diamond Sutra. Counterpoint, 2002.*

— *The Heart Sutra. Counterpoint, 2005.*

Rose, Fr. Seraphim. *Nihilism: the Root of the Revolution of the Modern Age. Platina: St. Herman of Alaska Brotherhood, 1994.*

— *Orthodoxy and the Religion of the Future. Platina: Saint Herman of Alaska Brotherhood, 1975.*

— *Orthodox Survival Course. Samizdat Press, 2019.*

— *The Place of Blessed Augustine in the Orthodox Church. Platina: Saint Herman of Alaska Brotherhood, 1983.*

— *The Soul After Death: Contemporary "After-Death" Experiences in the Light of the Orthodox Teaching on the Afterlife*. Platina: St. Herman of Alaska Brotherhood, 1988.

Rundle Clark, Robert Thomas. *Myth and Symbol in Ancient Egypt*. Thames & Hudson, 1999.

Rushdoony, Rousas John. *The One and the Many: Studies in the Philosophy of Order and Ultimacy*. Ross House Books, 2007.

Sandars, N. K. *The Epic of Gilgamesh*. Penguin Classics, 1960.

Sankaracarya. *Atmabodha. Swami Chinmayananda; Central Chinmaya Mission Trust*, 2018.

— *Brahma Sutra Bhasya*. Vedanta Press & Bookshop, 1965.

— *Upadesa Sahasri. Jagadananda, Swami; Sri Ramakrishna Math*, 2023.

Satchidananda, Sri Swami. *The Yoga Sutras of Patanjali*. Integral Yoga Publications, 2015.

Satyananda Saraswati, Swami. *Kundalini Tantra*. Yoga Publications Trust, 2016.

Schaff, Philip. *Ante-Nicene Fathers: Translations of the Writings of the Fathers Down to A.D. 325, Series - Vol I-IX . Enhanced Version (Early Church Fathers). Christian Classics Ethereal Library*; 1.1 edition, 2009.

— *Nicene and Post-Nicene Fathers Series 1 and 2 - Enhanced Version (Early Church Fathers). Christian Classics Ethereal Library*; 1.1 edition 2009

Schaya, Leo. *The Universal Meaning of The Kabbalah*. University Books, Inc.; 1971.

— *Universal Aspects of the Kabbalah and Judaism*. World Wisdom, 2014.

Scholem, Gershom. *Major Trends in Jewish Mysticism*. Schocken, 1995.

Schwab, Klaus. *COVID-19: The Great Reset*. World Economic Forum, 2020.

— *The Fourth Industrial Revolution*. Currency, 2017.

Segal, Alan F. *Two Powers in Heaven: Early Rabbinic Reports about Christianity and Gnosticism*. Baylor University Press, 2012.

Seneca, Lucius Annaeus. *Letters from a Stoic*. Penguin Books, 1969.

Shaw, Victor. *Lemegeton: The Complete Books I-V: Ars Goetia, Ars Theurgia Goetia, Ars Paulina, Ars Almadel, Ars Notoria*. Erebus Society, 2017.

Silesius, Angelus. *The Cherubinic Wanderer*. Lulu.com, 2023.

Singh, Jaideva. *Abhinavagupta: A Trident of Wisdom (SUNY Series in Tantric Studies). State University of New York Press, 1989.*

— *Pratyabhijnahrdayam: The Secret Of Self-Recognition. Motilal Banarsidass, 1987.*

— *Siva Sutras: The Yoga Of Supreme Identity - Text Of The Sutras And The Commentary Vimarsini Of Ksemaraja. Motilal Banarsidass, 2000.*

— *Spanda-Karikas: The Divine Creative Pulsation. Motilal Banarsidass, 2014.*

— *Vedanta And Advaita Saivagama Of Kashmir. Advaita Ashram, 2022.*

Smith, Huston. *The World's Religions: Our Great Wisdom Traditions. HarperOne, 1958. rev. ed. 1991.*

Sonam Rinchen, Geshe. *Atisha's Lamp for the Path to Enlightenment. Snow Lion, 1997.*

St. Athanasius Academy of Orthodox Theology. *The Orthodox Study Bible: Ancient Christianity Speaks to Today's World. Thomas Nelson, 2008.*

Staniloae, Dumitru. *Orthodox Spirituality: A Practical Guide for the Faithful and a Definitive Manual for the Scholar. St. Tikhon's Monastery Press, 2013.*

— *The Experience of God (Vol. I-VI). Holy Cross Orthodox Press, 1994.*

Tashi Gyaltsen, Shardza. *Heart Drops of Dharmakaya: Dzogchen Practice of the Bon Tradition. Snow Lion, 2002.*

Taylor, Thomas. *Collection of the Chaldean Oracles. Kshetra Books, 2015.*

— *Eleusinian and Bacchic Mysteries: A Dissertation. Wizards Bookshelf, 1997.*

— *Proclus: On the Theology of Plato: with The Elements of Theology. CreateSpace Independent Publishing Platform, 2017.*

— *The Orphic Hymns. Orpheus; Independently published, 2019.*

Teitaro Suzuki, Daisetz. *An Introduction to Zen Buddhism. Grove Press, 2007.*

— *Manual Of Zen Buddhism. Youcanprint, 2017.*

— *Mysticism: Christian and Buddhist. Routledge, 2017.*

— *Outlines of Mahayana Buddhism. Literary Licensing, LLC; 2014.*

— *The Lankavatara Sutra: A Mahayana Text. George Routledge & Sons, 1932.*

— *The Training Of The Zen Buddhist Monk. Cosimo, Inc.; 2004.*

the Areopagite, Dionysius. *Pseudo Dionysius: The Complete Works. Paulist Press, 1987.*

the Confessor, St. Maximus. *Disputations with Pyrrhus. St. Tikhon's Monastery Press, 2014.*

— Maximus the Confessor: Selected Writings. Paulist Press, 1985.

— On Difficulties in the Church Fathers: The Ambigua (Vol. I-II). Harvard University Press, 2014.

— On the Cosmic Mystery of Jesus Christ. St. Vladimirs Seminary Press, 2003.

— Quaestiones Ad Thalassium.Brepols Pub, 2018.

the Great, St. Basil. *On the Holy Spirit. St. Vladimirs Seminary Press, 2011.*

Thrangu, Khenchen. *Vivid Awareness: The Mind Instructions of Khenpo Gangshar. Shambhala, 2011.*

Trenham, Fr. Josiah. *Rock and Sand: An Orthodox Appraisal of the Protestant Reformers and Their Teachings. Newrome Press, LLC; 2018.*

Trismegistus, Hermes. *The Emerald Tablet of Hermes Hermes Trismegistus. Merchant Books, 2013.*

Valentin Andreae, Johann. *The Chymical Wedding of Christian Rosenkreutz. Zinc Read, 2023.*

Venkatesananda, Swami. *Vasiṣṭha's Yoga. SUNY Press, 2010.*

Vivekananda, Swami. *The Complete Book Of Yoga: Karma Yoga, Bhakti Yoga, Raja Yoga, Jnana Yoga. Rupa Publications, India 2022.*

Voegelin, Eric. *Science, Politics and Gnosticism: Two Essays. Gateway Editions, 1997.*

Von Rosenroth, Knorr (Author); MacGregor Mathers, Samuel Liddell (Editor). *Kabbala Denudata: the Kabbalah Unveiled. Containing the Following Books of the Zohar:the Book of Concealed Mystery, the Greater and Lesser Holy Assemblies. Isha Books, 2013.*

Walker, D.P. *Spiritual and Demonic Magic: From Ficino to Campanella. The Pennsylvania State University Press, 2001.*

Wallis Budge, E.A. *The Egyptian Book of the Dead: The Complete Papyrus of Ani. Clydesdale, 2021.*

Ward, Benedicta. *The Sayings of the Desert Fathers: The Alphabetical Collection. Liturgical Press, 1984.*

Williams, Paul. *Mahayana Buddhism: The Doctrinal Foundations. Routledge, 2008.*

Woodroffe, Sir John. *Introduction to Tantra Sastra. Productivity & Quality Publishing Private Ltd., 2004.*

Yampolsky, Philip B. *The Platform Sutra of the Sixth Patriarch. Columbia University Press, 2012.*

Yen, Sheng (Chan Master). *Attaining the Way: A Guide to the Practice of Chan Buddhism. Shambhala, 2006.*

— *Hoofprint of the Ox: Principles of the Chan Buddhist Path as Taught by a Modern Chinese Master. Oxford University Press, 2002.*

— *The Method of No-Method: The Chan Practice of Silent Illumination. Shambhala, 2008.*

Yeshe, Lama Thubten. *The Bliss of Inner Fire: Heart Practice of the Six Yogas of Naropa, Wisdom Publications 1998.*

Zaehner, R.C. *At Sundry Times. An essay in the comparison of religions. Faber & Faber, London, 1958.*

— *Hindu and Muslim Mysticism. Athlone Press, University of London, 1960.*

— *Hinduism. Oxford University Press, London, 1962.*

— *Mysticism: Sacred and Profane. Clarendon Press, Oxford University, 1957.*

— *The Dawn and Twilight of Zoroastrianism. Weidenfeld & Nicolson, London, 1961.*

— *Zurvan. A Zoroastrian Dilemma. Oxford University, 1955.*

A5. SUBJECT INDEX

About the Author

Jonathan Torralba Torrón

With half his time focused on science and engineering, and the other half fixated on the completely different but equally abstract concepts of mystical, esoteric, and religious worldviews, Jonathan decided to launch *The Metaphysical Compass Project* (book and website) in order to make it easier to understand these complex and increasingly popular topics.

After more than twenty years exploring the philosophy, metaphysics, and the solutions given by the different worldviews to the deepest and most complex questions in life, Jonathan conceived this project as a tool that provides a systematic and in-depth discussion on these matters, going beyond a mere introductory level.

The Metaphysical Compass is especially suitable for abstract and logically-minded people that, even if they are interested in such metaphysical issues, find it difficult to see the appeal of traditional spiritual or religious arguments.

This is because, while traditional arguments are usually more emotional in nature, this project aims at unraveling the fundamental philosophical questions underlying these matters.

Questions as basic as, for example, the problem of *the One and the Many* and its various solutions as proposed by the different worldviews, especially the uniquely non-dialectical one offered by Orthodox Christianity.